D1499398

Historical Writing in England
ii

Historical Writing
in England
ii

c. 1307 to the Early Sixteenth Century

Antonia Gransden

Routledge & Kegan Paul

London and Henley

*First published in 1982
by Routledge & Kegan Paul Ltd
39 Store Street,
London WC1E 7DD and
Broadway House,
Newtown Road,
Henley-on-Thames,
Oxon RG9 1EN
Set in Monophoto Baskerville
and printed in Great Britain by
Unwin Brothers Ltd*

British Library Cataloguing in Publication Data

*Gransden, Antonia
Historical writing in England.
2 : c. 1307 to the early sixteenth century
1. Great Britain—Historiography
I. Title
942′.007′2   DAI*

ISBN 0–7100–0480–X

To Katherine and Deborah

Contents

[vii]

Plates

[ix]

Introduction

At the beginning of the fourteenth century the tradition of historical writing in England was at a low ebb. As has been shown in volume i of this survey, *Historical Writing in England c.550–c.1307*, nearly all the chronicle sources for the reign of Edward I came to an end during the king's last years. It was hard to see in which directions the future of English historiography lay.

Nevertheless, the tradition did not die. Indeed, it continued through various vicissitudes until the eve of the reformation and survived to exercise an influence on historians during the Tudor period and later. The purpose of this volume is to examine the motives which impelled men to take up again the burden of historical enterprise, and to map the roads along which they travelled. The last reign for which the literary sources are discussed is that of Richard III, whose death in 1485 conventionally marks the end of the middle ages. However, since some of the works were not completed until the generation after the battle of Bosworth, the survey continues until the early years of Henry VIII's reign. The epilogue carries the story a little further; the final section of it attempts to show what became of the legacy of English medieval historiography later in the sixteenth century.

The medieval tradition of contemporary reportage survived throughout the fourteenth and fifteenth centuries. Every English victory in war, whether the battle of Halidon Hill or of Neville's Cross, the battle of Poitiers or of Agincourt, and every crisis, whether the deposition of Edward II or the Peasants' Revolt, the deposition of Richard II or the usurpation of Richard III, duly found its chroniclers.

However, despite the survival of the tradition itself, the classes of people who contributed to it changed. Monks, friars and regular canons lost their pre-eminence as the observers, recorders and commentators on public affairs. Despite a brief revival of monastic historiography in the reign of Richard II, the fourteenth and fifteenth centuries mark the final decline of the full-scale monastic chronicle. (Nevertheless, brief monastic annals were written until the end of the period—and one set of annals, which was started in the convent of the Grey friars of Newgate, London, was continued elsewhere until well after the reformation.)

As the main chroniclers of current events, the religious gave way to secular clerks in the fourteenth century. Then, in the fifteenth century, secular clerks in their turn gave precedence to laymen (both members of the chivalric classes and Londoners). This change in the categories of men writing history had an important corollary: first of all Latin was briefly replaced by Anglo-Norman as the usual language of historiography; and finally English gained dominance. These trends paved the way for the modern era, when historical writing is largely a matter for laymen, and English history is written in English.

But although the personnel of the chroniclers and the language they wrote in changed in the late medieval period, generally speaking the structure of chronicles and the nature of their contents did not: the vernacular London chronicles of the fifteenth century are annalistic in form and local in orientation, in much the same way as the Latin monastic chronicles had been. It must be admitted, however, that in the course of the fifteenth century the quality of reportage declined. The London chronicles do not compare as repositories of news with the monastic chronicles of the thirteenth century, or even with those of Richard II's reign. One result of the decline in quality is that the historian today has to fall back on continental chronicles for light on English history. (The most important of these are included in this survey.)

In the fourteenth and fifteenth centuries trends which had begun earlier in the medieval period gained momentum. The expanding power of king and government is reflected by an increase in their influence on historiography. Traces of government propaganda are found in an increasingly large number of chronicles. Such propaganda might be introduced because the author was persuaded that the official point of view was right, or because he wanted to curry favour with his audience. On the other hand it might be included as a result of a direct command from the centre of power.

Similarly, the growing importance of the nobility and other magnates in the kingdom found expression in the chronicles. Every monastery had its patron and its benefactors: these often both figure large and are praised in a house's chronicle. Every secular clerk and most laymen had at least one patron: a chronicle by such an author was intended to please the patron, and might be slanted with that end in view.

On their side, kings and nobles were increasingly interested in history. Two members of the aristocracy, Sir Thomas Gray of Heton, in Northumberland, and John Tiptoft, earl of Worcester, actually wrote quite ambitious histories themselves. And both royalty and noblemen liked to read or listen to history in the chivalric style, particularly because it was amusing—many owned sumptuous copies of such works. Moreover, history was useful. It could be used to persuade. As propaganda it was of service to the kings and to their opponents alike.

Though contemporary reportage survived under difficulty until the end of the medieval period, the study of past history gained some ground. This advance, however, was not made in general history. The most ambitious work in this field, and by far the most popular, was the *Polychronicon* by Ranulf Higden, monk of the Benedictine abbey of St Werburgh's, Chester, who wrote late in Edward II's reign and early in Edward III's. This was the first truly universal history to be written in England. Starting at the Creation, it embraces all aspects of human activity—social customs, technology, culture, learning and the like—besides geography and zoological lore.

As a serious study of the past, the *Polychronicon* has grave shortcomings. This amazing amalgam of fact and fiction appealed to men's taste for the weird and the wonderful rather than to their objective intellectual curiosity. It did little or nothing to promote sound research into England's distant past; indeed virtually no advance was made in the fourteenth and fifteenth centuries in that direction. For the history of ancient Britain, Geoffrey of Monmouth, with his stories of Brutus and King Arthur, ruled supreme as the one standard authority who seemed to make further investigation unnecessary. It was not until Polydore Vergil, an Italian humanist resident in England, wrote his *Anglica Historia* in the early sixteenth century, that the legend-laden British History was seriously challenged.

But on a local level the picture is different. As the monks and other religious abandoned their role as the main chroniclers of national events, they turned more and more to local history. They wrote monographs on local history, and devoted an increasing amount of space to local affairs in their annals. But particularly remarkable in the fifteenth century is the development of antiquarian studies. The monastic historian, spurred on by the desire to increase the prestige of his house, concentrated on proving its antiquity and elucidating its early years. In some cases this led to the proliferation of legends just as improbable as those of Geoffrey of Monmouth (with which they were often connected). But in others it resulted in excellent research on documents and in accurate first hand observation of antiquities. Later in the fifteenth century the scholarly study of antiquities was taken up by other historians—especially by the secular clerk, John Rous, and by two laymen, John Hardyng and William Worcester. Although these early antiquaries often betray the shortcomings of their times, at their best they show the merit which we have come to expect of all historians today, the painstaking search for the truth simply because it is interesting and important in itself.

The contents of this volume are arranged in the same way as in the previous one. Separate chapters are devoted to the two most important writers, in this case Ranulf Higden and Thomas Walsingham. The other writers are grouped chronologically, or according to their status (for example, whether monastic or secular, English or foreign), or according to the nature of their work (thus there is a chapter for the two antiquaries, John Rous and William Worcester, and another for the two humanist historians, Thomas More and Polydore Vergil). Such an arrangement overrides both a strictly chronological and a schematic distribution of material. To help the reader overcome this difficulty four indices are provided in Appendix H (pp. 499–503 below): first, a chronological index (similar to that in volume i) of the principal sources, arranged under reigns from 1307 to 1485; second, an index of the most important monastic annals; third, an index of the main local histories; and fourth, an index of those works which are primarily antiquarian in interest.

The fourteen plates (between pages 168 and 169) have been chosen to illustrate various aspects of this book. Two of the plates (II and XIII) are of autographs of well known scholars—Ranulf Higden and William Worcester—and one (VII) includes a note which may possibly be in the hand of the chronicler Henry Knighton. In addition, two plates (I and XIV) are pages from early drafts of chronicles. Four plates, of miniatures from *de luxe* books executed for royalty and the nobility, show the importance of patronage in the production of histories composed in the chivalric mode. One (IX) is from the copy of Jean de Waurin's chronicle executed for Edward IV; another (V) is from the copy of Jean Froissart's *Chroniques* executed for Edward's friend Lord William Hastings; and the last (VI) is from the copy of the history of Richard II's last years by Jean Creton which was executed for Charles III of Anjou. Also in the chivalric tradition is Chandos Herald's *La Vie du Prince Noir*; its frontispiece is reproduced in Plate III. The importance of the monastic patron, who figures largely in Thomas Walsingham's chronicles, is illustrated by a plate (IV) from Walsingham's *Liber Benefactorum*. Finally, a number of plates illustrate the antiquarian studies of the period. Two of these have already been mentioned in other contexts; they are Plate I, which includes a sketch of Old St Paul's, and Plate XIII, which is from William Worcester's notebook. The others, Plates X–XII, are from the works of Thomas Elmham, John Hardyng and John Rous.

This volume concludes this survey of English historiography from the mid-sixth century until the eve of the reformation. Having covered a period of nearly 1,000 years, it seemed appropriate to gather up the threads, and come to some general conclusions. This is done, therefore, in the epilogue, which assesses the outstanding characteristics and merits of the tradition of historical writing in England, and shows to what extent its influence survived into the modern era.

Nottingham, September 1978

Acknowledgments

In the course of research for this book I have incurred debts to many scholars, both past and present. For the latter half of the period covered, I have had the benefit of the late C. L. Kingsford's *English Historical Literature in the Fifteenth Century*; I cannot claim that my work has superseded his detailed study of the manuscript sources. I have also been helped by some recent editions of important chronicles, notably: N. Denholm-Young's *Vita Edwardi Secundi*, V. H. Galbraith's *Anonimalle Chronicle* and *St Albans Chronicle*, Frank Taylor's and J. S. Roskell's *Gesta Henrici Quinti*, A. H. Thomas' and I. D. Thornley's *The Great Chronicle of London*, C. A. J. Armstrong's edition of *The Usurpation of Richard III* by Dominic Mancini, R. S. Sylvester's edition of *The History of King Richard III* by Thomas More, and Denys Hay's edition of the *Anglica Historia* by Polydore Vergil. Moreover, the few recent studies of individual authors have been very helpful: John Taylor on Ranulf Higden, C. L. Kingsford on John Hardyng, E. F. Jacob on John Whethamsted, and Denys Hay on Polydore Vergil.

I am equally indebted to many scholars for assistance of a less formal kind. My colleague Dr Michael Jones has supplied me with bibliographical information on a variety of topics. In addition he has read some of the chapters in typescript and the whole in proof, thus saving me from a number of mistakes. I also owe a considerable debt to Mr Derek Turner, Deputy Keeper of Manuscripts in the British Library, who has answered numerous questions about the manuscripts in his care with unfailing helpfulness. Other scholars have given me information on particular subjects. I have acknowledged such debts in footnotes, but I must especially mention here Professor E. L. G. Stones and Professor P. E. Russell, for helping to solve problems raised by John Hardyng's chronicle; the Lord Sudeley, for sending me information about the fifteenth century chronicle roll of his family; Professor D. J. Sheerin, of the University of North Carolina, for sending me his research notes on Thomas Rudborne; and Professor R. B. Tate, for useful discussions and bibliographical help on renaissance historiography.

I should also like to record my thanks to those scholars who have allowed me to read their work in typescript in advance of publication: Dr J. J. N. Palmer for the typescript of his two articles on the French chronicles of Richard II's reign, which have since appeared in the *Bulletin of the John Rylands Library*, li (1978–9); Professor P. D. A. Harvey, Dr Felix Hull and the late Dr W. G. Urry, for the typescript of their respective pieces on Thomas Elmham's place in the early history of cartography and planmaking in England, which are to appear in *Local Maps and Plans from England*, ed. R. A. Skelton and P. D. A. Harvey (Oxford); and to Mr Nicholas Pronay for the typescript of his introduction to his edition of the second continuation of the Crowland chronicle, which is to be published in the series Oxford Medieval Texts.

In addition, I am particularly grateful to the staff of Nottingham University Library who with patience and courtesy have done all in their power to provide me with the books necessary for the preparation of this volume. I am also grateful to the staff of the students' room of the Department of Manuscripts in the British Library, and to the staff of Lambeth Palace Library, the library of the College of Arms, Cambridge University Library, the Bibliothèque Nationale, the Bibliothèque Municipale at Besançon and of Ghent University Library, for help when consulting manuscripts in their collections.

Finally I must thank: to the British Academy for a grant towards the cost of typing my manuscript and of the photographs for the plates Ms Elaine Donaldson of Routledge & Kegan Paul for the great care she has taken in the preparation of my book; and Professor and Mrs E. L. G. Stones for reading the index in proof and making a number of corrections and useful suggestions.

Abbreviations

AH, ed. Hay: *The Anglica Historia of Polydore Vergil A.D. 1485–1537*, ed., with an English translation, Denys Hay (Camden Soc., new series, lxxiv, 1950).

AH¹: Polydore Vergil, *Historia Anglica* (Basle 1534).

AH²: Polydore Vergil, *Historia Anglica* (Basle 1546).

AH³: Polydore Vergil, *Historia Anglica* (Basle 1555).

AL: *Annales Londonienses* in *Chrons Edw. I and II*, i. 3–251.

AM: the chronicle of Adam Murimuth in *Adae Murimuth Continuatio Chronicarum. Robertus de Avesbury de Gestis Mirabilibus Regis Edwardi Tertii*, ed. E. Maunde Thompson (RS 1889), pp. 3–219.

AP: *Annales Paulini* in *Chrons Edw. I and II*, i. 255–370.

AU: *Chronicon Adae de Usk A.D. 1377–1421*, ed., with an English translation, E. Maunde Thompson (London 1904).

Amund.: *Annales Monasterii S. Albani a Johanne Amundesham*, ed. H. T. Riley (RS 1870–1, 2 vols).

An.: *The Anonimalle Chronicle, 1333–1381*, ed. V. H. Galbraith (Manchester 1927).

Arrival: *Historie of the Arrivall of Edward IV in England and the Finall Recouerye of his Kingdomes from Henry VI, A.D. M.CCCC.LXXI*, ed. John Bruce (Camden Soc., original series, i, 1838).

BIHR: *Bulletin of the Institute of Historical Research*.

BJRL: *Bulletin of the John Rylands Library*.

Bel: *Chronique de Jean le Bel*, ed. J. Viard and E. Déprez (Soc. de l'Histoire de France 1904–5, 2 vols).

Ben: *John Benet's Chronicle for the Years 1400 to 1462*, ed. G. L. Harriss and M. A. Harriss (Camden Miscellany, xxiv, 1972).

Berm.: The chronicle of Bermondsey, 1042–1432, in *Annales Monastici*, ed. H. R. Luard (RS 1864–9, 5 vols), iii. 423.

Bridl.: The chronicle of Bridlington priory, 1307–1339, in *Chrons Edw. I and II*, ii. 25–151.

Brie, *Prosachronik:* F. W. D. Brie, *Geschichte und Quellen der Mittelenglischen Prosachronik the Brute of England oder the Chronicles of England* (Marburg 1905).

Brut: *The Brut or Chronicles of England*, ed. F. W. D. Brie (EETS, cxxxi, cxxvi, 1906, 1908, 2 vols, reprinted 1960).

But.: *The Register or Chronicle of Butley Priory, Suffolk, 1510–1535*, ed. A. G. Dickens (Winchester 1951).

CA: *Chronicon Angliae ab Anno Domini 1328 usque ad Annum 1388, auctore Monacho quodam Sancti Albani*, ed. E. Maunde Thompson (RS 1874).

CC: The chronicle of Crowland abbey, A.D. 616–1486, in *Rerum Anglicarum Scriptorum Veterum, Tom. I*, ed. William Fulman (Oxford 1684).

CCR: *Calendar of Close Rolls.*

CH: *La Vie du Prince Noir by Chandos Herald*, ed. D. B. Tyson (Beihefte zur Zeitschrift für Romanische Philologie, cxlvii, Tübingen 1975).

CH (P and L): *Life of the Black Prince, by the Herald of Sir John Chandos*, ed. M. K. Pope and E. C. Lodge (Oxford 1910, reprinted New York 1974).

CPR: *Calendar of Patent Rolls.*

CRSD: *Chronique du Religieux de Saint-Denys, contenant la Règne de Charles VI, de 1380 à 1422*, ed., with a French translation of the Latin text, L. Bellaguet (Paris 1839–52, 6 vols).

Cant.: the chronicle of Christ Church, Canterbury, 1346–1367, in *Chronica Johannis de Reading et Anonymi Cantuariensis 1346–1367*, ed. James Tait (Manchester 1914), pp. 99–186.

Chronicle of the Rebellion: *Chronicle of the Rebellion in Lincolnshire, 1470*, ed. J. G. Nichols (Camden Miscellany, i, 1847).

Chrons Edw. I and II: *Chronicles of the Reigns of Edward I and Edward II*, ed. William Stubbs (RS 1882–3, 2 vols).

Collections, ed. Gairdner: *The Historical Collections of a Citizen of London*, ed. James Gairdner (Camden Soc., second series, v, 1876).

Cont. NT: The continuation of the *Annals* of Nicholas Trevet, in *Nicholai Triveti Dominicani, Annales Sex Regum Angliae*, ed. Anthony Hall (Oxford 1719), pp. 1–29.

Creton: Creton, Jean, *Histoire du Roy d'Angleterre Richard, traictant particulièrement la rebellion de ses subiectz et prinse de sa personne: composée par un gentilhomme français de marque, qui fut à la suite dudict roy, avec permission du roy de France*, ed. J. A. Buchon (Collection des chroniques nationales françaises . . . , iii, Paris 1826).

Creton (Webb): Creton, Jean, op.cit., ed., with an English translation, John Webb in *Archaeologia*, xx (1824), pp. 13–423.

DC: the Dieulacres chronicle, in M. V. Clarke and V. H. Galbraith,

'The deposition of Richard II' in *BJRL*, xiv (1930), pp. 164–81. The article, together with the chronicle, is reprinted in M. V. Clarke, *Fourteenth Century Studies* (Oxford 1939), pp. 53–98.

Davies: *An English Chronicle of the Reigns of Richard II, Henry IV, Henry V, and Henry VI*, ed. J. S. Davies (Camden Soc., lxiv, 1856).

EETS: Early English Text Society.

EH: *Eulogium Historiarum sive Temporis: Chronicon ab Orbe condito usque ad Annum Domini M.CCC.LXVI a Monacho quodam Malmesburiensi exaratum*, ed. F. S. Haydon (RS 1858–63, 3 vols).

EHR: *English Historical Review*.

Emden, *Biographical Register*: A. B. Emden, *A Biographical Register of the University of Oxford to A.D. 1500* (Oxford 1957–9, 3 vols).

Eve.: *Chronicon Abbatiae de Evesham*, ed. W. D. Macray (RS 1863).

FH: *Flores Historiarum*, ed. H. R. Luard (RS 1890, 3 vols).

Fabyan: *The New Chronicles of England and France by Robert Fabyan, named by himself the Concordance of Histories*, ed. Henry Ellis (London 1811).

Flete: *The History of Westminster Abbey by John Flete*, ed. J. Armitage Robinson (Cambridge 1909).

Foedera: *Foedera, conventiones, litterae* . . . [1101–1654], ed. Thomas Rymer (London 1704–35, 20 vols).

Foedera (Rec. Comm.): *Foedera, conventiones, litterae* . . . [1069–1383], ed. Thomas Rymer, new edition by Adam Clarke, Frederic Holbrooke and John Caley (Record Commission, London 1816–69, 4 vols in 7 pts).

GASA: *Gesta Abbatum Monasterii Sancti Albani*, ed. H. T. Riley (RS 1867–8, 3 vols).

GB: *Chronicon Galfridi le Baker de Swynebroke*, ed. E. Maunde Thompson (Oxford 1889).

G.E.C., *Peerage*: G. E. C.[ockayne], *The Complete Peerage of England, Scotland, Ireland and Great Britain and the United Kingdom*, new edition by Vicary Gibbs *et al.* (London 1910–59, 13 vols).

GFC: *Chronicon ab Anno 1189 ad 1556, ex Registro Fratrum Minorum Londoniae* in *Monumenta Franciscana*, ed. Richard Howlett (RS 1882, 2 vols), ii. 143–260.

GHV: *Gesta Henrici Quinti*, ed., with an English translation, Frank Taylor and J. S. Roskell (Oxford Medieval Texts, 1975).

Gransden, *Historical Writing*, i: Antonia Gransden, *Historical Writing in England c. 550 to c. 1307* (London 1974).

HA: *Thomae Walsingham, quondam Monachi S. Albani, Historia Anglicana*, ed. H. T. Riley (RS 1863–4, 2 vols).

HG: *Historia et Cartularium Monasterii Sancti Petri Gloucestriae*, ed. W. H. Hart (RS 1863–7, 3 vols).

HK: *Chronicon Henrici Knighton vel Cnitthon Monachi Leycestrensis*, ed. J. R. Lumby (RS 1889–95, 2 vols).

Hardy, *Cat.*: T. D. Hardy, *Descriptive Catalogue of Materials relating to the History of Great Britain and Ireland to 1327* (RS 1862–71, 3 vols in 4 pts, reprinted New York 1963).

Herryson: John Herryson, *Abbreviata Cronica 1377–1469*, ed. J. J. Smith (Publications of the Cambridge Antiquarian Soc., i, 1840).

Historiae Dunelmensis Scriptores Tres, ed. Raine: *Historiae Dunelmensis Scriptores Tres, Gaufridus de Coldingham, Robertus de Graystanes et Willielmus de Chambre*, ed. James Raine, sn. (Surtees Soc., ix, 1839).

JB: *The Bruce by John Barbour Archdeacon of Aberdeen*, ed. W. M. Mackenzie (London 1909).

JF (K de L): *Oeuvres complètes de Froissart: Chroniques*, ed. Kervyn de Lettenhove (Paris 1868–77, 25 vols in 26 pts).

JF (SL): *Chroniques de Froissart*, ed. Siméon Luce, Gaston Raynaud, and Léon and Albert Mirot (Soc. de l'Histoire de France 1869–1975, 15 vols in 16 pts, in progress).

JG: *John of Glastonbury, Cronica sive Antiquitates Glastoniensis Ecclesie*, ed J.B.Carley (British Archaeological Reports, xlvii (i and ii), 1978, 2 vols).

JH: *The Chronicle of John Hardyng*, ed. Henry Ellis (London 1812, reprinted 1974).

JR: the chronicle of John of Reading in *Chronica Johannis de Reading et Anonymi Cantuariensis 1346–1367*, ed. James Tait (Manchester 1914), pp. 187–227.

JS: *The Chronicle of John Stone, monk of Christ Church, Canterbury, 1415–1471*, ed. W. G. Searle (Cambridge Antiquarian Soc. 1902).

JT: *Johannis de Trokelowe, et Henrici de Blaneforde monachorum S. Albani, necnon quorundam anonymorum, Chronica et Annales*, ed. H. T. Riley (RS 1866).

JW: *A Chronicle of the first thirteen Years of the Reign of King Edward the Fourth, by John Warkworth, D. D. Master of St. Peter's College, Cambridge*, ed. J. O. Halliwell (Camden Soc., original series, x, 1839).

Ker, *Libraries*: N. R. Ker, *Medieval Libraries of Great Britain* (second edition, London 1964).

Kingsford, *Hist. Lit.*: C. L. Kingsford, *English Historical Literature in the Fifteenth Century* (Oxford 1913, reprinted New York 1962).

Kingsford, *London Chrons*: C. L. Kingsford, *Chronicles of London* (Oxford 1905).

Lan.: *Chronicon de Lanercost, 1201–1346*, ed. Joseph Stevenson (Maitland Club, Edinburgh 1839).

Legge, *A N Lit.*: M. D. Legge, *Anglo-Norman Literature and its Background* (Oxford 1963).

Lond.: *Croniques de London*, ed. G. J. Aungier (Camden Soc., original series, xxviii, 1844).

Memorials Hen. V: *Memorials of Henry the Fifth*, ed. C. A. Cole (RS 1858).

Mon. Angl.: William Dugdale, *Monasticon Anglicanum*, ed. John Caley,

Henry Ellis, and Bulkeley Bandinel (London 1817–30, 6 vols in 8 pts).

NED: *A New English Dictionary,* ed. J. A. Murray *et al.* (Oxford 1888–1933, 11 vols in 21 pts).

Nicolas and Tyrrell: *A Chronicle of London from 1089–1483,* ed. N. H. Nicolas and E. Tyrrell (London 1827).

PC: *Philippe de Commynes, Mémoires,* ed. J. L. A. Calmette and G. Durville (Les Classiques de l'Histoire de France au Moyen Age 1924–5, 3 vols).

PV, EH: *Polydore Vergil's English History,* ed. Henry Ellis (Camden Soc., original series, xxix (1844), xxxvi (1846), 2 vols).

Pageant: *Pageant of the Birth, Life and Death of Richard Beauchamp Earl of Warwick K. G. 1389–1439,* ed. Viscount Dillon and W. H. St John Hope (London 1914).

Poly.: *Polychronicon Ranulphi Higden Monachi Cestrensis,* ed. Churchill Babington and J. R. Lumby (RS 1865–86, 9 vols).

Pseudo-Elmham: the so-called Pseudo-Elmham printed as *Thomas de Elmham Vita et Gesta Henrici Quinti,* ed. Thomas Hearne (Oxford 1727).

R III: Thomas More, *The History of King Richard III,* ed. R. S. Sylvester (*The Yale Edition of the Complete Works of St Thomas More,* ii, New Haven-London 1963).

RA: the chronicle of Robert of Avesbury in *Adae Murimuth Continuatio Chronicarum. Robertus de Avesbury de Gestis Mirabilibus Regis Edwardi Tertii,* ed. E. Maunde Thompson (RS 1889), pp. 279–471.

RR: the chronicle of Robert of Reading in *FH,* iii. 137–235.

RS: Rolls Series.

Reg. I: John Whethamsted's register, volume i, printed as *Annales Monasterii S. Albani a Johanne Amundesham, Monacho,* ed. H. T. Riley (RS 1870–1, 2 vols).

Reg. II: John Whethamsted's register, volume ii, printed *Registrum Abbatiae Johannis Whethamstede Abbatis Monasterii Sancti Albani,* ed. H. T. Riley (RS 1872–3, 2 vols).

Rot. Parl.: *Rotuli Parliamentorum* (printed in accordance with an order of the House of Lords dated 9 March 1767, 6 vols).

Rous: *Joannis Rousi Antiquarii Warwicensis Historia Regum Angliae,* ed. Thomas Hearne (Oxford 1716).

Rows rol: *This rol was laburd and finished by Master John Rows of Warrewyk,* lithographic fascimile, ed. William Courthope (London 1845–59; repr., with an introduction by Charles Ross, Gloucester 1980).

SA: Thomas Elmham, *Speculum Augustinianum,* printed as *Historia Monasterii S. Augustini Cantuariensis,* ed. Charles Hardwick (RS 1858).

St AC: *The St. Albans Chronicle 1406–1420,* ed. V. H. Galbraith (Oxford 1937).

Scala.: *Scalacronica by Sir Thomas Gray of Heton, knight,* ed. Joseph Stevenson (Maitland Club, Edinburgh 1836).

Strecche: Frank Taylor, 'The chronicle of John Strecche for the reign of Henry V (1414–1422)' in *BJRL*, xvi (1932), pp. 137–87.

TB: *Chronica Monasterii de Melsa, a Fundatione usque ad Annum 1396, Auctore Thoma de Burton, Abbate* . . . , ed. E. A. Bond (RS 1866–8, 3 vols).

TE: [*Thomae*] *Elmhami Liber Metricus de Henrico Quinto* printed in *Memorials Hen. V*, pp. 79–166.

TF: *Historia sive Narracio de Modo et Forma Mirabilis Parliamenti apud Westmonasterium Anno Domini Millesimo CCCLXXXVI, Regni vero Regis Ricardi Secundi post Conquestum Anno Decimo, per Thomam Fauent Clericum indictata*, ed. May McKisack (Camden Miscellany, xiv, 1926), pp. 1–27.

TL: *Titi Livii Foro-Juliensis Vita Henrici Quinti*, ed. Thomas Hearne (Oxford 1716).

T et M: *Chronicque de la Traïson et Mort de Richart Deux Roy Dengleterre*, ed., with an English translation, Benjamin Williams (English Historical Soc. 1846).

TR: Thomas Rudborne, *Historia Major . . . Ecclesiae Wintoniensis*, in Wharton, *Anglia Sacra*, i. 179–286.

TRHS: *Transactions of the Royal Historical Society.*

Thomas and Thornley: *The Great Chronicle of London*, ed. A. H. Thomas and I. D. Thornley (privately printed, London 1938).

Thorne's Chron.: *William Thorne's Chronicle of Saint Augustine's Abbey Canterbury*, translated by A. H. Davis, with a preface by A. Hamilton Thompson (Oxford 1934).

Thornton: Kathleen Major, 'The Thornton abbey chronicle (Bodleian Library, Tanner MS. 166), with extracts relating to the fabric of the abbey' in *Archaeological Journal*, ciii (1946), pp. 174–8.

Translator: the translation of Titus Livius' *Vita Henrici Quinti*, with additions, printed as *The First English Life of King Henry the Fifth*, ed. C. L. Kingsford (Oxford 1911).

Twysden, *Scriptores Decem:* Roger Twysden, *Historiae Anglicanae Scriptores Decem* (London 1652).

Usurpation: *The Usurpation of Richard III* [by Dominic Mancini], ed., with an English translation, C. A. J. Armstrong (second edition, Oxford 1969).

VCH: *Victoria County History.*

VE II: *Vita Edwardi Secundi*, ed., with an English translation, Noël Denholm-Young (Nelson's Medieval Texts 1957).

VR II: *Historia Vitae et Regni Ricardi Secundi*, ed. G. B. Stow (University of Pennsylvania 1977).

WG: C. E. Woodruff, 'The chronicle of William Glastynbury, monk of the priory of Christ Church, Canterbury, 1419–1448' in *Archaeologia Cantiana*, xxxvii (1925), pp. 121–51.

WT: the chronicle of William Thorne in Twysden, *Scriptores Decem,* cols 1753–2202.

WW: *William Worcestre, Itineraries,* ed. J. H. Harvey (Oxford Medieval Texts 1969).

Waurin: *Recueil des Croniques et Anchiennes Istories de la Grant Bretaigne . . . par Jehan de Waurin,* ed. William Hardy and E.L.C.P. Hardy (RS 1864–91, 5 vols).

Wharton, *Anglia Sacra:* Henry Wharton, *Anglia Sacra sive Collectio Historiarum de Archiepiscopis et Episcopis Angliae ad Annum 1540* (London 1691, 2 vols).

Political Poems, ed. Wright: *Political Poems and Songs relating to English History . . . from the Accession of Edward III to that of Richard III,* ed. Thomas Wright (RS 1852, 2 vols).

Ypodigma: *Ypodigma Neustriae a Thoma Walsingham,* ed. H. T. Riley (RS 1876).

1

Chroniclers of the Reign of Edward II

King Edward [II] was a handsome man, of outstanding strength, but his behaviour was a very different matter. For, underrating the company of the magnates, he was devoted to choristers, actors, grooms, sailors, and others skilled in similar avocations, and preferred the advice of foreigners to that of his own people. He was prodigal in giving, bountiful and splendid in living, quick and unpredictable in speech, most unlucky against the enemy, savage with members of his household, and passionately attached to one particular person, whom he cherished above all, showered with gifts and always put first; he could not bear being separated from him and honoured him above all others. As a result the loved one was hated, and the lover involved himself in odium and ruin. He promoted the unworthy and the unqualified to bishoprics —who afterwards did not stand by him in his troubles. Moreover, in his day there was a famine of all sorts of corn, and such a perpetual plague among men and murrain among animals as had never been seen before.[1]

Thus Ranulf Higden, writing about twenty years later, characterized Edward II and his reign. And, in varying degrees, it was the verdict of the other chroniclers. Treating Edward II's character and acts as central themes, the contemporary chroniclers deplored Edward's favouritism, his regard first for Piers Gaveston and then for the younger Hugh Despenser, which led to baronial rebellion. They also lamented the failure of Edward's Scottish campaigns, a result, in current opinion, of civil discord. In addition, the chroniclers were concerned, as a subsidiary theme, with the deeds of great nobles, men such as Thomas of Lancaster and Andrew Harcla, earl of Carlisle, who, supported by numerous retainers, played such a crucial role in the politics of the day. And the chroniclers repeatedly expiated on the natural catastrophes, the famine and plague which deci-

---

[1] *Poly.* viii. 298–300. For the *Polychronicon* see the next chapter. For the printed edition see p. 43 n. 1 below.

mated England (and Europe) from 1315 to 1317, aggravating Edward's troubles.[2]

Nevertheless, the chroniclers' estimates of the reign were not uniform. The attitude of each writer was at least partially conditioned by the prejudices of his class and the interests of his locality. Especially significant is the date when he wrote. Generally speaking the strictly contemporary writers were more pragmatic in their approach, and less theoretical and consistent than the writers of the next generation. This chronological factor is important because the comparatively late date of Higden's account of Edward II is by no means exceptional among the authorities for the reign.

The principal contemporary and near contemporary authorities can be divided into two groups: works by members of religious orders; and those by the secular clergy. Most of the chronicles written actually during Edward II's reign were by the religious. They represent, as it were, the tail end of the thirteenth century tradition of monastic historiography, using the term 'monastic' in this context to include chronicles by friars and Augustinian canons.[3] The monastic chronicle, as a historiographical mode, virtually lapsed in the reign of Edward II until its partial revival in the last half of the fourteenth century. For the most part the chronicles of Edward II's reign are short, factual records of events ('mere string[s] of notorious facts' in the words of William Stubbs).[4] However, nearly all preserve information not otherwise known, and have passages, combining succinct objectivity with vivid narrative, characteristic of the best monastic historiography. The following are the principal monastic chronicles: the St Albans chronicle, probably by William Rishanger and Henry of Blaneford, covering the period from 1307 to 1324;[5] the continuation, 1307 to 1318, of Nicholas Trevet's *Annals*, probably by a west country Dominican;[6] the continuation of Trevet, to 1339, written at the Augustinian priory of Bridlington in Yorkshire;[7] the continuation of the chronicle of the Franciscan friar, Richard of Durham, from 1297 to 1346, preserved in the Lanercost chronicle;[8] and the continuation of the *Flores Historiarum*

---

[2] For the famine see p. 7 and n. 32 below.

[3] See Gransden, *Historical Writing*, i. 404–86 passim.

[4] *Chronicles of the Reigns of Edward I and Edward II*, ed. William Stubbs (RS 1882–3, 2 vols), i. lxix. For an excellent short survey of the chronicle authorities for Edward II's reign, see T. F. Tout, *The Place of the Reign of Edward II in English History* (second edition, revised by Hilda Johnson, Manchester 1936), pp. 4–8.

[5] Printed in *Johannis de Trokelowe, et Henrici de Blaneforde monachorum S. Albani, necnon quorundam Anonymorum, Chronica et Annales*, ed. H. T. Riley (RS 1866), pp. 63–152.

[6] Printed in *Nicholai Triveti Dominicani, Annales Sex Regum Angliae*, ed. Anthony Hall (Oxford 1719), pp. 1–29.

[7] Printed in *Chrons Edw. I and II*, ii. 25–151.

[8] Printed in *Chronicon de Lanercost, 1201–1346*, ed. Joseph Stevenson (Maitland Club, Edinburgh 1839). For an English translation see *The Chronicles of Lanercost 1272–1346*, translated by Herbert Maxwell (Glasgow 1913).

(*Flowers of History*) to 1326, by Robert of Reading, monk of Westminster.[9]

More typical of the historiography of Edward II's reign than the monastic chronicles are the works by secular clerks and even one by a layman. The secular clergy and laity gained comparative importance as historians in the fourteenth century. In London someone connected with the Guildhall, perhaps Andrew Horn, an alderman, wrote contemporary annals to 1316, as a continuation to the *Flores Historiarum*.[10] Another continuation of the *Flores*, from 1306 to 1341, was produced, more or less contemporaneously with the events recorded, at St Paul's cathedral, apparently by more than one canon (whose names are unknown).[11] Another chronicle from St Paul's is not anonymous; in 1338 the canon Adam Murimuth started his continuation of the *Flores* which he carried on to 1346. Although Murimuth wrote in the next generation, he has some claim to contemporaneity for Edward II's reign because he used his own diary which he kept during that period.[12]

T. F. Tout picked out from this 'not very strong series of chronicles' the *Vita Edwardi Secundi* (*The Life of Edward II*),[13] an account of the reign to 1326 by an anonymous secular clerk, as 'the most human, most coloured, and in some way the most sympathetic and most critical.' This work is not a chronicle in the strict sense but a literary piece composed towards the end of the reign (or possibly later). Though it lacks the value of contemporaneity, subsequent research confirming its wise judgments and factual accuracy has added weight to the high regard in which Tout held it.

[9] Printed in *Flores Historiarum*, ed. H. R. Luard (RS 1890, 3 vols), iii, 137–235. There are also a number of monastic chronicles of less interest. (1) The part of Walter of Guisborough, 1307–12 (printed in *The Chronicle of Walter of Guisborough*, ed. Harry Rothwell (Camden Soc., third series, lxxxix, 1957), pp. 378–98). (2) The continuation of the *Flores Historiarum*, 1307–22 written at the Cistercian abbey of Tintern, which has some value particularly for the history of the Welsh border (printed in Luard, op. cit., iii. 328–48). (3) The Durham chronicle by Robert of Graystanes, 1214–1336, relating to local history (printed in *Historiae Dunelmensis Scriptores Tres, Gaufridus de Coldingham, Robertus de Graystanes, et Willielmus de Chambre*, ed. James Raine (Surtees Soc., ix, 1839), pp. 35–123, and see H. S. Offler, *Medieval Historians of Durham* (Durham 1958), pp. 14–16). (4) The *Historia Roffensis*, 1314–50, has some value for national events (see n. 13 below), but concerns mainly local history (printed in Wharton, *Anglia Sacra*, i. 356–77).

[10] Printed in *Chrons Edw. I and II*, i. 3–251.

[11] Printed in ibid., i. 255–370.

[12] Printed *Adae Murimuth Continuatio Chronicarum. Robertus de Avesbury de Gestis mirabilibus Regis Edwardi Tertii*, ed. E. Maunde Thompson (RS 1889), pp. 3–219.

[13] The most recent edition is *Vita Edwardi Secundi*, ed., with an English translation, N. Denholm-Young (Nelson's Medieval Texts 1957). See Tout, *Edward II*, p. 5. There are other chronicles of less importance than those mentioned above, which were written in Edward II's reign or soon after, almost certainly by secular clerks. (1) A brief chronicle, 1295–1322 (BL MS. Cotton Cleopatra D IX, ff. 83–5): it is pious in tone and slightly rhetorical in style, and has little value but shows some first hand knowledge of events in the north; printed G. L. Haskins (ed.), 'A chronicle of the civil wars of Edward II', in *Speculum*, xiv (1939), pp. 73–81. (2) The long version of the *Brut*, in French, 1307–33 (the French text is unpublished but the English translation, made between 1350 and 1380, is printed in *The Brut or the Chronicles of England*, ed. F. W. D. Brie (EETS, cxxxi, cxxxvi, 1906–8, reprinted 1960, 2 vols), i; for

The most important of the later authorities for Edward II's reign is Geoffrey le Baker, a clerk of Swinbrook in Oxfordshire.[14] He did not begin writing his chronicle, which covers the period from 1303 to 1356, until 1341, but, like his friend Adam Murimuth, he used earlier, contemporary material, notably for the battle of Bannockburn and for Edward's persecution and murder. It is questionable how far he is a reliable source. Certainly his dramatic representation of Edward II's end seems to belong to literature rather than historiography.

The monastic chronicles will be discussed first; then the secular ones; and lastly the chronicle of Geoffrey le Baker. (Those chronicles which extend into the reign of Edward III will be considered again below, in relation to that period.)

Historical writing was revived at St Albans after a forty year gap at the instigation of Abbot John de Maryns (1302–8). He commissioned the *Opus Chronicorum (A Chronicle Work)*, a brief chronicle from 1259 (when Matthew Paris stopped) to 1296.[15] It is anonymous, but may well have been by William Rishanger, the author of an account of Edward I's reign.[16] Rishanger also wrote in 1312 (at the age of sixty two) an account of the Baron's War,[17] and was probably the continuator of Paris' *Gesta Abbatum*

---

its value as a source for Edward II's reign see John Taylor, 'The French "Brut" and the reign of Edward II' in *EHR*, lxxii (1957), pp. 423–37) and p. 39 n. 241 below; for its value for Edward III's reign see pp. 73–7 below. (3) The chronicle in middle English by Thomas of Castleford, a Yorkshire cleric, from the earliest times to 1327 (unprinted; described by John Taylor, *Medieval Historical Writing in Yorkshire* (York 1961), pp. 18–19). (4) The so-called 'Pipewell' chronicle, an account of the events of 1327, printed M. V. Clarke, *Representation and Consent* (London 1936), pp. 194–5, from BL MS. Cotton Julius A 1, ff. 56–6ᵛ (the MS. is described by H. G. Richardson and G. O. Sayles, 'Early coronation records' in *BIHR*, xiv (1937), pp. 145–7). (5) The Lichfield chronicle (A.D. 349–1388, commenced 1323), Bodley MS. 956, pp. 164–214. For the value of (4) and (5) and of the *Historia Roffensis* (see p. 3 n. 9 above) as sources for the deposition of Edward II, see Clarke, op. cit, pp. 178–93 passim, and the same author's 'Committees of estates and the deposition of Edward II' in *Historical Essays in Honour of James Tait*, ed. J. G. Edwards, V. H. Galbraith and E. F. Jacob (Manchester 1933), pp. 27–43 passim, and B. Wilkinson, 'The deposition of Richard II and the accession of Henry IV' in *EHR*, liv (1939), pp. 223–8 passim.

[14] Printed *Chronicon Galfridi le Baker de Swynebroke*, ed. E. Maunde Thompson (Oxford 1889). Two other chronicles, the *Scalacronica* of Sir Thomas Gray and John Barbour's *Bruce*, written in the last half of Edward III's reign, used earlier sources for the reign of Edward II and have considerable value for the Anglo-Scottish wars. They are discussed with the other chronicles of Edward III's reign; pp. 80–3, 92–6.

[15] Printed in *JT*, pp. 3–59. The *Opus* (p. 4) begins: 'Incipit Liber Chronicorum, editus ad instantiam venerabilis patris nostri, Domini Johannis, Dei gratia, Abbatis huius Ecclesie.'

[16] The *Gesta Edwardi Primi* is printed in *Willelmi Rishanger . . . Chronica et Annales*, ed. H. T. Riley (RS 1865), pp. 411–24. The authorship of 'frater Willelmus de Rissanger, Chronicator' is stated at the beginning of the *Gesta*. For Rishanger's putative authorship of the *Opus* see *The St. Albans Chronicle 1406–1420*, ed. V. H. Galbraith. (Oxford 1937), p. xxx.

[17] Printed *The Chronicle of William de Rishanger, of the Barons' Wars: The Miracles of Simon de Montfort*, ed. J. O. Halliwell (Camden Soc., original series, xv 1840). The rubric at the beginning of the chronicle (reproduced in facsimile as a frontispiece in ibid.) reads: 'Memorandum quod ego frater Willelmus de Rishanger cronigraphus, die Inventionis Sancte Crucis,

Monasterii Sancti Albani (*Deeds of the Abbots of the Monastery of St Albans*).[18] These works are of interest not because of any intrinsic merit, but because they show the revival of historical writing at St Albans.

The St Albans chronicle covering Edward II's reign is ascribed in the text itself to two monks, John de Trokelowe[19] and Henry de Blaneforde. At the end of the annal for 1322 it has the colophon 'Hucusque scripsit Frater Johannes de Trokelowe' ('To here wrote Brother John de Troke-lowe'), and the annal for 1323 is headed 'Incipiunt Chronica Fratris Henrici de Blaneforde' ('Here begins the chronicle of Brother Henry de Blaneforde'). There is no problem in accepting Blaneforde's authorship of the chronicle from 1323,[20] for his name is included in Thomas Walsingham's list of St Albans chroniclers. Walsingham, writing at St Albans in about 1400, states that Matthew Paris succeeded Wendover, and after Paris 'William Risangre, Henry Blankfrount, Simon Bynham and Richard Savage successively (*successive*) wrote chronicles.'[21] The problematical omission from this list of John de Trokelowe has led to the suggestion that Trokelowe was merely the scribe, while Rishanger himself was the author.[22]

'Trokelowe' is not a well constructed chronicle and was apparently never properly revised. However, it contains some graphic passages with information not to be found in the other chronicles. Like Matthew Paris before him, the author profited from St Albans' prestige, its proximity to London and easy communication with the north (partly because of the abbey's cell at Tynemouth).

'Trokelowe's' political attitude is, predictably, pro-baronial. He bitterly

---

Anno gratie m. ccc. xii., qui est annus regis Edwardi filii regis Edwardi quintus, habui de ordine xlj. annos et in aetate lxij. annos.' Cf. Galbraith, op. cit., pp. xxix n. l, xxxii, xxxiii n. l.

[18] See *Gesta Abbatum Monasterii Sancti Albani*, ed. H. T. Riley RS 1867–8, 3 vols), ii. ix-xix.

[19] 'Trokelowe' is printed in *JT*, pp. 63–127.

[20] Printed in *JT*, pp. 131–52.

[21] *Annales Monasterii S. Albani a Johanne Amundesham*, ed. H. T. Riley (RS 1870–1, 2 vols), ii. 303. For a reference by Thomas Walsingham to 'the chronicles of William Rishanger' for material to be found in 'Trokelowe' see Walsingham's *Hist. Angl.* (for which see p. 125 n. 59 below), i. 165.

[22] See Galbraith, op cit., pp. xxx-xxxi. It should be noted that the *Opus*, Rishanger's account of the Barons' War and his *Gesta Edwardi Primi*, 'Trokelowe' and Blaneforde's chronicle are all in BL MS. Cotton Claudius D VI, a volume of historical pieces from St Albans. The same volume has an account of the trial by Edward I of the Scottish succession case, 1291–2, together with a collection of relevant official documents. The latter are originals and are not identical with those preserved in the Public Record Office. It has been suggested that they were acquired by the abbey from the royal notary, John de Caen, who was responsible for drawing up the official account of the proceedings; see *Edward I and the Throne of Scotland, 1290–1296: an Edition of the Record Sources for the Great Cause*, ed. E. L. G. Stones and G. G. Simpson (Glasgow 1978, 2 vols), i. 61–4. The historical items in Claudius D VI, which illustrate the revival of historical writing at St Albans, suggest the possibility that Rishanger was making drafts and collecting documents for a full-scale continuation of Matthew Paris' *Chronica Majora*, complete with a supplementary book of documents like the *Liber Additamentorum*. See Galbraith, op. cit., pp. xxix-xxxi, and Stones and Simpson, op. cit., pp. 64–5.

attacks Piers Gaveston who made civil discord inevitable by spending the king's treasure and alienating him from the queen, Isabella, and from the barons.[23] When Thomas of Lancaster became the baronial leader ('because a people without a head is like a flock without a shepherd'), 'Trokelowe' expatiates on Thomas's wealth, noble lineage and royal connections and ascribes his motivation in part to pity for the queen, who was his niece.[24] He asserts that Thomas's father-in-law, Henry de Lacy, earl of Lincoln, impressed on the earl that he had a responsibility for the defence of the liberty of the church and people in general, and of the Ordinances in particular.[25] However, though 'Trokelowe' deplores the bad influence of favourites and 'evil counsellors', he does not attack Edward personally. In fact 'Trokelowe' is the most tolerant of the strictly contemporary chroniclers. He remarks that in 1312 Edward's love of his new-born son helped him to forget Gaveston,[26] and comments on his bravery at Bannockburn, where the king fought like a lion to save his men.[27]

'Trokelowe's' tolerance was no doubt partly the result of his personality. He alone of the English chroniclers expressed sympathy for the Scots, whom he describes as fighting valiantly for their wives, children and possessions ('judging death martyrdom, and wounds salvation in such a cause'); and he comments on Robert Bruce's generosity to his soldiers and chivalrous behaviour to the vanquished.[28] But 'Trokelowe' probably liked Edward II because he was on good terms with St Albans. He describes a royal visit in 1314; Edward came with the queen and their son, commended himself to the monks' prayers, and when he heard that his father had intended to repair the choir gave the convent 100 marks of silver and also some timber.[29]

St Albans was a centre of affairs. One of the most interesting passages in 'Trokelowe' is the account of the negotiations with the barons, in January 1313, of the papal envoys, Arnaud Novelli, cardinal by the title of St Prisca, and Arnaud d'Aux, cardinal-bishop of Albano, who were staying at St Albans, for the return of Gaveston's horses and jewels.[30] The envoys wrote to the barons who replied that 'they had no knowledge of letters but were learned in war and in the use of arms', and refused to allow any foreigner to interfere in matters of state. The envoys were so scared that they returned to London, despite their previous intention of remaining at St

[23] *JT*, p. 68.
[24] *JT*, pp. 69–70, 75–6.
[25] *JT*, pp. 72–3.
[26] *JT*, pp. 79–80.
[27] *JT*, p. 86; cited by Tout, *Edward II*, p. 10.
[28] *JT*, pp. 84, 87.
[29] *JT*, p. 83.
[30] *JT*, pp. 77–9; cited in *Edward II, the Lords Ordainers and Piers Gaveston's Jewels and Horses (1312–1313)*, ed. R. A. Roberts (Camden Miscellany, xv, 1929), p. vii, where the report of the proceedings of the commission held by the two nuncios, 1312–13, and related documents are printed. For the proposed delivery of the jewels at St Albans see ibid., pp. 3, 13.

Albans for a month at least. 'Trokelowe's' account of the barons' failure to hand over the horses and jewels to the king's representatives at St Albans is confirmed by the report of the proceedings which the envoys sent to Pope Clement. 'Trokelowe' states that the royal officials, to protect themselves from the charge of negligence, committed the affair to writing. The document 'sealed by a public notary was read on two days in the church of St Albans before the prior and senior monks and all the people summoned there', and for greater security it was sealed with the convent's seal.[31]

Another passage derived from first hand knowledge of local affairs is the description of the famine which decimated the population of England (together with the rest of Europe) in 1315, 1316 and 1317. Edward on one of his visits to St Albans could scarcely find enough bread for his household. And everywhere magnates and monasteries had to reduce the number of their servants—those dismissed were forced to beg and steal. Lawlessness was endemic and people died of starvation. The bread available could not satisfy hunger because the grain had had no sun and was so badly soaked by the rain that it had to be dried before cooking. Dead bodies were so numerous that they could not be buried, and dysentery spread. There were even rumours of cannibalism.[32]

'Trokelowe' has some detailed information about London, for example an anecdote concerning the manner in which a letter was delivered to the king in 1317, when he was dining in Westminster Hall. The purpose of the letter was to remind the king of his duty to the nobles.[33] A woman, dressed like a stage-player, entered the hall mounted on a fine horse, suitably caparisoned; she circled the high table, as if acting, rode up the steps of the dais, placed the letter in front of the king, and, having greeted the company, rode out of the hall again. 'Trokelowe's' continuator, Henry de Blaneforde, gives the most detailed account of the escape of Roger Mortimer from the Tower of London in 1323, 'just as the blessed Peter escaped from the chains of Nero, led by an angel'.[34] Mortimer escaped through a hole in the wall of the palace kitchen, and over the roof to one of the castle wards. Then, by means of a cleverly made rope ladder previously supplied by a friend, he came to another ward, eventually reaching the Thames, where a light skiff awaited him. He crossed the Thames and made his way by land to a port, whence he embarked for France.

'Trokelowe's' knowledge of events in the north of England is well illustrated by the vivid account of the capture in 1317 of the brigand

---

[31] The sealing of the document with the convent's seal and its public reading is confirmed by ibid., p. 5.

[32] *JT*, pp. 92–6; cited by H. S. Lucas, 'The great European famine of 1315, 1316, and 1317' in *Speculum*, v (1930), pp. 351–7 and nn. passim.

[33] *JT*, pp. 98–9.

[34] *JT*, pp. 145–6. According to the long version of the *Brut* (see p. 3 n. 13 above), Mortimer drugged his guards; *Brut*, i. 231.

Gilbert of Middleton.[35] This knight and his comrades (who were called 'salvaldores') not only ravaged the property and neighbourhood of Tynemouth priory, but also seized and robbed two papal legates on their way to Scotland to negotiate a peace treaty between England and Scotland, and the bishop of Durham. In addition he imprisoned and held to ransom local gentry in his castle at Milford on the Wansbeck. The exasperated local barons approached Gilbert while his men were out plundering, as if to pay the ransoms, but instead they seized him.

The continuation of Trevet which was written in the west country, probably in a Dominican friary, resembles 'Trokelowe' in some respects. It too has little merit as a piece of historical writing, but contains a few graphic and informative passages. Its Dominican authorship is suggested by an anecdote under the year 1308 concerning a Dominican friar at the papal curia.[36] Its west country provenance (there were Dominican friaries at Salisbury, Wilton and Ilchester) is proved by a number of entries. For example there is a vivid description of a thunderstorm at Milton Abbas in Dorset on 2 September 1309, when the convent was at matins: lightning burnt and destroyed the belfry and bells, the church ornaments and the monks' books and archives.[37] The wind blew down innumerable trees and the church towers at Mudford and Yeovilton, both in Somerset, near Ilchester. And the chronicle records that on 17 January 1310 there was such a downpour of rain at Salisbury that the water in the cathedral washed the feet of the statues of kings by the west door of the choir, and no mass could be said there for days.

Of more general interest is the Dominican chronicler's unique account of the abduction of Alice, countess of Lancaster, from Canford in Dorset in 1317.[38] She was seized by Sir Richard of St Martin, a retainer of the earl of Surrey, who claimed he had married her before she married Thomas of Lancaster, which she admitted. The author describes how the band escorting the countess fled in terror between Alton and Farnham, leaving her unprotected, because they mistook a procession of priests for Thomas of Lancaster's men, but on realizing their mistake they returned to the countess. The chronicler, an ardent supporter of Thomas of Lancaster, laments the countess's adultery and consequent perdition.

The Dominican's sources of information reached beyond his own locality, even to Scotland. He is the sole authority for the capture at Bannockburn

---

[35] *JT*, pp. 99–101. Cf. May McKisack, *The Fourteenth Century* (Oxford 1959), pp. 40–1, 204.

[36] *Cont. NT*, p. 6. Another passage makes it unlikely that the author belonged to a property-owning order ('monachi nigri et canonici aliique religiosi possessiones amplas possidentes . . .'; ibid., p. 19.

[37] *Cont. NT*, p. 7. For further references relating to the fire at Milton Abbas see *VCH, Dorset*, ii. 59 n. 20.

[38] *Cont. NT*, pp. 20–2. This passage is cited in *G.E.C., Peerage*, vii, 392, from Thomas Walsingham's copy of it in *Hist. Angl.* (for which see p. 125 n. 59 below), i. 148.

of Roger de Northburgh, keeper of the king's privy seal, together with two of his clerks and the privy seal itself.[39] And he records that the privy seal was brought back to the king by Roger Mortimer, who was also captured in the battle, when he was released by the Scots.[40] The chronicler had some interest in and knowledge of the king's seals; he connects the loss of the privy seal at Bannockburn with Edward's adoption of another seal, the secret seal; he asserts that the new seal was to replace the lost one. Here the writer was inaccurate because the secret seal was in use before Bannockburn. However, even his limited knowledge of the king's seals shows that he must have had an informant close to the court, a man such as Robert Fitzpayne, steward of the royal household (1308–10) and keeper of the forests south of the Trent (1311–12), whose death and burial at Sherborne the chronicler notes under 1315.[41] The chronicler's interest in and knowledge of the Scottish war may well have been promoted by the fact that Robert Bruce's second wife, Elizabeth de Burgh, was imprisoned successively at Sherborne, Shaftesbury and Barking—for nearly six years according to the chronicler. (She was in English hands for eight years altogether, from 1306 to 1314.)[42]

Unlike the two chronicles just considered, which are of southern provenance, the two north country chronicles, the annals of the Augustinian canons of Bridlington and the continuation of the chronicle by the Franciscan, Richard of Durham, both survive only in later works. Nevertheless both have contemporary material for Edward II's reign. This material shows the writers' deep concern, almost obsession, with the Anglo-Scottish war, about which they provide unique information.

The tradition of historical writing was already well established in Bridlington priory. Besides having been the home of the chronicler Peter of Langtoft, it probably produced annals, which are now lost, in the late thirteenth and early fourteenth centuries.[43] The extant Bridlington chronicle covering the years from 1307 to 1339 (with short additional annals for some of the years between 1340 and 1377), was in its earliest form written fairly contemporarily with the events it records, but it survives only in a version composed late in Edward III's reign. It is not always clear which passages belonged to the original chronicle and which to the later rewrite. Obviously the verse prophecies of 'John of Bridlington' belong to the latter,[44] and it is likely that the passages exclaiming on the wickedness of the times are also insertions. On the other hand the sections of objective, often vivid, narrative read like contemporary reportage.

---

[39] *Cont. NT*, p. 15. For the value of this entry see Tout, *Edward II*, pp. 92 and n.1, 155 and n. 1.
[40] *Cont. NT*, p. 16.
[41] *Cont. NT*, p. 17. Cf. Tout, *Edward II*, pp. 315, 321.
[42] *Cont. NT*, p. 16. Cf. G. W. S. Barrow, *Robert Bruce* (London 1965), pp. 230, 330, 411.
[43] See *Guisborough*, p. xxvi.
[44] For the 'Bridlington' prophecies see p. 59 and n. 4 below, and *Chrons Edw. I and II*, ii. xxv-xxvii. For the later rewrite of the Bridlington chronicle see pp. 113–15 below.

The original, contemporary Bridlington chronicle was apparently pro-baronial in tone. It criticized the king for neglecting the advice of his magnates and following evil counsel, and refers to the sanctions of the king's coronation oath and the common consent of the people.[45] However, the author's pro-baronial views were modified by the Scottish war, because the English needed strong leadership against the Scots, and because some barons negotiated with the Scots: the author bitterly criticizes Andrew Harcla for failing to help Edward in his disastrous campaign in 1322, and for his proposed treaty with the Scots.[46]

The author of the Bridlington chronicle, writing in Edward II's reign and early in Edward III's, apparently used at least one literary source, a Life of Anthony Bek, bishop of Durham, which may previously have been used by Langtoft and Guisborough.[47] He probably borrowed from this work his full account of how Bek mediated between Edward I and the barons in 1297, which he inserted as a flashback after the obituary of Bek under the year 1311.[48] The author also used the archives of his house. He cites some documents *verbatim* but often refers the reader to the *Incidentia Chronicorum* (*A Supplement to Chronicles*) which must have been a register of documents similar to Matthew Paris' *Liber Additamentorum* (*Book of Additions*); it contained, for example, copies of public records such as the text of the Ordinances, besides papal bulls and other ecclesiastical documents.[49] But the author obtained much of his information from hearsay and from his own observation.

Some of the passages in the Bridlington chronicle which were composed more or less contemporaneously with events contain information not recorded in any other known source, and a few are written in vivid narrative prose suggesting the author's personal concern. Some of the unique information relates to the south, for example the statement that Piers Gaveston was tried at Warwick before William Inge and Henry Spigurnell, justices of gaol delivery, and convicted as a traitor.[50] But most of the facts not otherwise known relate to the north. Thus under 1317 the chronicle records that the king remonstrated with Thomas of Lancaster for holding private assemblies of magnates and for employing an unusual and excessive number of armed retainers ('whence the people were considerably frightened'),

---

[45] See *Bridl.* pp. 32–3, 34, 39–40, 42.

[46] *Bridl.* pp. 76, 81–3.

[47] For references to passages in Guisborough and Peter of Langtoft giving details about Anthony Bek's career see Gransden, *Historical Writing*, i. 480, 483.

[48] *Chrons Edw. I and II*, ii. xxviii; *Bridl.* pp. 38–9. Cf. *The Chronicle of Pierre de Langtoft*, ed. Thomas Wright (RS 1866–8, 2 vols), ii. 290, 292.

[49] *Chrons Edw. I and II*, ii. xxiv and n. 3, and, e.g., *Bridl.* pp. 40, 53, 78. For a notice of the *Incidentia Chronicorum* see V. H. Galbraith, *Historical Research in Medieval England* (London 1951), p. 32 n. 1.

[50] *Bridl.* pp. 43–4. The Bridlington chronicle has some value as a source for Edward II's deposition; see Wilkinson, 'The deposition of Richard II', p. 228.

and gives Lancaster's reply.[51] The chronicler adds details to his picture of north country society, dominated by powerful nobles—especially Thomas of Lancaster—under 1321. He records that Lancaster held an assembly at Pontefract where the magnates agreed, for themselves and their retainers, on mutual defence, the punishment of aggressors and the maintenance of peace. The chronicler follows this with the most detailed account known of Lancaster's 'parliament' at Sherburn in Elmet, including the text of the grievances read at the beginning of the proceedings and the clergy's reply to them.[52]

The Bridlington chronicle's most graphic passages describe the warlike condition of the north and the terror spread by the Scottish raiders. It has the best account of the defeat of the English, led by William Melton, archbishop of York, at Myton-on-Swale (near Boroughbridge in York-shire) in 1319. The Scots killed the mayor of York and many others, and took numerous prisoners, 'but the archbishop himself and the prelates with him (the bishop of Ely, the dean of York and the abbots of St Mary's, York, and of Selby) escaped. Moreover, the Scots failed to take the arch-bishop's banner, 'the staff of which was of silver and bore a gilded crucifix with the image of our Lord Jesus Christ.' The chronicler describes how it was saved :[53]

> [The cross-bearer] spurred his horse into the river and swam to the other side ; there, clinging to some willows he let his horse go and hid the archbishop's cross in an overgrown hollow, himself escap-ing in the dusk of evening. Not far from the place where the cross was concealed lived a certain poor man; he came that way after the clerk had gone, took the cross and hid it in bales of hay in his cottage, until afterwards it was looked for and restored to the archbishop.

In 1322, after a two years' truce, the Scots again delivered a savage attack into the heart of Yorkshire. And again the Bridlington chronicle gives details. It describes how Edward narrowly escaped capture near Byland and fled to Bridlington priory, where no doubt some of his company told the chronicler about the English defeat. Edward stayed one night, leaving next morning for Burstwick, conducted by the prior, Robert of Scarborough. 'What worse fate', the chronicle asks, 'could befall the English than to behold their king fleeing from place to place in his own realm in the face of the Scots?'[54]

---

[51] *Bridl.* pp. 50–2. This text is a Latin summary. The original French text is given by Adam Murimuth (*AM*, pp. 271–6). See J. R. Maddicott, *Thomas of Lancaster 1307–1322* (Oxford 1970), p. 192.

[52] *Bridl.* pp. 61–5. For the importance of this passage see *Chrons Edw. I and II*, ii. lxxxvii–xc, Tout, *Edward II*, p. 143, and Maddicott, op. cit., pp. 269–70.

[53] *Bridl.* p. 58. See Barrow, *Robert Bruce*, p. 342.

[54] *Bridl.* p. 79. See Barrow, op. cit., pp. 345–6.

The chronicler describes the panic in the priory caused by the Scottish onslaught. Fearing attack, the prior and all the convent except for eight canons left for the priory's church at Goxhill in Lincolnshire, taking with them the priory muniments and treasures packed in bags and loaded on carts. They stayed away for two weeks. Apparently the chronicler was one of the canons who stayed behind, for he notes that meanwhile Robert Bruce reached Malton, looting, burning and capturing men and animals. The canons still at Bridlington were so frightened that they sent one of their number, Robert de Baystone ('because his parents were with the Scots') to the Bruce at Malton to negotiate, so that the priory and its manors would not be burnt. Robert de Baystone returned with nine Scots, who took away bread, wine and ale loaded on to eighteen horses which they had brought with them. The canons feared that they would be excommunicated for making contact with the Scots (who were under sentence of excommunication); for the record, the chronicler gives a copy of a letter from the archbishop of York to the prior empowering him to deal with the canons concerned.[55]

The continuation of the chronicle of Richard of Durham[56] presents a problem similar to that posed by the Bridlington chronicle: it is not clear exactly what the text, now only preserved in the Lanercost chronicle, originally comprised. The continuation of Richard of Durham probably extended to 1346.[57] Into it the Lanercost writer inserted passages about his own priory, verses, pious reflections, embellishments in flowery prose (notably to describe the battle at Neville's Cross), and numerous documents.[58]

The continuation of Richard of Durham's chronicle was probably written in the Franciscan friary at Carlisle. This is suggested by the many references to Carlisle,[59] combined with its undoubted Franciscan provenance. Its author may well have been Thomas of Otterbourne, who some time before 1350 became lector of the Franciscans at Oxford. This is suggested by the fact that Sir Thomas Gray refers in the *Scalacronica* to Otterbourne as a famous Franciscan chronicler.[60] Whoever the author,

---

[55] *Bridl.* pp. 80–1. Unlike the 'Lanercost' chronicle, the Bridlington chronicle deals harshly with Andrew Harcla's attempted treaty with the Scots; see p. 10 and n. 46 above.

[56] For the chronicle of Richard of Durham, probably a friar of Haddington in East Lothian, see Gransden, *Historical Writing*, i. 494–501.

[57] See A. G. Little, 'The authorship of the Lanercost chronicle' in the same author's *Franciscan Papers, Lists and Documents* (Manchester 1943), p. 45, and V. H. Galbraith, *The Anonimalle Chronicle* (Manchester 1927), pp. xxiv-xxx. Cf. p. 116 n. 98 below.

[58] The conclusion that the documents and letters were inserted by the Lanercost writer is drawn from the fact that the Anonimalle chronicle, which is based from 1334 to 1346 on a now lost copy of the Franciscan chronicle, does not have them; see Galbraith, op. cit. pp. xxvi-xxvii.

[59] See *Lan.* pp. v-vi. For further evidence connecting the now lost Franciscan chronicle with Carlisle see Galbraith, op. cit., pp. xxix-xxx. See also pp. 15–17 below.

[60] The prologue to the *Scalacronica* has this passage: ' " . . . Et si est", fesoit Sebille, "le Cordeler

he was well informed, mainly about north country affairs but also about events in the south. He obtained his information from his own observation; by word of mouth, from documents and probably from newsletters. His outlook is typically Franciscan. He is interested in the history of his own order[61] and has sympathy for ordinary country people:[62] this sympathy sometimes conflicted with his pro-baronial sentiments, for the peasantry suffered from the depredations of Scots, king and barons alike.[63] He had little respect for Edward. He accuses him of improper familiarity with Gaveston,[64] and of being unwise[65] and unwarlike.[66] He gives an unflattering and fairly convincing character sketch of him:[67]

> From his youth he devoted himself in private to the art of rowing and driving carts, of digging ditches and thatching houses, as was commonly said, and also with his companions at night to various works of ingenuity and skill, and other pointless and trivial occupations unsuitable for the son of a king.

The Franciscan chronicler's sympathy for the barons appears, for example, in his indignation at Gaveston for calling the earl of Warwick ('a man of wisdom and integrity') the 'Black Dog of Arden' (to which Warwick replied, 'if he calls me a dog, be sure I'll bite him as soon as I get a chance').[68] The chronicler deplored the execution of Thomas of Lancaster without the advice of parliament, and notes that Pontefract became a place of pilgrimage because of the miracles reputedly worked at the earl's tomb.[69]

The author's knowledge of events reached south of the Trent. A newsletter or verbal information (or both) from a London Franciscan may

---

qe vous veistes suppuoillaunt leschel Thomas de Otreburn, vn mestre de diuinite et del ordre de Frers Menours, qi dez cronicles de cest isle se entremist, qe si tu pusses en cas ateindre toutes houres a les propretes de ditz bastouns du dist eschel, si cerchez lez cronicles du dist Thomas, qe bien moustrerount ta droit voy"'; *Scala*. pp. 3–4. Cf. pp. 94–5 below. For Thomas of Otterbourne's claim to authorship see Little, op. cit., p. 51. (The Franciscan Thomas of Otterbourne was not the author of the chronicle to 1420 printed by Thomas Hearne under the same name; see p. 196 and n. 18 below.)

[61] For entries relating to the Franciscan order see e.g. *Lan*. pp. 235, 245–6, 251–2, 264.

[62] The Lanercost chronicle notices, s.a. 1306, that the English executed 'simplices laici et rurales', and approves of Andrew Harcla's treaty with the Scots partly because it would save the country folk from the Scots' raids; *Lan*. pp. 204, 248, 249.

[63] The chronicle records that the Marchers ravaged the countryside like the Scots; *Lan*. p.217.

[64] *Lan*. p. 210.

[65] *Lan*. p. 215.

[66] *Lan*. p. 248.

[67] *Lan*. p. 236.

[68] *Lan*. p. 216. Cf. *RR*, p. 152, and p. 35 and n. 216 below. The long version of the French *Brut* gives more examples of the nicknames Gaveston gave the nobles; *Brut*, i. 206–7.

[69] *Lan*. pp. 244–5.

well have supplied the details of Edward II's deposition.[70] The chronicler's account does not entirely tally with Baker's (for example he says that the bishop of Winchester, not the bishop of Hereford, preached at Oxford on the text 'My head, my head'—the bishop of Hereford, according to him, preached on the text 'A foolish king shall ruin his people').[71] He states that at the queen's request no Franciscans were among those appointed to tell the king of his deposition, 'lest they should be the bearers of such bad news, because she loved the Minorites very much'.

The continuation of Richard of Durham's chronicle, like the chronicle of Bridlington, is primarily valuable for north country history. It confirms and adds further details to the depressing picture of conditions in the north given by the Bridlington annalist. It shows how widespread was the practice of towns and districts paying ransom money to the Scots in exchange for immunity from attack. In 1312 the citizens of Durham, despairing of royal protection, offered £2,000, but the Scots also insisted on a right of way through the bishopric.[72] In 1314 Coupland paid ransom, and in 1322 Furness abbey and Richmond followed suit.[73] Failure to pay meant devastation with fire and sword, as happened in Cumberland in 1314.[74]

The Franciscan chronicler had an especial interest in and knowledge of military history.[75] He gives an account of the battle of Myton-on-Swale which although not as detailed as the Bridlington chronicler's, is of some interest. He describes how the Scots met the inexperienced English forces which included many clergy and friars; the Scots formed themselves into a 'scheltron' (a closely packed body of men), and then letting out a loud shout, pursued the fleeing English on horseback with great slaughter ('if night had not come, hardly a single Englishman would have escaped').[76] The chronicler also has a full account, on the information of an eyewitness, of the battle of Bannockburn.[77] And he is particularly interested in sieges. He describes how the Scots took Edinburgh castle in 1314; one force attacked the south gate, causing the defenders to concentrate there, while the rest climbed the face of the rock on the north side and scaled the wall with rope ladders.[78] In his account of the siege of Berwick by Robert Bruce in

---

[70] *Lan.* pp. 257–8. For the importance of this account of Edward II's deposition see Clarke, *Representation and Consent*, pp. 183–8 passim, and Wilkinson, 'The deposition of Richard II', pp. 224–8 passim.

[71] 2 Kings iv. 19, and Ecclesiastes x. 3, respectively. See p. 40 and n. 246 below.

[72] *Lan.* p. 220. For these ransoms, and other examples, see Barrow, *Robert Bruce*, p. 282.

[73] *Lan.* pp. 229, 246, 242, respectively.

[74] *Lan.* p. 224.

[75] For the author's account of campaigns in Edward III's reign see pp. 115–17 below. It is possible that the author had been a knight before becoming a Franciscan friar. The chronicle mentions an example of such a man; *Lan.* p. 282.

[76] *Lan.* p. 239.

[77] *Lan.* pp. 225–8. For the value of this account see J. E. Morris, *Bannockburn* (Cambridge 1914), pp. 52–3, 57, 68, 71, 78–80, 88.

[78] *Lan..* p. 223. See Barrow, *Robert Bruce*, p. 278.

1312, the chronicler describes such rope ladders from his own observation:[79]

> The ladders, which they placed against the wall, were very ingenious, as I myself, who am writing this, saw with my own eyes. For the Scots made two long, strong ropes the height of the wall and knotted one end of both ropes. Then they made a wooden board, about two and a half feet long and half a foot wide, strong enough to carry a man, and at each end made a hole through which each rope could pass. Having passed the ropes through up to the knots, they made two more knots one and a half feet above, placing above them another similar board, and so on to the other end of the ropes. They also made an iron hook: one curved arm measured at least one foot and was intended to lie on top of the wall; the other arm, of the same length, hung down towards the ground, having at its end a round hole, through which a lance could be inserted, and two rings on each side on to which the ropes could be tied. When all this was ready, they took a strong spear as long as the wall was high and put its end into the iron hole, and two men lifted the ropes and boards with the spear and placed the iron hook (which was not round) on the wall; thus they could walk up the wooden steps just as if they were an ordinary ladder, and the heavier the climber the more firmly the iron hook lay on the wall. To prevent the ropes hanging too close to the wall and hinder the ascent, they made sort of discs at every third rung which held the ropes away from the walls.

Unfortunately for Berwick's assailants, a barking dog alerted the town and the Scots fled—leaving the ladders which the English derisively hung on a pillory.

Some of the author's most vivid descriptions relate to Carlisle. For example he gives a full account of the siege of Carlisle by the Scots in 1315. He describes the various types of siege engine and stratagem used unsuccessfully by the Scots who invested the city for ten days. They daily, and sometimes three times a day, attacked the three city gates, but were driven back by the rain of darts, arrows and stones. They tried the same stratagem as they had used at Edinburgh, attacking one gate as a diversion while men scaled the wall on the other side of the city; but despite covering shots from their archers, the defenders flung them and their ladders to the ground. The Scots set up a machine for throwing stones continually against the west gate, but killed only one man while the city replied with seven or eight stone throwers, besides 'springalds for discharging darts, and staves with sockets for casting stones'. The Scots tried to use a 'belfry' (a movable siege tower), but the city carpenters built an even higher wooden

---

[79] *Lan.* pp. 220–1.

tower on top of one of the wall towers from which the besieged could combat it—and in the event the belfry became stuck in the mud before reaching the wall. The Scots' attempts to scale the walls with ladders and sap the foundations under cover of a 'sow' (a movable structure with a strong roof used to protect sappers and miners during a siege), were frustrated, while the faggots made to fill the moat were too few, and the bridges on wheels which they constructed sank to the bottom. Eventually, on the eleventh day, at the approach of an army to relieve the besieged, the Scots 'marched off in confusion, leaving behind all their engines of war'.[80]

Perhaps the passage in the Franciscan chronicle which best reveals the author's humanity is the detailed account of the treachery and punishment of Andrew Harcla, earl of Carlisle, in 1322.[81] The main reason for the chronicler's knowledge of and interest in the affair was no doubt that Harcla made his last confession before his execution to the warden of the Franciscan friary at Carlisle, 'repeatedly, and concerning his whole life'; he had previously confessed to a parish priest, to a Dominican friar and to another Franciscan, 'and all justified him and acquitted him of the intention and taint of treason.' It is not, therefore, surprising that the chronicler treats Harcla with sympathy. He asserts that Harcla negotiated the treaty with the Scots because he saw that Edward was 'able neither to rule his realm nor to defend it against the Scots'. And so to prevent Edward losing his entire kingdom and to save the people suffering from capture, arson and plunder, Harcla decided that each king should recognize the rights of the other in his own country. The chronicler gives the terms of the treaty, pointing out that Harcla was acting without the consent of the king and parliament. He gives a graphic account of Harcla's consequent arrest; Sir Anthony de Lucy entered Carlisle castle with a select force as if on business, when he knew that Harcla's men were out, and arrested Harcla, who 'was sitting in the great hall dictating letters.' Harcla was tried at Carlisle and condemned to be drawn by horses from the castle to the gallows, and there hanged and beheaded. The chronicler gives an edifying description of his end:[82]

> With a steadfast face and, as it seemed to bystanders, with a brave spirit, he went to bear these sufferings; while being drawn through the city he had his hands clasped and raised and his eyes firmly fixed on heaven. At the gallows, his body unblemished, his spirit bold and his words brave, he explained why he had made an

---

[80] *Lan.* pp. 230–2. See Barrow, op. cit., p. 338.

[81] *Lan.* pp. 248–51. Professor Barrow also takes a lenient view of Harcla's treachery; Barrow, op. cit., p. 351.

[82] *Lan.* p. 251.

agreement with the Scots, and thus proceeded to undergo the aforesaid sentence.

The works so far discussed all conform more or less to the normal type of monastic chronicle. They comprise annals written up fairly close to the events they record. The authors' approach to politics tended to be factual and pragmatic, and despite an anti-royalist bias, they readily altered their opinions if circumstances demanded. The case with Robert of Reading, monk of Westminster, is different.[83] Although Robert arranged his material in chronological order, he treated it in literary fashion, writing rhetorical, florid (sometimes obscure) prose, to produce a flowing narrative with a strongly homiletic tone. Furthermore, he alone of the chroniclers criticizes Edward II with unremitting virulence. On the other hand he consistently supports Queen Isabella and Roger Mortimer. The thesis of the chronicle was apparently to prove that Edward II was unfit to rule, and, therefore, that the coup by Isabella and Mortimer was justified. The chronicle ends with an account of Edward II's 'voluntary' abdication. The king says: 'I greatly lament that I have so utterly failed my people, but I could not be other than I am; I am pleased that my son who has been thus accepted by all the people should succeed me on the throne.' And so 'the whole community of the realm gathered at Westminster, loudly praising God, immediately received the young Edward as king.'[84]

This evidence suggests that Robert of Reading wrote soon after the deposition, perhaps at the time of Edward III's coronation on 1 February

---

[83] For a writ of 1305 from Walter of Wenlock, abbot of Westminster, to his receivers to pay Brother Robert of Reading certain sums see *Documents Illustrating the Rule of Walter de Wenlok Abbot of Westminster, 1283–1307*, ed. B. F. Harvey (Camden Soc., fourth series, ii, 1965), pp. 95–6. For other references to Robert of Reading in the Westminster archives see T. F. Tout, 'The Westminster Chronicle attributed to Robert of Reading' in *EHR*, xxxi (1916) pp. 450–2 (the article is reprinted in *The Collected Papers of T. F. Tout* (Manchester 1932–4, 3 vols), ii. 289–304)., One of these references raises a problem, for it indicates that Robert of Reading was dead by 1317 (ibid., p. 452). Although Tout admits the possibility that there were two monks called Robert of Reading at Westminster, he challenges the attribution to him of the *Flores* from 1306 to 1326. His doubts about Robert's authorship are increased because the ascription of the work to him in the *Flores* s.a. 1326 is in a hand of the last half of the fourteenth century in the earliest copy (the Chetham MS.). Tout postulates that the *Flores* from 1299 to 1326 was by one author but not Robert of Reading (ibid., pp. 450–61 passim). However, although Tout raises some interesting questions, I am not convinced by his arguments and prefer the traditional attribution of the *Flores* from 1306 to 1326 to Robert of Reading. The fact that the *Flores* from 1299 to 1326 has stylistic similarities (which are also shared by the so-called Merton *Flores* and John Bever's *Lamentation* on the death of Edward I) surely proves only that this historiographical mode was current at Westminster. Nevertheless, the *possibility* must be borne in mind that one man (perhaps John Bever) did write the Westminster *Flores* from 1299 to 1326—and even the 'Merton' *Flores*. These matters are discussed in more detail in A. Gransden, 'The continuations of the *Flores Historiarum* from 1265 to 1327' in *Mediaeval Studies*, xxvi (Toronto 1974), pp. 472–80.

[84] *RR*, p. 235. For this passage see Gransden, op. cit., pp. 484–5, 488–9, and p. 18 n. 87 below.

1327, and before the fall of Isabella and Mortimer in October 1330. This raises the question whether Robert may not have written at the express request or command of Isabella and Mortimer (to whom the later chroniclers, such as Adam Murimuth and Geoffrey le Baker, are bitterly hostile), to provide an historical *pièce justificative* for the new régime. If this hypothesis is correct, and if, as I have suggested elsewhere, the so-called Merton *Flores Historiarum* was written at Westminster on the occasion of Edward II's coronation,[85] we have what is virtually an official history of the English kings from the reign of Henry III to the accession of Edward III.

There are possible objections to the view that Robert of Reading wrote soon after Edward II's deposition. In the annal for 1325 the chronicle states that 'Robert of Reading, formerly monk of St Peter's, Westminster, ended both his life and his chronicle.'[86] The last few pages were added, in the same style as the previous section, by a continuator (who borrowed from the chronicle of Adam Murimuth). Nevertheless, this passage is not an insuperable objection; it could merely signify the point at which Robert's death halted his work, not the date when he died. And possibly he left drafts for the concluding section.[87]

Another possible objection to the hypothesis that Robert's chronicle was a *pièce justificative* for Isabella and Mortimer is the fact that the Westminster monks had their own domestic reasons for hostility to Edward II which, it could be argued, might adequately explain Robert's venom. Thus Robert records that in 1320 Edward occupied, 'not without sacrilege', a cottage within the precincts 'called Borgoyne, preferring to have the title "of Borgoyne" rather than the titles used by his glorious predecessors'.[88] And Robert objected to the removal in 1319 of the royal exchequer and King's Bench from Westminster palace to York.[89] But these events hardly

---

[85] Gransden, op. cit., pp. 485–9, and the same author's *Historical Writing*, i. 459.

[86] 'Sicque frater Robertus de Redinge, quondam monachus ecclesiae beati Petri Apostoli Westmonasterii cronicarum, vitae quoque suae, finem conclusit'; *RR*, p. 232, and see Gransden, 'The continuations of the *Flores Historiarum* from 1265 to 1327', pp. 475–6.

[87] It may be suggested very tentatively that though the continuator, writing over ten years later, used Murimuth's chronicle, Murimuth himself may have used Westminster sources for this part of his work, at least for the account of Edward II's deposition (cited above). The fact that the deposition account in Murimuth so exactly corresponds with the theme of Robert of Reading's chronicle suggests the possibility that the postulated Westminster exemplar included a draft ending for Robert's chronicle. For Murimuth's use of Westminster material for the earlier part of his chronicle see p. 30 and n. 165 below.

[88] *RR*, p. 193. Miss Barbara Harvey, to whom I am indebted for the information in this note, believes that 'Borgoyne' was not only a cottage, but also a large garden. Miss Harvey also informs me that the Westminster monks had another local cause to complain of Edward II. When Edward restored the abbey's temporalities after the vacancy of 1315–16, he retained the manor of Eye, which he kept until his death. The manor extended roughly over the present day Pimlico and Mayfair and included the abbot's chief residence outside the abbey itself. Edward's retention of Eye from 1316 onwards is indicated by a gap in the accounts for the manor; they resume in 1327. See also *CCR, 1327–1330*, p. 4.

[89] *RR*, p. 191.

seem sufficient to account for the wholesale condemnation of Edward II's character and acts.

Robert of Reading's homiletic prose, replete with biblical citations and moral reflections, closely resembles that of the 'Merton' *Flores*, whose author, probably also a monk of Westminster, Robert surely knew.[90] Some of Robert's rhetoric has close parallels in the 'Merton' *Flores*. For example his lamentation on the sad state of England after the battle of Boroughbridge is reminiscent of that in the 'Merton' *Flores* on England's plight during the Barons' War. Robert writes:[91]

> Alas, the heirs of the nobles are afflicted with many griefs from unaccustomed and long imprisonment! Noble women grieve the loss of husbands and sons, children weep for the loss of parents, and citizens for the desolation of towns; the church bewails its own and the kingdom's sudden confusion which encompasses the community on every side; the free and the unfree, the rich and the poor, each has a fresh grief, and whoever seems to show a cheerful face, weeps inwardly, wetting his cheeks with secret tears. Thus the whole realm is involved in trouble; *the whole [earth] mourneth and languisheth*, and all the kingdom of England *is ashamed and hewn down* [Isaiah xxxiii. 9].

The parallel passage in the 'Merton' *Flores*[92] states that the Provisions of Oxford caused

> the division and desolation of the kingdom, contention and discord, looting and arson, the rape of churches, the persecution of the clergy, the besieging of castles, the tribulations of cities, the disinheritance of nobles, the groans of the poor, the extortion of ordinary folk, the ransoming of captives, the death of the old, the suffering of orphans, the violation and sighs of virgins, the tears and laments of widows, war and sedition, and every sort of damage and grief.

Robert of Reading expends some of his most eloquent rhetoric on Edward II's malefactions. Edward, 'paralysed by sloth, won disgrace not fame', losing the honour and prestige won by his famous ancestors whose noble deeds were extolled throughout the world. He was a coward in battle, fleeing with excessive terror from the Scots in 1322, 'spurring on his horse, trembling and defenceless'.[93] He habitually broke his word, 'forgetting

---

[90] See Gransden, 'The continuations of the *Flores Historiarum* from 1265 to 1327; pp. 476–8, and the same author's *Historical Writing*, i. 460.
[91] *RR*, p. 213.
[92] *FH*, iii. 248.
[93] *RR*, pp. 192–3, 210.

[19]

in the morning what he had promised in the evening'.[94] Robert accuses Edward of insatiable avarice, asserting that in 1323, by judicial exactions, he reduced many counties to penury ('so that they could hardly, if at all, recover their previous prosperity') ;[95] and, again, he *stretched forth his hands to vex* not *certain of the church* [Acts xii. 1] but every single prelate with his wicked ferocity.'[96] Robert also accuses Edward of stupidity and tyranny.[97]

Robert alleges that Edward planned to humble, even to exterminate, the aristocracy. Under 1321 Robert writes: 'In his insane fury he hated all the magnates with such wicked hatred that he plotted to overthrow, once and for all and without distinction, the great men of the realm together with the whole English aristocracy.'[98] Robert illustrates Edward's cruelty to the nobility with an account of the imprisonment of the Mortimers, father and son. He describes the escape of Roger Mortimer in words partly borrowed from the biblical account of St Peter's escape from Herod's prison (Acts xii. 4, 6–11) :[99]

> The king sent his detestable, cruel officials to the Tower of London, *intending to bring forth* the younger Roger after a few days *to the people* and condemn him to a violent death. *And when* the king *would have brought him forth*, behold *on the night* of St Peter ad Vincula, the Holy Ghost came ... and touching Roger's heart *raised him up, saying, 'Arise up quickly and follow me'*. And Roger, leaving, *followed him, which was done by* Christ; thus it was not that *he thought he saw a vision. When they were past the first and the second ward* they came to the river Thames.

Robert thought that the aristocracy had an important function in government. The barons had wisdom and magnanimity, and their strength and courage protected England's rights in war.[100] They were steadfast in support of their leader Thomas of Lancaster in 1321, preferring to die in the faith of Christ, for the liberty of church and realm, rather than violate their oath to uphold the Ordinances.[101] Thomas himself died a martyr to the cause; 'the manifold goodness of this famous man, the generous alms he gave, and his other pious acts when alive, and the merits of his posthumous miracles, worked by divine clemency' demand a special book of their own.[102]

[94] *RR*, pp. 222, 228.
[95] *RR*, p. 218.
[96] *RR*, p. 218.
[97] *RR*, pp. 201, 214, 221.
[98] *RR*, p. 200.
[99] *RR*, p. 217.
[100] *RR*, pp. 149, 188.
[101] *RR*, p. 204.
[102] *RR*, p. 214.

Robert not only disliked the frivolities of court life,[103] but also criticized Edward for making decisions 'in secret in his chamber with his intimates'.[104] He apparently appreciated parliament as an institution: under 1308 he says that there were many 'sophistical and quite absurd parliaments',[105] and he accuses Edward in 1323 of trying to circumvent opposition in parliament by delay so that the barons, worn out by work and expense, would agree to the aid he demanded.[106] Robert's support of Isabella, with concomitant Francophilia, is clearly shown. He alleges that in 1311 the queen pleaded with Edward to turn from his gossips (*confabulati*) 'to the excellence of the magnates, the wisdom of the clergy and the protection of the community', for the peace and tranquillity of the realm.[107] Later, in 1324, he says that Edward was cruel to the queen, depriving her of her household, and exclaims:[108]

> Oh! the insane stupidity of the king of the English, condemned by God and men, who should not love his own infamy and illicit bed, full of sin, and should never have removed from his side his noble consort and her gentle wifely embraces, in contempt of her noble birth.

Isabella's brother Charles IV was grieved at her ill treatment, and he and the whole nobility of France, full of admiration for her son's good manners and handsome appearance, promised to help her invade England.[109]

Robert's attitude to the church was partly conditioned by his attitude to Edward II. Robert inveighed against papal rapacity, especially when, in alliance with Edward's avarice, it resulted in taxation of the church.[110] But his attitude to the appointment of bishops was ambivalent. On the one hand he welcomed the succession of John XXII in 1316. This was because Pope John reserved for himself the right to nominate to all English bishoprics.[111] He did so because, in Robert's opinion, he was disgusted with the appointments made through Edward's agency—an example was the appointment of Walter Reynolds ('an illiterate layman who scarcely knew how to decline his own name', according to Robert), to

---

[103] For Robert's dislike of courtiers and court life see *RR*, pp. 191, 200, 211.

[104] S.a. 1323, Edward II summoned parliament 'sperabat namque firmiter infelices tractatus, quos clanculo seorsum in cameris cum suis agitabat in dispendium regni, ad finem pro voto perducere adoptatum'; *RR*, p. 219.

[105] *RR*, p. 143. The assemblies here referred to were not parliaments in any technical sense; see H. G. Richardson and George Sayles, 'The early records of the English parliaments' in *BIHR*, vi (1928–9), pp. 84–5.

[106] *RR*, p. 220.

[107] *RR*, p. 148.

[108] *RR*, p. 229.

[109] *RR*, p. 231.

[110] *RR*, pp. 179, 182. For disparaging remarks about Clement V see *RR*, p. 157.

[111] *RR*, pp. 175–6, 177. See Tout, *Edward II*, p. 208 and n. 4.

Canterbury in 1313.[112] On the other hand Robert condemns subsequent papal provisions to bishoprics, made in fact with Edward's connivance, of candidates regarded by Robert as totally unsuitable—of men such as Henry Burghersh ('a youth famous as a jouster'), who obtained the see of Lincoln in 1320.[113]

Robert of Reading's chronicle can, therefore, be best understood as a *pièce justificative* for Isabella and Mortimer, who held power from November 1326 until October 1330. Its interest, like that of the 'Merton' *Flores*, lies more in its argument than in the information it records. The reliability of the chronicle as a repository of facts is reduced not only by its bias, but also somewhat by Robert's credulity—he frequently refers to astral portents, supernatural occurrences and divine judgments.[114] Nevertheless, Robert's chronicle is not without factual value. He was well placed to collect news about the court, the government and events in London. Thus he could give pieces of court gossip, for example that Robert le Ewer, a 'prince of robbers' who entered the army in 1321, had previously been one of Edward I's courtiers, and had won the nickname 'Aquarius' because he excelled at water-jousting (in fact he was called 'Aquarius' because he held the office of king's waterbearer).[115] Robert's knowledge of the central government is shown by his statement that Sir Roger Bellers, baron of the exchequer, proposed in 1324 to divide the exchequer into two parts; here Robert is corroborated by official documents.[116] One of Robert's most interesting passages on events in London is the fully documented account of the dispute in the Dominican order vented at Blackfriars in 1314.[117] And he has useful information about events farther afield. For example, he asserts that at the battle of Bannockburn fierce rivalry broke out between Gilbert de Clare, earl of Gloucester, and Humphrey de Bohun, earl of Hereford, over the control of the army and the office of constable: the king, in contempt of Hereford, gave the office to Gloucester, though it belonged by hereditary right to Hereford.[118]

The influence of the Westminster historiographical tradition was strong on the second group of chronicles to be considered, those by secular clerks and the one by a layman. All except the *Vita Edwardi Secundi* were continu-

---

[112] *RR*, pp. 155–6.

[113] *RR*, p. 192. Cf. *RR*, pp. 182, 200.

[114] See e.g. *RR*, pp. 160, 171–2, 207.

[115] *RR*, p. 200. Cf. *VE II*, p. 117 and n. 4.

[116] See Tout, *Edward II*, p. 180, and in *EHR*, xxxi (1916), pp. 461–4 (see p. 17 n. 83 above).

[117] *RR*, pp. 161–7. Another (imperfect) version of the text copied by Robert is printed from a document in the Public Record Office (without a reference to Robert's copy) by A. G. Little, 'A record of the English Dominicans, 1314' in *EHR*, v (1890), pp. 107–12.

[118] *RR*, p. 158. See Morris, *Bannockburn*, p. 67. The earl of Hereford had been deprived of the office of constable but Edward II restored the constableship to him on 28 August 1311; see *G.E.C. Peerage*, vi. 468, and Clarke, *Representation and Consent*, p. 241.

ations of the *Flores*, and all (again with the possible exception of the *Vita*) were written in London.

William Stubbs tentatively attributed the *Annales Londonienses* (*The London Annals*) to the alderman and fishmonger, Andrew Horn, who was chamberlain of the city from about 1320 to 1328.[119] This attribution was based partly on the fact that the *Annales Londonienses* record the birth, baptism and death of John, son of Andrew Horn, in 1305[120] (but, as Stubbs notes, there is also an entry on the birth of twins to William le Cupere, and one on the death of a certain Joanna la Sausere).[121] Another piece of evidence which Stubbs interpreted as supporting Horn's claim to authorship is provided by the *Liber Custumarum* (*The Book of Customs*) and the so-called *Liber Horn* (*Horn's Book*), both city registers compiled by Andrew Horn and preserved in the Guildhall. These registers contain a number of documents which are also in the *Annales Londonienses*. (However, this proves only that the author of the *Annales* had access to the city archives.) Another clue detected by Stubbs was a reference in the *Liber Albus* (*The White Book*), a custumal of the city, to a story in the *Annales*, under 1285, as being from 'the chronicles of the Greater Liber Horn'. Therefore it is possible, even probable, that the *Annales* are a copy of the 'Greater Liber Horn', which may well be identified with the book *De Gestis* listed in Horn's will.

The *Annales Londonienses* (the text starts at 1194, the earlier part being lost) abbreviate the *Flores Historiarum*, interpolating material relating mainly to London, to the end of the thirteenth century (the annals from 1293 to 1301 are missing and the annal for 1307 seems incomplete). Thereafter until the end in 1316 they are independent of the *Flores*.[122] The *Annales* at least for the thirteenth century drew on some no longer extant London chronicle,[123] and the numerous references to St Paul's suggest the possibility that the author also used a chronicle compiled in the cathe-

---

[119] On Andrew Horn's claim to authorship see *Chrons Edw. I and II*, i. xxii–xxviii. He is accepted as author by Professor Williams, who also discusses Horn's *Liber Custumarum*; G. A. Williams, *Medieval London: from Commune to Capital* (London 1963), pp. 78, 174, 196, 259, 305, 312–13. The *Annales* were written for Horn's private use. Similarly, it seems likely that Arnold Fitz Thedmar wrote the *Cronica Maiorum et Vicecomitum Londoniarum* for his own use. Kingsford's contention (C. L. Kingsford, *Chronicles of London* (Oxford 1905), pp. v–vi) that both the *Annales* and the *Cronica* were composed for official civic use cannot be maintained. See D. C. Cox, 'The French chronicle of London' in *Medium Ævum*, xlv (1976), p. 207 (Appendix C). The *Mirror of Justices* is also attributed to Horn; see F. W. Maitland's introduction to *The Mirror of Justices*, ed. W. J. Whittaker (Selden Soc., vii, 1895), pp. xii–xv. Moreover, Horn was almost certainly the author of an invaluable contemporary account of the eyre of London of 1321; see *Year Books of Edward II, xxvi, pts. i and ii, the Eyre of London 14 Edward II, A.D. 1321*, ed. H. M. Cam (Selden Soc., lxxxv, lxxxvi, 1968, 1969, 2 vols), i. xii.

[120] *AL*, p. 137.

[121] *AL*, pp. 134, 147.

[122] There is a continuation for the years 1329 and 1330; *AL*, pp. 241–51.

[123] See *Chrons Edw. I and II*, i. xxi–xxii.

dral.[124] Although the *Annales* are of poor literary quality and not comparable in this respect with the chronicle attributed to Arnold Fitz Thedmar, they are a valuable source for English history from 1301 to 1316. The author was well informed and cites *in extenso* some important documents not found elsewhere.

The *Annales Londonienses* are a record of city affairs set against the background of national politics. The city itself played a vital part in the crises of the reign. The *Annales* are the best authority for the dealings of Edward II with the city and for the city factions in 1312.[125] They describe the appeal of the king, in fear and anger after the barons had murdered Gaveston, to the city for support. He appealed to the mayor and citizens, first at Blackfriars and then in the Guildhall, to defend the city for him (the *Annales* give the words of the citizen's loyal reply). And they describe the consequent disputes in the city resulting from this attempt to establish royal authority there.

The London of his day clearly had a visual impact on the author of the *Annales Londonienses*. His love of pageantry appears, for example, in his account of the welcome given by the city, which was 'bejewelled like a new Jerusalem', to Edward II and Isabella after their marriage in France in 1308.[126] And he gives a graphic description of the effects on London of the great frost of 1309:[127]

> There was such cold and such masses and piles of ice on the Thames and everywhere else that the poor were overcome by excessive cold, and bread covered with straw or otherwise protected was frozen so that it could not be eaten unless warmed. The crust of ice on the Thames was so thick that men could travel to London from Queenhithe in Southwark and Westminster; and it lasted so long that people put a piece of leather in the middle and wrestled on it by a fire they made, and caught a hare on the Thames, with dogs. London bridge only survived after great danger and damage.

Many of the documents, both ecclesiastical and secular, copied into the *Annales Londonienses* are of interest for general history. For instance there is a text of the charges laid against the Templars in 1311,[128] and the only known copy of the agenda of the ecclesiastical council held at St Paul's

---

[124] See e.g. *AL*, pp. 136, 138, 144. Perhaps the author's interest in ecclesiastical courts, especially in the court of arches, derived from this sources; see *Chrons Edw. I and II*, i. xxvi-xxvii, and *AL*, pp. 143, 147.

[125] *AL*, pp. 208–9. Cf. Williams, *Medieval London*, pp. 269–73 and nn., *passim*.

[126] *AL*, p. 152. Cf. the notice of the pageant of fishmongers, s.a. 1313; *AL*, p. 221.

[127] *AL*, p. 158.

[128] *AL*, pp. 180 and n. 1, 181–98. For this text see Clarence Perkins, 'The trial of the Knights Templars in England' in *EHR*, xxiv (1909), pp. 439–40 and n. 51, and the same author's 'The Knights Templars in the British Isles' in ibid., xxv (1910), p. 228.

in the spring of 1312.[129] There is also a copy of the letter of the barons to the pope, dated 6 August 1309, relating to abuses in the church.[130] The *Annales* have a unique account of the trial in London of William Wallace in 1305, including the royal commission to the justices (one of whom was John Blund, mayor of London) and the record of the proceedings.[131] They have a text of the interim ordinances first issued by the barons, giving the date of issue (19 March 1310) which is not found in the other copies,[132] and they are the only known source for the proposed terms of peace between the king and barons in 1312, and for the objections of the French lawyers to the Ordainers and all their acts.[133]

The *Annales Paulini* resemble the *Annales Londonienses* in many ways. They too mention local details (such as the jollities on the frozen Thames in 1309),[134] and show delight in public spectacles, whether a public execution (of Sir Henry le Tyeys who, wearing a gown quartered with green and purple, was dragged through the city to the gallows and hanged),[135] or a series of tournaments—at Kennington, Stepney, Cheapside and Smithfield (in 1308, 1309, 1330 and 1334).[136] But the *Annales Paulini* differ from the *Annales Londonienses* in so far as they lack the element of official city history and concentrate more on ecclesiastical affairs, especially those relating to St Paul's.

The *Annales Paulini* start with an abridgment of the *Flores Historiarum* interpolated with material mainly concerning St Paul's. They have additions to the annal for 1307, and continue to 1341. As the additional part of the 1307 annal and the annals for 1308 and 1309 contain information particularly concerning Westminster (and none about St Paul's), it is likely that the author either obtained the information for them directly from Westminster, or that he simply copied two pre-existing Westminster annals.[137] The relationship of the subsequent annals to 1341 to the chro-

---

[129] *AL*, pp. 176–8. Printed from this text in *Councils and Synods, with other Documents relating to the English Church*, ed. F. M. Powicke and C. R. Cheney (Oxford 1964, only vol. 2 in two pts, 1205–1313, published to date), ii. pt ii. 1369–71.

[130] *AL*, pp. 161 and n. 2, 162–5. This text is collated in Powicke and Cheney, op. cit., ii. pt ii. 1236–40.

[131] *AL*, pp. 139–42. Printed *Documents illustrative of Sir William Wallace*, ed. Joseph Stevenson (Maitland Club 1841), pp. 189–93. Cf. M. H. Keen, 'Treason trials under the Law of Arms' in *TRHS*, fifth series, xii (1962), p. 87.

[132] *AL*, pp. 172–3. See J. Conway Davies, *The Baronial Opposition to Edward II* (Cambridge 1918), p. 362 and n. 5. *AL* also have one of the only three known copies of the additional ordinances drawn up by a committee of the Ordainers; *AL*, pp. 198–202, and see Conway Davies, op. cit., p. 382.

[133] *AL*, pp. 210–15.

[134] *AP*, p. 268.

[135] *AP*, p. 303. For the author's/authors' love of public spectacles, with reference to Edward III's reign, see p. 63 below.

[136] *AP*, pp. 264, 267, 353–5, 361.

[137] Stubbs thought it possible that the section was written at Westminster, and Richardson considered this self evident; see *Chrons Edw. I and II*, i. xlvi, lxxvi, and H. G. Richardson, 'The *Annales Paulini*' in *Speculum*, xxiii (1948), p. 631.

nicle of Adam Murimuth, who was writing his own chronicle at St Paul's at this time, is problematical.[138] The two works have much common material in the annals from 1311 to 1320 and from 1332 to 1336, but it is uncertain which chronicle is derived from the other or whether both used a common source. The suggestion that Murimuth also wrote the *Annales Paulini* seems unlikely,[139] because each work begins the year on a different date (the *Annales* at Christmas and Murimuth on 25 March), and their interests do not coincide: the *Annales* alone show a close concern for St Paul's and do not share Murimuth's interest in royal and papal diplomacy. The problem also arises whether the *Annales* are a work of multiple authorship (it has been argued that there are changes of authorship at 1308/9, 1320/1 and 1331/2).[140] Nevertheless, William Stubbs's view that the *Annales* are by one author has much to recommend it; the same tastes and interests permeate the whole, and the unevenness of composition can be explained as reflecting the author's lack of literary skill when he moved from one batch of information to the next.

The author (or possibly authors) may well have been connected with the sacrist's office at St Paul's. This is suggested by the fact that the *Annales* show interest in matters which especially concerned the sacristy—in church ceremonies, and in the fabric, ornaments and lighting of the cathedral. Most of the ceremonies noted took place in St Paul's, but those in the annals for 1307 and 1308 were performed in Westminster abbey.

There is a detailed and obviously eyewitness account of the coronation of Edward II.[141] The crush of people in Westminster Abbey was so great that a wall fell on the high altar and pulpit, and killed a knight, John de Bakewell. Piers Gaveston, according to the *Annales*, provoked general indignation because he bore St Edward's crown. The *Annales* describe Gaveston's behaviour at the banquet:

---

[138] Stubbs leaves the question of the relationship between Murimuth and the *Annales Paulini* open, but Richardson states categorically that the *Annales* borrowed directly from Murimuth. Stubbs's more circumspect view seems preferable. See *Chrons Edw. I and II*, i. lxx-lxxii, and Richardson, op. cit., pp. 630–1, 638–40. It should be noted that from the annal for 1308 the manuscript of the *Annales Paulini*, Lambeth Palace MS. 1106, ff. 93–110, has the appearance of an early draft written shortly after the events which the annals record took place; there are spaces, comprising various numbers of blank lines, between the annals, marginal additions and changes of ink and possibly of hand (the page reproduced in Plate I below, chosen for its picture of old St Paul's, is tidier than many others; cf. p. 27 and n. 146 below). See also p. 64 below.

[139] See Stubbs, op. cit., i. lviii–lxxiv. Cf. p. 64 below.

[140] Richardson, op. cit., pp. 630 et seq.

[141] *AP*, pp. 259–62. For a full discussion of this narrative, particularly for its bearing on constitutional history, see Richardson, op. cit., pp. 631–7, where a severe view is taken of the historicity of the annals for 1307 and 1308. The *Annales Paulini* alone of the chronicles state that there was dissension between king and magnates before the coronation, and that, therefore, Edward made a placatory promise; its testimony is treated more sympathetically by R. S. Hoyt, 'The coronation oath of 1308' in *EHR*, lxxi (1956), pp. 373 et seq., and by B. Wilkinson, *Constitutional History of Medieval England 1216–1399* (London 1948–58, 3 vols), ii. 94–7, than by Mr Richardson.

He sought his own glory rather than the king's and, as if scorning the English, who came in cloth of gold, rode among the guests in purple silk embroidered with pearls, more splendidly dressed than the king.

The *Annales* vividly describe the illumination of the tombs of Eleanor of Castile and Henry III, and of the shrine of Edward the Confessor, in Westminster abbey on the occasion of a visit of the cardinal bishop, Peter of Spain, in 1307. Eleanor's tomb was surrounded by forty eight candles, each weighing sixteen pounds, and Henry's tomb was lit by twenty four similar candles. St Edward's shrine had twelve candles, each a pound in weight. The choir was illuminated with candles placed a foot and a half apart on beams fixed between the columns, and the congregation at mass, the religious from the city, the clergy and the laymen, all held candles of equal length.[142]

The *Annales* describe the translation of St Erkenwald in 1326,[143] and record the dedication of altars in 1314[144] and the reconciliation of the cathedral after pollution with blood in 1312, 1313 and 1329.[145] In addition, they are an important source for the history of the architecture and furnishings of St Paul's. For example, they state that in 1314 the spire with surmounting ball and cross was dismantled because of its dangerous condition, and a new spire surmounted by a golden ball and cross erected. This entry includes the measurements of the church and a pen sketch of the cathedral's west elevation.[146] Under 1325 the *Annales* record that when the great cross in the cathedral was taken down for painting, the workmen carelessly allowed the rood beam to fall on the altar, breaking the ornaments and statues and just missing the almoner, William, who was celebrating mass.[147] Under 1327 they note the removal of the pulpit from the nave, where it had been for seven years, to the new choir, because of danger from the spire.[148] And they note the repair of the cross and the ball in 1339, and describe the procession with the relics preserved in them which took place on this occasion.[149]

As a record of general history the *Annales Paulini* have value partly because they were written in the capital.[150] St Paul's itself was often the scene of public events. Ecclesiastical convocations were held there in 1319

---

[142] *AP*, pp. 255–6.

[143] *AP*, p. 311.

[144] *AP*, p. 276.

[145] *AP*, pp. 272, 274, 347.

[146] *AP*, pp. 276–7. See Plate I. Cf. G. H. Cook, *Old S. Paul's Cathedral* (London 1955), p. 42.

[147] *AP*, p. 310.

[148] *AP*, p. 338.

[149] *AP*, pp. 368–9. Cf. p. 71 below.

[150] Mr Richardson attacks the value of the *Annales Paulini* as an historical source, though he admits that the annals from 1321 to 1331 are 'a respectable compilation based upon documents and personal knowledge'; Richardson, op. cit., pp. 639. However, his strictures

and 1321,[151] and St Paul's was often used as a rostrum for public proclamations and political propaganda. Thus in 1311, as the *Annales* record, the Ordinances were read publicly in St Paul's churchyard, 'at the stone cross', by Master William de Maidstone, clerk, in the presence of Archbishop Robert Winchelsey and the magnates.[152] In 1318 the bishop of Norwich announced from the pulpit, 'by the great cross in the nave', in the presence of the king, archbishop and magnates, that the king promised to adhere to the counsel of his earls and barons.[153] In 1326 Archbishop Walter Reynolds had a papal bull excommunicating the invaders of England read 'in the church of St Paul's'; the bull had been issued seven years earlier and was intended against the Scots, but the archbishop's clerk, Thomas of Stowe, omitted the date so that the bull appeared to be aimed at Queen Isabella and her supporters.[154]

Sometimes the conflict of king and barons involved St Paul's in violence. The *Annales* describe how the king's treasurer, Walter Stapledon, bishop of Exeter, was dragged from the cathedral, where he had taken sanctuary, by the angry mob during the riots which accompanied Isabella's invasion in 1326. He was seized by the north door, struck on the head, pulled from his horse, and hauled across the cemetery to the market place in Cheapside, where he and his two esquires were beheaded. His head was sent to Queen Isabella in Bristol and 'his naked body', the *Annales* relate, 'was left for a whole day in the middle of the market place, a horrible sight to see.' Later the body was carried to St Paul's where it lay for the night, to be removed next day to St Clement Danes; from thence, as the rector would not allow its burial there, it was taken to the nearby church of the Holy Innocents, which was derelict; there the body stayed until at last it was claimed by the dean and chapter of Exeter, and Stapledon found a final resting place in his own cathedral.[155] The *Annales* also record the fate of the chancellor, Robert Baldock, on the same occasion.[156] Baldock, a canon of St Paul's, was imprisoned, and his treasure, which he kept in the cathedral, was seized by the mob.

Residence in London and proximity to Westminster explains the detailed information in the *Annales Paulini* on the city's relations with the king and

---

seem too severe in the light of present knowledge and do not in general have the concurrence of other scholars; see e.g. p. 26 n. 141 above, and p. 29 and n. 159 below.

[151] *AP*, pp. 286, 300.

[152] *AP*, p. 270. For the use of St Paul's Cross in the middle ages as a place for public proclamations and as a means of communication between king and people, etc., see Cook, op. cit., p. 68.

[153] *AP*, p. 282.

[154] *AP*, p. 315. For a similar occasion, in 1322, see *AP*, p. 302.

[155] *AP*, pp. 316–17. See Williams, *Medieval London*, pp. 295–6. An equally vivid account of disorder in London during Isabella's invasion is in the mid-fourteenth century French chronicle of London; see p. 72 below.

[156] *AP*, pp. 319–21.

the barons. They have a full account of the barons' negotiations with the city in 1321, and give the location of the troops quartered in the suburbs.[157] They also describe Edward's attempted procrastination in conceding the magnates' demands, and his ultimate capitulation in parliament (which he followed by a visit to St Paul's).[158] Presumably it was from baronial partisans staying in the neighbourhood that the author gained his knowledge of the barons' journey from Wales to Westminster. Therefore, his statement that on the way the barons 'had written, ordained and approved a certain tract on ancient custom' is probably correct: this tract has been identified as the work which still survives on the office of the steward.[159]

We may know little about the author (or authors) of the *Annales Paulini*, but much is known about Adam Murimuth. Unlike most of his contemporaries who wrote chronicles, Murimuth included a number of autobiographical details. His career can also be traced in official documents.[160] Murimuth was a man of some importance. He was born in 1274 or 1275 and died in about 1347[161] (he gives his age nine times in the chronicle). He belonged to the family of Murimuth settled at Fifield in Oxfordshire, and first appears in 1311 at the papal curia in Rome, as proctor of Oxford university in a suit against the Dominican friars. He continued his career as a clerical diplomat, in 1312 representing Archbishop Robert Winchelsey in the papal curia at Avignon, in a quarrel with the bishop of Coventry. In 1314 he was the king's envoy at the curia on behalf of John de Sandale, who had been nominated dean of St Paul's, and was still there in 1316. Similar work for Edward II (who in 1317 referred to him as 'our clerk in the Roman curia') and various ecclesiastics followed. In 1321 and 1322 he was at Avignon to obtain papal assent to a clerical aid. In 1323 he was on a mission to the king of Naples to press Edward's claims to various lands in France, and later in the same year Edward sent him to Rome in order to oppose the Scots in their attempt to obtain the removal of the interdict on Scotland. Murimuth was rewarded with ecclesiastical preferment, gaining a prebend in Hereford cathedral in 1320, one at St Paul's in

---

[157] *AP*, pp. 294–6. See Williams, op. cit., pp. 285 et seq.

[158] *AP*, pp. 296–7.

[159] *AP*, p. 293. For this passage see M. V. Clarke, *Representation and Consent*, p. 242. For the tract on the stewardship see L. W. Vernon Harcourt, *His Grace the Steward and Trial of Peers* (London 1907), pp. 144–52 passim (the text is printed in ibid., pp. 164–7; the MSS. are discussed in Clarke, op. cit., pp. 358–60). The *Annales Paulini* are also an important authority for the history of parliament; see H. G. Richardson and George Sayles, 'The early records of the English parliaments' in *BIHR*, vi (1928–9), pp. 85–8 passim.

[160] The fullest account of Adam Murimuth's life is by Stubbs in *Chrons Edw. I and II*, i. lx-lxvii, on which Maunde Thompson based his notice; *AM*, pp. ix-xiii.

[161] Murimuth's death in 1347 is noticed in the index to John le Neve, *Fasti Ecclesiae Anglicanae 1300–1541, v. St Paul's, London*, compiled by J. M. Horn (London 1963). (For an Adam Murimuth jun., who died in 1370, see ibid., p. 38, and *Chrons Edw. I and II*, i. lxi, lxvi.) However, the date of his death is not certain and Stubbs suggested the slight possibility that the version of his chronicle to 1347 was by a continuator; ibid., pp. lxvi-lxvii.

1325 and another, richer one there in 1328,[162] and in 1337 he obtained the rectory of Wraysbury.

In view of Murimuth's active and interesting career, his chronicle is disappointing. He began the chronicle, which extends in its longest form to 1346, before 1337, in which year he published the first edition. He subsequently continued the chronicle, publishing versions successively to 1341 and 1347 (and perhaps one to 1343).[163] To 1305 he used the *Flores Historiarum* which he found in Westminster abbey. Although he indicates that this completed his debt to Westminster sources,[164] it seems likely that he used Westminster material for his account of the funeral and for the assessment of the character of Edward I under 1307.[165] Murimuth was not writing contemporarily with events until 1338, but for the earlier years of the fourteenth century he drew both on his own memory, and on a journal he had kept.[166]

Unfortunately Murimuth's chronicle is very brief. This was partly because he was selective (he confesses that nothing happened in some years worth noting),[167] and may also have been the result of lack of literary talent and the pressure of his other activities. Nevertheless he is, as will be seen in a later chapter, an important authority for Edward III's reign, and notably for England's relations with the papacy and for the Hundred Years' War. In addition, he has some value for Edward II's reign, both for Anglo-papal relations and for home affairs, especially for the deposition and last days of Edward (his account of Edward's persecution and death provides some general confirmation of Geoffrey le Baker's detailed and graphic narrative, which will be discussed below).[168]

Murimuth's value for Anglo-papal relations may be illustrated by his information concerning appointments to English bishoprics. He tells how in 1320 the king obtained from the pope the appointment of Bartholomew Badlesmere's nephew, Henry Burghersh, to the see of Lincoln, disregarding the election of Anthony Bek. Badlesmere in the capacity of royal envoy at the papal curia spent more than £1,500, 'but he obtained nothing

---

[162] Murimuth successively held the prebends of Ealdstreet and Nesden; see Le Neve, op. cit., pp. 35, 49.

[163] For the recensions of Murimuth's chronicle see *Chrons Edw. I and II*, i. lxvi, and *AM*, p. xxii.

[164] *AM*, p. 3.

[165] See Gransden, *Historical Writing*, i. 459 and n. 161, 460, and p. 18 n. 87 above.

[166] 'Et ab anno Domini M.CCC. V, quo ego tantae eram aetatis quod facta praecipua ponderavi et ea scripsi breviter meo modo ex libro dierum meorum, scripsi ulterius ea quae mihi videbantur utilia ad scribendum ... '; *AM*, pp. 3–4.

[167] *AM*, pp. 29, 37.

[168] Murimuth notes Edward II's death and states that though many people were summoned to see the body, their inspection was superficial: 'dictum tamen fuit vulgariter quod per ordinationem dominorum J[ohannis] Mautravers et T[homae] de Gorneye fuit per cautelam occisus'; *AM*, p. 54. Cf. the account of Edward II's captivity at Berkeley; *AM*, p. 52.

useful to the king except the said Henry's promotion—who afterwards proved ungrateful.'[169] In 1323 Murimuth records that the pope provided John Stratford, a royal envoy to the curia on Scottish affairs, to the see of Winchester: the king was enraged because he had wanted to procure the bishopric for Robert Baldock, 'but by chance his letters to the curia arrived too late.'[170]

As would be expected in view of the period when he wrote, Murimuth is virulently anti-French—he makes the curious remark that many Frenchmen limp.[171] He is also anti-papal. He asserts that one of the cardinals who came in 1317 to arrange peace between England and Scotland, obtained benefices worth more than £1,000 a year 'not without cupidity and worldly ambition'.[172] And, on recording in the same year that the pope reserved first fruits throughout the world, contrasts the Germans' refusal to pay with the subservience of the English: 'the English, indeed, bearing like good asses whatever load is placed upon them, submitted to this and to other equally grievous burdens.'[173]

The *Vita Edwardi Secundi* stands apart from the chronicles so far considered. The fact that its (anonymous) author was undoubtedly a secular clerk, just possibly even a canon of St Paul's, would seem to bring it into closest relationship with the last two chronicles discussed. But in form the *Vita* most nearly resembles the chronicle of Robert of Reading. It too is a literary work rather than a chronicle in the technical sense, and was written soon after the last events recorded, not contemporaneously. Nevertheless, though the form of the *Vita* may be compared with Robert's work, it far excels it in quality. The author wrote clear, precise Latin prose (unlike the bombastic Robert), and was judicious, perceptive and highly educated.

The *Vita* is an account of Edward II's reign up to November 1325, when it ends abruptly, apparently without the author's final revision. It was probably written between its terminal date and September 1326, though the possibility of a later date cannot be discounted.[174] In the course of the work the author sometimes purposely gives the impression that he was writing contemporaneously with events;[175] this was probably a literary device, but it could reflect the use of a journal. The text as it survives today is incomplete—the annals from 1322 to 1324 are missing owing to the loss of leaves from the sole manuscript to survive the reformation

[169] *AM*, p. 31. See Tout, *Edward II*, p. 122 and n. 2. Henry Burghersh joined Queen Isabella in 1326. For Murimuth's familiarity with the papal curia see W. E. Lunt, *Financial Relations of the Papacy with England to 1327* (Cambridge, Mass., 1939), pp. 407, 479 nn. 6, 8, 567 n. 3.
[170] *AM*, p. 39. See Tout, *Edward II*, p. 210.
[171] *AM*, p. 25.
[172] *AM*, p. 27. For Murimuth's anti-papalism see also pp. 66–7 below.
[173] *AM*, p. 28. This passage is cited in Lunt, *Financial Relations*, i. 494. Cf. p. 67 below.
[174] The date of the *Vita* is fully discussed by Mr Denholm-Young; *VE II*, pp. xvi-xix. Cf. Stubbs in *Chrons Edw. I and II*, ii. xliv.
[175] See e.g. *VE II*, p. 39.

(which itself was burnt in the eighteenth century; its text is known only from a transcript made by Thomas Hearne).

This manuscript came from Malmesbury abbey. But there is no evidence supporting the view previously held by historians that the *Vita* was composed at Malmesbury.[176] On the contrary it was clearly the work of a secular clerk. The author shows no interest in any monastery or religious order, but has a long flashback on the defence of the church by Archbishop Winchelsey (who 'stood as a wall for the clergy') against Edward I's financial demands.[177] And he was knowledgeable about canon law, objecting, for example, to Henry Burghersh's provision to Lincoln because he was below the canonical age.[178] The author was obviously not an ecclesiastic of any importance: his sympathies were with the lower clergy, not the prelates. Thus he disapproved of the grant by the prelates of a tenth to the king, without papal authority, because 'the goods of the church are the goods of the poor.'[179]

The contents of the *Vita* indicate that the author came from the region of the Severn valley. He is particularly well-informed about people and events connected with Herefordshire and Gloucestershire and their vicinity. He gives a detailed account of the revolt of the community in Bristol against the ruling oligarchy.[180] Prominent among the numerous west country barons whom he mentions are the earls of Gloucester and Hereford and Sir Maurice de Berkeley.[181] He describes Gloucester's leadership of the barons,[182] has a minute account of his death at Bannockburn,[183] which he particularly laments because he died without male issue,[184] and describes the consequent division of the earldom.[185] He is at least as full on the earl of Hereford, whom he once calls 'our earl',[186] and regarded his death at Boroughbridge as a contributory cause of the baronial defeat.[187] The author records that in 1315 Maurice de Berkeley received custody of Berwick, and gives details of his attempted escape from Wallingford castle in 1323.[188]

The author's sympathies are not with the king but with the barons, though he was capable of charity to the former and of criticizing the latter. Therefore the evidence suggests that he may have had some connection

[176] *VE II*, p. xv.
[177] *VE II*, pp. 40–2. Cf. Ezekiel xiii. 5.
[178] *VE II*, pp. 104–5.
[179] *VE II*, p. 77.
[180] *VE II*, pp. 70–2.
[181] *VE II*, pp. xxii-xxiii.
[182] *VE II*, pp. 25–6, 39.
[183] *VE II*, pp. 52–3.
[184] *VE II*, p. 62.
[185] *VE II*, pp. 62–3, 94.
[186] *VE II*, p. 58.
[187] *VE II*, p. 124.
[188] *VE II*, pp. 59, 129–31. For other references to Sir Maurice de Berkeley see *VE II*, pp. 55, 73.

with one of the barons, perhaps with the earl of Hereford or Maurice de Berkeley, who both played an important part in the Scottish war, about which the *Vita* is extremely well informed. Mr Denholm-Young argues the claim to authorship of Master John Walwayn, canon of Hereford cathedral and of St Paul's, and a clerk in the service of the earl of Hereford, who failed to obtain the bishopric of Hereford in 1324 and died in July 1326.[189] However, the evidence seems insufficient to warrant more than a very tentative conclusion, especially as the *Vita* has nothing about St Paul's and practically nothing on London. But whoever wrote the *Vita*, he was a learned man, equally at home quoting the bible, the classics, canon and civil law, histories and medieval romance literature.

The *Vita* has a strongly homiletic tone. The author's edificatory intention influenced his presentation of events, resulting in the exaggeration of ills and the interpretation of evidence in accordance with moral values. The *Vita* has numerous references to and citations from the bible, and expiates on the sins of pride and avarice, favourite themes of medieval preachers.[190] It attributes the downfall of Piers Gaveston to his inordinate pride.[191] Similarly pride, the besetting sin of the English, was the cause of their defeat at Bannockburn.[192] Greed caused many evils. It was the motive behind the Despensers' wickedness.[193] Although usually pro-baronial, the *Vita* rails against the avarice of the barons in general and of Thomas of Lancaster in particular. He accuses the magnates of perpetually struggling to increase their property instead of living within their means. Thomas of Lancaster, seduced by greed, sold ('so it was said') his support to Robert Bruce for £4,000.[194] Thus avarice led to treachery, and treachery to Scottish victory. 'Cursed be avarice and its dealings because of which charity has departed and faith is exiled': there follows a long tirade against avarice, reinforced with an exemplary story and biblical references.[195] Venality in the central and local courts of justice led to corruption ('every man has his price'),[196] and to simoniacal appointments to bishoprics ('money rules at Rome'); Walter Reynolds obtained the see of Canterbury because King Edward paid the pope a large sum.[197] Moreover, the author expiates eloquently on the general corruption of the church in England— the illiterate clergy, the inarticulate preachers, the rapacious and ambitious

---

[189] See *VE II*, pp. xxiv-xxviii.
[190] G. R. Owst, *Literature and the Pulpit in Medieval England* (second edition, Oxford 1961), pp. 308–9 and passim (see the index in ibid., under 'Avarice' and 'Pride').
[191] *VE II*, pp. 3, 15–16, 28.
[192] *VE II*, pp. 56–7. On the pride of the English cf. *VE II*, p. 63.
[193] *VE II*, p. 108.
[194] For Thomas of Lancaster's negotiations with Robert Bruce in 1321 and 1322 see Barrow, *Robert Bruce*, pp. 343–4, 350–1.
[195] For this tirade see *VE II*, pp. 97–102.
[196] *VE II*, pp. 63–4. Cf. *VE II*, p. 74.
[197] *VE II*, pp. 45–6.

prelates; today there is no prudence and no humility.[198]

The *Vita*'s pessimistic view of the world is augmented by the author's use of literary devices such as paradoxes and aphorisms, commonly used by satirists writing in the classical tradition. For example he writes paradoxically of tournaments: 'it is the recognised rule of this game that he who loses most and is most frequently unhorsed, is adjudged the more valiant and the stronger.'[199] When writing in satirical style the author could take a cynical view of the barons. Their rapacity for the property of the king's favourites overthrown in 1321 'turned their right to wrong';[200] and, again, 'the love of magnates is as a game of dice, and the desires of the rich like feathers.'[201] Similarly, he elaborates on the magnates' susceptibility to flattery: 'by some depravity of nature the delicate ears of the rich more readily receive the blandishments of the lying tongue than the candid testimony of truth.'[202] He says that the barons' agreement with the king in 1313 was clinched with a banquet, 'as has become a custom in England',[203] and of their attempted revolt in general he comments: 'For an islander to rebel against an island king is as if a chained man were to strive with the warden of his prison.'[204]

The *Vita* has a number of citations from the Digest and Code—including the famous tag 'what touches all should be approved by all.'[205] Moreover, the author was fond of exemplary parallels from history—events from previous ages which could warn men of the possible results of their acts in the present. The author drew his examples from the bible, and from classical and later works. In a rhetorical passage he warns Thomas of Lancaster of the fate his treachery would bring upon him: Joab, despite his brave deeds, lost his reputation because of his treachery to Abner and Amasa; Philotas, a soldier of Alexander the Great, was sentenced as a traitor; Aeneas was exiled for betraying Troy; and in recent times Thomas Turbeville was sentenced for betraying England to France, and the earl of Atholl, Simon Frazer and William Wallace were executed as traitors.[206] Similarly, the men of Bristol ought to have remembered the fate of Bedford in 1224 and Kenilworth in 1266, when they dared resist the king.[207] The author was aware in discussing the baronial opposition

---

[198] *VE II*, pp. 105–7. For such tirades in medieval sermons see Owst, op. cit., chapter V ('The Preaching of Satire and Complaint, i'), passim.
[199] *VE II*, p. 2.
[200] *VE II*, p. 115.
[201] *VE II*, p. 8.
[202] *VE II*, p. 31.
[203] *VE II*, p. 44.
[204] *VE II*, p. 74.
[205] *VE II*, p. 16. For this dictum from the Code see A. Marongiu, *Medieval Parliaments*, translated and adapted by S. J. Woolf (London 1968), pp. 34–7.
[206] *VE II*, p. 98.
[207] *VE II*, p. 74.

to Edward II of the precedent in Henry III's reign. He states that in 1311 Edward gave way to the Ordainers lest he involved the country in civil war as Henry III had done. 'Civil war never yet had an acceptable end, of which the battle of Lewes is a manifest example, and the battle of Evesham an everlasting reminder, where the noble man Simon earl of Leicester laid down his life in the cause of justice.'[208] And what, the author asks, would have happened if in 1313 Edward had refused to concede the Ordainers' demands? He firmly believes, he asserts, that the barons would have kept Edward under restraint until the trouble-makers at court had been removed, just as Simon de Montfort had done with King Henry and his son Edward, but they would have risked the fate of Simon and other magnates who had opposed the king.[209]

The author of the *Vita* interpreted the politics of his own times in terms of personal relations and constitutional principles. In his view the root of the trouble between Edward and the barons was Edward's character. Edward was a fine figure of a man, handsome and strong, and if only he had expended as much energy on the use of arms as he did on 'rustic pursuits' he would have excelled Richard I in prowess.[210] But he was dilatory and unreliable in his dealings with the barons,[211] and worse still he allowed himself to be dominated by youthful courtiers (like Rehoboam he followed the advice of the young),[212] whose greed and power alienated the barons.[213] Particularly deplorable was his excessive love of Piers Gaveston which was greater than that of David for Jonathan, and of Achilles for Patroclus.[214] After Gaveston's execution Edward's attitude to the barons was determined by the desire to avenge his death. His bitterness, however, was somewhat lessened by the birth of his eldest son in November 1312, who provided him with an heir and a new object of affection.[215]

Gaveston, according to the *Vita*, was himself hated by the barons not only because he was a *parvenu*, but also because of his personality—his arrogance and flippancy (illustrated by his practice of nicknaming the barons).[216] His position was temporarily strengthened by his marriage to the king's niece, 'for it much increased the goodwill of his friends and restrained the hatred of the baronage.'[217] The Despensers had alienated the barons by

---

[208] *VE II*, p. 18.
[209] *VE II*, p. 44.
[210] *VE II*, p. 40.
[211] See e.g. *VE II*, p. 48.
[212] See *VE II*, pp. 18, 36. See A. Gransden, 'Childhood and youth in mediaeval England' in *Nottingham Mediaeval Studies*, xvi (1972), p. 10. For other pejorative references to young people see *VE II*, pp. 63, 105 (cf. p. 2), and Gransden, op. cit., p. 9.
[213] For the influence of courtiers on Edward II see *VE II*, pp. 40, 74–5.
[214] *VE II*, pp. 14–15, 30.
[215] *VE II*, p. 36.
[216] *VE II*, p. 25. Cf. p. 13 and n. 68 above.
[217] *VE II*, p. 2.

their ambition and greed. The *Vita* retails the particular grudges born by various barons against Hugh Despenser the younger in 1320; for example Thomas of Lancaster blamed him for the disgrace he had incurred at Berwick, the earl of Hereford hated him for procuring the disinheritance of his mother, and Roger Damory, who married a co-heiress of the earl of Gloucester, was his 'deadly rival' over the Gloucester inheritance.[218]

Although the *Vita* is an historiographical synthesis, showing the influence of a number of literary modes, it is a valuable source for the historian today. Besides recording a mass of accurate information, it reflects current attitudes to constitutional problems. Like all men of his time, the author believed in monarchy and he believed in the rights of the baronage: if the *status quo* were maintained all would be well. Both king and baronage should observe the law and charters, and keep their promises. The monarchy was necessary for the defence of the people. The author comments on the English defeat by the Scots in 1315: 'In truth, a leaderless people is easily dispersed, and the limbs fail when the head is removed.'[219] He attributes the king's failure in war to the lack of strong support by the baronage, and defends Edward's decision in 1319 to make a truce with the Scots, on the grounds that it was necessary for the safety of England during his absence in France.[220] He states that it is wrong to hold a castle against the king, and apparently agreed with Edward's assertion in 1311, contrary to baronial demands, that the king should be able to choose his own household (otherwise, 'the ordering of his whole house would depend on the will of an other, as if he were an idiot').[221]

The barons, on the other hand, were also an essential element in government. The author of the *Vita*, like other contemporary writers, laid great stress on noble birth. Just as he emphasized the king's famous lineage,[222] so he pointed out that Thomas of Lancaster became the baronial leader partly because of his aristocratic origins and royal connections.[223] Conversely, Gaveston won extra odium because he was a commoner. The author regarded the earls as a particularly privileged group, but in general used a more extended definition of baronage, to include the lesser nobility.[224] The barons are, he writes, 'a chief constituent of the monarchy, and without them the king cannot attempt or accomplish anything of importance.'[225] Edward would easily have defeated the Scots if he had followed the barons' advice: the bad advice of Gaveston and his successors in the royal house-

---

[218] *VE II*, p. 109.
[219] *VE II*, p. 62.
[220] *VE II*, p. 103.
[221] *VE II*, p. 21.
[222] *VE II*, pp. 36–7, 40.
[223] *VE II*, p. 28.
[224] See *VE II*, p. xx.
[225] *VE II*, p. 28.

hold ruined him.[226] The *Vita* is the only chronicle explicitly to mention the office of steward as a part of the baronial platform. He states that Thomas of Lancaster withheld military support from the king for his Scottish campaign in 1317 'because he was the steward of England, whose business it was to watch over the interests of the kingdom, so that if the king wished to take arms against anyone, he ought first to notify the steward.'[227]

The *Vita* expresses the opinion that royal officials should be changed annually.[228] It also seems to recognize parliament's importance as a focal point for the baronage. It states that in 1320 Lancaster refused to attend parliament because it was being held 'in cameris',[229] and that in 1325 the king's increasing severity so scared 'the great and the wise' that 'parliament, colloquies and councils decide nothing.'[230] In addition, the *Vita* shows that the barons used the king's coronation oath and oath to keep the Ordinances as sanctions against him. They only felt bound by their fealty if the king kept his coronation oath,[231] and Thomas of Lancaster would agree to nothing in 1317 without the observance of the Ordinances.[232]

The *Vita*, therefore, reflects the views of an intelligent, sensible man who lived through the events of Edward II's reign, but probably stopped writing before its tragic dénouement.

The last writer to be considered, Geoffrey le Baker, wrote from another chronological standpoint, in the next generation. Baker was a secular clerk, a native of Swinbrook, near Burford in Oxfordshire, who had some connection with Osney abbey (which lies within two miles of Oxford), with a local knight, Sir Thomas de la More, and with the Bohun family.[233] He began writing his *Chronicon* (*Chronicle*), which covers the period from 1303 to 1356, some time after 1341.

The *Chronicon* does not itself contain any attribution to Geoffrey le Baker. His authorship is established by comparing it with another work, the *Chroniculum* (*The Little Chronicle*),[234] a series of short annals from the Creation to 1336 which has a colophon explicitly stating that Baker was the author. The colophon reads:[235]

---

[226] *VE II*, pp. 40, 42–3.
[227] *VE II*, p. 81. This passage is cited in Tout, *Edward II*, p. 96, and in Clarke, *Representation and Consent*, p. 241.
[228] *VE II*, p. 139.
[229] *VE II*, p. 104.
[230] *VE II*, p. 136.
[231] *VE II*, pp. 10, 36.
[232] *VE II*, p. 85.
[233] For Geoffrey le Baker's life and work see *GB*, pp. v–xi.
[234] The *Chroniculum* is printed in *GB*, pp. 156–75.
[235] *GB*, p. 173.

> Be it remembered that Geoffrey le Baker of Swinbrook, clerk, wrote this little chronicle at the request of Sir Thomas de la More on Friday, on the feast of St Margaret the Virgin [20 July] 1347, being the twenty first year of the reign of King Edward III.

Sir Thomas de la More, Baker's neighbour at Northmoor, eleven miles from Swinbrook, was a member of parliament in 1340, 1343 and 1351. As will be seen, the *Chronicon* has two passages addressed to Sir Thomas, which suggests that it as well as the *Chroniculum* was written for him. If so, surely Baker must be the author of the *Chronicon*, because it seems unlikely that yet another historian besides Baker wrote to please Sir Thomas.

Geoffrey le Baker's *Chronicon* is chiefly valuable for its account of the Hundred Years' War (this aspect of it will be discussed in a subsequent chapter). Much of its material for Edward II's reign is derived from the chronicle of Adam Murimuth, probably his near neighbour in Oxfordshire. In addition Baker used another written source which still survives: his account of the battle of Bannockburn is mainly borrowed, as Baker acknowledges, from a poem by a Carmelite friar of Scarborough, Robert Baston.[236] Edward II took Baston on the Scottish campaign to celebrate in verse the expected English victory. But the Scots captured Baston, and Robert Bruce ordered him to write a poem to commemorate the English defeat. Baker probably obtained a copy of the poem from the Carmelite house in Oxford.

Some of the contemporary written sources which Baker used for Edward II's reign are not otherwise known. For example he used a lost charter of the Oxford Carmelites for his details about the endowment by Edward II (in fulfilment of a vow made on his flight from Bannockburn) of twenty four Carmelites to study theology.[237]

More remarkable is the information Baker derived verbally from eyewitnesses. He acknowledges that his account of Edward II's deposition was derived from Sir Thomas de la More:[238]

> You, noble knight, Sir Thomas de la More, with your wisdom and distinguished presence, being in attendance on the bishop

---

[236] *GB*, pp. 7, 186n. Robert Baston's poem is printed in *Joannis de Fordun Scotichronicon cum Supplementis et Continuatione Walteri Boweri*, ed. Walter Goodall (Edinburgh 1759, 2 vols), ii. 250–5. For its value as a historical source for the battle of Bannockburn see Morris, *Bannockburn*, pp. 50–1, 54, 61, 72.

[237] *GB*, pp. 9, 189n. See Tout, *Edward II*, p. 215, and *VCH, Oxford*, ii. 139. For Carmelites as Baker's informants for Edward III's reign see p. 77 and n. 120 below.

[238] *GB*, p. 27. The tract in French by Sir Thomas de la More describing Edward II's deposition does not survive. Nor is it known to what extent Baker relied on More's tract—presumably he also used verbal information from More and others. The *Vita et Mors Edwardi Secundi* current in the sixteenth century is not, as once was thought, a Latin rendering of More's tract, but merely an abbreviated and slightly altered extract from Baker's work. See *Chrons Edw. I and II*, ii. lviii-lix, lxiv-lxvi (the *Vita et Mors* is printed in ibid., ii. 297–319.)

of Winchester, were an ornament to the company (of those sent to
the king at Kenilworth); I am but the interpreter, as it were, of
what you saw and wrote down in French.

Baker claimed to have special knowledge of Edward's persecution and
death. He heard it 'after the great plague [of 1349] from William Bishop,
who was in charge of Edward's guards, which he confessed and repented,
hoping for divine mercy.'[239] Baker thought that the truth had been suppressed. Again addressing Sir Thomas he writes:[240]

> What we have written, Oh worthy knight! would be proclaimed
> in broad daylight if fear of the enemies of this devout king who
> are still living, did not forbid the declaration of the truth—which,
> nevertheless, cannot remain hidden for ever.

Baker also has unique information about Humphrey de Bohun, earl
of Hereford (1302–22), notably concerning his death fighting for the
barons at Boroughbridge.[241] Baker was usually royalist in his sympathies
but justified Earl Humphrey's baronial affiliations because this 'warlike,
courageous, energetic and circumspect hero' felt obliged, from the goodness
of his heart, to defend the interests, whether right or wrong, of his men,
'the guileless knights of his household', whom defeat threatened with
imprisonment, exile, or crippling ransom. The earl was killed by a Welsh
soldier stationed under the bridge who thrust a lance upwards through
an aperture in his armour into his abdomen, 'for knights, not expecting
to be struck from under the feet, do not protect their private parts.'

Baker's source for his knowledge about Humphrey de Bohun was probably oral, for the Bohuns were lords of Chadlington hundred, in which
Swinbrook lay.[242] Possibly Baker wrote partly to please the Bohun family.
This suggestion receives some support from the fact that the most authoritative extant manuscript of the *Chronicon* was almost certainly written for
a dependant of John de Bohun, earl of Hereford (1326–36), a secular clerk
called Thomas of Walmesford. Early in the fifteenth century the manuscript was in the hands of the family physician of Joan de Bohun, countess
of Hereford (the widow of Humphrey de Bohun, earl of Hereford from
1363 to 1373).[243]

---

[239] *GB*, p. 31.

[240] *GB*, p. 30.

[241] *GB*, pp. 13–14. A similar account of Humphrey de Bohun's death is in the long version
of the French *Brut* (see p. 74 and n. 99 below). For the possibility that the Ralph de
Bohun who wrote a *Brut* chronicle 'at the request of my Lord Henry de Lacy, earl of
Lincoln,' was a member of the Bohun family of the earls of Hereford and Essex, see Legge,
A-N Lit. pp. 280–3. See also p. 74 below.

[242] *GB*, p. ix. For the suggestion that Baker obtained his information on Roger Mortimer's
arrest from Humphrey de Bohun's son Edward see p. 78 n. 125 below.

[243] *GB*, pp. xiii-xvi.

The most moving pages in Baker's account of Edward II's reign are those describing the king's deposition, persecution and death; but to what extent they belong to English history as well as to English literature is hard to say. Baker obviously embroidered his informants' words—and they themselves probably exaggerated the facts and in any case may not have remembered them correctly. He collected and synthesized his information twenty years after the events. At that time the cult of Edward II was flourishing and legend was eroding historical accuracy, but, on the other hand, men wanted to dissociate the ruling king, Edward III, from the savage murder of his father for which his mother and her lover, both by then disgraced and the latter dead, were responsible. It is to be expected, therefore, that Baker would eulogize Edward II and denigrate Isabella and Mortimer and their supporters.[244]

Baker describes Isabella, whom he punningly calls Jezebel, as a woman with a heart of steel.[245] But his chief invective is expended on the pro-baronial bishop Adam of Orleton, the 'principal machinator', the 'architect of all the evil', and 'master of the queen's malice'. He gives a full account of the sermon Orleton preached at Oxford early in October 1326 in the presence of the queen, Mortimer and their 'satellites', on the text 'My head, my head', arguing that an ineffectual head should be removed from the body (here an analogue of the realm).[246]

Baker accuses Orleton of writing a letter containing an ambiguous phrase, 'Edwardum occidere nolite timere bonum est' to Edward's guards at Berkeley, Thomas Gurney and John Maltravers, which they interpreted as an instruction to kill the king. [247] Christopher Marlowe (whose ultimate source here was Baker's chronicle) explains in the words of Roger Mortimer:[248]

> *Edwardum occidere nolite timere bonum est:*
> Fear not to kill the king, 'tis good he die.

---

[244] T. F. Tout argues that Baker had no substantial information about Edward II's captivity and death beyond the brief statement he found in Adam Murimuth. He demonstrates the groundlessness of Baker's story of Orleton's ambiguous letter and Sir Thomas de Berkeley's last sad farewell to Edward in Berkeley castle; see T. F. Tout, 'The captivity and death of Edward of Carnarvon' in *BJRL*, vi (1921–2, reprinted in *The Collected Papers of T. F. Tout*, ii. 145–90), pp. 69–113 (see especially pp. 87–92).

[245] *GB*, pp. 21, 29.

[246] *GB*, p. 23. For Orleton's own account of this sermon see *The Register of Adam de Orleton, Bishop of Hereford 1317–1327*, ed. A. T. Bannister (Cantilupe Soc., ii, 1907–8), pp. xxxv–xxxvi. Bannister (op. cit., p. xxxv n. 2) accuses de la More of confusing this sermon with the one preached by John Stratford, bishop of Winchester, to parliament on 14 January 1327 (see *Lan.* p. 258). Cf. p. 14 and n. 71 above.

[247] *GB*, p. 32.

[248] *Edward II*, Act V, scene iv, lines 8–12. Marlowe's source here was Holinshed, who had the story from the *Vita et Mors* (see p. 38 n. 238 above) which was derived from Baker; *Edward II*, ed. H. B. Charlton and R. D. Waller (London 1930, reprinted New York 1961), p. 194 n. 6, and Hilda Johnstone in *The Times Literary Supplement*, 16 August 1928, p. 593.

But read it thus, and that's another sense:
Edwardum occidere nolite timere bonum est:
Kill not the king, 'tis good to fear the worst.

Whether Orleton ever wrote such a letter is extremely doubtful. Such oracular ambiguities have an ancient literary tradition.[249] Furthermore, Orleton was out of the country at the time, and was not charged with this particular piece of iniquity when accused in 1333 of instigating Edward II's deposition and murder.

Baker treats Edward II with compassion. He praises his loyalty to friends (that is to the Despensers whom Edward refused to sacrifice to baronial anger),[250] and his piety and patience in suffering, which Baker considered comparable to Job's.[251] The account of the king's last days is extraordinarily graphic. Having described Edward's attempt to escape to Lundy island (of which Baker gives a good topographical description),[252] he records his capture and the circumstances of the deposition. In the main his narrative on the deposition agrees with Murimuth's, but he adds some lifelike details, how Edward agreed, 'with tears and sighs', in a private conference with the bishops of Lincoln and Winchester to abdicate, and then 'wearing a black cloak' entered the room where the other baronial emissaries were assembled, and how he fainted with emotion and was lifted 'half dead' from the floor by the earl of Leicester and the bishop of Winchester.[253]

The details of Edward's journey from Corfe to Berkeley in the custody of Gurney and Maltravers are equally vivid. The 'satraps of Satan', fearing risings on Edward's behalf, travelled secretly and circuitously at night, and hoped by psychological torture and physical duress to end Edward's life. They allowed him only inadequate clothing and kept him perpetually awake, they fed him on food he did not like, contradicted everything he said and treated him with contempt. They crowned him with hay and shaved him with cold water from a stream ('"Despite your wishes", Edward said, "we shall have warm water", and wept copiously to supply it'). However, Edward's strong constitution survived hardship and humiliation.

Edward was put in Berkeley castle in a room above a charnel-house—

---

[249] Medieval examples of the use of 'occidere (or interficere) nolite timere bonum est' see G. C. Moore Smith in *The Times Literary Supplement*, 9 August 1928, p. 581. The story that Orleton procured Edward II's death by means of such a message is virtually dismissed as untrue by Tout (see p. 40 n. 244 above), and by R. M. Haines, *The Church and Politics in Fourteenth-Century England: the Career of Adam Orleton c. 1275–1345* (Cambridge 1978), p. 109.

[250] *GB*, pp. 16–18.

[251] *GB*, pp. 28–31 passim.

[252] *GB*, p. 22.

[253] *GB*, pp. 26–8.

with the intention that the stench would poison him. But though he complained bitterly to carpenters working outside his window, he again survived. Finally on the night of 22 September fifteen ruffians entered his room carrying ponderous cushions with which they suffocated him. To make his death certain 'they passed a red hot soldering iron, through a trumpet-like instrument (so that no visible mark would be left to be seen by any friend of justice) into his anus, through the intestines and into his windpipe. And so died this great soldier, with a terrible scream.' Those who heard the scream echoing throughout the castle and beyond, 'prayed with compassion for the departed soul. Thus he whom the world had hated, as previously it had hated his master Jesus, was received in heaven.'

Ranulf Higden

Little is known about the career of Ranulf Higden, the author of the *Poly-chronicon*.[1] He became a monk of the Benedictine abbey of St Werburgh's, Chester, in 1299, and remained there until his death some time in the 1360s. There is no evidence that he studied at Oxford or Cambridge, or that he travelled further afield than his own locality except on one occasion. By 1352 he had acquired sufficient reputation as an historian to be summoned to the king's council on 21 August, to come 'with all your chronicles and those in your charge to speak and treat with the council concerning matters to be explained to you on our behalf'. The wording of the summons suggests that he was *armarius*, that is keeper of the library at St Werburgh's, and head of the *scriptorium*. The occasion for the summons is unknown.[2]

Higden was the product of a monastic education and a monastic background. He had the use of an excellent library in the abbey, which perhaps he supplemented by loans from nearby monasteries. Not surprisingly his learning was traditional. He was apparently uninfluenced even by twelfth century scholasticism, but he has affinities with a number of twelfth century writers, notably John of Salisbury and Gerald of Wales. Various works have been attributed to him besides his best known, the *Polychronicon*, and he was certainly the author of two of them, the *Ars Componendi Sermones* (*The Art of Composing Sermons*) and the *Speculum Curatorum* (*A Mirror for Priests*).[3] Both works were designed as aids to preaching.

Although Higden's *Ars Componendi Sermones* enjoyed considerable popularity, his fame rested in his own day and still rests ultimately on the *Polychronicon*. Higden stands in the series of great English Benedictine historians—William of Malmesbury, Matthew Paris and Thomas Walsingham. Except for Bede's *Historia Ecclesiastica* and Geoffrey of Monmouth's *Historia Regum Britanniae*, no medieval history book rivalled the *Polychronicon* in popularity. Over 120 manuscripts survive, dating from the fourteenth

---

[1] For Higden's life see John Taylor, *The Universal Chronicle of Ranulf Higden* (Oxford 1966), pp. 1–2. The *Polychronicon* is printed *Polychronicon Ranulphi Higden Monachi Cestrensis*, ed. Churchill Babington and J. R. Lumby (RS 1865–86, 9 vols); see also p. 44 n. 5 below.
[2] See J. G. Edwards, 'Ranulf, monk of Chester' in *EHR*, xlvii (1932), p. 94.
[3] For these two works see Taylor, *Higden*, pp. 3–4, 183. See also Margaret Jennings, 'Monks and the "Artes praedicandi" in the time of Ranulph Higden' in *Revue Bénédictine*, lxxxvi (1976), pp. 119–28, and p. 53 below.

and fifteenth centuries, and the early date of some shows that the fame of the work spread during Higden's lifetime.[4]

As an historian Higden must be seen in his monastic context. The character sketch of Edward II quoted from the *Polychronicon* at the beginning of the previous chapter, is not typical of his work: despite the fact that he included the history of his own times, his primary concern was with past, not contemporary, history. His position as a monk of Chester may have encouraged the development of this dominant interest, for, while he had access to numerous books, he was remote from the centres of political affairs.

The *Polychronicon* is a universal history from the Creation until Higden's own day, in seven books. Moreover, it is an encyclopaedia. The first book describes the geography and natural history of the world, the various peoples and their customs. Throughout the work Higden interpreted his subject in the widest sense, to include social and intellectual history. He started writing the *Polychronicon* in 1327 or soon afterwards, and continued work on it until his death in the 1360s.

The stages of the development of the text of the *Polychronicon* can be roughly plotted by studying the manuscript written at St Werburgh's under Higden's supervision, now in the Huntington Library, California,[5] and by collating the numerous other manuscripts. It appears that Higden first wrote the *Polychronicon* to 1327; no copy of this version is known to survive. The next stage was the production of the so-called short version, which is ñot extant in its original form. Then Higden wrote the 'intermediate' version, which has revisions and additions. In accordance with an earlier intention,[6] he altered the initial letters of the chapters in Book I to produce the acrostic of his name. He also suppressed some passages in the light of new knowledge and reflection, but added many more. He subsequently produced two more versions, each longer than the one before. Most of the additional material was derived from Florence of Worcester's chronicle and the *Gesta Regum* of William of Malmesbury.[7] How Higden actually carried out this revision, by means of erasure, marginal notes and the like, can be seen in the Huntington manuscript, which represents the last and fullest recension of the *Polychronicon*. The different manuscripts of the *Polychronicon* end at various dates between 1340 and 1352. The

---

[4] See pp. 55 and n. 67, 56 below.

[5] Huntington Library MS. 132. Described by V. H. Galbraith, 'An autograph MS. of Ranulph Higden's *Polychronicon*' in *Huntington Library Quarterly*, xxiii (1959–60), pp. 1–18. See Plate II (a) and (b) below. The development of the text is discussed by Taylor, *Higden*, pp. 96–102.

[6] See *Poly.* ii. 76, Taylor, *Higden*, p. 94, Galbraith, op. cit., p. 11, and p. 47 below. For an example of an initial letter altered in order to produce the acrostic see Plate II (a) below.

[7] For the additional passages from Florence of Worcester, and from William of Malmesbury's *Gesta Regum*, see Taylor, *Higden*, p. 103. (For examples see *Poly.* v. 376 and n. 9; vii. 428 and n. 9, 454 and n. 9.) The Huntington MS. also has over twenty author's notes in the margins, each marked 'R'; see Galbraith, op. cit, p. 7, and Plate II (b) below.

Huntington manuscript shows that Higden wrote to 1340, and then someone, probably Higden himself, added brief entries from 1341 to 1352.[8]

Higden's originality as an author lay in his literary talent. He collected together a vast quantity of often disparate information and formed it into a comprehensible whole on which he impressed the seal of Christianity. To do this he used various literary devices. One was the concept of man as the microcosm of the world.[9] This idea was of great antiquity, going back to Pythagoras. Isidore describes man as a microcosm and Bernard Sylvester wrote a book on the subject of the world as the macrocosm of man and *vice versa*.[10] (The idea was often expressed in medieval iconography.)[11] Similarly John of Salisbury compares the kingdom to the human body.[12]

Higden applied this concept in a new way. He used it to link his first book, on geography, with the subsequent six books, on the history of mankind. Having described the physical appearance of the world, he turns from the greater world to the little world, man himself. As he says, 'the order of historical narrative requires that after the places of the world have been described, its acts should be described.' Since the greater world was made for the lesser world, and the greater should serve the lesser, the description of the greater world is usefully described first.[13] Higden, because the Creator had made man in the likeness of the great world, proceeds to compare the two. They resemble each other in three respects; in their dimensions, their composition, and their functions. The proportions of their measurements are the same; the distance in the world from zenith to nadir and from east to west are equal, as is the distance in man from head to foot and from one extended arm to the other. Their natural dispositions are similar: their parts and members correspond, and any dislocation

---

[8] See Galbraith, op. cit., pp. 15–16. Galbraith and Plate II (c) below reproduce the penultimate page of Huntington Library MS. 132, which shows the end of Higden's text in the latest recension, and the change of pen and ink with the additional annal for 1341.

[9] Higden's use of the concept of man as a microcosm of the world and the literary structure of the *Polychronicon*, are discussed at greater length in A. Gransden, 'Silent meanings in Ranulf Higden's *Polychronicon* and in Thomas Elmham's *Liber Metricus de Henrico Quinto*' in *Medium Ævum*, xlvi (1978), pp. 231–3, 238–9.

[10] For Isidore of Seville's familiarity with the concept of man as a microcosm of the universe see E. Brehaut, *An Encyclopedist of the Dark Ages: Isidore of Seville* (New York 1912), pp. 62–3. For the currency of the idea see J. K. Wright, *The Geographical Lore of the Time of the Crusades* (New York 1965), pp. 146–50, and Lynn Thorndike, *A History of Magic and Experimental Science* (New York 1923–58, 8 vols), ii. 153–4.

[11] For examples of the iconographic representation of man as a microcosm see Wright, op. cit., p. 149, and C. N. L. Brooke, *The Twelfth Century Renaissance* (London 1969), p. 62.

[12] *Policraticus*, v. 2; see *Ioannis Saresberiensis Episcopi Carnotensis Policratici*, ed. C. C. I. Webb (Oxford 1909, 2 vols), i. 282–4. For the use by some chroniclers of the analogy of the kingdom with the human body see pp. 36 and n. 219 above and 319 and n. 59 below.

[13] *Poly.* ii. 174–6.

causes disturbance in both; and both are composed of the same four elements, fire, water, earth and air. Finally, they resemble each other in their functions; both have childhood, youth and age, with their respective characteristics, and man's energies resemble those of the elements and the planets.[14] Thus by using the concept of man as the microcosm of the world Higden gives his work a cohesive theme, making the geographical section an integral part of the subsequent history. Moreover, Higden prepares the way for the history of mankind from the creation of Adam, by pointing out that in one respect man differs from the world. Although he was created at the same time as the earth, his condition was not, like the world's, static but subject to change. Before the Fall man was in perfect harmony with himself and was free from the corruption of the flesh; but after the Fall that harmony was lost and he became mortal.[15] The concept of man as a microcosm of the world not only helped give the *Polychronicon* thematic unity, but also placed its miscellaneous contents firmly in a biblical context.

Higden also used numerology to provide a theological framework for the *Polychronicon*, which he divided into seven books, 'after the example of the Creator who made all things in six days and rested on the seventh.' Numerology, an ancient literary device in which numbers assume an entirely symbolic quality, has been rather variously assessed as 'a superbly subtle instrument for the unification of knowledge', and as 'a static structure upon which scraps of knowledge of all sorts could be hung'.[16] Both assessments are true of the *Polychronicon*: numerology gives it structural unity, but of a rather artificial and rigid kind.

Higden used an elaborate numerological apparatus to discuss the nature and scope of history. (The passage in which he reflects on the subject incidentally shows the breadth of his approach.) Eight things, he writes at the beginning of Book I,[17] are necessary for the full knowledge of history. (Eight was treated by Plato as the number of perfection; to Christians it represented the seven days of the Creation and Heaven, and the Seven Ages of Man and his time in Heaven.) Higden enumerates the eight necessary things. First, descriptions of places. Second, kinds of society. Third, distinctions of times. Fourth, successions of governments. Fifth, variations of customs. Sixth, the passing of the ages. Seventh, the nature of actions. Eighth, the various ways of calculating the years. Higden then discusses each necessity in turn, still using numerology. Thus the first necessity is in the first book; as for the second, there are two kinds of society, that from the beginning of the world until Christ ('which is called of "deviation"'),

---

[14] *Poly.* ii. 176–86.
[15] *Poly.* ii. 212–18.
[16] Christopher Butler, *Number Symbolism* (London 1970), pp. 43, 44. For numerology in biblical exegesis see Beryl Smalley, *The Study of the Bible in the Middle Ages* (Oxford 1952), p. 5.
[17] *Poly.* i. 30–6.

and that from Christ until the end ('called of "reconciliation"'); with respect to the third necessity, it is noted that there are three distinctions of time, before the written law, under the written law and of grace. The fifth necessity provided Higden with an opportunity for a further numerological twist, four of the five kinds of customs (those of the Moslems), were discussed in his fifth book. And so on.

The same pattern of mind, which made such abstract structures congenial to Higden, reappears in the acrostic which stamps his name on the *Polychronicon*. The initial letters which begin each of the sixty chapters of Book I spell out: 'Presentem cronicam conpilavit frater Ranulphus Cestrensis monachus' ('Brother Ranulf, monk of Chester, compiled the present chronicle'). This is the first known use of an acrostic by an English historian (Higden added his name in acrostic to his other writings).[18]

Thus Higden's concept of a universal history had two elements: it included both geographical and anthropological information and the like, and a sequence of world events from the Creation until his own time. He had numerous precursors as an author of a universal history, many of them among his sources. For example, Isidore of Seville and Bartholomew Anglicus provided models for geographical and anthropological descriptions of the world. And Gerald of Wales, in the *Topographia Hibernica* and in the *Descriptio Cambriae*, had shown a close interest in the habits of the Irish and the Welsh.

The tradition of the chronological universal history goes back to Eusebius. More recently Marianus Scotus, one of Florence of Worcester's main sources, had written a massive universal history. In England Matthew Paris, to take only one example, began his chronicle at the Creation: although the comparative amount of space Paris devoted to universal history was small (he concentrated on English history as soon as the sources provided enough detail), he retained an interest in distant lands (for example in the Mongol empire).[19] The amalgamation of the geographical and historical elements typical of the fully developed universal history was achieved in the thirteenth century by Vincent of Beauvais.[20] He was an important source not only of Higden, but also of the English Dominican Nicholas Trevet, whose *Historia ab orbe condito ad Christi Nativitatem* (*History from the Creation of the World to the Birth of Christ*) was the immediate forerunner in England of the *Polychronicon*.[21]

Higden's chronicle is almost entirely a compilation, made up of borrowings from ancient and more recent authorities. History, Higden claims

[18] See p. 44 and n. 6 above. For acrostics in subsequent chronicles see pp. 94, 159, 405 below.
[19] See Gransden, *Historical Writing*, i. 362
[20] Vincent of Beauvais, *Speculum Historiale* (Balthazaris Belleri 1624). There are other early printed editions.
[21] Gransden, op. cit., i. 503–4.

in his prologue, immortalizes what would otherwise perish, and perpetuates in the memory what would otherwise be forgotten. He is, he admits, merely a compiler, but the writing of history by the method of compilation can be justified by excellent precedents. Either Virgil or Horace (Higden is not sure which) had an apt defence of such plagiarism: 'When he was accused by his enemies of borrowing verses by Homer and incorporating them in his own poems, and called a compiler of old writers, he replied, "It is a sign of great strength to wrest the club from the hand of Hercules".'[22]

The *Polychronicon* is a monument to Higden's extensive learning and to the library resources at his command. He used a wide variety of classical and Christian authorities.[23] They include among Roman writers, Valerius Maximus, Pliny (the *Natural History*), Suetonius (the *Lives of the Caesars*) and Eutropius. His early Christian authorities include Eusebius, St Augustine, Orosius and Isidore of Seville. Among his Dark Age and medieval authorities are Bede, Florence of Worcester, William of Malmesbury (the *Gesta Regum* and the *Gesta Pontificum*), Geoffrey of Monmouth, Henry of Huntingdon, John of Salisbury (the *Policraticus*), Alfred of Beverley, Gerald of Wales (the *Topographia Hibernica*, the *Itinerarium Cambriae*, the *Descriptio Cambriae*, the *De Principis Instructione* and the *Speculum Ecclesiae*) and Vincent of Beauvais.

Higden lists some of his authorities at the beginning of the *Polychronicon*,[24] and in the course of the work precedes many passages with the name of an authority (he prefaces his own remarks with 'Ranulphus'): sometimes it is hard to check the accuracy of such acknowledgments because he does not cite authorities *verbatim*, but paraphrases them. Both Higden's list and his notes of sources should be treated with caution. Higden lent heavily on medieval books of extracts and compendiums, and often cited works as if at first hand, which he only knew indirectly through an intermediate authority. For example he lists Livy as a source, but it is doubtful whether he had access to the work itself.[25] He also cites Cicero and Aulus Gellius but here his information was certainly second hand.[26] Conversely he used some authorities without acknowledging them. Thus many of the citations ostensibly from classical authors are in fact from two thirteenth century compilations, the *De Proprietatibus Rerum* by the Dominican Bartholomew Anglicus,[27] and the *Compendiloquium* by the Franciscan, John of Wales.[28]

Higden's treatment of his sources was in general uncritical. He trans-

[22] *Poly*. i. 10–12. Cited by Beryl Smalley, *English Friars and Antiquity in the Early Fourteenth Century* (Oxford 1960), p. 20.

[23] Higden's sources are discussed in Taylor, *Higden*, pp. 72–88.

[24] *Poly*. i. 20–4.

[25] *Poly*. i. 24. Cf. Taylor, *Higden*, p. 76.

[26] See ibid., p. 75.

[27] See ibid., pp. 82–3, and Thorndike, op. cit., ii. 401–35.

[28] See Taylor, *Higden*, pp. 74–80 passim, and Smalley, *English Friars and Antiquity*, pp. 51–5.

mitted from his authorities into his work a vast corpus of fiction which he treated on the same terms as factual history. The fictional element in the *Polychronicon* is not free fiction—it is not the product of Higden's creative imagination (Geoffrey of Monmouth's *Historia Regum Britanniae* was mainly fiction in this sense). It is traditional fiction, including myths, marvels and miracles, handed down by earlier writers, both pagan and Christian.

Higden admits in his prologue that equal credence cannot be given to all the statements in the *Polychronicon*, but he appeals to various ancient authorities to justify the inclusion of fictional material: St Augustine, who said that miracles should be wondered at and revered, not argued about; Jerome, who wrote that things might be incredible and improbable, but nevertheless true, because nothing contrary to nature was so marvellous as nature itself; and Isidore, who stated that though the origins of Rome are obscure, the origins of other cities are even more so, and therefore we should believe stories about them unless they are contrary to religion or known fact.[29]

Higden lived before the development of many techniques used by present day historians. He knew nothing about archaeology, philology, place-name studies or diplomatic. Hence he could not check a statement in a literary source against an objective, scientifically assessed piece of evidence. He did, however, sometimes apply one of two tests to a statement. He might compare it with another literary source, or he might question it on grounds of reason. For example he questioned the truth of Virgil's story of Aeneas and Dido, because according to other reputed authorities Dido had lived 300 years later,[30] and often discusses chronological problems caused by discrepancies between the literary sources.[31] His deference to written authority, without consideration of its relative worth, is clearly shown by his discussion about the foundation of Gloucester. He admitted that William of Malmesbury attributed its foundation to Julius Caesar, but argued that if William of Malmesbury had had the benefit of reading Geoffrey of Monmouth he would have accepted Bladud as the founder.[32]

Comparison with other sources and rational argument caused Higden to question Geoffrey of Monmouth's more extreme claims for King Arthur.[33] If, as Geoffrey writes, Arthur subdued France and Italy, why were all the Roman, French and English historians who recorded much less important things about much less important people, totally silent on his exploits? Higden also pointed out that no other authority mentions the continental

[29] *Poly.* i. 14–18.
[30] *Poly.* i. 166.
[31] For discussions of chronological problems see e.g. *Poly.* i. 32–40; ii. 220, 242–4; iii. 16, 104. The Huntington Library MS. shows that at a late stage in the revision of his text Higden was still interested in problems of chronology; see Taylor, *Higden*, p. 104.
[32] *Poly.* ii. 58.
[33] *Poly.* v. 334–8.

[49]

rulers whom, according to Geoffrey, Arthur conquered. Here Higden used literary authorities to good effect. Moreover, he offered a plausible explanation for Geoffrey's extravagances. Geoffrey, he asserts, like many other historians, was trying to increase the reputation of his own nation by extolling its national hero. The Greeks had lauded Alexander, the Romans Augustus, the English Richard I, and the French Charlemagne. And so the Britons praised Arthur. Sometimes Higden used reason to challenge fiction with less success, merely substituting one fiction for another. For example, he argued that Paradise could not be above the world because its weight could not be supported up there, and because the wall of flame dividing earth and moon would consume the vegetation. Moreover, if so situated it would cause eclipses of the moon, and no such eclipse had been observed. Therefore Higden, like other early geographers, placed Paradise in the extreme east of the world, protected by a wall of fire and a guard of angels.[34]

Thus the collation of literary sources and the use of reason only occasionally removed Higden from the realm of fiction. He cannot of course be criticized for not using historical techniques which have only developed in more recent times. However, he could have made greater use of first hand observation which had been employed to such good effect by earlier writers.[35] William of Malmesbury, one of Higden's principal sources, was an excellent topographer. Another of Higden's sources, Gerald of Wales, redeemed his often fictitious accounts of the Irish and Welsh with exact observations. And Matthew Paris' maps of England were genuine attempts, based on his own knowledge, to record the appearance of the country in his day.[36] But Higden turned to an authority if there was one. (This is well illustrated by his world map which has no value to the cartographer because it merely reproduces the traditional medieval view of the world.)[37] The lack of written sources is no doubt the main reason for Higden's comparatively brief treatment of his own times.

Despite Higden's reverence for authority, he did record a few observations at first hand which are of some interest to the historian today. He remarks on a few ancient monuments, for example on the massive ruins at Chester; he concludes that they must be the work of Romans or of

---

[34] *Poly.* i. 70–8. Cf. G. H. T. Kimble, *Geography in the Middle Ages* (London 1938), p. 185.

[35] See A. Gransden, 'Realistic observation in twelfth-century England' in *Speculum*, xlvii (1972), pp. 29–51.

[36] For the value of Gerald of Wales' descriptions of the Irish and the Welsh see Gransden, *Historical Writing*, i. 245, and Wright, op. cit., p. 120. For his geographical sense see ibid., pp. 337–45 passim, and Kimble, op. cit., p. 179. For the value of Matthew Paris' maps of England (which are orientated, like modern maps, from north to south) see Wright, op. cit., pp. 342–3, Kimble, op. cit., p. 189, and G. R. Beazley, *The Dawn of Modern Geography* (London 1897–1906, 3 vols), ii. 585.

[37] See p. 54 and n. 59 below.

giants, and not of the Anglo-Saxons. He notes the underground passages, the magnificent chambered halls, the monumental stones inscribed with archaic letters and the Roman coins found in the earth.[38] Similarly, he gives a careful account, based partly on Geoffrey of Monmouth and partly on his own information, of the course of the Roman trunk roads, the Fosseway, Watling Street, Ermine Street and Ryknield Street, and describes the course of Offa's Dyke, from the Severn valley, near Bristol, to Flint castle, near Chester.[39]

Moreover, Higden had some interest in contemporary society and economy. He records the folk lore of the Isle of Man, for example how the women sold wind to sailors (in the form of three knots which the sailors untied to bring the wind).[40] More generally, he discusses the different dialects in England, Scotland and Wales, and characterizes England and the English.[41] He follows William of Malmesbury's statement that the southern English could not understand people in the north, and adds that those living on the Welsh borders and in the midlands had no difficulty understanding each other.[42] He describes southerners as quiet and gentle in their habits, the northerners as fierce and restless, and the marchers and midlanders as being between the two extremes. The south of England was, he asserts, richer and more populous than the north, with larger cities and more commodious ports. He also remarks on the wool trade with Flanders: England produced the best wool, but it was dyed and made into cloth in Flanders. This was because in England there was water suitable for dyeing only in London and near Lincoln (where the best scarlet cloth was made).[43]

However, the *Polychronicon* is not primarily of value as a repository of facts. It is mainly important for the light it throws on Higden's opinions and tastes, which in their turn reflect those of his contemporaries. Higden wrote in an age when patriotism was in the ascendant. As will be seen,[44] the other chronicles of Edward III's reign reflect the development of national consciousness. Higden's universal history, therefore, raises the problem of his attitude to contemporary patriotism. At first sight the *Polychronicon* seems to be contrary to the current trend. Its universality is international rather than national. Although it does devote disproportionate space to British and English history and has some patriotic passages,[45] its interest in other countries makes it clear that Higden was not merely

[38] *Poly.* ii. 78–80.
[39] *Poly.* ii. 44–6, 34, respectively.
[40] *Poly.* ii. 42.
[41] *Poly.* ii. 156–66.
[42] Cf. *Poly.* ii. 34.
[43] *Poly.* i. 288.
[44] Chapters 3 and 4 below.
[45] See, e.g. the passages on England's natural prosperity and the numerous saints who were preserved uncorrupt· *Poly.* ii. 6, 12–30 passim.

providing a background to the Brutus story and its sequel. He even has a satirical tirade on the English character. He writes that although the English were invincible abroad they were easily conquered at home, and were excessively curious about foreign things and scornful of their own. He accuses them of perpetual dissatisfaction with their station in life, always aspiring to the next rank. He pours abuse—the English were 'actors in their deeds, playboys in address, tradesmen in business'. And he uses classical parallels to lend force to his accusations: the English are 'Tyrians in splendour, Argi in wealth, Tantali in labour, Daedali in court, Sardanapali in bed', and so on.[46] Higden's wish to write a balanced universal history also appears in his virtual suppression of local attachments. Although, in order to remedy William of Malmesbury's neglect, he mentions Chester's abundant natural resources (corn, meat, fish, especially salmon, and salt and iron), he spends only about two pages on its history[47] and makes no use of the work of its twelfth century local historian, Lucian, another monk of St Werburgh's.[48]

However, the *Polychronicon* is in a sense a patriotic work. It made a universal history available to readers in England, and ultimately became part of the vernacular literary tradition. Higden himself, despite his use of Latin, was interested in the English language. He lamented the dominance of French at the expense of English. Children, he states, were forced to learn French at school, 'contrary to the practice of other nations', so that their native tongue was neglected. The upper classes learnt French in their cradles and even country folk aspired to speak French.[49] Moreover, Higden tended to glorify the Anglo-Saxon past. He added to the King Alfred legend, which flourished in the fourteenth century, the story that Alfred founded Oxford university.[50] The *Polychronicon* became a part of English literature when John Trevisa translated it into the vernacular in the 1380s. It was translated again in the fifteenth century.[51] Both William Caxton and Wynkyn de Worde printed from Trevisa's English text.[52]

---

[46] *Poly.* ii. 168–74.

[47] *Poly.* ii. 76–8.

[48] For Lucian see Gransden, 'Realistic observation in twelfth century England', p. 4.

[49] *Poly.* ii. 158. At this point John Trevisa (see below) has an addition to Higden's text. He states that John of Cornwall, a master of grammar 'changed the lore in grammar school and construction of French into English', and that Richard of Penkridge (Staffs.) 'learned the manner of teaching of him and of other men of Penkridge, so that now, the year of our Lord 1385 . . . in all the grammar schools of England, children leaveth French and construeth and learneth in English': *Poly.* ii. 161. See p. 221 below.

[50] *Poly.* vi. 354. Taylor, *Higden*, p. 45. For the Alfredian legend in the fourteenth century see Smalley, *English Friars and Antiquity.* p. 208, and, for the legend that Alfred founded Oxford university, B.A. Lees, *Alfred the Great* (New York–London 1915), pp. 450–1.

[51] Trevisa's translation, which has additions to Higden's text, and the fifteenth century one, which slightly abbreviates Higden, are printed opposite the Latin text in the Rolls Series edition (p. 43 n. 1 above). Cf. Taylor, *Higden*, pp. 134–40.

[52] For the printed edition by Caxton, which has a continuation to 1461, see pp. 222 n. 10, 257 below, and for it and the edition by Wynkyn de Worde, see Taylor, *Higden*, pp. 140–2.

Although Higden successfully fitted all history into a theological frame-work (by treating man as a microcosm of the world and by the use of numerology), the amount of pagan material unavoidable in a universal history seems to have worried him. As a result he emphasized the edificatory purpose of the work. History, he writes, provides rules for living, models for behaviour and incentives to virtue.[53] Classical equally with Christian history could supply excellent *exempla*—anecdotes to show men how to behave and edifying life-stories which inspired emulation. Higden justified the intermixture of pagan with Christian material by an appeal to precedent.[54]

> If heathen fictions, pagan sayings and local marvels figure in this work, they serve the Christian religion. Thus it was legitimate for Virgil to seek the gold of wisdom in the dross of the poet Ennius, and for the children of Israel to despoil the Egyptians on the way to the Promised Land.

The numerous *exempla* and biographies in the *Polychronicon* show the strong influence on Higden of the homiletic tradition, of which they were an essential element. Higden himself was the author of two handbooks for preachers, the *Ars Componendi Sermones* (a selection of texts, notes on the division of sermons, and the like), and the *Speculum Curatorum* (which discusses such subjects as faith, virtues and vices, and the Lord's Prayer).[55] To cite only one *exemplum* borrowed by Higden from classical antiquity. He tells how Plato, enraged with a servant, ordered him to take off his tunic and bare his shoulders so that he could beat him, but he stopped because he became aware of his own blazing anger. On being questioned by Zeusippus he said that he who himself deserved punishment for his anger, was about to punish another. He asked Zeusippus to do it for him, lest he was more severe than he ought to be—'a servant should not be in the power of him who has not power over himself.'[56] In common with theologians of his day, Higden believed that a heathen could achieve virtue by following natural law, even though deprived of the help of the Christian faith. Therefore he gave a eulogistic account of Alexander the Great.[57] Similarly he regarded Lucretia as a model of female virtue and fidelity, and discusses the motives for her suicide.[58]

Higden's theocentric outlook is illustrated by the world map which he

[53] *Poly.* i. 4.
[54] *Poly.* i. 16. Cited Smalley, *English Friars and Antiquity*, p. 20.
[55] See Taylor, *Higden*, p. 4.
[56] *Poly.* iii. 348–50. For John of Wales' use of *exempla* from classical history, see Smalley, op. cit., pp. 52–3.
[57] *Poly.* iii. 392–478; iv. 2–16. For John of Wales' eulogy of Alexander the Great see Smalley, op. cit., pp. 52, 53.
[58] *Poly.* iii. 158–64. For the possible use of the story of the rape of Lucretia in a piece of political propaganda see p. 89 and n. 197 below.

prefixed to Book I of the *Polychronicon*.[59] His map resembles Matthew Paris' world map, and presumably it was cartographically like the three great wall maps, which were in London and its vicinity in Higden's time (at least one of them had been figured at Matthew's direction). Higden's map, like Matthew's, is in the tradition of the medieval *mappa mundi*. It places Jerusalem in the centre (Ezekiel v. 5), and was intended to illustrate the spread of Christianity. Palestine and the biblical lands are disproportionately large (they occupy about a third of the total map). Biblical places—Nineveh, Babylon and Jericho—are marked though they had long since vanished, while more recent cities are omitted. Like other map-makers of the period Higden orientated his map to the east. And in the east he depicted Paradise, the geography of which he also described in his chronicle. However, the map also shows classical influence: the world appears as a disc surrounded by a river; and it has classical cities and creatures of classical mythology—all, as it were, celebrating God's creation.

Nevertheless, despite its theological structure and its edificatory passages, the *Polychronicon* is not a solemn work. It has been described as 'a glorious jumble of fact, legend and marvel'.[60] God's creation in its infinite variety and often marvellous manifestations was the true witness of His omnipotence. Higden's unlimited curiosity and sense of wonder corresponded to his readers' tastes. He wrote partly to satisfy their curiosity, and to amuse and amaze them with marvels and good stories. The *Polychronicon* is full of fascinating information, some true and some fictitious. On the one hand Higden's wide coverage of social and cultural history includes, for example, a fairly accurate account, with diagrams, of the mathematical relations of musical sounds.[61] On the other hand he describes fabulous men, flora and fauna. There were Cyclops with one eye, Sciapodes who lay on their backs shading themselves from the sun with their feet, and Cynocephali, men with dogs' heads, who barked, were covered with hair and had sharp teeth. There were people of mixed gender, and women who conceived at the age of five and did not outlive their eighth year.[62] A remarkable tree was that which prophesied to Alexander the Great, telling him not to enter Babylon, and an extraordinary bird was the barnacle goose which grew on fir trees and which men could eat in Lent because it was not carnally conceived.[63] Such marvellous creations belonged

[59] Higden's map is discussed and a version reproduced in Taylor, *Higden*, pp. 63–8, and frontispiece. His map is also discussed, in the context of the medieval cartographical tradition, in, Kimble, *Geography in the Middle Ages*, pp. 185–7, and in Beazley, *The Dawn of Modern Geography*, ii. 585–6.

[60] Smalley, op. cit., p. 21.

[61] *Poly.* iii. 208–10.

[62] *Poly.* i. 80–2; ii. 202–10.

[63] *Poly.* i. 84 (cf. ibid., i. xxiv n. i.), 334–6.

to traditional medieval lore which had its origins in antiquity. They were described and depicted in bestiaries, moralized natural-history books, which were well known to Higden and his contemporaries.[64]

Higden tells many anecdotes with no apparent moral, some of which are earthy and consciously humorous. For example, he recounts that a Jew fell down a latrine in Tewkesbury on a Saturday, and would not allow himself to be pulled out on account of reverence for his sabbath. But Richard de Clare, earl of Gloucester, would not have him pulled out on Sunday—because of reverence for *his* sabbath. And so the Jew died. (Higden caps the yarn with an appropriate verse.)[65] Higden also has a joking riddle. Charlemagne asked Alcuin what was the difference between a Scot and a sot. Alcuin replied, 'Only the width of a table.'[66]

One of the *Polychronicon*'s principal contributions to historiography was its seminal potential. (In this respect it resembles Geoffrey of Monmouth's *Historia Regum Britanniae* and Matthew Paris' *Flores Historiarum*.) Copies were in the possession of numerous institutions and individuals in the fourteenth and fifteenth centuries: they provided the starting point for continuations and quarries of information.

Fourteenth century copies survive from many Benedictine houses besides St Werburgh's itself—Christ Church and St Augustine's, Canterbury, Westminster, Norwich, Gloucester, Glastonbury, Ely, Abingdon, Ramsey and Hyde. Copies were also owned by foundations of other orders; by the Carthusians of Sheen, and in the fifteenth century by those of Witham, by the Cistercians of Fountains and Whalley and by the Franciscans of London. A number of houses of Augustinian canons (Gloucester, Dunstable, Barnwell, Keynsham and Llanthony) are known to have had copies, and in the fifteenth century a copy was at St Victor's in Paris. The *Polychronicon* was almost as popular with the secular clergy. Copies were owned by various ecclesiastical institutions (for example the cathedrals of Lincoln, Exeter, Bath and Wells, the hospitals of St John's, Cambridge, St John's, Exeter, and St Thomas's, London, and by the churches of St Peter's, Cornhill, and St Sepulchre's, Newgate). In the late fourteenth and fifteenth centuries some individual clerics (including William of Wykeham, Adam of Usk and Thomas Gascoigne), and even a few laymen (for example Humphrey Stafford, duke of Buckingham, 1444–60) had copies.[67]

---

[64] For a reproduction of a medieval bestiary, of c. 1200, see *The Bestiary, being a Reproduction of the MS. Ii. 4. 26 in the University Library, Cambridge*, ed. M. R. James (Roxburghe Club 1928).

[65] *Poly.* viii. 246.

[66] *Poly.* vi. 262.

[67] The manuscripts are listed in Taylor, *Higden*, pp. 152–9. Their provenance, when known, is given in the list and discussed in ibid., pp. 105–9.

Continuations were written in a number of religious houses and else-where.[68] The continuation to 1352 written probably by Higden himself (in the Huntington manuscript) was the basis of a further continuation to 1377. This was written fairly close to the events recorded, and references to Ely suggest that it was composed in Ely abbey.[69] For the 1360s this continuation was either used by, or made use of, the chronicle written by the Westminster monk, John of Reading.[70] It in its turn was rewritten and expanded a number of times by various authors in Richard II's reign. A version was probably composed at St Albans, and certainly the continuation formed the basis of the chronicle of Thomas Walsingham, monk of St Albans.[71] Moreover, the *Polychronicon* was continued apparently at Whalley (from 1341 to 1430),[72] and at Worcester by the monk John of Malvern (from 1348 to 1377).[73] Malvern's continuation was further continued at Westminster (to 1394)[74] and, under the name *Historia Vitae et Regni Ricardi Secundi*, at Evesham (to 1402).[75] And Adam of Usk continued his copy (which included the continuation to 1377) to 1421.[76] These continuations were very different in style and content from the *Polychronicon*: they comprised annals recording events principally relating to English history, in the style typical of the monastic chronicle.

However, the *Polychronicon* did influence the form and content of some of the chronicles written in the fourteenth century. One author undoubtedly influenced by Higden was John of Tynemouth, who in the mid-fourteenth century composed the *Historia Aurea*, a massive history (seven times as long as the *Polychronicon*) of Britain to the 1340s.[77] Tynemouth used the version of the *Polychronicon* to 1327, and Higden himself used the *Historia Aurea* for the later recensions of the *Polychronicon*. A work similar to the *Historia Aurea*, which also made use of the *Polychronicon*, is the chronicle up to the end of Richard I's reign, which goes under the name of John

---

[68] These continuations are fully discussed by John Taylor, 'The development of the *Polychronicon* continuation' in *EHR*, lxxvi (1961), pp. 20–36 (this article is virtually reprinted in the same author's *Higden*, Chap. VII, sections i and ii).

[69] Taylor, 'The development of the *Polychronicon* continuation', p. 24.

[70] Ibid., p. 24. For John of Reading see pp. 105–9 below.

[71] Taylor, op. cit., pp. 28–33, and V. H. Galbraith, 'The *Historia Aurea* of John, vicar of Tynemouth, and the sources of the St Albans chronicle' in *Essays in History presented to Reginald Lane Poole*, ed. H. W. C. Davis (Oxford 1927), pp. 389–93. See p. 124 and n. 53 below.

[72] See p. 159 and n. *8* below.

[73] See Taylor, *Higden*, pp. 122, 128, and J. Armitage Robinson, 'An unrecognized Westminster chronicler, 1381–1394' in *Proceedings of the British Academy*, iii (1907), pp. 61–5.

[74] Printed *Poly*. ix. See Taylor, op. cit., pp. 127–9, and Robinson, op. cit., pp. 65–92.

[75] See pp. 157–8 and n. 4 below.

[76] See p. 160 below.

[77] The *Historia Aurea* is discussed by V. H. Galbraith in *Essays in History* (see n. 71 above), pp. 379–98 passim, and by the same author (with printed extracts) in 'Extracts from the *Historia Aurea* and a French "Brut" (1317–47)' in *EHR*, xliii (1928), pp. 203–6, 208–15. Cf. Taylor, *Higden*, pp. 143–4.

of Brompton, abbot of the Cistercian house of Jervaulx, who gave a copy to the conventual library.[78] Nevertheless, although these two works were influenced by the *Polychronicon*, they did not try to reproduce its universal scope—they were English histories. The same is true of two other works, the *Scalacronica* of Sir Thomas Gray[79] and the chronicle of Henry Knighton.[80] Both Sir Thomas Gray and Henry Knighton were concerned with the history of England, for which they borrowed extensively from the *Polychronicon*: the latter's stylistic influence appears in their use of an acrostic to declare their authorship.

Indeed, the only fourteenth century chronicle reminiscent of the *Polychronicon* in both style and content is the *Eulogium Historiarum*.[81] It was written by a monk of Malmesbury who completed the bulk of it by about 1362. It is a compilation from well known sources, one of them the *Polychronicon*, and is a universal history showing a breadth of interest and a homiletic fervour worthy of Higden.

---

[78] Printed Twysden, *Scriptores Decem*, cols 725–1284. See Taylor. *Higden*, pp. 23 and n. 4, 144. See p. 359 and n. 103 below.
[79] See pp. 93–4 below.
[80] See pp. 159–60 below.
[81] See pp. 103–4 below.

Chroniclers of the Reign of Edward III: the 'Seculars' and Laymen

Edward II had a bad press. Edward III had (until his last years) a good one. This was because of the successes of his Scottish and French campaigns. The chroniclers approved of his wars and stressed his hereditary right to supremacy over Scotland and to the crown of France. His reign was a period of patriotic fervour. This found its extreme expression in the political poems of the day, notably in those of Lawrence Minot,[1] a contemporary who celebrated in English verse the victories of Sluys, Neville's Cross and Crécy, and other triumphs. Like Langtoft he bitterly inveighs against the Scots,[2] and he writes of Edward III in patriotic strain. For example :[3]

> God that shaped both sea and sand
> Save Edward king of England,
> Both body, soul and life,
> And grant him joy withouten strife:
> For many men to him are wroth
> In France and in Flanders both:
> For he defends fast his right,
> And thereto Jesu grant him might,
> And so to do both night and day,
> That it may be to God's pay.

The same sentiments are expressed by the chroniclers. They denigrate the Scots and the French, and tend to eulogize the English army commanders (notably the Black Prince), not so much for their specific qualities but because they represented victory over the foreigner. As Edward III's

---

[1] The most recent complete edition of Lawrence Minot's known political poems, with a discussion of his identity (he was probably of a Yorkshire family), is *The Poems of Lawrence Minot*, ed. Joseph Hall (Oxford 1887). Four of his poems are in *Historical Poems of the XIVth and XVth Centuries*, ed. R. H. Robbins (New York 1959), pp. 30–9.

[2] Hall, op. cit., p. 5, and Robbins, op. cit., pp. xvii, 31.

[3] Hall, op. cit., p. 6.

reign neared its end this enthusiasm gave way to disillusion with the Hundred Years' War, because of military mismanagement and heavy war-time taxation. This disillusion is not only expressed by the chroniclers but also in the prophecies which go under the name of John of Bridlington.[4] (In fact at least the prose commentaries on the prophecies, which themselves are in verse, are by John Erghome, an Augustinian friar of York.) The purpose of the 'Bridlington' prophecies was to satirize the government and encourage the successful renewal of the conflict. They were written shortly after 1361 and dedicated to Humphrey de Bohun, earl of Hereford, son of the great army commander, and a stern critic of the government.

We are concerned here with chronicles composed by secular clerks and laymen (the monastic chronicles will be discussed in the next chapter). Three of the works in question concern Edward II's reign as well as Edward III's, and so have been considered in a previous chapter in so far as they relate to the earlier period. They are the *Annales Paulini*, the chronicle of Adam Murimuth and the chronicle of Geoffrey le Baker. The seven other works are: the chronicle of Robert of Avesbury;[5] the French chronicle of London;[6] the *Brut*:[7] John Barbour's *Bruce*;[8] the chronicle of Jean le Bel;[9] the chronicle of Jean Froissart;[10] Sir Thomas Gray's

---

[4] The 'Bridlington' prophecies are printed and described in *Political Poems and Songs relating to English History . . . from the Accession of Edward III to that of Richard III*, ed. Thomas Wright (RS 1852, 2 vols), i. xxviii-lv, 123–215. See also *Chrons Edw. I and II*, ii.xxv-xxvi. For the authorship of the verses and prose gloss see Paul Meyvaert, 'John Erghome and the *Vaticinium Roberti Bridlington*' in *Speculum*, xli (1966), pp. 656–64, and John Taylor, 'Higden and Erghome: two fourteenth-century scholars' in *Économies et Sociétés au Moyen Age: Mélanges offerts à Edouard Perroy* (Publications de la Sorbonne, série 'Études', v, Paris 1973), pp. 647–8. For Erghome's self-professed secrecy concerning his authorship see Wright, op. cit., i.123–4, and for the cryptic devices which he employed see Rupert Taylor, *The Political Prophecy in England* (New York 1911), pp. 5–7, 54–7. For the acrostic in which Erghome hid his name see M. R. James, 'The catalogue of the library of the Augustinian friars at York' in *Fasciculus Ioanni Willis Clark dicatus* (Cambridge 1909), pp. 10–11. For the inclusion of the prophecies in the Bridlington chronicle see pp. 9 above, 114 below.

[5] Avesbury's chronicle is printed in *Adae Murimuth Continuatio Chronicorum. Robertus de Avesbury de Gestis Mirabilibus Regis Edwardi Tertii*, ed. E. M. Thompson (RS 1889), pp. 279–471.

[6] Printed *Croniques de London*, ed. G. J. Aungier (Camden Soc., original series, 1844). Aungier's edition, the manuscript of the chronicle (BL MS. Cotton Cleopatra A VI. ff. 54–106ᵛ), and its subject matter are discussed in D. C. Cox, 'The French chronicle of London' in *Medium Ævum*, xlv (1976), pp. 201–8.

[7] The English *Brut* (see pp. 73–7 below) is printed *The Brut or Chronicles of England*, ed. F. W. D. Brie (EETS, original series, cxxxi, cxxxvi, 1906, 1908, 2 vols). The French *Brut* (see p. 73 below) has never been published in full but see p. 73 n. 90 below.

[8] A useful edition is *The Bruce by John Barbour archdeacon of Aberdeen*, ed. W. M. Mackenzie (London 1909).

[9] The standard edition is *Chronique de Jean le Bel*, ed. J. Viard and E. Déprez (Soc. de l' Histoire de France 1904–5, 2 vols).

[10] There are two standard editions of Froissart's chronicle: *Oeuvres complètes de Froissart: Chroniques*, ed. Kervyn de Lettenhove (Brussels 1868–77, 25 vols); *Chroniques de Froissart*. ed. S. Luce, G. Raynaud and L. and A. Mirot (Soc. de l'Histoire de France 1869–1975, 15 vols: unfinished: to date only Bks I, II and most of Bk III have been published). For an

Scalacronica;[11] and Chandos Herald's *Vie du Prince Noir* (*Life of the Black Prince*).[12] It should also be noted that the chronicle which formed the basis of the Anonimalle chronicle of St Mary's, York, which will be considered in the next chapter, may well have been by a secular clerk.

All these chronicles are bellicose in flavour, and some are little more than histories of Edward's wars, with detailed and graphic descriptions of sieges, battles and soldiers on the march. It is probable that England's resounding victories provided an incentive to historical composition. The fact that a number of the chronicles end with a victory suggests that the authors' intention was partly commemorative. Thus one version of the *Brut* ends with the battle of Halidon Hill.[13] The so-called Lanercost chronicle and Adam Murimuth end with Neville's Cross, and Robert of Avesbury and Geoffrey le Baker close with the battle of Poitiers.

Conversely, when enthusiasm for Edward III's campaigns declined the chronicle tradition lost its strength. One chronicle after another came to an end, not to be replaced by new works until Richard II's reign. Of the eleven chronicles here under consideration only half continue beyond 1360. Two of these, the *Scalacronica* and the chronicle of Jean le Bel, end in the 1360s (as do three monastic chronicles—John of Reading's, the *Eulogium Historiarum* and the Canterbury chronicle). The *Life of the Black Prince* by the herald of Sir John Chandos ends in 1376, and the now lost chronicle which was written in Edward III's reign and formed the basis of the Anonimalle chronicle (itself a product of the reign of Richard II) probably ended in the same year. Only Froissart's chronicle continued, ending at the close of Richard II's reign.

The chivalric tradition fostered interest in war and encouraged the literary glorification of army commanders. Chivalry flourished in the fourteenth century, as it had in the twelfth. When knights were not engaged in real battles, they fought in tournaments, and this was the age of the Order of the Garter and the Ordre de l'Étoile. Knights accepted the artificial chivalric code with its tradition of courtly love. However, chivalry was only a veneer on a basically violent and often barbaric society. Its

---

edition, with a useful introduction, of a short section of Froissart's chronicle see *Froissart, Voyage en Béarn*, ed. A. H. Diverres (Manchester 1953).

[11] The chronicle is printed from 1066 in *Scalacronica by Sir Thomas Gray of Heton, knight* [ed. Joseph Stevenson] (Maitland Club, Edinburgh 1836). An English translation is by Herbert Maxwell (Glasgow 1907). It is discussed as literature in Legge, *A-N Lit.* pp. 283–7.

[12] The standard edition is *La Vie du Prince Noir by Chandos Herald*, ed. D. B. Tyson (Beihefte zur Zeitschrift für Romanische Philologie, cxlvii, Tübingen 1975). This supersedes the previous three editions because it is based on a more authoritative manuscript (University of London Library MS. 1) than that used hitherto (Worcester College, Oxford, MS. 1). Miss Tyson collated the two manuscripts. See ibid., pp. 1–10. (For the frontispiece of the University of London Library MS. see Plate III.) However, Miss Tyson acknowledges the value and makes good use of the edition, which includes an English translation, by M. K. Pope and E. C. Lodge (Oxford 1910).

[13] See p. 77 below.

re-emergence as a dominant influence among the nobility was partly the result of the prevalence of war. On the other hand it stimulated the contemporary preoccupation with warfare and itself influenced the art of war. All the chroniclers, but especially the secular clerks and laymen, accepted chivalric values. Besides the chroniclers' taste for writing dramatic descriptions of battles, they loved to describe any colourful spectacle, such as a tournament or a procession.

In Edward III's reign there was a remarkable increase in the proportionate number of chronicles by secular clerks. Geoffrey le Baker, the author of the *Annales Paulini*, Adam Murimuth, Robert of Avesbury and almost certainly the author of the French chronicle of London and the *Brut* chroniclers, were all secular clerks. It is noteworthy that all except Baker and the *Brut* chroniclers worked in London, which demonstrates the rising importance of the capital in English cultural life. In addition two of the other chroniclers were secular clerks—Jean le Bel and Froissart, who, though both Hainaulters, have much material relating to Edward III's campaigns. Similarly another foreign writer whose work is of value for the history of Edward's reign, the Scot John Barbour, was a secular clerk. Some of these clerks wrote to please lay patrons. Baker may have written to please the Bohun family[14] and the author of the long version of the *Brut* perhaps partly wrote to please a member of the house of Lancaster. And, while the possibility cannot be discounted that Avesbury wrote to please Edward III himself, John Barbour certainly composed *The Bruce* in the interests of the Stewart dynasty.[15] The two Hainaulters also wrote for lay patrons, Jean le Bel for John of Hainault, uncle of Edward III's

[14] See p. 39 above. Another chronicle written to please a noble family is that which forms the basis of the chronicle written in the Augustinian abbey of Wigmore (in Herefordshire), of which the Mortimers, the earls of March, were patrons. The Wigmore chronicle comprises a copy of, and interpolations in, a continuation from 1340 to 1377 of the *Polychronicon*. This exemplar was composed in the 1360s and 1370s and was written in the interest of the earls of March; it contained their genealogy back to the legendary kings of Britain and entries concerning their family history. It also had information relating to other members of the higher aristocracy—the earls of Pembroke, Arundel and Warwick. The Wigmore chronicle is fully discussed and the text from 1360 to 1376 printed in John Taylor, 'A Wigmore chronicle, 1355–77' in *Proceedings of the Leeds Philosophical and Literary Society (Literary and Historical Section)*, xi (1964), pt v, pp. 81–94. The exemplar of the Wigmore chronicle was not intended as political propaganda except in a very general sense. It was not comparable in this respect with the genealogy which still survives, together with other historical material relating to the Mortimer family and Wigmore abbey, and is now preserved in Chicago University Library (MS. 224). This genealogy was intended to prove the claim of the earls of March to the throne. It was probably drawn up soon after 1385 when parliament proclaimed Roger Mortimer fourth earl of March successor to Richard II should the latter die without heir. Possibly it was composed under the direction of John Othelake, who had been appointed March Herald by Edmund, the third earl. See M. E. Giffin, 'A Wigmore manuscript at the University of Chicago' in the *National Library of Wales Journal*, vii (1951–2), pp. 321–4.

[15] For the suggestion, which however, is not convincingly substantiated, that the *Vie du Prince Noir* was written for Richard II see *CH*, pp. 30–3.

queen, Philippa, and Froissart for Queen Philippa herself and for a number of continental noblemen.

The development of lay patronage was the result of a taste for history among the nobility. The great men of the day liked listening to history books being read aloud. This in its turn encouraged composition in the vernacular. Therefore, the rise in the proportion of chronicles in French is not surprising. Nearly fifty copies of the *Brut* survive in French,[16] and the London chronicle is in French. Moreover, the Hainaulters Jean le Bel and Froissart, and the two lay authors, Sir Thomas Gray and Chandos Herald, all wrote in French. It should also be remembered that educated Englishmen were now trilingual, not bilingual. The English language was increasingly becoming a literary competitor to Latin and French. Between 1350 and 1380 the *Brut* was translated into English (more than 120 copies of the English translation are extant), while English words occur scattered through most Latin chronicles of the period. And John Barbour, by writing in English, became virtually the founder of vernacular literature for the English speaking regions of Scotland.

Literacy itself had reached the nobility. In England Henry of Grosmont, duke of Lancaster, wrote a pious book in French, perhaps at the order of his confessor, *Le Livre de Seyntz Medicines*.[17] It is an allegory on the wounds in Henry's soul, discussing the remedies to be supplied by the Divine Physician and his assistant, the 'Douce Dame', illustrated with personal reminiscences and contemporary anecdotes which show a lively imagination, a perceptive eye and some literary skill. Meanwhile in France Sir Geoffrey de Charny wrote a long poem on chivalry.[18] This spread of literacy among the nobility affected historiography in England. Sir Thomas Gray, author of the *Scalacronica*, was, as far as is known, the first English nobleman since Aethelweard the ealdorman to write a history. Interest in history among the nobility also prompted Chandos Herald to write his biography of the Black Prince.

The chronicles will be considered in turn: first, those written in London, the *Annales Paulini*, the chronicles of Adam Murimuth and Robert of Avesbury, and the French chronicle of London; second, other chronicles by English secular clerks, the *Brut* and the chronicle of Geoffrey le Baker; third, chronicles by foreign secular clerks, John Barbour, Jean le Bel and Jean Froissart; and finally the lay writers Sir Thomas Gray and Chandos Herald.

---

[16] For the *Brut* manuscripts see p. 73 n. 94 below.

[17] Printed *Le Livre de Seyntz Medicines*, ed. E. J. Arnould (Anglo-Norman Text Soc., ii, 1940). See also E. J. Arnould, *Études sur le Livre des Saintes Médecines du Duc Henri de Lancastre* (Paris 1948), the same author, 'Henry of Lancaster and his *Livre des Seintes Medicines*' in *BJRL*, xxi (1937), pp. 352–86, and Legge, *A-N Lit.* pp. 216–20.

[18] Geoffrey de Charny's book is described and extracts printed by Arthur Piaget, 'Le livre Messire Geoffroi de Charny' in *Romania*, xxvi (1897), pp. 394–411.

As has been seen, the author of the *Annales Paulini* and Adam Murimuth both wrote at St Paul's. Of all the chronicles to be discussed the *Annales* are the most locally orientated. Although they have value for general history, they are chiefly of interest for the history of St Paul's and London, especially for the cameos of life in the capital. The section for Edward III's reign shows the same concern as that for Edward II's reign[19] with the fabric of St Paul's and its liturgical ceremonies. The most graphic passages are the obviously eyewitness descriptions of the tournaments at Stepney and in Cheapside in 1331. The expenses of the latter were borne by Sir William Montacute who lodged in the bishop's palace.[20] The jousting area was enclosed with a strong timber fence and strewn with sand. In the procession before the tournament the knights were splendidly dressed and masked like Tartars, and each led by a silver chain 'a noble and beautiful lady in tunic of red velvet and cap of white cameline' (the king himself led his sister Eleanor who was 'a very beautiful girl'). They walked two by two, followed by their gorgeously caparisoned chargers, to the sound of trumpets 'and divers other instruments'. On the way through the city to the tournament at Stepney, the king and many magnates accompanied the twenty six knights, who wore masks and green tunics and mantles lined with red and embroidered with arrows of gold. They were followed by over fifty esquires, also masked, dressed in white tunics with the right sleeves of green cloth sewn with golden arrows. The company went to St Paul's and made an offering at the high altar.[21]

Perhaps it was from such chivalric visitors that the author obtained the anecdote concerning a near accident to Edward III. When riding from the field of a tournament held at Dartford in 1331, the king became irritated with his charger which, excited by the jousting, was pulling. He wanted to ride a palfrey but was dissuaded by a knight because 'it did not become his state to change horses on the field.' But as the horse made him more and more angry, he insisted on changing to the palfrey, which carried him quickly and safely to his lodgings. Meanwhile the man who had mounted the charger was nearly drowned, because it, being tired and hot, plunged into the river for a swim—the king in his armour would never have survived.[22]

The annalist's residence at St Paul's also enabled him to acquire more serious news. For example, in January 1329 Henry earl of Lancaster and

---

[19] For the section of the *Annales Paulini* concerned with Edward II's reign see pp. 25–9 above.
[20] *AP*, pp. 354–5. The three tournaments of 1331, at Dartford, Stepney and Cheapside are noticed, with references to the *Annales Paulini* and other contemporary authorities, by Dietrich Sandberger, *Studien über das Rittertum in England vornehmlich während des 14. Jahrhunderts* (Berlin 1937), pp. 45–6 and nn.
[21] *AP*, pp. 353–4.
[22] *AP*, pp. 352–3.

other magnates, both lay and ecclesiastical, met at St Paul's, as the *Annales* record in some detail, to discuss what to do about the misgovernment of the kingdom, and agreed 'on certain ordinances for the benefit of the king and realm of England'.[23] The author's interest in Edward III's Scottish campaign of 1333 may well have been sharpened by the day of thanksgiving held in London for the surrender of Berwick: he records that there was a solemn procession of all the clergy and people from St Paul's to the church of Holy Trinity.[24]

The narrative of events from 1332 to 1337 in the *Annales* is almost the same as that in Adam Murimuth's chronicle. The exact relationship between the two works is obscure.[25] However, it is likely that the *Annales* were written before Murimuth's work and, therefore, that if one chronicler borrowed directly from the other, Murimuth must have been the borrower. Murimuth's account of the reign of Edward III, like his account of that of Edward II discussed above,[26] shows that he was a very different writer from the author of the *Annales*. His centre of interest is not local affairs but the government and national politics, especially diplomatic relations with the papacy and France, and the Hundred Years' War. Murimuth is a terse, factual writer, meticulous about names and dates, with no gift for literary narrative. But he did more than record facts: he interpreted evidence and expressed views on events. His opinions are almost invariably pessimistic and even cynical.

Murimuth has some information about the king's council (he refers specifically to the 'privy' or 'secret' council)[27] and government deliberations, though his knowledge was, as he himself admits,[28] far from complete. His information about business transacted in the king's council mainly concerns papal negotiations. This suggests that he obtained it from a clerk (or clerks). He has, for example, exact information concerning the reception of the two cardinals sent in 1337 to mediate peace. Having described their reception outside London by the archbishop of Canterbury, the duke of Cornwall and other magnates, he records that the king met them 'at the entrance of the lesser hall at Westminster and conducted them into the painted chamber'.[29] Similarly Murimuth has a full account of Andrew Ufford's report to the council in 1343, after his return from Avignon. Ufford described the attempted peace negotiations between the English

[23] *AP*, pp. 343–4.
[24] *AP*, pp. 358–9.
[25] *Chrons Edw. I and II*, i. lxxii–lxxiv. See p. 26 and n. 138 above.
[26] Adam Murimuth's career and the section of his chronicle concerning Edward II's reign are discussed above, pp. 29–31.
[27] *AM*, pp. 119 ('*privatum concilium*'), 159, 162, 170, 177 ('*secretum concilium*'). For the 'privy' or 'secret' council, with reference to Murimuth's evidence, see J. F. Baldwin, *The King's Council in England during the Middle Ages* (Oxford 1913), pp. 104–5 and nn.
[28] *AM*, pp. 153, 158–9, 199.
[29] *AM*, p. 81.

and French envoys before the pope, and gave the pope's objections to Edward III's claim to the French crown.[30] And in 1346 Murimuth records that the news of the glorious English victory at Neville's Cross was announced to the king's council.[31]

Adam Murimuth was a patriot. He ends his chronicle with the battle of Neville's Cross, and his opinions about contemporary politics are best understood by taking his patriotism, already apparent in his annals for Edward II's reign,[32] into account. He approved of Edward III's claim to the French crown, which he discusses from both the English angle and the French angle, in greater detail than any other chronicler, illustrating his argument with a genealogical tree.[33] (He also stresses that the French were opposing the 'true heir' in Brittany.)[34] He consistently refers to Philip as Philip de Valois rather than as king of France, and he has numerous descriptions of military and naval engagements in the Hundred Years' War. A good example of his factual literary style is his account of an attack on the coast of France by sailors of the Cinque Ports in 1340:[35]

> Having collected many well armed small ships and little boats, the men of the Cinque Ports landed at Boulogne in cloudy weather, and burnt nineteen galleons in the lower part of the town, and in addition four large ships and twenty small ones, with all their arms. [They] also [burnt] the houses on the sea shore, among them a large house full of oars, sails, arms and arblasts sufficient for the number of men needed to man the nineteen galleons. Many were killed from both sides, but most from Boulogne.

Murimuth derived most of his news about the war from newsletters, some of which he copied in full. Thus he has a version of the letter of Michael de Northburgh, one of the king's councillors, and a version of the letter of the king's confessor Richard de Winkley, both on the 1346 campaign.[36] One such letter copied by Murimuth, which applauded the successful raids carried out by a few bands from the great host immediately after it landed at La Hougue in July 1346, was from the chancellor of St Paul's 'to his friends in London'.[37] Patriotic fervour was no doubt fanned at St Paul's by a sermon which Archbishop John Stratford delivered in the churchyard on 12 August 1346: he included a reading of the conven-

---

[30] *AM*, pp. 147–8. For Master Andrew Ufford's career, with a reference to this passage in Murimuth, see. Baldwin, op. cit., p. 82 and n. 9.
[31] *AM*, p. 218.
[32] See p. 31 above.
[33] *AM*, pp. 100–1.
[34] *AM*, p. 121.
[35] *AM*, pp. 103–4.
[36] *AM*, pp. 212–17. See also p. 69 and n. 65 below.
[37] *AM*, pp. 201–2.

tion between King Philip and the Normans for the invasion of England, a copy of which had been captured at Caen. Murimuth cites the convention *verbatim* and states that the purpose of the archbishop's sermon was 'to stir the people of the realm to love the king more ardently and pray more diligently for the success of his expedition—the king who preserved his people unharmed from the machinations of the French, exposing himself and his men to danger on land and at sea.'[38]

Nevertheless, though Murimuth supported the war, he severely criticized the way it was run. He blamed Edward III for allowing the season for warfare to pass in 1339 while he waited in Brabant for allies and money.[39] Again in 1344 the king procrastinated ('to the great damage of the king-dom'), staying in England during futile peace negotiations, so that the supplies collected for the campaign were wasted.[40] Murimuth considered that the earls of Salisbury and Suffolk were captured in 1340 because of their 'senseless audacity',[41] and regarded the truce of Tournai, although unavoidable, as 'useless to the king and his men'.[42]

Murimuth's sympathies lay with the ordinary Englishman, whether layman or cleric. He bitterly disapproved of Edward's financial expedients to raise money for the war and had some knowledge of his manipulation of the wool trade. He records the king's purchase from the merchants of the country's wool clip in 1337 and its transportation for sale in Brabant. Unfortunately the vessels waited the whole summer and autumn in the Thames blocking all other ships so that commerce was 'iniquitously' brought to a virtual standstill.[43] Murimuth records parliament's grant of wool to the king in 1338, 'to the great injury of the people',[44] and the excessively severe inquiry into the collection of taxes in 1341.[45] He also disapproved of the 'very burdensome and unprecedented' inquiry into military service held in 1346.[46]

Murimuth's antagonism to the papacy and the ecclesiastical 'establish-ment' in England was largely the result of his patriotism. He objected to papal provisions in part because they could result in the appointment of unsuitable candidates to bishoprics, but his objection was reinforced by his anti-French, anti-foreign sentiment. Thus he criticized the transla-tion by the pope of Adam of Orleton from Worcester to Winchester in 1333 because it was done at the request of the king of France and regardless of Edward III's nominee. Edward was angry because 'it seemed to him

[38] *AM*, pp. 205–12.
[39] *AM*, pp. 90–1.
[40] *AM*, p. 160.
[41] *AM*, pp. 104–5.
[42] *AM*, p. 116.
[43] *AM*, p. 80.
[44] *AM*, p. 85.
[45] *AM*, p. 118.
[46] *AM*, p. 192.

that his requests, not those of the king of France, ought to be listened to concerning bishoprics and dignities in England.'[47] Murimuth's dislike of papal provisions was accentuated because they resulted in the draining of money from England, money which was needed to finance the Hundred Years' War. He gives a full account, with copies of documents, of the proceedings in parliament which culminated in the statute of provisors of 1343. The statute was intended to check papal provisions which were 'to the grave prejudice of king and kingdom'.[48] But Murimuth had little faith in statutes. Under 1344 he notes that, despite the statute of provisors, the pope provided William Bateman to Norwich, and records other appointments by papal provision, including that of a cardinal to the archdeaconry of Ely: thus, comments Murimuth, 'benefices in this realm are always given to foreigners'—he attributes such disregard of the statute to the influence of 'lords and ladies'.[49] He has a long tirade against the cupidity of the Roman curia with an historical résumé of papal exactions in the first half of the fourteenth century.[50] And he deplores the docility of the English, asserting that there was a saying in the papal curia that the English were good asses who would bear whatever intolerable burden was placed on them. And he laments the inability of the prelates to protect the people from the injury and oppression resulting from the pope's demands, which he attributed to the fact that nearly all the bishops were appointed by the pope.[51]

Robert of Avesbury was, like Murimuth, a patriot, but, as will be seen, he expressed his patriotism differently. Little is known about Avesbury's life, the only evidence being his chronicle and his will, which is dated 27 January 1359, and was entered on the rolls of the court of hustings on 10 February 1359.[52] The title of the chronicle states that the author was Robert of Avesbury, registrar of the court of the archbishop of Canterbury (at Lambeth), and the interest it shows in the riots at Oxford in 1355 suggests the possibility that he had studied at the university.[53] His will shows that he married a lady called Milicent, that they lived in Ivy lane in the parish of St Faith in the crypt (of St Paul's), and had two sons, John

[47] AM, p. 70.

[48] AM, pp. 138–46.

[49] AM, pp. 157–8. John of Reading held a similar view on the ineffectiveness of the statute of provisors; see p. 107 and n. 34 below.

[50] AM, pp. 173–5.

[51] AM, pp. 82, 175. For a similar comment on the docility of the English see p. 31 and n. 173 above.

[52] Maunde Thompson comments on the lack of evidence for Avesbury's life (RA, p. xxii), but he overlooked the will, a synopsis of which is printed in Calendar of Wills proved and enrolled in the Court of Hustings, London, A.D. 1258–A.D. 1688, ed. R. R. Sharpe (London 1889–90, 2 vols), ii. 7. Cf. C. L. Lethbridge, 'Robert de Avesbury' in EHR, xxii (1907), p. 292.

[53] RA, pp. 421–3. Avesbury's account is noticed in H. Rashdall, The Universities of Europe in the Middle Ages, ed. F. M. Powicke and A. B. Emden (Oxford 1936, 3 vols), iii. 98 n. 1.

and William. It also shows that Milicent predeceased him and was buried in Pardon churchyard at St Paul's, and that he himself wished to be buried next to her.

Avesbury's chronicle is virtually a military history of Edward III's reign. He describes victory after victory granted to the English by Christ, 'the mightiest of athletes', 'who is always on the side of justice',[54] culminating in the battle of Poitiers. He asserts that Edward III was in the right in all his wars. Avesbury states that France was Edward's by right of inheritance, and that it had been violently occupied by Philip de Valois.[55] He also demonstrates Edward III's right to overlordship of Scotland with a flashback, compiled 'from the ancient chronicles', recapitulating Anglo-Scottish relations from the time of Brutus to the coronation of Robert Bruce.[56] And he asserts that Edward invaded Brittany in support of his vassal, the lawful heir, John de Montfort, and carefully explains the latter's hereditary right.[57] Avesbury's patriotism also appears in his denigration of the character of John II of France; he accuses him of adultery, incest and fornication—even nuns were not spared from his lust.[58]

However, unlike Murimuth, Avesbury was not critical of the running of the war. On the contrary he concentrates on eulogizing Edward III in chivalric terms.[59] His royalist bias is so strong as to suggest the possibility that he wrote specifically to please the king. His purpose was, he writes in the preface, to record 'the wonderful deeds of the magnificent king of England, the Lord Edward the third after the Conquest, and of his nobles'. Edward's achievements are set against the background of his predecessor's failures (Avesbury begins with a brief recapitulation of the events of Edward II's reign). Edward III himself is praised as a chivalric hero. He is magnificent, generous and merciful, always ready to spare a captive or make a just peace. Above all he is brave. His bravery appears in the dramatic account of the battle near Calais in 1350, when he and the Black Prince fought to save the town from a surprise attack by the French. In the course of the fighting the king, with hardly thirty men at arms and only a few archers, became separated from the rest of his troops. Seeing this Geoffrey de Charny began to approach with a large company of French knights. 'Then the said king, situated in such great danger, did not lose heart but, like an experienced and great hearted warrior, drew his sword and shouted at the top of his voice "A Edward, seint George! A Edward, seint George!"'[60] The French were so terrified by this

---

[54] *RA*, pp. 377, 296–7.
[55] *RA*, pp. 302–3.
[56] *RA*, pp. 286–96.
[57] *RA*, p. 339.
[58] *RA*, p. 414.
[59] For praises of Edward III see e.g. *RA*, pp. 285, 390–1, 396, 413, 451, 455.
[60] Avesbury gives Edward's words in French. cf. p. 262 below. For instances of the use of English by Avesbury see *RA*, pp. 433, 468.

war-cry that reinforcements had time to rush to Edward's assistance.[61]

Nevertheless, despite Avesbury's panegyrical tone, he is an indispensable authority for the Hundred Years' War. It is, for example, likely that the account just quoted of the engagement near Calais is substantially true, especially as it was based, according to Avesbury, on the information of a captured French knight. Similarly Avesbury has a unique account of Henry of Grosmont's proposed expedition to help the king of Navarre in 1355.[62] Some of his information was taken from newsletters written by people present at the campaigns. For instance the account of Philip's retreat from the neighbourhood of Calais without offering battle in 1347 is clearly derived in part from King Edward's letter to the archbishop, a copy of which follows Avesbury's narrative.[63] The chronicle derives much of its value from copies of such newsletters, some of which (for example the letters from the Black Prince and Sir John Wingfield to the bishop of Winchester on the prince's raid from Bordeaux to Narbonne in 1355)[64] are not known to survive elsewhere. Avesbury copied a few letters which were also transcribed by Murimuth; both chroniclers have copies of the letter of Michael de Northburgh and that of Richard de Winkley on the 1346 campaign.[65] Possibly Avesbury used the same texts as Murimuth. He certainly had access to the archives at St Paul's. This is proved by the fact that he copied two letters addressed to the dean and chapter of St Paul's. One is the letter of submission by the competitors for the Scottish throne in 1291 to the judgment of Edward I.[66]

The other letter addressed to the dean and chapter of St Paul's which Avesbury copied is the *Libellus famosus*, Edward III's accusations against Archbishop John Stratford in 1341.[67] For this crisis Avesbury certainly used the archiepiscopal archives: he has a copy of Stratford's letter to the king stating his case.[68] The crisis itself presented Avesbury with a problem. He could not, as an official of the archbishop of Canterbury, neglect it,

---

[61] *RA*, pp. 409–10. Chandos Herald emphasizes the part played by the Black Prince in this combat; see p. 98 below.

[62] *RA*, pp. 425–7. For the value of this passage see Kenneth Fowler, *The King's Lieutenant, Henry of Grosmont, first Duke of Lancaster 1310–1361* (London 1969), pp. 147, 278 n. 5, and H. J. Hewitt, *The Black Prince's Expedition of 1355–1357* (Manchester 1958), pp. 38, 179 n. 157.

[63] *RA*, p. 391.

[64] *RA*, pp. 434–45. For a modern account of the raid, partly based on Avesbury's information, see Hewitt, op. cit., pp. 43–77, 181–3 nn. passim.

[65] *AM*, pp. 212–17 (cf. p. 65 and above); *RA*, pp. 358–63. Murimuth gives a Latin translation of Northburgh's letter, which Avesbury has in French. Avesbury gives only the beginning of Winkley's letter which is in Latin in both works.

[66] *RA*, p. 291.

[67] *RA*, pp. 330–6. For the 'Libellus famous' see T. F. Tout, *Chapters in the Administrative History of Medieval England* (Manchester 1923–35, 6 vols), iii. 128 and n. 1.

[68] *RA*, pp. 324–7. Stratford's letter is printed from Avesbury's text, in an English translation, in Bertie Wilkinson, *The Constitutional History of England 1216–1399* (London-New York 1948–58, 3 vols), ii. 190–3.

but it did not conform with his intention of praising Edward III because the king was on this occasion in conflict with the archbishop. Moreover, Avesbury especially lauded Edward by recording his victories—but the Stratford crisis was immediately preceded by the truce of Tournai. Thus Avesbury had both to exonerate Edward III from the attack on the archbishop and to justify the truce. Avesbury pointed out that Edward only agreed to the truce because of the lack of supplies[69]—which he attributed to the failure of his ministers, particularly Stratford. And to exonerate the king from the attack on the archbishop Avesbury put the blame on Edward's close advisers: the king's anger with Stratford was roused by the envy of his confidential clerks (*secretarii*) ;[70] the *Libellus famosus* itself, with its indiscriminate invective, was, 'many people said', concocted by Stratford's bitter enemy, Adam of Orleton, bishop of Winchester.[71]

Avesbury relied mainly on hearsay and documents for evidence. There are very few passages in his chronicle which have the touch of a personal impression. One passage which may be based on his own observation is the account of Archbishop Stratford's sermon at St Paul's (also mentioned by Murimuth), in which the archbishop read the convention drawn up between the French and the Normans in 1338 for the invasion of England, and exhorted the people to pray for protection.[72] But the only description which is obviously drawn from life is of the Flagellants who arrived in London in 1349. Avesbury's amazement at the remarkable spectacle they presented evoked his most exact piece of descriptive prose :[73]

> Over 120 men, coming from Zealand and Holland by way of Flanders, reached London about the feast of St Michael. They went in procession twice daily, sometimes at St Paul's and sometimes in other places in the city, one after the other with bare feet in view of all the people. [Each was] covered from thigh to ankles in a linen cloth but was otherwise bare, wore a cap signed with a red cross on the front and back, and carried a whip in the right hand with three thongs, a knot bristling with sharp needles on every thong. They beat one another on their bare,

[69] *RA*, p. 317.

[70] *RA*, p. 324.

[71] *RA*, p. 330. This passage is cited by G. T. Lapsley, 'Archbishop Stratford and the parliamentary crisis of 1341' in *EHR*, xxx (1915), p. 194 n. 79. Besides Avesbury two other important authorities for the Stratford crisis are the London chronicle (see p. 72 below), and the *Vitae Archiepiscoporum Cantuariensium* (printed in Wharton, *Anglia Sacra*, i. 1–48), pp. 19–41, which has been wrongly ascribed to Stephen Birchington; its authorship is discussed in Tait's edition of the Canterbury chronicle, (for which see p. 101 n. 1 below), pp. 63–6.

[72] *RA*, pp. 363–4. The text of the convention follows, as in Murimuth.

[73] *RA*, pp. 407–8. In places in this passage the Latin construction is obscure and I am grateful to Professor Robert Markus for help with the translation. A useful account of the Flagellants (who are first heard of at Perugia in 1260), with a picture of them from the chronicle of Gilles le Muisit, is in *The Catholic Encyclopaedia* (London 1907–22, 12 vols), vi. 89–92.

bleeding bodies, four singing in their own language and the rest making responses to these four, like a litany sung by Christians. And on three occasions during the procession they all together threw themselves to the ground, their hands outstretched in the sign of the cross. Continually singing, as has been mentioned, whoever was the last one in the line of those thus prostrate, [stood up] first, and took a step past the man in front, striking him with his whip as he lay at his feet. And so he went from one to the next until he had done it to the total number of those prostrate. The same ritual was repeated until everyone had had a turn. Then they all dressed in their everyday clothes, and, still wearing their caps and carrying their whips, they went to their lodgings. It was said they did the same penance every night.

The last chronicle written in London to be considered here is the French *Croniques de London*. The surviving text starts with the year 1259, although it is likely that it originally began, like other London chronicles, in 1189,[74] and ends in 1343. It is the only one of this group of London chronicles which may have a direct connection with the city. Perhaps its author held some civic office, as had Fitz Thedmar and the author of the *Annales Londonienses*. Each annal starts by recording the names of the mayor and sheriffs, and the use of French may also indicate that the author held an official position, since French was the language normally used for the collections of documents compiled in the city.[75]

However, the principal reason for the author's use of Norman French was undoubtedly his debt to the French *Brut* chronicle, the short version of which was his main source of information for national events down to 1333. For local history he probably used two now unidentified London chronicles, one reaching to the 1280s and the other to 1327.[76] Thus the chronicle is an original authority, independent of other known literary works, for national history from 1333, and for local history from 1327.

The *Croniques de London* have a number of entries of specifically local interest, for example the detailed account of the relics found in the cross of St Paul's steeple when it was repaired in 1314, which Robert de Clothale showed to the people before they were put back.[77] But notwithstanding such local news, the main objective of the chronicler, who was an enthusiastic supporter of Edward III's French war, was to record events of national importance. He has a graphic account of the English naval victory at Sluys; he records the brave part taken by 'a ship from London, belonging to William Haunsard', and praises King Edward who 'greatly encouraged

[74] See D. C. Cox, 'The French chronicle of London' in *Medium Ævum*, xlv (1976), pp. 205–6.
[75] See Ralph Flenley, *Six Town Chronicles of England* (Oxford 1911), p. 9.
[76] For the sources of the *Croniques de London* see Cox, op. cit., pp. 203–5 passim. For the *Brut* and its versions see pp. 73–7 below.
[77] *Lond.* p. 38. Cf. p. 27 above.

the men in the combat'.[78] He justifies the truce of Tournai by pointing out that Edward did not want to spill Christian blood.[79] Conversely he hated King Philip, 'a coward and a recreant knight'.[80]

The London chronicler deplores the raising of the siege of Tournai ('a great grief to our people') which he attributes to the failure of the 'false guardians in England' to find supplies. He has a vivid account of the 1340 crisis with details not found elsewhere. He describes how Edward suddenly returned to England, summoned the mayor and ordered the arrest of the defaulting officials. Next he rode to St Albans and searched the abbey and discovered 'a great quantity of treasure'. Later he went to Ditton, a manor belonging to Sir John Moleyns, 'and there he found armour for eighty men and great plenty of valuables and treasure which Sir John had put in small, well tied sacks; these in turn he had put in large sacks, carefully corded up, and plunged in a deep well.'[81]

The principal accused were ecclesiastics, and the London chronicler records that the king swore 'he would never again have a cleric as chancellor or treasurer, or holding any other great office in his service, but only such persons as he could cause to be drawn, hanged and beheaded if they were attainted of felony.'[82] The chronicler also gives details of how Stratford was finally admitted to parliament to defend himself.[83]

Although the London writer has a strong patriotic, royalist bias his point of view differs from Avesbury in one respect. He was a Lancastrian in sentiment. This appears in his treatment of Thomas of Lancaster and Henry of Lancaster. He records that Edward II had the candle in St Paul's removed 'where offerings were made out of devotion to the martyr', Thomas of Lancaster, but comments that the people's veneration for him was by no means diminished by this action.[84] He also notes the removal at Edward II's order of the tablet which Earl Thomas had placed in St Paul's to commemorate the Ordinances, and its replacement when Isabella and Mortimer seized power (he has an excellent account of the riots in London which accompanied Edward II's deposition).[85] He regarded Henry of Lancaster as 'the chief guardian of the king [Edward III] by common assent of all the realm, from the time of the coronation', and, therefore, as having an obligation to check the excessive power of Isabella and Mortimer.[86]

[78] *Lond.* p. 77 and n.
[79] *Lond.* p. 82.
[80] *Lond.* p. 81.
[81] *Lond.* pp. 82–7.
[82] *Lond.* p. 86. Cited Wilkinson, *Constitutional History*, ii. 177 n. 5.
[83] *Lond.* p. 90. The incident is discussed and the passage printed in an English translation in Wilkinson, *Constitutional History*, ii. 180–1, 193–4.
[84] *Lond.* p. 46. See May McKisack, *The Fourteenth Century* (Oxford 1959), p. 85 and n.
[85] *Lond.* p. 54.
[86] *Lond.* p. 62.

A pro-Lancastrian bias is even more characteristic of the *Brut* chronicle. The *Brut* survives in two main versions and in three languages (French, English and Latin).[87] It and Higden's *Polychronicon* were without exception the most popular fourteenth century chronicles. The first *Brut* to be composed was the French one, which was written probably early in the fourteenth century. (However, there is a version ending in 1272 which may have been written towards the end of the thirteenth century.)[88] It was compiled from various well known authorities;[89] two of them, Gaimar and Wace, were writers in the romance tradition indebted to Geoffrey of Monmouth. It also used (for the twelfth and thirteenth centuries) some chronicle closely related to the Waverley annals, and, for Edward I's reign, a lost version of Peter of Langtoft. Towards the mid-fourteenth century the *Brut* was continued: this continuation is in two main versions:[90] one, the short version, ends shortly before the battle of Halidon Hill; the second, the long version, with which we are concerned here, ends with the battle of Halidon Hill itself (1333).[91]

The *Brut* to 1333 is the earliest known work beginning with the Brutus legend to be written in Anglo-Norman prose—its precursors, the works by Gaimar, Wace and Peter of Langtoft, were in verse. The long version was translated into English some time between about 1350 and 1380, probably in the east midlands, and was continued (in English) to 1377.[92] Here again it was apparently innovatory; it is the earliest known history since the Anglo-Saxon Chronicle to be written in English prose (the thirteenth century chronicle of Robert of Gloucester is in English verse).[93]

Of the over 160 copies of the *Brut* extant nearly three quarters are in English; the rest, excluding four Latin texts, are in French.[94] Its translation

---

[87] The textual tradition and composition of the *Brut* are discussed in detail by F. W. D. Brie, *Geschichte und Quellen der mittelenglischen Prosachronik the Brute of England oder the Chronicles of England* (Marburg 1905).

[88] See ibid., pp. 13, 43–4.

[89] For the sources of the *Brut* to 1307 see ibid., pp. 32–46.

[90] Ibid., p. 17. For a third version, which is known in only one manuscript (Corpus Christi College, Oxford MS. 78) and which continues to 1397, see ibid., pp. 24–5, 51. It is discussed and extracts are printed by V. H. Galbraith, 'Extracts from the *Historia Aurea* and a French "Brut" (1317–47)' in *EHR*, xliii (1928), pp. 206–7, 215–17.

[91] The long version is discussed by John Taylor, 'The French "Brut" and the reign of Edward II' in *EHR*, lxxii (1957) pp. 423–37. Mr Taylor produces convincing evidence proving that the traditional ascription of this version to William Pakington (Brie, *Prosachronik*, pp. 47–51) is ill founded and argues that from the latter part of Edward II's reign it was written more or less contemporarily with the events recorded. I suggest here a slightly later date, soon after the battle of Halidon Hill. Mr Taylor also emphasizes the historical value of this version of the *Brut* for the reign of Edward II (cf. p. 3 n. 13 above).

[92] See Brie, *Prosachronik*, pp. 54–5. The continuations of the *Brut* from 1333 are discussed on pp. 222–7 below.

[93] Robert Mannyng of Bourne had translated Langtoft's chronicle into English in 1338; see p. 220 and n. 1 below.

[94] For a list of manuscripts of the *Brut* in French, English and Latin, see Brie, *Prosachronik*, pp. 1–5. See also M. D. Legge and G. E. Brereton, 'Three hitherto unlisted MSS. of the

into English and the proliferation of the English version demonstrate the *Brut*'s popularity with the laity. And its chivalric tone, combined with its use of such phrases as 'now you shall hear', indicates that it was intended to be read aloud to the knightly class. It has a number of colloquial 'popular' touches, for example the nickname given to Joan of England on her marriage with David of Scotland ('Make peace'),[95] and the lampoon composed by the Scots on the English: 'Long beard heartless, painted hood witless, gay coat graceless, maketh Englishmen thriftless.'[96]

The strong Lancastrian bias of the *Brut* suggests that it was written to please a member (or members) of the house of Lancaster. This Lancastrian connection may also be indicated by the fact that an abridgment of the *Brut* was made in 1310 at the request of Henry de Lacy, earl of Lincoln (1258–1311), whose daughter Alice had married Thomas of Lancaster in 1294. The abridgment was by a Master Ralph de Bohun, perhaps a member of the aristocratic Bohun family.[97] As has been pointed out above, Geoffrey le Baker may have had a Bohun patron.[98] Moreover, there may be some literary connection between Baker's chronicle and the *Brut*. This possibility is suggested by the similarity in both works of the account of the death of Humphrey de Bohun at Boroughbridge[99] and of the murder of Edward of Carnarvon.[100]

The *Brut* eulogizes Thomas of Lancaster and Henry of Lancaster and has detailed knowledge about them. It has a full account of the capture of Thomas (variously described as 'noble', 'gentle' and 'good') at Boroughbridge and of his execution.[101] (However, the details are so highly coloured that they should not be relied on.) Thomas, on being called on to surrender at Boroughbridge, went into a chapel and prayed: 'Almighty God, to thee do I me yield, and wholly put me into Thy mercy.' The *Brut* continues: 'Villains [and] ribalds leapt about him, on every side that gentle earl, as tyrants and... tormentors', took off his armour and clothed him in his esquire's livery. He was taken to York where he was pelted with snowballs—but the 'gentle earl' suffered in silence. After a trial in his own hall ('he had made therein many a fair feast, both to rich and to poor'), his persecutors 'set they upon his head in scorn an old chaplet, all rent and torn, that was not worth a halfpenny; and after they set him upon a lean

---

French prose *Brute Chronicle*' in *Medium Ævum*, vii (1938), pp. 113–17, and J. Vising, *Anglo-Norman Language and Literature* (London 1923), pp. 74–5.

[95] *Brut*, i. 257.

[96] *Brut*, i. 249. For abusive verses provoked by the Anglo-Scottish wars see Gransden, *Historical Writing*, i. 484–6 and nn.

[97] See Legge, *A-N Lit.* pp. 280–3, 348. Cf. p. 39 n. 241 above.

[98] P. 39 above.

[99] Cf. *GB*, p. 14, and *Brut*, i. 219. See p. 39 and n. 241 above.

[100] Cf. *Brut*, p. 253, and *GB*, p. 33. For another possible parallel between the two works see p. 78 n. 125 below.

[101] *Brut*, i. 217–24.

white palfrey, full unseemly, and...all bare, with an old bridle', to lead him to his execution. On the way he prayed: 'Now, the King of Heaven give us mercy, for the earthly king hath us forsaken.' Just before the execution he clung in terror to the Dominican friar who accompanied him saying, 'Fair father, abide with us till that I be dead; for my flesh quaketh for dread of death.' He wanted to die on his knees facing east, but 'the ribald that men called Hugh of Moston' forced him to face north, in token of his alleged complicity with the Scots.

The *Brut* has a full account of the cult of 'St Thomas', of the pilgrimages to Pontefract and of the king's attempt to stop them.[102] And it states that Edmund, earl of Kent, tried to obtain Earl Thomas's canonization.[103] Moreover, it has details about the 'traitor', Sir Robert de Holand, who betrayed Thomas at Boroughbridge. It asserts that the earl had raised him from nothing (he 'nourished him in his butlery, and gave him 2,000 marks of rent by year').[104] Later it records that he was murdered near St Albans by Sir Thomas Wither, a retainer of Henry of Lancaster, in 1327.[105] The *Brut* states that Isabella's supporters, who enabled her to seize power, had been of Thomas's 'alliance',[106] and emphasizes the importance of Henry of Lancaster in the new reign. It was Henry who tried to check the power of Mortimer and Isabella in 1328; the *Brut* has a particularly detailed and valuable account of the objectives of the Lancastrian party on that occasion.[107]

The chivalric element in the *Brut* appears in a number of passages. The author describes coats of arms worn by the barons at the parliament of Westminster in 1321 ('wherefore that parliament was called "the parliament with the white bend" ');[108] he asserts that the battle of Boroughbridge brought shame on 'the gentle order of knighthood';[109] and he writes that because of the treacherous advice of the Despensers Edward II caused the

---

[102] *Brut*, i. 228–31. The cult of Thomas of Lancaster is briefly discussed (without reference to the evidence of the *Brut*) by J. C. Russell, 'The canonization of opposition to the king in Angevin England' in *Haskins Anniversary Essays in Mediaeval History*, ed. C. H. Taylor (Boston-New York 1929), pp. 284–5.

[103] *Brut*, i. 263. The commons petitioned for Thomas of Lancaster's canonization in the parliament of February/March 1327; *Rot. Parl.* ii. 7. See also William Stubbs, *The Constitutional History of England* (Oxford 1891–3, 3 vols), ii. 387, and J. R. Maddicott, *Thomas of Lancaster 1307–1322* (Oxford 1970), p. 329.

[104] *Brut*, i. 216–17. For Sir Robert de Holand's long service with Thomas of Lancaster and the favours received by Holand from Lancaster, see Maddicott, op. cit., pp. 48, 62, 76.

[105] *Brut*, i. 257. Cf. p. 179 n. 125 below.

[106] *Brut*, i. 246–7.

[107] *Brut*, i. 268–72. Stubbs, *Chrons Edw. I and II*, i. cxix-cxx, cites Joshua Barnes, *The History of...Edward III* (Cambridge 1688), pp. 31–2, as his authority for the objectives of Lancaster's party in 1328; Barnes himself was citing the English *Brut* for this and other information on Edward III's reign.

[108] *Brut*, i. 213. Cited Maddicott, op. cit., p. 279.

[109] *Brut*, i. 220.

death of 'the flower of chivalry'.[110] He considers it ridiculous that Roger Mortimer should try to emulate King Arthur by holding a Round Table— for King Arthur 'was the most worthy lord of renown that was in all the world', and conquered France.[111] And, with reference to the reign of Edward II, the author has a long passage on the prophecies of Merlin.[112] Moreover, the *Brut* has vivid battle scenes. The author's enthusiasm for warfare was stimulated by his patriotism. The treaty of 1328 with Scotland provokes an indignant outburst. The author writes that thereby Edward II was disinherited, through the bad influence of Isabella and Mortimer: no such treaty should have been made without the 'common assent of England'. He adds that 'from the time that Brutus had conquered Albion, and named the land after his own name Britain ... so was the realm of Scotland holden of the realm of England.'[113] The *Brut* attributes the disharmony ('unkindness') in the English nation (which resulted in the battle of Boroughbridge) to the unhappy mixture of various peoples in England. The author apparently objected both to the English living side by side with people of foreign birth, and to intermarriage with foreigners. He writes:[114]

> the great lords of England were not all of one nation, but were mixed with other nations, that is some Britons, some Saxons, some Danes, some Poitevins, some Frenchmen, some Normans, some Spaniards, some Romans, some Hainaulters, some Flemings, and of other diverse nations, the which nations accord not to the kind blood of England. And if the great lords of England had been only wedded to English people, then should peace have been, and rest amongst them, without envy.

The *Brut* has considerable value for the history of the Anglo-Scottish war. It has details relating to Edward Balliol's expedition in 1332, the siege of Berwick and the battle of Halidon Hill. After describing Edward III's encampment at Berwick it mentions his use of firearms which is not recorded elsewhere. Edward made 'many assaults with guns and with other engines', destroying houses and churches with the stones thus projected.[115] The *Brut* is also the only known authority for the composition

---

[110] *Brut*, i. 224.
[111] *Brut*, i. 262.
[112] *Brut*, i. 243–7.
[113] *Brut*, i. 256.
[114] *Brut*, i. 220.
[115] *Brut*, i. 281. Cited Ranald Nicholson, *Edward III and the Scots* (Oxford 1965), p. 121 and n. 6. It is evident from record evidence that firearms could have been used at this early date; see T. F. Tout, 'Firearms in England in the fourteenth century' in *EHR*, xxvi (1911), p. 669 (the article is reprinted in *The Collected Papers of T. F. Tout* (Manchester 1932–4, 3 vols), ii. 233–75).

of the Scottish battles at Halidon Hill.[116] It ends triumphantly with the English victory:[117]

> There might men see the doughtiness of the noble King Edward and of his men, how manly they pursued the Scots, that flew for dread. And there might men see many a Scottish man cast down unto the earth dead, and their banners displayed, and hacked into pieces, and many a good habergeon of steel in their blood bathed.

With patriotic exaggeration the author estimates that the English, though outnumbered by five to one, lost only seven foot soldiers, while the Scots lost 35,712.

Although the chronicle of Geoffrey le Baker[118] never achieved a popularity at all comparable with that of the *Brut*, there are points of resemblance between the two works. Both are patriotic in tone and were influenced by the chivalric tradition, and both are a vital source for military history. Baker concentrates particularly on the Hundred Years' War, but without neglecting the war with Scotland. Nevertheless, despite his primary interest in warfare, Baker included entries on other matters, mainly relating to English domestic history.[119] He assiduously collected information from hearsay and written sources, in the same way as he had done for the reign of Edward II. Again he obtained news from Carmelite friars: he cites the testimony of one Carmelite by name, Thomas de Lavyngtone, for the death of James Douglas.[120] For Edward III's campaigns he must have questioned returned soldiers, and he certainly used official documents,[121] newsletters,[122] casualty lists,[123] and itineraries.[124] Some of his information is similar to Murimuth's.

Although Baker was capable of drawing rational deductions from his

---

[116] *Brut*, i. 283–5. Cited Nicholson, op. cit., p. 124 n. 3.

[117] *Brut*, i. 285. See Nicholson, op. cit., p. 137 and n. 9 (cf. ibid., p. 129 and n. 2, on the exaggeration in the *Brut* and other English chronicles of the size of the Scottish army).

[118] For Geoffrey le Baker's career, patrons, works and value as an authority for Edward II's reign see pp. 37–42 above.

[119] For example Baker gives a full account of the alleged plot of Edmund earl of Kent in 1330 (*GB*, pp. 43–4, and the next note), of the arrest of Mortimer (see below), and of the Black Death—including a description of the clinical symptoms of bubonic plague (*GB*, pp. 98–100).

[120] *GB*, p. 41. Cf. p. 38 and n. 237 above. The fact that members of the Carmelite order were accused of complicity in the earl of Kent's alleged plot, suggests the possibility that Baker derived at least part of his information about the affair from a Carmelite monk; see *GB*, p. 44. He also, having noticed the death in Calais from the plague of the captain and another man, records that both were buried with the London Carmelites which suggests that a Carmelite may again have been his informant; *GB*, p. 99.

[121] E.g. the text of the truce of 1347; *GB*, pp. 92–5.

[122] See, for example, the account of the Breton campaign of 1352; *GB*, pp. 120, 286 n.

[123] E.g. *GB*, pp. 154–5, 313 n.

[124] For Baker's use of itineraries see p. 79 and nn. 137, 138 below.

evidence, he loved good stories, many of which probably display his talent as a raconteur more than his integrity as an historian. His narrative powers can be illustrated by the dramatic account of the arrest of Roger Mortimer in Nottingham castle.[125] The king and his companions were led a considerable distance at night by men with torches 'through a secret passage underground' into the castle, and so to the queen's chamber. Leaving the king outside the door, 'lest his mother saw him', the knights entered with drawn swords and found Isabella and Mortimer ready for bed. They took Mortimer out into the hall, with Isabella (who suspected Edward's presence) at their heels crying 'Good son, good son, have pity on the gentle Mortimer!' Another dramatic anecdote occurs in the description of the battle of Halidon Hill.[126] Before the engagement a champion came from the Scottish camp, a formidable giant, 'a very Goliath', who was called in English Turnbull ('Turnebole'), and challenged any Englishman to single combat. At length a Norfolk knight called Robert de Benhall accepted the challenge and rode towards the champion with drawn sword. On the way, he cut in two a black mastiff 'which accompanied and supported' the champion: the latter was so maddened by the slaughter of his dog that Benhall succeeded in cutting off his left hand and then his head.

Baker's patriotism is frequently and fervently expressed. It appears, for example, in his account of how in 1350 King Edward asked the pope for a cardinal's hat for an English ecclesiastic. Edward was amazed that no Englishman had been so honoured because there were 'many excellent clerks who have graduated in arts in both the universities of his kingdom, and they were equally distinguished by their excellent characters.' Baker notes that the pope told the king to nominate two candidates—but none the less created eleven French cardinals.[127]

Baker's patriotism is most evident in connection with the French war. He ends almost immediately after a graphic account of the Black Prince's victory at Poitiers, with the peace negotiations. Already, on recording the birth of the prince in 1331, he foresees his future military success: 'Divine clemency will allow us to praise him and to describe in due course his magnificent triumphs which he achieved, among others the capture of the king of France.'[128] The Black Prince exhorted his troops before the battle of Poitiers (Baker admits that he has not reported the harangue *verbatim*) in patriotic terms. The soldiers should fight for honour, love of

---

[125] *GB*, p. 46. For a similar account of Mortimer's arrest see the *Brut*, i. 269–71. Baker could have derived his information through his connection with the Bohun family, because one of Edward III's companions on this occasion was Edward de Bohun, son of Earl Humphrey (who was killed at Boroughbridge) and brother of John de Bohun, earl of Hereford. Baker records Edward de Bohun's death by drowning; *GB*, p. 57.

[126] *GB*, p. 51.

[127] *GB*, pp. 111–12.

[128] *GB*, p. 48.

their country—and for spoil. If they survive, they shall continue in stead-fast comradeship; if they die they shall have eternal fame and heavenly joy.[129] Baker eulogizes the Black Prince: he was a wise commander ('prudens imperator'),[130] eager for battle because of the peace which would follow.[131] Baker also praises Edward III whose 'glorious deeds' he under-takes to describe.[132] Conversely Baker's patriotism appears in his abuse of the French. Philip de Valois was a 'pseudo-king' ('seudo-rex') and tyrant who planned to annihilate England:[133] he, and indeed every Frenchman, was bloated with pride.[134]

The influence of contemporary chivalry appears in a number of passages in Baker's chronicle. He has a long account of the foundation of the Order of the Garter in 1350. He describes the composition of the order, names its members, and gives details of their dress (each knight wore a russet coloured gown embroidered with blue garters resembling the garter worn on his right leg, and a blue mantle with scutcheons of St George).[135] And Baker's account of the heroic death of Sir Thomas Dagworth in Brittany is in true chivalric style. Dagworth, wounded five times in the face by bolts from French crossbows and blinded by a blow from a lance, his men prostrate around him, would not surrender but continued to wound and kill his adversaries until he himself was slain by a sword blow.[136]

As a military historian Baker, besides giving vivid descriptions of skir-mishes, sieges and battles, has numerous apparently authentic details not found elsewhere. He is the principal source for the itinerary of the Black Prince's first raid, from Bordeaux to Narbonne, in 1355.[137] He also gives the itinerary of Edward III from La Hougue to Calais in 1346, which has value when used in conjunction with other accounts of the same journey.[138] Baker obviously had an interest in and knowledge of military tactics. For example he comments that the English, imitating the Scots, fought on foot for the first time at Halidon Hill.[139] And he explains how at the battle of Poitiers Sir William Douglas persuaded John king of France to make many of his men-at-arms fight on foot (sending their horses into town to prevent their use in flight) because, as Sir William informed him,

[129] *GB*, pp. 145–6.
[130] *GB*, 146, cf. ibid., p. 140.
[131] *GB*, p. 141.
[132] *GB*, p. 39.
[133] *GB*, pp. 54, 55.
[134] Baker refers to the 'fastus pompaticus Gallicorum' and the 'pompatica nobilitas Galli-corum'; *GB*, pp. 123, 143.
[135] *GB*, pp. 108–9, 278–9 nn.
[136] *GB*, pp. 101–2.
[137] *GB*, pp. 128–39, 292–8 nn. For the value of this passage see Hewitt, *The Black Prince's Expedition of 1355–1357*, pp. 43–77 passim, 180–3 nn. passim.
[138] *GB*, pp. 79–81, 249–59 nn.
[139] *GB*, p. 51. In fact the English had fought on foot at Dupplin Moor; see Nicholson, *Edward III and the Scots*, pp. 87, 133.

it was the custom of the English in those days to fight on foot in imitation of the Scots.[140] And Baker is the only authority for the statement that at Crécy the English dug pits, one foot deep and one foot wide, to trip the French cavalry.[141]

The next group of chronicles to be considered, those by foreign writers, reflects the chivalric values of the fourteenth century to an even greater extent than the preceding works. The main influence on this group was romance literature. Knightly heroes and deeds of chivalry are the authors' principal concern, and often their patrons take the centre of the stage. The literary tradition of France, the home of chivalric culture, helped determine the tone of these chronicles. The connection between the historiography of England and of France and its neighbours was close at this period: similar historiographical modes, the annalistic type of chronicle and romance-style biography in vernacular verse, flourished on both sides of the channel.[142] And Scotland had close cultural affinities not only with England but also with France. Moreover, the authors derived much of their information from a cosmopolitan society, from knights and heralds involved in the wars of the period and in touch with various royal and noble courts. And they travelled: both Jean le Bel and Froissart visited England. As will be seen, the lay writers in the chivalric tradition had similar cross channel contacts; Sir Thomas Gray fought in the English army on the continent, and Chandos Herald, although probably Flemish by birth, chose to write the biography of an Englishman—the Black Prince. Hence it is not surprising that a number of continental chronicles contain considerable information on Edward III's wars,[143] but the most notable are those by Jean le Bel and Froissart. Similarly the chronicle by the Scot, John Barbour, has essential information for the Anglo-Scottish war.

John Barbour's *Bruce* was written under the influence of both French

---

[140] *GB*, p. 143. Baker's statement that King John made most of his men-at-arms fight on foot is confirmed by Froissart; *JF* (K de L), v. 411–12. Froissart, however, states that it was at the suggestion of Eustace de Ribemont, not William Douglas. Baker's account of the battle of Poitiers is the best of those in the chronicles written in England: see A. H. Burne, 'The battle of Poitiers' in *EHR*, lv (1938), pp. 21–52 passim.

[141] *GB*, pp. 83, 260 n. Noticed Charles Oman, *A History of the Art of War* (London 1898), p. 606.

[142] The interrelation of the fourteenth century chronicle traditions of England and France is briefly discussed by Denys Hay, 'History and historians in France and England during the fifteenth century' in *BIHR*, xxxv (1962), pp. 111–15.

[143] For an example of a chronicle written in the annalistic style in Flanders at this time, which contributes to our knowledge of the Hundred Years' War, see *Chronique et Annales de Gilles le Muisit, Abbé de Saint-Martin de Tournai (1272–1352)*, ed. H. Lemaître (Soc. de l'Histoire de France 1906). An example of a chronicle in vernacular verse written in the romance style, which is a valuable source for the Breton war, is the *Chronique de Bertrand du Guesclin par Cuvelier*, ed. E. Charrière (Paris 1839); the latter was written by a trouvère probably in Paris (ibid., pp. lxiv-lxv, 4) and covers the years from 1324 to 1380.

and English historiographical traditions. It is a life of Robert Bruce (king of Scotland from 1306 to 1329), with the life of Lord James Douglas (d. 1330) as a secondary theme, and concerns the years from 1290 to 1332. Although it is primarily of importance for the Anglo-Scottish war in the reigns of Edward I and Edward II,[144] it will be considered here because it was composed during Edward III's reign and illustrates historiographical features characteristic of that period: it is a vernacular work probably intended for a lay patron; it is written in the romance style; and it is very patriotic in tone.

John Barbour was born in about 1325 of a family with property in Aberdeen.[145] By 1357 he was archdeacon of Aberdeen. He studied at Oxford in 1357 and again in 1364. In 1365 he was at St Denis, Paris, and was also in France from 1368 to 1369. Subsequently he held various offices under Robert II: he was clerk of audit in Robert's household in 1372 and was auditor of the Scottish exchequer in 1382, 1383 and 1384. He received a number of grants in reward for his services. One of these grants, £10 from the customs collected at Aberdeen, was made in 1377, soon after the completion of *The Bruce*. This suggests that Barbour wrote to please Robert II. Such a work would have been particularly *à propos* because Robert II was, through his mother Marjorie, the grandson of Robert Bruce. Barbour may also have written the genealogy, now lost, of the Stewart family, for Robert, who was the first Stewart king. In addition, Barbour was probably the author of two romances, the *Trojan War* and the *Buik of Alexander*, a *Brut* chronicle which is apparently lost, and perhaps of a *Life of St Ninian*.[146]

Probably Barbour wrote in vernacular verse because this style was the most acceptable to Robert II. The language is the Middle English dialect spoken in southern Scotland. In fact Barbour can claim to be the virtual founder of Scottish vernacular literature. Moreover, *The Bruce* has a pre-

---

[144] The gist of *The Bruce*'s romantic story of the origin of the rising of Robert Bruce in 1306 is corroborated by a letter of Edward I to the pope; *JB*, pp. 14–20. See G. W. S. Barrow, *Robert Bruce* (London 1965), pp. 197–9. Similarly, a letter of Edward III .corroborates Barbour's account of Bruce's deathbed request to James Douglas that his heart should be buried in the Holy Land (for a parallel passage in Jean le Bel, see pp. 86–7 and n. 177 below); *JB*, p. 365 (bk XX, ll. 191–5), and see Barrow, op. cit., pp. 445–6, and A. A. M. Duncan, 'The *Acta* of Robert I' in *Scottish Historical Review*, xxxii (1953), p. 22. Moreover, Barbour is an authority of primary value for the battle of Bannockburn; see J. E. Morris, *Bannockburn* (Cambridge 1914), pp. 50, 59, 63, 66–7, 70, 85–92. For the value of *The Bruce* to the historian see also *JB*, pp. xx-xxiii, Barrow, op. cit., pp. 431–2, and *The Buik of Alexander*, ed. R. L. G. Ritchie (Scottish Text Society, xii, xvii, xxi, xxv, 1921–9, 4 vols), i.ccxxvi-ccxliv and nn., passim.

[145] For John Barbour's career see *JB*, pp. xvi-xix, and Ritchie, op. cit., i.clxxiii-ccxxi.

[146] For these works attributed to Barbour see *JB*, pp. xix-xx, and, for the *Buik of Alexander*, *JB*, pp. 505–6; Barbour's authorship of the latter is accepted by Ritchie, op. cit., i. passim, and in *The Oxford Book of Scottish Verse*, chosen by J. MacQueen and T. Scott (Oxford 1966), pp. 5–6, where an extract is printed. Ritchie, op. cit., i.ccxvi and n. 15, argues that the Stewart genealogy is to be identified with Barbour's *Brut*.

eminent place in Scottish historiography: it is the first extant history in literary form written in Scotland. Only one other history of any substance survives which had previously been written there, the chronicle of Melrose abbey.[147] The next surviving Scottish chronicle, the *Scotichronicon* by John of Fordun, another clerk of Aberdeen (d. 1384), was written a few years later,[148] while Andrew of Wyntoun[149] and Walter Bower[150] belong to the fifteenth century. However, it is likely that a biography of Robert Bruce earlier than *The Bruce* once existed. This was apparently used by Jean le Bel and possibly by Barbour himself.[151]

John Barbour had literary pretensions. He was influenced by the *Brut* and by the romances so popular in France.[152] Robert Bruce is represented as a chivalric hero. He was 'valiant, strong and wise', and generously rewarded loyal service.[153] He started the battle of Bannockburn with a 'doughty deed' worthy of any chivalric warrior. The Bruce was charged by Sir Henry de Bohun, 'a good and bold knight, clad in fine strong armour', who thought that he could easily vanquish the Bruce because the latter was mounted on a light palfrey. But when they met, Barbour writes, Sir Henry missed the king, and the Bruce, standing in his stirrups dealt him such a mighty blow with his keen, strong axe that neither hat nor helmet could withstand it. The heavy stroke that he gave clove skull and brain; the axe-handle shivered in two; and Bohun crashed lifeless to the

---

[147] For the Melrose chronicle (which covers the years from 731 to 1270) see Gransden, *Historical Writing*, i. 319 n. 7. The only other known monastic chronicle compiled in Scotland is the so-called Holyrood chronicle covering the period, very briefly, from the invasion of Julius Caesar to 1189, with later additions (for 1266, 1286, for some years between 1296 and 1318, and for 1355 and 1356). To 1128 the 'Holyrood' chronicle was compiled from English sources and has no particular bearing on Scottish history. From that date it drew on Scottish sources. Material relating to the Augustinian abbey of Holyrood occurs from 1150 to 1171–2, between which dates the chronicle has some value for Scottish history. From 1164 begin entries relating to the Cistercian abbey of Coupar-Angus which probably acquired the Holyrood chronicle some time between 1171 and 1186. The only two texts of the 'Holyrood' chronicle which survive contain the Coupar-Angus version, with continuation. The 'Holyrood' chronicle is printed, translated and exhaustively discussed in *The Chronicle of Holyrood*, ed. M. O. Anderson, with some additional notes by A. O. Anderson (Scottish History Soc., xxx, 1938). For a twelfth century historical collection, possibly from the Augustinian abbey of Jedburgh, see J. M. Todd and H. S. Offler, 'A medieval chronicle from Scotland' in *Scottish Historical Review*, xlvii (1968), pp. 151–9.

[148] Printed *Chronica Gentis Scotorum*, ed., with an English translation, W. F. Skene (Historians of Scotland, i, iv, Edinburgh 1871, 1872, 2 vols); see also n. 150 below.

[149] His chronicle is printed *The Original Chronicle of Andrew of Wyntoun*, ed. F. J. Amours (Scottish Text Soc., Edinburgh-London 1903–14, 6 vols).

[150] His chronicle is printed as a continuation to Fordun's chronicle in the editions of Fordun by Thomas Hearne (Oxford 1722, 5 vols), and Walter Goodall (Edinburgh 1759, 2 vols).

[151] See p. 86 below.

[152] For references to the heroes of classical and romance literature, and to biblical figures, see e.g. *JB*, pp. 12–16 passim (bk I, ll. 395, 465, 525–6, 537, 549 respectively). Cf. B. W. Kliman, 'The idea of chivalry in John Barbour's *Bruce*' in *Mediaeval Studies*, xxxv (Toronto 1973), pp. 477 et seq. For *The Bruce* as literature see also *JB*, pp. xv-xvi, and Ritchie, op.cit., i.ccxxi-ccxliv.

[153] *JB*, p. 23 (bk II, ll. 173–5).

earth.[154] Barbour praises James Douglas, Bruce's friend and supporter, for his unwavering loyalty to his lord. Love of loyalty, he asserts, is a gracious thing: through loyalty men live righteously; with the virtue of loyalty a man may come to be of high account; and without it no one, however strong or wise he be, may win renown.[155]

Patriotic fervour permeates *The Bruce*. John Barbour's patriotism exceeded that even of such writers as Murimuth, Baker and the author of the long version of the *Brut*. This was probably because Scotland was, in contrast to England, a beleaguered nation. Scottish nationalism developed because it was frustrated. Thus Barbour gives extreme expression to national ambitions, and shows how the Scots regarded the war with England. He rejoiced at Edward II's defeat in 1322, when Edward was 'discomfit in his own country'.[156] Scottish raids into England, though confessedly they led to no deed of chivalry, meant riches for the soldiers ('prisoners and cattle, riches, and many fair jewel'), since England abounded in wealth.[157] Above all Robert Bruce, like Maccabeus, fought to free his people from bondage. Barbour writes a timeless paean on freedom, part of which, paraphrased in modern English, reads:[158]

> Freedom is a noble thing. Freedom gives man choice. Freedom gives man all solace. He that lives free, lives at ease. A noble heart can have no ease, nor any pleasure, if freedom fails. For liberty to please oneself is desired above all things. Nor may he who has lived free well know the actual state, the affliction and the wretchedness, that are coupled to vile thraldom. But if he has tried it, then he should understand it with his whole heart, and should think freedom more to be praised than all the gold in the world.

We turn now from the Scot, John Barbour, to the two continental writers who are at least equally important as sources for Edward III's wars, namely Jean le Bel and Froissart. Both were secular clerks from Hainault whose connection with England resulted from Edward III's marriage with Philippa of Hainault in 1328. Jean le Bel's patron, John of Hainault (lord of Beaumont and brother of William I count of Hainault), was Philippa's uncle, and Philippa herself was patroness of Froissart.

Although Jean le Bel was a cleric he moved in chivalric society. He was born of a good burgher family of Liège in the late thirteenth century.[159]

---

[154] *JB*, pp. 210–11 (bk XII, ll. 25–61).
[155] *JB*, p. 11 (bk I, ll. 365–70). For praise of Douglas see also *JB*, pp. 9–10 (bk I, ll. 305–13).
[156] *JB*, p. 338 (bk XVIII, l. 568).
[157] *JB*, pp. 246–7, 337–8 (bk XIII, ll. 740–4; bk XVIII, ll. 559–62).
[158] *JB*, p. 7 (bk I, ll. 225–40). The whole passage on freedom and thrall is printed in the *Oxford Book of Scottish Verse*, pp. 10–11.
[159] For Jean le Bel's life and works see the introduction to the standard edition of his chronicle p. 59 n. 9 above); *Bel*, i. i–viii.

His father was burgomaster of Liège in 1304, and his brother an alderman of the city. By 1313 Jean was apparently a canon of St Lambert in Liège, but he retained his status in the world and love of good living. A contemporary who knew him well described his magnificent clothes, studded with pearls and gems, his numerous retinue (he went to church with sixteen, or even twenty attendants), and his lavish hospitality (on solemn feast days he banqueted at least forty, sometimes fifty people).[160] He loved hunting and hawking and jousting, and had two sons, John and Giles, 'by a young lady of rank', Marie des Prés. And he was a close friend and companion of John of Hainault.

The prince-like Jean le Bel had literary taste and ability. He wrote songs and virelays, and in 1352, at the request of John of Hainault,[161] he began his chronicle in French prose, which when completed covered the period from the late thirteenth century to 1361. His primary theme was the wars of Edward III. He aimed at recording 'the notable perilous adventures and battles, feats of arms and prowess' since Edward III's coronation.[162] He wanted to perpetuate the memory of the chivalric heroes, especially of Edward III but also of other valiant men, such as John of Hainault himself, the Black Prince, the duke of Lancaster, and the famous Hainault knight Walter Manny. His work was intended to replace with authentic history the romance verse accounts of the campaigns, which he said were so full of lies and flights of fancy that they made a mockery of the subject. Le Bel showed the first thirty nine chapters (which record events to the middle of 1340) to John of Hainault: the latter 'and others present' corrected it 'as they wished, without fiction'. And Le Bel presented a copy of the same thirty nine chapters to John of Hainault. The chronicle ultimately had 109 chapters, but Le Bel did not start the continuation until after John's death in March 1356.[163]

The first recension of the chronicle contains its most interesting and unusual section, the account of Edward III's Scottish campaign in the summer of 1327.[164] Jean le Bel wrote as an eyewitness for he accompanied his patron John of Hainault on the campaign. It is hard to parallel in other sources of the period the realism of this section. Jean le Bel minutely describes what he saw and also records the feelings of many of Edward III's

---

[160] See Jacques Hemricourt, *Le Miroir des Nobles de Hesbaye*, printed in *Oeuvres de Jacques de Hemricourt*, ed. C. de Borman, A. Bayot and E. Poncelet (Brussels 1910–31, 3 vols), i. 226–8.

[161] That Le Bel wrote at the request of John of Hainault is stated by Jean d'Outremeuse: Jean d'Outremeuse, *Ly Myreur des histors, Chronique de Jean des Preis dit d'Outremeuse*, ed. Stanislas Bormans (Brussels 1864–87, 7 vols), vi. 322–3.

[162] *Bel*, i. 1–4 (prologue).

[163] See *Bel*, i. viii and n. 2, ix–x.

[164] *Bel*, i. 39–77. Froissart copied this section of Le Bel almost word for word. For full modern accounts of the campaign see Ranald Nicholson, 'The last campaign of Robert Bruce' in *EHR*, lxxvii (1962), pp. 233–46, and the same author's *Edward III and the Scots*, Chap. III.

unfortunate soldiers. Thus he gives a unique picture of the problems and sufferings imposed on an English army by the terrain and climate of the northern regions of Britain, and by the Scots' guerrilla tactics.

John of Hainault and his company joined Edward III at York on 28 May.[165] Le Bel describes the Hainaulters' excellent billets in the suburbs of York. There was plenty of wine, from Gascony and the Rhine, and food was cheap: a daily market was held before their lodgings where 'a large capon cost only three shillings—the best was only four shillings—and two large fowl cost three shillings, and twelve herring one shilling.'[166] But unfortunately the English hated the foreigners and a riot broke out between the English archers and the young Hainaulters. Le Bel witnessed the fighting which he vividly describes, estimating that 316 of the archers were killed before the rest finally fled. Henceforth the Hainaulters lived in fear, staying indoors in the daytime, armed even at night, and protected by scouts detailed to report trouble in the town, and by patrols who guarded the fields and roads.[167]

After three weeks the army left York, on 10 July, to march northwards against the Scots. Le Bel describes the wild Northumberland countryside[168] and the characteristics of the enemy.[169] The Scots, he writes, were a tough and hardy people, experienced in war. The knights and esquires rode fine horses, and the rest small cobs. They did not take carts through the mountains and no bread or wine, but drank river water and seized animals *en route*, roasting the meat in its skin. They carried a large metal plate and a sack of meal between the saddle and panel. After eating the ill-cooked meat they put the stone plate on the fire, mixed the meal with water and made a little flat cake 'to comfort their stomachs'.

The problem facing the English army was how to confront the Scots, who avoided open battle but moved unseen from place to place pillaging and ravaging. The English advanced northwards guided by the smell of burning. Their progress was disorganized; the soldiers, arms at the ready, lost contact with their lords and fellows in the rough country, and were hindered by rocks and marshes. Sometimes they all rushed forward hearing a cry which they mistook for an encounter with the enemy— only to find that it was caused by deer or other wild animals fleeing from the advancing army. The soldiers camped, with no idea of their whereabouts, by the river Tyne in almost total darkness and without shelter. Only a few knights had brought candles on pack horses and hardly anyone had an axe to make some sort of covering. The soldiers spent the night

[165] *Bel*, i. 39.
[166] *Bel*, i. 47. See also for the prices paid by the army for provisions, high in these instances, *Bel*, i. 60, 70.
[167] *Bel*, i. 44–6. For the Hainaulters' fear of the English archers see also *Bel*, i. 71
[168] *Bel*, i. 49.
[169] *Bel*, i. 51–2.

fully armed holding their horses as they could not see to tether them. They had nothing to drink but river water, and nothing to eat but the bread they had carried behind their saddles, which was soaked with the horses' sweat. And it poured with rain so that they could not light camp fires, or cross the river because it became so swollen.[170]

Eventually the English located the Scots encamped on a hill just south of the river Wear. They struck camp at the foot suffering the same privations as before. The Scots refused a pitched battle, and the English could see their huge fires and hear their hullaballoo the night long ('it seemed as if they were devils come from hell to murder us').[171] The Scots had no bread, wine or salt but roasted the innumerable animals they had taken. Jean le Bel discovered this for himself, because he was one of the party from the English army who rode to the top of the hill to look around after the Scots had slipped away one night unseen. They found the carcasses of 500 animals, besides 400 cauldrons made of hide with the hair still on, hanging on stakes over the fire, full of water and meat, and over 1,000 spits with meat on them. And they also found more than 10,000 old shoes made of raw leather—and five wretched English prisoners tied to trees, two with their legs broken.[172]

The rest of Jean le Bel's chronicle is less remarkable than this description of Edward III's Scottish campaign of 1327. Henceforth Le Bel gives a competent though on the whole pedestrian account of Edward's wars and diplomacy. Towards the end of the chronicle he was writing more or less contemporarily with the events he recorded.[173] He clearly retained his interest in Anglo-Scottish relations on which he writes at some length. He was well informed on them and, in contrast to the English chroniclers, expresses admiration for 'the noble king' Robert Bruce, 'who had been most valiant and suffered much against the English'.[174] He recalls how Edward I had forced Robert Bruce into the forests where he hunted him with dogs. For this passage Le Bel cites the authority of 'a history made by the said King Robert'.[175] As has been suggested above, this work, which no longer survives, may also have been used by John Barbour.[176] It seems possible that Le Bel obtained a copy, directly or indirectly, from someone in the entourage of James Douglas who stayed at Sluys for twelve days in the autumn of 1329 on his way to the Holy Land carrying Robert Bruce's heart. Le Bel has a full account of Robert Bruce's deathbed request to

---

[170] *Bel*, i. 55–60.
[171] *Bel*, i. 66–7.
[172] *Bel*, i. 73.
[173] For the stages in which Le Bel composed the chronicle see *Bel*, i. xiv–xvi.
[174] *Bel*, i. 5, 36.
[175] 'Et aucune fois, ce dit on, et le treuve on en hystoire faitte par le dit roy Robert, le fist chasser le bon roy Edowart par ces grands forests, par l'espace de iii jours ou de iiii par chiens et limiers pour ce affaictiez et acharnez . . .'; *Bel*, i. 111.
[176] See p. 82 above.

Douglas to carry his heart to fight the enemies of Christ and of Douglas' promise to do so.[177] He describes Douglas' stay at Sluys, his festivities aboard ship with his companions and all comers,[178] and he records Douglas' decision to go to Spain instead of Jerusalem, and his death there.[179]

Le Bel's narrative of Edward III's wars in France and Brittany was mainly based on oral information. He learnt about the battle of Crécy from a number of combatants, including 'my lord and friend John of Hainault and ten or twelve knights and companions of his household, who were in the battle with the valiant and gentle king of Bohemia, and had their horses killed under them.'[180] Occasionally Le Bel has to admit ignorance—at least once because his informant 'was not in the secret counsel of the lords.'[181] He is particularly full on the Breton war, showing especial interest in the gallant exploits of Sir Walter Manny. Some of his information for Breton history before the spring of 1342 may well have derived from contact with the household of the count of Hainault. The count was with Edward III, having come to England at Easter, 1342, for a tournament, when the king received messengers from the duchess of Brittany appealing for aid against Charles of Blois.[182] Le Bel records the embassy. He also has accurate details concerning an embassy from Bordeaux which reached Edward at the same time, also asking for help, and describes the plight of the city.[183] (Although Le Bel concentrates mainly on Edward's wars, he shows some interest in conflicts in his own locality; for instance he gives an account of the war between the bishop of Liège, and the populace of Liège and that of Huy in 1347.)[184]

Despite his taste for exact historical narrative, Le Bel was influenced by the romance literary tradition. Edward III is his principal hero and John of Hainault, his patron, the secondary one. He tends to exaggerate the importance of John of Hainault in public events. Queen Isabella and the other exiles from England in 1326 appealed for help to John, then 'in the flower of his youth'. And, because 'all good knights must help and comfort all ladies and damsels in distress', he promised aid.[185] Isabella

---

[177] *Bel*, i. 83–5. A similar account of Robert Bruce's deathbed request to James Douglas concerning his heart and Douglas' consequent expedition, is in John Barbour's *Bruce*; see p. 81 n. 144 above. Le Bel's account is fully collated with Barbour's in *JB*, pp. 490–4 nn; cf. *JB*, p. 511.

[178] Le Bel states that Douglas went to Sluys with the hope of meeting someone going to Jerusalem, but while there heard of the war in Spain; *Bel*, i. 86–7. Douglas' visit to Sluys is not mentioned by Barbour; see *JB*, p. 493 n. However, there seems no reason to doubt the truth of Le Bel's statement.

[179] *Bel*, i. 87–8. Cited *JB*, pp. 493–4 n.

[180] *Bel*, ii. 105.

[181] *Bel*, ii. 7. Cf. *Bel*, ii. 21

[182] *Bel*, ii. 3–4.

[183] *Bel*, ii. 4–6, and nn.

[184] *Bel*, ii. 140–4.

[185] *Bel*, i. 14–17.

conquered England with the assistance of John and his troops. He stayed in England until after Edward III's coronation, receiving great honour and much admiration from 'countesses, ladies and damsels'.[186] Similarly Le Bel emphasizes the honour done to John of Hainault by Edward III at York in 1327, before and after the Scottish campaign,[187] and attributes to him an important part in arranging the marriage of his niece, Philippa of Hainault, whom he conducted to London, to King Edward.[188]

Jean le Bel also eulogizes the 'valiant, gentle king' Edward, whose court was comparable to King Arthur's, and whom men could not praise and honour too much.[189] Never had a Christian prince fought on so many fronts at once and borne such heavy expense.[190] Le Bel elaborately justifies himself for calling Edward 'the noble king', while referring to Philip simply as 'the king of France'. It was not, he claimed, because of favouritism or bias, but because Edward deserved more honour. Edward took good counsel, honoured his nobles, defended the realm, conquered and fought on his subjects' behalf at home and abroad, paying his soldiers and allies generously. On the other hand Philip allowed his country to be ravaged in order to save his own skin and avoid danger, took the advice of clerks and prelates, not of his lords (some of whom he executed and disinherited), oppressed his people with taxes and did not pay his soldiers well. Therefore he was hated by his subjects, while Edward was loved.[191] Nevertheless, despite his attitude to the two kings, Le Bel neither loved Englishmen in general nor hated France. He writes that 'we did not much mind' when some English soldiers were drowned during the 1327 Scottish campaign.[192] And he praises France for excelling all countries in chivalry and wealth.[193]

Notwithstanding Jean le Bel's tendency to eulogize Edward III, he tells one story which reflected discredit on the king. It is unlikely that this story is true and Le Bel may well have derived it from some propaganda tract probably written in France under provocation of the Hundred Years' War, as a deliberate 'smear' on Edward III.[194] 'Now', Le Bel begins, 'I must tell you something very bad done by the king which I have heard; he must be blamed for it because he was a person of no small consequence.'[195] He relates how Edward (allegedly) raped the countess of Salisbury (Kathe-

---

[186] *Bel*, i. 25–33.

[187] *Bel*, i. 39, 43, 75–6.

[188] *Bel*, i. 78–81.

[189] *Bel*, i. 115, 118, 119; ii. 173.

[190] *Bel*, ii. 168.

[191] *Bel*, ii. 65–7.

[192] *Bel*, i. 62.

[193] *Bel*, ii. 66–7.

[194] See A. Gransden, 'The alleged rape by Edward III of the countess of Salisbury' in *EHR*, lxxxvii (1972), pp. 333–44.

[195] 'Or vous vueil je conter le villain cas que fist le roy Edowart, dont on le pouoit blasmer, car il ne fut pas petit, ainsy que je l'ay ouy dire'; *Bel*, ii. 30.

rine, wife of William de Montagu, earl of Salisbury 1337–44). Edward fell in love with the countess when he stayed at Wark castle, which she was holding for her husband during the Scottish campaign in the autumn of 1341. Le Bel describes Edward's infatuation in romantic terms. Edward considered the countess the most beautiful woman he had ever seen and was so enamoured that he did not join his men in their feasting. When the countess remonstrated with him, he declared his love, but she, fearing dishonour, repulsed him. Later, in 1342, he again visited her at Wark, having sent the earl of Salisbury off to the Breton war. Edward stayed the day, and at night when everyone was asleep except the chamberlains whom he ordered not to disturb him, he entered the countess's bedroom, locking the door to exclude her ladies in waiting. He put his hand over her mouth before she had time to scream more than two or three times, and raped her. He left her in a faint, bleeding from nose, mouth 'and another part'. Next day he rode to London. Le Bel gives a highly coloured account of the earl of Salisbury's sad confrontation with his wife after the event, and his reproaches to the king, and states that the earl subsequently died at the siege of Algéciras.[196] This tale is full of improbabilities and impossibilities, and its author may well have taken as a literary model Livy's story of the rape of Lucretia.[197] The first writer known to have cast doubt on its veracity was, as will be seen, Jean Froissart.

Jean le Bel's chronicle formed the basis of Jean Froissart's *Chroniques*. Moreover, Le Bel's patron, John of Hainault, was one of Froissart's patrons. Froissart was born at Valenciennes in Hainault in the 1330s.[198] He had early connections with England. Possibly he was educated as a child in the English court. He may have visited England from 1359 until the spring of 1360, and was certainly there from the autumn of 1360 and until 1366, visiting Scotland in 1365. In 1362 he became a clerk of Queen Philippa and she remained his patron until her death in 1369. In her service he extended his knowledge by travel. He was in Bordeaux in 1367, then in England again, and in 1368 went to Italy with Lionel duke of Clarence. After the death of Queen Philippa, her brother-in-law Robert of Namur became his patron. From him Froissart obtained the cure of Estinnes-au-Mont where he lived for ten years. His patrons in later life were Wenceslas, duke of Brabant (d. 1381), for whom he wrote a poem on the Round Table, and John of Hainault's grandson, Guy II of Châtillon, count of Blois. Froissart visited England again in 1395 and died some time between 1404 and 1410.

[196] For the story see *Bel*, ii. 30–4.
[197] See Gransden, op. cit., pp. 342–4.
[198] For Froissart's life and work see *JF* (K de L), i. pt i. 3–464, and F. S. Shears, *Froissart Chronicler and Poet* (London 1930). His connections with England are discussed by Margaret Galway, 'Froissart in England' in *University of Birmingham Historical Journal*, vii (1959–60), pp. 18–35. [Since my book went to press the following scholarly collection of studies on Froissart has appeared: *Froissart: Historian*, ed. J. J. N. Palmer (Bury St Edmunds 1981).]

This series of patrons whom Froissart gained in the course of his eventful career profoundly influenced his historical writing. He wrote his first work for one of them, Queen Philippa. This work, now lost, was apparently an account in French prose or verse of 'the wars and adventures' of Edward III from the battle of Poitiers (1356) to 1359/60. He presented a copy to the queen, 'who kindly and obligingly received it from me and made me great profit.'[199] This work was the germ of his *Chroniques*, a history in French prose of events, mainly military, in western Europe from 1327 to 1400. The style of the work, with its innumerable lifelike anecdotes and colourful prose, was well suited to the tastes of Froissart's patrons.

The chronicle survives in three main redactions, each written at a different stage in Froissart's career and having considerable variations from the others. Each expresses a different point of view, reflecting Froissart's response to his current situation and calculated to please whomever was his patron at the time.[200] The first redaction of Froissart's chronicle follows Jean le Bel to 1361 (where Le Bel ends) often word for word, and has a eulogy on him in the prologue. His dependence on Le Bel decreases as he nears 1361, and he continues to 1369. Froissart composed this redaction immediately after his return from England and he revised it about ten years later. He wrote at the request of Robert of Namur, who married Isabella of Hainault, sister of Queen Philippa, in 1354, and was an ally of Edward III—he fought in Edward's campaigns and received a pension from him. Froissart wrote the second redaction of his chronicle after 1376. By that time his connection with England was ended; he was the court poet of Wenceslas and chaplain of Guy count of Blois who was an ally of the king of France. This redaction follows Le Bel less closely, and replaces the eulogy of him in the prologue by a brief acknowledgment. Froissart collected additional material from numerous sources, mainly using oral information derived from French knights and heralds. The tone of the work is changed—Guy of Blois is eulogized, and the French

---

[199] See *JF* (SL), i.x. One result of the fact that Froissart wrote for, and consequently that his work was popular with royalty and the nobility, was that a number of the surviving texts were sumptuously produced, with lavish illumination. See, for example, the copy, which is now incomplete (it contains only vol. iv), executed in Flanders for Edward IV, BL MS Royal 18 E II. A copy, also now incomplete (it contains vol. ii), very similar in style was executed, presumably at about the same time, for Edward's chamberlain and companion during his exile in Flanders, 1470–1, William Lord Hastings; BL MS. Royal 18 E I (see Plate V below). King Edward and Hastings both stayed in Flanders with Louis de Bruges, seigneur de Gruthuyse, himself the owner of a fine library; see p. 291 and n. 21 below. Cf. Margaret Kekewich, 'Edward IV, William Caxton, and literary patronage in Yorkist England' in *Modern Language Review*, lxvi (1971), p. 483.

[200] For the evolution of Froissart's chronicle and his patrons' influence on it I have followed the clear explanation by Luce; *JF* (SL), i. vii et seq. His views are also accepted in general in G. T. Diller, 'La dernière rédaction du premier livre de *Chroniques* de Froissart: une étude du Reg. Lat. 869' in *Le Moyen Age*, 4e série, xxv (1970), pp. 91–125 passim (see especially pp. 92, 102, 104). Professor Diller, op. cit., discusses in detail the manuscript, literary structure and historical content of bk I of the third redaction.

more favourably treated than formerly, and the English less so. However, this second redaction never achieved the popularity of the first which survives in about fifty manuscripts, as opposed to two copies of the second one. Finally after 1400 Froissart revised the chronicle again. He now substituted original narrative for the passages borrowed from Jean le Bel. His outlook had become serious, even sombre, and very critical of the English, no doubt reflecting disillusion with England after his visit in 1395.

It can be seen from the above that Froissart is only an independent authority (discounting a few additions) after Jean le Bel ends in 1361. His chronicle as a whole is primarily a source for the continental wars, including Edward III's campaigns. But, even after Froissart's direct connection with England ended in 1369, he retained an interest in English affairs and has considerable value for the reign of Richard II (for example, he is, as will be seen in Chapter 6, an authority for the Peasants' Revolt). However, the credibility of his chronicle raises problems.[201] Froissart wrote in the highly coloured chivalric style and undoubtedly presents a romanticized view of events. Moreover, he relied much on oral information—which can amount to little more than gossip and rumour. Nevertheless, he included many passages based on his own observation and clearly had historical judgment: his statements deserve careful consideration.

Both Froissart's inimitable gift as a raconteur and also his ability to weigh evidence are well illustrated by his treatment of Jean le Bel's story concerning the rape of the countess of Salisbury. In the first redaction of his chronicle he suppresses Le Bel's account of the rape altogether.[202] In the second redaction he inserts a paragraph questioning Le Bel's allegations. He writes:[203]

> I have stayed long and had many conversations in England, principally in the king's court and in the courts of the great lords of that country, but never have I heard speak of such a wicked deed; and when I have asked many people who would have known, they were completely ignorant of it.

He comments that any such idea would dishonour the king, the noble lady and her husband. On the other hand Froissart adds in the second redaction the celebrated story of the game of chess played by the king and countess. The story is obviously fictional, but, unlike the rape story, it is not scurrilous. It has a conversation between the parties which shows Froissart's ability to write realistic dialogue:[204]

---

[201] For a discussion of the style and value to the historian today of the *Chroniques* see *Froissart, Voyage en Béarn*, ed. Diverres, pp. xiii-xxvii.
[202] *Bel*, ii. 30–4 (see p. 88 and n. 194 above); see *JF* (SL), ii. 135.
[203] *JF* (SL) iii. xviii n. 5, 293.
[204] *JF* (SL), ii. 135. Diverres, op. cit., pp. xxvi-xxvii, states that Froissart differed from his

Edward said to the countess, laughing, 'Lady what will you be
pleased to adventure on the game?'
She replied, 'Sir, and what will you?'
The king took a ring with a large ruby from his finger and
placed it on the board.
The countess then said, 'Sir, Sir, I have no ring so rich as yours.'
'Lady', said the king, 'such as you have put it forth; I shall not look
too closely.'

And she put down a gold ring, not of great value. They played, and
'ever between the turns he regarded the lady so that she was ashamed and
made false moves.' But he, wishing her to have his ring, made false moves
on purpose. Eventually the countess won and Edward insisted she took
the ring. However, she sent one of her 'damsels' to return it when he
was leaving—but he gave the ring to the girl 'so that it might remain
there.'

John Barbour, Jean le Bel and Froissart were all much travelled secular
clerks. All three, but especially Le Bel and Froissart, were closely connected
with chivalric society. This connection is reflected in the subject matter
and style of their works. It also illustrates the growing interest of laymen in
this kind of history which was written under the influence of romance
literature. As has been seen, other works besides these three were composed
for lay patrons, and an increasing proportion of chronicles was in the
vernacular, for the benefit of a lay audience.

The enthusiasm of the chivalric class for history in the romance style
cannot be better demonstrated than by the two chronicles by laymen,
Sir Thomas Gray's *Scalacronica* and Chandos Herald's *Life of the Black
Prince*.

Sir Thomas Gray of Heton was, as far as is known, the first nobleman
since Æthelweard to write a chronicle. He belonged to an old family in
Northumberland. His father, also called Thomas,[205] served Edward I
and Edward II in their Scottish campaigns and was captured at Bannockburn. He subsequently received many rewards from the king for his services
and in 1318 he was appointed constable of Norham castle and sheriff of
Norham. Thomas, junior, the chronicler,[206] appears in 1338, in letters
of protection to accompany William de Montagu, earl of Salisbury,

---

contemporaries, who wrote formalized dialogue, in his gift for writing realistic talk;
however, Le Bel attempted to write the conversation of Edward and the countess realistical-
ly; *Bel*, ii. 30–1.

[205] For an account of the career of Sir Thomas Gray, sr., who died in about 1343, from the
Scalacronica and official records see *Scala*. pp. xv–xxvii, and Charles Moor, *Knights of Edward
I* (Harleian Soc., lxxx–lxxxiv, 1929–32, 5 vols), ii. 155 (here spelt Grey).

[206] For the career of Sir Thomas Gray, jr, see *Scala*. pp. xxvii–xxxii.

beyond the sea.[207] He fought at Neville's Cross, and later held a number of official positions: for example, he was appointed sheriff and constable of Norham in 1345, and was appointed to treat with the Scots in 1348. In 1355 Norham was attacked by the Scots and Gray was captured. Having insufficient money to pay the ransom, he petitioned Edward III. He was released in 1359 and accompanied the Black Prince to France. In 1367 he was appointed keeper of the marches, and probably died a few years later.

It was while Sir Thomas Gray, junior, was in captivity that he began his chronicle, the *Scalacronica*. The Scots imprisoned him in Edinburgh castle, and there he found an excellent library of history books, presumably collected by the English during their occupation of the castle from 1296 to 1314. He writes of himself (in the third person) in the prologue:[208]

> He perused books of chronicles, in verse and prose, in Latin, French and English, concerning the deeds of our ancestors, at which he was astonished. And it weighed heavily upon him that he had not previously known more about the sequence of the centuries. So, as he had hardly anything to do with his time, he became curious and contemplated how he might deal with and convert into more succinct form the chronicles of Great Britain and the deeds of the English.

The *Scalacronica* is a history of England and its wars from the time of the early Britons to 1363, in Anglo-Norman prose. Gray compiled it to the end of the thirteenth century from various well known authorities which he lists in the prologue. He used Gildas, Bede, the English *Brut*, Florence of Worcester (to whom he refers as Marianus Scotus), William of Malmesbury, Henry of Huntingdon, Roger of Howden, the *Polychronicon*, John of Tynemouth and Thomas of Otterbourne ('a master of divinity and member of the order of Friars Minor').[209] From the reign of King John onwards the *Scalacronica* contains some material not found in these sources and, although Gray lived well after the reign of Edward II, his account of it has some value for the Anglo-Scottish war. In writing of Edward III's reign, Gray is principally concerned with the Hundred Years' War. Unfortunately the text as it survives today is incomplete: part of the annals for 1339 and 1356, and all the annals from 1340 to 1355 are missing. Their content is only known from an abstract made by John Leland before the loss of the leaves.[210]

---

[207] *Foedera*, ii. pt ii, 1048.
[208] *Scala*. p. 2.
[209] See p. 12 and n. 60 above.
[210] Leland's abstract of the complete chronicle is printed in *Scala*. pp. 259–315. An English translation of his abstract of the annals from 1340 to 1355 is in Maxwell, op. cit. (see p. 60 n. 11 above), pp. 112–20.

Sir Thomas Gray was a well educated man and capable of thinking in abstract terms. Thus he discusses in the *Scalacronica* the relative merits of war and peace. A good peace, based on virtue and a desire to please God, cannot but be beneficial. But a peace founded on indolence and love of comfort is bad. A king should fight for his just claims and not be deflected from his purpose by lack of money, lack of perseverance, or because of growing old. War fought boldly brings honour, profit and cheerfulness, and soldiers should be liberally rewarded.[211] This passage illustrates Gray's preoccupation with chivalric values. As a writer he reflects the chivalric society to which he belonged, and was influenced by romance literature. He relates tales of knights errant and courtly love. For example he tells how, in 1318, Sir William Marmion, ordered by his lady-love to go to the most dangerous place in Britain to win fame for his helmet, arrived at Norham castle. A group of marcher knights came from Berwick to combat him. Marmion, 'glittering with gold and silver, marvellously attired in finery, with the helmet on his head', charged his opponents but was unhorsed and hurt. Sir Thomas Gray, senior, then warden of the castle, came to his aid, remounting him on his own horse. He scattered the enemy, captured fifty horses, and killed 'a Fleming called Cryn, a piratical sea captain'.[212] Gray ends his chronicle on a chivalric note. He records the marriage of David Bruce to Margaret de Logie, 'a lady who had been married already, and who had lived with him for some time. This marriage was made solely on account of love, which conquers all things.'

Sir Thomas Gray's chivalric outlook determined the form of the *Scalacronica*. The chronicle has a poem in the prologue which not only spells out his name ('Thomas Grai'), indicating each letter by numerical reference to its place in the alphabet, but also describes the Gray blazon of arms.[213] And the title, *Scalacronica*, is an allusion to the family motif, a scaling ladder. Sir Thomas relates in the prologue that he dreamed that the Sibyl and a

---

[211] *Scala.* p. 198.

[212] *Scala.* pp. 145–6.

[213] The arms of Sir Thomas Gray are hard to reconstruct exactly from the verses (*Scala.* p. 1);

> Autre cote auoit afoebler,
> Lestat de soun ordre agarder,
> Qe de fieu resemble la colour;
> Et desus, en purturature,
> Estoit li hardy best quartyner
> Du signe teynt de la mere;
> Enviroun palice un mure,
> De meisme peynt la colour.

The arms here described do not seem to correspond to those given for Sir Thomas, sn., in Moor, op. cit., ii. 155, and certainly not to those reproduced in Maxwell, op. cit., as the frontispiece. For the crest of the Gray family see *Boutell's Manual of Heraldry*, revised and illustrated by V. Wheeler-Holohan (London 1931), p. 297, and J. Burke and J. B. Burke, *Encyclopaedia of Heraldry* (London 1847), under 'Gray' and 'Grey'.

Franciscan friar gave him a ladder to scale a city wall (from the top of which he observed various allegorical phenomena) and instructed him to call his work *Scalacronica*. To some extent the chronicle is a family memoir. Gray undoubtedly wrote partly to record his father's and his own chivalric exploits, set in their historical context.

Sir Thomas Gray, like most chivalric writers, loved a good yarn. These stories usually show, for the amazement and amusement of posterity, how a knight overcame adversity by courage and endurance, by a clever ruse—or by a stroke of sheer good luck. Gray recounts a number of tales about his father, which give a graphic picture of the life of a marcher lord during the Scottish war. He records how in 1297 William Wallace attacked and slew the sheriff of Clydesdale at Lanark. Sir Thomas Gray, senior, was in his service and was left stripped as if dead in the mêlée. He lay all night naked and would have died of exposure if it had not been for the heat of two burning houses on either side. At daybreak he was found and revived by William de Lundy.[214] The chronicler's father had another near escape at the siege of Stirling castle in 1304. When dragging his lord, Sir Henry de Beaumont, clear of a hook thrown by an enemy machine, he was struck on the head with a bolt from a springald and fell unconscious just beneath the walls. Sir Thomas's body was rescued and 'a party was paraded to bury him', but he suddenly moved and opened his eyes.[215]

The chronicler tells a number of stories of his father's heroism. For example, when, after attending Edward II's coronation, Sir Thomas, senior, returned to the castle of Cupar in Fife, of which he was then warden, he was ambushed by Robert Bruce. Sir Thomas, who had a company of not more than twenty six soldiers, was forewarned but instead of avoiding the ambush, charged with such determination that the enemy fled, abandoning their horses: being unable to catch any of the horses, Sir Thomas drove them to the castle.[216] On another occasion Sir Thomas, spurring on his charger, managed to re-enter the castle through the midst of about 100 of Bruce's men.[217] The *Scalacronica* asserts that Sir Thomas held Norham castle against the Scots for eleven years, surviving two sieges, while the rest of Northumberland succumbed partly because of treachery.[218] 'It would take too long to relate all the combats and feats of arms and hardships caused by lack of provender, and the sieges which befell him.'[219]

---

[214] *Scala.* pp. 123–4.
[215] *Scala.* p. 127.
[216] *Scala.* pp. 138–9.
[217] *Scala.* p. 139.
[218] *Scala.* pp. 145, 147.
[219] *Scala.* p. 145. Sir Thomas Gray, sr, who was captured by the Scots at Bannockburn, apparently passed on to his son one piece of information learnt in the Scottish camp which is only known from the *Scalacronica*: the latter records that a Scottish knight in English service, Sir Alexander Seton, came to Robert Bruce on the night before the battle and

Despite the loss of the full text of the *Scalacronica* for the years from 1339 to 1356, it is an important source for Edward III's continental wars. Gray, writing in the chivalric style, interspersed his historical narrative with numerous feats and exploits. His chronicle becomes particularly valuable after the notice of the battle of Poitiers. From then onwards he could derive information from eyewitnesses and, for 1359–60, from his own observation, because he himself took part in Edward III's last expedition to France. He shows a close interest in the situation in France which was nearing anarchy. He describes the revolt of the Jacquerie in Paris, how the commonalty chose a leader for themselves, calling him the 'provost of the merchants', and captured the dauphin, clapping 'a cap of his colours' on his head.[220] Gray describes the bands of young Englishmen which roamed the French countryside fighting and looting. These young men had started their careers as archers and become knights or even captains. Some of them subsequently joined the Great Company, a band composed of men of various nationalities.[221] But Gray is particularly valuable for Edward III's campaign itself. He was in the Black Prince's division and is the principal authority for the itinerary from Calais to Reims in the winter of 1359.[222] Later, in January 1360, he describes the Black Prince's plight when, having left his father's route for lack of forage for his horses, he encamped at Egleny near Auxerre. Gray writes that 'several of his knights and esquires were killed at night in their quarters and his foraging parties were taken in the fields.' However, the situation was relieved by at least one feat. Five almost unarmed English esquires, who were attacked while foraging in a corn mill by fifty French men-at-arms, so successfully defended themselves that they took eleven prisoners: 'wherefore even the French of the other garrisons called this in jest the exploit of the fifty against the five.'[223] Gray also describes the hardships endured by the king's army. Edward withdrew from Paris in April 1360 because of the need to find fodder for his horses, and marched towards the Beauce. Gray writes:[224]

> The weather was very bad, with rain, hail and snow, and so cold that many weakly men and horses perished in the field. They abandoned many vehicles and much of the baggage because of the cold, the wind and the wet, which was worse at this season than memory could recall.

---

advised him to attack because the English had lost heart; *Scala.* pp. 141–2 (cf. Barrow, *Robert Bruce*, p. 319).
[220] *Scala.* pp. 178–9.
[221] *Scala.* pp. 178, 180, 188, 200, 201.
[222] *Scala.* pp. 187 et seq. See Fowler, *The king's Lieutenant, Henry of Grosmont* (p. 69 n. 62 above), p. 202.
[223] *Scala.* p. 189. See Fowler, op. cit., p. 204.
[224] *Scala.* pp. 193–4. See Fowler, op. cit., p. 206.

The other layman who wrote a well known chivalric work relating to the reign of Edward III was the herald of Sir John Chandos. His *Life of the Black Prince* is a biography of Edward, prince of Wales (d. 1376), treated in its historical context, in French verse. Although the herald composed the work at least ten years after the Black Prince's death he based his account on personal observation, the information of eyewitnesses, contemporary documents, and possibly on some literary source.[225] Heralds were in a favourable position to accumulate historical information (Froissart questioned numerous heralds to obtain news) : they were in their masters' confidence and kept their records; they acted as messengers,[226] and were in close contact with other lords.

The identity of Chandos Herald is obscure. He may, like Froissart, have been born in Valenciennes.[227] He probably entered the service of Sir John Chandos in 1360.[228] Froissart mentions the herald of Sir John Chandos in his account of the negotiations between Sir John and the count of Foix for the passage of the Great Company in 1366, and again in 1369 when Froissart records that the herald took a message from Sir John and Sir Robert Knolles to the Black Prince.[229] Froissart used the *Life of the Black Prince* for the second redaction of his chronicle. His account of the Black Prince's campaign in the second redaction follows that of Chandos Herald closely. The account of the campaign in the first redaction apparently used information in common with Chandos Herald's work: this suggests the possibility that Froissart may have recorded a verbal description of the campaign given by the herald.[230]

The *Life of the Black Prince* belongs to the same literary genre as the *History of William the Marshal*,[231] but it lacks the literary quality and the realistic, personal touches of the earlier work.[232] (Its inferiority in these respects can be seen by comparing the account of the death of William the Marshal with that of the Black Prince.)[233] Unlike the author of the *History of William the Marshal* Chandos Herald probably did not know his hero personally, certainly not intimately. His work also resembles Barbour's

---

[225] For the sources of the *Life* see *CH* (P and L), pp. lv-lx passim.

[226] Chandos Herald records that a herald who delivered a letter from the Black Prince to Henry the Bastard 'was glad and merry at heart and made great rejoicings, for they bestowed on him fine jewels, ermine robes and furred mantles'; *CH*, 11. 2953–7. For another notice of a herald acting as messenger see *CH*, 11. 2437–40. For heralds as informants and authors in general see *CH*, pp. 33–4.

[227] Miss Tyson concurs with the suggestion made by Miss Pope and Miss Lodge that Chandos Herald's birthplace was Valenciennes or its neighbourhood. See *CH*, p. 14, and *CH* (P and L), pp. xxxii, xlvii-xlviii, and the linguistic introduction in ibid.

[228] For the career of Chandos Herald see *CH*, pp. 14–18, and *CH* (P and L), p. liv.

[229] *JF* (SL), vi. 216; vii. 146.

[230] *CH* (P and L), p. lix; cf. *JF* (SL), vii. iii n. 1.

[231] See Gransden, *Historical Writing*, i. 345–55.

[232] For the literary quality of the *Vie du Prince Noir* see *CH*, pp. 34–43.

[233] *CH*, 11. 4093–4178. For William the Marshal's death see Gransden, op. cit., i. 354.

Bruce. Both the herald and John Barbour wrote under the influence of romance literature and of the contemporary chivalric social code. And both authors have a secondary hero—in the herald's case his master, Sir John Chandos.

Chandos Herald eulogizes the Black Prince,[234] and, to a lesser extent, Sir John Chandos. He begins with fulsome praise of the prince in chivalric terms. The prince was the perfect model of all honour, nobleness, wisdom, valour and bounty. He upheld chivalry—none was more valiant than he. He loved the church (being particularly devoted to the Holy Trinity).[235] He was adored by his wife who, because of her fortunate union, holds sway over the whole world.[236] And he was comparable to the great heroes of romance, Alexander, Julius Caesar, Arthur, Oliver and Roland.[237] Whenever the prince fought, he took a prominent part in the battle. At Crécy he led the vanguard: he bore himself so valiantly that it was a marvel to behold—and by his courage the field was gained.[238] The herald apparently exaggerated the prince's part in the relief of Edward III at Calais in 1349–50.[239] He may even have purposely suppressed a fact concerning the battle of Nájera in order to exaggerate the glory of the prince's victory: he does not mention that Henry the Bastard left a favourable position where he was encamped with his army, and marched to the open plain facing Navarrete in order to have no unfair advantage.[240]

The herald's account of the battle of Nájera eulogizes Sir John Chandos as well as the Black Prince. It describes how Chandos obtained the prince's permission to raise his own banner for the first time; he fought under it with his companions, and acquired great renown.[241] The herald relates a valiant feat performed by Sir John. During the battle Sir John was thrown from his horse and a Castilian 'of great stature' fell upon him trying to wound him through his vizor. But Sir John stabbed him with a dagger, leapt to his feet and plunged into the fray with his sword, 'fierce and terrible and marvellous to behold'.[242] When the herald records his master's death in 1370, he asserts that the French rejoiced at the passing of so redoubtable an enemy.[243]

Notwithstanding the chivalric style and eulogistic tone of the *Life of the Black Prince*, it has value to the present day historian. As Sir John

---

[234] For Chandos Herald's bias in favour of the Black Prince see *CH*, pp. 35–6, 38.
[235] *CH*, 11. 1–106 passim; cf. *CH*, 11. 660–4, 1611–38, 4176–8.
[236] *CH*, 11. 3587–95.
[237] *CH*, 11. 51–2, 2796, 3383, 4099, 4100.
[238] *CH*, 11. 326–7, 355–7.
[239] *CH* (P and L), 11. 429–33 and p. 187 n. Avesbury stresses the king's prowess on this occasion; see pp. 68–9 and n. 61 above.
[240] *CH*, (P and L), 11. 3060–2 and p. 212 n.
[241] *CH*, (P and L), 11. 3121–51 and p. 213 n.
[242] *CH*, 11. 3275–94 (cf. 3255–6).
[243] *CH*, 11. 3967–72.

Chandos' herald, the author had knowledge of and was present at a number of important events. Although he did not write strictly contemporaneously with what he recorded and gives few dates, he has much information not found in the other literary authorities. For example, he gives a full account of the negotiations which preceded the battle of Poitiers: as he himself mentions, Sir John was one of the deputation to the French camp.[244] However, the herald cannot give first hand information on the Black Prince's French campaigns—his principal value is for the Spanish campaign of 1366–7.[245] According to the herald, Sir John Chandos and Sir Thomas Felton, both of the Black Prince's 'most privy council', advised the prince to accede to Peter of Castile's request for assistance.[246] And he records that Sir John went to the Great Company to obtain help for the prince (it was in these negotiations that, as Froissart records, the herald himself took an active part).[247] Moreover, after the battle of Nájera Sir John negotiated with the king of Aragon to allow the English army to return to France through his territory.[248]

Chandos Herald has the best literary account extant written from the English side of the battle of Nájera. He has a number of realistic details, and graphically describes the Castilian defeat. He mentions that the Black Prince camped before the battle near Logroño in an orchard, under the olive trees, while Henry camped in a vineyard by the river.[249] After the English victory the grand master of the order of Calatrava was captured in a cellar; the master of the order of Santiago and the prior of the order of St John were taken hiding behind a wall.[250] Describing the flight of the Castilians the herald writes:[251]

> The battlefield was on a fair and beautiful plain, whereon was neither bush nor tree for a full league round, by the side of a fine river, very rapid and fierce, which caused the Castilians much damage that day, for the pursuit continued right up to the river—more than 2,000 were drowned there. On the bridge in front of Nájera, I can assure you, the pursuit was hot and deadly. There you might see knights leap into the water for fear, and die one on top of the other; and it was said that the river was red with the blood that flowed from the bodies of dead men and horses.

Chandos Herald does not end with this English victory but with the

[244] *CH* (P and L), 1. 881 and p. 193 nn.
[245] See *CH* (P and L), pp. lvii-lx, 198–9 n.
[246] *CH*, 11. 1910–20.
[247] See p. 97 and n. 229 above.
[248] *CH*, 11. 3722 et seq.
[249] *CH*, 11. 2897–905.
[250] *CH*, 11. 3455–67.
[251] *CH*, 11. 3425–45.

death of the Black Prince, on a note of sadness and disillusion. The prince fell sick on returning to Aquitaine, with the result that his administration began to fail and 'his friends became his enemies.'[252] The English campaign seemed doomed to disaster and, with the deaths of Sir John Chandos and Sir James Audley, he lost two of his best friends and supporters.[253] To Chandos Herald as to other writers, it must have seemed that the golden age of chivalry was past.

[252] *CH*, 11. 3825–6.
[253] *CH*, 11. 3941–62.

4

Chroniclers of the Reign of Edward III: the 'Religious'

While a growing number of secular clerks and laymen wrote histories during the reign of Edward III, the number of chroniclers who were members of religious orders diminished, and, although in general the quality of secular and lay historiography improved, that of the monastic chronicle deteriorated. The practice of keeping a chronicle as part of the archives of a religious house had more or less lapsed before the end of the reign: it seems likely that this reflects a general decline in monastic morale and *esprit de corps*. Only the chronicles written at Christ Church, Canterbury,[1] and at Westminster (by John of Reading),[2] both covering the period from 1346 to 1367, sustained the old tradition of contemporary annals at all competently. The *Eulogium Historiarum (A Eulogy of Histories)*[3] written in Malmesbury abbey, which starts with Brutus and ends in 1366, is disappointingly brief on contemporary history. Although the Anonimalle chronicle[4] of St Mary's, York, continues to 1381 and is detailed for its last five years, it is a compilation and not a true monastic chronicle. Indeed there is no incontrovertible evidence that it was composed at St Mary's at all, and the possibility cannot be discounted that from 1346 it relied at least in part on some secular chronicle.

Earlier in the reign there is evidence of two good chronicles composed by the religious. One was the chronicle of Bridlington to 1339, and the other a Franciscan chronicle to 1346. The originals of both these chronicles are lost, but the Bridlington annals were copied (with alterations) and sporadically continued at Bridlington until late in Edward III's reign,[5] and the Franciscan chronicle was used both by a canon of Lanercost for

---

[1] Printed in *Chronica Johannis de Reading et Anonymi Cantuariensis 1346–1367*, ed. James Tait (Manchester 1914), pp. 187–227. For a monastic chronicle written in Edward III's reign, that of Wigmore abbey, which is not discussed here, see p. 61 n. 14 above.

[2] Printed in Tait, op. cit., pp. 99–186.

[3] Printed *Eulogium Historiarum sive Temporis: Chronicon ab Orbe condito usque ad Annum Domini M.CCC. LXVI. a Monacho quodam Malmesburiensi exaratum*, ed. F. S. Haydon (RS 1858–63, 3 vols). For a continuation of the *Eulogium* from 1366 to 1413 see pp. 158 and n. 5, et seq. below.

[4] Printed *The Anonimalle Chronicle 1333–1381*, ed. V. H. Galbraith (Manchester 1927).

[5] For the Bridlington chronicle as an authority for Edward II's reign see pp. 9–12 above. For the printed edition see p. 2 n. 7 above.

the chronicle of his house,[6] and by the author of the Anonimalle chronicle for the annals from 1334 to 1346:[7] the reliance of these two authors on the Franciscan chronicle illustrates the weakness of the monastic historiographical tradition (the Lanercost writer made no attempt to continue his exemplar).

Nevertheless, the tradition of the monastic chronicle did just survive. It owed its tenuous existence to a number of factors. It seems possible that at least in the south the homiletic tradition encouraged the writing of chronicles. Monks themselves sometimes preached, for example at the solemn inaugurations of chapters and visitations, and on occasion a monk was chosen to preach at the inauguration of an ecclesiastical synod. It is possible that they learnt how to preach in the monastic schools, and they certainly studied the art at university: since an increasing number of monks attended university in the fourteenth century (they did not necessarily take a degree), this may partly explain the growing interest of monks in homiletics. As mentioned above, Ranulf Higden wrote a tract on the art of preaching.[8] It is not, therefore, surprising that some chroniclers were influenced by the homiletic tradition. The author of the *Eulogium* and John of Reading wrote their most passionate prose in tirades against contemporary fashions in dress.

However, the most important factor keeping the monastic chronicle alive at least in the first half of the fourteenth century was undoubtedly the enthusiasm for Edward III's wars; the monastic chroniclers shared (though in a rather limited degree) the patriotic fervour of the non-monastic ones—and their love of fine spectacles. Early in the reign the Scottish war provided an incentive for writing history, and then the war with France attracted most attention. John of Reading, the Canterbury chronicle and the Anonimalle chronicle all have valuable information about the French campaigns. But as Edward's reign proceeded, the Hundred Years' War declined in popularity and, therefore, ceased to provide chroniclers with a patriotic motive for recording its progress. Patriotism engendered by the war is especially characteristic of the north country chronicles: the canon of Lanercost may well have copied the Franciscan one merely as an introduction to the glorious victory of Neville's Cross which he describes in grandiloquent terms.

To a certain extent the tradition of monastic historiography was self

---

[6] For the Lanercost chronicle as an authority for Edward II's reign see pp. 12–17 above. For the printed edition and translation see p. 2 and n. 8 above.

[7] See p. 111 and n. 60 below.

[8] P. 43 above. For the monks as preachers see David Knowles, *The Religious Orders in England*, ii (Cambridge 1955), p. 244, *Documents illustrating the Activities of the General and Provincial Chapters of the English Black Monks, 1215–1540* (Camden Soc., third series, xlv, 1931, xlvii, 1933, liv, 1937, 3 vols), ii. 11–12; iii. 28–9, and Margaret Jennings, 'Monks and the "Artes praedicandi" in the time of Ranulf Higden' in *Revue Bénédictine*, lxxxvi (1976), pp. 119–28.

perpetuating. Established traditions in individual houses encouraged the keeping of chronicles. The author of the *Eulogium*, writing at Malmesbury, was well aware of his famous predecessor, William of Malmesbury, and the Canterbury chronicler must have known the earlier chronicles written at Christ Church. Both John of Reading (at Westminster) and the Bridlington annalist continued pre-existing chronicles kept in their houses. The Franciscan chronicle on which the Lanercost chronicle (which extends to 1346) is based, had been started in the late thirteenth century, and it is possible that a chronicle written in Guisborough priory, which had a strong historiographical tradition, underlies the Anonimalle chronicle of St Mary's abbey in York.[9] Another factor which contributed to the survival of the monastic chronicle was the influence of Higden's *Polychronicon* and of the *Brut*. The *Polychronicon* helped determine the structure of the *Eulogium*, while the *Brut* formed the starting point of both the *Eulogium* and the Anonimalle chronicle.[10]

The chronicles will be discussed in the following order: the *Eulogium*; John of Reading's chronicle; the Canterbury annals; the Anonimalle chronicle; the chronicle of Bridlington; and finally the so-called Lanercost chronicle.

The author of the *Eulogium* asserts that he wrote to dissipate the boredom of his life:[11]

> I often sit bored in the cloister, my senses dull and faculties idle, plagued with wicked thoughts, because of the length of the lessons and the monotony of the prayers, and because of the vain boastings and evil ways of the world (their pleasure and general acceptance, and what is worse their numerousness). Therefore I wondered how I could extinguish such burning darts which try to inflict a multitude of wounds on the meditations of a monk. And I decided, at the request of my superiors, to prepare a work from various authors for the information of posterity.

The *Eulogium* is divided into five books: Book I contains a world history from the Creation to the Ascension of Christ; Book II has the journeys of the apostles and a papal history up to Innocent V; Book III comprises an account of the empires of the world, including a history of the emperors of western Europe up to Frederick II of Germany; Book IV is a geographical description of the world; and Book V is a history of England, starting with the *Brut* and continuing to 1366. Until the author's own time, the

---

[9] See p. 111 and n. 62 below.
[10] For the influence and continuations of the *Polychronicon* and *Brut* see pp. 55–7, 71, 73–4 above, respectively.
[11] *EH*, i. 2.

Eulogium is almost entirely a compilation from standard works. The first four books are mainly extracted from the *Polychronicon*. Nevertheless, the author abuses Higden. (The modern editor of the *Polychronicon* accuses the author of adding 'calumny to larceny.')[12] One reason why he wrote was undoubtedly a sense of competition with 'this new compiler, the besotted monk of Chester'. He bitterly criticizes him for daring to contradict such famous authorities as Jerome, Isidore and Bede—on the reason for Ireland's lack of snakes and goats, and William of Malmesbury—on the characteristics of Chester.[13]

From about 1354 the continuation of the *Brut* in Book V of the *Eulogium* was written more or less contemporarily with the events it records.[14] However, this part of the *Eulogium* is meagre as a political history. Although the author shows some concern for Edward III's wars (he includes a detailed account of the Black Prince's itinerary from Bergerac to Poitiers in 1356 copied from some now lost source[15]), his interest, like Higden's, in contemporary politics was limited. His most immediate response to his own times was elicited by moral indignation at certain aspects of social life. He was particularly outraged at the fashionable clothes worn by some of his fellow countrymen. One of his few additions to the *Polychronicon* is to Higden's unflattering sketch of the national character: he claims that the fickleness of the English is well illustrated by the annual change in dress fashions.[16] And one of his most eloquent passages is a tirade, in full homiletic style, against such fashions.

The tirade against fashionable dress occurs in the annal for 1362,[17] and includes exact descriptions of laymen's clothes. This shows that his zeal for the moral reformation of society made the author take a close look at the world around him. It also suggests that his visual sense was more developed than Higden's. The passage is of interest both for sartorial history and also for the history of the English language since the vernacular names of garments are included. The chronicler especially attacks the effeminacy of men's clothes: he describes the 'gowns' which were not open in front as was suitable for men, and which from behind made men look like women; these 'gowns' had hoods which buttoned under the chin in feminine fashion, were decorated on top with jewels and gold and silver thread, and had

[12] *Poly.* i. xlii.

[13] *EH*, ii.130–1. His prologue, in which he declares himself incapable of aspiring to the high objectives of history (which are stated in the prologue to the *Polychronicon*) is in effect another sneer at Higden; *EH*, i. 1.

[14] For the date of composition see *EH*, ii. viii–xxii; for the author's autograph manuscript (Trinity College, Cambridge, MS. R.7.2.), see ibid, i.v et seq.

[15] *EH*, iii. 215–22. For the value of this passage see H.J. Hewitt, *The Black Prince's Expedition of 1355–1357* (Manchester 1958), p. 185 nn. 2, 3.

[16] *EH*, ii.170–1.

[17] *EH*, iii.230–1. For similar tirades against contemporary fashions in the Westminster chronicle see p. 105 and n. 23 below.

long pointed ends reaching to the ankles 'in the style of a buffoon'. The author describes the hose called 'harlots' attached by latchets to the short coat or sleeved doublet known as a 'paltok' ('and so one harlot serves another'), and the beaked shoes called 'crakows' ('talons for devils rather than ornaments for men'). The author appeals rather speciously to the bible to support his view that the 'paltok' was more suitable for a priest than a layman: King Solomon had never worn one.[18] Reflecting on the frivolous, worldly characters which such fashions betrayed, the author prays for God's mercy and forgiveness, lest divine punishment result.

John of Reading, a monk of Westminster who successively held the offices of *custos ordinis* and infirmarer and probably died in 1368 or 1369, only started his chronicle within three years of his death.[19] He continued the *Flores Historiarum* from 1346 to 1367. (An anonymous Westminster monk had continued Robert of Reading's continuation of the *Flores* from 1326 to 1345, relying mainly on the chronicles of Adam Murimuth and Robert of Avesbury.)[20] In the preface John apologizes for his 'lack of education and skill', an apology which is appropriate because his chronicle has no literary merit and the Latin is sometimes ungrammatical. Nevertheless, John's very lack of literary pretension contributes to the value of his work to the present-day scholar, for as a result of it, he explains, he had to rely 'more on common talk than on his own study or the works of great men, and nowhere cited ancient writings.' Hence John did not study the distant past but turned instead to 'the prolixity of recent events', and apart from a slight debt to Higden and Avesbury, did not, as far as is known, extract from the works of other chroniclers.[21] Instead he relied for information on documents and conversation, and at least from the mid-fourteenth century on his own memory. Other chroniclers were indebted to his work: it was an important source of the *Polychronicon* and *Brut* continuations, and was used at St Albans by Thomas Walsingham.[22]

John of Reading has the censorious doom ridden pessimism character-istic of some preachers, and aims his invective against most sections of society. He has a tirade against the fashionable clothes of his day which rivals in fervour that in the *Eulogium*: it is in the annal for 1365 and adds the information that 'harlots' were also called 'gadelinges' and 'lorels', and that men wore long knives hanging between their legs, and caps shaped like hose or a sleeve.[23] John dwells on the moral depravity of his contempo-

---

[18] The earliest examples cited in the *NED* of the words 'crakow' and 'paltock', and, as applied to hose with long, pointed toes tied to an upper garment, 'harlot', are from the *Eulogium*; see *NED*, ii. pt ii. 1131; vii. pt i. 408; v. pt i. 94, respectively. For 'crakows' cf. p. 165 and n. 37 below.

[19] For John of Reading's career see *JR*, pp. 10–12.

[20] For a description of and extracts from the Westminster *Flores* from 1325 to 1345 see *JR*, pp. 5–7, 18, 77–90.

[21] For John of Reading's sources see *JR*, pp. 24–33.

[22] For the debt of later chroniclers to John of Reading see *JR*, pp. 42–62.

[23] *JR*, p. 167.

raries. He regarded the disease 'called in English pokkes' which visited this country in 1365 as divine vengeance for the extravagant fashions and for the depravity of manners and morals,[24] and the great plague itself was a punishment for the greed, arrogance and malice of Englishmen.[25] John asserts that the statute of labourers in 1351 was intended to curb these same vices of arrogance and malice among the workers, who now 'work less and their work is worse done' than formerly.[26] He lamented that the plague of 1360–1 did not make men sad but resulted in an outburst of immorality; widows gave birth to 'false heirs' by strangers and relatives, and fornication, incest and adultery were regarded as fun not sin.[27] The avarice of merchants was the cause of the extortionate price of wax in 1362 (1s.6d.per 1b.), and it was for the convenience of the merchants and not for the benefit of the realm that the staple was established in Calais.[28]

John did not confine his invective to laymen; he used the same moralistic tone to write of the religious and the secular clergy. He particularly hated the friars. (Westminster had a particular cause of complaint, because Queen Isabella had been 'seduced' by the Franciscans to bequeath her body to them, although she had previously intended to be buried in the abbey.)[29] The monks indeed might be tainted by mammon, but the friars were mortally corrupted—if they did not burn now as heretics, they would assuredly burn later in hell.[30]

Moreover, John criticized the secular clergy. Archbishop Islip deserved opprobrium (like Pharaoh), because he removed the feasts of some saints from the liturgical calendar.[31] More especially John was critical of certain aspects of papal administration. He considered that the two cardinals who came to England in 1357 to mediate peace with France achieved nothing beyond conferring churches and prebends 'for their own benefit'.[32] And he deplored the practice of papal provisions by which episcopal elections were overridden. Commenting on William of Wickham's appointment to Winchester he writes that the papacy was moved more by fear than affection:[33]

[24] *JR*, p. 167. This 'pock' disease was smallpox according to J.F.D. Shrewsbury, *A History of Bubonic Plague in the British Isles* (Cambridge 1970), p. 133.

[25] *JR*, pp. 110–11.

[26] *JR*, p. 113.

[27] *JR*, p. 150. For the 1360–1 plague and its impact on contemporaries see Shrewsbury, op. cit., pp. 127–8.

[28] *JR*, pp. 152, 153; cf. *JR*, p. 297n.

[29] *JR*, pp. 128–9.

[30] *JR*, pp. 109–10, 119.

[31] *JR*, p. 154.

[32] *JR*, p. 127. The Anonimalle chronicle criticizes in similar terms Cardinal Simon Langham's attempts to mediate peace in 1371; *An.* p. 70.

[33] *JR*, p. 178.

Alas! the mammon of iniquity raises the unworthy to be prelates. The Saviour of old founded the church on solid rock, but now its columns, that is many of its prelates, are appointed not because of virtuous life or learning, but by gold and silver.

Despite the homiletic tone of John of Reading's chronicle it has value because it reflects current attitudes and has some information not found elsewhere. John was interested in the government's legislation—though he thought it achieved little. He was opposed to the statute of provisors because though he disliked papal provisions he hated royal influence even more. (The pope might provide a suitable candidate to a bishopric, but the king was only interested in promoting his own officials.)[34] John is the only authority for the decision in 1365 that Peter's Pence should not be paid.[35] He discusses the legislation of 1351, which attempted, for example, to fix wages; all was ineffectual 'because of the money and favour of lords'.[36] He describes fairly accurately the statute of purveyance of 1362, and (rather inaccurately) the ordinances of 1363 fixing prices: his account of the government's attempt at enforcing the latter against local opposition is not found elsewhere.[37] John had some knowledge of the royal court. He was able to record, for example, a remark made by King John of France on the occasion of 'an over-sumptuous feast' given in his honour by Edward III in 1358: King John said, laughing, that he had never seen or heard of such a magnificent affair paid for by tallies, without gold or silver.[38]

Predictably, John of Reading is well informed about affairs in London. He records some anecdotes; for example concerning certain 'unknown devils' who beheaded and dismembered a priest at a tournament in 1363.[39] He also records some information crucial for the history of the city. Under 1366 he gives a unique account of how the king deposed the mayor, Adam de Bury. Edward ordered the election of someone 'more faithful' but the commons strongly objected, eventually agreeing to the election of a successor by a representative body of citizens. Bury fled abroad but was later restored, after he had regained royal favour by bribing courtiers.[40]

John of Reading's knowledge was not confined to London. Despite his captiousness he was patriotic and took a close interest in Edward III's wars. English victories redounded to England's glory ('Blessed be the

---

[34] *JR*, pp. 163, 322–4n.
[35] *JR*, p. 163.
[36] *JR*, p. 117.
[37] *JR*, pp. 155, 157–8, 303n, 311n. Cf. *JR*, pp. 160, 315–6n.
[38] *JR*, p. 130.
[39] *JR*, pp. 156–7.
[40] *JR*, pp. 169–70, 331–2n.

Lord' he exclaims after the battle of Poitiers).[41] He has a eulogy on the Black Prince who followed wise counsel, never preferred secular affairs to the divine office and his honour, and who liberally endowed the church and kept his marriage vows.[42] John has a full account of the preliminaries to the Black Prince's Spanish campaign and follows his account of the battle of Nájera with verses celebrating the victory and praising the prince.[43] John's interest in these wars was no doubt increased by royal connections with Westminster abbey. In 1346, John records, Edward III granted the monks a charter of privilege in return for their twice weekly prayers for the success of his French campaign.[44] In 1359 the king visited Westminster among other shrines to pray for his cause, and John records his speech on the occasion, asking to be buried in the abbey along with Edward the Confessor, Henry III and Edward I (that 'most illustrious and courageous soldier, and most prudent statesman').[45] Similarly the Black Prince visited Westminster in 1355 to pray for his expedition to France.[46]

John had some interest in European affairs even if they were only indirectly connected with England. This is illustrated by one of his most vivid passages, the description of the progress of the emperor Charles IV through Avignon to the papal palace, where he was to negotiate concerning the suppression of the companies in France, preparatory to the pope's return to Rome. Here John, who gives details not found elsewhere, must have relied on some eyewitness account, perhaps a newsletter. He writes:[47]

> The emperor Charles came to Avignon with 500 knights. He enter-
> ed the first church on his route and had himself clothed in a red
> alb and cope. A sumptuous mitre was placed on his head, bearing
> two gold crowns decorated with gems and two labels hanging
> down the back and another two by the ears. And so he mounted
> a small palfrey. He was preceded by members of religious orders
> and a great number of other ecclesiastics, and knights—among
> them a knight who carried a live eagle, continually fluttering,
> perched on a spear before him. Another knight carried the
> imperial sceptre on a lance, and a third bore his shield with a lance
> on his left. In front of him a certain duke dressed as a monk, bore
> the [imperial] sword, drawn; and over him and over the two
> cardinals riding with him, eight marquises and counts who were

[41] *JR*, p. 126.
[42] *JR*, p. 173.
[43] *JR*, pp. 184–5.
[44] *JR*, p. 103.
[45] *JR*, p. 132–3.
[46] *JR*, p. 120.
[47] *JR*, pp. 165, 326n.

on foot bore a canopy worked or woven with gold. Two splendidly caparisoned war horses followed.

The Canterbury chronicle, though of a rather higher literary standard and of greater accuracy than John of Reading's work, resembles the latter in some respects. It also ends in 1367 and was written contemporarily with the events recorded for the last few years. And it too was interested in the Hundred Years' War. Like John of Reading, the Canterbury chronicler profited from his house's location in his search for information. Famous people came to St Thomas's shrine, and Christ Church was in close touch with London because of the archbishop's residence there, and with Dover through its cell, the priory of St Martin's—and by way of Dover the chronicler could obtain news from Calais.

The Canterbury chronicle is singularly well informed about Geoffrey de Charny's attempt to surprise Calais in 1350 (it is the only chronicle to give the exact day and other details),[48] and about the escape of Louis count of Anjou, John II's son, while on parole at Calais in 1363, on pretext of a hunting expedition.[49] It has unique information about the composition of the French army at Poitiers[50] and is an important source for the list of casualties at Auray.[51] It is also fairly full on the Black Prince's Spanish campaign and the only authority to assert categorically that Peter king of Castile made the prince his heir.[52]

The chronicle has a more detailed account of the first treaty of London (of 8 May 1358) than any other chronicle.[53] The author may have derived his information from someone either in the archbishop's household or in King John's. This is suggested by the fact, recorded by the chronicler, that the two cardinals, Elie Talleyrand de Périgord and Nicholas cardinal priest of St Vitalis, who had been sent to negotiate the peace with France, both passed through Canterbury on their way to London (Talleyrand lodged at St Augustine's). The chronicler describes their reception in London by the archbishop and Edward III.[54] Then two years later, in May 1360, King John himself stayed a day at Christ Church on his journey to Dover after three years' captivity. The chronicler records that he gave St Thomas a beautiful jewel worth 200 marks or more, and St Mary a 'nouche' (a necklace, bracelet or brooch) of gold set with precious stones.[55]

---

[48] *Cant.* pp. 194–5, 359n.
[49] *Cant.* pp. 214–15, 365–6n.
[50] *Cant.* pp. 196, 360–1n.
[51] *Cant.* pp. 219–20, 368–9n.
[52] *Cant.* pp. 223, 370n. The Canterbury chronicler used a newsletter, which was also used by the author of the Anonimalle chronicle, for his account of the Nájera campaign; *An.* pp. 171–2n. (Cf. *Cant.* p. 371n.)
[53] *Cant.* pp. 208, 362–3n.
[54] *Cant.* pp. 206–7.
[55] *Cant.* p. 208.

Similarly, the source of the chronicler's unique details concerning the negotiations between Louis II of Flanders and King Edward for the marriage of Louis' daughter Margaret with Edward's son Edmund of Langley, earl of Cambridge, in 1364, is fairly certain.[56] The writer must surely have obtained his information from someone connected either with the court or with the king, because the negotiations took place in Dover castle where Louis stayed. The chronicler records that Edward arrived while Louis was at supper and that they talked amicably all night. The negotiations, which were attended by the duke of Lancaster and Edmund of Langley, lasted from Monday to Wednesday (14–16 October). On Thursday the party came on pilgrimage to St Thomas's shrine. They left the next day after lunch, reaching Dover at night, whence Louis sailed on Sunday. The chronicler is the only authority to record that Lancaster, Langley and the bishop of London came to Canterbury on 27 October and on 28 October sailed for Flanders. (The marriage did not take place because the pope refused a dispensation.)

The author's love of precise itineraries appears in two passages which are perhaps the most remarkable in the Canterbury chronicle. One relates to King John's arrival in England in 1357 at the beginning of his captivity,[57] and the other to his visit in 1364 to negotiate ransoms for the French hostages.[58] The chronicler's graphic description of the reception of the Black Prince and King John by the Londoners must surely be based on an eyewitness account. They were met outside the city by the mayor, aldermen and citizens and numerous members of the guilds on horseback. They were conducted through the city (by way of St Paul's, Ludgate and Fleet street) to Westminster palace, the men of the guilds riding in order, amidst great rejoicing and free wine for all. The goldsmiths had erected a platform in the Cheap, adorned with silk streamers, on which they had stationed two beautiful girls who showered leaves of gold and silver down on the riders' heads.

When King John came to England in January 1364, he landed at Dover and travelled to London by way of Canterbury and Ospringe. He stayed at the Savoy where he fell ill. Therefore 'he was allowed to eat meat during Lent', and Edward III, much grieved, frequently visited him. On his death his body was embalmed and after lying in St Paul's it was carried to Dover. The Canterbury chronicler gives the exact itinerary with places and dates, and describes its reception at Canterbury.[59]

An account of King John's reception in London in 1357 which equals the Canterbury chronicle's in vivid detail is in the Anonimalle chronicle.

[56] *Cant.* pp. 220–1, 369n.
[57] *Cant.* pp. 204–6.
[58] *Cant.* pp. 215–16.
[59] *Cant.* pp. 216–17.

Here the author probably used a newsletter, or perhaps the testimony of an eyewitness; it is unlikely that he wrote at first hand because he almost certainly lived in the north of England. The provenance of the Anonimalle chronicle, which covers the period from Brutus to 1381 and is in Anglo-Norman French prose, presents problems.[60] The only surviving medieval manuscript of it belonged to St Mary's abbey in York. The chronicle has a few particular references to St Mary's: these, however, are not sufficient to prove that it was composed there, because they could be interpolations into a pre-existing chronicle which had been copied for St Mary's. The chronicle uses the French *Brut* to 1333, and thence to about 1346 it borrows from the same Franciscan chronicle which forms the basis of the chronicle of Lanercost. From 1346 the author may have extracted from some now lost Latin chronicle. The annals for the last five years are very full, and the chronicler clearly used London material, perhaps a chronicle or newsletters, or oral information: from it were derived the remarkable, probably eyewitness accounts of the Good Parliament (of 1376) and Peasants' Revolt.[61] In fact there is not enough evidence to be certain about the provenance of the Anonimalle chronicle. Possibly it was compiled at St Mary's, or perhaps, as a detailed entry under 1377 concerning porpoises stranded at Guisborough seems to suggest,[62] it was written in Guisborough priory. There is, however, no conclusive evidence that it was a north country composition at all, or even that it was by a monk or a regular canon—it could equally well have been by a secular clerk.

The Anonimalle chronicle from 1346 to 1376 is patriotic in tone and mainly concerned with Edward III's wars. Its lost Latin original was apparently written up fairly close to events, and its attitude to the army commanders usually appears to be impartial.[63] This gives it especial value because no other contemporary chronicle covers the last years of Edward III's campaigns and writers of the next generation were subject to strong bias. (For instance Thomas Walsingham is virulently prejudiced against John of Gaunt, while Henry Knighton unduly favours him.)

The Anonimalle chronicle has numerous details derived from newsletters[64] and presumably from oral testimony about King Edward's

---

[60] For the provenance and the composition of the Anonimalle chronicle see *An.* pp. xviii, xxiv-xxxvi, J.G. Edwards' review of Professor Galbraith's edition in *EHR*, xliii (1928), pp. 103–9, and A.F. Pollard, 'The authorship and value of the "Anonimalle" chronicle' in *EHR*, liii (1938), pp. 577–605.

[61] For these two narratives see *An.* pp. xli, xliii–xlv, 79–94, and pp. 166–7 below.

[62] *An.* p. 118. For the burial of Lord William Latimer in Guisborough priory see *An.* p. 133. J.G. Edwards argues the case for the Guisborough provenance of the Anonimalle chronicle, op. cit., passim. For the historiographical tradition of Guisborough priory in the late thirteenth and early fourteenth century, see Gransden, *Historical Writing*, i. 470–6.

[63] See *An.* pp. xl–xli, 174n., 177–8n.

[64] For the use of newsletters in the Anonimalle chronicle see *An.* pp. xxxiv–xxxv, 165n. For its

campaigns, which are not found in the other chronicles. For example it alone mentions Edward's pilgrimage with his companions to St Edmund of Pontigny on the 1359 expedition.[65] There are also unique details concerning the battle of Poitiers,[66] Edward III's itinerary in 1360 after the treaty of Brétigny[67] and Sir Robert Knolles' expedition in 1370.[68]

The tone of the chronicle is both chivalric and patriotic. The chivalric element appears in references to noble exploits and in amusing anecdotes. There is for instance the story of how King Edward arranged for a band of 500 men, dressed in green coats and mantles, to ambush the king of France like robbers, on his arrival in England in 1357, telling him that these were men of the forest who lived by hunting and were habitually thus clothed.[69] The author's chivalric outlook is also apparent in the graphic account of the French soldiers of Poitiers ('their heads without basinets but covered by chaplets of ostrich and falcons' feathers'),[70] and in the romantic account of the reception of John of Gaunt and his bride, Constance, 'the lovely daughter' of the king of Spain, in London: they were escorted through London by many lords and knights, and by the mayor and citizens 'splendidly dressed and nobly mounted'; in Cheapside they were met by a great crowd of 'lords, ladies and damsels come to see the beauty of this young lady'.[71]

The author's patriotism explains his disapproval of the treaty of Brétigny. He laments the consequent cession by the English of towns and castles, 'which they had won with so much effort'. This was, he comments, 'to the great loss and damage of the king of England and his heirs, for all time, because nearly the whole community of France was in his power, and the captains and their men could quickly have conquered the kingdom of France for the king of England if he had let them.'[72] The chronicler's hatred of the French is expressed when he accuses Charles V of treachery and inquity for disavowing the treaty.[73] Sometimes patriotism resulted in the distortion of truth. For example the chronicler exaggerates the ease with which the English captured Romorantin in 1356: he fails to distinguish the capture of the town on 31 August from the capture of the donjon on 3 September; he implies that both were captured at once, representing the

---

use of a newsletter in common with the Canterbury chronicle see p. 109 n. 52 above. For the use of newsletters by chroniclers see the index under 'newsletters' below.

[65] *An.* pp. 45, 167n.
[66] *An.* pp. 36–9, 165n.
[67] *An.* pp. 47, 168n.
[68] *An.* pp. 63–5, 175–6n.
[69] *An.* p. 41.
[70] *An.* p. 37.
[71] *An.* p. 69.
[72] *An.* p. 49.
[73] *An.* p. 59.

previous eight days, in fact occupied with fighting, as a period of truce generously conceded by the Black Prince.[74]

Nevertheless, the Anonimalle chronicle demonstrates the disillusion with the army command in the last decade of Edward III's reign. This is especially evident in the account of Sir Robert Knolles' Breton expedition in 1370 and in that of John of Gaunt's expedition in 1373. The writer describes how Knolles retreated to 'Conk' (probably Concarneau); he went to the castle with his men-at-arms, but told the rest of the soldiers to leave the town with their horses and equipment. When they had gone he locked the gates and 'deceitfully' had it proclaimed that those who wished to cross to England should go to the coast where they would find some large ships to carry them. But there were only two small ships which would not take more than 200 men, and the rest, finding themselves locked out of the castle and the town, were slaughtered or driven into the sea by the enemy.[75] Similarly, Gaunt's soldiers suffered in Aquitaine at the end of his campaign. Many soldiers and horses died of hunger because the duke forbade foraging without payment; nor would he allow his men to return to England. Eventually he disbanded the army in Bordeaux, leaving them without their horses, ill clothed, ill equipped and penniless, so that they could neither pay their passage home nor buy food: many died, and the others only survived because of the charity of the citizens and other good people of the neighbourhood.[76]

The other two north country chronicles, both produced by Augustinian houses, the Bridlington annals and the Lanercost chronicle, are principally of value to the historian today because of their first hand information about Edward III's Scottish war, though they also show interest in the French campaigns. Each, like the Anonimalle chronicle, owes its contemporary value for Edward's reign to an earlier work it incorporates and not to the author of the extant text. And both reflect strong patriotic and royalist feelings provoked especially by bitter antagonism to the Scots.

The Bridlington chronicle was, as pointed out above,[77] written in its present form towards the end of Edward III's reign, but its historical content derives from a lost chronicle begun late in Edward II's reign, and continued to 1339 contemporarily with the events it records. The author of the present text interpolated this factual chronicle with the

---

[74] *An.* pp. 35, 164n.

[75] *An.* pp. 65, 176n. Professor Galbraith attributes the Anonimalle chronicle's vindictive attitude to Sir Robert Knolles to the fact that he had secured a grant of the manor of Whitgift, an old possession of St Mary's; *An.* pp. xxxvii, 63, 72, 175, 178. However, as the St Mary's writer may merely have interpolated a pre-existing chronicle, the opinion about Knolles' campaign could be that of the author of the earlier chronicle.

[76] *An.* pp. 74–5. See also the plight of the besieged in Bécherel in 1371, and the account of the surrender by the English of St Sauveur-le-Vicomte in 1374; *An.* pp. 68, 77–8, 181n.

[77] P. 9 above.

prophecies of 'John of Bridlington'[78] and edifying reflections on the politics of his time. Thus, though the account of Edward II's reign in the original chronicle was pro-baronial, the later 'editor' interjected laments on the reversal by the barons of the natural order of government. Writing of the barons' proceedings against the Despensers in 1321, he exclaims:[79]

> What an amazing sight! See how the members cut themselves off from the head! The magnates dealt with the case in parliament without even seeking the king's assent; the members, acting as judges, wanted to destroy those who had been judged, and the head, the judge, who had not been called to hear the case, tried to protect the condemned by using the plenitude of royal power. . . . [The magnates], the founders of laws, became the corruptors of the very laws they had established.

The same writer added a prophecy which, he asserts, was made to Edward I by a certain magnate of Gascony. The latter said to the king:[80]

> A king of England will not only gain lands by conquest but even win the crown of France, because the day will come when the king of France is greedy, cruel, foolish, hateful and oppressive, while at the same time the king of England is generous, merciful and courageous, a brave conqueror of his enemies, courteous to and loved by everyone at home and abroad.

Surely, the writer remarks, this must have referred to the young King Edward III! He, like King Arthur, started to rule when still a boy, and venerated the blessed virgin Mary. The author ends the passage with verses on Edward III's love of St Mary and another prophecy.

Although the point of view of the later Bridlington writer is of interest, the value of the Bridlington chronicle both as a source for contemporary opinion and for facts derives from its dependence on the earlier work. The original Bridlington chronicle apparently expressed anti-French feelings similar to those of the later writer but in more restrained terms: it emphasized Edward's hereditary claim to the crown of France and accused King Philip of refusing a peaceful settlement.[81] However, the earlier writer was more deeply concerned than the later one with the Scottish war. He hated the Scots, whom he frequently accused of treachery ('to seek faith among the Scots is like trying to find a knot in a rush').[82] He was convinced of the justice of the English cause—Edward Balliol and

---

[78] See p. 59 and n. 4 above.
[79] *Bridl.* pp. 70, 73.
[80] *Bridl.* pp, 94–5.
[81] *Bridl.* pp. 133, 138, 140–7.
[82] *Bridl.* p. 110. Cf. *Bridl.* pp. 120, 127, 128.

his followers invaded Scotland in 1332 to claim their rightful inheritance.[83] The chronicler linked the French war with the Scottish one, pointing out that the French helped the Scots in 1338 with arms and supplies; Edward III, attacked by enemies on all sides, had to take arms 'in defence of holy church and of the lands subject to his rule'.[84] In the same year the chronicler recorded that the archbishop of York ordered masses to be said and processions to be held in all churches in his province for Edward's success in his wars: in this way the church encouraged patriotism.[85]

Patriotism sometimes caused the Bridlington chronicler to misrepresent facts. His astronomical figures for the Scots' losses at Dupplin Moor ('the dead were stacked in heaps fifteen feet high') is surely an exaggeration,[86] while his estimate that English casualties at Halidon Hill amounted to only one knight, an esquire and 'a few foot soldiers' must be an underestimate.[87] Nevertheless, despite its occasional inaccuracies, its brevity and the fact that it only survived in a later, 'edited' version, the Bridlington chronicle is a primary authority for the early years of Edward III's reign. Although it does not neglect affairs in southern England, it is most valuable for the Anglo-Scottish war, especially for Edward Balliol's invasion of Scotland in 1332.[88]

The 'Lanercost' chronicle is another important source for Anglo-Scottish relations in Edward III's reign, but it is more detailed and vividly written than the Bridlington one. The section for Edward III's reign continues that for Edward II's without a break, and, like the previous section, is based on a lost chronicle by a Franciscan probably of Carlisle,[89] which the Lanercost writer interpolated with documents, information about his own priory, pious reflections and the like. As in the case of the Bridlington chronicle, the value of the Lanercost chronicle as a source derives primarily from the fact that it preserves the substance of the earlier work. The Franciscan writer was both patriotic and royalist. He excused Edward III for the treaty with Scotland in 1328 on grounds of his youth, blaming Mortimer and Isabella,[90] and chauvinistically asserted that no other Christian prince could equal Edward's power at sea.[91]

However, the Franciscan writer's approach to history was in general pragmatic, not theoretical. He loved describing battles, sieges and military exploits, and was particularly well informed when an event involved Carlisle, its bishop or neighbouring lords. Edward Balliol spent the Christ-

---

[83] *Bridl.* p. 105.
[84] *Bridl.* pp. 133, 135.
[85] *Bridl.* pp. 136–7.
[86] *Bridl.* pp. 105–7. See Ranald Nicholson, *Edward III and the Scots* (Oxford 1965), p. 89.
[87] *Bridl.* p. 116. See Nicholson, op. cit., p. 137.
[88] *Bridl.* pp. 103–5. See Nicholson, op. cit., pp. 82 et seq. and nn.
[89] See p. 12 and n. 59 above.
[90] *Lan.* p. 261.
[91] *Lan.* p. 286.

mas of 1332 in the house of the Franciscans at Carlisle after his coronation,[92] and was there again in January 1334 to assemble his forces for a raid on Scotland.[93] The chronicler described in detail the raid by Sir Anthony Lucy into Scotland by way of Carlisle in 1332, with the loss of two esquires who were buried in Carlisle; Sir Anthony himself was wounded in the foot, eye and hand, but recovered.[94] The Franciscan gave an especially graphic account of the behaviour of the Scots at Carlisle in October 1337 on their way to raid Allerdale and Coupland: they had the temerity to march around the town in three bands daring anyone to engage them, and they burnt the hospital of St Nicholas in the suburbs and destroyed the bishop's manor of Rose; although Sir Anthony Lucy attacked them, no effective relief came until the arrival of Henry Percy and Ralph Neville on the third day, by which time the Scots had left. The chronicler mentioned a rumour that such successful Scottish raids were the result of secret information supplied by 'a certain north-country noble'.[95]

The chronicler told some good anecdotes about the Franciscans in Scotland. He related that after the capture of Berwick Edward III ordered the Scottish inmates of the Franciscan friary to be replaced by English friars—but, while the newcomers were being well entertained at dinner, the Scottish friars wrapped up the books, chalices and vestments and absconded with them saying that they had been deposited there by Earl Patrick of Dunbar.[96] And he told how the sailors from Newcastle burnt the Franciscan house at Dundee in 1335, and carried off their great bell—which the Dominicans of Newcastle most unjustly bought for ten marks.[97]

In one respect the Lanercost writer's treatment of the Franciscan chronicle resembles the Bridlington writer's treatment of the earlier Bridlington chronicle. He too imposed an ultra-patriotic mould on the pre-existing work. The climax of the Lanercost chronicle is the battle of Neville's Cross in 1346. Apparently the Lanercost writer rewrote in florid prose, with numerous biblical references, the Franciscan's factual record of the English victory.[98] His long-winded eloquence suggests that one motive for copying the Franciscan chronicle was to provide an historical introduction to this splendid victory. The English triumph was particularly gratifying to a canon of Lanercost because in the raid preceding it

[92] *Lan.* pp. 271. See Nicholson, op. cit., p. 105.
[93] *Lan.* p. 279. See Nicholson, op. cit., p. 186.
[94] *Lan.* p. 273.
[95] *Lan.* p. 292–3.
[96] *Lan.* p. 275.
[97] *Lan.* p. 282. See Nicholson, op. cit., p. 207 and n. 6.
[98] *Lan.* pp. 344–51. The last paragraph (p. 352) of the Lanercost chronicle is in a factual style which suggests the Lanercost writer here returned to his Franciscan exemplar which probably continued after this point (see p. 12 above). The rewriting at Lanercost of the Franciscan's account of the battle of Neville's Cross is discussed by V.H. Galbraith; *An.* p. xxvii.

the Scots had attacked Lanercost priory, the home of 'venerable men and servants of God', and robbed the church of its treasures. They also sacked the Augustinian priory at Hexham.[99] The writer calls King David another Ahab who was deceived by an evil spirit,[100] and the Scots were the sons of iniquity, the cursed children of Belial.[101] William Zouche, archbishop of York, commander of the English forces, is compared with 'that noble priest, the mourning Mathathias, with his five sons, Abaron, Apphus, Gaddis, Thasi and Maccabaeus'—here taken to represent Henry Percy, John Mowbray, Ralph Neville, Henry Scrope and Thomas Rokeby.[102]

Praising the archbishop's courage, the Lanercost chronicler writes, with allusions to John x. 12–14, that the archbishop, 'having chosen from the north skilled men, eager for war, did not *flee* like a *hireling* but like the *Good Shepherd* went forth against the wolves to save his sheep from the jaws' of the Scots.[103] The chronicler ends with the description of the battle, with more biblical allusions, this time to Psalm vii. 16:[104]

> The Scots fled, our men slaying them. Praise be to the Most High! On that day the English were victorious. And thus through the prayers of the blessed Virgin Mary and Saint Cuthbert, confessor of Christ, [King] David and the flower of Scotland, by God's just judgement, are *fallen into the ditch which* they themselves *made*.

It can, therefore, be seen that despite the general decline in the quality and quantity of historiography produced by members of the religious orders, the monks and friars still on occasion produced chronicles of value as sources and of interest as examples of historical writing. It is also evident that, although these chroniclers had more taste for homiletic prose than their 'secular' and lay counterparts, they shared to some extent the latter's predilections: they too loved good spectacles and were, at least until towards the end of the reign, ardent supporters of Edward III's wars.

---

[99] *Lan.* p. 346.
[100] 'David, diabolico spiritu deceptus ut alter Achab'; *Lan.* p. 344. Cf. 1 Kings xxii. 20–22; 2 Chronicles xviii. 19–21. For other pejorative comparisons of David with biblical personages see *Lan.* p. 349.
[101] *Lan.* p. 344.
[102] *Lan.* p. 347. Cf. 1 Macc. ii passim.
[103] *Lan.* p. 347. Cf. John x. 11–16.
[104] *Lan.* p. 351.

5

Thomas Walsingham

Until nearly the end of Edward III's reign the tradition of historical writing founded at St Albans by Roger of Wendover and Matthew Paris only just survived. In the early fourteenth century William Rishanger wrote annals on English history and brought the *Gesta Abbatum Monasterii Sancti Albani* (*Deeds of the Abbots of the Monastery of St Albans*), the abbey's domestic history, up to date. He was succeeded by one or two annalists whose work is now all but forgotten.[1] It fell to Thomas Walsingham, a monk of St Albans who became precentor in 1380, to revive the languishing tradition and to restore it to a flourishing state similar to that in Matthew Paris' day. Once more St Albans became the most important centre of historiography in England. This renewed vitality lasted well into Henry V's reign, but when it ended in 1422, there was no further important revival.[2]

It is necessary to say something about the milieu in which Thomas Walsingham wrote. A picture of St Albans abbey in the fourteenth century is given in Walsingham's own works, notably in his continuation of the *Gesta Abbatum Monasterii Sancti Albani*. Figuratively, and sometimes literally, the abbey in the fourteenth century resembled a beleaguered castle. Its most immediate enemy lay just outside the precinct walls: it was the vill of St Albans. From the rule of Abbot John de Hertford (1235–63) conflict between the abbey and the townsmen was perennial. The abbot had to defend the house's liberties against the encroachments of the townsmen, who resisted, for example, his insistence that all corn should be ground in his mill. Sometimes dispute led to violence. (The abbey obtained a royal licence to crenellate in 1357.)[3] On one occasion the marshal and an esquire of Abbot Richard de Wallingford (1328–36) were involved in a fracas in the vill, in which a townsman and the esquire were killed.[4] On another occasion the bedel of Abbot Richard's chamberlain was beaten up.[5] And during the abbatiate of Thomas de la Mare (1349–96), some time before the Peasants' Revolt, a townsman called

---

[1] For William Rishanger and his immediate successors see pp. 4–8 above.
[2] See pp. 342–3, 412 and n. 147 below.
[3] *CPR, 1354–1358*, p. 574; *Gesta Abbatum Monasterii Sancti Albani*, ed. H.T. Riley (RS 1867–9, 3 vols), iii. 122.
[4] *GASA*, ii. 217–18. For Richard of Wallingford see p. 122 and note 40 below.
[5] *GASA*, ii. 263

William Grindcob assaulted two monks who were carrying out a survey of town property.[6] Predictably violence was aggravated in times of national crisis. When Edward II was deposed, the townsmen besieged the abbey, demanding specific liberties.[7] They rose again during the Peasants' Revolt, ripping up the pavements in the abbey church, tearing down houses, freeing the prisoners from the abbot's gaol and demanding the delivery of the abbey's muniments so that they could burn them.[8] William Grindcob, embittered by the penance for assault which he had had to undergo naked in the chapter-house, was one of the ringleaders.[9]

Moreover, the abbot of St Albans came into conflict with the tenants on his estates and with neighbouring landlords. (Similar tensions prevailed in respect of the priories dependent on St Albans, at Hertford, Wymondham, Binham, Belvoir and Tynemouth.) One enraged neighbour, Sir Philip de Limbury, put John de la Moote, cellarer under Thomas de la Mare, in the pillory.[10] The pious Abbot Thomas himself starved fifty animals to death rather than cede a point to an opponent.[11] This almost anarchic situation is well illustrated by two anecdotes which Thomas Walsingham records. One tells how a plausible looking esquire visited Abbot Hugh de Eversden (1310–27) and asked to confer with him in private. As soon as they were alone he extorted £20 by threats of violence. The moral drawn by the chronicler is that the abbot should never allow himself to be alone, without any of his household, with unknown persons.[12] The other anecdote is about a clever ruse in the time of Abbot Richard de Wallingford, by a lady, Petronilla de Banstede, who was so afraid of burglary that she deposited a large treasure chest, which was in fact filled with lead and sand, in the abbey as if for safe-keeping: thus, comments Walsingham, she gained a reputation for both wealth and wisdom.[13]

However, most of the abbots' battles were fought in the law courts. All the fourteenth century abbots of St Albans were tireless in their legal defence of the abbey's property and privilege, but Thomas de la Mare was especially notable. He was, with God's help, a veritable St Martin in his struggle against secular encroachment, and 'most prudently freed his church from tyrannical servitude and extortion'.[14] Argument was met with argument. The townsmen contended that when King Offa founded the monastery of St Albans he gave the townsmen the vill with certain

---

[6] *GASA*, iii. 369.
[7] *GASA*, ii. 156 et seq.
[8] *GASA*, iii. 287–96.
[9] *GASA*, iii. 369. Cf. *Chronicon Angliae*, pp. 300–1. For the printed edition of the *Chronicon Angliae* see p. 125 n. 59 below.
[10] *GASA*, iii. 4.
[11] *GASA*, iii. 6.
[12] *GASA*, ii. 176–7.
[13] *GASA*, ii. 366.
[14] *GASA*, iii. 3, 100.

liberties, which later the monks abrogated.[15] The monks countered this claim with evidence from Matthew Paris' *Gesta Abbatum* (which states that Wulsin, the sixth abbot, founded the vill)[16] and from the *Life of St Ethelwold* (which showed that the vill was called Verulamium up to the reign of King Edgar).[17] The abbey's opponents sometimes resorted to forgery. The tenants at Redbourn in Richard de Wallingford's time fabricated a charter to support their claim to exemption from tallage, but the monks detected the forgery because although the charter purported to belong to Edward the Confessor's reign, it was partly in French, 'as it is spoken at the present time, and which has been in use from the Conquest when our language was corrupted by the Norman settlement.'[18] Under Abbot Michael de Mentmore (1336–49) the men of Barnet, attempting to prove that their land was freehold, made their forged charter look old by smoking the parchment up a chimney.[19]

The beleaguered position of St Albans abbey had two interrelated results: it made the friendship of influential people necessary; and it increased the abbey's burden of debt. Abbot Hugh de Eversden's lack of learning was compensated for, according to Walsingham, by his sociability which enabled him to make friends in high places.[20] Abbot Richard de Wallingford was to be praised for his 'renewal of friendships especially among the religious, the gentry and liege men of the neighbourhood'.[21] Thomas de la Mare had the advantage of noble birth, which meant that he had numerous relatives among the aristocracy and influential gentry.[22] To be on good terms with the royal court was particularly useful to the abbey. Richard de Wallingford gave four books to Richard de Bury, keeper of the privy seal (a notable book-collector and author of the *Philobiblon*), in order to promote the abbey's interests at court.[23] Both Edward II[24] and Edward III paid friendly visits to the abbey. On one occasion Edward III reprimanded Richard de Wallingford for spending lavishly on constructing a grand clock instead of repairing the fabric of the abbey.[25] Thomas de la Mare was especially friendly with Edward III who held him in high esteem.[26]

Friendship cost money. One method of ensuring the support of a lord

[15] *GASA*, iii. 365–7.
[16] See *GASA*, i. 22.
[17] *GASA*, iii. 366.
[18] *GASA*, ii. 261–2.
[19] *GASA*, ii. 317–18.
[20] *GASA*, ii. 113.
[21] *GASA*, ii. 202. For the abbey's powerful friends see pp. 144–6 below.
[22] *GASA*, ii. 371–2.
[23] *GASA*, ii. 200. Richard de Bury (bishop of Durham 1333–1345) was keeper of the privy seal from 1329 to 1334, and chancellor in 1334.
[24] For Edward II's generosity to St Albans see *GASA*, ii. 123–4, 179.
[25] *GASA*, ii. 281–2. For Richard de Wallingford's clock, see p. 122 n. 40 below.
[26] *GASA*, ii. 389–90, 405.

was to grant him a pension. For example, Abbot Hugh de Eversden, on a visit to the house of a neighbour, Sir Simon Hethersett (Hetyrsete), granted a pension to his baby son and heir, Edmund, which burdened the abbey for fifty years.[27] Hospitality itself was expensive. Visits from royalty and the nobility were frequent partly because St Albans was only twenty miles from London and on the royal road from London to Chester.[28] Moreover, there was the cost of the abbot's litigation. Thus the insecurity of the times necessitated expenditure which increased the abbey's indebtedness. Debts were also incurred for other reasons, for example because of royal and papal taxation.

Debt was not the only problem in internal administration faced by the fourteenth century abbots of St Albans. There was at least one instance of threatened violence within the cloisters themselves. Richard de Wallingford suffered from leprosy so that in his last years he could hardly fulfil his duties as abbot. A monk of Abingdon, Richard de Ildesle, tried to supplant him, but he was driven from St Albans by the angry monks with threats against his life. ('There were at that time men of great height and strength in the monastery'.)[29] And Abbot Richard fearing treachery sent those monks who had relatives or close friends among the hostile population of the vill to the priories dependent on the abbey.[30]

Nevertheless, despite trouble in external relations and in internal administration, the abbots made serious attempts at reform. Besides composing prayers[31] Richard de Wallingford wrote treatises on statutes issued by papal legates and by the general chapters of the English Benedictines.[32] He also enforced observance of the Rule in the priories dependent[33] on St Albans. His work was continued by Michael de Mentmore who enforced statutes issued for the Benedictines[34] and drew up his own regulations for the abbey and its dependent priories.[35] He was a president of the general chapter of the English Benedictines, in which office he was succeeded by Thomas de la Mare.[36] The latter himself was a rigorous disciplinarian—some monks left because of the strictness of his regime.[37] He reformed the customs of the monastery, composed a new ordinal, and

[27] *GASA*, ii. 178.
[28] Thomas Walsingham remarks on the expense of visits by royalty and the nobility which resulted from proximity to London; *GASA*, iii. 414.
[29] *GASA*, ii. 292.
[30] *GASA*, ii. 202.
[31] *GASA*, ii. 294–9.
[32] *GASA*, ii. 196.
[33] *GASA*, ii. 201.
[34] *GASA*, ii. 301–2, 304.
[35] *GASA*, ii. 304–15.
[36] *GASA*, ii. 402–3. See *Documents Illustrating the Activities of the General and Provincial Chapters of the English Black Monks, 1215–1540*, ed. W.A. Pantin (Camden Soc., third series, xlv, xlvii, liv, 1931–7, 3 vols), iii. 34.
[37] *GASA*, ii. 415.

reformed the nearby nunnery of St Mary de Pré.[38] (To the indignation of the precentor of St Albans he presented the nuns, whom he insisted should be literate, with six or seven of the monks' service books.) And, at the request of Edward III, he held a visitation of the royal abbeys (Eynsham, Abingdon, Battle, Reading, Chester and Bury St Edmunds).[39]

Furthermore, St Albans was a centre of intellectual activity. Most outstanding of all the monks was Abbot Richard de Wallingford, a distinguished mathematician and astronomer. He wrote numerous highly technical treatises and, besides constructing the great clock at St Albans, made astronomical instruments.[40] Michael de Mentmore studied at Oxford,[41] while Thomas de la Mare was noted for his learning in the scriptures; his writings, though in a crabbed (deformis) hand, in English, Latin and French, were, according to Walsingham, both fluent and highly valued. During his abbacy monks whom he had educated at St Albans made their names at Oxford.[42] His successors, Abbot John de la Moote (1396–1401) and William Heyworth (1401–20) rebuilt the hostel of the St Albans' monks at Oxford, replacing the 'restricted and unpleasant' building which overlooked a kitchen, with a more commodious stone one near the hostel of the monks of Norwich.[43] Another inmate of St Albans, Simon Southerey, was well known as a scholar. He was 'an eminent poet, very skilled in astronomy and most learned in poetry,'[44] and a friend of a London grammar master, John Seward, the author of treatises on Latin prosody. Southerey also acquired a reputation for preaching and writing against Wycliffism.

The promotion of learning at St Albans is shown by the abbots' accumulation of books and by some of their building activities. Abbot Michael de Mentmore bought back from the executors of Richard de Bury some of the thirty two books which Richard de Wallingford had sold to help pay his debts.[45] Thomas de la Mare increased the abbatial library.[46] The

---

[38] GASA, ii. 395, 401–2.

[39] GASA, ii. 405–6. See Pantin, op. cit., iii. 34.

[40] See GASA, ii. 201, 207. Richard of Wallingford's treatises are edited, with English translations and full critical apparatus, in Richard of Wallingford, ed. J.D. North (Oxford 1976, 3 vols). For the text of his treatise on the mechanics of his clock see ibid., i. 441–526; for the manuscripts of, and a synopsis and commentary on the text, followed by an assessment of the importance of his clock, see ibid., ii. 309–70. A picture of Wallingford with his clock is reproduced from Thomas Walsingham's Book of Benefactors, BL MS. Nero D VII, f. 20 (for which see p. 123 and n. 52 below), as Plate I at the end of ibid., iii. A detailed biography of Wallingford is in ibid., ii. 1–16.

[41] GASA, 182. For Mentmore see Emden, Biographical Register, ii. 337.

[42] GASA, iii. 409–10.

[43] GASA, iii. 447–8, 496.

[44] Annales Monasterii S. Albani a Johanne Amundesham, Monacho, ed. H. T. Riley (1870–1, 2 vols), ii. 305. Cf. V. H. Galbraith, 'John Seward and his circle' in Medieval and Renaissance Studies, i (Warburg Institute, 1941), 93–4, and Emden, op. cit., iii. 1734.

[45] GASA, ii. 200.

[46] GASA, iii. 389.

provision of studies for the monks was begun by Mentmore[47] and continued by Thomas de la Mare. Abbot Thomas built studies and a chapel in the cloisters, with a library above and a vault for the monastic archives below.[48] He also built himself a study at Redbourn (the priory used by the monks for vacations) out of the monks' communal latrine, which he replaced by new, individual lavatories.[49] Moreover, Abbot Thomas built a new scriptorium. This is recorded by Walsingham who here mentions himself:[50]

> The scriptorium was built at the abbot's expense and by the efforts of Thomas Walsingham then precentor and chief scribe; the books there written by him and his staff, the books bought, and those repaired, were allocated to the convent's library and to the library of the abbot's study.

The date when Thomas Walsingham became a monk of St Albans is unknown. He held the office of precentor for fourteen years after his appointment in 1380, and then in 1394 Abbot Thomas made him prior of Wymondham. When John de la Moote became abbot in 1396, he recalled Thomas Walsingham and Simon Southerey, prior of Belvoir, 'at their request and urgent entreaty, for they were weary with worldly cares'.[51] Walsingham spent the rest of his life, until his death in about 1422, as a cloister monk at St Albans. His earliest known work is the *Liber Benefactorum (Book of Benefactors)*, a list with brief notes of the benefactors of St Albans: it is arranged in sections for different categories of people (kings, queens, popes, bishops and laymen), and richly illustrated with stylized portraits.[52] The fact that the book has a list of the monks of St Albans in 1380 indicates that it was written in that year. Walsingham's own name ('Thomas Walsingham, precentor, who compiled this book') is twenty second in the list of fifty four monks: this suggests that he was already fairly senior. The list also has the name of the scribe (William de Wyllum) and of the artist (Alan Strayler).

At about this time Walsingham started writing history with the conscious

[47] *GASA*, ii. 302.

[48] *GASA*, iii. 442.

[49] *GASA*, ii. 399.

[50] *GASA*, iii. 392–3.

[51] *GASA*, iii. 436. Thomas Walsingham's life and works are discussed in *The St. Albans Chronicle 1406–1420*, ed. V. H. Galbraith (Oxford 1937), pp. xxxvi-xlv.

[52] Ibid., pp. xxxvi-xxxvii, and Plate IV below. The *Book of Benefactors* is in BL MS. Cotton Nero D VII. The list of monks of St Albans and other short extracts are printed in *Mon. Angl.* ii. 208. Perhaps this was the *Book of Benefactors* kept on the high altar; see p. 401 and n. 73 below. A shorter version, perhaps written in 1394, is in Corpus Christi College, Cambridge, MS. 7 (see Galbraith, op. cit., pp. xxxix, lv, lviii); it is printed in *JT*, pp. 427–64. For other minor works, perhaps by Walsingham (in BL MS. Cotton Claudius E IV), some of which are printed as Appendices E-K in *Amund.* ii. 296–363, see *St AC*, p. xxxviii and p. 127 n. 69 below.

intention of reviving the tradition established by Matthew Paris. Although
he may have begun his career as an historian by writing the St Albans
continuation of Higden's *Polychronicon* to 1377,[53] his principal work was a
massive history of England to 1392 written as a continuation to Matthew
Paris' *Chronica Majora* (*Greater Chronicle*). To 1306 Walsingham used the
continuation of the *Chronica Majora* attributed to William Rishanger.
From 1308 to 1343 he compiled his work from 'Trokelowe', Blaneford,
Nicholas Trevet, the *Polychronicon* and Adam Murimuth. He then used
the St Albans continuation of the *Polychronicon* to 1377,[54] when his chronicle
become a full-scale contemporary history written up within three or four
years of the events it records.[55] The form of this section shows the influence
of Matthew Paris. Originally Walsingham, following Matthew Paris'
example, began each annal with a notice of where the king spent Christmas
and ended with a summary characterizing the year. (Some of these entries
were omitted in the later copies of the chronicle.)[56] Walsingham also
continued Matthew Paris' *Gesta Abbatum Monasterii Sancti Albani*, using
Rishanger's continuation to 1308. From that date Walsingham used oral
information and numerous documents (chapter ordinances, charters,
public records and the like). He intended to continue the *Gesta* to the death

---

[53] The continuation of the *Polychronicon* from 1343 to 1377 printed in *Adami Murimuthensis Chronica*, ed. Thomas Hog (English Historical Soc. 1846), pp. 174–227, was almost certainly written at St Albans and may well be by Walsingham himself. If it is not by Walsingham, but was written at St Albans, it proves that history was being written in the abbey from the mid-fourteenth century. For this continuation see V. H. Galbraith, 'The *Historia Aurea* of John, vicar of Tynemouth, and the sources of the St Albans chronicle (1327–77)' in *Essays in History presented to Reginald Lane Poole*, ed. H. W. C. Davis (Oxford 1927), pp. 391–2, and John Taylor, *The Universal Chronicle of Ranulf Higden* (Oxford 1966) pp. 118–21. This continuation was a source used by Walsingham for his chronicle. In its turn Walsingham's own writings were used as a source by the authors of other continuations of the *Polychronicon*; see Taylor, *Higden*, pp. 121–2. Cf. p. 56 and n. 71 above.

[54] For this continuation of the *Polychronicon* see the previous note. For the sources of Walsingham's *Chronica Majora* to 1377 see *St AC*, pp. li-liii, and Galbraith, 'The *Historia Aurea* . . . and the sources of the St Albans chronicle', pp. 379–95.

[55] Professor Galbraith states that Walsingham wrote within two or three years of the events recorded; see *St AC*, pp. lvii-lviii, lxiii. However, at least in some cases three or four years elapsed before writing; thus the annal for 1377 has a prognostication of the Peasants' Revolt; *Chron. Angliae* (for which see p. 125 n. 59 below), p. 146. The dates when Walsingham compiled his chronicles is uncertain. Galbraith argued that Walsingham completed the *Chronica Majora* shortly after April 1394, before he went to Wymondham, and that he probably wrote the short chronicle between 1394 and 1397. Nevertheless, any attempt at exact dating would be misguided because Walsingham constantly altered and revised the two chronicles, and both were certainly available in some form to the author of the first part of the Evesham chronicle who wrote some time between 1390 and 1393. See V. H. Galbraith, 'Thomas Walsingham and the St Albans chronicle, 1272–1422' in *EHR*, xlvii (1932), pp. 17–18, *St AC*, pp. 1–li and n. 1, and the comments of Professor Stow in *VR II* (for which see p. 158 and n. 4 below), pp. 13–20 and nn., passim.

[56] It is noteworthy that almost all the numerous manuscripts extant of Walsingham's chronicle were written *c*. 1420–30. In the course of transmission his text was continually modified: no surviving manuscript is an exact copy of another and no known manuscript contains the full text to 1420. See *St AC*, pp. xii, xiv-xv, liii, lxiii.

of Thomas de la Mare,[57] but stopped in about 1393 (presumably because of his removal to Wymondham). To the same period belongs Walsingham's short chronicle of the world, from the Creation to 1392, a compilation which roughly corresponds with Matthew Paris' *Abbreviatio Chronicarum* (*Epitome of Chronicles*).[58]

While at Wymondham Walsingham wrote a short version of his *Chronica Majora*,[59] in the same way as Matthew Paris had produced a short version, the *Historia Anglorum* (*History of the English*), of his great work. On Walsingham's return to St Albans in 1396 his interest in English history apparently cooled. Instead he turned his attention especially to classical studies. He wrote the *Archana Deorum* (*Secrets of the Gods*), a commentary on Ovid's *Metamorphoses* together with an account of the origins of the ancient gods, which he dedicated to the prior, Simon Southerey.[60] He became interested in ancient history, composing a version of the fourth century history of the Trojan war by Dictys Cretensis,[61] and the *Historia Magni Principis Alexandri* (*History of Alexander the Great*), an account of Alexander based on Julius Valerius and a twelfth century St Albans compilation.[62]

Walsingham resumed writing chronicles probably in the late fourteenth

---

[57] *GASA*, ii. 109. See *St AC*, p. xxxviii.

[58] *St AC*, p. xlvii n. 1. Professor Galbraith notes that new copies of Matthew Paris' own chronicles were made at St Albans in the early fifteenth century; *St AC*, p. lxix.

[59] The title as applied to Thomas Walsingham's long chronicle is a courtesy title derived from the fact that it is a continuation of Matthew Paris' *Chronica Majora*. No complete manuscript of this work exists. It has been hypothetically reconstructed from the existing manuscripts by Professor Galbraith, who points out that none of the printed editions contains its unadulterated text; on the contrary they all print combinations of Walsingham's long chronicle and his short one. The printed editions are: *Chronicon Angliae, 1328–1388*, ed. E. M. Thompson (RS 1874); the *Historia Anglicana, 1272–1422*, ed. H. T. Riley (RS 1863–4, 2 vols); *Annales Ricardi II et Henrici IV* in *JT*, pp. 155–424, and *St AC*. For an analysis of the printed editions in relation to the long and short chronicles see *St AC*, p. xlvi. (In the discussion of Walsingham's chronicle below, reference is made to the long chronicle.) Professor Galbraith discusses the manuscript tradition fully in his introduction. I have here accepted Professor Galbraith's conclusion that Walsingham is the sole author of the two versions of the St Albans chronicle from 1272 to 1420 and 1422 respectively (*St AC*, pp. lxvi-lxxi).

[60] See *St AC*, pp. xli-xlii, and F. W. Hall, 'An English commentary on Ovid' in *Classical Quarterly*, xxi (1927), pp. 151–3 (the latter prints Walsingham's preface). There was already before Walsingham's time a tenuous tradition of classical scholarship at St Albans. By the thirteenth century a twelfth century copy of the *Comedies* of Terence, derived from some ancient archetype, with pictures of actors which are crucial evidence in the history of the Roman theatre, was in the abbey library. The MS. is now Auct. F. 2.13 (formerly 27603) in the Bodleian Library, Oxford; see Falconer Madan *et al.*, *Summary Catalogue of Western Manuscripts in the Bodleian Library at Oxford* (Oxford 1895–1953, 7 vols in 8). v. 297–8. Matthew Paris himself was interested in classical studies. He extolled the knowledge possessed by John of Basingstoke, archdeacon of Leicester, about Greek and Latin literature, and reproduced in facsimile the Greek numerals, copies of which John had brought back from Athens where he had studied; *Chronica Majora*, ed. H. R. Luard (RS 1872–83, 7 vols), v. 284–6. It may also be noted that Matthew's drawings include one of Socrates and one of Plato; see Francis Wormald, *More Matthew Paris Drawings* (Walpole Soc., xxxi, 1942–3), pp. 109–12 and Plate XXVII b.

[61] See *St AC*, pp. xlii-xliv.

[62] See *St AC*, pp. xliv-xlv.

or early fifteenth century. He continued the *Chronica Majora* to 1420 and the shorter chronicle to 1422: both continuations are less full and rather less satisfactory than the previous sections.[63] Moreover, between 1419 and 1422 he wrote the *Ypodigma Neustriae*, a chronicle from 911 to 1419, which has been compared with Matthew Paris' *Flores Historiarum* (*Flowers of History*).[64] The title, which may be translated roughly as *The Symbol of Normandy*, calls for comment. The word *Ypodygma* (as Walsingham spelt it) testifies to his classical studies: he coined it from the Greek word $\dot{v}\pi\acute{o}\delta\varepsilon\iota\gamma\mu\alpha$, meaning a sign, token, mark, or a pattern. He used *Neustriae* to qualify it because he wished to commemorate the conquest of Normandy by Henry V, to whom he dedicated the work.[65] For the same reason he began with Rollo's conquest of Normandy in 911, and recorded Henry V's conquest at some length. However, the *Ypodigma* has very little other information about Normandy, being mainly a history of England. It is compiled from various well known authorities such as William of Jumièges, Ralph Diceto, Nicholas Trevet, the *Polychronicon* and Adam Murimuth, besides for the contemporary period Walsingham's own chronicles.[66]

It can, therefore, be seen that at least in certain respects Walsingham revived the historiographical tradition established at St Albans by Matthew Paris. His great work, the *Chronica Majora*, provided full-scale coverage of English history of nearly half a century: this achievement certainly bears comparison with Matthew Paris' *Chronica Majora* which gives a detailed account of the first two thirds of Henry III's reign. Furthermore, Walsingham adopted a technique for this, his principal chronicle, similar to that used by Matthew Paris. And finally the overall scheme of Walsingham's total corpus resembles Matthew Paris'. It remains to consider how far Walsingham's range of interests emulated, and to what extent his concept of history and his views on contemporary society and politics resembled, those of his predecessor.

Walsingham's interests were by no means narrow, and yet they were not as wide as Matthew Paris'. He did not share the latter's taste for the illustrated chronicle—nor did he have his gift as an artist. Although his *Book of Benefactors* is enlivened with coloured portraits, these are not by him but by Alan Strayler (none of Walsingham's other works is illustrated). Walsingham's lack of visual sense is apparent in other contexts; his works do not have the graphic descriptions of, for example, works of art which characterize Matthew Paris' writings. He showed no interest in heraldry, a subject on which Matthew Paris was an expert. Nor can he compete with

---

[63] See pp. 139–44 below.
[64] Printed *Ypodigma Neustriae a Thoma Walsingham*, ed. H. T. Riley (RS 1876). See *St AC*, pp. lx–lxi.
[65] *Ypodigma*, pp. x and n. 1, 3–5.
[66] For the sources see *Ypodigma*, pp. xv–xxxvi.

Matthew Paris' interest in natural history (his description of the habits of the dolphin, evoked by the capture of one in the Thames in 1391, is copied from Pliny's *Natural History*).[67] Walsingham's credulity with regard to animals appears in his account of a dragon which allegedly appeared near Sudbury in Suffolk in 1405. It was enormous, he writes, had 'a crested head, serrated teeth and a tail of excessive length', and killed a shepherd and many sheep. Arrows rebounded with a clatter from its metal-like scales, but they did scare it into flight—it vanished into the marshes never to be seen again.[68]

However, although Walsingham did not share Matthew Paris' knowledge of cartography, he did have some interest in geography. The passages relating to geography show preoccupations typical of the fourteenth century. Walsingham was influenced by both Higden and by *Mandeville's Travels*. The latter, commonly attributed to Sir John Mandeville, was written in 1356 or soon after. Its author claims that he was born and educated at St Albans, which may well be true.[69] Walsingham was clearly intrigued by his colourful account of foreign lands. A copy of the *Travels* made some time before 1400 was bound with a copy of one of Walsingham's chronicles, and it has been suggested that the translation of the work from French into Latin in the late fourteenth century was done in the abbey. Like Higden and the author of the *Travels*, Walsingham combined a love of prodigies and marvels with a genuine curiosity about foreign lands. Thus he gives in his version of Dictys Cretensis an account of the wonders of Ethiopia, its people and its animals, 'for the amusement of those who do not know about that race and country'.[70] His interest in distant countries was stimulated by the expansion of Europe. He gives a realistic description of the Canaries which 'sailors from Spain, sailing the vast expanses of the southern oceans for trade, piracy or fishing, unexpectedly discovered at about this time.' (Walsingham puts the description in the annal for 1404.) He writes:[71]

---

[67] *HA*, ii. 204 and n. 3, 205.

[68] *JT*, p. 402.

[69] For the connection of the author of the *Travels* with St Albans and Walsingham's interest in the work see J. A. W. Bennett, *The Rediscovery of Sir John Mandeville* (New York 1954), pp. 211 et seq. The only complete English version of the *Travels*, BL MS. Egerton 1982 (see ibid., pp. 237 et seq.) which was written in the fifteenth century, was owned by St Albans abbey; Ker, *Libraries*, p. 166. The Latin text owned by St Albans is bound with Walsingham's chronicle from 1272 to 1393, in BL MS. Royal 13 E IX (see Bennett, op. cit., p. 211 and nn.). Sir John Mandeville, whose claim to authorship of the *Travels* is defended by Bennett, op. cit., passim, is in the biographical list of famous men connected with St Albans, perhaps compiled by Walsingham (see p. 123 n. 52 above), in BL MS. Claudius E IV; *Amund.* ii. 306 (Appendix E). See also p. 323 and n. 112 below.

[70] Quoted *St AC*, p. xliii.

[71] *JT*, pp. 389–90. Walsingham has confused the dates here. The Canaries were rediscovered by the Portuguese in 1341, but in 1344 Don Luis of Spain obtained the grant of them (the Fortunate Isles) from Pope Clement VI. Don Luis apparently did nothing to consolidate his gain. Eventually, after other ineffectual expeditions, two Frenchmen, Jean de Béthen-

There goats and sheep abounded, and people of both sexes, black and naked but dangerously swift of foot. They have nothing made of iron nor of any other metal, and they live on the flesh of goats and sheep. They protect themselves against the winter cold with cow hide, but in the summer they need no clothing. The women carry their sons tucked under the arm, suckling them meanwhile (so that a baby's head is at its mother's breast while the rest of the body and feet hang next to her back). They have woods and groves to which they flee when strangers come. They fend off the latter from the shores by hurling stones so hard that a blow from a large one is deadly. They have no houses but live in caves and pits. They catch fish to eat, not with iron hooks but with goats' horn sharpened with fine chips of flint, and heated slightly to soften the horn as required. They make lines or ropes with goats' hair, to which the hooks are tied, for throwing out deep. When fishing they stay on the rocks and often catch fine fish. They skin goats and sheep with stone knives or chips of flint, drying the flesh in the sun and wind to eat when fish are short.

Walsingham also has a description of Denmark which he derived by word of mouth from the envoys who accompanied Henry IV's daughter Philippa there in 1406 for her marriage to Eric IX. The king, they reported, was handsome enough, and witty and friendly, but the country was harsh and uncultivated. No wheat apparently grew and grain had to be imported. The sterility of the countryside and the neglect of agriculture was attributable to the ravages of the Danish soldiers whom the queen mother allowed to live off the land, because she could not afford to pay their wages.[72]

Although in general Walsingham did not rival Matthew Paris in breadth

---

court and Gadifer de la Salle, conquered the islands with an expedition which set out in 1402. Possibly Walsingham conflated Don Luis' expedition with the French one. The source of his description could well be a letter of an Italian seaman who sailed with the Portuguese in 1341, or of an Italian trader. Boccaccio based his account of the Portuguese expedition on such letters. See C. R. Beazley, *The Dawn of Modern Geography* (Oxford 1897–1906, 3 vols), iii. 424 and n. 4. Alternatively he could have seen some newsletter relating to the French expedition. It is noteworthy that one of the two authors of the narrative of the French conquest (which in its earliest form was completed in 1404) was a Benedictine of St Jouin de Marnes, Pierre Boutier, chaplain of Gadifer de la Salle. See ibid., iii. 445, 448. Walsingham's description of the Canaries is clearly not derived either from Boccaccio or from the narrative of the French conquest, though it has similarities with both as is to be expected in realistic descriptions of the same place. See the printed edition, with an English translation, of the narrative of the French conquest, *The Canarian . . .* , ed. R. H. Major (Hakluyt Soc. 1872), especially pp. 92–3, 130–9, and the English translation of Boccaccio in ibid., pp. xiii-xix. Cf. the short description of the Isles in Murimuth; *AM*, p. 162.
[72] *JT*, p. 420.

of vision, his ideas and opinions in some ways resemble his predecessor's. A key to the understanding of Matthew Paris' ideas is his Christian faith and his piety towards the Benedictine order.[73] The same is true of Thomas Walsingham. Like Matthew Paris he was influenced by the tradition of preaching. Some passages in his chronicles have a strongly homiletic tone. He writes tirades against the moral failings of great men, with frequent animadversions on the sins of pride, avarice and adultery. Thus he attacks Edward III for his greed and for his adultery with Alice Perrers: 'Oh! all England must lament the king's levity, cupidity and unworthiness', who has become the servant of the flesh and of a woman![74] He inveighs with especial vehemence against 'the adulterous and proud' John of Gaunt in the annal for 1376. Addressing Gaunt, Walsingham writes:[75]

> Oh! unhappy and unfortunate duke! Oh! those whom you should lead in war you betray by your treachery and cowardice, and those whom you should lead in peace by the example of good works, you lead astray, dragging them to ruin! ... Think, unhappy man, you who regard yourself as prosperous and believe yourself most blessed, how your miseries oppress you and your lust tortures you, never satisfied with what you have, never fearing the none too distant future! Knowledge of your evil-doing pricks your conscience—if only you were terrified by fear of law and judgment like other people; then indeed you would mend your ways, even if reluctantly.

Similarly Walsingham inveighs against William Latimer's immorality in the account of his trial in 1376. Latimer, writes Walsingham, was proud and cruel and unmindful of God; he 'abandoned his wife and spent the nights with whores in a London brothel, ... lavishly spending what he had extorted through avarice from his wretched tenants'.[76] And again, Walsingham has an eloquent tirade against the bishops, because they did not excommunicate Alice Perrers (which he attributed to venality and subservience to the king).[77]

The idea of history as a manifestation of the divine will was of course central to medieval historiography. Nevertheless, some chroniclers emphasize it more than others, and only the Evesham chronicler (to be discussed in the next chapter) among Walsingham's contemporaries rivalled his homiletic tone. (Earlier John of Reading had written in similar vein.) Walsingham particularly exploited the commonplace that God rewards the good and punishes the bad. He abused in moral terms those people

[73] See Gransden, *Historical Writing*, i. 367–74 passim.
[74] *CA*, p. 105.
[75] *CA*, p. 75.
[76] *CA*, p. 84.
[77] *CA*, pp. 104–5.

of whom he disapproved politically, implying that divine retribution would ensue. The political troubles of Edward III's last years were the result of the king's moral decline. Edward, being a slave of his own vices and unable to rule himself, was unworthy of the name of lord and could not hope to rule the free.[78] Latimer fell because of his moral turpitude and John of Gaunt was only saved by a dramatic repentance. When writing of the year 1381, Walsingham was faced with the fact that Gaunt was no longer the villain of the political scene, but a man of worth and loyalty. To justify a *volte-face* in his own attitude, Walsingham alleges that Gaunt turned to religion and confessed both in public and in private the sins of his past life (to which the duke ascribed his troubles at that time).[79]

Walsingham explicitly attributes some events to divine vengeance. Thus he asserts that the murder of Robert Hawley in Westminster abbey in 1378 was God's revenge for the murder of Thomas Becket.[80] Even more notable is his long disquisition on the causes of the Peasants' Revolt.[81] Some say, he asserts, that the revolt was divine vengeance for the laxity of the clergy, who allowed the dissemination of the heresies of John Wyclif. Others ascribed it to the nobles who were 'tyrants to their inferiors, envious of their equals, treacherous to all, incestuous, adulterous, and destroyers of the church'. And some ascribed the revolt to the general immorality of the English, their drunkenness, perjury, quarrelsomeness, falsity, fornication and adultery. (Walsingham's words are reminiscent of Higden's and John of Reading's on the same subject.)[82] Walsingham himself decided that the revolt was God's judgment for the sins of the English, but especially for those of the mendicant friars, who, forgetful of their rule, aspired to accumulate possessions, and seduced princes by flattery and the people by lies.

Walsingham's theocentric view of history also appears in his many references to portents and prophecies. In 1385 an earthquake presaged discord between the kings of England and France;[83] the dolphin in the Thames was an omen of the trouble between Richard II and the Londoners in 1392;[84] the drying up of the river Ouse near Bedford was a portent of the political division in the kingdom in 1399;[85] and the severe weather accompanying the accession of Henry V foretold the strictness of his rule.[86] An example of an event regarded as the fulfilment of a prophecy is the

---

[78] *CA*, pp. 105–6.
[79] *CA*, p. 328. Walsingham describes another dramatic repentance of John of Gaunt s.a. 1389; *HA*, ii. 194. Cf. Henry Knighton, cited p. 180 and n. 134 below.
[80] *CA*, p. 209.
[81] *CA*, p. 310–12 (cf. pp. 285, 301–2).
[82] See pp. 52, 105–6 above.
[83] *HA*, ii. 130.
[84] *HA*, ii. 211.
[85] *HA*, ii. 229.
[86] *St AC*, p. 69.

capture of Richard Scrope, archbishop of York, and of Thomas Mowbray, earl of Norfolk and earl marshal, in 1405; Walsingham stated that these events occurred in accordance with a prophecy of John of Bridlington.[87] And an example of a miracle is the claim that the land where Archbishop Greenfield was executed became marvellously fertile.[88]

In considering whether Walsingham's views on contemporary society and politics resemble those expressed by Matthew Paris, it must of course be remembered that Walsingham lived in a very different world. Abroad he witnessed a tragedy for western Christendom, the Great Schism, and at home saw the rise of the first heretical sect in England, the Lollards. And he survived two crises in English history, events which for many must have been traumatic experiences, the Peasants' Revolt and the Lancastrian coup in 1399. In keeping with his religious preoccupations Walsingham had a consistent interest in both the schism and in Lollardy. And his recognition of the crucial importance of the Peasants' Revolt and the 1399 revolution is abundantly proved by the full coverage he gave them.

Walsingham describes and documents the beginning of the schism,[89] traces its course,[90] and has a full account of the council of Constance.[91] He accuses the cardinals who elected Clement VII of reducing the church to turmoil, of sowing tares, of seducing the innocent into error and of rocking St Peter's boat.[92] His anti-French feeling engendered by the Hundred Years' War added fuel to his religious fervour. On the protection afforded to Clement by Charles V in 1379, Walsingham exclaims:[93]

> Oh! detestable, profane, damnable malice (not ignorance) of that king! he is not ignorant how unjust, invalid and null is the title of the pseudo-pope, but none the less strives to adore, worship and exalt that idol, not only to the destruction of his own soul but to the death and damnation of many.

Walsingham expends his bitterest invective against John Wyclif ('or rather Wykbileve'), as an 'angel of Satan and forerunner of Antichrist', 'the mouthpiece of the devil, the enemy of the church, the confuser of common folk, the idol of heretics, the mirror of hypocrisy, the incitor of schism, the sower of hatred, and the inventor of lies'.[94] Walsingham regarded the spread of Lollardy with almost hysterical abhorrence. He deplores

[87] *JT*, p. 407.
[88] *JT*, p. 410.
[89] *CA*, pp. 212–19.
[90] See e.g. *HA*, ii. 121–5; *St AC*, pp. 3–21 passim, 43, 45, 50–1.
[91] *St AC*, pp. 104–9.
[92] *CA*, p. 216.
[93] *CA*, p. 224.
[94] *CA*, p. 281; *HA*, ii. 119. Henry Knighton is the other main chronicle authority for the Lollards; see pp. 170–1 below.

that the authorities of Oxford university failed to crush the heresy.[95] He accuses the Lollards of misleading innocent, ignorant people[96] and asserts (in fact wrongly) that John Balle, one of the leaders of the Peasants' Revolt, was influenced by Wyclif's doctrines.[97] Walsingham was also enraged by the contamination of the nobility and of the knightly class. Wyclif, that 'execrable heretic, led astray the greatest in the land as well as those of least importance.'[98] He describes at length the parliament at Gloucester, in 1378, when John of Gaunt produced Wyclif himself, so that the heretic could state the justifications for the taxation of the clergy.[99] Walsingham describes Sir John Oldcastle, whose heretical career he traces, as inflated with pride—Oldcastle asserted at his trial that after his execution he would rise on the third day and give peace to his sect.[100]

Undoubtedly Walsingham felt strongly about Wycliffism, as did his fellow monk Simon Southerey. Nevertheless his words have the exaggerated tone of a preacher, and his attitude may in fact have been more rational and less emotional than appears at first sight. Like many good preachers he carefully states his opponents' views, and quite often he copies the texts of Wyclif's and his followers' conclusions in full, ostensibly so that the reader could see for himself the enormities of the heretical doctrines.[101] He once even uses an argument reminiscent of the Wycliffite doctrine of lordship: he asserts that Edward III's authority as a ruler had been underminded by his moral depravity.[102] And on one occasion he treats Lollardy with apparent humour. He tells how a Lollard knight rushed home from holy communion with the sacramental bread, which he thereupon ate with wine, onions and oysters.[103]

Heresy struck at the fabric of medieval society. On a theoretical level the Lollards undermined authority by denying the right of kings, nobles and ecclesiastics to have dominion if they were in a state of sin. And in actuality they tended to become involved in sedition and even in insurrection.[104] Belief in a static, hierarchic society is a characteristic of Matthew Paris' work.[105] It is equally apparent in Walsingham's chronicles, although expressed in the terms of his own time. Walsingham particularly emphasiz-

[95] CA, pp. 173–4, 341, 341–5.
[96] HA, ii. 188.
[97] CA, p. 321. See Margaret Aston, 'Lollardy and sedition, 1381 1431' in Past and Present, xvii (1960), pp. 4–5.
[98] CA, p. 335. For the support of Wycliffism by the knights and nobility see CA, pp. 115 et seq., HA, ii. 157–9, and JT, pp. 174, 182, 347.
[99] CA, pp. 115 et seq.
[100] St AC, p. 117. Cf. pp. 209–10 and n. 106 below.
[101] See e.g. CA, pp. 181–3, 184–9, 336–44 passim; JT, pp. 174–82, 347–8; St AC, pp. 47–55.
[102] CA, pp. 105–6. For Wyclif's doctrine of lordship see H. B. Workman, John Wyclif (Oxford 1926, 2 vols), i. 257–66.
[103] CA, p. 282.
[104] See St AC, pp. 70, 89, and Aston, op. cit., pp. 1–44 passim.
[105] See Gransden, Historical Writing, i. 373–4, and pp. 165–6 below.

ed the necessity of people remaining in their social groups. Already Higden had deplored the ambitions of the lower orders to emulate their social superiors, and the same preoccupation appears in the works of a number of Walsingham's contemporaries.[106] He seems to have been especially interested in the problem of movement between social groups.

The principal division of society was between lords (*domini*) and their social inferiors whom Walsingham variously calls *servi*, (*servus* usually means a villein but it can mean a servant), *plebei* and *populares*, and, with reference to the Peasants' Revolt, *rustici*, *nativi* (villeins) and *bondi* (another word for villeins). Already in Edward III's last years Walsingham lamented that the king (because of his failure to rule himself) deserved 'to be called a servant (*servus*) and not a lord'.[107] Walsingham's interest in this social definition was stimulated by the Peasants' Revolt. Then the 'rustics whom we call *nativi* or *bondi* ... began to struggle for liberty and to achieve equality with the lords.'[108] He writes of those who invaded the Tower: 'Those villeins (*servi*) who were previously of the most lowly condition behaved like lords',[109] and thus 'order was reversed and turned topsy-turvy, for villeins ruled lords.'[110] Walsingham explains John Balle's view of society at some length.[111] Balle preached on the proverb:

> When Adam delve[d] and Eve span,
> Who was then a gentle man?

Balle tried to prove that all forms of servitude were the result of unjust oppression introduced by man, for God had created all men equal; if He had intended that there should be lords and unfree men, He would have created men of both groups. Walsingham saw the restoration of order after the Peasants' Revolt as the salvation of the two-tier medieval society. Richard II, he asserts, delivered a powerful address to the men of Essex, saying: 'Rustics you have been and are; and you shall remain in bondage, not as heretofore but incomparably more vilely. ... We shall keep you down as an example to posterity.'[112] Walsingham regarded the harsh treatment of the rebellious townsmen of St Albans, who called themselves 'the nobility of the towns', with satisfaction. The townsmen had surreptitiously taken down from the gallows the bodies of their fellows whom the royal justices had hanged. The king, angry at their insubordination, forced them to dig up the stinking, putrifying and verminous corpses and to hang them up again. Thus 'he forced a degrading and abominable servi-

---

[106] See p. 52 above, and pp. 165–6 below.
[107] *CA*, p. 105.
[108] *CA*, p. 285.
[109] *CA*, p. 291.
[110] *GASA*, iii. 309.
[111] *CA*, pp. 320–2.
[112] *CA*, p. 316.

tude on those who had struggled for liberty.' Moreover, as the townsmen used the chains of their dogs to suspend the corpses, the victims became, Walsingham comments, viler than the dogs which went free.[113]

Although Walsingham's interest in the grades of society is most marked in the account of the Peasants' Revolt, it also appears in the later part of his chronicle. On one occasion his belief in the traditional structure of society conflicted with his patriotism, and resulted in an ambivalent attitude to some 'rustics' who failed to keep to their traditional place in society. Walsingham records that in 1404 the common folk, both men and women, of Dartmouth and the neighbouring countryside defeated a force of French raiders with remarkable bravery, fighting not only with swords, but also with whips and various agricultural implements. Being unable to understand French, they killed many of the enemy who would have surrendered and paid ransom. Nevertheless they did capture a number. And so, Walsingham comments, 'nobles were taken according to the law of war by those who were not of noble birth, lords, or rather men in positions of authority, but by rustics of inferior fortune, and servants ruled masters.' The victors drove the captives 'like cattle' to Henry IV, who was both amazed and delighted. He thanked them and filled their purses, but kept the prisoners, 'because,' he said, 'although you must not think that I would seize your prize, I know who they are better than you do, and it is in your best interests to take my advice in this matter.'[114]

Clearly Walsingham was most preoccupied with the great division of society between lords and *plebs*. However, he was also interested in other social groups, the stability of which was necessary to the medieval hierarchy. He deplored the 'revolution' in the city of London in 1382, whereby those who had been inferiors gained supremacy, and those who had had power, lost it.[115] Similarly he criticized the knights on the 'crusade' in 1383 led by Henry Despenser, bishop of Norwich, because those who ought to have been the bishop's 'subjects' became his 'masters'.[116]

Moreover, Walsingham reflects the medieval attitude to youth and age; each age-group had its own attributes and consequent functions in society.[117] The medieval view was ambivalent. The young were good because they were strong and daring, but they had the demerits of rashness and impetuosity. The old were good because they had experience and perhaps wisdom; but they had the disadvantage of progressive decrepitude. Walsingham often writes of a man in relation to his age-group. He regarded Edward III's passion for Alice Perrers as particularly deplorable because of

[113] *CA*, pp. 325–6. Cf. *GASA*, iii. 355–6.
[114] *JT*, pp. 383–6.
[115] *CA*, p. 350. A reference mainly to the attack on the fishmongers' monopoly. See pp. 152 and n. 246, 184 below.
[116] *HA*, ii. 98.
[117] See A. Gransden, 'Childhood and youth in medieval England' in *Nottingham Mediaeval Studies*, xvi (1972), pp. 3–19 passim.

his advanced years. (Edward was in his sixties.) Edward was moved by frenzy not love, for 'a lustful young man sins, but a lustful old man raves'.[118] His last illness was not one natural to old age, but 'one which is said to be often endemic among the young because of the inordinate indulgence of their lasciviousness'.[119] (Walsingham also blames John de la Moote, abbot of St Albans, for retaining youthful impulses in old age.)[120]

Walsingham often mentions Richard II's youth and innocence in the early years of his reign.[121] Initially Walsingham thought that the young king's innate goodness would bring peace, but he soon began lamenting that the king, because of his youth, followed the counsel of the young,[122] and was deceived by courtiers[123] and misled by John of Gaunt.[124] He cites the bible: 'Woe to thee, O land, when thy king is a child.'[125] Walsingham gives a graphic description of Richard's coming of age. In 1389 Richard suddenly entered the council chamber and asked how old he was. The councillors replied that he was twenty. 'Therefore,' Richard said, 'I am of full age to govern my home, household and realm. It seems wrong to me that my condition should be worse than that of the least important of my subjects. For when any heir in my kingdom attains his twentieth year, he is allowed, on the death of his parent, to manage his own affairs freely.' Thereupon he demanded that the great seal should be handed to him, and began ruling 'according to his own will and power'.[126]

Sometimes Walsingham praised youth, and sometimes he criticized it. He praised the bravery of Prince Henry, 'although a boy', in the battle against Henry Percy ('Hotspur') in 1403,[127] and he praised the courage of 'the young and brave' Henry Despenser, bishop of Norwich, in face of the rebels in Norfolk during the Peasants' Revolt.[128] But he also called Despenser a 'headstrong and insolent youth', when he infringed the liberties of the priory at Wymondham,[129] and accused him of acting like Rehoboam (who followed the unwise counsel of young men) when, on a visit to Lynn, Despenser insisted, although discouraged by the aldermen, on receiving the same honours as the mayor.[130] And when some young monks of St Albans

---

[118] CA, p. 98.
[119] CA, pp. 103–4.
[120] GASA, iii. 465–6.
[121] See e.g. CA, pp. 150, 163.
[122] HA, ii. 126. Other chroniclers remark on Richard II's dependence on the counsel of the young; see, for example, VR II (for which see p. 158 and n. 4 below), pp. 152–3, and Usk (for which see p. 160 and n. 12 below), p. 83.
[123] CA, pp. 353–4.
[124] CA, p. 197.
[125] Eccl. x. 16, cited HA, ii. 97.
[126] HA, ii. 181–2.
[127] JT, p. 368.
[128] CA, p. 306.
[129] CA, p. 258.
[130] CA, pp. 139–40. Cf. 1 Kings xii. 8; 2 Chrons x. 8.

accepted papal chaplaincies in 1387, Walsingham said that they acted with youthful 'light-headedness'.[131]

It can, therefore, be shown that the medieval concept of a static, hierarchic society appears in Walsingham's work, as it had in Matthew Paris', although, because of the circumstances of the times, it was very differently applied.

Similarly, contemporary conditions and events influenced Walsingham's political attitudes. He, like Matthew Paris, held 'constitutional' views but in a rather different form. Matthew had believed that if the rights and privileges, as defined by charters and ancient custom, of all people and institutions were observed, England's political troubles would be ended. A corollary to such a concept was the limitation of authority, whether of king or pope; but in Matthew's day the means by which such a limitation was to be achieved was uncertain. However, by the late fourteenth century the 'community of the realm' as represented in parliament had gained enough power to be able on occasion to impose its wishes on the government. Besides responding to the development of parliament, Walsingham was profoundly influenced by the revolution of 1399. In general it can be argued that until the Lancastrian coup, his 'constitutionalism' bears comparison with Matthew Paris', though moulded by different contemporary conditions. But after the coup Walsingham's 'constitutionalism' seems to have a less secure theoretical basis than Matthew Paris'—he was less consistent, and has with some justification been accused of being a time-server.[132]

Walsingham identifies himself with the commons in his account of the Good Parliament of 1376. The knights stood for the good of the realm against the government, which was controlled by John of Gaunt. (The Black Prince, Walsingham intimates, favoured the knights.)[133] The speaker of the commons, Sir Peter de la Mare, was Walsingham's hero:[134]

> God filled Sir Peter's heart with abundant wisdom from his own unlimited supply, and had endowed him with the courage to fulfil what his mind conceived, and with surprising eloquence. Moreover, He gave him perseverance and constancy, so that he neither feared the threats of his opponents, nor was disturbed by the plots of his rivals. Sir Peter was always ready to suffer everything for truth and justice, that is he who had laid foundations on a firm rock, in accordance with his name, was immovable in the face of his adversaries. He yielded to no threat of the magnates, he was softened by no gifts, but followed the straight way of justice.

[131] *GASA*, ii. 418.
[132] See Kingsford, *Hist. Lit.* p. 15.
[133] *CA*, pp. 86–7.
[134] *CA*, pp. 72–3.

Walsingham had personal contact with at least one member of parliament, Sir Thomas de la Hoo. Sir Thomas told Walsingham of a dream he had when lying in bed. He had been wondering 'how or by what means the king could be brought to lead a better life and benefit from wise counsel, and how the present abuses in the kingdom could be rooted out'. Then Sir Thomas slept and had a dream which indicated that the Holy Spirit had given seven gifts to him and his colleagues who had met for the benefit and reform of the kingdom.[135]

Walsingham became critical of Richard II even during his minority, in the 1380s. He expresses disapproval of the king's practice of frequently moving from place to place like 'a vagabond'.[136] Richard's visits with large retinues were a heavy financial burden on the abbeys, especially because he and his queen expected rich gifts. On one visit to St Albans (in 1383) Richard borrowed the abbot's palfrey but did not return it. On this occasion Walsingham criticized Richard for excessive impetuosity; he was hurrying to London because Henry Despenser, bishop of Norwich, had sent asking for help for his 'crusade'. But by the time Richard reached London his ardour had cooled, and the bishop had to make peace with the French. Thus, comments Walsingham, citing Horace, 'the mountains heaved, and gave birth to a ridiculous mouse.'[137]

Walsingham also blames Richard for his 'obscene' affection for Robert de Vere, earl of Oxford (whom he made duke of Ireland in 1386).[138] This criticism is reminiscent of charges made against Edward II. Other criticisms recall the days of Henry III and Matthew Paris' invectives. Walsingham accuses Richard of favouring foreigners, notably the Bohemians in the entourage of Queen Anne. According to him they found their position at court so pleasant that they forgot their native land.[139] The opposition of Richard Scrope to favouritism towards foreigners and others at court, and especially to the consequent gifts of crown property, was, in Walsingham's opinion, the reason why the king dismissed him from the chancellorship in 1382. Scrope had been 'chosen by the community of the realm with the assent of the lords', and his dismissal angered the magnates and the 'community of the realm' because it was contrary to the customs of the kingdom.[140] Also reminiscent of Henry III's reign is Walsingham's attack on evil counsellors. Richard took the advice of malicious courtiers and hated his 'natural and faithful magnates'.[141] In the constitutional crisis

---

[135] CA, pp. 70–2. For Thomas de la Hoo's dream and career see Anthony Goodman, 'Sir Thomas Hoo and the parliament of 1376' in *BIHR*, xli (1968), pp. 139–49. For Walsingham's other informants, and for his written sources see pp. 149–51 below.

[136] *HA*, ii. 96.

[137] *HA*, ii. 103. Cf. Horace, *De Arte Poetica*, 1. 139.

[138] *HA*, ii. 148; *JT*, p. 185.

[139] *HA*, ii. 119.

[140] *CA*, pp. 353–4.

[141] *CA*, p. 354; *HA*, ii. 149, 152.

of 1387 and 1388 Walsingham records that the lords appellant, acting 'for the good of the king and kingdom', demanded the removal of the 'traitors whom the king kept with him', and threatened to choose another king, who would take the advice of his magnates.[142]

Walsingham complains about the king's treatment of parliament. He asserts in the annal for 1382 that statutes made in parliament by the community and nobility of the realm were of no effect, because they were changed and abrogated by the king and his private council.[143] And under 1387 he records that Richard tried to persuade the sheriffs to allow no knight of the county or shire to be elected to parliament unless chosen by the king and his council. But the sheriffs replied that they had not the power to oppose the 'commons', who insisted on maintaining the established custom of election of knights by the 'commons' themselves.[144]

Walsingham's bitterest invective was reserved for John of Gaunt, the virtual ruler of England in the early years of Richard II's minority. Walsingham abuses him eloquently and was prepared to record rumour and scandal to Gaunt's discredit. For example, he tells the story that Gaunt was not the son of Edward III; the baby born to Queen Philippa in Ghent died and was replaced by a Flemish infant.[145] Gaunt, the protagonist against Peter de la Mare in the Good Parliament, acted with unbridled malice and greed, fearing neither God nor man, and supporting the traitors.[146] He also tried to subvert the liberties of the city of London in 1377,[147] supported the heretic John Wyclif,[148] planned to extort money unjustly from the church and people in 1378,[149] and, in the same year, behaved like a coward when commanding the expedition to St Malo.[150] Walsingham's abuse peters out after the dramatic description of Gaunt's repentance in 1381.[151]

On the basis of this evidence it seems just to describe Walsingham's attitude to the politics of Richard II's minority as 'constitutional': he persistently criticized king and government, and supported the attempts by the magnates and parliament to limit royal power. The question arises whether Walsingham's views were the result of reason and principle, or whether he arrived at them on account of ulterior motives. It is true that he might have hated Richard because he took the abbot's palfrey. And he might have hated John of Gaunt because the duke took thirty oak

[142] HA, ii. 172.
[143] CA, p. 333.
[144] HA, ii. 161.
[145] CA, p. 107. For Walsingham's later modification of his abuse of Gaunt see pp. 142–3 below.
[146] CA, pp. 79, 87.
[147] CA, p. 115.
[148] CA, pp. 115 et seq.
[149] CA, p. 211.
[150] CA, p. 205.
[151] See p. 130 above.

trees from one of the abbot's estates for works on his castle at Hertford (the abbot said he would have gladly paid £30 to save them).[152] It is also true that Walsingham had a friend and informant whose interests were opposed to John of Gaunt's. This was Sir John Philpot, a rich citizen and mayor of London (1378–79), who defended the liberties of the Londoners against Gaunt in 1377, and brought about the subsequent reconciliation between the king and citizens.[153] (Moreover, there is the remote possibility that Sir Peter de la Mare was a relative of Thomas de la Mare, abbot of St Albans: if so, it is reasonable to suppose that a chronicler of St Albans would sympathize with him politically.)[154]

Nevertheless, these factors do not justify the dismissal of Walsingham's 'constitutionalism' as unidealistic. There is no reason to suppose that this part of his chronicle is not a fairly accurate reflection of the views of many of his contemporaries. The violent attacks on John of Gaunt in 1377, when the Londoners paraded his arms reversed, and during the Peasants' Revolt in 1381, when his palace of the Savoy was sacked, show that feeling against him ran high.[155] Walsingham implies that there was a decline in Richard's popularity as the reign proceeded. He does not abuse him at the beginning of the reign. On the contrary, he hoped that the reign would be a success,[156] and admired Richard's heroism during the Peasants' Revolt. Richard met the rebels at Smithfield on 15 June, and behaved 'with an understanding and bravery beyond his years'. When, on the murder of their leader, Wat Tyler, the rebels threatened to shoot, Richard said: 'What are you doing, my men? Surely you do not wish to shoot at your king? Do not quarrel nor grieve the death of a traitor and a scoundrel, for I will be your king, your captain and your leader.'[157] And in the course of the revolt Richard went daily to Blackheath to inspect his troops: 'he, armed, rode first among the armed, on a great war horse, with his banner carried before him; he loved to be seen in the army and to be recognized as lord by his men.'[158] In fact Walsingham most probably reflects a change in contemporary opinion: as Richard's popularity declined, John of Gaunt's rose.

Walsingham's treatment of the political crisis from 1397 to 1399 is

---

[152] *CA*, p. 164.

[153] *CA*, pp. 120–1, 147. Walsingham's sympathy for Sir John Philpot in London politics was no doubt strengthened by the fact that Philpot's rival, John of Northampton (mayor 1381–3) favoured Wycliffism; *HA*, ii. 65–6, 71. For Philpot as an informant of Walsingham see pp. 149–50 below.

[154] Professor Roskell considers it very unlikely that Sir Peter de la Mare and Abbot Thomas were relatives, especially as Walsingham never mentions their kinship; see J. S. Roskell, 'Sir Peter de la Mare, speaker for the commons in parliament in 1376 and 1377' in *Nottingham Mediaeval Studies*, ii (1958), p. 26.

[155] *CA*, pp. 125, 288–9.

[156] *CA*, pp. 150–1.

[157] *CA*, p. 297.

[158] *CA*, p. 313.

different. His antagonism to the expansion of royal authority remains, but it is expressed in a more extreme form, and the narrative of events is less convincing. He wrote this section after the revolution of 1399, and adopted the Lancastrian point of view. He used as a source the new régime's official account of the deposition, the 'record and process', which was enrolled on the rolls of parliament.[159] (St Albans was one of the monasteries to provide Henry with chronicle material to justify his coup.)[160] Moreover, Walsingham used the 'record and process' elsewhere in his account. The text from the end of the annal for 1396 is a highly coloured narrative of Richard's arbitrary rule, apparently written as an historical introduction to the account of the deposition itself. Some passages are copied word for word from the articles accusing Richard of misgovernment, which were included in the 'record and process'. (For example, the articles are the source of the statement in Walsingham in the annal for 1397 that Richard persuaded parliament in 1398 to delegate its powers, and that he had entries on the parliament rolls altered and deleted.)[161]

Other passages in the section from 1397 to 1399, which are not derived from the 'record and process', have such an exaggerated, romantic tone that their melodramatic details are hard to believe.[162] It will be suggested in the next chapter that the moving description of Gloucester's arrest was part of a tract designed to arouse the reader's admiration for the duke and indignation at Richard II.[163] The account of the earl of Arundel's execution is in a similar style.[164] It tells how Arundel asked, when he reached Charing Cross on the way from Westminster palace to the Tower, where he was to be executed, that his hands should be unbound so that he could give alms to the poor—which he did with great devotion. Then, his hands cruelly tied again, he was pushed forward by the Cheshire guards and escorted to the Tower. People deeply lamented the fate of such a famous, rich nobleman, whose chivalric renown had spread far and wide. He piously confessed his sins, but vehemently denied that he was a traitor. When ready for execution he looked sharply at Thomas Mowbray, earl of Nottingham, and Thomas de Holand, earl of Kent, who were standing

---

[159] For the 'record and process', which was copied on to the rolls of parliament, see p. 186 and n. 167 below. Walsingham's version (*JT*, pp. 252–86) corresponds closely with the official printed text (*Rot. Parl.* iii. 416, no. 10 to 424, no. 60), but has one significant addition (*JT*, p. 282 and see n. 3); see H. G. Richardson, 'Richard II's last parliament', in *EHR*, lii (1937), p. 41.

[160] *JT*, p. 252.

[161] *JT*, p. 222; *Rot. Parl.* iii. 418, no. 25 (and *JT*, pp. 263–4). For other examples of passages in Walsingham's narrative for 1397 derived from the 'record and process' see: *JT*, p. 225, *Rot. Parl.* iii. 419, no. 27 (and *JT*, p. 264); *JT*, p. 226, *Rot. Parl.* iii. 419, no. 28 (and *JT*, p. 265); *JT*, pp. 236–7, *Rot. Parl.* iii. 420, no. 44 (and *JT*, p. 271–2); *JT*, p. 239, *Rot. Parl.* iii. 420, no. 41 (and *JT*, p. 270).

[162] See p. 141 below.

[163] *JT*, pp. 203–6. See p. 187 and n. 180 below.

[164] *JT*, pp. 216–18.

nearby 'impatient for his death', and said: 'Indeed, you ought not to be here on this occasion. For I educated, enriched and exalted you, and you shamefully turn on me, with ingratitude. Without doubt, God willing, the time will come and shortly, when there will be as much wonder at your misfortune as at my present predicament.' He then forgave and kissed the executioner, asked him to make quick work of it, and tested the blade of the sword. He was beheaded at one blow, 'but', writes Walsingham, 'his headless trunk raised itself to its feet and stood, with no assistance, for the space of time it takes to say the Lord's prayer.' This passage, with its eulogistic tone, its apparent prediction of the fate of the two earls (Nottingham was exiled for life by Richard II in 1398, and Kent was executed by Henry IV in 1400), and its tale of the miraculous behaviour of Arundel's dead body, cannot be sober reportage: it is surely Lancastrian propaganda.

Similarly, in order to give Henry IV's coronation an especial sanction, Walsingham inserted another passage which reads like Lancastrian propaganda. He alleges that once, when Richard II was rummaging among the various chests stored in the Tower ('because he was very inquisitive about the relics of his ancestors'),[165] he found a phial of sacred unction which had been owned by St Thomas of Canterbury. Hoping it would make him 'glorious and victorious', he asked the archbishop to anoint him with it. But the archbishop, 'as though with divine foresight', refused, unwilling that Richard should be anointed twice. Nevertheless, the king carried the phial with him whenever he was in danger, and on his capture by the Lancastrians in 1399 he handed it to the archbishop. Therefore, this sacred oil, 'sent as it were from heaven', was used for the first time at the coronation of Henry IV; many people, Walsingham wrote, thought that God had purposely reserved the oil for him whom He had chosen, with the promise of more grace than any of his predecessors had enjoyed.[166]

---

[165] Another example of Richard's antiquarian interests is recorded on the patent rolls. In 1386 he granted, under his signet (which indicates his personal interest), £11. 18s. 0d. 'old sterlings' found during repairs in the ground under the high altar of the chapel of St Hilda, co. York, on condition that 'they are brought and the king that he may look at them'; *CPR, 1385–1389*, p. 162. I owe this reference to Dr John Palmer.

[166] *JT*, pp. 297–300. See P. E. Schramm, *A History of the English Coronation*, translated by L. G. Wickham Legg (Oxford 1937), pp. 131–3, 137 and n. 5. For the story treated as Lancastrian propaganda, together with evidence for the use of the sacred oil of St Thomas for the coronations of the succeeding Lancastrian kings, Henry IV and Henry V and Henry VI, and of Richard III and possibly of Edward IV, see J. W. McKenna, 'The coronation oil of Yorkist kings' in *EHR*, lxxxii (1967), pp. 102–4, and cf. Walter Ullmann, 'Thomas Becket's miraculous oil' in *Journal of Theological Studies*, new series, viii (1957), pp. 129 et seq. and the same author's edition of the *Liber Regalis* (Henry Bradshaw Soc. 1961), p. 90 n. 3. The same story, clearly from the same source, is in the *Eulogium Historiarum; EH*, iii. 380. This story, considered in conjunction with the panegyrical passages on Thomas Arundel's life, raises the question whether it did not form part of a propagandist biography of the archbishop similar in style to the biography postulated above of his brother Richard, earl of Arundel, and also to that of the duke of Gloucester; cf. pp. 181 n. 137, 187–8 n. 180, 199 n. 38 below. A recent scholar, however, argues, in my view unconvincingly, that the

Thus there is ample evidence proving that Walsingham wrote the section from the end of 1396 up to the autumn of 1399 after Henry's coup. It may also be suggested tentatively that he wrote the annals from 1393 to 1396 at the same time. He stopped composing his *Chronica Majora* when he went to Wymondham as prior in 1394. The exact date when he recommenced work on the chronicle after his return in 1396, is unknown. It can be argued that he started again after the 1399 revolution: the need to put the revolution in historical perspective provided a direct incentive to bring the chronicle up to date. Furthermore, it was at this time that Walsingham revised the earlier part of the *Chronica Majora*, to make it more acceptable to the Lancastrian dynasty.[167] As has been seen, the section from 1369 to about 1381 has bitter abuse of Henry IV's father, John of Gaunt. (Walsingham had revised one copy before he went to Wymondham, to modify the scurrilous attacks on Gaunt, because it was intended for Gaunt's younger brother, Thomas of Woodstock, duke of Gloucester.)[168] The full-scale revision carried out after the revolution involved the suppression of some passages injurious to Gaunt's reputation and the modification of others. Derogatory remarks on his greed, lust, cruelty and cowardice, and the aspersions on him for his hatred of the Londoners and possible connivance with the French, are omitted, or subtly altered to remove the venom.[169] An example of such an alteration is in the account of Gaunt's unsuccessful expedition to St Malo in 1378.[170] Walsingham originally wrote with reference to the offer of peace by the people of St Malo:

> The duke, not knowing how to use a peace divinely granted to him and his men, when he had heard the generous terms, soon swelled with pride, and became so arrogant at heart that he spurned the proffered peace. The duke, indeed, because reputedly it was his practice to say not 'come' but 'go', ordered his men to try their strength against the townsmen, while he himself kept at a distance, to watch the course and outcome of events.

After revision this same passage read:

---

[167] story of St Thomas's oil was not part of official Lancastrian propaganda; see T. A. Sandquist, 'The holy oil of St Thomas of Canterbury' in *Essays in Medieval History presented to Bertie Wilkinson*, ed. T. A. Sandquist and M. R. Powicke (Toronto 1969), pp. 339–44.

[167] For the approximate date of this revision see V. H. Galbraith, 'Thomas Walsingham and the St Albans chronicle (1272–1422)' in *EHR*, xlvii (1932), pp. 21–5, and *St AC*, p. li.

[168] This copy is Bodley MS. 2752 (now 316) in the Bodleian Library, Oxford. BL MS. Harley 3634 was originally part of the same volume which contained the *Polychronicon* and the St Albans chronicle from 1328 to 1388. It was written in or soon after 1388 for Thomas of Woodstock. See *CA*, pp. xiv-xviii, xxvi-xxvii, xxxii, and F. Madan *et al.*, *A Summary Catalogue of Western Manuscripts in the Bodleian Library at Oxford* (Oxford 1895–1953, 7 vols in 8), ii. pt i, pp. 527–8.

[169] See e.g. *CA*, pp. 79 and n. 1, 99 and n. 1, 108 and n. 3, 168 and n. 1, 197 and nn., 211 and nn., 223 and nn. 5–7.

[170] *CA*, pp. xxiv, 205.

The duke judging that the citizens' submission was madness, as many said, when he had heard the generous terms, did not receive [the citizens] but completely rebuffed them, and so spurned the proffered peace. The duke, indeed, when he had collected the army and what was necessary for attacking the town, ordered his men to go and try their strength against the townsmen, while he himself stayed at a distance to watch the warriors and reward the best according to their merits.

Walsingham maintains a pro-Lancastrian bias, although in an attenuated form, until the end of the *Chronica Majora* in 1420. He gives the Lancastrian version of Richard II's death: Richard died of starvation because he was so saddened by the death of his brother John de Holand, earl of Huntingdon, that he refused to eat, and when at the persuasion of his friends he tried to break his fast, his throat was too constricted to swallow.[171] Walsingham praises Henry IV for his (supposedly) courteous treatment of the captive Richard,[172] for his refusal later to benefit from Richard's property,[173] for his staunch support of the church[174] and for his bold defiance of the French in 1412. ('I believe', Walsingham writes, 'that he could have taken France if the strength of his body had equalled the strength of his spirit.')[175] In the dedication of the *Ypodigma Neustriae* to Henry V, Walsingham describes him as 'the most magnificent and illustrious Henry, king of the French and the English, conqueror of Normandy, most serene prince of Wales and lord of Ireland and Aquitaine, by the grace of God, everywhere and always victorious.'[176] Walsingham eulogizes him for his virtues and conquests and wise rule. He asserts that on his accession Henry V became a new man, 'honest, modest and serious, aspiring to every possible virtue'.[177] He praises his bravery and piety;[178] he records Henry's three religious foundations at Sheen, his especial veneration for the Virgin Mary and his good treatment of monks in France during the war.[179]

Walsingham's attitude to politics from 1397 must be regarded as 'Lancastrian' rather than 'constitutional'. The Lancastrian party itself can only be regarded as 'constitutional' if two dubious premises are accepted: that Richard II tried to dispense with parliament in 1398; and that the Lancastrians upheld parliamentary authority.[180] Walsingham himself

---

[171] *JT*, pp. 330–1.
[172] *JT*, p. 251.
[173] *JT*, p. 335.
[174] *St AC*, p. 56.
[175] *St AC*, p. 64.
[176] *Ypodigma*, p. 3.
[177] *St AC*, p. 69.
[178] *St AC*, p. 96.
[179] *St AC*, pp. 82, 121, 110.
[180] See e.g. J. G. Edwards, 'The parliamentary committee of 1398' in *EHR*, lv (1925), pp. 321–33; G. Lapsley, 'The parliamentary title of Henry IV' in *EHR*, xlix (1934), pp. 423–49,

shows no particular regard for parliament in his account of the Lancastrian kings. In fact he criticizes Henry IV for keeping parliament in session so long that the knights were put to inordinate expense, and he criticizes the knights themselves for planning to despoil the church.[181] On the other hand St Albans had close connections with magnates supporting the opposition to Richard. Abbot Thomas de la Mare was apparently the duke of Gloucester's godfather, and both Gloucester and the earl of Warwick were the abbey's benefactors.[182] There is even evidence suggesting that in the political crisis of 1386–8 Thomas de la Mare was involved in a plot with the duke of Gloucester, the earl of Warwick and the earl of Arundel, against Richard.[183] It seems that the parties met first at St Albans and then in Arundel castle, before they were betrayed to the king.[184]

It can, therefore, be seen that Walsingham had many features in common with Matthew Paris, whose work he undertook to continue. His technique and distribution of material into separate books, his idea of history and his attitude to contemporary society and politics are all reminiscent of Matthew Paris'. On the other hand, inevitably his historiography was influenced by the preconceptions and conditions of his own time. Although he shared Matthew Paris' desire to maintain the social and political *status quo*, the method he advocated for doing so, the preservation of the traditional social group was characteristic of the fourteenth century and not of the thirteenth. Similarly, his 'constitutionalism' resembles Matthew Paris' only in a very general sense. And some aspects of Walsingham's historiography are so characteristic of his own day that a comparison with Matthew Paris would be unprofitable.

While a recurrent theme in Matthew Paris' chronicles is the wickedness of all enemies of St Albans, Walsingham is more preoccupied with the abbey's friends. His chronicles are strongly biased in favour of these friends,

---

577–606. For a summary of the arguments see B. Wilkinson, *The Constitutional History of Medieval England 1216–1399* (London 1948–58, 3 vols), ii. 284–304.

[181] *JT*, p. 418; *St AC*, pp. 56–7. *JT*, p. 414; *St AC*, p. 52.

[182] Both Thomas Beauchamp, earl of Warwick, and Thomas of Woodstock, duke of Gloucester, have entries in the *Book of Benefactors* (for which see p. 123 and n. 52 above); *JT*, p. 434; Nero D VII, ff. 109, 110.

[183] The evidence is in the continuation of the *Eulogium Historiarum* and in the chronicle of Adam of Usk (for the printed editions see pp. 158 n. 5 and 160 n. 12 below, respectively); *EH*, iii. 375, and *AU*, pp. 16–17. The full and largely fictional account in the *Traïson et Mort* (for the printed edition see p. 162 n. 27 below) of a plot in 1397, in which the author alleged the abbot of St Albans took part (by then John de la Moote was abbot, Thomas de la Mare having died in 1396), probably derives ultimately from knowledge of the plot ten years earlier; *T et M*, p. 122, and see J. J. N. Palmer, 'The authorship, date and historical value of the French chronicles on the Lancastrian revolution in *BJRL*, li (1978–9), pp. 400–8.

[184] *T et M*, pp. 3–6. It is also noteworthy that Richard's supporter Thomas Merks, bishop of Carlisle, was entrusted to the custody of the abbot of St Albans at the time of the deposition in 1399: ibid., p. 71, and *JT*, p. 314; cf. p. 150 below.

whose names he inscribed in the *Book of Benefactors*. Among the principal ones (besides the duke of Gloucester and the earl of Warwick, who have already been mentioned) were Sir John Philpot, Thomas Percy, earl of Worcester (1397–1403), Sir Robert Knolles and Thomas Arundel, archbishop of Canterbury (1396–7, 1399–1414). Walsingham records, often with laudatory comments, a number of facts about Philpot's career. He tells how Philpot, 'a man of outstanding gifts and extraordinary wealth', put to shame John of Gaunt and other lords, 'who ought to have provided for the defence of the kingdom', by personally financing a fleet to defeat a combination of Scottish, French and Spanish pirates in 1378.[185] By so doing Philpot won the praise of everyone with the exception of his enemies, the nobles; in Walsingham's opinion Philpot's action was justified because his objective was not gain, but to relieve the sufferings of the people. Again in 1380 Philpot earned Walsingham's praise by paying the debts contracted by the force destined for the expedition in aid of John duke of Brittany, and by redeeming the arms, armour and the like which the soldiers had pawned in order to buy food. And in 1383 Philpot provided transport for Henry Despenser's 'crusade'.[186] On recording Philpot's death in 1384 Walsingham writes that 'he was a most noble knight and citizen, who had laboured more than any for the good of the realm, and had often helped the king and kingdom with money and support.'[187] Similarly Walsingham records facts about the career of Thomas Percy ('a most zealous friend of our monastery')[188] in flattering terms. For example, he records that only Percy achieved anything laudable in the naval war against the French in 1378, and that he and Sir Hugh Calverley (in contrast to Sir John Arundel) compensated those who had suffered from the marauding soldiers before the army sailed for the Breton expedition of 1379.[189] Walsingham follows the military career of Sir Robert Knolles, a generous benefactor, with equal interest. Recording his death, he writes:[190]

> [Sir Robert] was an invincible knight, whose arms harassed the kingdom of France for many years, who frightened the duchy of Brittany and terrified the realm of Spain. Besides deserving praise for his deeds in war, he constructed a magnificent bridge near Rochester over the Medway, endowed the Carmelite house in London, founded a chantry at Pontefract, and completed many other works, which would have exhausted a royal treasury.

---

[185] *CA*, pp. 199–200. For the entry relating to Philpot in the *Book of Benefactors* see *JT*, p. 460, and Nero D VII, f. 106ᵛ. For the influence of patrons and benefactors on other chroniclers of this time see pp. 178–85 below.

[186] *CA*, pp. 266–7; *HA*, ii. 96.

[187] *HA*, ii. 115.

[188] *JT*, p. 437.

[189] *CA*, pp. 192, 249–50.

[190] *St AC*, p. 22. For other references see the index to *HA*, ii. See also *JT*, p. 453; Nero D VII, f. 109ᵛ.

Walsingham has a considerable amount of information about Archbishop Arundel, 'a most generous friend of this place'.[191] (Arundel himself was an acquaintance of Sir John Philpot, who had served his father in an official capacity.)[192] Walsingham represents Arundel as a champion of the church, describing how he reprimanded Henry IV because the king and his knights insufficiently venerated the eucharist,[193] how he thwarted the attempts of the knights in parliament to despoil the church[194] and how he battled against Lollardy.[195]

Like many other fourteenth century writers, Walsingham was patriotic. He considered that England was degraded by weak government. He seems to have had a perennial fear that the country would again be reduced to anarchy as it had been during the Peasants' Revolt.[196] This preoccupation was closely linked with his concern, which has already been discussed, that people should keep in their own social groups. Walsingham's fear of anarchy was one reason why he wanted strong government. He criticized Richard II partly because of his failure to keep order in the kingdom. Describing how in 1384 Thomas of Woodstock burst into the king's chamber threatening with death anyone who accused his brother John of Gaunt, Walsingham comments that this would have been a capital offence if the country had been properly governed.[197] And in the annal for 1399, with reference to Richard's aspiration to be elected Holy Roman emperor,[198] Walsingham asserts that two or three electors demurred because they did not think that Richard, who was unable to keep order in England, could possibly rule the empire effectively:[199] perhaps Walsingham was here expressing his own view. He deplored the effects of lawlessness on the poor—their sufferings as a result of marauding soldiers, whether the enemy or English soldiers living off the land.[200]

Moreover, weak government at home left England defenceless. Walsingham laments the degradation of England in 1378, when the country was weakened by internal corruption and was exposed to attack from abroad.[201] Walsingham wholeheartedly supported the French war. He defended the justice of the English king's claim to the throne of France,[202] and one of the criticisms he levelled against Richard II and

[191] JT, p. 443; Nero D VII, f. 87.
[192] See Margaret Aston, Thomas Arundel (Oxford 1967), pp. 17, 195.
[193] JT, p. 395.
[194] St AC, pp. 1–2.
[195] JT, pp. 414–15.
[196] See e.g. HA, ii. 126.
[197] HA, ii. 114–15.
[198] For Richard II's proposed election as emperor, see, with reference to the passage in Walsingham, E. Perroy, L'Angleterre et le Grand Schisme d'Occident (Paris 1933), pp. 342–3 and nn.
[199] JT, p. 199.
[200] See e.g. CA, p. 275.
[201] CA, p. 196.
[202] CA, p. 267.

John of Gaunt and their advisers was that they planned to cede England's possessions in France.²⁰³ His attitude to the French is chauvinistic. He calls them 'grave robbers' because of their excessive, as he thought, love of loot.²⁰⁴ He accuses them of cowardice, cruelty and impiety,²⁰⁵ and expresses the view that the people of France would have preferred English to French rule, because their own government imposed such heavy taxes on them.²⁰⁶ He also blames the French nobility for failing to defend the poor against hostile armies.²⁰⁷

Moreover, Walsingham's patriotism appears both in his criticism of the English and in his praise of them. He admired the virtues of bravery and self discipline. When writing of exploits in battle, he shows the influence of the chivalric tradition. He bitterly deplores any occasion when the English did not fight creditably, and particularly criticizes the nobility for any failure to defend the poor. For example, he blames the earl of Arundel for not defending Lewes castle, and John of Gaunt for abandoning Pevensey castle in face of French invaders in 1377: he alleges that Gaunt said of the castle 'they may destroy it to its foundations—I have the power to build it up again'.²⁰⁸ Walsingham also accuses other classes besides the nobility of cowardice, remarking in general that the English, who not long ago had equalled leopards in courage, were now effeminate.²⁰⁹ When the rebels in 1381 stormed the Tower of London, he writes that the guard of 600 men-at-arms and 600 archers were powerless to resist, and nearly died of fright, forgetting the brave deeds and glory of their forefathers.²¹⁰ Similarly, he accuses the Londoners of panic ('they behaved as if drunk ... and fled and hid like rabbits and mice') under threat of French invasion in 1386.²¹¹ Walsingham particularly inveighs against those knights who fell short of the chivalric ideal. He writes of the failure of the knights in England to help Henry Despenser on his 'crusade':²¹²

> Alas! Oh land, which formerly produced men respected by all at home and who inspired fear abroad, now spews up effeminate men, objects of ridicule among the enemy and of common talk among their fellow citizens!

Again in 1385 the 'effeminate' English knights, 'once brave, now cowardly, once stout-hearted, now spiritless and effete', thought only of flight

---

²⁰³ *HA*, ii. 170, 174 (s.a. 1387); cf. *JT*, p. 236 (s.a. 1399).
²⁰⁴ See *St AC*, pp. 97, 99, 113.
²⁰⁵ See *CA*, p. 277; *HA*, ii. 107, 120; *St AC*, p. 99.
²⁰⁶ *CA*, p. 277.
²⁰⁷ *CA*, pp. 276–7.
²⁰⁸ *CA*, pp. 168–9.
²⁰⁹ *CA*, p. 203.
²¹⁰ *CA*, p. 290.
²¹¹ *HA*, ii. 145.
²¹² *HA*, ii. 104.

when the French attacked the south coast. (It was left to the men of Portsmouth and Dartmouth to retaliate with fearless attacks on the French coast.)[213] Walsingham considered the knights at the royal court especially degenerate. They were, he writes, 'more valiant in bed than in battle, better armed with words than with the lance'. And they were a bad influence on the young Richard II, because they did not instruct him in arms, or in other occupations (such as hunting and hawking) which were suitable and honourable for a king in peacetime.[214]

Nevertheless, Walsingham sometimes praises English soldiers. The Black Prince was for him, as for many of his contemporaries, the flower of chivalry. On the prince's death he writes:[215]

> While he lived none feared enemy invasion; when he was there, none feared hostile attack, nor was any evil deed or martial deficiency allowed—as was said of Alexander the Great, he attacked no people without conquering them, and laid siege to no city without taking it.

Walsingham had especial praise for individual knights, heroes like Sir Hugh Calverley ('who was always, even in the direst straits, the most faithful comrade and loyal companion'),[216] and Sir John Hawkwood ('of world renown ... whose unbelievable deeds of valour deserve a book of their own').[217] Some of Walsingham's most vivid prose describes chivalric exploits. He also explicitly praises the English nobles who fought in Brittany, for their bravery, good discipline (they did not allow their soldiers to loot) and for 'their clean living and innocent hearts'.[218] And he more than once mentions the success of the English archers.[219]

Walsingham's most patriotic passages relate to Henry V's victories in France. He expatiates, for example, on the hardships suffered by the English army on the way to the battle of Agincourt, their hunger, thirst and cold, and on their piety before the battle itself (they spent the night praying and confessing). He describes the battle (with citations from Virgil, Lucan, Persius and Statius), in which the king 'fought not as a king, but as a knight, leading the way, the first to assail the enemy, giving and receiving cruel blows'. The knights themselves rivalled the king in valour.[220] Walsingham gives this account of Henry's reception in London after the battle:[221]

---

[213] *HA*, ii. 127–8.
[214] *HA*, ii. 156.
[215] *CA*, p. 91.
[216] *HA*, ii. 100.
[217] *JT*, p. 171.
[218] *CA*, p. 275.
[219] See e.g. *HA*, ii. 92; *St AC*, p. 96.
[220] *St AC*, pp. 93–7.
[221] *St AC*, pp. 97–8.

It is impossible to describe the joy, the rejoicing and the triumph with which [King Henry] was welcomed by the Londoners, because the elaborate arrangements, the enormous expenditure, the variety of spectacles would need a short book to themselves. When [the king] approached the church of St Paul's he was met by a solemn procession of twelve mitred bishops who led him to the high altar. After he had completed his devotions, he returned to the cemetery (where meanwhile the horses had been assembled) and, mounting his charger, rode through the centre of London to Westminster. He was met by an extraordinarily large crowd—it seemed to comprise everyone in London. The abbot and convent of Westminster received him with a magnificent procession and led him to the church.

It remains to consider the value of Walsingham's work as source material for the historian today, and its literary merit. Walsingham's great gift was as a reporter of current events. He was excellently informed and wrote close in time to the events he recorded—and thus reflects the opinions of at least some of his contemporaries. He often wrote in considerable detail, in clear, expressive prose, and sometimes gave reasonable explanations for what happened.

As an historian Walsingham benefited from the location of St Albans on a royal road within twenty miles of London, and from its importance as a centre of affairs. Numerous official documents, both secular and ecclesiastical, reached St Albans, many of which Walsingham copied into his chronicle (unlike Matthew Paris he did not compile a *Liber Additamentorum*). He may also have used an occasional newsletter.[222] It has been mentioned above that Walsingham expounded at length the tenets of John Wyclif and his followers, because he believed in stating even opponents' views.[223] For the same reason he copied two cryptic letters in English circulated by the rebels during the Peasants' Revolt.[224] He also used written sources for his account of Henry IV's coronation—books kept at Westminster and those in the keeping of the archbishop of Canterbury.[225]

Walsingham obtained much of his information by word of mouth. Occasionally he names his informants. As has been seen, Sir Thomas de la Hoo, a member of the Good Parliament, told him about his vision.[226] Sir John Philpot informed him concerning the money he had contributed

---

[222] See p. 127 n. 71 above. Walsingham may also have used a newsletter for his account of the capture of Pontoise in 1419; see *St AC*, p. 123. However, Professor Galbraith did not identify any surviving newsletter as having been used by Walsingham for his chronicle from 1406 to 1420; *St AC*, p. xxii.

[223] See p. 132 and n. 101 above.

[224] *CA*, p. 322. See R. B. Dobson, *The Peasants' Revolt* (London 1970), pp. 380–1.

[225] *JT*, p. 292.

[226] P. 137 and n. 135 above.

to the expedition to France in 1380.[227] Walsingham met Augustine, bishop of Oslo, when the latter visited England on an embassy to negotiate the marriage of Henry IV's daughter Philippa to Eric IX:[228] he records that he discussed the life of St Alban with the bishop.[229] Sometimes Walsingham merely states that he heard of an event from those who were present, but often he gives the reader no explicit indication of the source of his information.

A number of people stayed at St Albans from whom, or from whose *entourage*, Walsingham must have heard news. During the suppression of the Peasants' Revolt the king visited St Albans, and his justices tried the malefactors there.[230] John Balle, of whom Walsingham gives a full biography, was brought to St Albans where he was tried and executed.[231] Walsingham may have collected some of his information about the revolt in London from such judicial proceedings and from those against townsmen who went to join the rebels in London. His knowledge of the rising in East Anglia may have derived from William de Ufford, earl of Suffolk, who fled to St Albans to escape from the rioters at Norwich after an unwelcome invitation to be their leader.[232] At other crises important men stayed at St Albans.[233] For example, in 1399, the duke of York came to St Albans to summon forces against Henry Bolingbroke,[234] then Henry himself, with Richard II under guard, stayed two nights there on the way from Wales to London,[235] and finally Thomas Merks, bishop of Carlisle, who was charged with having conspired against the duke of Gloucester, was lodged in the abbey for safety, because of the hostility of the populace.[236] And in February 1400, the body of Richard II rested in the abbey church for a night on the way to its burial at Langley: Walsingham observes with apparent reticence that though Richard was recognizable, only his face, from brow to throat, was exposed to view. (The abbot of St Albans attended the funeral, which was held 'without pomp and with only a few people'.)[237] Walsingham had the opportunity of gaining information on many other occasions. Perhaps he was already a monk in the abbey when King John II of France stayed in the abbey during his captivity in England.[238]

Moreover, the monks of St Albans and of the dependent priories were

---

[227] *CA*, pp. 266–7.
[228] See p. 128 above.
[229] *JT*, p. 412.
[230] *CA*, pp. 320 et seq.
[231] *CA*, p. 322.
[232] *CA*, p. 305.
[233] For a visit by Richard II during a crisis over Henry Despenser's 'crusade' see p. 137 and n. 137 above.
[234] *JT*, p. 244.
[235] *JT*, p. 251.
[236] *JT*, p. 314. Cf. p. 144 n. 184 above.
[237] *JT*, p. 331.
[238] *GASA*, ii. 408.

often directly involved in events. The best example of such involvement was during the Peasants' Revolt, when the perennial conflict with the townsmen reached a crisis. Again, Walsingham obviously learnt the details of Henry Despenser's 'crusade' from the seven monks (whom he names) of St Albans and its priories, who joined the bishop; one died and although the other six returned their health had been permanently impaired by the heat and bad water.[239] Walsingham obviously found the collection of some material relating to the Lollards easy, because St Albans was in an area where they were active. The Lollards were antagonistic to the abbey, a stronghold of monastic 'possessioners'. In 1414, after the suppression of the rising led by Sir John Oldcastle, a roll belonging to the precentor of St Albans was found in Lollard hands, which listed the monks whom they hoped to eliminate.[240] In 1417 the Lollards distributed pamphlets in the town (and also in Northampton and Reading).[241] But especially significant is the fact that in the same year Oldcastle hid for many days 'in the house of a rustic' on the abbot's demesne. On hearing this members of the abbot's household hurried there one night, only to find that Oldcastle had fled. However, they found 'books written in English and some old books beautifully illuminated and illustrated with figures; the heads of these figures, in accordance with their false doctrines, had the haloes erased, as were all the saints' names in the litanies and the name of the Blessed Virgin as far as the verse *Parce nobis, Domine.*' They also found blasphemous writings about the Virgin Mary. The abbot sent one of the books which had been damaged by erasure to the king, who sent it to the archbishop of Canterbury, so that he could exhibit it in his sermons at St Paul's Cross, in order to convince the citizens of the enormities of the Lollards.[242]

Walsingham showed some intelligence in dealing with the massive quantity of material he was able to collect. Despite his edificatory, homiletic tone, he was capable of rational deduction. The fact that he regarded the Peasants' Revolt as divine retribution for the sins of the English in general and of the friars in particular, should not blind the reader to the fact that he also treated its causation rationally. He explicitly gives the poll tax of 1379 as the immediate cause of the rising,[243] and indicates the more long-term reasons for discontent. He particularly mentions the rebels' angry frustration on account of servile obligations: he notices their hatred of lawyers (because they enforced such obligations), and of the educated (because they wrote the deeds which defined the obligations), and the rebels' desire to destroy all archives and so to commit to oblivion all record

[239] *GASA*, ii. 416.
[240] *St AC*, p. 79. See Margaret Aston, 'Lollardy and sedition, 1381–1431' in *Past and Present*, xvii (1960), p. 20.
[241] *St AC*, p. 104.
[242] *St AC*, p. 115.
[243] *CA*, p. 281. See May McKisack, *The Fourteenth Century* (Oxford, 1959), pp. 405–6.

of their burdens. Walsingham also explains the popular belief in the equality of man.[244] Walsingham's rationality appears in other contexts. For example, he shows some understanding of the economic situation in his day. He bitterly condemned the Londoners for murdering a Genoese merchant, who planned to develop Southampton as a port, 'which no other port in western Europe would equal' and which would have facilitated the import of goods from the near east.[245] He also deplored the prohibition by the London authorities of trade by fishmongers from outside London in the area around the city; instead they had to sell to the Londoners at a fixed price, with the result that the Londoners had plenty of fish and their neighbours virtually none.[246]

However, it is not for rationality that Walsingham deserves his reputation. He deserves it for his gift of recording contemporary events in vivid prose. In cases where his sources of information were good, few chroniclers can rival his dramatic narrative. Parts of four passages from his *Chronica Majora* and one from the *Gesta Abbatum Monasterii Sancti Albani* can be cited to illustrate his talent. For three at least of these passages, the account of the shipwreck of Sir John Arundel in 1379, that of Henry Despenser's 'crusade', and the description of how the duke of Clarence facilitated the capture of Caen in 1417, Walsingham relied for his information on eyewitnesses. Possibly he also relied on others for his account of Richard II's coronation, though he may have been there himself. The last passage to be cited, the description of the death of Abbot Thomas de la Mare, was of course based on Walsingham's own observation.

Much of Walsingham's account of Richard II's coronation derives from the *ordo* for the ceremony, but his vivid description of the pageantry and the decoration of London for the procession from the Tower to Westminster on the day before the coronation, are original:[247]

> The king on a large charger suitable for such a person and royally caparisoned, rode after [the earl marshal, Henry Percy, and the steward, John, duke of Lancaster]. His sword was born aloft before him by Simon Burley, and Sir Nicholas Bonde, on foot, led him by the rein. Knights and his contemporaries, and members of his household followed him. There was no lack of musical accompaniment with horns and trumpets: the procession itself was preceded

---

[244] See *CA*, pp. 287, 308, 321. See also p. 133 above.

[245] *CA*, p. 238. For this plan to make Southampton a great port, which was apparently supported by John of Gaunt because it would reduce the commercial power of London, see Ruth Bird, *The Turbulent London of Richard II* (London 1949), p. 50.

[246] *CA*, pp. 350–1. For the attack led by the mayor John of Northampton on the monopoly of London fishmongers see Bird, op. cit., pp. 75–8. John of Northampton, a draper, was the opponent of Walsingham's friend John Philpot, who was a grocer and therefore supported the victualling misteries. Cf. p. 184 and n. 158 below.

[247] *CA*, p. 155.

by its own trumpeters, and the Londoners had stationed trumpeters on the water conduit[248] and on the tower which they had built in honour of the king in the same market place, who blew their instruments when the king arrived—the combined noise was wonderful indeed!... In the king's honour the citizens had ordered that wine should flow continually in the pipes of the conduit during the procession, that is for over three hours. They had also built a castle with four towers in the top part of the market place known as the Cheap, from which wine flowed abundantly in two places. On each of the four towers there was a beautiful maiden clad in white, of the same height and age as the king. When the king approached the four maidens scattered golden leaves in front of him, and when he came nearer they threw golden coins and fake pieces down on him and his horse. When he reached the castle they took golden cups, filled them with wine at the pipes of the castle, and handed them to the king and lords. On top of the castle, between the four towers, was a dome on which was placed a golden angel holding a golden crown; it was so ingeniously made that it seemed to be offering the crown to the king with a bow as he approached.

After the coronation Richard was so exhausted that 'he was carried on the shoulders of one of the knights to the royal palace [at Westminster], led into his chamber, and there, after eating a little, he rested.'[249]

Sir John Arundel was shipwrecked off the Irish coast. Walsingham gives a graphic description of the storm which overtook his fleet, and explains that Sir John, against the advice of the captain Robert Ruste, insisted on sailing his ship towards a small island. The sailors ran the ship on to the sand, and tried to jump to safety. Walsingham writes of Sir John's death:[250]

At length Sir John Arundel jumped and reached the sand. But he appeared to be over confident of his safety, for he stood on the sands as if there was nothing to fear, and began wringing out his clothes which were soaked with sea water. When Robert Ruste saw this, and realized the danger from which Sir John could never escape, he went down to the sands, seized his hand, and tried to drag him from his perilous position. But Ruste cared too much for the safety of another and he neglected his own. Hence he lost his life—when he tried to drag Sir John away with him, an immense wave reared up, broke and flowed forward; it knocked

[248] 'The first Cesterne of leade castellated with stone in the Citty of London, was called the great Conduit in West Cheape, which was begunne to bee builded in the yeare 1285'; John Stow, *A Survey of London*, ed. C. L. Kingsford (Oxford 1908, 2 vols), i. 17.
[249] *CA*, p. 161.
[250] *CA*, p. 252.

both men down, and drew them back into deep waters as it retreated. And so they met their end.

Walsingham then describes how many of the others were drowned, continuing:[251]

> A few escaped and reached the island but without their clothes, or if by chance they had any they were drenched with water: this caused even worse cold, since they could find no houses there, and they died of exposure. The rest endeavoured by running and wrestling to overcome the cold by every possible means. They survived there in great misery from Thursday until the ninth hour on the next Sunday, when, the sea having become calm, some Irish boarded their little boats and sailed to the island. They brought the survivors to the mainland, and revived them as best they could—they were half dead from starvation.

Walsingham has a detailed account of Henry Despenser's 'crusade'. One of the most graphic passages concerns the recruits who hurried to join the bishop when they heard of his capture of Gravelines and Dunkirk, and saw the booty brought home by those who were on the campaign:[252]

> Without careful consideration, many London apprentices, mostly of servile condition, putting on white hoods, and red crosses on their right sides, and red scabbards for swords on their left, set forth against the wishes of their masters and lords. Others from almost all over England followed their example, leaving their parents and relatives and beloved families, and started out unarmed except for swords, bows and arrows. And not only laymen did this, but the religious of every sort presumed as if of one mind to undertake the journey, having sought but not obtained permission. It was to their great shame and detriment that they decided to go on pilgrimage not so much for the sake of Jesus, but in order to see the countryside and the world.

This crowd, amounting, Walsingham estimated, to 60,000 men, was transported by Sir John Philpot. Despenser in despair asked Philpot to bring him no more such recruits, and said to the men, 'Why do you come here? To consume the food which barely suffices for those who will fight? You are "extras, born to eat the fruit";[253] it would have been better for you to have stayed at home, free from care, sitting over the fleshpots.'[254]

Walsingham's description of how in 1417 the duke of Clarence occupied

---

[251] *CA*, p. 253.
[252] *HA*, ii. 95.
[253] *HA*, ii. 96. Cf. Horace, *Epist.* i. 2. 27.
[254] Cf. Exodus xvi. 3.

the monastery of St Stephen's, Caen, a vantage point from which the English could capture the town, is equally vivid. The French soldiers who should have guarded the abbey robbed and deserted it, and it seemed that they planned its total destruction. Walsingham continues:[255]

A certain monk named Gerard heard this whispered, and fearing the destruction of the monastery, boldly exposed himself to danger; in the evening of the same night he crawled on hands and knees through the enemy, through fire and hostile weapons, until he came to the place where the duke of Clarence, the king's brother, was observing the siege. Having discovered an entrance he found the duke lying fully armed on the grass in an orchard, his head resting on a rock. The monk immediately fell on his knees, and tearfully besought the duke to save his monastery from ruin, which would indeed immediately be destroyed if he did not come at once. 'You', the monk said, 'should most especially serve our house because you descend from the line of kings who founded, built and endowed it. Therefore, let me without delay lead the way, and I will guide you, and our community will rejoice!' Without hesitation the duke did as he was asked, and, taking a ladder, came to a place which was unguarded—only a handful of men, who were unarmed, had been left there, more for appearances than for defence. They were terrified at the duke's arrival. He captured them or allowed them to leave, considering them unworthy of his sword because they were peasants and of low estate. ... Thus the duke obtained a foot-hold, and next morning brought King [Henry] there. The king was overjoyed, because from the walls and towers of the monastery he could see everything happening in the town. He could also use the place to erect and station his guns (which the French call cannon), with which he could make a more powerful onslaught on the town.

Probably the strongest influence on Walsingham's life was Abbot Thomas de la Mare, the architect of the intellectual revival at St Albans: his achievement did not long survive his death in 1396. Walsingham gives many biographical details about him which, notwithstanding their eulogistic tone, sound true, and he describes his last illness in moving terms:[256]

His illness was such that for five days or more in every fortnight he could neither sleep nor retain food ... which often all but killed him. His screams, coming from unbearable suffering,

[255] St AC, pp. 111–12.
[256] GASA, iii. 420–1.

were so loud that they reached the ears of the cloister monks and those in the nearby offices. They unnerved those serving him as priests to such a degree that they often did not know when they made a mistake in the divine office: but the abbot himself burnt with such fervour for the Lord, that despite his illness he both heard and spoke, and could himself tell those who had forgotten exactly what they should say, and where they had gone wrong.

After his death Abbot Thomas's body was laid out in the abbey church, publicly on view to all:[257]

The body was clothed according to the custom for deceased monks, and also in the vestments of an abbot with pontifical mitre, gloves, ring and sandals, the hands lying on the breast as in prayer, the pastoral staff bound under the left arm, and the thin face covered with a silken shroud.

[257] *GASA*, iii. 422.

6

Chroniclers of the Reign of Richard II

No other chronicler in the reign of Richard II produced a corpus of works comparable with Thomas Walsingham's. Nevertheless, more chronicles were written under Richard II than under Edward III. Monastic historiography underwent a marked revival, and a number of good chronicles were produced by secular clerks. In addition, some chronicles were written by foreigners, mostly Frenchmen, which either wholly or partly concern affairs in England.

The Benedictines played an important part in this revival. A monk of St Mary's, York, apparently compiled the Anonimalle chronicle soon after 1381, which incorporates a narrative of the Peasants' Revolt written in London.[1] A monk of Westminster wrote, more or less contemporaneously with the events he recorded, a continuation of the *Polychronicon* from 1377 to 1394.[2] Another continuation of the *Polychronicon*, the *Historia Vitae et Regni Ricardi Secundi* (*History of the Life and Reign of Richard II*, usually known as the *Life of Richard II*), comes from Evesham. The monks had a copy of the *Polychronicon* with a continuation from 1348 to 1377 by John of Malvern, a monk of Worcester who became the prior of Worcester in 1395.[3] One

---

[1] See pp. 101, 111–13 above, and pp. 160 and n. 17, 166–7 below.

[2] Printed *Poly.* ix. 1–283. This chronicle is anonymous, but there has been speculation about its authorship. J. Armitage Robinson, 'An unrecognized Westminster chronicler, 1381–1394' in *Proceedings of the British Academy*, iii (1907), pp. 61–77, passim, argues the claim of John Lakyngheth, candidate for the abbacy of Westminster in 1380. He had been appointed warden of the abbot's household in 1362, and then held the offices successively of treasurer and cellarer in the convent. John Taylor, *The Universal Chronicle of Ranulf Higden* (Oxford 1966), p. 128, considers it more likely that the author was William of Sudbury. This suggestion arises from the fact that the Westminster chronicle shows particular interest in the regalia (see *Poly.* ix. 45, 77–8, 222–3, 260–1, and cf. p. 182 below), about which Sudbury wrote a treatise. (The treatise was incorporated by Richard of Cirencester into his *Speculum Historiale*, bk III, c. 3. See *Speculum Historiale de Gestis Regum Angliae* (*A.D 447–1066*), ed. J. E. B. Mayor (RS 1863–9, 3 vols), ii. 26–39, and cf. Robinson, op. cit., pp. 68, 73–4.) However, this is not a strong argument because any monk of Westminster might be expected to be interested in the regalia. Mr Taylor also considers the possibility that Richard of Cirencester (who d. *c.* 1401) was himself the author of the chronicle.

[3] For John of Malvern see Taylor, op. cit., pp. ·122–3, 127. The Evesham copy of the *Polychronicon* has additions, probably made at Evesham, to Higden's text which from the early thirteenth century are substantial: some provide important source material, notably for the

[157]

of the monks of Evesham (perhaps Nicholas Herford, prior of Evesham from 1352 to 1392) used this book and the chronicles of Thomas Walsingham to compile a chronicle from 1377 to 1390, adding some information of his own; and in the reign of Henry IV another Evesham monk continued the chronicle to 1402.[4] This continuation appears to be independent of other known sources, except for its account of the parliament of 1397 which is nearly the same as that in Adam of Usk. In the late fourteenth and early fifteenth century a continuation was added of the *Eulogium Historiarum*, which to 1366 was the work of a monk of Malmesbury. The continuation reaches to 1413, and its authorship is unknown.[5] Its contents show a strong Franciscan interest and also a connection with Canterbury. This evidence makes it fairly certain that the continuation was by a Franciscan friar who was possibly a member of the convent of Grey Friars in Canterbury.

Three Cistercian abbeys produced useful, if short and jejune, chronicles. A monk of Kirkstall in Yorkshire wrote a chronicle covering the period

---

constitutional crisis of 1297; see J. H. Denton, 'The crisis of 1297 from the Evesham chronicle' in *EHR*, xciii (1978), pp. 260–79.

[4] The Evesham chronicle is printed, and its authorship, composition and relationship to the chronicle of John of Malvern and to the chronicles of Thomas Walsingham are discussed, in *Historia Vitae et Regni Ricardi Secundi*, ed. G. B. Stow (Haney Foundation Series, University of Pennsylvania, xxi, 1977). This definitive edition, which is based on the earliest known version (BL MS. Cotton Claudius B IX), collated fully with another early manuscript (BL MS. Cotton Tiberius C IX), and partially collated with the ten other known manuscripts, supersedes that of Thomas Hearne (Oxford 1729) which used only one manuscript. The chronicle's value for political history is discussed at greater length in G. B. Stow, 'The *Vita Ricardi* as a source for the reign of Richard II' in *Research Papers* (Vale of Evesham Historical Society, iv, 1973), pp. 63–75.

[5] Printed *EH* iii. 333–421. A modern unpublished edition is by S. N. Clifford, 'An edition of the continuation of the *Eulogium Historiarum*, 1361–1413' (M. Phil. thesis, University of Leeds 1975). Kingsford, *Hist. Lit.* p. 28, expresses the view that the continuation of the *Eulogium* is a composite work compiled after 1428. However, two recent scholars have made a convincing case for accepting that the continuation was written by one author fairly contemporarily with the events it records from the late fourteenth century onwards (the entry concerning the exhumation of John Wyclif in 1428 is probably an interpolation); see J. I. Catto, 'An alleged great council in 1374' in *EHR*, lxxxii (1967), pp. 764–5, and Clifford, op. cit., pp. 26–8. Haydon on the basis of internal evidence concluded that the continuation was written at Canterbury, but did not mention that the author was almost certainly a Franciscan; *EH*, iii. lii n. (Kingsford accepted the possibility of a Canterbury provenance; Kingsford, *Hist. Lit.* pp. 29, 127 and n. 1.) For the latter conclusion see Catto, op. cit., pp. 765–6. Clifford accepts Catto's view and corroborates it, but underestimates the obvious Canterbury connection; Clifford, op. cit., pp. 29–37, 236–8. For an unconvincing attempt to prove that the continuation was by John Trevor, bishop of St Asaph (1395–?1410) see E. J. Jones, 'The authorship of the continuation of *Eulogium Historiarum*: a suggestion' in *Speculum*, xii (1937), pp. 196–202. The value of the *Eulogium* to the historian today does not of course end with Richard II's reign but continues to its close in 1413. For the value of its account of the trial of some minorites for treason in 1402 (*EH*, iii. 389–94) see 'Clergy and common law in the reign of Henry IV', ed. R. L. Storey in *Medieval Legal Records edited in memory of C. A. F. Meekings*, ed. R. F. Hunnisett and J. B. Post (London 1978), pp. 353–7 passim. For the *Eulogium* from the Creation until 1366, written in Malmesbury abbey, see pp. 101, 103–5 above.

from the thirteenth century to 1400, using a Franciscan chronicle at least for some entries between 1231 and 1385.[6] Some time before 1413 a monk of Dieulacres in Staffordshire wrote a chronicle of the years from 1337 to 1400. (Another monk of Dieulacres continued it to 1403.)[7] Moreover, a continuation of the *Polychronicon* to 1430 was owned by Whalley abbey in Lancashire.[8] Of much greater scope and literary quality than these Cistercian works is the chronicle of Henry Knighton, an Augustinian canon of the abbey of St Mary of the Meadows at Leicester.[9] With the exception of Walsingham's, his is the only monastic chronicle which is not anonymous. However, nothing is known about his life apart from the fact that he gave some books to the abbey library, was granted a royal pardon in 1370 for harbouring two criminals and went blind in his last years.[10] He died in or about 1396. His chronicle extends from the tenth century to 1395. (There are no annals for the years from 1366 to 1377.) It seems most likely that Knighton began writing the history of his own times (from 1377) in about 1390, and subsequently compiled, showing some historical discrimination, the preceding section which he only completed up to 1366: his principal source was the *Polychronicon*, from which he presumably borrowed the idea of giving his name (Cnitthon) in an acrostic

---

[6] The so-called 'short chronicle' of Kirkstall is printed *The Kirkstall Abbey Chronicles*, ed., with an English translation, John Taylor (Thoresby Soc. xlii, 1952), pp. 52–85, 98–129. For its sources and importance see ibid., pp. 25–6, 42–6. The chronicle is also discussed and extracts printed in M. V. Clarke and Noël Denholm-Young, 'The Kirkstall chronicle, 1355–1400' in *BJRL*, xv (1931), pp. 100–37. (This article is reprinted in M. V. Clarke, *Fourteenth Century Studies*, ed. L. S. Sutherland and May McKisack (Oxford 1937), pp. 99–114.) For a twelfth century chronicle of Kirkstall see Gransden, *Historical Writing*, i. 287, 295.

[7] Printed in M. V. Clarke and V. H. Galbraith, 'The deposition of Richard II' in *BJRL*, xiv (1930), pp. 164–81. (This article is reprinted in Clarke, op. cit., pp. 53–98.)

[8] The Whalley chronicle is a continuation of the *Polychronicon*, one manuscript of which, now BL MS. Harley 3600, belonged to Whalley abbey. It ends in 1430. It has some value as a source for Richard II's reign, particularly for the deposition; this part is discussed and extracts printed in Clarke and Galbraith, op. cit., pp. 144–5, 157. The fifteenth century section is printed in Kingsford, *Hist. Lit.* pp. 279–91.

[9] Printed *Chronicon Henrici Knighton vel Cnitthon Monachi Leycestrensis*, ed. J. R. Lumby (RS 1889–95, 2 vols). The composition of Knighton's chronicle, with especial reference to the earliest manuscript, now BL MS. Cotton Tiberius C VII, is fully discussed in V. H. Galbraith, 'The chronicle of Henry Knighton' in *Fritz Saxl 1890–1948: a Volume of Memorial Essays from his Friends in England*, ed. D. J. Gordon (London 1957), pp. 136–45. Tiberius C VII was copied, probably from Kinghton's own draft, by a number of scribes. It contains numerous corrections and additions not apparently in Knighton's hand. Perhaps he was only able to supervise the copying and revision on account of his blindness (see below and the next note). However, two short additions may be in his autograph; see ibid., p. 142, and Plate VII below.

[10] Six books entered in the late fifteenth century catalogue of the library of St Mary's, Leicester, have a note that they were acquired through Henry Knighton; see M. V. Clarke, 'Henry Knighton and the library catalogue of Leicester abbey' in *EHR*, xlv (1930), pp. 103–4. For the pardon granted to Knighton for harbouring two felons see *CPR, 1370–1374*, p. 4; cf. A. Hamilton Thompson, *The Abbey of St. Mary of the Meadows Leicester* (Leicester 1949), p. 37. Knighton laments the sudden onset of blindness is some Latin verses in Tiberius C VII (f. 3); cf. Galbraith, op. cit., pp. 136, 142.

in the prefatory book. He also used a now lost chronicle of Leicester until 1326.[11]

A number of chronicles on Richard II's reign were by clerks who had connections either with the central government or with a magnate. The most important such chronicle was by Adam of Usk,[12] a clerk attached to the court of the archbishop of Canterbury.[13] He included a full account of Richard II's reign in his continuation of the *Polychronicon* from 1377 to 1421 which, although written under Henry V, will be discussed here because it was partly based on earlier reminiscences.[14] Thomas Favent, the author of the *Historia sive Narracio de Modo et Forma Mirabilis Parliamenti* (*The History or Narrative of the Mode and Form of the Wonderful Parliament*),[15] a tract on the Merciless Parliament of 1388, written in favour of Richard's opponents, the Appellant lords, was apparently a clerk in minor orders, and was acquainted with one of the two clerks of the crown, Geoffrey Martin.[16] The author of the account of the Peasants' Revolt preserved in the Anonimalle chronicle was probably a clerk attached to the royal chancery.[17] Two poets also wrote history. William Langland, who was in orders and lived in London, wrote a chronicle in verse on Rich-

---

[11] See ibid., p. 144; *HK*, i. 442.

[12] Printed *Chronicon Adae de Usk A. D. 1377–1421.* ed., with an English translation, E. Maunde Thompson (second edition, London 1904).

[13] For Adam's career see *AU*, pp. xi–xxxiv, and pp. 175 and n. 97, 176–7 and n. 108 below.

[14] See *AU*, pp. xxxv–xxxvii.

[15] Printed *Historia sive Narracio de Modo et Forma Mirabilis Parliamenti apud Westmonasterium Anno Domini Millesimo CCCLXXXVIII Regni vero Regis Ricardi Secundi post Conquestum Anno Decimo, per Thomam Fauent Clericum indictata*, ed. May McKisack (Camden Miscellany, xiv (1926), 1–27). A short chronicle of events from the beginning of the parliament which opened on 1 October 1386, to the end of the Merciless Parliament, which favours the Appellants and has some value for the battle of Radcot Bridge, is in the register of Henry Wakefield; *A Calendar of the Register of Henry Wakefeld Bishop of Worcester 1375–95*, ed. W. P. Marett (Worcestershire Historical Soc., new series, vii, 1972), pp. xxxi–xxxiii, 144–9 passim. See R. G. Davies, 'Some notes from the register of Henry de Wakefield, bishop of Worcester, on the political crisis of 1386–1388' in *EHR*, lxxxvi (1971), pp. 547–58.

[16] For what little is known concerning Favent see *TF*, p. vi. For Geoffrey Martin see *TF*, p. viii and nn., 15.

[17] For references in the account of the Peasants' Revolt which show particular knowledge of chancery see pp. 166 and n. 47, 167 and n. 48 below. For suggested identifications of the author of this section see A. F. Pollard, 'The authorship and value of the 'Anonimalle' chronicle' in *EHR*, liii (1938), pp. 577–605, and V. H. Galbraith, 'Thoughts about the Peasants' Revolt' in *The Reign of Richard II, Essays in Honour of May McKisack*, ed. F. R. H. Du Boulay and C. M. Barron (London 1971), pp. 48–51. Another man, William Ferriby, who was probably a chancery clerk and may have been the notary of that name commissioned to hear Richard II's renunciation in the Tower, wrote a lament on the death of Richard which was copied into 'Giles's' chronicle. This chronicle is a compilation of earlier material made in about 1460 covering the reigns from Richard II to Henry VI, and was edited by J. A. Giles, *Incerti Scriptoris Chronicon Angliae de Regnis trium Regum Lancastrensium Henrici IV, Henrici V, et Henrici VI* (London 1848); Giles, however, omitted the section on Richard II's reign because of its close resemblance to the Evesham chronicle. On its additions (including Ferriby's lament) to the Evesham chronicle and its other features, see Kingsford, *Hist. Lit.* pp. 24–8 passim, 155–7, and Clark and Galbraith, 'Deposition', pp. 149–52. It should also be remembered that the poet, Thomas Hoccleve (1368–1437), was a clerk in

ard's tyranny and downfall,[18] and John Gower, a citizen of London, wrote a verse chronicle on the reign.[19] (The author of the chronicle which formed the basis of the *Brut* for this period was also a Londoner.)[20]

A group of chronicles, especially relating to Richard's last year as king, was written by Frenchmen who took a close interest because of Richard's marriage (in March 1396) with Isabella, daughter of Charles VI of France. By far the best of these is by Jean Creton,[21] a French esquire who came to England with a friend in the spring of 1399 for the sake of 'amusement and to see the country'.[22] He joined Richard for his Irish expedition in the summer of that year, but returned to England with the advance

---

the privy seal office, which he entered in 1387; see A. Compton Reeves, 'Thomas Hoccleve, bureaucrat' in *Medievalia et Humanistica*, new series, v (1974), pp. 201–14.

[18] The chronicle, *Richard the Redeless*, is printed and its authorship discussed in *Piers the Plowman and Richard the Redeless*, ed. W. W. Skeat (Oxford 1886, 2 vols), i. 603–28; ii. lxxxii–lxxxvi.

[19] Gower's *Cronica Tripertita* (see p. 185 below) is printed in *The Complete Works of John Gower*, ed. G. C. Macaulay (Oxford 1899–1902, 4 vols), iv. 314–43. Although the chronicle is in verse, it has historical commentary in prose in the margins.

[20] See pp. 221, 225–7 below.

[21] Creton's *Histoire du Roy d'Angleterre Richard, traictant particulierement la rebellion de ses subiectz...* is printed from Bibliothèque Nationale MS., nouvelles acquisitions fr. 6223, formerly St Victor's MS. 275, in J. A. C. Buchon, *Collection des Chroniques nationales françaises*, xxiv (Paris 1826), pp. 321–466. A translation is by J. Webb in *Archaeologia*, xx (1824), pp. 13–239. The French text from BL MS. Harley 1319 (for which see p. 189 n. 186 below) s printed in ibid., pp. 295–423. After my draft of this chapter had been typed, I read the article by J. J. N. Palmer, 'The authorship, date and historical value of the French chronicles on the Lancastrian revolution', which Dr Palmer kindly sent me in advance of publication (it has since appeared in two parts in *BJRL*, lxi (1978–9), pp. 145–81, 328–421). Most of the views I had expressed agreed with his. I concur with Dr Palmer in accepting Jean Creton's authorship of the chronicle despite the doubts cast on it by E. J. Jones, 'An examination of the authorship of *The Deposition and Death of Richard II* attributed to Creton' in *Speculum*, xv (1940), pp. 460–77, who argues in favour of the authorship of John Trevor, bishop of St Asaph (1395–?1410); Dr Palmer disposes of Trevor's claim very thoroughly. The evidence for Creton's authorship is all but conclusive: (1) The St Victor's MS., one of the three known medieval manuscripts of the chronicle (all three manuscripts are closely related and none is an autograph), ends 'Explicit lystoire du Roi Richart d'Engleterre co[m]posee p[ar] Creton' (BN MS. n.a.fr. 6223, cf. Jones, op. cit., p. 466; (2) Philip the Bold, duke of Burgundy, paid Creton for a book on King Richard; it seems likely that the 'livre faisant mencion de la prinse de feu le roy Richart' for which Philip the Bold (cf. p. 174 below) paid to Jean Creton 60 écus by letters patent dated 16 July 1402, was Creton's chronicle. See Pierre Cockshaw, 'Mentions d'auteurs, de copistes, d'enlumineurs et de libraires dans les comptes généraux de l'état Bourguignon (1384–1419)' in *Scriptorium*, xxiii (1969), p. 135 no. 50. Jones, op. cit., pp. 469–70, cites a similar entry in the library list of the dukes of Burgundy, where the sum paid is 'neuf escus d'or' (Jones gives the year 1401). Creton is known to have been deeply concerned about Richard's fate after his deposition, which accords with the chronicler's evident esteem, even affection, for the king (see pp. 173–4 below). Dr Palmer (op. cit., pp. 153–4, 173) adduces the additional evidence of Creton's letter to Richard II written after the deposition (see p. 173 and n. 89 below); Creton states that he will bring the 'history' (which he describes in terms representing it as similar to the extant chronicle). This almost amounts to proof unless the letter is a forgery; see Palmer, op. cit., pp. 151–4. See also p. 190 n. 193 below.

[22] *Creton*, p. 411.

party at the express wish of its commander John de Montagu, earl of Salisbury, who wanted his company 'for merriment and song'.[23] Creton, still with the earl, rejoined Richard at Conway, went with him to London after his capture by Henry Bolingbroke, and left England for France shortly before Richard's deposition on 29 September. The earl of Salisbury, when captured with King Richard in Wales, had asked Creton to write the history of the tragic events.[24] This Creton did after he returned home (he wrote at some date between November 1401 and March 1402),[25] adding an account of the deposition, of Queen Isabella's return to France and of Richard's death.[26]

The *Chronique de la Traïson et Mort de Richart Deux Roy Dengleterre* (*Chronicle of the Betrayal and Death of King Richard II of England*) was written shortly after Creton's chronicle. It was probably by a Burgundian who at the time in question was attached temporarily to the household of John de Holand, duke of Exeter (this is indicated by the interest it shows in the duke and his relatives).[27] The *Traïson et Mort* survives in four different versions of varying lengths. It seems most likely that the shortest was written first and that the subsequent versions were produced in order of length, the longest being the last. The short version is apparently independent of other historical works. It contains a dramatic and mainly fictional narrative of the last year of Richard's reign and of his deposition and death. (The other versions gain their greater length because of the insertion of material from Creton's history.) Clearly, therefore, because of the nature of its composition, the *Traïson* has little source-value to the historian today. The other French chronicle which has information on this period is the *Chronique du Religieux de Saint Denys* (*Chronicle of the Monk of St Denis*), an account of Charles VI's reign (1380–1422) by an anonymous monk of St Denis, who, like the author of the *Traïson et Mort*, drew heavily on Creton.[28] Finally, the Hainaulter, Jean Froissart, included abundant information about Richard's reign in his chronicle of European history.[29]

The principal reason for the revival of historical writing in England in Richard's reign was undoubtedly the occurrence of two traumatic

---

[23] *Creton*, p. 345.

[24] *Creton*, p. 465.

[25] See Palmer, op. cit., p. 154.

[26] See pp. 173, 191–2 below.

[27] Printed *Chronicque de la Traison et Mort de Richart Deux Roy Dengleterre*, ed., with an English translation, Benjamin Williams (English Historical Soc. 1846). The authorship, date, composition and historical value of the chronicle are fully discussed in Palmer, op. cit. Dr Palmer's suggestion that Creton was responsible for the two recensions of the *Traïson et Mort* which contain the most material from his own chronicle (Palmer, op. cit., pp. 159–63) does not seem to be sufficiently supported by evidence to carry conviction.

[28] Printed *Chronique du Religieux de Saint-Denys, contenant le Regne de Charles VI, de 1380 à 1422*, ed., with a French translation, L. Bellaguet (Paris 1839–52, 6 vols). Discussed in Palmer, op. cit., pp. 145–6, 158–9, 171, 173.

[29] For Froissart and his chronicle see pp. 59 and n. 10, 89–92 above.

events—the Peasants' Revolt and the deposition of Richard II. As has been seen, these events absorbed Thomas Walsingham's attention, and their impact and the fear and amazement they aroused stimulated others to write history. The chroniclers, sure of an avid audience, wanted to record such stirring events. Moreover, besides the desire to satisfy contemporary curiosity, there was the wish to point the moral: here was ample scope for the chroniclers' propensity for homiletic moralization, which had been a feature of historiography in Edward III's reign. The Peasants' Revolt provided numerous salutary lessons on the necessity of maintaining an ordered, stratified society. And Richard II's deposition supplied examples particularly useful to princes but also of interest to others: it was interpreted by the English as demonstrating the dangers of tyranny, and by the French as showing how treachery and rebellion put the very institution of monarchy in jeopardy. In addition, other chroniclers besides Walsingham reacted with consternation to the rise of the Lollard heresy: in their eyes the Lollards posed a threat both to the Christian faith and also to all orderly government.

Preoccupation with the Peasants' Revolt, Richard's deposition and Lollardy eclipsed interest in warfare which had dominated the minds of chroniclers in Edward III's reign. This trend was encouraged by the fact that the Hundred Years' War was by now discredited. Inevitably the chroniclers' three principal themes led them to concentrate on social and political history. They examined the social causes and manifestations of the Peasants' Revolt and of Lollardy, and they wrote about the political implications of Richard's rule and deposition.

The chronicles' value to the social historian today does not depend solely on the authors' interest in their environment. It is increased by the taste of some for autobiographical details. This taste is especially characteristic of the two foreign authors, Creton and Froissart, but it is also evident in the chronicle of Adam of Usk. Undoubtedly the most important reason for the inclusion of autobiographical material was the stimulus of foreign travel: Creton and Froissart felt impelled to record their response to what they saw and heard on their travels. Similarly Adam of Usk wrote at length about his experiences in France and Italy. However, an additional motive for self expression was the result of the dramatic and sometimes frightening times in which the chroniclers lived. Creton describes both his fear as a member of the royal entourage after Richard's capture and his compassion for the king. Even Adam, although a Lancastrian at heart, describes with feeling Richard's sadness in the Tower.

The chroniclers wrote at length about the deposition and the events leading up to it not only because of their irresistible news-value, but also as a result of outside pressure; in varying degrees the chroniclers were susceptible to the pressure of Lancastrian propaganda immediately after the coup. A number wrote to justify the new régime, even including propaganda material emanating from the government. However, the government was not the only influence on the chroniclers; their political attitudes were also partly determined by their patrons.

The chronicles, as relevant, will be discussed, first, in relation to social history, second, for their autobiographical features and, third, as political histories.

The most important chronicles for social history are: the Anonimalle chronicle (for the Peasants' Revolt); the Westminster continuation of the *Polychronicon*; and the chronicle of Henry Knighton. Also of value are the Evesham *Life of Richard II* and the chronicles of Adam of Usk, Froissart and Creton.

The information on social history contained in these works must be considered in the context of the poetry and sermons of the time. To this period belongs the first great English poet, Chaucer, besides several lesser poets, and there was a flourishing tradition of homiletic literature. The poets wrote (often in satirical vein) and the preachers inveighed against the evils of society. Verses (both in English and in Latin) attacked the corruption of the church, the pride of the nobles and the tyranny of the royal court,[30] themes also popular with the preachers. (The *Eulogium* records that Archbishop Thomas Arundel preached to the king's court in 1397, before his exile, on the contamination of the kingdom by the luxurious living of the great lords, and by the avarice and pride prevalent in their households.)[31] The chroniclers, who themselves heard sermons, and no doubt read contemporary poems, shared the same attitudes. The chronicler of Evesham writes in a homiletic tone, frequently interrupting his historical narrative with pious tirades, for example on the sin of avarice to which Richard II succumbed, and on the worthlessness of worldly success and prosperity in the face of fickle fortune.[32] Adam of Usk's homiletic tirades are aimed at the corruption of the papal court.[33]

Writers virulently attacked extravagant fashions in dress, in the same way as John of Reading, writing at Westminster, and the author of the *Eulogium Historiarum*, writing at Malmesbury, had done in Edward III's reign.[34] Some verses (with alternate lines in English and Latin), probably composed in 1388, criticize the artificially broad shoulders and wide, high collars of men's clothes, the boots with long pointed toes,

---

[30] For examples see *Political Poems*, ed. Wright, i, passim. (The two poems by John Gower, printed under the headings 'On the vices of the different orders of society' and 'On King Richard II' in ibid., i. 356–63, are also printed in *The Complete Works of John Gower*, ed. Macaulay, iv. 355–64.)

[31] *EH*, iii. 376–7.

[32] *VR II*, pp. 150 (cited Stow, 'The *Vita Ricardi* as a source for the reign of Richard II', p. 71), 151 (line 3582), 165 (line 4068).

[33] *AU*, pp. 78, 87–9 passim.

[34] See pp. 104–6 above.

and the long spurs, and hose of such elegance that the wearers dared not kneel for fear of damage—hence the wearers were not only themselves prevented from praying in church, but also distracted the devout by standing throughout divine service.[35]

The monk who wrote the second part of the Evesham chronicle, from 1390 to 1402, felt equally strongly about contemporary fashions. He feared God's vengeance on the kingdom because of the 'insolent clothes', especially the cloaks with wide long sleeves called 'pokys ... made in the form of a bagpipe, which indeed would more correctly be called receptacles for devils, because anything furtively taken can easily be hidden in them.' Some sleeves, he writes, are so long 'that they reach to the feet, or at least the knees, full of slashes and devils.' They had the disadvantage that when a servant waited on his master at table, they trailed in the food and drink ('thus tasting the drink before the lord'); and so man became the slave to his clothes, which should have served him.[36] The previous Evesham chronicler, compiler of the section from 1377 to 1390, tells a story how, in the course of a quarrel between William Courtney, archbishop of Canterbury, and the bishop of Exeter over the right of metropolitan visitation, the archbishop forced the members of the bishop's household to eat their 'crakows' (shoes with pointed toes), in retaliation because the bishop had made the archbishop's emissary eat his mandate, complete with seal.[37]

One of the Evesham chronicler's objections to extravagant fashions in dress was that they blurred the distinctions between social groups. The servants in all their finery looked like their masters.[38] Henry Knighton made the same point when writing of the renewal in 1388 of the statute of labourers:[39]

> The pride of the lower orders has so blossomed forth and grown these days in fine dress and splendid display—in the variety of fashions—that one can hardly distinguish one person from another, because of their gorgeous clothes and accessories. The humble cannot be distinguished from the great, the poor from the rich, the servant from his master, nor the priest from anyone else, but each imitates the other and strives to introduce some new fashion and to excel his superior by wearing even grander clothes.

This interest in dress, seen as a means whereby social barriers were broken down, reflects the contemporary obsession, already discussed with refer-

---

[35] *Political Poems*, ed. Wright, i. 270–8.
[36] *VR II*, pp. 168–9.
[37] *VR II*, pp. 82–3. For the Evesham chronicler on the introduction of 'crakows' into England by the Bohemians who accompanied Queen Anne see *VR II*, p. 134. Cf. p. 105 and n. 18 above.
[38] *VR II*, p. 168.
[39] *HK*, ii. 299. For reference to ladies' extravagant dress see *HK*, ii. 58.

ence to Thomas Walsingham, with the structure of society, the conviction that in a happy society each man keeps in his place.[40] The form of Chaucer's *Canterbury Tales* depends on the conception of society as a hierarchy of groups, and Gower's *Vox Clamantis* describes the condition of society and the various degrees of men. This structure had already been threatened, in Henry Knighton's view, by the improved status of villeins resulting from the shortage of labour created by the Black Death.[41] Froissart commented on the comparative prosperity of the lower orders, to which he partly attributed the Peasants' Revolt.[42] The revolt itself was undoubtedly the most serious challenge to established society. Gower writes in the *Vox Clamantis* that during the revolt 'slaves were raised on high and nobles brought to the ground', servants became masters, and masters servants.[43] Henry Knighton reiterated the theme: tenants began to rise against their lords in many places, for as it is written, 'no one is more violent than the humble who raises himself on high'.[44]

The best authorities for the Peasants' Revolt are (besides Thomas Walsingham) the Anonimalle chronicle, Henry Knighton, the Westminster chronicler and the continuator of the *Eulogium Historiarum;* and Froissart, despite his love of imaginative dramatization, has some value. Their evidence is complementary and often mutually confirmatory.[45] The Anonimalle chronicle is particularly full on events in London, although it is also informative on the revolt in East Anglia. The author of the section on the revolt was clearly an eyewitness of some of the events he describes, having especially detailed knowledge of the king's movements, and concerning the chancery and its officials. Thus he gives an account of Richard's behaviour in the Tower during the revolt, relating, for example, that 'when the rebels dispersed the king went to his wardrobe to rest after his great exertions.'[46] He records the destruction by the rebels of the chancery remembrancer rolls,[47] and that, after the murder of the chancellor,

---

[40] See pp. 132–4 above.

[41] *HK*, ii. 63–4.

[42] *JF* (SL), x. 94.

[43] *Vox Clamantis*, i. 8 (11. 659–660); vii. 4 (1. 235): *Complete Works of John Gower*, ed. Macaulay, iv. 40, 278.

[44] *HK*, ii. 141–2.

[45] In addition, there is a good account of the Peasants' Revolt at Bury St Edmunds in the *Electio Johannis Tymworth (The Election of John Timworth)* by John Gosford, almoner of St Edmund's abbey. The conflict at Bury was particularly violent. It was exacerbated by the fact that it coincided with the disputed election to the abbacy of John Timworth, the internal candidate; his opponent was Edmund Bromfield, a papal nominee, who was supported by the townsmen, who were always ready to attack the abbey. The complaints of the convent against the townsmen for their 'diverse transgressions and horrible malefactions' during the revolt are rehearsed in another tract, the *Articuli sive Punctus (The Articles or Details)*. Both tracts are printed in *Memorials of St Edmund's Abbey*, ed. Thomas Arnold (RS 1890–6, 3 vols), iii. 113–43.

[46] *An.* p. 150.

[47] *An.* p. 140.

Archbishop Simon Sudbury, Richard entrusted the seal temporarily to Thomas Arundel. (And 'all that day [the king] caused the various clerks to write out the charters, patents and letters of protection', which he had been forced to grant to the rebels, 'without taking fines for sealing or transcription'.)[48] The chronicle also has a unique account of the defence of the bridge at Huntingdon against the rebels by William Wightman ('Wyghmane' in the text), spigurnel of chancery, Walter de Rudham, and 'other good men of the town'.[49]

The Anonimalle chronicle has some excellent reportage. An example is its description of the sacking of Fleet street and of John of Gaunt's palace, the Savoy:[50]

> In Fleet street the commons of Kent broke open the Fleet prison and released the prisoners, letting them go where they would. They then stopped to pull down and set alight a chandler's shop and another belonging to a marshal which stood in the middle of the street (it is thought that there will never again be a house on that spot), thus destroying the street's appearance. Afterwards they went to the Temple to despoil the occupants, and they pulled down the houses and ripped off all the tiles so that the houses were left roofless and derelict. They went to the church and took all the books, rolls and remembrances kept in the cupboards of the apprentices of the law in the Temple, and carried them to the high road and burnt them. .... At last they came to the Savoy where they broke open the doors and entered. They went to the wardrobe and took all the torches which they could find, and lit them and burnt all the clothes, coverlets, beds and head-boards of great value (one of which, decorated with heraldic shields, was said to be worth 1,000 marks). They carried all the napery and other goods which they could find into the hall and burnt them with the torches. They also set fire to the hall, and to the rooms and apartments within the gates of this palace ... which the commons of London had left unguarded. It is said that they found three barrels of gunpowder; thinking the gunpowder was gold or silver, they threw the barrels on to the fire, so that they exploded and made the flames in the hall blaze more fiercely than ever.

The Westminster chronicler, writing close to one of the principal areas of the revolt, has a full account of events in London, which corroborates that in the Anonimalle chronicle, and adds some new details.

---

[48] *An.* pp. 146.
[49] *An.* pp. 150. Cf. *CPR, 1381–1385*, p. 120.
[50] *An.* pp. 141–2.

For example, he describes King Richard's visit to Westminster abbey on 15 June, before he met the rebels at Smithfield. By means of this royal visit St Edward, according to the chronicler ('to the exaltation of his own sanctity and the consolation of the kingdom'), was able to avenge the injury done him by the rebels, who had violated his sanctuary (they had dragged the fugitive steward of the marshalsea, Richard Imworth, from it in order to murder him). The king came, accompanied by lords, knights and citizens, to pray for help. He was met by a procession of the monks, and prayed with his companions who made generous offerings at the shrines. 'And as they rose from their devotions, each received hope and reassurance that all would be well.'[51]

Henry Knighton was well informed about the revolt, both in London and elsewhere, but like the Westminster chronicler he writes particularly vividly with reference to his own home. He describes the preparations made by the men of Leicester against the expected arrival of the rebels from London, who intended to destroy John of Gaunt's manor there.[52] The mayor was uncertain whether to resist, risking his and his men's lives, or to collaborate with the rebels, and face the possibility of punishment afterwards as an accomplice. After taking advice he decided to stand firm, and, therefore, ordered everyone to arm. About 1,200 men assembled, 'some good and some less so'. Meanwhile Gaunt's keeper of the wardrobe[53] arrived, loaded the duke's possessions in the castle on to carts, and brought them to St Mary of the Meadows for safekeeping. But as the abbot was too frightened to accept custody, they were deposited in the cemetery of St Mary of the Castle. However, the precautions proved unnecessary because the rebels never came.

The chroniclers all wrote about the Peasants' Revolt from the point of view of the established order. All were equally appalled by the anarchy. Nevertheless, it is possible to detect some sympathy for the rebels. The Anonimalle chronicle, Henry Knighton and the *Eulogium*, giving the poll tax as the immediate cause of the revolt, describe the activities of the tax commissioners as excessively oppressive. The Anonimalle chronicle asserts that no benefit, only evil and suffering, came to the realm from the heavy taxation of the poor and the impoverishment of the commons.[54] Both it and Henry Knighton relate how the men of Fobbing in Essex finally led the commons to revolt.[55] (The *Eulogium* has a similar account, but does not give the name of the actual place.)[56] Knighton writes: 'when

---

[51] *Poly.* ix. 4–5.
[52] *HK*, ii. 142–3.
[53] Here called 'custos gardropiae' (*HK*, ii. 143). For Gaunt's clerk of the wardrobe, William Oke, see *John of Gaunt's Register, 1379–1383*, ed. R. Somerville (Camden Soc., third series, lvi, lvii, 1937, 2 vols), i. xxxviii et seq.
[54] *An.* p. 133.
[55] *An.* p. 134; *HK*, ii. 130–1.
[56] *EH*, iii. 351.

PLATE I   The *Annales Paulini:* the annals from 1314 to 1316, with a marginal drawing of the west front of Old St Paul's, and an addition inserted at the end of the annal for 1315. (Lambeth Palace Library MS. 1106, f.96ᵛ.) See pp.26 and n.138, 27 and n.146.

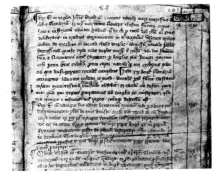

PLATE II   Ranulf Higden's *Polychronicon*, autograph, *c*.1352. (Huntington Library and Art Gallery, San Marino, California, MS. HM 132, ff.32, 103, 281, respectively.) See pp.44 and n.7, 45 and n.8. (a) An erased and rewritten initial letter: part of the revision required in order to insert Higden's name in acrostic; 'L' is changed to 'P', for the 'p' in 'Ranulphus'. (An enlarged ultra-violet photograph.) (b) A marginal addition by Higden, with his mark, 'R'. (An enlarged ultra-violet photograph.) (c) Part of the penultimate page: the text of the latest recension of the *Polychronicon* ends at 'discessum est'; the continuation for 1341 proceeds with a change of pen and ink. (A reduced photograph.)

PLATE III Chandos Herald's *La Vie du Prince Noir:* the frontispiece; above, the Holy Trinity; below, the Black Prince praying. Late 14th century. (University of London Library MS.1, f.3ᵛ.) See p.60 n.12.

PLATE IV Thomas Walsingham's *Liber Benefactorum*, 1380: a page with pictures of the benefactors; a self portrait of the artist, Alan Strayler (right). BL MS. Cotton Nero D VII, f.96ᵛ, 108, respectively.) See p.123 and n.52.

PLATE V Jean Froissart's *Chroniques*: a miniature from a richly illuminated copy executed in Flanders for William Hastings, Baron Hastings, c.1460–80. The Peasants' Revolt; John Balle (marked 'Jehan Balle') addresses the rebels led by Wat Tyler (marked 'Waultre le Tieulier'). (BL MS. Royal 18 E I, f.165ᵛ.) See p.90 n.199.

(a)

(b)

PLATE VI Jean Creton's *Histoire du Roy d'Angleterre Richard:* miniatures from a copy executed in France for Charles III of Anjou, count of Maine and Mortain (d.1472). (BL MS. Harley 1319, ff.7ᵛ, 44, respectively.) See p.189 and n.186. (a) (Top) Relief ships bringing provisions to Richard II's troops in Ireland, 1399. (b) (Bottom) The capture of Richard II near Conway, 1399.

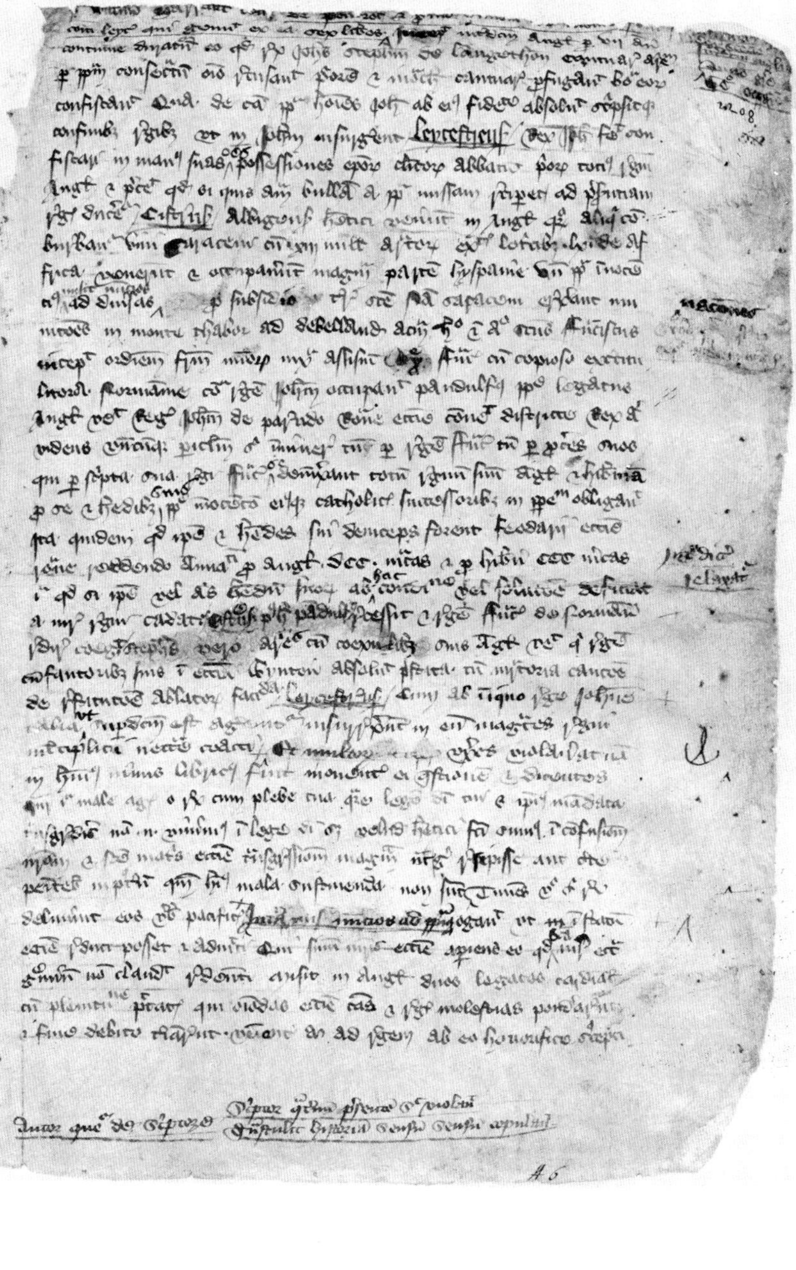

PLATE VII The chronicle of Henry Knighton: a page from an early text revised, by inter-lineal and marginal correction, under the author's supervision, with a note and two lines of verse in the bottom margin possibly in the author's own hand; *c.*1395. (BL MS. Tiberius C VII, f.62.) See p.159 n.9.

PLATE VIII The *History of the Arrival of Edward IV*: a miniature from an illuminated copy executed in Flanders, *c.*1471; the battle of Barnet. (University of Ghent MS. 236, f.2.) See pp.265, 482–3, 487–9.

PLATE IX Jean de Waurin's *Recueil des Croniques*: a miniature from the illuminated copy executed in Flanders for Edward IV, c.1470–80; the author presenting his book to the king, whose arms are in the lower border. (BL MS. Royal 15 E IV, f.14) See p.291 n.20.

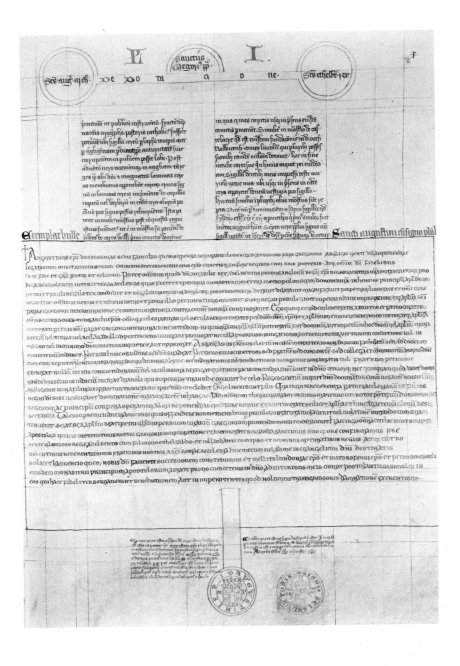

PLATE X   Thomas Elmham's *Speculum Augustinianum*: his facsimile of St Augustine's 'bull' to the abbey of St Augustine, Canterbury, *c*.1410. (Trinity Hall, Cambridge, MS. 1, f.24.) See p.353 and nn.60, 61.

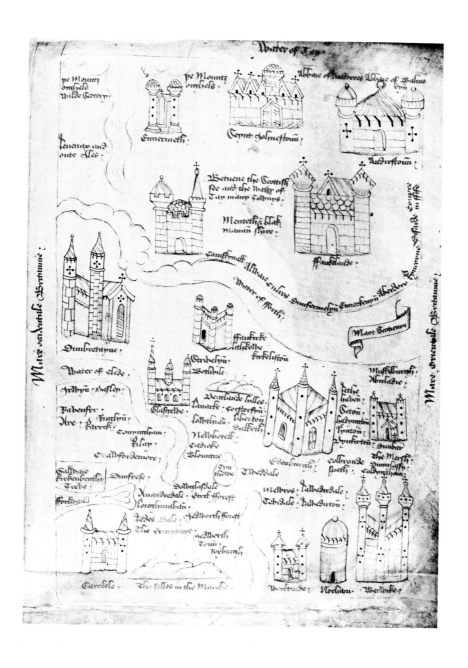

PLATE XI Map of the lowlands of Scotland, from John Hardyng's *Chronicle*, c.1464. (BL MS. Harley 661, f.187.) See p.286 and n.278.

(a) Arthgallus.

(b) Ufa.

PLATE XII   Illustrations from John Rous's Warwick Rolls, 1477–1485. ((a)–(e) are from the 'Lancastrian' roll, BL MS. Additional 48976, and (f) is from the 'Yorkist' roll in the College of Arms.) See p.327 and nn.133–5.

(c) William de Newburgh
(d.1184).

(d) Waleran de Newburgh
(d.1203 or 1204).

(e)   Thomas Beauchamp II
(d.1401).

(f)   Richard Neville (d.1471).

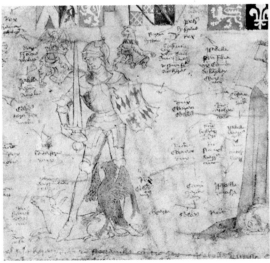

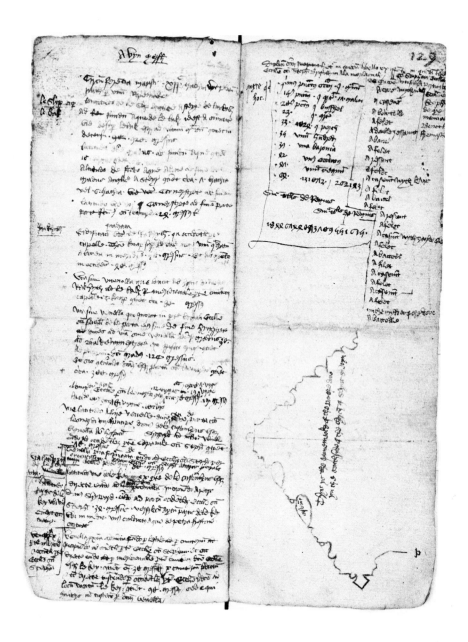

PLATE XIV   The chronicle of the Grey friars of Newgate, London: the annals from 1537 to 1540. It will be noticed that there is no change in the handwriting at 1538, the year of the friary's dissolution. (BL MS. Cotton Vitellius F XII, f.352.) See pp.421 n.238, 422.

the commons saw themselves thus harshly treated, and that ever increasing burdens were placed on them, they were unable to bear it any more, and consulted to find a remedy.'[57] The fact that these chroniclers, like Thomas Walsingham, explain the insurgents' case in such detail, suggests that they had at least some understanding of their troubles. Moreover, Knighton includes copies of vernacular verses current among the rebels, similar to those quoted by Walsingham.[58] And Froissart has such a powerful rendering of John Balle's sermon to the rebels on the equality of man, that it is hard to believe he did not appreciate its content. The sermon (in Lord Berners' translation) is as follows:[59]

> Ah, ye good people, the matters goeth not well to pass in England, nor shall not do till everything be common, and that there be no villeins nor gentlemen, but that we may be all uni[t]ed together, and that the lords be no greater masters than we be. What have we deserved, or why should we be kept thus in servage? We be all come from one father and one mother, Adam and Eve: whereby can they say or shew that they be greater lords than we be, saving by that they cause us to win and labour for that they dispend? They are clothed in velvet and camlet furred with grise, and we be vestured with poor cloth: they have their wines, spices and good bread, and we have the drawing out of the chaff and drink water: they dwell in fair houses, and we have the pain and travail, rain and wind in the fields; and by that that cometh of our labours they keep and maintain their estates: we be called their bondmen and without we do readily them service, we be beaten. . . .

Although the Peasants' Revolt was beyond dispute the most serious challenge to the social order in medieval England, another force was beginning to undermine it in Richard's reign. This was Lollardy. Knighton asserted that Lollardy set servant against master,[60] and both he and Thomas Walsingham believed that John Balle acquired his egalitarian views from Lollard teaching,[61] although in fact such opinions were commonplace in the sermons of the time. Nevertheless, some of John Wyclif's tenets, for example his theory of dominion (that authority could only be exercised by those in a state of grace), and his belief in the sole sufficiency of the bible, which should be open to everyone, do have egalitarian tendencies.

Both the author of the *Eulogium* and Henry Knighton deplore the

[57] *HK*, ii. 130.
[58] *HK*, ii. 138–40. See p. 133 above.
[59] *The Chronicles of Froissart translated by John Bouchier, Lord Berners*, ed. G. C. Macaulay (London 1913), p. 251. Cf. *JF* (K de L), ix. 388.
[60] *HK*, ii. 187.
[61] *HK*, ii. 151, 170. See p. 132 above.

Lollards' dissemination of the gospels and of religious books in English, which in their view could only result in the corruption of literate laymen as well as those of humbler birth.[62] Knighton appealed to the thirteenth century theologian and controversialist William of St Amour, who had included changes made in the text of the gospels among the signs portending the end of the world.[63] The support given by the nobility to the Lollards was a cause of concern. John of Gaunt's active partisanship posed a problem for Henry Knighton because the Lancastrians were the patrons of his house. Therefore he represents the 'pious' duke as having been seduced, like many others, by the wiles of the Lollards.[64]

Of all the chroniclers Henry Knighton shows the greatest interest in and knowledge of the Lollards. This was because Leicester was one of their centres. Wycliff himself held the rectory of Lutterworth less than thirteen miles away, and a group of Lollards occupied the chapel of St John the Baptist just outside Leicester.[65] One Lollard, John Aston, preached in the town on Palm Sunday 1382[66] and another, William de Swinderby, not only preached and lived there, but even for a while had a room, food and pension in the abbey because the canons temporarily believed in his sanctity.[67] In 1388 the king wrote to various dignitaries in Leicester ordering them to exterminate the heresy,[68] and in 1389 a number of Lollards did public penance in the market place.[69]

It is not, therefore, surprising that Lollardy elicited some of Knighton's best descriptive writing. He treats the subject biographically, perhaps influenced by the hagiographical tradition, and includes illustrative documents. Thus he described the heretical careers of Nicholas of Hereford, John Purvey, William Smith and William de Swinderby.[70] His first-hand observation appears, for example, in his description of the Lollards' dress: they wore 'russett coloured clothes, as if they were proving their simplicity of heart to the outside world'.[71] similarly, he describes some of the Lollard leaders. John Purvey, 'a simple chaplain, who dressed like a common man, was mature in gesture and appearance, and was of a more saintly aspect than the others; he devoted himself tirelessly to the labour

---

[62] *EH*, iii. 355; *HK*, ii. 152–6, 188, 263, 313.

[63] Knighton cites chapter eight, and gives the chapter headings of William of St Amour's tract against the mendicants, *De Periculis novissimorum Temporum* (printed *Fasciculus Rerum expetendarum* ..., ed. Edward Brown (London 1690, 2 vols), ii. 18–41, and elsewhere); *HK*, ii. 152–6.

[64] *HK*, ii. 193.

[65] *HK*, ii. 182. The chapel of St John the Baptist was in the eastern suburbs of Leicester; see *VCH*, *Leics*. ii. 40.

[66] *HK*, ii. 176.

[67] *HK*, ii. 190.

[68] *HK*, ii. 263–5.

[69] *HK*, ii. 313.

[70] *HK*, ii. 170–98 passim.

[71] *HK*, ii. 184.

of preaching.'[72] William Smith, on the other hand, was 'insignificant and deformed in appearance'. Knighton tells how when forbidden to preach in the chapel of St John, Swinderby used 'a pair of millstones which stood by the royal road nearby' as a pulpit from which to preach to the people.[73]

Knighton's account of William Smith's and William de Swinderby's lives at Leicester is particularly vivid. Smith, according to Knighton, was rejected by a pretty girl, and, therefore, turned to religion, renouncing women together with linen, meat, fish, wine and beer, and went for years barefoot. He and another Lollard held meetings of the sect in St John's chapel. One day, having no fuel to cook a cabbage, they chopped up a statue of St Katherine to burn, 'thus making her suffer martyrdom again', saying that they would only spare and adore her if she bled.[74] (Knighton remarks on the Lollards' hatred of images; apparently they called St Mary of Lincoln the 'witch of Lincoln', and St Mary of Walsingham the 'witch of Walsingham'.)[75] Smith, with some others, did penance for this at Leicester in 1388; 'he walked around the market place dressed only in a shirt carrying a crucifix in his right hand and an image of St Katherine in his left.'[76]

Knighton thought William de Swinderby unstable because he had tried various modes of life. At first Swinderby lived in Leicester but preached with such immoderate venom against the weakness and pride of women, that the good matrons threatened to stone him out of town. He next became a hermit in the duke of Lancaster's woods where, maintained by the alms of John of Gaunt and the pious people of Leicester, he gained a reputation for sanctity. Then, after his stay in St Mary's abbey, he joined William Smith in St John's chapel. In 1382 he was convicted of heresy by the bishop of Lincoln, and condemned to be burnt. However, through Gaunt's intervention his punishment was commuted: he had to declare his errors and heresies publicly in Lincoln, Leicester and elsewhere, and promise not to preach without the bishop's licence. He remained for a while in St John's chapel but, being now deserted by all his followers, he fled to Coventry, thus passing from Knighton's view.[77]

The autobiographical element (the authors' record of events in their lives, their impressions and feelings) which is a characteristic feature of the chronicles of Froissart, Creton and Adam of Usk, both foreshadows the renaissance autobiographies, and is reminiscent of some twelfth century

[72] *HK*, ii. 178–9.
[73] *HK*, ii. 180, 192.
[74] *HK*, ii. 180–2.
[75] *HK*, ii. 183.
[76] *HK*, ii. 313.
[77] *HK*, ii. 189–98.

writers, for example Gerald of Wales. It is especially marked when the authors wrote fresh with the impression of novelties experienced on their travels abroad.

Ireland had the same fascination as in the days of Gerald of Wales. Froissart learnt from an esquire, Henry 'Crystède', who had an Irish wife, about the Irish methods of guerrilla combat, and how Edward III educated four Irish kings in English manners and customs after their submission to him.[78] But Creton gained his information at first hand. He describes vividly the people and terrain, both of which amazed him. Having noted the arrival of King Richard's fleet at Waterford, he writes: 'The wretched and filthy people, some in rags, others girt with a rope, lived in holes or huts: they were forced to carry great burdens, and to go into the water up to their waists, in order to unload the boats from the sea quickly.' He comments on the wildness of the country; there were no roads, and the bogs were so deep that, if you were not careful, you would sink up to the waist or wholly disappear. Creton declares that he 'never saw a wilder people than the Irish', who feared the arrows of the English, but could do much injury on their fast horses which 'scoured the hills and valleys fleeter than deer'. He himself saw the submission of the uncle of Art Mac-Murrough, king of Leinster, to Richard II, 'with a halter round his neck and a drawn sword, together with many others naked and barefoot'. And Creton, referring the reader to a portrait on the opposite page, describes Art MacMurrough: his horse 'was so fine and good that without saddle or harness it cost him, they say, 400 cows (because there is little money in the country, the only currency is animals), . . . and [Mac-Murrough] carried in his right hand a great long dart, which he cast with much skill'.[79]

Creton expresses his discomfort during the Irish campaign,[80] which was only alleviated by the arrival of provisions when the army moved to Dublin.[81] Sometimes, he observed, four or six soldiers had to share a single loaf, while some had nothing to eat for five days together. The horses were weakened by the sparse diet of green oats, and by the rain and cold. 'For my part I should have been heartily glad to have been penniless in Poitiers

---

[78] *JF* (K de L), xv. 168 et seq.

[79] *Creton*, pp. 326–331 passim, 334–5. For a picture of Art MacMurrough or MacMurchad (1357–1417) see **BL MS.** Harley 1319 (for which see p. 189 n. 186 below), f. 9 (reproduced in E. Maunde Thompson, 'A contemporary account of the fall of Richard II' in *Burlington Magazine*, v (1904) pp. 160–72, 267–70, Plate II and, in lithograph, in *Creton* (Webb), Plate IV). A recent scholar considers that of chronicle sources Froissart and Creton are the most useful for Richard II's Irish expeditions; see J. F. Lydon, 'Richard II's expeditions to Ireland' in *Journal of the Royal Society of Antiquaries of Ireland*, xciii (1963), p. 149.

[80] The contemporary poets also on occasion expressed their own feelings. For example, John Gower describes his terror during the Peasants' Revolt; *Vox Clamantis*, i. 16–21 passim (*Complete Works*, ed. Macaulay, iv. 59–81).

[81] *Creton*, pp. 331–3.

or Paris, because here there was no amusement or mirth, only trouble, toil and danger.'

Creton gives an equally exact description of his emotions in his account of political history. When Richard's fortunes declined, Creton pitied his sufferings. 'I declare', he writes, referring to the king's wanderings from castle to castle in north Wales (Richard had to sleep on straw for lack of furniture), 'that I wept for him a hundred times.'[82] Richard's capture moved Creton to even deeper sympathy, and he was delighted when the native Welsh harried Henry duke of Lancaster's army on its way through the marches of Wales to London.[83] However, eventually his fear proved stronger than his sympathy for the fallen king. When Henry took Richard to Chester, Creton writes 'I do not think that I ever was so much afraid as I was at that time.' Therefore, he and his companion obtained an interview with Duke Henry, told him who they were and pleaded for their lives.[84] Henry promised them safety, but when they reached London, being 'sad and sick at heart', they asked leave to return to France.[85]

Creton's esteem and sympathy for Richard survived his return home. Having written his chronicle to record Richard's tribulations, he completed the work with details of the deposition itself, which he heard from an eyewitness,[86] and with an account of the king's death by voluntary starvation. He upbraided the English for their treacherous cruelty, and included a ballad inciting the chivalry of Europe to avenge Richard's sufferings:[87] his final words were: 'Princes and kings, knights and barons, French, Flemings, Germans and Bretons should attack you [the English] for you have done the most horrible deed that ever man committed.'

Meanwhile Creton was uncertain about Richard's ultimate fate, and began to suspect that the king was not dead. Already in the chronicle he had expressed doubt as to whether the body buried on 12 March 1400 was actually that of the former king,[88] and rumours must have reached him that Richard was alive and in Scotland. Then late in 1401 or early in 1402 Creton addressed a letter to Richard expressing his joy at learning that the king was alive and his wish to visit him soon; he promised to bring Richard a copy of his history.[89] Shortly afterwards Charles VI and Philip the Bold, duke of Burgundy, sent Creton to discover the truth, whether

---

[82] *Creton*, p. 372.
[83] *Creton*, p. 416.
[84] *Creton*, pp. 410–11.
[85] *Creton*, p. 418.
[86] *Creton*, p. 422.
[87] *Creton*, pp. 419–20.
[88] *Creton*, pp. 451–2.
[89] The letter, which is undated, is printed in P. W. Dillon, 'Remarks on the manner of the death of King Richard the Second' in *Archaeologia*, xxviii (1840), pp. 87–9, from Bibl. Nat. MS. n.a. fr. 6223 (for which see p. 161 n. 21 above). For the date of the letter see Palmer, op. cit., p. 154.

Richard was alive or not.[90] Creton returned with the knowledge of Richard's murder and wrote a moving letter, including a ballad, to Philip the Bold (whom he had supplied with a copy of his chronicle),[91] exhorting him and the nobles of France to revenge Richard by force of arms.[92]

Creton's chronicle, therefore, reflects its author's feelings. In a similar way Froissart combined notices of events in his life with comments on his reactions to them. He describes his experiences and feelings on his visit to England in 1395, his first visit for twenty seven years.[93] He especially wished to meet King Richard whose baptism he had attended at Bordeaux in 1367. Before leaving Flanders he collected numerous letters of recommendation, and had some of his love poems bound in a presentation volume. He arrived at Canterbury, and was told that the king was coming there as a pilgrim. Froissart, therefore, went to Ospringe, where he joined Sir William Lisle, with whom he rode to Leeds castle. He was at last introduced to the king, but did not give him the book because Richard 'was so sore occupied with great affairs'. Froissart rode with the court from Leeds to Eltham, on the way questioning Sir William Lisle and Sir John de Grailly about recent political events in England, and 'memorizing their words'. At Eltham he met an old acquaintance, Sir Richard Stury (a friend of Chaucer's) whom he had not seen since his previous stay in England. He obtained information from him on recent events as they 'walked in the galleries, where it was right pleasant and shady, for those galleries were at the time covered with vines.'

Stury and another old acquaintance, the duke of York, and Sir Thomas Percy explained Froissart's business to the king, who asked for the book which he had brought; '[King Richard], therefore, saw it in his chamber, for I laid it ready on his bed. When the king opened it, it pleased him well, for it was fair illumined and written, and covered with crimson velvet, with ten buttons of silver and gilt, and roses of gold in the midst, with two great gilt clasps, richly wrought.' In reply to Richard's questions, Froissart

---

[90] Jean Creton was paid 20 francs by John the Fearless, duke of Burgundy (1404–19) 'pour soy en aller au pays d'Escoce par devers le roy Richart' by a mandate dated 11 November 1407; Cockshaw, op. cit., p. 138 no. 69. He was also paid 200 francs by Charles VI 'pour et en recompensation d'un Voyaige que par nostre commandement et ordonnance il fist pieca au pays d'Escoce pour savoir et enquerir la vérité de nostre très cher et très ame fils le Roy Richart d'Angleterre que l'on disoit lors estre en vie audict pays d'Escoce'; the mandate, printed in Dillon, op. cit., p. 94, is dated 29 July 1410. The receipt, printed in ibid., p. 95, is dated 7 August 1410. Jones, op. cit., p. 468, prefers to call this document 'a record of a transaction' rather than a receipt. He discusses (ibid., pp. 467, 468) both documents printed by Dillon, but was not acquainted with the extracts from the Burgundian accounts which Cockshaw later printed. Cf. Palmer, op. cit., p. 153.

[91] See p. 161 n. 21, above.

[92] The ballad and letter, which is undated, is printed from Bibl. Nat. MS. n.a. fr. 6223 (for which see p. 161 n. 21 above) in Dillon, op. cit., pp. 90–4. For the date of the letter see Palmer, op. cit., p. 154.

[93] *JF* (K de L), xv. 140–67.

explained the subject of the book. The king read some passages ('for he could speak and read French very well') and then had the book taken by a knight of his chamber called Sir Richard Credon into his 'secret chamber'. Although later Froissart strongly disapproved of Richard's political behaviour, he continued to appreciate his kindness. When he left court after a stay of about three months, Richard gave him 'a goblet of silver and gilt weighing two mark of silver, and within it 100 nobles, by which', Froissart comments, writing after the king's deposition, 'I am as yet the better, and shall be as long as I live.'

Adam of Usk scatters his personal reminiscences throughout his chronicle, recording the stages of his career and his reactions to the tribulations he endured. He was born in about 1352 at Usk in Monmouthshire,[94] and went to study at Oxford. As a student he seems to have been rather a hothead, but in 1388 he learnt to 'fear the king and his laws': he led the Welsh students against the north country ones, when the latter besieged their lodgings for two days— 'and on the third day we put them to flight with help from Merton Hall'; he was among those indicted by the royal justices, and scarcely escaped conviction by the jury.[95] During the 1399 revolution Adam was again involved in violence. He was in the train of Archbishop Arundel during the march to Chester, and records with satisfaction that, when Bolingbroke's army was camped at Coddington, 'I spent a not uncheerful night in the tent of Lord Powis.' He also records that he was with those who searched for loot 'in water-cisterns and other hiding places'.[96]

Adam became a traveller after his flight from England in 1402. He does not explain why he left, but other evidence suggests that it may have been for fear of royal anger incurred because of an allegation that he had stolen a horse.[97] He describes the hardships of his journey to Rome. He crossed the Alps through the St Gotthard pass: 'I was drawn in an ox-waggon half dead with cold and with my eyes blindfold lest I should see the dangers of the pass.'[98] In Rome he was appointed a chaplain and auditor in the papal court, but had to escape in 1405 on the expulsion of Innocent VII. Having hidden for eight days dressed as a Dominican friar, he fled 'like the beggar I was—for a merchant had taken my money at the first excuse.' He made his way down the Tiber dressed as a sailor, and going through

---

[94] *AU*, p. xi.

[95] *AU*, pp. 7 8.

[96] *AU*, p. 26. For Lord Powis see p. 176 below.

[97] Adam of Usk was indicted for stealing a black horse with saddle and bridle, and 100s and 14 marks from a certain Walter Jakes in Trinity, 1402. He was granted a pardon for the felony on 18 January and 16 June, 1403; see *CPR 1401–1405*, pp. 188, 234. Professor Storey, however, believes that he was the victim of a false indictment; see 'Clergy and common law in the reign of Henry IV', ed. Storey (p. 158 n. 5 above), p. 362. Cf. *AU*, p. xxi and n. 1.

[98] *AU*, pp. 74–5.

Ostia and Albano joined the pope at Viterbo. There he was jeered at for his disguise and nearly died of poison (administered 'by the envious', in his opinion).[99]

Adam spent the next five years, from 1405 to 1411, in the north of France and in Flanders trying to win Henry IV's favour so that he could return to England. But Henry was implacable, apparently because Adam was in touch with English traitors abroad.[100] Therefore, at great risk, 'hunted like a hare by so many hounds', Adam sailed for Wales, ostensibly to seek the protection of Owen Glendower, but in fact hoping for the help of Sir Edward Charleton, lord of Powis. He landed at Barmouth and proceeded, hiding in woods, caves and thickets, to Charleton's castle at Pool. There he lived for a while, a penniless chaplain, avoided by his relatives and former friends: 'I led a sorry life, God knows.'[101]

Adam was pardoned in 1411. Afterwards he visited some old friends from whom he obtained two horses and 100 shillings which enabled him to hire a servant. 'I was like one new-born, and began to some extent to recover the position I had had before my exile.' He went to England, regained his post in the archbishop's court, and 'sat with the other doctors in parliament.' And so gradually 'with God's help I enlarged my heart and spirit ... and like another Job, collected together servants, books, garments, and household goods, blessed be God!'[102]

A portrait emerges from Adam's chronicle of a conceited, boastful, perhaps rather paranoic man, piqued at his misfortunes and tenacious in his struggle for rehabilitation, but also of a learned scholar and acute observer. Adam probably exaggerated his influence on famous people. It was, he claims, through his intervention that Henry Bolingbroke spared the town of Usk in 1399 from the vengeance provoked by the resistance of the wife, Eleanor, of its lord, Sir Edward Charleton.[103] (Eleanor was the daughter of Richard II's half-brother, Thomas de Holand, earl of Kent.) And Adam asserts that in the same year he obtained the release from prison of Thomas Prestbury, a monk of Shrewsbury and a former fellow student at Oxford, and his promotion to the abbacy of his house.[104]

Adam tended to parade his learning and boast about his professional achievements. In 1401 when ambassadors came to arrange a marriage between Louis, duke of Bavaria, and Henry IV's daughter Blanche, Adam talked at such length and with so much erudition about the election of the emperor, that the bishop of Hereford had to tell him to be silent.[105]

[99] *AU*, pp. 99–100.
[100] *AU*, pp. 105, 117.
[101] *AU*, pp. 117–18. Sir Edward Charleton succeeded to the lordship of Powis in 1401: *AU*, pp. 70; G.E.C., *Complete Peerage*, iii. 21–2.
[102] *AU*, pp. 118–19.
[103] *AU*, pp. 25, 174 n. 4.
[104] *AU*, pp. 25–6, 175 n. 2; *CPR, 1396–1399*, pp. 592, 594 (cf. ibid., p. 584).
[105] *AU*, p. 59.

And he asserts that on becoming auditor in the papal court, he immediately settled thirty important legal cases.[106] He was ambitious in his career and resented the fact that the pope did not provide him to the bishopric of St Davids—which he attributed to the intrigues of his enemies.[107]

Adam was obviously a man of considerable learning. In England he was counsel to a number of prelates and lay magnates,[108] and he was one of the scholars appointed by Henry in 1399 to find legal justifications for the deposition of Richard II: Adam regarded Richard's misrule as reason enough and quoted the decretals to support his opinion.[109] In 1400 he was among those who advised Archbishop Arundel, having examined 'the corpus of law and the chronicles', on the violation of ecclesiastical liberties by the temporal power.[110]

As an historian, Adam had an insatiable curiosity. He questioned anyone he met from foreign parts, whether about the Greek dynasty at Constantinople, or about the origins of the monastery of St Mary of Scotland in Vienna.[111] He ransacked chronicles,[112] in order to give historical precedents for contemporary events, and to draw typological parallels between the great men of his own day and those of the past.[113] Adam was interested in the contemporary scene. When in Rome he observed the customs of the people, which he describes in some of his best passages. He gives detailed and vivid accounts of the games played by the Romans on Quinquagesima Sunday, and of the ceremonies observed in Holy Week.[114]

On a more personal level Adam shows, besides loyalty to his patrons,[115] a strong affection for his home town of Usk. He lists his own generous gifts to the church at Usk (three copes bearing his arms, and five service books 'newly written'), and while in Rome he obtained papal indulgences for those who had made gifts to the nunnery in Usk which was impoverished by the Welsh war.[116]

Information in the chronicles concerning the politics of Richard II's reign is plentiful, but its reliability is often hard to assess. This is because

---

[106] *AU*, p. 75.

[107] *AU*, p. 92.

[108] Adam was, for example, counsel to the following: John Okendon, prior of the London Charterhouse from 1397–1412 (*AU*, p. 60, and for Okendon see W. St J. Hope, *The History of the London Charterhouse* (London 1925), p. 148); Tideman de Winchcomb, bishop of Worcester (*AU*, p. 64); Lord Walter Fitz Walter (*AU*, p. 78); and 'many bishops, abbots and [other] great men in Flanders, France, Normandy and Brittany' (*AU*, p. 104).

[109] *AU*, pp. 29–31. Cf. pp. 183–4 below.

[110] *AU*, p. 44.

[111] *AU*, pp. 96–7, 101–2.

[112] For example while staying in Flanders in 1406, Adam examined chronicles in the monastery of Eeckhout; *AU*, pp. 107, 110.

[113] See, e.g., *AU*, pp. 18, 29, 43, 133.

[114] *AU*, pp. 95–8.

[115] See pp. 181–2 below.

[116] *AU*, p. 56.

all the chroniclers, with the possible exception of Froissart, are biased either against Richard or, more rarely, in his favour.[117] The bias is on occasion so strong that it leads to misrepresentation. This bias was partly the result of the influence exercised by the king and great magnates, usually as patrons, on the chroniclers, and partly the result of deliberate government propaganda. The influence of patrons is most significant in the accounts of the first important political crisis of the reign, from 1386 to 1388, and the influence of government propaganda was strongest during the last and final crisis, Richard's bid for autocracy and his de-position.

Henry Knighton, the author of the continuation of the *Eulogium Histori-arum*, and Adam of Usk, all had baronial patrons and wrote from the baro-nial point of view. The earls of Leicester and dukes of Lancaster were the patrons of Knighton's home, the abbey of St Mary of the Meadows. Henry of Grosmont (earl of Leicester 1345–61 and duke of Lancaster from 1351) in particular was an active benefactor. Knighton records that in 1352 he gave the abbot and convent a licence to make a park of its woods, stocking it with animals from his own park, and appropriated two churches to the abbey, 'the duke mediating in person with the pope' to gain the necessary papal assent.[118] Henry was also the benefactor of the town of Leicester. In 1353 he transformed the hospital of the Annun-ciation of St Mary in the Newarke, founded by his father in 1331, into a college, of the same dedication, with a dean and ten canons, and 'ten strong women to care night and day for 100 poor and infirm old people'.[119] And in 1360 Leicester obtained, through Duke Henry's intervention with the king, a licence to hold an annual fair.[120] Thus Knighton's bias in favour of and interest in the house of Lancaster were mainly the result of his loyalty to St Mary's abbey and to the town of Leicester. His affection for the abbot, William de Cloune, whose rule from 1345 until 1377 covered one of the abbey's best periods, is evident in the eulogy which accompanies the notice of his death.[121]

Knighton records numerous facts concerning the careers of Thomas of Lancaster (earl of Lancaster and Leicester 1296–1322), Henry of

---

[117] Bias in the fourteenth and fifteenth century chronicles which cover Richard II's reign is the subject of L. D. Duls, *Richard II in the Early Chronicles* (The Hague-Paris 1975). The author groups the chronicles (including those written abroad) into three categories, Lancastrian, Ricardian and Yorkist. Her purpose is to try to explain the ambivalent attitudes of the sixteenth century historians, poets and dramatists to Richard II and to other great personages of his reign, and their divergent views.

[118] *HK*, ii. 74.

[119] *HK*, ii. 115–16. See A. Hamilton Thompson, *The History of the Hospital and the New College of the Annunciation of St. Mary in the Newarke, Leicester* (Leicester 1937), chapters 1–3, and the same author's 'Notes on the colleges of secular canons in England' in *Archaeological Journal*, lxxiv (1917), pp. 139–239.

[120] *HK*, ii. 112.

[121] *HK*, ii. 125–6. Cf. Galbraith, 'The chronicle of Henry Knighton', p. 136.

Lancaster (earl of Leicester 1324–45 and of Lancaster from 1326), Henry of Grosmont, and John of Gaunt (duke of Lancaster 1362–99).

Although Knighton wrote towards the end of the fourteenth century, he has interesting details about Thomas of Lancaster and Henry of Lancaster which he derived from the earlier, now lost, chronicle of Leicester abbey,[122] from the archives preserved by the canons,[123] and from men's reminiscences. He has unique information about the baronial revolt against Edward II, including an apparently verbatim record of negotiations at Leicester between the king and Thomas of Lancaster in the summer of 1318.[124] Some of his information concerning the capture and execution of Thomas of Lancaster is also in the *Brut*,[125] but the account of how Henry of Lancaster, a partisan of Queen Isabella, acquired the possessions of Hugh Despenser, earl of Winchester, in 1326, is not recorded elsewhere: Despenser's servant, Sir John de Vaux, brought Despenser's priceless treasure, with his horses ('among the best in the realm') and their fine harness to Leicester abbey, for safe keeping; but, when he was besieged by Henry of Lancaster's men, he took it all to Leicester castle, and gave it to Henry, who three days later joined the queen's forces at Dunstable.[126] In 1328 Henry revolted with other lords against Isabella and Mortimer; the latter, Knighton records, came to Leicester and ravaged it for eight days, forcing Henry to submit.[127]

Knighton is particularly full on Henry of Grosmont's campaigns abroad, which he describes in eulogistic terms. For example, he gives an account of Henry of Grosmont's part in the capture of Calais, on 4 August 1347, after which Henry, then at the height of his power, was in charge of the town until the truce was concluded with France on 28 September in the same year. Henry had under his command 700 men-at-arms and 2,000 archers. The duke 'held such hospitality that his expenses each day amounted to £100 and eight or nine marks; when he returned after the truce it was estimated that he had spent over £17,000 of his own money besides the money he received from the king.'[128] Knighton has an especially vivid account of Duke Henry's reception at Avignon when he came as ambassador

---

[122] See p. 160 and n. 11 above.

[123] See e.g. the letter concerning the siege of Calais in 1347, cited *HK*, ii. 48. See also below and the next note.

[124] *HK*, i. 413–21. See J. R. Maddicott, *Thomas of Lancaster 1307–1322* (Oxford 1970), pp. 221, 337.

[125] For similarities between Knighton's chronicle and the *Brut* (for which see pp. 73–7 above) for the period from the end of Edward II's reign to the beginning of Edward III's see, for example: the account of Isabella's and Mortimer's autocracy, *HK*, i. 447, *Brut*. i. 257; the account of the career, capture and murder of Sir Robert de Holand (who betrayed Thomas of Lancaster), *HK*, i. 449, *Brut*, i. 216, 257 (cf. p. 75 above).

[126] *HK*, i. 435.

[127] *HK*, i. 450–1.

[128] *HK*, ii. 54. Cf. Kenneth Fowler, *The King's Lieutenant, Henry of Grosmont, First Duke of Lancaster, 1310–1361* (London 1969), pp. 70–1.

[179]

in 1353 to negotiate a truce. He arrived with 200 horses, thirty two of them fully caparisoned, and was met by bishops, nobles and citizens, in all numbering about 2,000 on horseback—so great a crowd that they could scarcely cross the bridge. He was received by the pope in the papal palace, and then went to his lodgings. There he feasted all comers (100 tuns of wine had been put ready in the cellars for his visit), 'and he showed such generosity to all, especially to the pope and cardinals, that everyone said: "he has no equal throughout the world." '[129]

Knighton is equally interested in John of Gaunt's career. He describes the hard treatment Gaunt received during the Peasants' Revolt because of the animosity he had aroused.[130] Gaunt himself was refused hospitality by the earl of Northumberland, who feared the rebels' hostility, and his wife Constance was refused admittance to his own castle of Pontefract. Therefore, the 'pious and gentle' duke, 'a lover and maker of peace', acting 'wisely, not rashly or with anger', stayed safely in Scotland where he had been negotiating a truce. Knighton concludes with a comment: 'Lest any reader wonder why I always call the duke pious, it is because in all his troubles he never sought revenge but, bearing everything with equanimity, pardoned offences to anyone who asked; he would not even allow the servants who stole his silver to be hanged, provided that they abjured his household and the king's, and the households of his brothers.'[131]

Knighton was also well informed about Gaunt's activities abroad. He has a stirring account of his siege of Brest (1386–7),[132] and reports news he heard from a member of the duke's household concerning the wealth Gaunt acquired on the marriage of his daughter Katherine with the infante, Henry, son of Juan I, king of Castile and Leon, in 1388: he states that King Juan sent forty seven mules laden with gold for the second part of the payment. ('I did not ask about the first part.')[133]

Knighton's attitude to John of Gaunt was inevitably ambivalent. He wanted to praise him as a Lancastrian, but there were two obstacles: John of Gaunt was immoral—he had a mistress, Katherine Swinford; and he abetted heretics—he supported John Wyclif and his followers. Knighton countered the first difficulty by asserting that at the time of the Peasants' Revolt, Gaunt, seeing his troubles as divine vengeance for his immorality, renounced Katherine.[134] With regard to the second obstacle,

---

[129] *HK*, ii. 78–9. Cf. Fowler, op. cit., pp. 136–7.

[130] See p. 168 above.

[131] *HK*, ii. 143–50 passim.

[132] *HK*, ii. 209. Cf. Michael Jones, *Ducal Brittany 1364–1399* (Oxford 1970), p. 103.

[133] *HK*, ii. 208. Cf. S. Armitage-Smith, *John of Gaunt* (London 1904), p. 330. For the payments owed by Juan I to the duke of Lancaster and Constance according to the agreement for the marriage of Henry and Katherine see *Cronicas de los Reyes de Castilla ... por D. Pedro Lopez de Ayala*, ed. Eugenio de Llaguno Amirola (Madrid 1779–80, 2 vols), ii. 273–4.

[134] *HK*, ii. 147–8. Walsingham has a similar account of Gaunt's repentance; see p. 130 and n. 79 above.

Knighton alleged that the duke was 'deceived, like many others, by the plausible words and appearance' of the Lollards.[135]

The loyalty of the Franciscan continuator of the *Eulogium Historiarum* was not to a secular magnate, nor exclusively to one ecclesiastic. However, probably because he had some connection with Canterbury, the continuator shows a marked regard for the archbishop. His attachment becomes particularly apparent towards the end of the fourteenth century, the period when he began writing. He has a close interest in and knowledge of Thomas Arundel, the brother of the appellant lord, Richard earl of Arundel (1376–97), and archbishop of Canterbury from 1396 to 1397, and again from 1399 to 1414.

The continuator gives a graphic description, with direct speech, of the archbishop's reluctant part in the arrest of his brother, the earl of Arundel, in 1397. The king asked Archbishop Arundel to bring the earl to him, but the archbishop replied, 'You will do him harm if he comes.' Eventually, at the king's insistence, the archbishop consented, and led the frightened earl into the royal presence. King Richard at once handed him over to Thomas Mowbray, earl of Nottingham, who took him into another room, closing the door. The archbishop 'waited until evening, and then sadly returned to his house at Lambeth.'[136] The continuator describes in similar style how Archbishop Arundel was exiled in the same year. The archbishop was grieved at the sentence, but the king promised his early recall and undertook that no successor should be appointed in his absence.[137] And the author has a full account of Archbishop Arundel's part in Richard II's deposition.[138]

Adam of Usk, a secular cleric, was influenced by more than one patron. His patrons included Archbishop Thomas Arundel, from whom he received a number of livings. His loyalty to the archbishop is reflected in his chronicle. He commemorates his death with a panegyric,[139] and has a number of details, which are not found elsewhere, relating to the archbishop's career. Particularly vivid is his account of Archbishop Arundel's return to Lambeth palace after Henry IV had restored him to the primacy in October 1399. Adam describes how he noticed when dining with the archbishop that Roger de Walden, to whom King Richard (despite his promise to Arundel not to appoint a successor) had given the archbishopric during Arundel's exile, had removed all the ornaments from the hall and

---

[135] *HK*, ii. 193.

[136] *EH*, iii. 371–2.

[137] *EH*, iii. 376. For the sermon he preached at Henry IV's accession, which is also recorded by the chronicler, see p. 183 and n. 150 below. For the possibility that these biographical passages relating to the archbishop originally formed part of a biography written in the Lancastrian interest see p. 141 n. 166 above and pp. 187 n. 180, 199 n. 38 below.

[138] *EH*, iii. 382–4 passim.

[139] *AU*, pp. 121–3.

other rooms, including the Arundel coat of arms, which he had replaced by his own. 'However,' Adam writes, with reference to Walden's arms, 'they did not last long for, taking them down, my Lord Thomas again restored his own arms and badges which had been most skilfully woven in textile. And when the arms of the said Roger were thus taken down, I saw them lying under the benches, objects of mirth, to be cast and flung out of the window by the servants.'[140] In addition, Adam had secular patrons, the earls of March. Roger Mortimer, the fourth earl of March (1381–98) gave Adam a studentship in civil and canon law at Oxford, and Philippa, countess of March and widow of Edmund, the third earl (1360–81), gave him the living of West Hanningfield. Adam has a number of notices concerning the family; he includes a eulogy on Earl Edmund, a genealogy from Adam the first man through the British kings to the earls of Adam of Usk's own day, and other details of family history.[141]

The patrons of Henry Knighton, the continuator of the *Eulogium* and Adam of Usk were all supporters of the baronial cause. The patron of the Westminster chronicler was, on the contrary, the king himself. Besides describing a number of visits paid by Richard II to Westminster abbey, the chronicler notices with gratitude the king's munificence to the monks. He records, for example, his gift of a ruby ring 'of great value' to St Edward's shrine in 1388, and that after the king had attended the exequies of his half sister Matilda, countess of St Pol, at Westminster in 1392, he gave the monks the rich banners erected around the bier.[142]

The chronicler especially praises Richard for defending the abbey's privilege of sanctuary. As a result of the flight of Sir Robert Tresilian, the chief justice, to the sanctuary of Westminster abbey in 1388, the barons called the privilege in question. The chancellor (Thomas Arundel) decided that a fugitive should be taken from the sanctuary. Otherwise, he argued, even someone killing the king could never be brought to justice. However, the king himself thought such an idea ridiculous, and said that those who had dragged Tresilian from Westminster should be excommunicated. The chronicler concludes his account with a panegyric on Richard:[143]

> See how the king venerates and loves the church of God, with what affection and assiduity he struggles to defend and preserve her liberties. Truly no bishop is so zealous for the rights of the church as he!

Clearly the political views of the chroniclers were influenced by those of their patrons. Knighton, the continuator of the *Eulogium*, and Adam of

---

[140] *AU*, p. 38.
[141] *AU*, pp. 19–23, 54–5.
[142] *Poly.* ix. 200, 265.
[143] *Poly.* ix. 174. For other references to the sanctuary see ibid., pp. 9, 47, 247, 271.

Usk held 'constitutional' opinions, while the Westminster chronicler had a royalist bias.[144] (Creton, who, like Froissart, favoured King Richard, partly because he had been a guest at his court, will be considered separately, as a special case.) Knighton's point of view appears in his account of Edward II's reign, and lasts throughout his chronicle. He represents Thomas of Lancaster as dying for the 'justice of church and realm',[145] and asserts that Henry of Lancaster was made 'chief keeper and supreme councillor of the king by common consent of the great men and magnates of the realm' at Edward III's coronation.[146] (He has little on John of Gaunt's political role, concentrating on his campaigns and relations with the Lollards.) He reiterates that both Edward II and Richard II were seduced by evil counsellors, and has a full account of the constitutional crisis of 1386–8, describing the Appellants as 'friends of the king and kingdom, defenders of the truth, and stalwart guardians, with God's help, of the poor'.[147]

The continuator of the *Eulogium* expresses equal hostility to Richard II's rule, although in less theoretical terms. He refers to 'flatterers' at court, accuses the king of extortion, and states that the proceedings of the parliament of 1397 were in accordance with civil law and not with the laws of England.[148] He gives an unfavourable account of Richard's behaviour in the annal for 1398. He describes how on state occasions he had a throne prepared in his chamber on which he sat in silence from lunch time until evening, staring at the company—whomever he looked at, of whatever rank, had to genuflect to him.[149] The continuator gives a full account of Archbishop Thomas Arundel's part in the final climax of the reign, reciting his speech on Richard's misrule at the deposition and specifying the theme of his sermon at Henry's accession.[150]

Similarly Adam of Usk is unfavourable to Richard. His patron, Roger earl of March, was, as Adam points out, the victim of the king's anger in 1398.[151] Furthermore, Adam took an active part in Richard's deposition: he was one of the commissioners appointed to examine its legal justification; he decided, on studying the chronicle evidence, that Richard's mis-

---

[144] In addition, Richard of Maidstone, a Carmelite friar who wrote an account in verse of the king's reconciliation with the Londoners in 1394, and was probably in royal service, shows a strong bias in favour of King Richard. His poem is discussed and printed in *Political Poems*, ed. Wright, i. lxxiii-lxxvii, 282–300.

[145] *HK*, i. 426.

[146] *HK*, i. 447. According to Knighton, Isabella and Mortimer made peace with Scotland 'without the counsel and assent of the community of the realm and of the lords', while the lords opposed Richard II in 1386 'with the common consent of lords and commons': *HK*, i. 448; ii. 215.

[147] *HK*, ii. 244. For 'evil counsellors' see *HK*, i. 435, 442; ii. 236, 242–3.

[148] *EH*, iii. 367, 372, 373.

[149] *EH*, iii. 378.

[150] *EH*, iii. 382–4.

[151] *AU*, p. 19.

government, not the law of inheritance, justified Henry Bolingbroke's succession.[152] Adam's antagonism to Richard appears throughout his chronicle. He deplores the influence that sycophants had over Richard, criticizing their self indulgence and extravagance and attributing their power partly to the king's youth.[153] And he states that in 1398 Richard oppressed his people, notably by employing 400 Cheshire guards whose unbridled excesses brought about the king's ruin.[154]

The attitude of the Westminster chronicler to Richard II is ambivalent. Although he praises Richard as the abbey's patron, his opinion of him as king is only a little higher than that of the other chroniclers. He includes criticism of Richard, asserting, for example, that the king followed the advice of evil counsellors, did not keep his promises to the lords, did not live exclusively on his own income and kept 'superabundant' retainers.[155] And he has graphic descriptions of Richard's hot temper: he relates how the king reduced parliament to amazed silence, when he shouted at Richard, earl of Arundel (who had accused him of misrule), calling him a liar and telling him to go to the devil.[156] On another occasion the king was restrained with difficulty by the earl of Buckingham from striking William Courtney, archbishop of Canterbury, with his sword, having leapt into his boat when they met on the Thames. Richard was angry because the archbishop had accused him of taking evil counsel and conniving at a plot to murder John of Gaunt.[157] One reason why the Westminster chronicler criticizes Richard, his abbey's patron, was probably city politics, which he describes in detail. The chronicler sympathized with John of Northampton, a draper, mayor from 1381 to 1383, who tried to break the monopoly of the victuallers, especially of the fishmongers. Richard opposed and imprisoned Northampton, appointing his own nominee, Nicholas Brembre, a grocer, to the mayoralty.[158] On this matter, therefore, the Westminster chronicler represented different interests from the king's. The same reason may also partly account for his consistently favourable attitude to John of Gaunt, the principal supporter of John of Northampton.[159]

---

[152] *AU*, pp. 29–31.

[153] *AU*, pp. 4–5. For the influence of youthful counsellors on Richard see *AU*, p. 36.

[154] *AU*, p. 23.

[155] *Poly.* ix. 57 and 103, 109, 73, 83, respectively.

[156] *Poly.* ix. 33. However, the previously held view that Richard threw his shoes and cloak out of the window in a fit of rage when a Carmelite friar, John Latimer, accused John of Gaunt of treachery, is now known to have been based on a misreading of the manuscript: *Poly.* ix. 34; cf. L. C. Hector, 'An alleged hysterical outburst of Richard II' in *EHR*, lxviii (1953), pp. 62–5.

[157] *Poly.* ix. 58–9.

[158] *Poly.* ix. 29–31, 45–9, 51, 68–9, 74–5, 238–9, 243. See Ruth Bird, *The Turbulent London of Richard II* (London 1949), pp. 63–85. Cf. p. 152 and n. 246 above.

[159] For passages in favour of John of Gaunt, particularly as a peace maker, see *Poly.* ix. 219, 238, 267.

In the same way patronage helped determine John Gower's political outlook. He originally dedicated the *Confessio Amantis* (*The Confession of a Lover*) to King Richard, and praised him in it. However, when he revised the poem in about 1390, he dedicated it to Henry Bolingbroke, his patron. Henceforth he was increasingly critical of Richard, partly no doubt because he was disillusioned with his rule, but partly because relations between Richard and Henry Bolingbroke were deteriorating. He revised the *Vox Clamantis* (*The Voice of One Crying*), adding an account of the Peasants' Revolt and a history of Richard's fall in an appendix, the *Cronica Tripertita* (*The Tripartite Chronicle*). Gower regarded the deposition as divine punishment for the king's failure to take notice of the warning supplied by the Peasants' Revolt.[160] (Langland's *Richard the Redeless* is also bitterly hostile to Richard.)

Patronage is not the only factor to be taken into consideration when explaining a chronicle's political complexion. Some chronicles were deliberate attempts at propaganda. An early example is almost certainly Thomas Favent's tract on the Merciless Parliament of 1388, the *History ...of the Wonderful Parliament*, a work which survives in only one post-medieval copy.[161] The strength of its bias in favour of the Appellants indicates that it was composed to justify their harsh acts.

Favent's *History* is unlike the other chronicles because it is written in highly coloured rhetorical prose, with numerous biblical allusions and a homiletic tone, and has a dominant theme. Favent claims that the three 'most noble lords', the Appellants (whom he compares with the persons of the Holy Trinity), were inspired by our Merciful Lord to lead the realm in the path of peace, and to protect the statutes of England, with the support of 'the whole community of parliament'.[162] Conversely, he calls the king's favourites 'pseudo lords' and asserts that they had hidden, like Adam and Eve, from God 'in the dark places of the palace and in secret lairs'.[163] At the persuasion of the devil, they had lived viciously, embracing the iniquity of mammon, and had deluded the king, gaining control of the government. Under the shadow of such sinners the king had impoverished the realm with oppressive taxes and imposts.[164] Favent compares the purge of the government carried out by the Appellants, not only to the eradication of thistles, thorns and tares, but also to the sudden destruc-

---

[160] For the *Confessio Amantis* see Gower, *Complete Works*, ed. Macaulay, ii. xxi-xxvi; for the *Cronica Tripertita* see ibid., iv. xxviii, xxxi, lvii.

[161] Possibly early copies were deliberately destroyed during Richard II's tyranny in 1397, or the work may have been intended for very limited circulation.

[162] *TF*, pp. 2, 11, 21. For the analogy of the Holy Trinity in fifteenth century political thought see E. H. Kantorowicz, *The King's Two Bodies, A Study in Mediaeval Political Theology* (London-Princeton 1957), p. 227.

[163] *TF*, pp. 8–10.

[164] *TF*, pp. 1–2.

tion of a 'squalid nest' in a tree, which put the 'badly injured birds' to flight.[165]

The political protagonists clearly recognized the value of historical works as propaganda. Later evidence alleges that John of Gaunt even commissioned the forgery of a chronicle, which he distributed to a number of monasteries, to promote the claim to the throne of his son Henry Boling-broke; apparently the chronicle 'proved' that Edmund Crouchback was Henry III's eldest son, and, therefore, that Bolingbroke, a descendant of Edmund through the female line, had a better claim than the earl of March.[166]

The deposition of Richard II and Henry's accession resulted in the composition of official history by the Lancastrian party. The official account of events, the so-called 'record and process', was copied on to the rolls of parliament. Here Richard is represented as voluntarily promising at Conway to renounce the crown, and abdicating in the Tower of London 'with a cheerful countenance'.[167] He read his renunciation to an assembly of the estates and people, which gladly acclaimed Henry's accession. This account illustrates the worst aspect of official history, deliberate falsifica-tion: comparison with other sources shows that it gives an erroneous impression of events. Adam of Usk and the Evesham chronicler say nothing of Richard's alleged cheerfulness at the abdication.[168] On the contrary, Adam describes an occasion on 21 September 1399 when he saw Richard dining in the Tower; Adam 'marked [the king's] mood and bearing', heard him talk on the fate of kings in England and left much saddened, 'perceiving the trouble of his mind'.[169]

Especially illuminating are those chronicles written at a distance from the centres of Lancastrian influence. The chronicle of Dieulacres states that Henry's envoys to Richard at Conway, far from claiming the throne for Henry, merely asked for the hereditary stewardship of England for him and a free parliament, and that Henry swore that Richard should 'keep his royal power and dominion'. In addition, it asserts that Richard when in the Tower demanded a hearing in parliament.[170] The chronicles of Kirkstall and Whalley make it clear that Henry alone was responsible

---

[165] *TF*, pp. 13–14.
[166] The allegation concerning this forged chronicle is made by John Hardyng; see p. 279 below.
[167] *Rot. Parl.* iii. 416–32. For the 'record and process' see M. V. Clarke and V. H. Galbraith, 'The deposition of Richard II' in *BJRL*, xiv (1930), pp. 124–55; H. G. Richardson, 'Richard II's last parliament' in *EHR*, lii (1937), pp. 40–2; B. Wilkinson, 'The deposition of Richard II and the accession of Henry IV' in *EHR*, liv (1939), p. 219. For Thomas Walsingham's use of the 'record and process' see p. 140 and n. 159 above.
[168] *AU*, pp. 31–2; *VR II*, pp. 157–8. Cf. Clarke and Galbraith, op. cit., pp. 145–6.
[169] *AU*, p. 30. Cf. G. T. Lapsley, 'The parliamentary title of Henry IV' in *EHR*, xlix (1934), pp. 436–7.
[170] *DC*, pp. 173, 179. Cf. Clarke and Galbraith, op. cit., pp. 144, 146, and Wilkinson, op. cit., pp. 218–19.

for the decision to make Richard a captive at Flint.[171] The French authorities, although not wholly reliable because of their bias (to be discussed below) in favour of Richard II, corrobate the evidence of these chronicles. Creton states that while at Conway Richard promised Henry his inheritance, and describes how he was captured on leaving Conway, and taken to Flint.[172] The *Traïson et Mort* mentions Richard's demand for a hearing in parliament, and gives the impression that the assembly which heard Richard's renunciation and acclaimed Henry's accession was little better than a rabble.[173]

The Lancastrian régime did not only preserve the 'record and process' on the parliament rolls, it also distributed copies to the chroniclers.[174] Thus the text of the 'record and process' was used by Thomas Walsingham (as has been seen),[175] and also by the continuator of the *Eulogium*[176] and by the Evesham chronicler, who synthesized it with other sources and with his own rhetorical moralizations.[177] Adam of Usk, although a supporter of Henry, did not copy the 'record and process'. However, it is possible that Adam used other propaganda material. His account of the parliament held by Richard at Westminster in September 1397, as part of the king's bid for autocracy, is almost identical with that used by the Evesham chronicle,[178] which suggests that both chroniclers were copying some Lancastrian hand-out. It was suggested above that Thomas Walsingham's highly coloured description of the earl of Arundel's arrest, trial and execution were copied from a tract written in the Lancastrian interest.[179] The object of such a propaganda tract written in almost hagiographical style would obviously have been to denigrate Richard by stimulating sympathy for his victims. Moreover, Walsingham includes (as already mentioned) an account of the arrest of the duke of Gloucester in similar dramatic vein. It seems likely that this passage was the beginning of a tract on Gloucester's fate. The final section is probably preserved by the Evesham chronicler:[180] the latter has a blood-curdling description of Glou-

---

[171] *KC*, p. 123. The relevant extract from the Whalley chronicle (for which see p. 159 and n. 8 above) see Clarke and Galbraith, op. cit., p. 144, and Wilkinson, op. cit., p. 217 n. 3.

[172] *Creton*, pp. 376, 398–401.

[173] *T et M*, pp. 68–9.

[174] The use of the 'record and process' by the chroniclers is discussed in the articles cited above, p. 186 n. 167.

[175] P. 140 above.

[176] *EH*, iii. 382–4.

[177] *VR II*, pp. 157–61.

[178] *AU*, pp. 9–18; *VR II*, pp. 138–48. The similarity of the texts is noticed in Stow, 'The *Vita Ricardi* as a source for the reign of Richard II', pp. 70–1.

[179] See pp. 140–1 above.

[180] P. 140 above; *VR II*, pp. 160–1. There is evidence suggesting the possibility that other propaganda tracts were written in Richard II's reign and shortly after his deposition. It is possible that the highly coloured passages relating to Archbishop Thomas Arundel in

cester's murder which he copied, he states, from some now lost work. He writes: 'We will insert this story, these extraordinary or rather execrable proceedings, which will utterly astound any reader.'

Similarly, the chronicles written by Frenchmen concerning the deposition contain propaganda—but it is in favour of Richard. Creton's invective against Richard's murderers at the end of his chronicle and in the two ballads, was probably not simply the result of his spontaneous regard for the king.[181] It must also have had a propagandist purpose—to promote the war against the English. Creton wrote no doubt to please Charles VI of France and Philip the Bold of Burgundy, both of whom he served as valet-de-chambre.[182] He is eloquent on the treachery of the English, whose treatment of Richard was 'neither loyal nor right',[183] and emphasizes the mutual antipathy between the English and the French.[184] He even alleges that it was Richard's affection for his father-in-law, Charles VI, which caused his downfall.[185]

The suggestion that Creton's chronicle had a propaganda purpose is corroborated by the fact that it was fairly widely disseminated. A number

---

the continuation of the *Eulogium* (p. 181 and n. 137 above, p. 199 n. 38 below) derived from such a tract. It has also been suggested above (p. 141 n. 166) that the story of St Thomas' holy oil, with which Henry IV was anointed, had a similar origin. Moreover, a recent scholar has argued that the account of the alleged Great Council of 1374 in the continuation of the *Eulogium*, was copied from a propaganda tract; see A. Gwynn, *The English Austin Friars in the Age of Wyclif* (Oxford 1940), pp. 218–21. The account is in rhetorical style and gives the arguments presented by the various theologians and canon and civil lawyers to the Black Prince and Archbishop Whittlesey in the sacristy at Westminster, that the pope had no temporal dominion (and, therefore, no right to levy taxes, etc. for his wars). Pre-eminent importance is given to the part played by the Franciscan John Mardeslay, who was to become, or was already, minister-provincial in England. Gwynn and other scholars following him, have dismissed the narrative as fictitious. Dr Catto, however, has convincingly defended its historicity, but dated the council to 1373, not 1374. Nevertheless, the evidence does not seem to warrant Dr Catto's corollary that the passage, therefore, was not copied from a propaganda tract; such a tract, though in propagandist style, might well have been based on an actual event. See J. I. Catto, 'An alleged Great Council of 1374' in *EHR*, lxxxii (1967), p. 771.

[181] See p. 173 and n. 87 above. The use of literature for the purpose of political propaganda was prevalent in fifteenth century France. For its use by John the Fearless, duke of Burgundy, see C. C. Willard, 'The manuscripts of Jean Petit's *Justification*: some Burgundian propaganda methods of the early fifteenth century' in *Studi Francesi*, xiii (Società Editrice Internazionale, Turin, 1969), pp. 271–80.

[182] Creton is referred to as Philip the Bold's 'varlet de chambre' in two entries in the ducal accounts, of 1402 and 1403; Cockshaw, op. cit., pp. 135 (no. 50), 137 (no. 61), and see p. 161 n. 21 above. He appears as Charles VI's 'varlet de chambre' in the mandate of 29 July 1410 printed by Dillon, op. cit., p. 94 (see p. 174 n. 90 above). An earlier reference to 'Jehan Creton escuyer' in the royal accounts, a receipt for wages for service in war, is dated 7 October 1357; printed Dillon, op. cit., p. 86 (cited Jones, 'An examination of the authorship of *The Deposition and Death of Richard II* attributed to Creton', p. 468, who gives the date 1354). In view of the early date of this receipt, it is highly unlikely that this esquire was the Jean Creton with whom we are concerned.

[183] *Creton*, p. 421.

[184] *Creton*, p. 422.

[185] *Creton*, p. 452.

of manuscripts survive. An exceptionally beautiful copy, with sixteen miniatures illustrating the narrative, was owned by Charles III of Anjou[186] (Charles, the brother of King René, was born in 1414, became count of Maine and Mortain in 1440, and died in 1472). As already mentioned, Philip the Bold himself seems to have owned another copy.[187]

The *Traïson et Mort* is a clearer example of propaganda. The fact that numerous copies survive,[188] and that it reflects the official French attitude to Henry's coup, suggests the probability that it was written at the command of Charles VI or of one of his nobles. Its representation of Richard as the protagonist of peace with France, the opponent of the war-mongering English lords, was calculated to appeal to the French in the early fifteenth century. Moreover, the *Traïson et Mort* could be read as an object lesson: Charles VI's bouts of insanity were a potential threat to the French monarchy; the example overseas of a king deposed by his subjects must have increased the consequent anxiety. The author puts a rhetorical exhortation addressed to the French nobility into Richard's mouth: 'O noble lords of France ... preserve the honour of chivalry, for never was it known that such treason was committed against any of the noble kings of France as my own cousins and kin have committed against me.'[189]

The *Traïson et Mort* begins with the duke of Gloucester's opposition to Richard's cession of Brest. (The king handed it over to the duke of Brittany in order to achieve peace with France.) As a result Gloucester prepares to rebel, to prevent the king losing the cities won by his ancestors.[190] The Anglo-French alliance remains the central theme of the work. In Richard's eloquent lamentation on his plight after his capture, he invokes 'our dearest Isabella of France, our dearest father of France, our dear uncles of Berry and Burgundy, our dear cousin of Brittany', and other French nobles, to avenge the wrong done to him. He asks the 'noble and mighty' king of France 'to show the same compassion for our dearest companion Isabella as the Saviour had for mankind.'[191]

---

[186] BL MS. Harley 1319. See Plate VI (a) and (b). The miniatures are reproduced and fully described in E. Maunde Thompson, 'A contemporary account of the fall of Richard II' in *Burlington Magazine*, v (1904), pp. 160–72, 267–70. Lithographs of them are in *Creton* (Webb). The illustrations must have been in the earliest copy because the text refers to one of them (see p. 172 and n. 79 above). Of the copies in the Bibliothèque Nationale (fr. 1668, fr. 14645, n.a. fr. 6223) only one is illustrated; fr. 14645 has a rather coarsely executed full-page miniature illustrating Richard's departure for Ireland. For Charles III of Anjou see Gustave Dupont-Ferrier, *Gallia Regia* (Paris 1942–66, 6 vols), iii. 13393, 13396, 13413, 13718, 14018.

[187] Pp. 161–2 n. 21, 174 above.

[188] Thirty seven manuscripts of the *Traïson et Mort* are listed in Palmer, 'The authorship, date and historical value of the French chronicles on the Lancastrian revolution', pp. 180–1.

[189] *T et M*, p. 55. For the fifteenth century Frenchman's fascination with the regicidal proclivities of the English see P. S. Lewis, 'Two pieces of fifteenth-century iconography' in *Journal of the Warburg and Courtauld Institutes*, xxvii (1964), pp. 319–20.

[190] *T et M*, pp. 1–3.

[191] *T et M*, pp. 53–6 (cf. pp. 66–7).

Besides emphasizing Richard's francophilia, the author dramatizes events—often at the expense of truth—in order to arouse anti-English sentiment. He gives a long, detailed and gruesome account of the hanging, drawing and quartering of Sir Thomas Blount, who, allegedly, remained loyal to Richard throughout his protracted last agonies; the details were clearly the product of the author's imagination, not observation.[192] His graphic account of the murder of King Richard himself not only lacks historical foundation, but is also contrary to the other evidence. He asserts that Sir Peter Exton disturbed Richard at dinner, and killed him by striking him twice on the head with an axe.[193]

Similarly, the other chronicle written in France which describes Richard's deposition, the *Chronique du Religieux de Saint Denys*, reflects throughout the attitude of the French government. A product of the abbey of St Denis, written at the order of the abbot shortly after 1422, it may have been intended as the basis of the *Grandes Chroniques*, the official history of the French monarchy, for Charles VI's reign. The identity of the author is unknown, although he records that he visited England on the abbey's affairs at the time of the Peasants' Revolt.[194] However, he had close connections with Charles VI's court, and it has been suggested that he was a royal secretary. He certainly attended the marriage of Richard II and Isabella, and was engaged on other official business. His chronicle reflects the considerable interest in France in Anglo-French relations and events in England.

The deposition, the monk of St Denis writes, concerns him because it was a cause of sorrow to his sovereign lord, King Charles.[195] Like the author of the *Traïson et Mort*, which was his principal source, he emphasizes that Isabella's marriage should have brought the much desired peace between England and France.[196] He deplores the sufferings of Isabella in England, and lays stress on the antipathy between the two nations.[197] He expresses horror at the deposition and, apparently thinking of the English conquests

[192] *T et M*, pp. 90–1. Dr Palmer deals severely and at length with the dramatic style and extreme bias of the *Traïson et Mort*, to which the author sacrificed his veracity; Palmer, op. cit. pp. 398–412. For another example see p. 144 and n. 182 above.

[193] Richard's (alleged) murder by Exton is the subject of a miniature (of mediocre quality) in one fifteenth century manuscript of the *Traïson et Mort;* Bibliothèque Nationale MS. fr. 5625, f. 1. The Exton story is discussed in Palmer, op. cit., pp. 399–400. In order to explain the fact that Froissart attributed the story to Creton (which has been used as an argument against Creton's authorship of the *Histoire* since the latter does not have the story), Dr Palmer suggests that Creton, once convinced of Richard's death, extracted the story from the *Traïson et Mort* and circulated a tract containing it; see Palmer, op. cit., pp. 161–2. However, Froissart may simply have made a mistake, perhaps misled because, on account of the *Histoire*, he connected Creton with works on Richard II.

[194] For a recent attempt to identify the author of the *Chronique* see N. Grévy-Pons and E. Ornato, 'Qui est l'auteur de la chronique latine de Charles VI, dite du Religieux de Saint-Denis?' in *Bibliothèque de l'école de chartes*, cxxxiv (1976), pp. 85–102.

[195] *CRSD*, ii. 670.

[196] *CRSD*, pp. ii. 414, 476.

[197] *CRSD*, ii. 704.

in France in his own day, expresses the hope that 'the kings of England, who, blinded by the favour of Fortune, measure their prestige by their prosperity, will find a lesson in the fall of Richard, cease to boast of their good luck, and deplore less bitterly their unhappiness when they fall from power.'[198] The author admits that Richard had faults as a king: he mentions his reliance on the counsel of the low born rather than on that of the nobility, his oppressive taxation, and his propensity to break promises.[199] He also shows some regard for Henry IV, mentioning his popularity with the French when in exile before his accession,[200] and he records that before Henry invaded England, he undertook to recover the priory of Deerhurst for St Denis.[201]

It can, therefore, be seen that the chronicles of Richard II's reign must be treated with caution as sources for political history, because, as a result of the influence of patrons and government, they were subject to strong bias. Nevertheless, most chroniclers occasionally reveal in their accounts of political events and in their descriptions of public figures, the same power of acute observation and the same talent for objective reportage, as they show in other contexts. For example the monk of St Denis has an eye-witness description of the marriage of Isabella and Richard in 1396, which took place between Calais and Ardres.[202] He includes a description of the tents and pavilions. The French had 120 tents supported by strong ropes and staves, surrounded by a palisade, with one large and especially magnificent square pavilion in front. The English had the same number on the Calais side, with an enormous round pavilion supported by a rope attached to a huge post near the king of France's pavilion: because the post was centrally placed, the two kings met there.

Even the *Traïson et Mort*, despite its general unreliability, has some apparently authentic details about Isabella's life in England. It describes the arrangements made by Richard for Isabella's household at Windsor before his departure for Ireland, and certainly its account of how Richard and Isabella walked hand in hand from the castle to St George's chapel, for what proved to be their final leave-taking ('I never saw so great a lord makes so much of, nor show such affection for a lady as did king Richard for his queen'), has the air of truth.[203] Adam of Usk himself watched Isabella, then ten years old, leave London for France in 1401, and there is no reason to disbelieve his description: she departed, 'clad in mourning weeds, giving King Henry angry and malignant looks and scarcely opening her lips, as she went on her way'.[204]

---

[198] *CRSD*, ii. 702.
[199] *CRSD*, i. 494–6; ii. 670, 674–6.
[200] *CRSD*, ii. 674.
[201] *CRSD*, ii. 706.
[202] *CRSD*, ii. 452.
[203] *T et N*, pp. 24–7.
[204] *AU*, p. 63.

Creton apparently saw her handed over to the French emissaries, in a chapel at Leulinghem ('what [the chapel] is like', comments Creton, 'everyone knows who has seen it'). After the formal ceremony, both parties wept at the separation. However, Creton records,[205]

> When they left the chapel, the queen, whose heart was filled with goodness, led all the English ladies, who made sore lamentation, to the French tents where they intended to dine together. And so, it seems, they did. After dinner the queen had a quantity of jewels brought, and gave them to the great ladies and to the lords of England, who wept for sorrow. The queen comforted them and said goodbye, but when she had to leave they renewed their expressions of grief.

Thomas Favent, despite his florid prose style, has some touches which suggest personal observation. For example he describes how the Appellants entered parliament arm in arm, dressed in cloth of gold.[206] His account of the capture of the chief justice, Sir Robert Tresilian, is an example of excellent reportage no doubt based on first hand information. Tresilian had fled at the opening of the parliament, and was spotted hiding on the gutter of a roof, whence he watched the lords entering and leaving Westminster hall. Knights were sent to arrest him, and he was eventually caught under a round table, hidden by the table-cloth. He was disguised in 'a cloak of well-worn russet reaching to the middle of his legs, red stockings and shoes "of Joseph", so that he looked more like a pilgrim or a beggar than a king's justice.' He was taken to parliament amidst shouts of: 'We have him! We have him!'[207]

Creton has some exact details concerning Henry's expedition against Richard in north Wales in 1399. He describes, for example, the capture of Holt. The castle was 'so strong and safe' because of its mountainous situation, 'that it could not have been taken by force in ten years.' However, although it had sufficient soldiers to garrison it:[208]

> The [soldiers] were not diligent in keeping good guard at the entrance, nor of the pass which is narrow and must be ascended on foot, step by step: but faint hearted and cowardly as they were, they surrendered it to Duke [Henry], who quickly entered, more delighted than ever; for it contained 100,000 marks sterling in gold, or more, which King Richard had ordered to be stored there,

---

[205] *Creton*, p. 462. Creton describes, though briefly, a number of castles in North Wales: see pp. 345, 354 (Conway); 370 (Beaumaris and Caernarvon); 383–4 (Rhuddlan); 378–9, 409, 414 (Chester).

[206] *TF*, p. 14.

[207] *TF*, p. 17.

[208] *Creton*, pp. 379–80.

besides a great quantity of other treasure. By Saint Maur! I heard it said that what could be found there might safely be reckoned at 200,000 marks. The duke took it all away with him.

The Evesham chronicle has a graphic account of the treatment by the people of Cirencester of the rebel lords in January 1400. (The author probably obtained his news from the Augustinian abbey in the town.) When the rebels came to Cirencester to muster support, they were attacked and put under guard in the priory. There they plotted to escape by creating a distraction—arson committed by their servants. But the townsmen heard of the scheme, and were so enraged that they immediately executed the lords.[209]

Such passages show that the chroniclers when stirred could transcend propaganda, and describe political events with the same verve as they applied to the social scene and, on occasion, even to their own experiences and feelings.

---

[209] *VR II*, pp. 163–4.

7

The Biographies of Henry V

The Englishman's idea of Henry V is fixed by Shakespeare who gives a timeless portrait of this 'mirror of all Christian kings'[1] and 'true lover of the holy church'.[2] Henry was a just man, who fought the French in order to pursue his legitimate claim to the crown of France.[3] Above all he was a brave soldier and great army commander. Shakespeare describes the English and French before the battle of Agincourt: turning from the 'confident and over-lusty French' to the English with their 'lank-lean cheeks and war-worn coats', their army merely 'a ruined band', he depicts 'the royal captain' as he walked 'from watch to watch, from tent to tent' and cheered his men ('Upon his royal face there was no note/How dread an army hath enrounded him').[4] The duke of Exeter and the earl of Salisbury both comment on the 'fearful odds' of 'five to one', while Henry proudly disdains the earl of Westmoreland's wish that they had 10,000 more men, saying:[5]

> If we are marked to die, we are enow
> To do our country loss; and if to live,
> The fewer men, the greater share of honour.

Henry attributed the victory itself to God.[6]

Shakespeare represents the marriage of Henry and Katherine, which sealed the peace between England and France, as a love match, and stresses the princess's modesty during the courtship in romantic terms.[7] Moreover, he has stories which, though apparently based on actual events, show the accretions of legend in the process of transmission, and which formed part of a body of traditional lore about Henry. There is, for instance, the story of the transformation of the wild Prince Hal, who repudiated his boon companions and became an exemplary king.[8] And there is the

---

[1] *King Henry V*, Act II, chorus.
[2] Ibid., Act I, scene i.
[3] Ibid., Act I, scene ii.
[4] Ibid., Act IV, chorus.
[5] Ibid., Act IV, scene iii.
[6] Ibid., Act IV, scene viii.
[7] Ibid., Act V, scene ii.
[8] *Henry IV, Pt II*, Act V, scene V.

story of how the dauphin scornfully sent Henry tennis balls (with the inference that he was only capable of trivial pastimes); Henry remarked:[9]

> When we have matched our rackets to these balls,
> We will, in France, by God's grace, play a set
> Shall strike his father's crown into the hazard.

Shakespeare created his Henry V from a pre-existing legend. He derived his material indirectly from the fifteenth century biographies, as transmitted by Holinshed, and from now unidentified sources, and probably from oral tradition.[10] Henry's career evoked numerous biographies. There are still extant three biographies in Latin prose written during his lifetime and in the following generation, and one in verse. The earliest is the anonymous *Gesta Henrici Quinti* (*The Deeds of Henry the Fifth*), covering the period from Henry's accession, in 1413, until 1416, written between 20 November 1416 and July 1417.[11] Shortly afterwards Thomas Elmham wrote his *Liber Metricus de Henrico Quinto* (*A Book in Verse on Henry the Fifth*), a history of the reign until 1418.[12] In 1437 Titus Livius Frulovisi, 'poet and orator' of Humphrey duke of Gloucester, wrote his *Vita Henrici Quinti* (*Life of Henry the Fifth*), which starts with Henry's birth and ends with his death,[13] and towards the middle of the century an anonymous author (the so-called Pseudo-Elmham) wrote a Life covering the same period.[14] Nor did these works exhaust interest in Henry V. In the sixteenth century

---

[9] *Henry V*, Act I, scene ii.

[10] Shakespeare's sources are fully discussed in Geoffrey Bullough, *Narrative and Dramatic Sources of Shakespeare* (London-Columbia 1957–73, 7 vols), iv. 351–75. For parallels between Shakespeare's account of Henry V and his reign and the fifteenth century biographies see pp. 196 n. 18, 200 and n. 49, 201 n. 54, 205 n. 80, 207 and n. 90, 212 and nn. 122–3 below. The detailed description of the biographies, from Titus Livius to Raphael Holinshed and John Stow, by C. L. Kingsford, 'The early biographies of Henry V' in *EHR*, xxv (1910), pp. 58–92, is still of value although now partially superseded (Kingsford's view, for example, that Thomas Elmham wrote the *Gesta Henrici Quinti* (ibid., pp. 60–1) is no longer accepted; see below). For a brief survey of historians' views of Henry V from the fifteenth century to modern times, tested against the reality of the king's personality and reign, see C. T. Allmand, *Henry V* (Historical Association pamphlet no. 68, 1968). McFarlane's 'personal portrait' of Henry V, based partly on Henry's household accounts, tends to corroborate the favourable views of the fifteenth century writers; K. B. McFarlane, *Lancastrian Kings and Lollard Knights* (Oxford 1972), pp. 114–33.

[11] Printed *Gesta Henrici Quinti*, ed., with an English translation, Frank Taylor and J. S. Roskell (Oxford Medieval Texts 1975). This edition supersedes that by Benjamin Williams (London 1850). For the date of the *Gesta* see J. S. Roskell and Frank Taylor, 'The authorship and purpose of the *Gesta Henrici Quinti*: Part I' in *BJRL*, liii (1970–1), p. 428 and n. 3. (The contents of the two articles by Roskell and Taylor on the *Gesta*, *BJRL*, liii (1970–1), pp. 428–64, and ibid., liv (1971–2), pp. 223–40, are summarized in their edition, pp. xviii-xxviii.)

[12] Printed in *Memorials of Henry the Fifth*, ed. C. A. Cole (RS 1858), pp. 79–166.

[13] Printed *Titi Livii Foro-Juliensis Vita Henrici Quinti*, ed. Thomas Hearne (Oxford 1716). For the date of the *Vita* see Kingsford, *Hist. Lit.* p. 51.

[14] Printed *Thomae de Elmham Vita et Gesta Henrici Quinti*, ed. Thomas Hearne (Oxford 1727). This Life is called the Pseudo-Elmham because Hearne (groundlessly) attributed it to Thomas Elmham; see Kingsford, op. cit., pp. 61–2.

a Life was written in English in 1513 or 1514,[15] and another, by Robert Redmayne in Latin some time between 1574 and 1578.[16] These biographies were not all independent of each other. The Pseudo-Elmham used Titus Livius which was also translated by the author of the English Life to form the basis of his work. Thomas Elmham almost certainly used a now lost prose Life which he himself had composed using the *Gesta* as his source. Moreover, there is evidence suggesting the previous existence of one more early biography; the Translator of Livius used some work which is now lost.[17] And there are other, shorter pieces about the king, for example the account of his reign (to 1420) in the chronicle of Thomas of Otterbourne[18] and the contemporary panegyric on him in Latin verse by a monk of Westminster.[19]

No other medieval king of England was honoured with such an abundance of literature. There was virtually no tradition of royal biography in England, although the kings occupy a prominent place in the chronicles.[20] Excluding the pre-conquest royal biographies, there were William of Poitiers' *Gesta* of William the Conqueror, the two biographies of Richard I, based on a Norman source,[21] and more recently Robert of Avesbury's

---

[15] Printed *The First English Life of King Henry the Fifth*, ed. C. L. Kingsford (Oxford 1911). Titus Livius' Life was translated as a result of the chivalric tastes of the early sixteenth century; see A. B. Ferguson, *The Indian Summer of English Chivalry* (Durham, North Carolina, 1960), pp. 160–2. See p. 476 and n. 137 below.

[16] Printed *Memorials Hen. V.*, pp. 3–59. See R. R. Reid, 'The date and authorship of Redmayne's "Life of Henry V"' in *EHR*, xxx (1915). pp. 691–8.

[17] For the lost sources of Elmham and the Translator of Livius see pp. 206–7, 217 below.

[18] Printed *Duo Rerum Anglicarum Scriptores Veteres viz. Thomas Otterbourne et Johannes Whethamstede*, ed. Thomas Hearne (Oxford 1732, 2 vols), i. The identity of this Thomas of Otterbourne, who *floruit* in the early fifteenth century (and, therefore, is not to be confused with the Franciscan chronicler of the same name mentioned in Sir Thomas Gray's *Scalacronica*, for whom see p. 000 and n. 60 above) is unknown. However, he was probably a northerner and may have been the clerk of that name who became rector of Chingford in 1393; see Kingsford, *Hist. Lit.* p. 21. His chronicle is a brief compilation, starting with the legendary history of Britain and continuing to 1420. From the reign of Richard II to the end it is fairly detailed, and is mainly derived from a rather fuller text of the St Albans chronicle than that in the printed works of Thomas Walsingham; see *St AC*, pp. xvi, xviii. For the reigns of Henry IV and Henry V it has additions. Some of them suggest that the chronicle has a north country connection and three relate to Henry V: the first describes his quarrel as prince with his father in 1412; the second concerns the dauphin's gift of tennis balls in 1414 (see p. 195 and n. 9 above and p. 207 and n. 90 below); the third describes how Vincent Ferrier preached before Henry at Caen in 1418 (see p. 218 and n. 153 below); *Otterbourne*, pp. 270–1, 274–5, 280–1. Cf. Kingsford, *Hist. Lit.* p. 23. For the chronicle of John Strecche which ends in 1422 and has some value for Henry V's reign see pp. 405–8 below, and for an account of the Hundred Year's War, from 1415 to 1429, see pp. 329–30 and nn. below.

[19] Printed *Memorials Hen. V.* pp. 63–75. This work mainly concerns Henry's piety and his benefactions to Westminster abbey.

[20] The kings are especially prominent in the 'Merton' version of the *Flores Historiarum;* see A. Gransden, 'The continuations of the *Flores Historiarum* from 1265 to 1327' in *Mediaeval Studies*, xxxvi (Toronto 1974), pp. 472–92.

[21] For William of Poitiers and the biographies of Richard I see Gransden, *Historical Writing*, i. 99–102, 238–42 respectively. For a brief survey of biographies of the kings of England see

Gesta of Edward III.[22] All these works treated their subjects eulogistically. Such treatment is a marked characteristic of the biographies of Henry V. None, even the earliest, describes him in exact terms. This does not mean that they necessarily contain falsehoods, merely that the authors selected material and sometimes exaggerated to give a consistently flattering picture of Henry. They present the accepted view of the king, and have anecdotes which men loved to repeat and embroider—they show how even during Henry's lifetime the legend began to evolve which Shakespeare was to inherit.

It is necessary to discover why for over a century Henry V's reputation evoked so much panegyrical literature, both written and oral. One reason undoubtedly was that Henry was a hero in real life: he won resounding victories against the French. In addition his piety is well attested. He founded three religious houses and issued regulations to stop his soldiers looting churches or molesting the clergy and other non-combatants. And he was a ruthless represser of heresy in England, supporting with the secular arm the church's action against Lollardy. He could, therefore, be praised as an exemplary king by patriotic Englishmen and by zealous churchmen. The desire of some authors to praise Henry was fostered by a literary mode new to England. Titus Livius was an Italian humanist and the author of the Pseudo-Elmham was also influenced by continental humanism. The renaissance produced numerous works in praise of princes.

But there was a more powerful motive for glorifying Henry V: propaganda. Three crucial works, the *Gesta Henrici Quinti*, Titus Livius' *Vita* and its first English translation, were all written to promote the policy of the central government. The first two were specifically intended to stimulate enthusiasm for the war with France, and nearly a century later the translator of Livius wrote to encourage Henry VIII in his French war. Such propaganda pieces had numerous parallels on the continent in the fifteenth century. In France, besides the official history of the French kings which was still written (although intermittently) at St Denis and at the royal court even towards the end of the century, tracts were produced by secretaries connected with the royal court to justify the opposition of the French monarchy to the English claims during the Hundred Years' War. Some of these tracts, which were aimed at stirring patriotism, achieved wide currency.[23] However, except for the biographies of Henry V, England

---

A. Gransden, 'Propaganda in English medieval historiography' in *Journal of Medieval History*, i (1975), pp. 371–4.

[22] See pp. 67–71 above.

[23] See Denys Hay, 'History and historians in France and England during the fifteenth century' in *BIHR*, xxxv (1962), pp. 111–27, P. S. Lewis, 'War propaganda and historiography in fifteenth-century France and England' in *TRHS*, fifth series, xv (1965), pp. 1–21, and C. C. Willard, 'The manuscripts of Jean Petit's *Justification*: some Burgundian propaganda methods of the early fifteenth century' in *Studi Francesi*, xiii (Società Editrice Internazionale, Turin, 1969), pp. 271–80.

produced very little literature of this kind.[24]

Although the fifteenth century biographies of Henry V are eulogistic and propagandist in tone, they cannot be dismissed as valueless panegyrics. They throw light on the political attitudes of the times, and they contain excellent, often eyewitness accounts of Henry's battles and sieges. The series of descriptions of warfare covers the whole reign (to 1416 in the *Gesta*, from 1416 to 1420 in Titus Livius and from 1420 to 1422 in the Pseudo-Elmham): it is almost the last manifestation of the chivalric historiographical tradition in medieval England.[25]

The Lives of Henry V will be considered in turn in chronological order.

The name of the author of the *Gesta Henrici Quinti* is unknown, but clearly he was a royal chaplain.[26] He mentions the royal chapel explicitly on a number of occasions. He describes how the chaplains walked, fully vested, in procession to the walls of Harfleur after its surrender.[27] He records that during the battle of Agincourt the royal chaplains, 'who were to celebrate divine office and make fervent prayer for King Henry and his men', waited with the baggage behind the battle lines, in accordance with the king's instructions.[28] He gives precise liturgical details of the prayers of thanks offered by the clerks of the chapel after the relief of Harfleur in 1416,[29] and he records that a storm blew down the tent used for the chapel during the negotiations between King Henry, the emperor Sigismund, Charles VI and John the Fearless, duke of Burgundy, at Calais in 1416.[30]

In addition, the author of the *Gesta* mentions himself personally in a number of contexts. He records how during the march to Calais 'I who am writing and many others prayed to the Virgin Mary and to St George', that the English army should be 'snatched from swords of the French'.[31] At the battle of Agincourt he was one of the priests ordered by the king to stay with the baggage, and he described how he sat on a horse and prayed with the others. Later, when he toured the battle field after the English victory and saw the extent of the carnage the English had wrought with God's help, the piles of the defeated, most dead, some still alive, as high as a man, he could not help grieving: 'I think none could have seen the death of so many Christians without tears.'[32] The author mentions himself again

---

[24] For a few fourteenth and fifteenth century examples see Gransden, 'Propaganda', pp. 373–5.

[25] The subsequent example in the medieval period appears to be John Hardyng's chronicle; see pp. 274–87 below. For the revival of the chivalric tradition in the late fifteenth and sixteenth centuries see pp. 475–6 below.

[26] The authorship of the *Gesta* is fully discussed in Roskell and Taylor, 'The authorship and purpose of the *Gesta Henrici Quinti*: Part I', pp. 428–64.

[27] *GH V*, p. 50.

[28] *GH V*, p. 84.

[29] *GH V*, p. 150.

[30] *GH V*, p. 164.

[31] *GH V*, p. 66.

[32] *GH V*, pp. 84, 92.

when describing the negotiations at Calais: he writes that they treated for three days, 'but what conclusion these secret talks had was locked in the royal bosom, guarded by the discretion with which he kept his counsel', and admits that he had only heard the current rumours.[33]

These passages, besides some graphic descriptions which could only have been written by an eyewitness, prove that the author was at the siege of Harfleur, on the march to Calais and at the battle of Agincourt. He also attended the pageant held in London on Henry's return in November 1415, and was at Calais during the peace talks. Other passages show that although the author was not cognisant of the government's inner counsels, he had a good knowledge of its more routine affairs. Thus he records the appointment of 'the venerable and widely known' Master Henry Ware as keeper of the privy seal,[34] and has specific references to two stewards of the royal household, Thomas Erpingham (steward from 1413 to 1417) and Walter Hungerford (steward from 1415 to 1421 and again in 1424).[35] Furthermore, he often refers the reader for the text of documents to an official collection of records.[36] He also refers to the archives of the archbishop of Canterbury,[37] and seems to have had a special regard for Archbishop Thomas Arundel. Recording Arundel's condemnation of John Wyclif's tenets he writes:[38]

> [the archbishop was] a man of exalted ancestry and profound intelligence, and was a noble defender of the church, whom prosperity could not raise up, nor adversity throw down; none from the earliest times was braver in fighting the battles of Christ and in opposing the sedition of men.

The author of the *Gesta*, therefore, wrote close to the centre of affairs. His work contains the government's justification for its policy towards France. King Henry's standpoint was elaborated by Henry Beaufort, bishop of Winchester, in his opening speech to the parliament held at Westminster in March 1416.[39] (Similar speeches were made to the parliaments of 1415, 1417 and 1419.)[40] The bishop said that the king wanted peace, but a just peace which would recognize his legitimate claims in France: the king had tried to achieve this objective by negotiation, but he

---

[33] *GH V*, p. 172. For further references to the author see *GH V*, pp. 10–11, 78–9.

[34] *GH V*, p. 158 and n. 2.

[35] *GH V*, pp. xxvii n. 4, xxxiv, 78 and n. 2, 170, 171 and n. 3. Cf. ibid., p. xlv n. 2.

[36] See e.g. *GH V*, pp. 14, 18, 56. Cf. *GH V*, pp. xxxix–xliii.

[37] *GH V*, pp. 8–9.

[38] *GH V*, p. 4. The tone of this passage suggests the possibility that it was extracted from a eulogistic Life, now lost, of Thomas Arundel: it was tentatively postulated above (pp. 141 n. 166, 181 and n. 137, 187 n. 180) that such a Life was the source of the eulogistic passages about the archbishop in the continuation of the *Eulogium*.

[39] *Rot. Parl.* iv. 94.

[40] Ibid., iv. 62, 106, 116.

was unsuccessful because the French were full of pride. Therefore, King Henry had to resort to the sword. The great victories at Harfleur and Agincourt proved that God favoured the English. The bishop concluded with the text: 'We make war so that we may have peace, because the end of war is peace.'[41] The *Gesta* has a fuller version of this same speech. The bishop, according to the *Gesta*, said that three divine judgments proved that God upheld 'the right of the crown of England to the realm of France': the naval victory of Sluys in the reign of Edward III; King Edward's victory at Poitiers; and King Henry's victory at Agincourt. (The author then specifies three advantages gained by the English as a result of these victories.)[42]

The theme expounded by the bishop of Winchester runs through the *Gesta*. Above all Henry wanted a just peace; he only fought because he failed to achieve one by negotiation.[43] (The *Gesta* has a detailed account of the peace talks in 1416.)[44] But negotiation was never successful because of the pride and duplicity of the French.[45] With reference to the siege of Harfleur, the author states that King Henry acted in accordance with the law of Deuteronomy (xx. 10–14):[46] first, the king offered peace to the besieged on condition that they surrendered the town, which, Henry claimed, was part of the inheritance of the English crown and of the duchy of Normandy; then, because they would not surrender, Henry reduced the town to submission, punishing the men but sparing the women and children. (Henry quoted the same text in Deuteronomy in a letter of July 1415 to Charles VI.)[47] The author of the *Gesta* frequently emphasizes that God was on the English side. Writing for instance of the victory at Agincourt he says: 'May our people not attribute our triumph to their own glory or bravery, but to the Lord alone.'[48] He stresses Henry's adherence to this view. When the king at Agincourt scorned the suggestion (here made by Sir Walter Hungerford and not by the earl of Westmoreland, as in Shakespeare) that the English must wish for 10,000 more archers, the *Gesta* gives his reply thus:[49]

> You speak stupidly, because by the God of heaven, in whose grace I am, and in whom I place my firm hope of victory, I would not have a single man more than I do, even if I could. For those I have here are the people of God, whom He has deigned to give

---

[41] Ibid., iv. 94.
[42] *GH V*, p. 122.
[43] See e.g. *GH V*, pp. 2–3, 34–5, 132–3. Cf. *GH V*, p. xxix and n. 4.
[44] *GH V*, pp. 126–32 passim.
[45] *GH V*, pp. 134–6.
[46] *GH V*, pp. 34, 48. Cf. ibid., pp. xxx and n. 2, 154.
[47] See *GH V*, p. xxx n. 2.
[48] *GH V*, p. 98. Cf. above and n. 42.
[49] *GH V*, p. 78. Cf. p. 194 and n. 5 above.

me at this time. Do you not believe that the Almighty can at will by means of these humble few defeat the pride of the French, who glory in their great number and their strength?

And the *Gesta* describes Henry's humility on his return to London, his self effacing bearing during the pageant which welcomed him; he rode with few followers and downcast eyes, thus indicating that he did not claim for himself credit for the victory, but rather attributed it to God.[50]

While emphasizing the moral turpitude of the French on the one hand, the author of the *Gesta* stresses Henry's piety and humanity on the other (God would more readily bestow his favour on the morally excellent).[51] He states that Henry attended lauds and mass before the battle of Agincourt, and that the army confessed.[52] The author records that Henry prohibited any attack on women and unarmed clergy, and that the king also forbade looting,[53] summarily putting to death a soldier who stole a gilded pyx (probably thinking it was solid gold) from a church.[54] He gives full details of the liturgical commemorations which Henry ordered his chaplains to recite in gratitude for the relief of Harfleur in 1416,[55] and mentions thanksgivings after the battles of Cany and Agincourt.[56] He asserts that Henry's policy at home was to enrich the church and establish peace in the realm.[57] He stresses the king's personal piety, noting his foundation of three religious houses,[58] and starts the work with a full account of Henry's suppression of the Lollard revolt led by Sir John Oldcastle (whose career the author sketches).[59]

The unifying theme of the *Gesta* is easily explicable if the work was a propaganda piece written preparatory to Henry's renewal of the French war in the summer of 1417. Specifically Henry needed financial aid from parliament, and more generally he wanted support from the country at

---

[50] *GH V*, p. 112.

[51] See e.g. *GH V*, p. 146; 'Et noluit Deus non audiri, tantae humilitatis et confidentiae in precibus, principem.' Cf. *GH V*, p. 154.

[52] *GH V*, pp. 82–4 passim.

[53] *GH V*, pp. 26, 60.

[54] *GH V*, pp. 68. A pyx is the vessel in which the consecreted bread is kept. The same incident is mentioned by Titus Livius (*TL*, p. 13), who was probably the source of Shakespeare's story that Bardolph was executed for stealing a pax (i.e. a tablet bearing a picture of the Crucifixion which worshippers kissed at mass) 'of little price'; *Henry V*, Act III, scene vi. Cf. Bullough, op. cit., iv. 353, 361 and n. 1. The Pseudo-Elmham also mentions this incident, and in addition records that Henry executed 'a certain foreigner' who stole a pyx from the abbey of St Faro during the siege of Meaux in 1422; *Pseudo-Elmham*, pp. 53, 318–19, respectively.

[55] *GH V*, p. 150.

[56] *GH V*, pp. 120, 178.

[57] *GH V*, pp. 2, 12, 98.

[58] *GH V*, pp. 12, 154, 186–7.

[59] *GH V*, pp. 2–11. Henry's action against Oldcastle and the Lollards is, as one would expect of someone writing in the Protestant era, passed over by Shakespeare.

large, in the form of both money and prayers.[60] (The clergy conducted processions and services appealing for divine help against the French.)[61] The same propagandist motive may account for the prominence given in the *Gesta* to the emperor Sigismund and to the Anglo-imperial alliance: here was proof of Henry's diplomatic success. The author describes the part played by the 'most Christian and superillustrious' Sigismund, who stayed in England from April to August 1416 as mediator in the peace negotiations with France, and he lays especial emphasis on the cordial relations between Henry and the emperor, whom Henry had made a knight of the Garter.[62] For example the *Gesta* has a moving description of how Henry and Sigismund, having left Dover in order to sail separately to Calais for the resumption of negotiations, were reunited on the opposite shore: Sigismund was waiting impatiently to 'see again the beloved face of the king', and when the latter landed, they rushed into each other's arms.[63] And it describes their final tearful parting after the unsuccessful talks in Calais. Henry's officials and everyone else allegedly said of Sigismund that 'no better and kinder prince, no better behaved and more gracious household could ever have entered England nor left with greater honour and love.'[64] For his part Sigismund on leaving England had distributed leaflets which bore his farewell, blessing and praises in four lines of verse (including an anagram on 'Anglia').[65]

The *Gesta* ends with the Anglo-imperial alliance (Henry and Sigismund had signed an offensive and defensive treaty against France at Canterbury on 15 August 1416),[66] and the renewal of the French war. Its interest in Sigismund suggests that as a piece of propaganda it was intended for a wider audience than England alone. Sigismund left the peace negotiations in Calais in the autumn of 1416 to go to the council of Constance (he arrived on 27 January 1417). Perhaps Henry sent a copy of the *Gesta* to the council in order to strengthen his case against France and also to improve the status of the English delegation.

Henry did not regard his foreign policy and the fortunes of the council as unconnected. He considered that the former was in the interests of the latter: the French were not only his enemies, who refused overtures of peace, but also the church's because they favoured the schism. Sigismund, on the other hand, was dedicated to restoring the unity of the church. Already in 1415 Henry had ordered to be copied 'treaties and conventions

---

[60] See *GH V*, pp. 84–6, and p. 197 above. In general my conclusions as to the purposes of the *Gesta* coincide with those of Professor Roskell and Dr Taylor; see ibid., pp. xxiv–xxviii.
[61] For an example of the clergy supporting the king's (in this case Edward III's) war effort with masses and processions see p. 115 above.
[62] *GH V*, p. 132.
[63] *GH V*, p. 156.
[64] *GH V*, p. 174.
[65] *GH V*, p. 156.
[66] See the treaty of Canterbury; *Foedera*, ix. 377–81.

formerly agreed between the most serene king of England, Henry IV, his progenitor, and certain magnates of France, relating to the divine right and conquest of the duchy of Aquitaine from which, contrary to their own oaths, signatures and seals, they had had the temerity to recede.' He had sent the transcripts to the council, as well as to Sigismund and various princes, 'so that all Christendom would know how the duplicity of the French had forced him to rebel.'[67]

Shortly after concluding the treaty of Canterbury Henry took steps to make the Anglo-imperial alliance more effective. In December 1416 he authorized his representatives at the council to win the support of the electors and princes of the empire.[68] Sigismund worked for the same end,[69] and showed his friendship for the English in other ways. On 29 January he gave a private audience to the English delegation (the English 'nation'), on which occasion he praised all that he had seen in England. Henry's delegates were gratified that he wore the robes of the Order of the Garter at high mass on Sunday, 31 January (after which they entertained him at a banquet).[70]

It is not, therefore, unlikely that Henry would have commissioned a work to promote the Anglo-imperial alliance. Nor is it unlikely that he would have commissioned one to increase the prestige of the English delegation at the council of Constance. The political quarrels of Europe were reproduced in the arena of the council. An example of Anglo-French antagonism occurred in March 1417, when the French tried to prevent the recognition of England as one of the four 'nations' represented in the council. The constitutions of Benedict XII had recognized four 'nations', the Italian, German, French and Spanish. Therefore, England ought to be added to the German 'nation', or the other nations should be divided according to their respective governments. However, the only result of the French objection was a vindication put forward by the English of their own country's right to be a 'nation'. They argued on geographical and historical grounds that England was superior to France.[71]

[67] *GH V*, pp. 16–18. Henry V had this collection of documents made while staying in the abbey of Titchfield. Dr John Palmer has called my attention to a similar collection which still survives, and is now E 36/188 in the Public Record Office. It was made by David, archbishop of Bordeaux, in response to a request by Henry, and is dated 4 April 1419. It contains documents relating to Henry's right to Aquitaine, beginning with the treaty of Paris, 1259, and including the treaty of Brétigny and that of Calais (both 1360). Such collections made at Henry's request show that the king based his claims in France on history. For the claims of Henry IV, Henry V and Henry VI to overlordship of Scotland, which they also derived from history, see pp. 275 and n. 186, 276–7 below.

[68] See J. H. Wylie and W. T. Waugh, *The Reign of Henry the Fifth* (Cambridge 1914–29, 3 vols), iii. 32 and n. 2.

[69] See C. J. Hefele, *Histoire des Conciles*, ed. and translated into French H. Leclercq and others (Paris 1907–38, 20 vols, in progress), vii. pt i. 448 n.

[70] See M. Creighton, *A History of the Papacy from the Great Schism to the Sack of Rome* (London 1907–11, 6 vols), ii. 66–7.

[71] Ibid., ii. 76–81 passim.

The contents of the *Gesta* corroborate the suggestion that as a piece of propaganda it was intended for a continental audience as well as an English one. This would account for the eulogy of Sigismund and the emphasis on his friendship with Henry. Sigismund played an important role at the council of Constance, and was president of the fourteenth session (15 June 1415). Most of the issues under discussion at the council are stressed in the *Gesta*. The council's primary objective, to end the schism, is mentioned in the *Gesta* as Sigismund's dearest wish.[72] The council was also concerned with suppressing heresy: the tenets of John Wyclif were condemned in the eighth session and those of John Hus in the fifteenth session. (Hus was burnt as a heretic on 6 July 1415.) As has been seen, the *Gesta* describes Henry's activity in putting down the Lollard revolt of 1415. The council aimed at promoting ecclesiastical reform throughout Christendom; perhaps this encouraged the author of the *Gesta* to stress Henry's acts of piety. The possibility cannot be discounted that the sole purpose of the *Gesta* was to support Henry's policy abroad: if so, the paucity of manuscripts would be explained (only two medieval texts, one of which is a copy of the other, are known).[73]

As has been stated above, the propagandist tone of the *Gesta* does not seriously reduce its historical value. In keeping with the chivalric historiographical tradition, it has authentic details about warfare. It gives full accounts both of the siege of Harfleur and of the battle of Agincourt.[74] The former description is especially exact. It includes a topographical account of Harfleur and its neighbourhood. The author describes the marshy land (today submerged by the sea) where the English army landed. The soldiers were hindered by the ditches and pits which the tidal river filled, by the enemy's defensive earthworks and by the rocks and the narrowness of the tracks. He describes Harfleur itself, through which the Seine flowed out into the sea, the river being diverted into two walled channels which operated two mills. He also describes the town's fortifications, its walls, gates and towers and its circular barbican built of wood and earth. He ends with the port:[75]

> The harbour is fortified to receive ships, which can sail right into the middle of the town, with an enclosing wall on both sides of the channel which is higher than the walls of the town, and has suitable defensive towers at intervals. There are two beautiful towers at its entrance, between which the water ebbs and flows. One is high and very large, fortified both on top and half way up. The other is smaller and fortified only on top. Both prevent, by

---

[72] *GH V*, pp. 12, 126.
[73] BL MSS. Cotton Julius E IV, ff. 113–27, and Sloane 1776, ff. 50–72. See *GH V*, pp. xv–xvii.
[74] *GH V*, pp. 26–54, 80–98.
[75] *GH V*, p. 30.

a chain between them, any ship entering or leaving without permission. The farsighted enemy had fortified the entrance and much of the wall on the side which was open and exposed to ships at high tide, with piles and tree trunks thicker than a man's thigh fixed very close together, one end pointing inwards towards the town and the other outwards towards the river. Thus if our ships came in on the tide to attack by way of the harbour or to make an assault on the walls, they would either retreat on seeing the piles or if they did not care about their safety or if the piles were covered by the tide, would be dashed against them and wrecked.

The *Gesta* gives graphic details about the siege itself. It describes how the besieged put mud on the streets to cushion the fall of missiles, and prepared jars of sulphur and boiling oil to throw from the walls,[76] and how the English dug defensive trenches [77] and protected their guns and siege engines with screens.[78] At Agincourt it records that Henry ordered complete silence so that the French thought the English had retreated. The English could hear the French calling their servants and friends 'as usual',[79] and meanwhile Henry cheered the soldiers.[80] It also states that Henry made the archers fix staves in front of them for protection against the French cavalry.[81]

Again in accordance with chivalric tastes, the author of the *Gesta* loved a splendid spectacle. He gives a long description of the pageants which welcomed Henry on his return to London.[82] They consisted of a series of tableaux. The first Henry reached, to the sound of trumpets, was on the tower at the entrance to London bridge: there was a statue of a giant, of immense size, holding a great sword in his right hand, as if fighting, and keys in his left representing him as janitor of the city. On his right was a statue of a woman, almost equally large, in a scarlet cloak, bedecked with jewels. The tower itself was decorated with banners bearing the royal arms and the words 'Civitas Regis Justitiae'. Next Henry came to models of his armorial supporters, an antelope with the royal arms on a shield round its neck, holding a sceptre in its right hoof, and a lion holding the king's standard in its right paw, each on a wooden column covered with cloth painted to look like marble. In a nearby house innumerable boys dressed to represent the hierarchy of angels sang hymns as the king appro-

---

[76] *GH V*, pp. 38–40.
[77] *GH V*, p. 36.
[78] *GH V*, p. 36.
[79] *GH V*, p. 80.
[80] *GH V*, p. 78. Cf. Shakespeare, *Henry V*, Act IV, chorus.
[81] *GH V*, p. 82.
[82] *GH V*, p. 102–12. For the propaganda purpose of such ceremonial pageants staged to welcome kings of England in the fifteenth century see J. W. McKenna, 'Henry VI of England and the dual monarchy: aspects of royal political propaganda, 1422–1432' in *Journal of the Warburg and Courtauld Institutes*, xxviii (1965), pp. 159–62.

ached. The writer goes on to describe in detail the other tableaux, the water conduits transformed into castles and the like.

As pointed out above, the *Gesta* is an official history of Henry V's reign written by one of the king's chaplains. It was no doubt through his connection with the royal court that Thomas Elmham obtained a copy of the *Gesta*. He apparently used it as the basis of the now lost Life of Henry V in Latin prose,[83] which he wrote in addition to the surviving Life in Latin verse. Elmham started his career as a monk of St Augustine's, Canterbury.[84] In 1414 he became prior of the Cluniac monastery of Lenton in Nottinghamshire, and in 1415 he was appointed vicar-general of the Cluniacs in England and Scotland. He must have known Henry V, to whom he dedicated the metrical Life, because Henry refers to him as 'capellanus noster' in a letter to the abbot of Cluny, dated 24 November 1414.[85] Besides the two Lives of Henry V which are to be considered below, Elmham wrote a history of St Augustine's, the *Speculum Augustinianum* (*The Mirror of St Augustine's*),[86] and, in 1416, the *Cronica Regum Nobilium Angliae* (*A Chronicle of the Noble Kings of England*).[87] The *Speculum* will be discussed in Chapter 8. The *Cronica* is a genealogy of the kings of England from Brutus to Richard II, with a few small illustrations (mainly conventional pictures of cities) and brief historical notes.

It has been suggested that Elmham was himself the author of the *Gesta*.[88] This suggestion was made partly because of the reference to him as Henry's chaplain. However, he cannot have been attached to the royal chapel in the same way as the author of the *Gesta*, because it was staffed with secular priests. Moreover, it is unlikely that the prose work to which Elmham refers the reader of his metrical Life for further details, and which he claims to have written, was the *Gesta*. Comparison of the metrical Life with the *Gesta* shows that there are important variants of fact between the two works.[89] Furthermore, the section in the metrical Life covering the years from 1416 to 1418, a period not reached by the *Gesta* which ends in 1416, has a different emphasis from the previous part: Henry V is less central

---

[83] For Thomas Elmham's claim to have written a prose Life of Henry V, see *TE*, p. 79. Cf. Roskell and Taylor, 'The authorship and purpose of the *Gesta Henrici Quinti*: Part I', pp. 453–5.

[84] For Thomas Elmham's career see ibid., pp. 455–61, and Kingsford, *Hist. Lit.* pp. 45–6.

[85] Roskell and Taylor, op. cit., p. 433.

[86] See pp. 345–55 below.

[87] BL MS. Claudius E IV, ff. 2–32. For this chronicle see F. Taylor, 'A note on Rolls Series 8' in *BJRL*, xx (1936), pp. 379–82.

[88] This was suggested by various scholars in the past; see Roskell and Taylor, 'The authorship and purpose of the *Gesta Henrici Quinti*: Part I', pp. 431–3. However, recently the attribution has been challenged, and Roskell and Taylor produce convincing evidence, which is rehearsed below, against it; see ibid., pp. 434–64.

[89] It should be noticed that there are two versions of the metrical Life (Cole published a conflated version), a longer and a shorter one; see ibid., pp. 441 and n. 3, 442.

to the theme. This change surely reflects the point at which Elmham could no longer rely on another author but had to write independently. Thus the evidence indicates that Elmham used the *Gesta* as the source for his prose Life and then used his prose work as the source for the metrical *Life*. This view is corroborated by the fact that, as far as is known, he was not on the 1415 campaign in France.

Besides correcting the *Gesta* on some points, Elmham amplified it. (For example he added the story of the dauphin's gift of tennis balls to Henry V.)[90] In general, however, he reproduced its factual content. He also reproduced its political outlook in so far as Henry dominates the scene in his work (until 1416). Nevertheless, although it, like the *Gesta*, stressed Henry's piety and rectitude—Henry fought the French only to achieve a just peace—it gives more weight to the king's suppression of Lollardy. This aspect of the reign dovetailed well into the Life's eulogistic framework. The Lollards had a dual role: they were both heretics and conspirators against established authority. It was Henry's duty as a Christian prince to wipe out heresy; and it was his duty as a good king to put down sedition. The new emphasis in the metrical Life, if considered in conjunction with its style, which is totally different from that of the *Gesta*, suggests that part of Elmham's intention was to write a polemic against Lollardy.

The style of the metrical Life is deliberately obscure. Elmham admits in the preface that he chose to write verse, not prose, because its meaning is less immediately clear.[91] In addition, he used various kinds of cryptogram, figure and word-play.[92] His own name appears in an acrostic in the proem, and he explains in the preface that the year-dates occur in letter-numerals at the beginning of each annal and elsewhere. A sample passage containing both anagrams and a chronogram relates to the plot hatched at Southampton by Richard, earl of Cambridge, Henry Lord Scrope and Sir Thomas Gray, in 1415.[93] Putting the significant letters in capitals and representing the letter 'U' as 'V' where necessary, it reads:

> SCrVtans Conspirat, RiMatVr OLentia PLEbi;
> Rumpe Iugo CoR AVens, Res Dabit Ultra Sonum.
> EIA! Ruunt GenS Aucta Malis, Opus Hoste. Triumphant. ...

The anagram in the first line is Scrope, that in the second Ricardus, and

[90] *TE*, p. 101. Cf. Kingsford, *First English Life*, p. xliii, and p. 196 n. 18 above.
[91] *TE*, p. 80.
[92] Recent scholars have tended to neglect the cryptic element in the metrical Life. See A. Gransden, 'Silent meanings in Ranulph Higden's *Polychronicon* and in Thomas Elmham's *Liber Metricus de Henrico Quinto*' in *Medium Ævum*, xlvi (1978), pp. 235–8, 240 nn.
[93] *TE*, p. 105. Cf. the next note. For a slightly different interpretation of the cryptograms see *Pseudo-Elmham*, pp. 376–7. No doubt many cryptograms in Elmham's Life remain undetected.

that in the third, in reverse, Thomas Graie. The elucidation of the chronogram requires the rearrangement of letters and some arithmetic. The numerals are C V C V L L C V M, which rearranged is M C C C L L V V V: by adding the pair of Ls to make 100, and the three Vs to make fifteen, the date 1415 is arrived at.

Elmham was not the first historian in England to adopt a cryptic style. More than one fourteenth century author had given his name in an acrostic, starting with Higden who also used numerology and literary iconography.[94] Elmham explains in the preface why he adopted this style. He states that he wrote so that Henry V's subjects would appreciate the king's great achievements. But he was faced with a difficulty because Henry's pious humility was such that he did not like his victories praised, lest God should think he attributed them to his own effort rather than to divine power. This prevented Elmham asking the nobles at court for information.[95] As a result of Henry's attitude Elmham resolved to put the meaning of his work beyond the understanding of most men: only the learned, who would appreciate Henry's desire for reticence, would fully understand it.

However, Elmham may well have had other motives for adopting a cryptic style. He probably intended to write a book especially for the ecclesiastical élite—the cryptograms would beguile the hours (as crossword puzzles do today).[96] But the style served a more serious purpose. By multiplying levels of meaning it reinforced both praise and blame. It was especially appropriate for discussing underground movements—sedition and conspiracy (such as, in the passage cited, the Southampton plot): secrets in real life found an analogue in literary occultism. In addition hidden meanings had mysterious power. (This aspect is illustrated by the use of lucky and unlucky numbers.)

It seems likely that Elmham considered the cryptic style particularly suitable for attacking the Lollards. It implicitly undermined their explicit claim that ordinary men could read and understand books,[97] for here was a book beyond their comprehension. And not only did Elmham add force to his invective by adopting the style, but he was also, as it were, pitting his magic against theirs. Any reference to Sir John Oldcastle is accompanied by a spate of cryptograms.[98] He plays on the name of Oldcastle's master,

[94] See pp. 44 and n. 6, 47 above. Sir Thomas Gray, Henry Knighton and John Strecche also gave their names in acrostics; pp. 94, 159–60 above, p. 405 and nn. 104, 105 below.

[95] TE, p. 80.

[96] For examples of the use of cryptograms involving numbers as puzzles in middle English secular literature see Edmund Reiss, 'Number symbolism and medieval literature' in Medievalia et Humanistica, new series, i (1970), p. 167. For the use of number symbolism in general in such literature see ibid., pp. 165–9 and nn.

[97] For a reference to Oldcastle's distribution of tracts see TE, pp. 147–8.

[98] The cryptic passage already cited concerning the Southampton plot relates, though rather remotely, to the Lollards, because Sir John Oldcastle was reputedly implicated; see E. F. Jacob, The Fifteenth Century (Oxford 1961), p. 246.

Wyclif, which he gives as Mala Vita (Wicked Life),[99] and renders the name of Oldcastle's captor, Lord Powis, in an acrostic.[100] He ends the passage with some numerological reflections on the lucky number five: in Henry V's fifth year constancy triumphed with the capture of Oldcastle; Christ had five wounds; the name Maria has five letters; there follow five lines in each of which the name Maria appears in acrostic; and so on.[101] After this section on Oldcastle there are a few brief entries on general history and then the work ends with the *Te Deum* adapted as an address to the Virgin Mary. In the course of the work is the description of the suppression of the revolt led by Oldcastle in 1413, treated in a similar cryptic style,[102] besides other information about the Lollards.[103]

Elmham used biblical imagery for the same purpose as cryptograms, that is to strengthen his polemic against the Lollards. In the tirades against Oldcastle which virtually begin and end the work, Oldcastle, the Antichrist, is put in juxtaposition to Henry, the Christ figure; he is the great dragon,[104] identified as the devil, of the book of Revelation (xii. 4, 14):[105]

> This little book of history ... includes in its five year span the dawn of glory, of the psalter, of the cithara of our Catholic prince and king, [who came] to defeat the shadows of evil, so that his glory might be acknowledged by the people to the Lord, and cover the whole earth. [It includes] the rise and fall of the already broken head of the dragon (*his tail* drawing with it *the third part of the stars*), that is of that satellite of hell, John Oldcastle, heresiarch and arch-Lollard. It is well known that his vile stench (like that of a dungheap) reached the noses of Catholics after the schism had been crushed, by means of which it is thought that he was raised *for a time, and times, and half a time:* however, as will be shown in the work below, he perished in the end.

Elmham describes Oldcastle's capture and execution in similar terms. Again Oldcastle appears as the great dragon, and also as two other biblical types of the devil, Behemoth and the Leviathan (Job xl and xli). Elmham alludes to Psalm lxxiv. 15–17, in his satirical comments on Oldcastle's execution by burning: it was, he writes, commonly believed that Oldcastle regarded himself as another Elijah, and claimed that he would rise again after three days; and, indeed, the heresiarch did go, like Elijah,

---

[99] *TE*, p. 156.
[100] *TE*, p. 156.
[101] *TE*, p. 161. For the especial association of the number five with the Virgin Mary see Reiss, op. cit., p. 165.
[102] *TE*, pp. 96–100.
[103] See e.g. *TE*, p. 151.
[104] Cf. Psalm lxxiv. 13.
[105] *TE*, p. 82. See also Gransden, 'Silent meanings', pp. 237–8.

to his death in a chariot (that is in a wooden cart), and did leave this earth by fire.[106]

Elmham's metrical Life, by content and style, was admirably suited to an ecclesiastical audience. If he meant to amuse as well as to edify, he had some success, for his work was fairly popular: nine fifteenth century copies are known.[107]

Unlike Elmham's metrical Life, the three Lives still to be considered, that by Titus Livius, the Pseudo-Elmham and the English translation of Titus Livius, were not intended primarily for a clerical audience. They were written, as was the *Gesta*, for the nobility and for those closely connected with the royal court. Moreover, the first two Lives can be further distinguished from both the *Gesta* and Elmham's metrical Life: the latter were, in their different ways, typically medieval works but Titus Livius' Life and, to a lesser extent, the Pseudo-Elmham were products of renaissance humanism.

Titus Livius was born at Forli, forty miles from Ferrara, some time after 1400.[108] He joined the household of Humphrey duke of Gloucester probably in 1436 (the duke applied for his denization in 1437) as his *'poeta et orator'*.[109] Apparently he held a position similar to that of a scholar in an Italian court. He helped introduce Duke Humphrey's circle to Italian books and learning, but he soon applied to the chancellor, John Stafford, for a post, and, being unsuccessful, left England in 1438 or 1439, pleading poverty.[110] He travelled to Milan, Toulouse and then to Barcelona where he was in 1442 pursuing the career of a continental humanist.

Before Titus Livius left for Italy Humphrey, duke of Gloucester, asked him to write the Life of Henry V.[111] At about the same time he wrote an account in Latin verse of the duke's campaign in Flanders against Philip

---

[106] *TE*, pp. 151, 158.

[107] See *TE*, pp. xlv–xlvi, and Roskell and Taylor, 'The authorship and purpose of the *Gesta Henrici Quinti*: Part I', p. 441 n. 3. Cole prints in footnotes to the text a gloss on the cryptograms from the manuscript (BL MS. Cotton Julius E IV, ff. 89–112) which has the fullest version of it.

[108] For Titus Livius' career see: Kingsford, *First English Life*, p. xiv; the same author's 'The early biographies of Henry V', pp. 58–60; C. W. Previté-Orton, 'The earlier career of Titus Livius Frulovisiis' in *EHR*, xxx (1915), pp. 74–8; Roberto Weiss, 'Humphrey duke of Gloucester and Tito Livio Frulovisi' in *Fritz Saxl 1890–1948; a Volume of Memorial Essays from his Friends in England*, ed. D. J. Gordon (London 1957), pp. 218–27; the same author's *Humanism in England during the Fifteenth Century* (Oxford 1957), pp. 41–8. Seven comedies, a political tract (*De Republica*) and an encomium on John Stafford (see below and note 110) by Livius are printed and discussed in *Opera hactenus inedita T. Livii de Frulovisiis de Ferrara*, ed. C. W. Previté-Orton (Cambridge 1932).

[109] Titus Livius is so described in the letters of denization; *Foedera*, x. 661–2.

[110] See Livius' encomium of sixty three hexameter lines addressed to John Stafford, then bishop of Bath and Wells, in BL MS. Cotton Claudius E III, f. 353ᵛ, printed *Opera hactenus inedita*, ed. Previté-Orton, pp. 390–2.

[111] *TL*, p. 2.

the Bold, duke of Burgundy; he covered the period from the congress of Arras in 1435 to Duke Humphrey's triumphant homecoming in August 1436.[112] This poem, the *Humfroidos*, resembles works by other Italian humanists, for example Francesco Filelfo's *Sfortias*, Porcelio Pandone's *Feltria* and Tito Vespasiano Strozzi's *Borseide*.[113] Such works were expected of humanists at Italian courts. Both the Life and the *Humfroidos* show their renaissance affinities. The Life is in classical Latin, while the *Humfroidos* has numerous borrowings from classical authors such as Virgil, Statius and Horace, and begins with a discussion in the underworld (a device inspired by Claudian's *In Rufinum*, Book I[114]) on the decline in the number of those killed in battle, because there was no war.

Titus Livius wrote both works primarily as propaganda in favour of Duke Humphrey. The duke, whose position in the regency was strengthened by the death of the duke of Bedford in 1435, wanted to consolidate his position and renew the war with France by leading an expedition against the duke of Burgundy. The purpose of the Life was to rehearse Henry V's triumphs, in order to spur his son to emulation. Livius addresses the work to Henry VI and urges the king to fight,[115]

> not because I prefer you to have war instead of peace, but because you cannot have a just peace. You should resolve to imitate that divine king your father in all things, seeking peace and quiet for your realm by using the same methods and martial valour as he used to subdue your common enemies.

The *Humfroidos* sought to prove by recounting Duke Humphrey's campaign in Flanders and relief of Calais, that the duke was a worthy successor to Henry V as a military commander, capable of reviving England's glory.[116]

Although Duke Humphrey is not the hero of the Life, he occupies an important place in it. Livius begins with a panegyric on him:[117] he remarks that King Henry was committed as a child to the care of 'the most noble' duke, his uncle, who watched over his education and religious development, just as Lycurgus had had charge of his nephew, the son of Polydectes, king of the Lacedaemonians.[118] And he comments on the duke's pre-eminence as a student of letters 'both human and divine', his patronage of

---

[112] This poem is discussed and the first and last twenty-five lines printed in Weiss, 'Humphrey duke of Gloucester and Tito Livio Frulovisi', pp. 221–7.

[113] Vittorio Rossi, *Il Quattrocento* (Milan 1933), in *Storia Letteraria d'Italia* (Milan 1929 onwards), pp. 244–5.

[114] Claudian's *In Rufinum* opens with a council of Furies in Hades deploring the just rule of Theodosius the Great and plotting to disturb the peace; *In Rufinum*, bk I, lines 28–117. Cf. Alan Cameron, *Poetry and Propaganda at the Court of Honorius* (Oxford 1970), p. 459.

[115] *TL*, pp. 2–3.

[116] Weiss, 'Humphrey duke of Gloucester and Tito Livio Frulovisi', pp. 224–5.

[117] *TL*, pp. 1–2.

[118] See Plutarch, *Lives*, *Lycurgus*, iii.

Livius himself and his request that Livius should write the Life. In the course of the work Livius records the duke's part in Henry V's campaigns. One such notice, which is about the battle of Agincourt, is detailed: the duke was badly wounded in the groin and fell with his feet towards the enemy; Henry stood over him fighting fiercely until Humphrey could be carried to safety.[119]

Undoubtedly one of Livius' principal sources of information was Duke Humphrey himself. Livius also used the *Brut*, a London chronicle, official documents[120] and a contemporary poem on the siege of Rouen (in 1418) by an eyewitness, John Page.[121] His description of Henry's 1415 campaign is very like that in the *Gesta* in many particulars. However, since there is no evidence that Livius used the *Gesta*, these similarities must be taken as mutually confirmatory and as indications that both works derived from the probably oral account accepted at court. For the section covering the years from 1418 to 1422 Livius is the earliest chronicle authority. Furthermore, although Elmham continues after 1416 when the *Gesta* ends, until 1418, Livius is much the fullest authority for these two years. He describes the negotiations preceding the treaty of Troyes (of 21 May 1420), and has details which became part of the tradition inherited by Shakespeare: Henry's love of Katherine[122] and her modesty when he gave her a kiss ('the kiss of peace').[123]

The most graphic passages in Livius' Life describe the sieges and battles in which Duke Humphrey participated.[124] Perhaps the best is the description of the siege of Cherbourg which the duke commanded in the spring and summer of 1417.[125] Livius describes the site of the town, on sandy levels at the foot of the steep hills by the estuary of the river Divette. The castle was inside the town walls which were almost totally surrounded by water at high tide, partly by the sea and partly by the defensive ditches. The besiegers were harassed by the constantly shifting sand which the wind blew hither and thither, and by missiles from the town. To protect the English from the latter, Duke Humphrey sent his soldiers at night in groups of three to the nearby woods to load sledges with brushwood and great stakes. The timber was used to construct a defensive palisade, but

[119] *TL*, p. 20.

[120] See Kingsford, *Hist. Lit.* pp. 53–4.

[121] John Page's poem is printed in *Collections*, ed. Gairdner (for which see pp. 228 n. 51, 232 and n. 81), pp. 1–46, and elsewhere. See J. H. Wylie and W. T. Waugh, *The Reign of Henry the Fifth*, iii. 125–6. For its use (perhaps indirectly) by Titus Livius see ibid., p. 126 n. 1, and Kingsford, *Hist. Lit.* p. 118. For Page's poem see also pp. 224, 232 below.

[122] Titus Livius asserts that because of French obstruction the peace negotiations would have foundered 'nisi quod visae regiae Katherinae quaedam amoris flamma Martium regem tunc primum accendit'; *TL*, p. 75.

[123] 'Anglicus rex Gallorum, ut dicunt, reginae prius, inde Katherinae filiae virgini pacis osculum dedit, quod sine rubore virginis esse nequivit'; *TL*, p. 75.

[124] *TL*, p. 52. Cf. Wylie and Waugh, *Henry V*, iii. 108.

[125] *TL*, pp. 52–5.

though the townsmen were amazed to see it in the morning, they soon destroyed it and everything in its vicinity with fire balls. The English rebuilt the palisade protecting it with water, and fortified their huts as well as they could. Duke Humphrey even tried to divert the river, but it broke back into its old channel during the spring tides. He also raised huge mounds, higher than the town walls, from which the English could attack, but again they were defeated by the enemy's missiles. Eventually, however, the duke's blockade succeeded, and famine forced the town to submit.

The next work to be considered, the Pseudo-Elmham, resembles Livius in some respects: it too combines the humanist with the chivalric literary tradition, and derives its information from a source near the royal court. The text survives in two recensions, the latest having been written some time between 1445 and 1446. The date of the earlier recension is unknown although it was obviously after Henry V's death. This recension was written, as the preface states, at the command of Walter Lord Hungerford, to whom it is addressed.[126] Lord Hungerford was an important man in Henry V's service.[127] Besides being steward of the household from 1415 to 1421, he was employed on various diplomatic missions: to the emperor Sigismund in 1414; to the council of Constance from 1414 to 1415; to Theodoric archbishop of Cologne in 1416; and to the French court in 1417. He took part in the peace negotiations with France in 1419. He also fought in Henry V's campaign of 1415 (at Agincourt he made the inapposite remark to the king cited above), and in the 1418 campaign. He was, as the Pseudo-Elmham records, an executor of Henry V's will. Sir Walter retained his importance under Henry VI. He was a member of the council of the protector Humphrey, duke of Gloucester, in 1422, and steward of the household again in 1424, and treasurer from 1426 (in which year he became Baron Hungerford) until 1432. Furthermore, judging from his foundation of a number of chantries and from his other religious endowments, he was a pious man. He died in 1449.

Although the name of the author of the Pseudo-Elmham is unknown, he was clearly much influenced by the humanist movement. The work is in classical Latin and has rhetorical passages. For example Fortitude and Compassion exhort Henry V not to be overwhelmed by grief at the news of the death of the duke of Clarence.[128] When Henry succumbed to his

---

[126] The Pseudo-Elmham is discussed in Kingsford, *Hist. Lit.* pp. 56–63. The address in the first recension to Lord Hungerford is printed in ibid., p. 58 n. 3.

[127] For Sir Walter Hungerford's career see J. S. Roskell, 'Three Wiltshire Speakers' in *Wiltshire Archaeological and Natural History Magazine*, lvi (1955–6), pp. 301–41. His religious benefactions are noticed in ibid., p. 334. See also K. B. McFarlane, *The Nobility of Later Medieval England* (Oxford 1973), pp. 126–8.

[128] *Pseudo-Elmham*, pp. 305–7.

last illness, the author apostrophizes Disease, accusing it of hastening to despoil the world of its principal treasure, to destroy the castle of all virtue and the splendour of cities and kingdoms, to unite the world in universal sadness and prevent the growth of perfect peace, and to deprive rich and poor alike of all joy, and so on. The author ends his harangue:[129]

> Oh cruel Disease! Do you not know whom you have presumed to fill with such fearful poison? whom you have afflicted with such terrible torments? whom you rejoice at removing from a grieving world? The king, indeed, is the glory of kings, the model of magnanimity, the mirror of chivalry, the champion of justice, the zealot of equity, the victor of France and Normandy. Now for shame, you intend to conquer him, and do not hesitate to torture such an illustrious king, allowing, in your outrageous excess, not one hour's rest to so great a prince. In your blind presumption you fail to distinguish between a prince and a pauper.

The humanist tone of the Pseudo-Elmham is even more evident in the second recension which is dedicated to John Somerset, the physician of Henry VI from 1428 to about 1432.[130] Somerset remained in royal service until 1450, when he was disgraced as a partisan of William de la Pole, duke of Suffolk. He died in about 1455. Somerset was a learned man; he had studied medicine in London and Paris, became a fellow of Pembroke College, Cambridge, and wrote medical treatises and perhaps a work on grammar. He also collected a library, which he bequeathed to his own college and to Peterhouse. Humphrey duke of Gloucester left him the custody of his books after his death (in 1447). His piety is attested by the foundation in 1446 of a hospital (for nine poor men), chapel and guild of SS. Raphael, Gabriel, Michael and All Angels, at Brentford End in Middlesex.[131]

This foundation is mentioned in the epilogue to the second recension of the Pseudo-Elmham. The epilogue is a typically humanist composition modelled on Martial.[132] The writer apostrophizes his 'foolish, unpolished, beggarly little book', telling it to seek a patron. He recommends John

---

[129] Ibid., pp. 331–2.

[130] Ibid., pp. 338–43. For Somerset's career see Emden, *Biographical Register*, iii. 1727–8.

[131] Henry VI's licence to Master John Somerset, chancellor of the exchequer, to found a hospital and guild in honour of All Angels, next to the chapel he had built (the foundation stone of which Henry himself had laid) at Brentford End, just south of the highway from Brentford to Hounslow, dated 12 October 1446, is enrolled on the patent rolls; *CPR, 1446–1452*, p. 29. For the full text of the licence, in an English translation, and for the subsequent history of the foundation see G. J. Aungier, *The History and Antiquities of Syon Monastery, the Parish of Isleworth, and the Chapelry of Hounslow* (London 1840), pp. 215–25.

[132] Martial, *Epigrams*, bk III. 2–5. Catullus used the same form of dedication (which has Hellenistic precedents): Catullus, *Carmina*, 1; see C. J. Fordyce, *Catullus: a Commentary* (Oxford 1961), p. 83.

Somerset who will clothe it in purple cloth,[133] bestow on it abundant treasure and make its rough prose sparkle with his fluent rhetoric. Commenting on Somerset himself, the author extols his knowledge of astronomy, of 'the demonstrations of Aristotle, and the aphorisms of Hippocrates,' and asserts that Somerset gave the king's mind the riches of learning and virtue, and preserved the king's body from sickness. Next the author instructs the book how to find Somerset. He tells it not to seek him at court, because there he is fully occupied with helping the poor, working for the good of the country and advising the king. Rather the book should go to Somerset's own home:[134]

> When you begin your journey, take the king's highway and follow it for a few miles until you come to a path on the right (easily seen because worn with use), not far from a very beautiful chapel of royal foundation, formerly built at [Somerset's] expense in honour of SS. Raphael, Gabriel, Michael, and All Angels. There, when you see the footprints made by the bare feet of the poor who crowd to his house, and find the shoe marks made when they return after his alms have given them leather shoes, and when you see the poor, the hungry and the wretched hurrying to his house along the same path, and meet them clothed, fed and happy on account of his liberal charity, you will know that this must inevitably be the most direct way to his abode.

The epilogue ends with instructions on how the book was to present itself to Somerset, in the company of the poor and supplicating him with a panegyric in verse.

It will be noticed that both Lord Hungerford and John Somerset had connections with Humphrey, duke of Gloucester. Therefore, the author of the Pseudo-Elmham presumably obtained a copy of Titus Livius' Life of Henry V, which was his principal source, from the duke's library. He follows Livius' factual content closely, although with considerable rhetorical embellishment, until 1420. Then he writes more fully, and gradually becomes an independent authority. He almost certainly derived the information for his detailed and lively description of the siege of Meaux, which lasted from October 1421 until May 1422, from Lord Hungerford himself (Hungerford was at that time steward of the royal household).[135] Meaux is on an isthmus of the river Marne, and on the south bank opposite the town was the suburb called The Market, which was protected on three sides by the Marne and on the fourth by an artificial channel. The town

---

[133] 'Purpura et bysso quibus te vestiat'; *Pseudo-Elmham*, p. 339. Cf. Martial, *Epigrams*, bk III. 2.

[134] *Pseudo-Elmham*, p. 340.

[135] Ibid., pp. 315–28. Cf. Wylie and Waugh, *Henry V*, iii. 337–57.

and The Market were connected by a long bridge, and were strongly defended by walls, towers and ditches. The Market offered the stiffest resistance to the English forces. The Pseudo-Elmham describes some of the siege machines. There was a great wooden structure ingeniously devised by King Henry which was dragged on wheels to face the drawbridge: it overhung both water and drawbridge, thus enabling the besieged to attack the walls. There was a tall wooden tower, also the product of Henry's ingenuity, erected on top of two large boats which were bound together with massive beams. The masts of the boats formed the corner posts of the tower, and the tower itself was divided into storeys, the upper one being taller than the highest part of The Market's fortifications and having a bridge across which armed men could storm the ramparts. In the event a truce was made before this construction could be floated against the walls, but afterwards it was tried out as an experiment, apparently successfully. The Pseudo-Elmham records that Hungerford was in command of the forces on the west where 'the fighting was the fiercest and most serious because of the very great number of ballistic and other machines assigned to him'.[136] It describes how, at the king's order, a bridge of boats was constructed on the west side which enabled the English to build shelters near the walls to protect their sallies and bombardment.

As the Pseudo-Elmham records, Henry V when on his deathbed put Lord Hungerford, together with Thomas Beaufort, duke of Exeter, in charge of his son, the young Henry.[137] Therefore, perhaps it was from him that the Pseudo-Elmham derived the authentic details in the long passage (which is mainly fulsome rhetoric) on Henry's last days and death. The king fell ill in the summer of 1422 when on a campaign in Picardy. He went to the castle of Bois de Vincennes, but then tried to set out to relieve Cosne. However, he was too ill to ride and had to be taken, as the Pseudo-Elmham records, in a horse-litter. He lay ill for several days at Corbeil, but as his condition worsened it was decided to take him back to Vincennes. He went by boat down the Seine to Charenton, where, to reassure the people, he tried to ride, but 'after a few paces, from the agony of excessive pain, he could not stay on the horse', and went the rest of the way in a litter. He was put to bed in Vincennes, never to get up again.[138]

The account of Henry's actual death in the Pseudo-Elmham is rhetorical, but there are realistic touches in the subsequent passage. Henry's corpse was so emaciated by illness that there was scarcely any flesh to putrify. Therefore, it was allowed to remain intact, complete even with intestines.

---

[136] *Pseudo-Elmham*, p. 324.
[137] Ibid., p. 333. The Pseudo-Elmham is the only authority for this statement; see Wylie and Waugh, *Henry V*, iii. 417 n. 5.
[138] *Pseudo-Elmham*, pp. 329–31.

It was steeped in aromatic herbs and balsam, enveloped in waxed linen and lead, and placed, wrapped in a silk cloth, in a wooden coffin. This was carried in a funeral carriage draped with black, and on top lay a large effigy of the king in royal vestments wearing a crown and holding a sceptre. Thus, escorted by princes and magnates, it set out for England.[139]

It can, therefore, be seen how the view of Henry V which was taken over by the Tudors evolved in the Lives discussed above. These biographies, all by men closely associated with the royal court or with Humphrey duke of Gloucester's circle, expressed the authors' natural admiration for a victorious king. The tendency to eulogize was encouraged in the case of Titus Livius and the Pseudo-Elmham by the humanist tradition of panegyric. Moreover, eulogy was a necessary part of those Lives which had a propaganda purpose, whether to promote the French war or counter Lollardy. In this way the traditional view of Henry V developed. The last work to be considered, the English translation of Titus Livius' Life, links the fifteenth century biographies directly with the Tudor period.

The Translator wrote between June 1513 and the autumn of 1514.[140] His principal source was Titus Livius, though he also used Enguerran de Monstrelet's chronicle and the version of the *Brut* in Caxton's *Polychronicon*.[141] But he made important additions to this well known material from some lost book of reminiscences or some Life of Henry V by an author who derived his information from James Butler, fourth earl of Ormonde.[142] The earl was born in 1392 and succeeded his father in 1405. He was a friend of Thomas, duke of Clarence, whom he accompanied on his expedition to France in 1412. He was also on the 1415 campaign with Henry V and fought at Agincourt. He was at the siege of Rouen in 1418, but early in 1420 he was appointed lieutenant of Ireland. Ormonde served in France in the 1430s, but he spent most of Henry VI's reign until his death in 1452, as deputy in Ireland. On two occasions, in 1439 and in 1446, he was accused of treason in connection with his administration, but each time he was pardoned. He seems to have been a man of scholarly tastes, with a particular liking for history and heraldry.

Thus Ormonde had plenty of opportunity to learn about Henry V. The work for which he supplied the information was apparently compiled after 29 June 1455, the date of the canonization of St Vincent Ferrier which it mentioned,[143] but not much later, because it was written when memories were still fresh. It included a collection of stories nearly all

---

[139] Ibid., pp. 336–8. For references to other accounts of the embalming of Henry's body and the funeral cortege see Wylie and Waugh, *Henry V*, iii. 420–2.

[140] For the date of the translation see *Translator*, pp. ix-x.

[141] Ibid., pp. xiv-xvi.

[142] Ibid., pp. xvi-xx.

[143] Ibid., p. 130. Cf. pp. xviii-xix, xxxvi.

connected with Henry. The Translator gives ten stories which probably all derived ultimately from Ormonde, although the source is not mentioned in all instances. They represent only a proportion of the tales, many of which may well have contained a grain of truth, about Henry current in the fifteenth century; other examples are preserved in the *Brut* chronicles and elsewhere.[144] They are: (1) concerning Henry's continence before marriage;[145] (2) how in 1412 Henry disguised himself 'in a gown of blue satin or damask made full of eyelets or holes, and at every eyelet the needle wherewith it was made hanging there by the thread of silk, and about his arm he wore a dog's collar set full of esses of gold and the terrets of the same also of fine gold', and was reconciled with his father;[146] (3) the death-bed scene of Henry IV;[147] (4) Prince Henry's riotous youth, and how he, together with a band of friends, would rob his own receivers, later giving them acquittances for what they had lost and rewarding the man who had resisted best;[148] (5) Henry's conversion from his wild ways on his accession, and his dismissal of his youthful companions;[149] (6) Henry's foundation of a house of Celestines at Isleworth;[150] (7) how Humphrey duke of Gloucester waded into the sea at Dover with sword drawn, to prevent the emperor Sigismund landing until he had declared that he claimed no imperial right over England;[151] (8) how Henry only kept 'a goodly French book' from the spoils acquired after the capture of Caen in 1417;[152] (9) how Vincent Ferrier rebuked Henry (probably in May 1418) for causing so much suffering by war, but was convinced by Henry's arguments;[153] (10) the combat between Henry and the Sire de Barbasan in the mines at Melun.[154]

It remains to consider why the Translator wrote. Once again in the Translator's day the example of the victorious Henry V was used to promote war against France. The Translator began work during Henry VIII's French war but finished after peace had been made. He writes:[155]

> the principal cause of this my pain (for as much as we then laboured in war) was that our sovereign Lord by the knowledge and sight of this pamphile should partly be provoked in his said war

[144] Ibid., pp. xxxviii-xlvi.
[145] Ibid., pp. xx, 5.
[146] Ibid., pp. xx-xxvii, 11–13. For the use made by Shakespeare of this story and of nos 3–5 see ibid., pp. l–lvi.
[147] Ibid., pp. xxvii–xxix, 13–16.
[148] Ibid., pp. xxix, 17.
[149] Ibid., pp. xxix-xxxii, 19.
[150] Ibid., pp. xxxii-xxxiii, 20.
[151] Ibid., pp. xxxiii-xxxiv, 67–8.
[152] Ibid., pp. xxxiv, 92.
[153] Ibid., pp. xxxiv-xxxvi, 130–2. See also p. 196 n. 18 above.
[154] Ibid., pp. xxxvi-xxxviii, 167–71.
[155] Ibid., p. 4. Cf. p. 190.

to ensue the noble and chivalrous acts of this so noble, so virtuous, and so excellent a prince, which so followed, he might the rather attain to like honour, fame, and victory.

In addition the Translator had a more general purpose; to instruct Henry VIII on how to rule well by showing him the example of his ancestor Henry V. He expresses the hope that[156]

his Grace, hearing or seeing, or reading the virtuous manners, the victorious conquests, and the excellent sages and wisdoms of the most renowned prince in his days, King Henry the Fifth, his noble progenitor (of whose superior in all nobleness, manhood, and virtue, to my pretence, it is not read nor heard amongst the princes of England since William of Normandy obtained the government of this realm by conquest) his Grace may in all things concerning his person and the regiment of his people, conform himself to his life and manners, which he used after his coronation, and be counselled by the example of his great wisdom and discretion in all his common and particular acts.

---

[156] Ibid., p. 4. A good example of a passage aimed at instructing 'all princes' follows the story of Henry's conversion from his riotous youth after his coronation. The Translator points out that anyone keeping bad company becomes a party to their offences, and that such friendships prevent a prince from dispensing justice impartially; ibid., p. 19.

8

The *Brut* Chronicles and the Chronicles of London in the Fifteenth Century

Perhaps the most remarkable historiographical development in the fifteenth century was the rise of the vernacular chronicle. At no time since the Anglo-Saxon period had the vernacular chronicle achieved such importance. Previously as far as it known only one chronicle, that of Robert of Gloucester, written in the thirteenth century, had been actually composed in English. Then in 1338 Robert Mannyng of Bourne had translated parts of Peter of Langtoft's chronicle, supplementing it with extracts from Wace to produce a consecutive history.[1] And in 1387 John Trevisa, a graduate of Oxford university and vicar of Berkeley, completed his translation of Higden's *Polychronicon* (with a continuation to 1360),[2] undertaken at the request of his patron Thomas Lord Berkeley.[3]

In the fourteenth century English gained ground as the written language of the secular clergy and of educated laymen—noblemen, lawyers, merchants and the like. Trevisa, who himself translated a number of other Latin works besides the *Polychronicon*,[4] defended the principle of translation, because it made famous works available to those who knew no Latin. Moreover, he believed that 'the gospel, and prophecy, and the right faith of holy church' should be made accessible in the same way: therefore, preaching in English 'is good and needful.'[5]

[1] See Gransden, *Historical Writing*, i. 477 and n. 304.

[2] For Trevisa and his works see p. 52 above, John Taylor, *The Universal Chronicle of Ranulf Higden* (Oxford 1966), pp. 134–42, D. C. Fowler, 'John Trevisa and the English bible' in *Modern Philology*, lviii (1960), pp. 81–98, and the same author's 'New light on John Trevisa' in *Traditio*, xviii (1962), pp. 289–317.

[3] Thomas, Lord Berkeley, of Berkeley castle, d. 1417. Cf. Taylor, *Higden*, pp. 135–6.

[4] For an account of Trevisa's translations see *Dialogus inter Militem et Clericum . . . by John Trevisa*, ed. A. J. Perry (EETS, original series, clxvii, 1925), pp. lxxvii-cxxvi. See also Fowler, 'New light', pp. 315–16 and n. 108.

[5] See Trevisa's *Dialogue between a Lord and a Clerk on Translation* which he prefixed to his translation of the *Polychronicon*. The work is unedited but the text in modern English is printed in A. W. Pollard, *Fifteenth Century Prose and Verse* (Westminster 1903), pp. 203–8 (extracts are in Taylor, *Higden*, p. 136, and Fowler, 'John Trevisa and the English bible', pp. 97–8). See Fowler, 'New light', p. 316 n. 108.

Trevisa also provides evidence that even before his time English had become influential in grammar schools. When he translated the passage in which Higden deplored the neglect of English in favour of French since the Norman Conquest, he added a piece of information and a comment relating to his own day: he records that John of Cornwall, a school master in Oxford (in the mid-fourteenth century) taught his boys English grammar 'so that now, in the year of Our Lord 1385 ... , in all the grammar schools of England, children leaveth French and construeth and learneth in English.'[6] The last half of the fourteenth century was of course the first period to produce outstanding English poets—Geoffrey Chaucer, John Gower and William Langland, all laymen writing in London. Official recognition of the growing importance of the English language in national life was given by a parliamentary statute of 1362: it enacted that in future all pleading and judgments in law courts should be in English, although they were to be enrolled in Latin. (In fact, however, French held its own against English in the law courts well after this date.)[7]

Trevisa's translation of the *Polychronicon* retained some influence throughout the fifteenth century, and contributed to the survival of the taste for universal histories in the sixteenth and seventeenth centuries. In 1482 it was printed by William Caxton, who added his own continuation up to the accession of Edward IV.[8] Nevertheless, it was not a widely popular work (there is evidence for the existence of only about a dozen manuscripts of it).[9] Although the geographical sections appealed to the age of the expansion of Europe, in general Higden's work was too recondite and dealt with periods too remote in time for the average fifteenth century reader. Most people preferred vivid contemporary history, especially if it was associated with their own environment. As contemporary history the vernacular continuations of the *Polychronicon* had drawbacks: Trevisa's continuation was slight, and it was based on well known contemporary sources, the *Brut* chronicles and the chronicles of London, which themselves far excelled the *Polychronicon* in popularity.

The fifteenth century *Brut* and London chronicles have features in common with each other, and are in fact directly related, because the *Brut* chronicles were partly derived from the London ones. They survive in many versions but their complete textual history can never be known

[6] *Poly.* ii. 161. Cited *Dialogus inter Militem et Clericum*, ed. Perry, p. lxxxvi, and Taylor, *Higden*, p. 61. For John of Cornwall see Nicholas Orme, *English Schools in the Middle Ages* (London 1973), pp. 95, 96, 99, and p. 52 n. 49 above. Cf. Emden, *Biographical Register*, i. 490. Cf. p. 52 n. 49 above.
[7] For the 1362 statute see *Rot. Parl.* ii. 273, and *Statutes of the Realm*, i. 375–6. S. B. Chrimes, *Sir John Fortescue de Laudibus Legum Anglie* (Cambridge 1949), p. 194, writes 'This act is evidence of the growing importance of English, but it caused no appreciable change in practice.' See also P. H. Winfield *The Chief Sources of English Legal History* (Cambridge 1925), p. 9, and W. Holdsworth, *A History of English Law* (London 1909–72, 17 vols), ii. 477–82.
[8] See Taylor, *Higden*, pp. 140–2.
[9] Ibid., p. 139.

because of the loss of numerous copies. Their authors, nearly all of whom are anonymous, lived in London, and their chronicles express their civic pride. In politics they were, as one would expect of Londoners, Yorkist. They favoured the French war, which brought lucrative business to the merchants, whether victualling the troops or financing the king, and supported the Yorkist interest partly because it promoted the war. It is notable that although ultimately all the *Brut* and London chronicles are based on excellent contemporary sources of evidence, a number were written up in their present form at one sitting, so to speak, in 1461 or soon after; they emphasize the Yorkist claim throughout, and end on a note of triumph with the accession of Edward IV, which had clearly provided an incentive for their composition.[10]

Nevertheless, distinctions can be drawn between the *Brut* and the London chronicles. The *Brut* chronicles all grew from one stock, the Brutus legend, while the London chronicles evolved, as will be seen, from notes added to lists of the mayors and sheriffs of the city. Moreover, in very general terms the two groups appealed to different, though overlapping, audiences: the *Brut* chronicles with their patriotic and chivalric tone, which is still discernible in the annals for the fifteenth century, appealed especially to the noble and knightly classes; the London chronicles suited the tastes of the city oligarchy.

The development of the *Brut* chronicles in the late thirteenth and in the fourteenth century has been discussed above.[11] The English versions belong to the late fourteenth century and to the fifteenth century, when they eclipsed the French and Latin versions in importance. Their popularity is attested by the survival of over 120 medieval copies and by the numerous continuations.[12] As far as is known the first continuation covered the years from 1377 to 1419 and was probably written in about 1430.

[10] The version of the *Brut* printed by Davies (see the next note and p. 225 and nn. below) and one of the versions printed by Brie (*Brut*, ii. 491–533, and see p. 225 and n. 37 below), both end at 1461. Cf. F. W. D. Brie, *Geschichte und Quellen der mittelenglischen Prosachronik the Brute of England oder the Chronicles of England* (Marburg 1905), p. 109, and Kingsford, *Hist. Lit.* p. 115, 119, 127–9, 133. The *Brut* derived from the London chronicles (see p. 226 and n. 41 below); for a London chronicle ending in 1461 see Robert Bale's chronicle (p. 233 and n. 84 below). Caxton's continuation to the *Polychronicon* (see p. 52 above), and his *Brut* (see p. 223 below) end in 1461: both works were based on the lost Main City Chronicle (see p. 230 below); however, two recent scholars have denied that this proves that 1461 marks a stage in the evolution of the Main City Chronicle, and argue that Caxton stopped in that year merely for 'personal and prudential reasons'; see *The Great Chronicle of London*, ed. A. H. Thomas and I. D. Thornley (London, privately printed, 1938), p. lxx. Cf. p. 257 below.

[11] Pp. 73–7 above. The fifteenth century versions are in the second volume of the edition cited on p. 3 n. 13 above, though it should be noted that the chronicle therein printed in Appendix F (*Brut*, ii. 456–90) is a London chronicle. Another fifteenth century version of the *Brut* is printed as *An English Chronicle of the Reigns of Richard II, Henry IV, Henry V, and Henry VI*, ed. J. S. Davies (Camden Soc., original series, lxiv, 1856).

[12] For a list of the manuscripts known to Dr Brie of the English *Brut* see Brie, *Prosachronik*, pp. 2–5. For descriptions of them see ibid., pp. 51–115 passim.

Two others end in 1430 and 1436 respectively; both were written almost contemporarily with events for the last years they record. Then there was a gap in composition until some time after August 1464 when a continuation to 1461 was written. Another continuation to 1475 was composed in 1478/9.[13] The continuators apparently rewrote the earlier sections, adding and omitting material (in rather the same way as a monastic chronicler might do), so that he produced a new version to precede his continuation. The *Brut* to 1461 was first printed by William Caxton in 1480. Four other editions were printed subsequently in the fifteenth century, and at least seven in the early sixteenth century. And so the *Brut* reached the Tudors, to be plundered by the historians Edward Hall and Raphael Holinshed and through them to provide Shakespeare with copy.[14]

To some extent the *Brut* retained the liveliness and chivalric tone of the original work until the end of the fifteenth century. The authors loved a good story and often added a legendary element to their account of events. For example one version tells how an astrologer warned Richard II that he would be destroyed by a toad; therefore, after seeing Henry Boling-broke wearing a gown embroidered with toads, Richard was struck with fear, and as a result later exiled Henry for ten years.[15] There are also stories about Henry V in the *Brut*—the story of his riotous youth and that of the tennis balls, and a tale of how when eating oysters he settled a dispute between two lords by saying that he would execute them if they did not come to an agreement before he had finished his meal.[16] A number of stories relate to war. For example one version gives an anecdote to explain the rebellion of Sir Henry Percy in 1403; it alleges that Percy asked Henry IV for wages for guarding the marches and, on receiving a slighting answer, said that the king did not treat him as he ought because 'he never had been king of England.' Henry thereupon struck him on the cheek at which Percy exclaimed, 'In faith! this shall be the dearest-bought buffet that ever was in England', and rode off to raise war.[17] The chivalric tone of the *Brut* appears in the descriptions of jousts (for instance those in 1388 when twenty four ladies led twenty four knights on horseback to the venue at Smithfield),[18] and in the graphic descriptions of warfare,[19] and in the record of the deaths of famous soldiers.[20]

---

[13] The versions and continuations are fully described by Brie, op. cit., pp. 51–115 passim. For a more concise account see Kingsford, *Hist. Lit.* pp. 114–15.

[14] For the influence of the *Brut* see ibid., pp. 113, 135–7.

[15] *Brut*, ii. 590.

[16] *Brut*, ii. 593–5, 374–5, 595, respectively.

[17] *Brut*, ii. 548.

[18] *Brut*, ii. 343. For other examples of notices of tournaments see *Brut*, ii. 366, 369–70, 451.

[19] See for example the detailed accounts of the siege of Rouen in *Brut*, ii. 394–422 (see also *Brut*, ii. 387–91, and p. 224 below), and of the Picard war of 1436 in *Brut*, ii. 572–80.

[20] E.g. the death of Sir Robert Knolles (in 1407), and of Thomas, earl of Salisbury (in 1428); *Brut*, ii. 367, 434 (and 454), respectively.

As in the earlier part, the *Brut* continuations describe the Hundred Years' War in patriotic terms. The accounts of Henry V are both patriotic and eulogistic: he was 'a worthy king, and a gracious man, and a great conqueror'.[21] The authors took their descriptions of Henry's siege of Rouen from the poem of John Page, an eyewitness, quoting him either *verbatim* or in paraphrase. Page clearly reflected the contemporary attitude to Henry:[22]

> And as he is king most excellent,
> And to God, but to none other, obedient,
> That reigneth here in earth by right,
> But only to our Jesu full of might
> And within himself emperor,
> And also almighty king and conqueror. . . .
> He is manful, when war doth last,
> And merciful when it is past;
> Manhood, meekness, wit and grace,
> Is contained with him in little space. . . .

After describing Henry's capture of Rouen, one version of the *Brut* asserts that the poor in the city actually preferred him and the English to their French lords, saying among themselves: 'Ah! Almighty God, the Englishmen be of good and true heart! Lo, how here this excellent prince and king that we thought never to obey unto, nor never proffer nor do him homage, now hath he on us more pity and compassion by a thousand than hath our own nation; therefore, our Lord God, that art full of might, grant him grace to win and get his true right.'[23] The *Brut* emphasizes Henry's claim to the territories in France by 'true title of conquest, and right heritage'.[24] Its concern for England's commercial interests abroad is shown by the very detailed account of the defence of Calais against the French and Flemings from 1435 to 1436, when Humphrey duke of Glouces-ter was captain of the town, which ends with verses mocking the Flemings and rejoicing at their discomfiture.[25]

However, this tone of triumphant patriotism could not last. Well before the mid-fifteenth century victory was superseded by defeat,[26] and the government, dominated by William de la Pole, earl of Suffolk, adopted a peace policy. The *Brut* supported the continuance of the war. Recording the capture of Dieppe and Harfleur by the French in 1436 it sadly com-

---

[21] *Brut*, ii. 373. Cf. the eulogy of Henry on his death; *Brut*, ii. 493–4.
[22] *Brut*, ii. 405, 406. For John Page's poem see p. 212 n. 121 above.
[23] *Brut*, ii. 403.
[24] *Brut*, ii. 374.
[25] *Brut*, ii. 572–84.
[26] See Kingsford, *London Chrons*, pp. xli–xlii.

ments: 'And thus Englishmen began to lose a little and a little in Normandy.'[27] It particularly deplores the cession of Anjou and Maine, 'the key of Normandy', as part of the marriage settlement made on Henry VI's marriage to Margaret in 1445.[28] It regards the marriage itself as a violation of an undertaking made on Henry's behalf to marry a daughter of John count of Armagnac; one version remarks that 'from this time forward, King Henry never profited nor went forward; but Fortune began to turn from him on all sides, as well in France, Normandy [and] Guienne, as in England.'[29]

The *Brut* is hostile to the earl of Suffolk because he was the author of the peace policy,[30] and conversely praises his opponent, Humphrey duke of Gloucester.[31] One version strengthens this anti-Lancastrian bias by dwelling on the government's maladministration: the common people, it asserts, cursed because of misrule and heavy taxation,[32] and the rising in Kent in 1450 was the result of 'the malice and the tyranny' of the treasurer, James Butler, earl of Wiltshire.[33] The same version quotes a ballad praying Jesus to send Richard, duke of York, to avenge the wicked sons of Satan who had reduced the land to misery:[34] it regards Duke Richard as the rightful heir to the throne, by lineal descent from Richard II (whose crown had been usurped by Henry IV),[35] gives the text of the agreement between Henry VI and Duke Richard,[36] and ends with the accession of Richard's son as Edward IV. Another version ending with Edward's accession concludes with a prayer for him: 'I beseech God to preserve, and send him the accomplishment of the remnant of his rightful inheritance beyond the sea, so that he may reign in them to the pleasure of Almighty God, health of his soul, honour and worship in this present life, and well and profit of all his subjects. . . . '[37]

The London provenance of the *Brut* it demonstrated by its detailed knowledge of the city. For example there is the full account of the attack on London by Jack Cade and his fellow insurgents from Kent. It includes a vivid description of the fighting on London Bridge between the rebels

---

[27] *Brut*, ii. 504.

[28] *Brut*, ii. 510. Cf. Davies, p. 61.

[29] *Brut*, ii. 511.

[30] See e.g. *Brut*, ii. 516, and Davies, p. 62.

[31] See e.g. *Brut*, ii. 512, and Davies, p. 62.

[32] See Davies, pp. 79, 95. See also Davies, pp. 86–90, for the manifesto issued by the Yorkist lords against the king's supporters (this is the only known text of the manifesto; see William Stubbs, *The Constitutional History of England* (fifth edition, Oxford 1891–1903, 3 vols), iii. 187–8).

[33] Davies, p. 91.

[34] Davies pp. 91–4.

[35] Davies, p. 99. Richard duke of York's hereditary claim is set out in full in the agreement between him and the king; see below and the next note.

[36] Davies, pp. 100–6. *Rot. Parl.* 374–82.

[37] *Brut*, ii. 533. For the Yorkist bias in the *Brut* see also p. 222 and n. 10 above.

and the citizens, who had summoned various people to help, among them Matthew Gough, 'a captain of Normandy' :[38]

> the mayor, aldermen and the commons of the city [and others] . . . came to London bridge, into Southwark, ere the captain [i.e. Jack Cade] had any knowledge thereof; and there they fought with them that kept the bridge. And the Kentish men went to harness, and came to the bridge, and shot and fought with them, and got the bridge, and made them of London to flee, and slew many of them, and this endured all the night, to and fro, till nine of the clock in the morn. And at last they burnt the drawbridge, where many of them of London were drowned. In which night, Sutton, an alderman, was slain; Roger Hesant, and Matthew Gough, and many other.

The *Brut* describes the Londoners' reactions to Queen Margaret and her forces when they encamped at St Albans in 1461 in similar graphic terms :[39]

> Then the queen and her party . . . sent anon to London, which was on Ash Wednesday, the first day of Lent, for victual. . . . The mayor ordained . . . that certain carts laden with victual should be sent to St Albans to them. And when the carts came to Cripplegate, the commons of the city that kept that gate, took the victuals from the carters, and would not suffer it to pass. Then were there certain aldermen and commoners appointed to go to Barnet for to speak with the queen's council for treaty, that the northern men should be sent home unto their country again; for the city of London dread for to be robbed and despoiled if they should come.

These same two passages have particular details about one rich London citizen, the alderman, Philip Malpas; his house was robbed by the Kentish insurgents, and in 1461 he fled to Antwerp 'fearing the coming of the queen'.[40]

The *Brut* chronicles are, therefore, London chronicles in the sense that they were written in London. Moreover, the authors used as sources chronicles closely related to the extant London chronicles.[41] Hence much that can be said of the *Brut* is also true of the London chronicles and *vice versa*. Although the *Brut* was probably 'the most popular and widely read

---

[38] *Brut*, ii. 519. Cf. Davies, p. 67.

[39] *Brut*, ii. 531.

[40] *Brut*, ii. 518, 532. For Philip Malpas see Kingsford, *London Chrons*, p. 314.

[41] For the use of the London chronicles as a source for the *Brut* see Brie, *Prosachronik*, pp. 66–8, and Kingsford, *Hist. Lit.* pp. 70, 72, 78, 85–6, 99, 108, 115, 118, 121, 133–4, and Thomas and Thornley, pp. xxxi-xxxiii.

history of England'[42] in the late middle ages, the London chronicles deserve closer analysis than the *Brut* because they formed the basis of the *Brut* continuations from 1377.

The vernacular London chronicles date from about 1414 but developed from a well established tradition of Latin chronicles which was based on chronicles written in London from the thirteenth century onwards. The earliest extant London chronicle in Latin is the *Cronica Maiorum et Vicecomitum Londoniarum* written in Henry III's reign probably by Arnold Fitz Thedmar, an alderman.[43] The next is the *Annales Londonienses*, a continuation of the *Flores Historiarum*, probably by the alderman Andrew Horn.[44] To the fourteenth century belongs the French chronicle of London covering the years from 1189 to 1343.[45] These surviving examples represent only a fraction of the London chronicles in Latin and French actually written.[46]

   This chronicle tradition began with historical notes added to lists of the city's chief officials, in much the same way as monastic chronicles had originated with notes entered on Easter tables.[47] The fifteenth century London chronicles can be distinguished from the *Brut* (or any other chronicle) because they begin at 1189, with the accession of Richard I (during whose reign the mayoralty and commune developed), and each annal is headed with the names of the officials for the year—of the bailiffs to 1207,[48] and subsequently of the mayor and sheriffs: each year is dated from the mayoral election which was (and is) held on 29 October. Because of the authors' close interest in the city's history, and because of the abundant

---

[42] Kingsford, *Hist. Lit.* p. 110.

[43] Printed *De Antiquis Legibus Liber: Cronica Maiorum et Vicecomitum Londoniarum*, ed. Thomas Stapleton (Camden Soc., original series, xxxiv, 1846), pp. 1–177. Cf. Gransden, *Historical Writing*, i. 509–17.

[44] Pp. 3 and n. 10, 23–5 above.

[45] P. 59 and n. 6, 71–2 above.

[46] For lost London chronicles see Kingsford, *London Chrons*, pp. vii-viii, xxiii, and his *Hist. Lit.* p. 71 and n. 4.

[47] For the early history of the London chronicles see Gransden, *Historical Writing*, i. 508–9, and pp. 23–5 above. Other towns of course also kept list of officials, and on a few of these historical entries were made. Thus Bristol started keeping lists in 1216, and from 1440 the town clerk, Robert Ricard, began entering notes on local and national events. This chronicle continues until 1497, from which date only the names of the city officials are given until the chronicle was resumed in 1522: regular yearly entries continue until 1543, and then there are occasional entries until 1698. The chronicle is printed *The Maire of Bristowe is Kalendar by Robert Ricart*, ed. Lucy Toulmin Smith (Camden Soc., second series, v, 1872). A roll of the mayors and bailiffs of Northampton from 1381 to 1461 has a few notes on national history. However, most of these town chronicles, which are of minor importance, belong to the sixteenth century or later. See Ralph Flenley, *Six Town Chronicles of England* (Oxford 1911), pp. 27–36.

[48] The statement that the rulers of the city were but keepers and bailiffs until the ninth year of John (1207–8) is an error shared by all versions of the London chronicle (the mayoralty developed in the reign of Richard I) which proves that they had a common archetype; see Thomas and Thornley, p. xxxiii.

supply of a wide variety of material, most of the London chronicles expanded far beyond the length of brief annals.

The account of events up to the end of the fourteenth century is fairly homogeneous in the fifteenth century London chronicles, which clearly descend for this period from Latin originals.[49] Thereafter divergences between the copies multiply. Apparently a prospective chronicler would borrow a copy or copies of the London chronicle and in the course of transcription add his own information, omit some passages and alter others; in fact he treated his sources in the same way as a monastic chronicler did. In this way the London chronicle grew in the process of transmission. The authors' method is revealed in one passage: 'Here is no more of the siege of Rouen: and that is because we wanted the true copy thereof; but whosoever owns this book may write it out in the hinder end of this book, or in the farther end of it, when he gets the true copy.'[50] As copyists the London chroniclers do not rank high; they made numerous errors and sometimes exaggerated facts in order to give extra credit where they considered it due (for example one copyist increased the number of Scots which a force of 2,000 Englishmen defeated in 1332, from 12,000 to 40,000).[51] Although some sections of the extant copies demonstrably descend from common originals which were ultimately based on contemporary material, many of the texts in their present form are later; they may well represent conflations of various copies of the London chronicle, and without doubt reflect the political views of the age to which they belong. Despite the close relationship between the copies and their consequent similarities, some preserve fuller accounts of particular events than others, and also have passages peculiar to themselves.

The interrelation of the extant copies of the London chronicles can be demonstrated by reference to the more important ones.[52] These are: the chronicle to 1432 in Cotton MS. Julius B II in the British Library (to be referred to as JB II);[53] the chronicle to 1439 in Cotton MS. Vitellius F IX (VF);[54] the chronicle to 1443 in Harley MS. 565 in the British Library (H);[55] the chronicle, also to 1443, in Cotton MS. Cleopatra C IV (C);[56] the so-called Short English Chronicle, to 1465, in Lambeth Palace Library

[49] For the Latin originals behind the vernacular London chronicles see Kingsford, *London Chrons*, pp. vii–viii, and Thomas and Thornley, p. xxx.

[50] Cited from BL MS. Egerton 650 in Kingsford, *Hist. Lit.* p. 86 and n. 1.

[51] See *The Historical Collections of a Citizen of London*, ed. James Gairdner (Camden Soc., second series, xvii, 1876), p. xix.

[52] In addition to the printed editions of the London chronicles to be noted in this paragraph, attention should be called to the five short texts printed in Flenley, *Six Town Chronicles*, pp. 99–201. Cf. p. 233 and nn. 84, 85 below. See also p. 222 n. 11 above.

[53] Printed in Kingsford, *London Chrons*, pp. 1–116.

[54] See ibid., pp. xiii–xiv.

[55] Printed *A Chronicle of London from 1089* [*sic*] – *1483*, ed. N. H. Nicolas and E. Tyrrell (London 1827).

[56] Printed in Kingsford, *London Chrons*, pp. 117–52.

MS. 306 (S) ;[57] Gregory's Chronicle, to 1469 (Greg.) in BL MS. Egerton 1995;[58] the chronicle to 1483 in Julius B I (JB I) ;[59] the chronicle to 1509 in Vitellius A XVI (VA) ;[60] and the Great Chronicle of London, to 1512 (GC).[61]

Stated very briefly and bearing in mind that each copy has some unique material, these texts are related thus: JB II resembles H; VF resembles JB I to 1431, and thereafter is like H; H resembles JB II, although it is fuller, and then C and VF; C is identical with S from 1416 to 1420, and then resembles JB II most closely; S is very abbreviated to 1445, but resembles both C and JB I; Greg. is almost identical with VA to 1440 (from which date it is independent) ; JB I is like VF to 1439, and then like S until 1459 (it is independent though brief from 1459 to 1483) ; VA resembles Greg. to 1440; GC resembles JB I and JB II; and from 1440 VA and GC are very similar.[62]

Attempts have been made to group the extant copies of the London chronicles into versions.[63] However, because of the loss of numerous copies such an undertaking is hazardous. In the words of two recent scholars working in collaboration:[64]

> The mere fact that two or more chronicles, using the same mater-
> ial, draw apart at a definite date, or that other chronicles come
> to a close in the same year, does not appear ... to be sufficient
> warrant for grouping widely different works as one version or

[57] Printed in *Three Fifteenth Century Chronicles*, ed. James Gairdner (Camden Soc., new series, xxviii, 1880), pp. 1–80.

[58] Printed in *Collections*, ed. Gairdner, pp. 57–239.

[59] Julius B I resembles Harley 565 to 1443 (when the latter ends) and has a continuation from 1443 to 1483; its variants to 1443 and the continuation are printed in Nicolas and Tyrrell, op. cit. Cf. Kingsford, *London Chrons*, pp. xiii-xv.

[60] Printed in ibid., pp. 153–263.

[61] Printed Thomas and Thornley, with an invaluable introduction and (at the end of the volume) footnotes. The manuscript of the Great Chronicle was formerly in the possession of Mr William Bromley-Davenport at Baginton Hall, Warwickshire (*Historical MSS. Commission*, second report, Appendix, p. 80) and was sold as lot 326 ('Fabian (Robert) Chronicle') in the sale of the library of Baginton Hall, 'by order of the Trustees of the late William Bromley-Davenport', at Sotheby's on 8 and 9 May 1903. It was purchased by Quaritch for £5 15s (I owe this information which is recorded in the copy of Sotheby's sale catalogue in the Department of Manuscripts, British Library, to Mr D. H. Turner, deputy keeper of manuscripts). It was purchased in 1933 by Viscount Wakefield of Hythe (Charles Cheers Wakefield, lord mayor of London 1915–16) who in the same year presented it to the Guildhall library, where it is now MS. 3313. The manuscript was consulted by Kingsford while at Quaritch's, and is noticed in his *Hist. Lit.* pp. 70–1 and n. 1 (the reference to the *Hist. MSS. Comm. Report* is wrong), 82–3. Kingsford mentions a forthcoming edition by Mr E. H. Dring (ibid., p. 71 n. 1) and lists it as published in 1913 (ibid., pp. ix, 80) ; however, this edition never appeared.

[62] For detailed accounts of these relationships see Kingsford, *London Chrons*, pp. ix-xvii passim, and Thomas and Thornley, pp. xxiv-xxxix.

[63] See Kingsford, *London Chrons*, pp. xviii-xxii, and his *Hist. Lit.* pp. 75–108.

[64] Thomas and Thornley, p. xxxix. For their comments on Kingsford's overprecision in grouping copies of the London chronicle into versions see ibid., pp. xxv-xxviii.

recension. Each compiler appears to have been a law unto himself and the result of his labours was a version unto itself irrespective of dates and passages shared with others.

Nevertheless, despite the idiosyncrasies of the individual chroniclers and the multiplicity of their sources, it is occasionally possible to detect one 'master chronicle' behind their work. Thus the similarities between VA and GC from 1440 onwards betray their use of a lost chronicle, the so-called Main City Chronicle, which originally extended to 1496 but was subsequently continued to 1503.[65] This lost chronicle was also used by Robert Fabyan for his *New Chronicles of England and France*, which (because it is not purely a London chronicle) will be considered later.[66]

The authors of the London chronicles belonged to the merchant class and probably many held office in the city. This can be deduced from those few authors who can be identified and from the tone of the chronicles. Of the London chronicles already specifically referred to, all are anonymous except two—and the authorship of even these presents problems. Gregory's Chronicle is in part almost certainly by William Gregory, skinner, sheriff of London from 1436 to 1437 and mayor from 1451 to 1452. The evidence for Gregory's authorship is in the annal for 1450/1 which has the entry:[67]

And that year came a legate from the pope of Rome with great pardon, for that pardon was the greatest pardon that ever came to England from the Conquest unto this time of my year, being mayor of London, for it was plenary indulgence.

However, William Gregory, mayor in the year in question, cannot have written the chronicle as it stands because Gregory died in 1467 while the chronicle continues to 1470. Furthermore, from 1450 until nearly the end it has individual touches, which indicate the work of one man:[68] the first of these occurs in the full and apparently first hand account of Jack Cade's rising, and the last in the annal for 1468/9. It should also be noted that up to 1452, with the exception of the passage on Cade's rising,

---

[65] For the Main City Chronicle see ibid., pp. lxix–lxxii passim, where views expressed by Kingsford (*Hist. Lit.* pp. 99–101) are revised. It will be noticed that passages quoted *verbatim* below are from VA although many are also in GC (because both works derive from a common source, notably the Main City Chronicle); VA is cited as the most easily accessible printed text and references are given to corresponding passages in GC in the footnotes if the citation is of any length; see pp. 235–44 nn. 95–165 passim below.

[66] Pp. 245–8 below. For notes indicating that Fabyan was using a common source/sources with GC see pp. 238 n. 111, 241 nn. 132, 136, 242 nn. 143–4, 243 nn. 155–6, 244 n. 158, below.

[67] *Collections*, ed. Gairdner, p. 197.

[68] Gairdner suggests that Gregory wrote the chronicle up to the year of his own mayoralty and then stopped, and that his chronicle was continued by someone else; ibid., p. v. Kingsford, *Hist. Lit.* p. 97, suggests that Gregory merely added the note on his mayoralty to a copy of the London chronicle which he owned.

the chronicle seems to resemble other London chronicles.[69] Then there is a gap, the annal for 1453/4 being omitted, before the chronicle resumes with an independent account of events. The evidence, therefore, suggests that Gregory wrote the chronicle to 1452, but not the passage on Cade's rising which may well have been inserted by the anonymous author who continued the chronicle to 1469.

The other chronicle to which an author can be tentatively ascribed is the *Great Chronicle of London*. Its modern editors have made a strong case for the authorship of Robert Fabyan,[70] who also wrote the already men-tioned *New Chronicles of England and France*. Fabyan was an alderman, a member of the drapers' company, and, in 1493, a sheriff of London. In 1496 he was appointed one of the citizens deputed to petition the king for the redress of grievances resulting from the embargo on English cloth in the territories of Philip archduke of Austria and duke of Burgundy;[71] in 1497 he was appointed to help hold the city gates against the Cornish rebels, and was also an assessor in London for the tax of a fifteenth. He retired in 1502, resigning the alderman's gown on grounds of poverty, and completed the *New Chronicles* in 1504.[72] He died in 1513. At least three sixteenth century scholars—John Stow, John Foxe and Richard Hakluyt—attributed the Great Chronicle to Fabyan as well as the *New Chronicles*.[73] Their testimony is supported partly by the manuscript itself, partly by the style of the text and partly by its content. The manuscript was written in the early sixteenth century, and is in the same hand as the two volumes which comprise the *New Chronicles*.[74] Both works share stylistic peculiarities, and both have the same interests and points of view (the Great Chronicle is more outspoken on politics, but this is to be expected of a later work).[75] The Great Chronicle shows considerable knowledge of civic government; it is well established that Fabyan made extensive use of the city records.[76] Moreover, the one passage it contains in which the author speaks of himself shows that he was a member of the drapers' company.[77] The chronicler records that in 1468 Sir Thomas Cooke, an alderman and a draper, was appealed of treason 'by one named Hawkins', and states that as a warning to wise men he will explain the cause of the appeal and the result, 'for in

[69] Kingsford, op. cit., p. 96.

[70] Thomas and Thornley, pp. xl-lxix passim. It should, however, be noted that the references in GC to Fabyan are reticent, which suggests the possibility that GC is by a collaborator rather than by Fabyan himself; see ibid, pp. lxvi-lxvii.

[71] For Fabyan's career see ibid., pp. xliv-xlvi, and *The New Chronicles of England and of France*, ed. Henry Ellis (London 1811), pp. i-iii. For the embargo on English cloth see p. 244 and n. 160 below.

[72] See ibid., p. 681, and Thomas and Thornley, pp. lxii-lxiii, lxx.

[73] Ibid., pp. xli-xliii.

[74] Ibid., pp. xliii-xliv.

[75] Ibid., pp. lxv-lxvi.

[76] Ibid., p. lxvii.

[77] Ibid., pp. xl-xli.

the time of his first trouble I was his apprentice and about the age of seventeen or eighteen years and thereabout.'[78] He ascribes Cooke's misfortunes partly to the enmity of the duchess of Bedford, who had wanted to buy a piece of arras at her own price: it was 'wrought in most richest wise with gold of the whole story of the siege of Jerusalem; ... I heard the foreman of my master say that it cost in barter when my said master bought it £800.'[79] Cooke was freed in 1469 but in 1471 was again in trouble—this time for supporting the Lancastrians—and fled the country. He was finally pardoned in 1472 and returned to London. It is unlikely that the author of the chronicle stayed in his service throughout these vicissitudes; it is more probable that he transferred to another master.

A number of the London chronicles are in common-place books, that is in volumes containing a miscellany of useful, curious and literary items. The earliest known such compilation by a London citizen is the *Liber de Antiquis Legibus*,[80] a book mainly of customs relating to London, which includes the *Cronica Maiorum et Vicecomitum Londoniarum*. Gregory's Chronicle is among the fifteenth century chronicles preserved in a common-place book. This volume has various items besides the chronicle, including a version of the English poem called 'The Seven Sages of Rome', notes on venery, a treatise on how to keep in good health, a poem on blood-letting, the assize of bread and ale, a list of the churches of London, John Page's poem on the siege of Rouen and John Lydgate's poem, *The Kings of England*.[81]

The names of the owners of two other, though later, common-place books which contain chronicles of London are known. Richard Arnold, merchant and haberdasher, included a short chronicle to 1502 in a miscellaneous volume also containing civic ordinances and oaths for city officials, besides public records and tracts on such matters as grafting trees and making ink.[82] In the reign of Henry VIII Richard Hill, merchant and grocer, compiled a similar volume, with a chronicle to 1536 and a collection of English folk songs, carols, lyrics and religious poems.[83] The authorship

---

[78] Ibid., p. 205.

[79] Ibid., pp. 207–8.

[80] Printed *De Antiquis Legibus Liber*, ed. Stapleton. See Gransden, *Historical Writing*, i. 510–11. Cf. p. 227 and n. 43 above.

[81] This common-place book is printed *Collections*, ed. Gairdner. For a list of its contents see ibid., pp. i-ii. Gairdner only prints two other items besides Gregory's chronicle, John Page's verses on the siege of Rouen (pp. 1–46), and John Lydgate's verses on the kings of England (pp. 49–54). For further references to common-place books see p. 254 below.

[82] For Richard Arnold see Flenley, *Six Town Chronicles*, p. 25 (who calls him Robert Arnold in error). His book was first printed in Antwerp in ?1503 and subsequently as *The Customs of London*, ed. F. Douce (London 1811). Its most important item is a copy of the articles and arbitrament of 1425–6 between Henry Beaufort and Humphrey, duke of Gloucester (ibid., pp. 287–300); see Kingsford, *Hist. Lit.* pp. 88, 263 (Kingsford, ibid., p. viii, erroneously attributes Douce's edition to Sir Henry Ellis).

[83] *Songs, Carols and other Miscellaneous Poems from the Balliol MS. 354, Richard Hill's Commonplace-book*, ed. Roman Dyboski (EETS, extra series, ci, 1907). Cf. Flenley, op. cit., pp. 25–6.

of two earlier common-place books which include chronicles is more problematical. One, with a chronicle from 1437 to 1461,[84] has been attributed
to Robert Bale, a public notary, civil judge and citizen of London, but the
evidence is weak. The other has among its contents items which suggest
that the compiler was a goldsmith and city chamberlain; it gives the oaths
taken by the officials of the goldsmiths' company (but not those of the other
crafts), and it has the oath taken by the chamberlain (but not those of the
other city officials). The compilation was probably made in the reign of
Edward IV; the chronicle it contains ends, although incomplete, in 1471
(an annal relating to the trial of Perkin Warbeck in January 1496 has
been added in another hand). The author, therefore, could be either William Philip or Miles Adys, who each held the office of chamberlain, from
1474 to 1479 and from 1479 to 1484 respectively.[85] Previously, in 1419
another member of the same class is known to have compiled a common-
place book, the *Liber Albus*,[86] which comprises laws and customs of London;
he was John Carpenter, the town clerk: his volume, however, does not
contain a chronicle.

It is likely that the compilers of the common-place books were also the
authors of the chronicles in them. If so, this supports the view that the
chroniclers formed a fairly homogeneous group. Even if the compilers did
not compose the chronicles, the common-place books themselves demonstrate the spread of literacy in the merchant class.

The anonymity of the majority of the London chronicles is reflected in
their tone. With only one exception they reveal nothing of the author's
personality: the exception is Gregory's Chronicle, the continuator of
which leaves traces of his sense of humour and of some connection, perhaps
a friendship, with an individual, Doctor William Ive of Wickham College,
Winchester. In describing the defences prepared by the insurgents on
Blackheath in 1450, the author comments humorously that the rebels
behaved as if in a 'land of war, save only they kept order among them,
for as good was Jack Robin as John at the Noke, for all were as high as pigs-
feet. ... '[87] Similarly the author has a quip in the annal for 1461: he
records that victuals and money were collected in the city for the queen
when she and her forces were approaching London, but the commons took
the victuals and divided them among themselves; 'but as for the money,
I wot not how it was [divided]; I trow the purse stole the money.'[88] And

---

[84] The chronicle is printed in ibid., pp. 114–53. The volume (Trinity College, Dublin, MS.
E.5.9) is described and Bale's authorship discussed in ibid, pp. 66–74. Cf. Kingsford,
Hist. Lit. pp. 95–6.

[85] The volume (Bodleian Library MS. Gough London 10) is described and its authorship
discussed in Flenley, op. cit., pp. 74–81. The chronicle is printed in ibid., pp. 153–66.

[86] Printed in *Munimenta Gildhallae Londoniensis*, ed. H. T. Riley (RS 1859, 3 vols), i.

[87] *Collections*, ed. Gairdner, p. 190.

[88] Ibid., pp. 214–15.

again in the annals for 1468/9 he has a joke. He describes how mean the Flemings were to the English who attended the wedding of Edward IV's sister Margaret to the duke of Burgundy:[89]

> meat and drink was dear enough as though it had been in the land of war, for a shoulder of mutton was sold for 12*d*. And as for bedding, Lyard my horse had more ease than had some good yeomen, for my horse stood in the house and the yeomen sometimes lay without in the street, for less [than]4*d* a night should not have a bed at night. Lo how soon they could play the niggards!

One of these humorous passages relates to Doctor William Ive.[90] The author tells how once (in Lent 1458) Ive came to Coventry to preach before the king. There was a rule that anyone preaching before Henry VI should submit his sermon in writing to an arbiter: failure to do so meant forfeiture of costs and sustenance. Ive submitted his sermon and was told to omit some passages. However, when he came to deliver it, he did so in full and 'said the truth', and also told the king how the sermons he usually heard were censored so that 'their purpose was all turned upside down'. The author concludes: 'The great reward that he had for his labour was the riding of 160 miles in and out for his travail, and all his friends full sorry for him.'[91]

Obviously the author had a close interest in Doctor William Ive. This conclusion is confirmed by two other passages. One is a long account of the controversy in the 1460s between 'this noble doctor Ive' and the friars on the question of the mendicancy of Christ, the former denying the proposition and the latter defending it.[92] At this time Doctor Ive 'kept the schools at St Paul's that is under the chapter house.' An English friar at Rome had written a treatise asserting that Christ begged, copies of which were distributed in Rome and some brought to England. The controversy came to the pope's notice and Ive wrote him a letter of explanation. The pope thereupon imprisoned the friar. The author continues:[93]

> And ever his friends and the friars looked after his coming home, but he may not, for he hath bound himself unto the pope by an iron obligation fast sealed about his two heels. And then he lacked money and friendship, [and] submitted him to the pope, but when he shall come home I wot not.

---

[89] Ibid., p. 238.

[90] For William Ive see Emden, *Biographical Register*, ii. 1008–9.

[91] *Collections*, ed. Gairdner, p. 203, where the incident is in the annal for 1458; but cf. Emden, op. cit., ii. 1008–9.

[92] Ibid., pp. 228–32. For this controversy, with reference to the passage in Greg., see F. R. H. Du Boulay, 'The quarrel between the Carmelite friars and the secular clergy of London, 1464–1468' in *Journal of Ecclesiastical History*, vi (1955), pp. 156–74.

[93] *Collections*, ed. Gairdner, p. 232.

The other passage concerning Doctor William Ive relates to a gang who stole the pyxes from many of the London churches. The author gives a detailed account of the affair, and of how one of the thieves could not see the sacrament at mass until he had confessed his crime in Newgate after his arrest: Ive was one of the four doctors who heard the last confessions of the culprits.[94]

The London chroniclers, writing at the centre of affairs and in close touch with the city government, if not actually civic officials, were extremely well informed. Ultimately much of their information rested on the evidence of eyewitnesses, whether of the author himself or of an informant. The chronicles have a wealth of graphic descriptions which can only rest on first hand authority. For example there is the account in VA of how Edward IV entertained the mayor, William Haryot, and his fellows in 1481/2:[95]

> And this year King Edward, for the great favour he had to this mayor, he commanded him to await upon him with a certain of his brethren, the aldermen, and certain commoners, to go with him on hunting in the forest of Waltham; where, when the mayor and his company was comen, there was ordained for them a pleasant lodge of green boughs, and thither was brought all things necessary for them. And the king would not go to dinner till they were served of their meat. And they were served well and worshipfully. . . . There was also wine couched,[96] red, white, and claret, whereof they had good plenty. And after dinner they went on hunting with the king, and slew many deer, as well red as fallow; whereof the king gave unto the mayor and his company good plenty. And after, the king sent the mayors and their sisters[97] two harts and six bucks, and a tun of wine to make them merry with, which was eaten in Drapers' Hall.

Equally vivid is the account in VA of the reception in London of Katherine of Aragon for her marriage with Prince Arthur in 1501.[98] The ceremony took place in the consistory of St Paul's on a round platform 'covered with red worsted, and overlaid with carpets', and was watched by the king, queen, the queen-mother and others of high estate from a 'latised closet'. 'And almost against the king's closet was ordained for the mayor and his

---

[94] Ibid., p. 235.

[95] Kingsford, *London Chrons*, p. 189. Similar passages are in GC and Fabyan; Thomas and Thornley, pp. 228–9, 435, and *Fabyan*, p. 667.

[96] I.e. laid down.

[97] The mayors and their sisters: i.e. the mayor, aldermen and their wives; see Kingsford, op. cit., p. 320.

[98] Kingsford, op. cit., pp. 248–9. Cf. the closely related account of Katherine's reception, marriage and wedding feast in GC; Thomas and Thornley, pp. 310–12, 447–9.

brethren a stand, where Sir John Shaa, then mayor, stood without sword showing, in crimson velvet, and all his brethren, the aldermen, in scarlet beholding the said solemnity.' Afterwards the bride, her white satin train borne by the queen's sister, the Lady Cecily, and her ladies processed to the choir along 'a scaffold railed upon both sides unto the choir door, and the rails covered with red worsted, the which scaffold was man height from the ground.' They were followed by the mayor, his sword borne before him, and by the aldermen, who sat in the choir during mass. The author continues:[99]

> Wonderful it was to behold the riches of garments and chains of gold, that that day were worn by lords, knights and gentlemen; among the which two specially were to be noted, that is to say Sir Thomas Brandon, knight, and master of the king's horse, the which wore that day a chain of gold valued at £1,400; and the other was William de Rivers, Breton, and master of the king's hawks, which wore a chain of gold valued at £1,000.

After mass the princess was taken, led by the duke of York and 'a legate of Spain', to the bishop's palace for the feast:[100]

> And the mayor and his brethren were set in the entry of the palace, where they might behold the said princess with all the foresaid noble companies pass by them. And that done the said mayor and his brethren were by Master Richard Croftes, steward of my lord prince's house, conveyed unto the great hall, and there set at the board upon the right hand of the said hall, and served honourably with three courses: the first course with twelve dishes, the second with fifteen dishes, and the third course with eighteen dishes; and by the officers well and courteously attended, served and cheered, to the great honour of the prince.

By no means all the passages based on eyewitness evidence relate to events in London. There are many graphic accounts of campaigns in France, some of which must have been derived from soldiers and others questioned by the chroniclers. The citizens were in close touch with the English army abroad, because London merchants provided victuals and Londoners served as soldiers. An error in C under 1437 betrays the use of oral information. It records that the dauphin laid siege to Montereau-faut-Yonne, but spells the name Montrewe-in-fort-Jon;[101] the author must here have been writing phonetically. In the annal for the previous year C records that the city of London sent reinforcements to Calais,

[99] Kingsford, op. cit., p. 249.
[100] Ibid., pp. 249–50.
[101] Ibid., pp. xxiv, 143.

to defend it against the duke of Burgundy:[102] possibly it was from among these men that the author found an informant. Similarly there can be little doubt that the account of the surrender of Harfleur in C derives from oral information. It describes with precise details how the French who came to deliver the town were received by Henry V:[103]

> Our king was in his tent, with his lords and with his gentlemen, and sat in his estate as royal as did ever any king; and, as it is said, there was never Christian king so royal, neither so lordly sat in his seat as did he. And the king had assigned certain lords and knights to take them in and to bring them before the king; and when the Frenchmen were come, a knight in the midst of them brought the keys [of the town] in his hands, and when they came to the tents they kneeled all down together, but there had they no sight of the king; and then they were brought into other tents, and there they kneeled down forthwith for a long time, but sight of our king had they none; and there they were took and brought into an inner tent, and there they kneeled long time, and yet saw not our king; and then they were after took up, and brought where our king was, and there they kneeled long time and then our king would not reward them with none eye, till they had long kneeled, and then the king gave them a reward with his look, and made a countenance to the earl of Dorset, that should take of them the keys, and so he did, and there were the Frenchmen taken up and made cheer.

Some of the chroniclers' information was derived from public proclamations. Important matters of state might be publicized at St Paul's Cross and elsewhere. Thus VA records under 1483 that it 'was declared at Paul's Cross, that King Edward's children were not rightful inheritors unto the crown, but that the duke of Gloucester's title was better than theirs.'[104] In the annal for 1492 it states:[105] 'my lord of Canterbury, chancellor of England, [showed] how the king of Spain had conquered the city and country of Granada, and after was there a solemn procession general and a noble sermon. And after *Te Deum* solemnly sung in St Paul's choir. And in the said sermon was showed, that the same year in Rome was found in an old wall a piece of the Holy Cross.' Similarly the annal for 1497

---

[102] Ibid., p. 141.
[103] Ibid., pp. 118–19.
[104] Ibid., p. 190. A similar passage is in GC; Thomas and Thornley, pp. 231–2. For the use of St Paul's Cross for public and private pronouncements see C. A. J. Armstrong, 'Some examples of the distribution and speed of news in England at the time of the Wars of the Roses' in *Studies in Medieval History presented to F. M. Powicke*, ed. R. W. Hunt, W. A. Pantin and R. W. Southern (Oxford 1948), pp. 442, 443.
[105] Kingsford, op. cit., p. 197. A similar passage is in GC; Thomas and Thornley, pp. 246–7.

records that the peace between England and Scotland was proclaimed in Leadenhall and throughout the city.[106]

Bills exhibited in the city were another source of evidence. Unlike proclamations, bills did not normally express the policy of the government but of rebels and dissidents, and voiced popular protest. The practice of bill posting was already well established in the fourteenth century. H records that in 1326 Queen Isabella and Prince Edward before coming to London, sent a letter to the Londoners expounding their policy and asking for support: copies were posted on the cross in Cheapside and to many doors and windows in the city. (The letter refers to a previous letter announcing their landing; it states that as they had received no reply, they did not know the attitude of the commonalty of London.)[107] The chronicles record a number of examples of bill posting in the fifteenth century. VA states that in 1470 the duke of Clarence caused 'much to do for bills that were set up in divers places of the city',[108] and Gregory's Chronicle mentions bills posted against the Flemings (in 1425) and against Doctor William Ive.[109] The latter also records that during Jack Cade's rising 'many strange and wonderful bills were set in divers places, some at the king's own chamber door at Westminster, in his palace, and some at the hall door at Westminster, and some at [St] Paul's church door, and in many other divers places of London.'[110] The text of the Lollards' Petition (otherwise called the Lollards' Bill), which is given in full in three of the London chronicles, was presumably obtained from copies circulated in the city.[111]

The chroniclers' close contact with the city government enabled them to benefit from news transmitted to the mayor either orally or in writing. VA often gives as its source 'tidings brought to the mayor'. For example the author was informed in this way concerning the insurrection of the

---

[106] Kingsford, op. cit., p. 222. A similar passage is in GC; Thomas and Thornley, p. 286. Edward IV's flight abroad in 1470 had also been published throughout the city; see Armstrong, op. cit., p. 442 and n. 6.

[107] Nicolas and Tyrrell, p. 50.

[108] Kingsford, op. cit. p. 180. A similar passage is in GC; Thomas and Thornley, p. 209. For seditious bills in the fifteenth century and the government's attempts to suppress them, see Armstrong, op. cit., pp. 434–5. However, some bills merely contained factual information on battles, etc.; see ibid., pp. 432–3 and nn. See also pp. 251–2 below.

[109] *Collections*, ed. Gairdner, pp. 158, 229.

[110] Ibid., p. 195.

[111] The full text is in Julius B II (Kingsford, *London Chrons*, pp. 65–8), GC (Thomas and Thornley, pp. 88–90), and in Longleat MS. 53 (for which see ibid., pp. xxxi, xxxiv). The Lollards' Petition, which was aimed against the retention of possessions by religious communities, was deliberately removed from the rolls of parliament, and this is the earliest extant text. The Petition is mentioned and a Latin text of the opening clause given by Walsingham (*Hist. Angl.* ii. 282–3), and a later English abstract is in Fabyan (*Fabyan*, pp. 575–6). Jack Sharpe revived the Petition, with variants, in 1431 and posted copies in London and other towns; see Thomas and Thornley, pp. 409–10, Kingsford, *Hist. Lit.* pp. 16, 82–3, 88, 105, and his *London Chrons*, pp. xxxvii-xxxviii, 295–6.

[238]

'commons' of Cornwall, and the attack by Perkin Warbeck and the rebels on Exeter in 1497.[112] News of Perkin's capture was sent by the king himself to the mayor, from whom no doubt the chronicler obtained his information.[113]

Not infrequently the chroniclers used newsletters written to the mayor and aldermen. It is probable that at least since the reign of Henry III the king and men powerful in the government considered it expedient to keep the city informed of their political activities.[114] Henry VII specifically stated at the end of a letter to the mayor and aldermen that 'as other news come we shall advertise you of the same.' This passage is at the end of a letter giving an account of Henry's negotiations with Archduke Philip in 1500 which VA and GC quote in full. [115] However, generally the chroniclers do not copy the text of the letters, and it is often not clear what information derives from newsletters, although much, especially that relating to foreign affairs, must come from them. The fairly numerous copies of newsletters extant in fifteenth century common-place books suggest that there was ready access to them. Some at least were read to the city magnates: VA records that on 9 November 1492 'was read in the Guildhall before the mayor, aldermen, and common council, a letter sent from the king unto the city, of the conclusion of the peace between the kings of England and of France for the term of either of their lives and for a year after of him that longest lived.' (Other terms of the treaty follow.)[116]

The London chroniclers used the legislative, financial and judicial records of the city government. They made use of the ordinances of the common council: for example C records under 1439/40 that 'all the strumpets that might be take in London were made to wear ray hoods and to bear a white rod in their hands,'[117] and under 1491/2 VA specifies various regulations 'enacted by a common council' to protect orphans' property. [118] Under 1499 VA states that a common council granted a tax of a fifteenth and a half to pay for the pageants put on to receive Katherine of Aragon,[119]

---

[112] Ibid., pp. 213, 217. A similar passage is in GC; Thomas and Thornley, pp. 276, 281.

[113] Kingsford, *London Chrons*, p. 218. A similar passage is in GC; Thomas and Thornley, p. 283.

[114] See for example the letter of Richard of Cornwall (of 1258) to the mayor and citizens announcing his coronation as Holy Roman Emperor and his victory at Boppard over the archbishop of Trier, and his letter (of 1271) informing them of the murder of his son Henry of Almain, in the *Liber de Antiquis Legibus* (ed. Stapleton, pp. 26–9, 134–5). For the use of newsletters in fifteenth century England, see Armstrong, op. cit., p. 432 and pp. 252, 263–4 below.

[115] Kingsford, *London Chrons*, pp. 229–31, and Thomas and Thornley, pp. 292–4, 447.

[116] Kingsford, op. cit., p. 197. A similar passage is in GC; Thomas and Thornley, p. 247.

[117] Kingsford, op. cit., p. 146. A similar entry is in Greg; *Collections*, ed. Gairdner, p. 182. 'Ray' is a kind of striped cloth.

[118] Kingsford, op. cit., p. 196. A similar passage is in GC; Thomas and Thornley, pp. 246, 439.

[119] Kingsford, op. cit., p. 229. A similar passage is in GC; Thomas and Thornley, pp. 292, 447.

and elsewhere gives exact details of the citizens financial dealings with the king.[120] The chroniclers methodically record the punishment of offenders in London—of fraudulent bakers and the like in the pillory[121] and of heretics at the stake.[122] Moreover, the details of repairs and building operations in the city probably come at least in part from official records.[123]

Presumably it was from the city records that the chroniclers obtained copies of those statutes of parliament and decrees of the king's council which especially affected Londoners. There are, for example, regulations concerning aliens in the city: C has details of the parliamentary statute of 1439 relating to the domicile and trading of alien merchants,[124] and VA and GC of the decree issued by the king and council in 1499 to control the number of foreign brokers.[125]

The chroniclers copied a few official documents *verbatim*. One of those in both VA and GC was a bond of the mayor himself, by which he undertook to observe the treaty (the so-called Magnus Intercursus) of 1496 between England and Flanders.[126] The other documents given in full relate to general history but were presumably preserved in the city archives. The principal ones are: the official 'process' of the deposition of Richard II;[127] the Lollards' Petition of 1410;[128] the treaties for the surrender of Falaise and Rouen to Henry V and the treaty of Troyes; the treaty for the surrender of Pont Meulan to Henry VI and the articles of alliance between the duke of Bedford, regent of France, and the dukes of Burgundy and Brittany;[129] the articles and arbitrament settling the dispute between Humphrey, duke of Gloucester, and Henry Beaufort, bishop of Winchester, of 1425/6;[130] and Perkin Warbeck's confession.[131]

---

[120] See p. 243 below. Kingsford, op. cit., pp. 186, 212, 213.

[121] E.g. ibid., pp. 187, 210–11, 257.

[122] E.g. ibid., p. 200; *Collections*, ed. Gairdner, p. 171.

[123] See for example the account of the repair of the city walls, 1476–8, and the extensions to the Guildhall in 1501; Kingsford, op. cit., pp. 187–8, 257. A similar passage is in GC; Thomas and Thornley, pp. 225–6, 319–20.

[124] Kingsford, op. cit., pp. 146–7. Cf. *Statutes of the Realm*, ii. 303–5, and E. Lipson, *The Economic History of England* (London 1920–31, 3 vols, 9th edition of vol. i, London 1947), i. 529.

[125] Kingsford, op. cit., pp. 225, 331; Thomas and Thornley, pp. 289–90, 446.

[126] Kingsford, op. cit., pp. 209–10; Thomas and Thornley, pp. 263–4, 442–3. The treaty itself is printed in *Foedera*, xii. 578–91. Cf. Lipson op. cit., i. 587–8.

[127] What appear to be English translations of an official Latin document corresponding closely to that on the parliament rolls (*Rot. Parl.* iii. 416–45), are in Julius B II (Kingsford, op. cit., pp. 19–62), GC (Thomas and Thornley, pp. 51–83), and in Longleat MS. 53 (cf. p. 238 n. 111 above). See Thomas and Thornley, pp. 404–8.

[128] See p. 238 and n. 111 above.

[129] All these documents relating to the Hundred Years' War are in GC; Thomas and Thornley, pp. xxxvi, 97–115 passim, 124–8. For references to copies in other London chronicles see ibid., pp. xxxvi, 412–13 passim, 415.

[130] Ibid., pp. xxxvii, 138–49. For references to copies in other London chronicles see ibid., pp. 416–17.

[131] Ibid., pp. 284–6, 445. Warbeck's confession is also in VA; Kingsford, op. cit., pp. 219–21.

The chroniclers also used documents for less solemn matters. The descriptions of the pageants staged in the city to welcome notabilities are based on official records. The accounts of the pageants put on for Henry VI on his return from Paris in 1432 cite in full, or derive almost entirely from, the poems composed by John Lydgate (who devised the pageant) to be recited on the occasion.[132] Similarly the account of the pageant welcoming Katherine of Aragon includes the text of the verses.[133] Furthermore, it is likely that the description of the jousts which follows the eyewitness account of the marriage and banquet (cited above),[134] may be partly derived from an official narrative like the one still extant in the College of Arms.[135] State banquets were another kind of public function which interested the chroniclers and here again they used documents. Some chronicles have the order of sitting and the menu for the feast held on the coronation of Katherine in 1421, and give the menu and 'subtlety' accompanying each course at Henry VI's coronation feast.[136] (The account in Greg. of the coronation itself is based on the official order.)[137]

Despite the excellent sources used by the London chroniclers, they were held in poor esteem by at least one sixteenth century writer. In Thomas Nashe's view they were but 'poor Latinless authors . . . so simple they know not what they do . . . lay chronographers that write of nothing but the mayors and sheriffs and the dear year, and the great frost.'[138] Certainly they do not compare in quality to the best chronicles of the previous centuries. Nevertheless, they preserve much of value in a period when the monastic chronicle and the chivalric history were nearing extinction.

Since London was the centre of national events, the chroniclers benefited not only from news brought to the city, but also from the opportunity of observing events which took place there. Thus they could give excellent first hand accounts of such events as the trial of Eleanor Cobham,[139] Jack Cade's rising[140] and the Yorkist coup of

---

[132] See VA, GC and Fabyan: Kingsford, op. cit., pp. 97–116, 301–4; Thomas and Thornley, pp. xxvii, 156–70, 419; *Fabyan*, pp. 603–7.

[133] See VA and GC: Kingsford, op. cit., pp. 234–48, 332–4; Thomas and Thornley, pp. 297–309, 447–8.

[134] Pp. 234–5 above.

[135] Printed in F. Grose and T. Astle, *The Antiquarian Repertory* (London 1807–9, 4 vols), ii. 248–322. Cf. Kingsford, op. cit., p. 332.

[136] *Collections*, ed. Gairdner, pp. 139–41, 169–70; Thomas and Thornley, pp. 152–4, 418–19; *Fabyan*, pp. 599–601. A 'subtlety' in this sense is defined in *NED*, ix. pt ii. 69, under 'Subtlety', 5, as: 'A highly ornamental device, wholly or chiefly made of sugar, sometimes eaten, sometimes used as a table decoration.'

[137] *Collections*, ed. Gairdner, pp. 165–8. Kingsford, op. cit., pp. 273–4.

[138] Thomas Nashe, *Pierce Penilesse ; The Works of Thomas Nashe*, ed. R. B. McKerrow (London 1904–10, 5 vols), i. 194. Cf. Kingsford, *Hist. Lit.* pp. 74–5.

[139] *Brut*, ii. 478–9. For references to accounts in other London chronicles see Thomas and Thornley, p. 422.

[140] See especially *Collections*, ed. Gairdner, pp. 190–4. For references to accounts in other London chronicles see Thomas and Thornley, p. 424.

1461.[141] And the London chronicles are, of course, indispensable sources for the history of the city. They provide factual information, and are at least equally valuable as mirrors of the tastes and opinions of the Londoners. They reflect the citizens' love of pageantry and their civic pride. However, it should be remembered that because they were quasi-official productions, the interests they show and the views they express were those of the ruling oligarchy.

There is no evidence that any of the chroniclers was actually commissioned by the mayor, but, as has been seen, much of the material they used proves a close association with the Guildhall. The chroniclers tend to put the mayor in the centre of the stage, whether meeting the king, ordering the repair of the city walls, or sealing a treaty with Flanders. They record many facts in the history of the mayoralty: William Askham, mayor from 1403 to 1404, 'was prentice to William Walworth, sometime mayor, that was prentice sometime with John Lovekyn; and all the sheriffs and mayors each after other [were] in one house';[142] Robert Clopton was chosen mayor for 1441/2 by the mayor and aldermen in preference to Ralph Holland, a tailor, who had been nominated for election by the commons of the city, but when he was presented to the city 'certain taylors and other craftsmen cried "Nay, nay, not this man but Ralph Holland"'—they were, therefore, imprisoned in Newgate;[143] and John Norman on his election in 1452, was the first mayor to travel with the aldermen to Westminster by water, instead of processing through the streets—'wherefore the watermen of the Thames made a song of this John Norman, whereof the beginning was "Row thy boat Norman"'.[144] The lost Main City Chronicle apparently laid especial emphasis on the importance of the mayor. It almost certainly included the text of a ballad composed, probably by the Scottish poet William Dunbar, on the occasion of the feast held by the mayor Sir John Shaa for the ambassadors from Scotland in 1501. The poem praises London in general and the mayor in particular. It ends:[145]

> Thy famous mayor, by princely governance,
> With sword of justice thee ruleth prudently;
> No lord of Paris, Venice, or Florence

---

[141] See e.g. the account in GC; Thomas and Thornley, pp. 193–6. For further references see ibid., pp. 426–7.

[142] Nicolas and Tyrrell, pp. 88–9.

[143] Kingsford, *London Chrons*, pp. 154–5. Similar passages are in GC and Fabyan: Thomas and Thornley, pp. 175–6, 422–3; *Fabyan*, p. 615.

[144] Kingsford, op. cit., p. 164. Similar passages are in GC and Fabyan: Thomas and Thornley, pp. 186–7, 425; *Fabyan*, p. 628.

[145] The poem is in VA and GC: Kingsford, op. cit., pp. 253–5; Thomas and Thornley, pp. 316–17. For other copies of it see ibid., p. 449. The poem is printed and its attribution to Dunbar discussed in *The Poems of William Dunbar*, ed. W. Mackay Mackenzie (London 1932), pp. 177–8, 240–1 (see also ibid., pp. 230–1), and in C. F. Bühler, '*London Thow art the Flowre of Cytes all*' in *Review of English Studies*, xiii (1937), pp. 1–9.

> In dignity or honour goeth to him nigh;
> He is exemplar, loadstar, and guide,
> Principal patron and rose original,
> Above all mayors as master most worthy:
> London, thou art the flower of cities all.

The Yorkist sympathies of the London chroniclers are evident through-out.[146] They praise Humphrey, duke of Gloucester,[147] and denigrate the earl of Suffolk, deploring the loss of Normandy and Anjou.[148] Although they treat Henry VI himself with tolerance,[149] they disapprove of Queen Margaret[150] and applaud the Yorkist succession.[151] They hate any popular movement, but show some compassion for the sufferings of the lower orders (provided the common man did not seek violent remedies),[152] and praise the Yorkists' attempts to remedy oppression.[153] They are consistently opposed to the Lollards, whose executions and other punishments they often record.[154]

The chronicles reproduce the financial and commercial preoccupations of the ruling oligarchy. They give the assessments of the citizens for a num-ber of royal taxes and other impositions. For example VA records under 1474/5 that the king persuaded the city to give him 'a certain money toward his voyage into France'; the mayor contributed £30, some aldermen 20 marks, and others £10, while the commons paid the wages 'for half a man for a year after, 6d by the day'.[155] Under 1487/8 it gives details of contri-butions to a prest assessed on the guilds; the mercers, grocers and drapers paid £1,615, and the goldsmiths, fishmongers and tailors £946 13s 4d.[156]

The rich citizens' commercial interests also occupy the chroniclers' attention. There are a number of entries recording prices and other facts

---

[146] See p. 222 and n. 10 above.

[147] For favourable epithets applied to Humphrey, duke of Gloucester, see e.g. Nicolas and Tyrrell, p. 82, *Collections*, ed. Gairdner, pp. 189, 193, Kingsford, *London Chrons*, p. 158, and Thomas and Thornley, pp. 179, 180.

[148] *Collections*, ed. Gairdner, pp. 189–90; Kingsford, op. cit., p. 158; Thomas and Thornley, p. 180.

[149] See especially the sympathetic estimate of Henry VI's character in GC; Thomas and Thornley, p. 212. VA describes him as 'a ghostly and a good man [who] set little by worldly matters'; Kingsford, op. cit., p. 184. One London chronicle has a story illustrating Henry's sanctity, telling how as a baby he refused to travel on a Sunday; ibid., pp. 279–80.

[150] See e.g. *Collections*, ed. Gairdner, p. 209.

[151] See e.g. ibid., p. 215. A favourable estimate of Edward IV is in GC; Thomas and Thornley, pp. 229–30.

[152] See e.g. *Collections*, ed. Gairdner, p. 216.

[153] See Greg. on the Yorkists' undertaking to remedy oppression in 1460; ibid., p. 206. Cf. p. 225 and nn. above.

[154] See e.g. Kingsford, *London Chrons*, pp. 69, 211. See also p. 240 and n. 122 above.

[155] Kingsford, op. cit., p. 186. Similar passages are in GC and Fabyan; Thomas and Thornley, p. 223; *Fabyan*, p. 665.

[156] Kingsford, op. cit., p. 194. Similar passages are in GC and, more briefly, in Fabyan; Thomas and Thornley, p. 242; *Fabyan*, p. 683.

concerning the commercial life of the capital. For example C records under 1442/3 that it 'was cried that all men that would adventure any corn or victual to Bordeaux or Bayonne, or to any place of that coast, . . . should go custom free',[157] and VA states under 1443/4 that 'it was ordained that the Sunday should be held high and holy, and that no manner of victual should be brought to the town and sold, neither by the citizens nor by foreigners.'[158] Similarly they record government action to control trade, for example the statute of 1439 regulating the activities of foreign merchants in London,[159] the embargo imposed on trade with Flanders, and the expulsion of all Flemings from England in 1493 (in retaliation the Emperor Maximilian and Philip archduke of Austria and duke of Burgundy, prohibited the import of English cloth and yarn),[160] and the treaty of 1496 between England and Flanders.[161] The chroniclers' interest in the merchant adventurers occasionally led them to preserve information of wider interest. Thus VA and GC contain the earliest information concerning the discovery of Newfoundland. This occurs in two entries which were almost certainly the source of the well known statements of John Stow[162] and Richard Hakluyt.[163] The first passage is about John Cabot's second voyage. In VA it is under 1498 and reads:[164]

> This year the king at the busy request and supplication of a stranger Venician, which by a chart made himself expert in knowing of the world, caused the king to man a ship with victual and other necessaries for to seek an island, wherein the said stranger surmised to be great commodities; with which ship by the king's grace so rigged went three or four more out of Bristol, the said stranger being conductor of the said fleet, wherein divers merchants, as well of London as of Bristol, adventured goods and slight merchandises; which departed from the West Country in the beginning of summer, but to this present month came never knowledge of their exploit.

The second passage is under 1502 in VA and reads:[165]

---

[157] Kingsford, op. cit., p. 152.

[158] Ibid., p. 156. Similar passages are in GC and Fabyan; Thomas and Thornley, p. 177; *Fabyan*, p. 617.

[159] See p. 240 and 124 above.

[160] Kingsford, op. cit., p. 200; Thomas and Thornley, p. 253; Cf. *A Bibliography of Royal Proclamations of the Tudor and Stuart Sovereigns, 1485–1714*, ed. Robert Steel (Oxford, Bibliotheca Lindesiana, v and vi, 1910, 2 vols), i. 3, no. 22, and Lipson, *Economic History of England*, i. 587 and n. 6.

[161] See p. 240 and n. 126 above.

[162] John Stow, *Chronicles of England* (London 1580), p. 875.

[163] *Divers Voyages touching the Discovery of America*, ed. J. W. Jones (Hakluyt Society, vii, 1850), p. 23.

[164] Kingsford, op. cit., pp. 224, 327–30; Thomas and Thornley, pp. 287, 445–6.

[165] Kingsford, op. cit., pp. 258, 337–8; Thomas and Thornley, pp. 320, 450.

This year three men were brought out of an island, found by merchants of Bristol, far beyond Ireland; the which were clothed in beasts' skins, and ate raw flesh, and [were as] rude in their demeanor as beasts.

Robert Fabyan's *New Chronicles of England and France* was the principal vehicle by which the historiographical tradition and factual content of the London chronicles was transmitted to Tudor England. By its means both tradition and content reached not only Stow and Hakluyt but also such scholars as Edward Hall and Raphael Holinshed (and so indirectly William Shakespeare).[166] The *New Chronicles* covers the period from the Creation to the accession of Henry VII in 1485. It is divided into seven books, and includes the history of France as well as that of England: chapters on French history alternate with those on English history. Fabyan completed the work in 1504, and later a brief continuation to 1509 was added, possibly but not certainly by him.[167] It was first published (without the continuation) by Richard Pynson in 1516, and then (with the continuation) by William Rastell in 1533, and subsequently twice more in the sixteenth century (in 1542 and 1559).

Fabyan, who, as has been seen,[168] was probably the author of the Great Chronicle of London, wrote the *New Chronicles* from the point of view of a Londoner; his civic pride permeates the work. The prologue which is in verse includes lines in praise of London:[169]

> And for that London, that ancient city,
> Hath ever persevered in virtuous nobless,
> To the great honour, as may considered be,
> Of all this land in wealth and great largess,
> Therefore I think somewhat to express,
> Of their good order, and civil policy,
> That they so long have ruled their city by.

The last book, Book VII, which covers the period from the Norman Conquest onwards, reveals Fabyan's preoccupation with London. It begins with the statement:[170]

Now, for as much as we be coming to the time that officers were chosen and charged with the rule of the city of London, it

---

[166] For the influence of the *New Chronicles* on the Tudor historians see Kingsford, *Hist. Lit.* pp. 106, 254, 255, 262, 265–9 passim, 273.

[167] For evidence suggesting that the continuation from 1485 to 1509, which was probably written between 1509 and 1513, was by Fabyan, see Thomas and Thornley, pp. xlvi-xlvii, lxix-lxxi, lxxv-lxxvi.

[168] See also pp. 231–2 and nn. above.

[169] *Fabyan*, p. 4.

[170] *Fabyan*, p. 293.

is necessary that here we do show what officers there were, and of the name that to them was admitted and given.

Book VII proceeds with a notice of the city's earliest charter, more eulogistic verses on London, and lists of its parish churches, religious houses, colleges, chapels and the like. Fabyan's debt to the London chronicles is manifest. From the accession of Richard I the *New Chronicles*, in so far as it relates to English history, is arranged like a London chronicle; each annal begins with the names of the bailiffs and then later, when the bailiffs were superseded, with those of the mayor and sheriffs for the year. Fabyan makes some use of the London chronicles as sources from the late twelfth century onwards, and from the early fifteenth century relies principally on them for English history. He used various versions, including the Main City Chronicle,[171] and also added material from his own knowledge.[172]

However, Fabyan's contribution to historiography was not limited to the transmission of the London chronicles to the modern period. He was a learned and ambitious historian who attempted to take over and pass on the whole of the English medieval tradition of historical writing. He used numerous medieval authorities, such as Bede, William of Malmesbury, Henry of Huntingdon and Roger of Howden.[173] His debt to the *Brut* is obvious because, though he begins at the Creation, the early part of his work principally comprises the legendary British history. Moreover, the division of his work into seven books shows the influence of Higden's *Polychronicon*. Possibly his attempt at giving the work universal scope, by beginning at the Creation and including French history, was likewise partly the result of the *Polychronicon's* influence. (For the history of France he mainly relied on Robert Gaguin's *Compendium super Francorum Gestis* which was printed in Paris in 1497.)[174]

Nevertheless, although Fabyan was influenced by his medieval predecessors, he was equally influenced by contemporary trends. Unlike Higden he did not adopt the sevenfold division of his work in order to represent the Seven Ages of the World, but rather to commemorate the Seven Joys of the Virgin Mary: each book of the *New Chronicles* ends with an English verse translation of the appropriate verse of her Joys,[175] and the prologue includes a prayer to the Blessed Mary to help the author

---

[171] See Kingsford, *Hist. Lit.* pp. 99–101, and Thomas and Thornley, p. lxix.

[172] For Fabyan's use of the Guildhall records see p. 231 and n. 76 above.

[173] For a list of his authorities see *Fabyan*, pp. xiii–xvi.

[174] See Kingsford, *Hist. Lit.* p. 105. For Fabyan's use of another French chronicle, Guildhall Library MS. 244, see Thomas and Thornley, pp. xxii–xxiii, xlvi.

[175] Pynson's edition of the *New Chronicles* and the manuscript of it (British Library MS. Cotton Nero C XI), which is imcomplete at the end owing to the loss of leaves, do not conclude Book VII with the verses for the seventh Joy. However, Rastell's edition does so (*Fabyan*, p. 681) which suggests the probability that this was the original ending in Nero C XI (which Rastell apparently used, presumably before the final leaves were lost); why Pynson should have omitted the ending is obscure: see Thomas and Thornley, pp. lxii–lxiii.

in his undertaking. In this way the work reflects the popularity of the cult of the Virgin in his day.

Above all, Fabyan illustrates the political outlook of early Tudor England. Henry VII had promoted friendly relations with France, and his commercial treaties won the favour and support of the city oligarchy: Fabyan undoubtedly wrote partly to celebrate the rapprochement with France. This intention must be the principal reason for his inclusion of French history. He expiates in the prologue on the damage caused by the Hundred Years' War, now happily replaced by peace.[176] Similarly, Fabyan saw the history of the past century from the point of view of a loyal subject of the new régime. He was an ardent supporter of Henry VII, a descendant of the House of Lancaster. Therefore, although Fabyan made extensive use of the London chronicles, he did not adopt their political outlook. Instead of giving his work a Yorkist bias, he gave it a Lancastrian one. Queen Margaret becomes 'that noble and most bounteous princess, of whom many and untrue surmise was imagined and told',[177] and Edward IV is regarded as a usurper.[178] Fabyan's attitude to the last Yorkist king, Richard III, is so hostile that it has a propagandist ring,[179] while the conqueror, Henry VII, 'that virtuous prince', is described as the legitimate heir to the English throne.[180] Fabyan writes at the end of his account of Richard's defeat at Bosworth,[181]

> And thus with misery ended this prince, which ruled mostwhat by rigour and tyranny, when he in great trouble and agony had reigned or usurped by the space of two years, two months and two days. And then was the noble prince Henry admitted for king, and so proclaimed king by the name of Henry VII.

Of that 'magnificent and excellent prince' Henry VII himself, Fabyan (or his continuator) writes:[182]

> sufficient laud and praise cannot be put in writing, considering the continual peace and tranquillity which he kept this his land and commons in, with also this subduing of his outward enemies of the realms of France and Scotland, by his great policy and wisdom, more than by shedding of Christian blood or cruel war; and over ruled so mightily his subjects, and ministered to them such justice, that not alonely they loved and dread him,

[176] *Fabyan*, p. 4. For Henry VII's rapprochement with France see S. B. Chrimes, *Henry VII* (London 1972), pp. 237, 279, 282, 283, 288–9.
[177] *Fabyan*, p. 640.
[178] *Fabyan*, p. 662.
[179] *Fabyan*, pp. 669–70.
[180] *Fabyan*, p. 672.
[181] *Fabyan*, p. 673.
[182] *Fabyan*, pp. 678, 690. Cf. Thomas and Thornley, pp. lxi and nn. 4, 5, lxx-lxxi, 338–9, 453.

but all Christian princes hearing of his glorious fame, were desirous to have with him amity and alliance. . . . His acts passed the noble acts of his noble progenitors since the Conquest, and [he] may most congruously, above all earthly princes, be likened unto Solomon king of Israelites, and be called the second Solomon, for his great sapience and acts. . . .

9

Chroniclers of the Wars of the Roses: English

One modern scholar has written that 'the waning interest felt by English-men in the French wars under Henry VI is reflected in the scarcity of chroniclers.'[1] Another has written of Edward IV's reign that 'For no other reign in English history since Henry III do we possess less strictly con-temporary information, save perhaps that of Henry VI.'[2] And for the reign of Richard III we have to rely mainly on later accounts.

Nevertheless, despite the dearth of chronicle sources, the period was rich in the variety of historiographical genres. As has been seen, the *Brut* chronicles and the chronicles of London underwent remarkable develop-ment, providing important contemporary evidence of events especially in the capital. And, as will be shown in a subsequent chapter, the period is distinguished by the growth of antiquarian studies. Moreover, although the tradition of the monastic chronicle (which will be discussed later) was nearing extinction, some houses were still producing historical works of interest, particularly on local history. Even the chivalric tradition of histo-riography, although by no means flourishing, survived.

In this period the chroniclers belonged to a wider range of social groups than formerly. The importance of the merchant class has been discussed already, in relation to the London chronicles. In addition, works were produced by those connected with the royal administration. The authors (or author) of the two 'official' histories to be considered, the *Chronicle of the Rebellion in Lincolnshire, 1470*,[3] and the *History of the Arrival in England of Edward IV and the Final Recovery of his Kingdoms from Henry VI, 1471*,[4] were royal servants (or a royal servant). A royal official was also almost certainly the author of the section on Edward IV's reign which is in the chronicle

---

[1] B. J. H. Rowe, 'A contemporary account of the Hundred Years' War from 1415 to 1429' in *EHR*, xli (1926), p. 504.

[2] Charles Ross, *Edward IV* (London 1974), p. 429.

[3] Printed *Chronicle of the Rebellion in Lincolnshire, 1470*, ed. J. G. Nichols (Camden Miscellany, i, 1847).

[4] Printed *Historie of the Arrivall of Edward IV in England and the finall Recoverie of his Kingdomes from Henry VI, A.D. 1471*, ed. John Bruce (Camden Soc., original series, i, 1838). For the version in French see pp. 264 and n. 107, 265 and n. 108 below. For the possibility that the *Chronicle of the Rebellion* and the *Arrival* were by the same author see pp. 262, 270 below.

of Crowland abbey.[5] (This part of the Crowland chronicle, the so-called second continuation, will be considered here, on account of its secular authorship, although the rest of the work will be discussed below, with the monastic chronicles.) It should also be noted that one of the antiquaries, William Worcester, was an official of a member of the baronage, Sir John Fastolf.[6] A soldier, John Hardyng, was responsible for keeping the tradition of chivalric historiography alive in England.[7] And a beneficed and resident priest, John Benet, vicar of Harlington in Bedfordshire (1443–71), wrote a chronicle.[8] (The antiquary, John Rous, was chaplain of Guy's Cliff, near Warwick.) Benet was probably educated at Oxford (John Rous certainly was), and Cambridge produced two writers to be discussed in this chapter, John Herryson[9] and John Warkworth, who was master of Peter-house.[10] This diversity of authorship reflects widespread curiosity about the recent and remote past, a curiosity not yet satisfied by historians writing under the influence of the renaissance. The variety both of historiographical genres and of authorship may have been one factor accounting for the breadth of the chroniclers' interests.

All the chroniclers respected the tradition of historical writing establish-ed in the middle ages. Benet and Herryson wrote as continuators of the *Polychronicon*; Warkworth appended his chronicle to a version of the *Poly-chronicon* conflated with the *Brut*;[11] and Hardyng started with the *Brut* (as did the continental writer Jean de Waurin who will be discussed in the next chapter), and he (like Waurin), adopted for his continuation the chivalric style of the pre-fifteenth century section of the *Brut*. Even those chronicles which were not written as continuations of earlier ones in tradi-tional form, were indebted to medieval historiography. Benet's chronicle is closely related to the London chronicles,[12] while Hardyng, like Rous and Worcester, used an impressive array of medieval sources—indeed one of the most notable achievements of these three authors, none of whose professions entailed adequate library facilities, was their success in obtain-ing access to books.[13]

---

[5] For the printed edition see p. 265 and n. 109 below.

[6] For the antiquaries John Rous and William Worcester see pp. 309–10, 328–32 below.

[7] For John Hardyng's career see pp. 274–6 below. For the editions of his chronicle see p. 274 n. 174 below. For a chronicle of the French war (1415–29) by two soldiers, see pp. 329–30 below.

[8] For John Benet's probable connection with Oxford see *John Benet's Chronicle for the Years 1400–1462*, ed. G. L. Harriss and M. A. Harriss (Camden Miscellany, xxiv, 1972), p. 171.

[9] For Herryson (or Harryson), who was not, as has been supposed, chancellor of the university, see A. B. Emden, *A Biographical Register of the University of Cambridge to 1500* (Cambridge 1963), p. 290.

[10] See *A Chronicle of the first thirteen Years of the Reign of King Edward the Fourth, by John Warkworth, D. D. Master of St Peter's College, Cambridge*, ed. J. O. Halliwell (Camden Soc., original series, x, 1839), p. ix.

[11] See pp. 257–8 below.

[12] P. 255 below.

[13] Pp. 254, 310, 322, 328–9, 331 below.

The Crowland continuator is one of the only two chroniclers to treat the politics of his day with a fairly open mind. The other writer to achieve some degree of objectivity was John Warkworth. Although he wrote under Edward IV, between 1478 and 1482, he expresses sympathy for Henry VI and criticizes Edward.[14] But the rest of the chroniclers responded to the political situation. None seems to have had idealistic loyalty to either Yorkist or Lancastrian dynasty, but all supported whichever was in power, though they provided rational justification for their allegiance.[15] John Benet, writing between 1461 and 1471, and John Herryson, who wrote in about 1469, were both Yorkist. Other chroniclers changed sides with remarkable facility. John Hardyng presented the first recension of his chronicle down to 1437, to Henry VI. But when he continued it to 1464, he revised the chronicle in the Yorkist interest for presentation to Edward IV. And as will be seen, John Rous's and William Worcester's changes of allegiance were reflected in their works in much the same way.[16]

The chroniclers were subjected to government propaganda and to propaganda from the opposing factions. Because of the insecurity of their dynasties, both Lancastrians and Yorkists used all known means to rally popular support, particularly that of the expanding middle classes.[17] The spread of literacy made written propaganda more effective than ever before. As mentioned above, dissident factions made especial use of bills posted on church doors and elsewhere, to justify their acts, explain their intentions and announce their victories.[18] And the government used them for the same purposes. Bills took the form of both letters and tracts. An example of a dissident bill is the propagandist letter addressed by Clarence and Warwick to the 'worshipful, discreet, and true commons of England'.[19] In it they accuse the government of oppression and injustice, and promise reform and to 'redeem for ever the said realm from thraldom of all outward nations, and make it as free within itself as ever it was heretofore'. This letter was apparently exhibited in Cheapside, on London Bridge and on

---

[14] P. 259 below.

[15] Pp. 254, 257, 277–9 below. It should be noted that the Augustinian Friar, John Capgrave, a theologian, hagiographer and chronicler (d. 1464), shows a similar change of opinion in his historical works; see pp. 389 and n. 1, 390 below. For the changes of allegiance of Sir John Fortescue, first a Lancastrian propagandist and then a Yorkist one, see p. 252 n. 24 below.

[16] See pp. 315–17, 331 below.

[17] For propaganda methods used by the Lancastrians and Yorkists to help stabilize their dynasties see J. W. McKenna, 'Henry VI of England and the dual monarchy: aspects of royal political propaganda, 1422–1432' in *Journal of the Warburg and Courtauld Institutes*, xxviii (1965), pp. 145–62 and Plates XXVI-XXIX, the same author's 'The coronation oil of the Yorkist kings' in *EHR*, lxxxii (1967), pp. 102–4, and the same author's 'Popular canonization as political propaganda: the cult of Archbishop Scrope' in *Speculum*, xlv (1970), pp. 608–23. See also pp. 252 and n. 24, 280 and n. 233 below.

[18] P. 238 above.

[19] Printed in *Original Letters illustrative of English History*, ed. Henry Ellis, second series (London 1827, 4 vols), i. 135–7.

various church doors elsewhere in England in advance of the landing of Clarence and Warwick.[20] At the same time a propagandist tract was produced in support of Warwick, *The Manner and Guiding of the Earl of Warwick at Angers from the fifteenth day of July to the fourth of August, 1470, which day he departed from Angers*, describing the earl's proceedings in France, notably how he had obtained the pardon of Queen Margaret and Prince Edward.[21] Besides such letters and tracts which were heavily biased in the interests of propaganda, newsletters were written; these contain fairly objective reportage, but nevertheless served a propagandist purpose because of the nature of the news they conveyed. Thus after the first battle of St Albans in 1455 the Yorkist party distributed a newsletter giving an account of their victory.[22] (A letter can, of course, contain news of public events but not be propagandist at all, if addressed privately to an individual; for example John Paston sent his mother details of the marriage of Edward IV's sister Margaret to Charles, duke of Burgundy, in 1468.)[23]

Among the means of propaganda adopted by the Lancastrians and Yorkists not least important was the appeal to history. The period shows a marked development in the use of history as a propaganda instrument, both to persuade and to inform.[24] It produced the first two indisputably 'official' histories, that is histories commissioned by the government, to be written in England, the *Chronicle of the Rebellion in Lincolnshire*, and the *History of the Arrival in England of Edward IV*. Conversely history was used to influence the government. John Hardyng wrote his chronicle partly to persuade Henry VI and Edward IV to subdue Scotland. (Similarly, William Worcester composed the *Boke of Noblesse* to urge Henry VI to the conquest of France.)[25] In rather the same way Titus Livius had earlier written the *Vita Henrici Quinti* and the *Humfroidos* as propaganda in support of Humphrey duke of Gloucester, who in 1435 wanted to renew the French war.[26]

---

[20] Ibid., p. 138.

[21] Printed ibid., pp. 132–5. See also p. 261 n. 79 below.

[22] Printed in *The Paston Letters 1422–1509 A.D.*, ed. James Gairdner (Edinburgh 1910, introduction and 3 vols), i. 327–31 (no. 239). See *The Stonor Letters and Papers*, ed. C. L. Kingsford (Camden Soc., third series, xxix, xxx, 1919, 2 vols), i. 52, and C. A. J. Armstrong, 'Politics and the battle of St Albans, 1455' in *BIHR*, xxxiii (1960), pp. 1–2, and passim.

[23] *Paston Letters*, ed. Gairdner. ii. 317–19 (no. 585).

[24] It should be noted that historical evidence constituted an important element in Sir John Fortescue's polemical writings in defence of the Lancastrian claim to the throne, which he composed while in exile with Henry VI in Scotland from 1461 to 1464. And subsequently, when Fortescue had had to reconcile himself to Edward IV's restoration in 1471 and wrote as a Yorkist propagandist, he again used the evidence of history (he asserted that he now had access to more accurate chronicles and documents than previously) as one means of refuting the arguments he had put forward in the Lancastrian interest. See P. E. Gill, 'Politics and propaganda in fifteenth-century England: the polemical writings of Sir John Fortescue' in *Speculum*, xlvi (1971), pp. 339, 342–6.

[25] Pp. 330–1 below.

[26] P. 211 above.

Some of the nobility and gentry had intellectual interests and built up good libraries[27] (notable examples are Humphrey duke of Gloucester and John duke of Bedford).[28] At least one nobleman, John Tiptoft, earl of Worcester, himself wrote a chronicle. This work, which is now lost,[29] covered the period from Brutus to 1429 and was mainly a compilation from well known sources, notably the *Brut*. And noble families tended to be interested in their own history. For example, in the mid-fifteenth century the Sudeleys and Botelers of Sudeley castle had a roll chronicle made for them.[30] It comprises: a history of England from Edward the Confessor to Henry VI (each reign is described in a Latin summary and English verses); a royal pedigree with portraits of the kings in roundels; and the pedigree of the Sudeleys and Botelers, with heraldic shields. This chronicle was undoubtedly compiled for the entertainment of the family, and perhaps for the instruction of the children. Such an interest in history among the nobility undoubtedly encouraged men in aristocratic employ to write chronicles, and improved a chronicler's chance of finding a generous patron. Moreover, a highly placed patron added to a chronicler's sources of information: he would be well informed about public affairs and would have access to collections of documents. (John Hardyng obtained valuable information about Henry Bolingbroke's coup in 1399 from the earl of Northumberland.)[31]

[27] For the education of the fifteenth century nobility in England see K. B. McFarlane, *The Nobility of Later Medieval England* (Oxford 1973), pp. 228–78. For the intellectual interests of Humphrey, duke of Gloucester, and his circle see K. H. Vickers, *Humphrey, Duke of Gloucester* (London 1907), Chaps IX and X passim, and Appendix A, and R. Weiss, *Humanism in England during the Fifteenth Century* (second edition, Oxford 1957), pp. 39–70. For John Tiptoft see below and n. 29.

[28] See K. B. McFarlane, 'William Worcester: a preliminary survey' in *Studies presented to Sir Hilary Jenkinson*, ed. J. Conway Davies (Oxford 1957), p. 205 and n. 2, Vickers, op. cit., pp. 345–6, and E. F. Bosanquet, 'The personal prayer-book of John of Lancaster duke of Bedford, K. G.' in *The Library*, fourth series, xiii (1932–3), pp. 148–54. See also, with further references, Weiss, *Humanism in England*, pp. 37 and n. 4, 61 and n. 4, 67 n. 66.

[29] For the chronicle attributed to John Tiptoft, formerly Phillipps MS. 11301, see p. 480, Appendix A, below. For Tiptoft's intellectual interests in general see R. J. Mitchell, *John Tiptoft, 1427–1470* (London 1938), especially Chaps XI and XIII, and Weiss, op. cit., pp. 109–22.

[30] The roll is fully described and discussed in Lord Sudeley, 'Medieval Sudeley. Part I. The Sudeleys and Botelers of Sudeley Castle' in *Family History, the Journal of Heraldic and Genealogical Studies*, x (1977), pp. 9–20, and D. Winkless, 'Medieval Sudeley. Part II. The fifteenth century roll chronicle of the kings of England, with the Sudeley and Boteler pedigree. The Latin text and the roundels' in ibid., pp. 21–39. Mrs Winkless suggests that the text, which derives from well known sources, was composed in the abbey of Bury St Edmunds. However, the evidence is far from conclusive. The roll is now in the New York Public Library, Spenser Collection MS. 193. It was formerly Phillipps MS. 26448; see *Bibliotheca Phillippica, Medieval MSS.*, new series, pt vii (Sotheby and Co.), 21 November 1972, lot 556. For a reference to a similar roll chronicle of the Sudeleys and Botelers, now in the College of Arms, see *Herald's Commemorative Exhibition 1484–1934 . . . catalogue* (London 1936), p. 38, no. 68. I am indebted to the Lord Sudeley for sending me an offprint of his and Mrs Winkless's articles, and for drawing my attention to the roll in the College of Arms.

[31] P. 283 below. Similarly William Worcester acquired documents concerning the Hundred

The principal chronicles of this period will be discussed individually: first the *Polychronicon* and *Brut* continuations; next the 'official' histories and the second continuation of the Crowland chronicle, and finally the chronicle of John Hardyng.

The three *Polychronicon* and *Brut* continuations have little merit as pieces of historical writing. Nevertheless they illustrate the intellectual tastes of their authors, men of comparatively humble rank—a vicar and two otherwise obscure academics. And two of the continuations have some value as contemporary sources in a period when these are not plentiful. The chronicle of John Herryson does not share this advantage. It consists of brief annals from 1377 to 1469, becoming slightly fuller from 1460 and containing references to London towards the end which suggest the use of some London source.[32] In general the annals are objective, but the description of Edward IV as 'our most serene king' and of the duke of Clarence as that 'most mighty and sagacious prince' indicate Yorkist affiliation.[33] The most interesting entries in the chronicle concern the history of Cambridge university and the careers of some of its graduates.[34]

John Benet's chronicle is a much more substantial piece of work. It is in a common-place book assembled and partly copied by Benet, which shows the breadth of his intellectual interests. He incorporated, for example, a copy of the tract *De Bello* by John of Legnano, and some thirteenth century annals of north country provenance.[35] He himself transcribed various political ballads, religious poems, historical notes, documents and memoranda. The chronicle ends abruptly in 1462 in the middle of a quire, the remaining nine pages of which are filled with miscellaneous notes mostly of 1471; this proves that the chronicle was written before that date.[36]

The popularity of common-place books at this period was the result of a combination of circumstances: the growing desire for knowledge and the shortage of books—to copy an extract was to keep it.[37] The rarity value of a book is testified by the inscription in Benet's volume anathematizing anyone who purloined it.[38] This inscription has led the modern editor of Benet's chronicle to suggest that Benet belonged to a 'book lending circle'.[39] Possibly Benet borrowed books from Dunstable priory, the

Years' War and the English administration in France from his patron, Sir John Fastolf; see p. 329 below.

[32] Herryson's chronicle is printed *Abbreviata Cronica 1377–1469*, ed. J. J. Smith (Publications of the Cambridge Antiquarian Soc., i, 1840).

[33] *Herryson*, pp. 12, 14.

[34] Ibid. pp. 11, 12.

[35] The contents of the volume are described in the printed edition (see p. 250 n. 8 above), pp. 153–7.

[36] *Ben.* p. 156.

[37] For common-place books see also pp. 232–3 above.

[38] *Ben.* pp. 153, 157. See also p. 258 and n. 66 below.

[39] *Ben.* p. 173.

patron of his living at Harlington. He may also have had access to books at Toddington, in the next parish, where there was a chapel and hospital founded in 1433 by John Broughton, who is known to have been a book collector.[40] Benet must have been on good terms with Broughton, because in 1471 the latter presented him to the rectory of Broughton (which Benet occupied until his death in 1474). Benet's interest in books is demonstrated by an entry in his chronicle: under 1439 he records the gift by Humphrey duke of Gloucester of books 'worth more than £1,000' to Oxford university library.[41]

Benet's chronicle cites other medieval sources besides the *Polychronicon*— Bede, Florence of Worcester, Geoffrey of Monmouth and probably some version of the *Brut*, in addition to other now unidentified works; it only acquires independent value from about 1440.[42] The evidence that Benet himself was the author of the chronicle is inconclusive. The chronicle's unity of style and the homogeneity of the interests it displays suggest that it was composed by one man. In addition, particular references to Oxford indicate that the author was a student at the university,[43] and passages relating to London, which occur from 1447 onwards, suggest the possibility that he was resident in the capital.[44] These indications can be regarded as obstacles to the acceptance of Benet as author: he was not an Oxford MA and from 1443 was at Harlington, after he was presented to the living. However, these obstacles are not insuperable. Benet might have studied at Oxford without graduating, and acquired information about London indirectly,[45] perhaps even acquiring a chronicle from London into which he worked his own material. He could have had indirect contact with London either through Dunstable priory (which was on a main road and little more than thirty miles from the capital) or through John Broughton (who purchased books there).[46]

One of the most graphic passages in Benet's chronicle is the account of the riot in Oxford on 29 and 30 August 1441, between the southern students and the northern ones:[47]

> On the night after the feast of the decollation of St John the Baptist sixty southern men, well armed, rose suddenly in Oxford, apparently without cause. They violently broke a window of Master William Wytham, doctor of civil law and then principal of White hall in Catte street; they shouted and called everyone

---

[40] *Ben.* p. 173.
[41] *Ben.* p. 186.
[42] For the sources of Benet's chronicle see *Ben.* pp. 159–62.
[43] *Ben.* pp. 158, 162–4, 171, 186–7. See below.
[44] *Ben.* pp. 166–7, 194–5, 198–204, 215, 221–3 passim.
[45] See *Ben.* pp. 162, 169, 172–3.
[46] *Ben.* p. 173.
[47] *Ben.* pp. 186–7.

belonging to that hall 'Scots dogs', and bawled 'Fire, fire, fire'. Moreover, when the doctor opened the gate, they shot in 200 arrows—but by God's protection no one inside was hurt. On the following afternoon, soon after two o'clock (that is on Wednesday, the feast of Saints Felix and Audactus), the two parties, both well armed, met in the High street before the gate of the hall commonly called Broadgates in the parish of All Saints, despite an order of the chancellor, who was assisted by the mayor of Oxford, Thomas Bailey. There they fought fiercely, and many of the southerners were wounded and laid low. The thirty hiding within the hall did not dare show their faces for fear of death. The northerners, about eighty of them, hurried jubilantly to Carfax, where they met thirty Welshmen coming to defend Broadgates hall. They wounded some, felled others, and put others to flight, and one, alas! was struck in the neck by an arrow and died eight days later. But none of the northerners suffered any injury, by God's protection.

Another vivid passage is the description of Jack Cade's rebellion in London in 1450. It includes an account of Lord Saye's execution by the rebels. When Saye was indicted before the justices he claimed the right to trial by his peers. At this the commons wanted to execute him there and then:[48]

But one of the little captains said they should let [Lord Saye] have a confessor. After he had confessed, the little captain together with the men of Kent dragged him from the Guildhall and led him to the standard in Chepe, and there without delay they cut off his head. Then the captain himself came with two heads on spears and put Lord Saye's head on a longer spear; he stripped his body, tied his feet to the saddle of a horse and dragged him naked, with arms outstretched, from the standard outside Newgate and thus through the Old Bailey and by Ludgate into Watling street, and so through Candlewick street to the bridge. There he circled round a big stone striking it with his sword; he placed the three heads on the Tower and dragged the body to the hospital of St Thomas in Southwark.

Benet's chronicle shows the interests to be expected of a cleric. Like the London chronicles, it notes the burning of heretics—but unlike them it gives in two instances their heretical tenets, which are not recorded elsewhere.[49] Similarly it describes Reginald Pecock's beliefs and gives the

[48] *Ben.* pp. 200–1.
[49] *Ben.* p. 187, 194–5.

text of his abjuration and confession.[50] And the chronicle shows compassion for the sufferings of the common people under oppressive government.[51]

The chronicler's political sympathies are consistently Yorkist.[52] Suffolk is 'the wicked duke'.[53] Somerset is also wicked: as a result of his negligence, England ignobly lost Normandy, to her irreparable damage; and under his rule the king did not prosper and the realm nearly perished.[54] On the other hand, the duke of Gloucester was that 'most faithful prince',[55] and the duke of York is favoured. When in 1455 the latter resigned his office as protector to the king, the chronicle records: 'He had ruled the whole kingdom of England for a year most excellently and nobly, and pacified all rebels and malefactors according to the law and without great rigour in a wonderful manner.'[56] The chronicle ends with the deposition of Henry 'because he had ruled tyrannously', and the coronation of the triumphant Edward IV 'with God's favour'.[57]

John Warkworth's chronicle is both less learned and less partisan than Benet's. Little is known about Warkworth himself. He was elected a fellow of Merton College, Oxford, in 1446.[58] In 1453 he was principal of Neville's Inn[59] and a chaplain of William Gray, bishop of Ely, one of the early humanists in England.[60] Gray appointed him master of Peterhouse, Cambridge, in 1473, which position he held until his death in 1500.

The only known copy of Warkworth's chronicle, Peterhouse MS.190, is appended as a continuation (from 1460) to a handwritten copy of the second edition of Caxton's version of the *Brut* (that is his *Chronicles of England*) published on 8 October 1482. This is stated in the final colophon to Warkworth's chronicle, but in fact to some extent the text of Caxton's *Brut* has been conflated with that of Caxton's *Polychronicon*, published on 2 July 1482. At the point where Warkworth's chronicle departs from Caxton's text (Peterhouse MS. 190, f. 214^v), it cites the colophon to Caxton's *Polychronicon*, not that to his *Brut*.[61] The whole volume is by two scribes, the

---

[50] *Ben.* pp. 219–20.

[51] *Ben.* pp. 202–3.

[52] See *Ben.* pp. 168–9.

[53] E.g. *Ben.* pp. 195–8 passim.

[54] *Ben.* pp. 202, 212–13.

[55] *Ben.* p. 192.

[56] *Ben.* p. 212. Cf. *Ben.* pp. 202–7 passim, 210–17 passim.

[57] *Ben.* p. 230.

[58] G. C. Brodrick, *Memorials of Merton College* (Oxford Historical Soc., iv, 1885), p. 236. A useful survey of Warkworth's life is by James Gairdner in the *Dictionary of National Biography*, xx. 844–5.

[59] Brodrick, op. cit., p. 236.

[60] For Gray see Weiss, *Humanism in England*, pp. 86–96. Gray gave Warkworth some books which may have been among those Warkworth gave to Peterhouse; ibid., pp. 94 and n. 13, 95.

[61] Peterhouse MS. 190 is described in M. R. James, *A Descriptive Catalogue of the Manuscripts in the Library of Peterhouse* (Cambridge 1899), p. 221. James notes that the MS. is a fair copy in two hands (the second hand starts on folio 196^v). James states correctly that the chronicle

second of whom started work before the end of Caxton's *Brut* and proceeded with Warkworth's chronicle until its conclusion in 1474. A note by the scribe of the text following Caxton's colophon (to the *Polychronicon*) indicates that the copy was made at Westminster, where Caxton had his press ('ffinyshed and ended after the copey of Caxton then in Westmynster'). A further note proves that the text of Warkworth's chronicle in the Peterhouse MS. was copied from another text, now lost. This note is clearly a directive which the scribe copied in error from his exemplar. It instructs him where to find the continuation when he had finished copying the *Brut*. It reads: '[A]s for alle thynges that folowe referre them to my copey in whyche is wretyn a remanente' (i.e. a continuation).[62]

Although the use of the second edition of Caxton's *Brut* proves that the exemplar of the Peterhouse MS. was copied after 8 October 1482, it provides no solution to the problem of when Warkworth's chronicle was composed.[63] The chronicle reads like a fairly contemporary record, but it was probably written after 18 February 1478, the date of the duke of Clarence's murder, to which it has an oblique reference: recording Clarence's desertion of the Lancastrians in 1471, the chronicler comments that this resulted in his 'destruction'.[64] Moreover, the chronicle must have been completed before the date in 1483 when Warkworth presented the volume to his college.[65] The ex libris inscription, possibly in Warkworth's own hand, is in fact the only evidence connecting him with the volume. It reads: 'Liber Collegii Sancti Petri in Cantabrigia, ex dono Magistri Johannis Warkworthe, Magistri dicti Collegii, sub interminacione anathematis nullatenus a libraria ibidem alienandus.'[66]

It is uncertain, therefore, whether Warkworth composed the chronicle, or whether he acquired and transcribed it (or had it transcribed), or whether he commissioned it. One feature could be interpreted as strengthening his claim to authorship. As will be seen, the chronicle shows an interest in and knowledge of north country affairs. This would be explained if the

---

follows the second edition of Caxton's *Brut*, published on 8 October 1482, but he does not remark that the colophon cited on f. 214ᵛ is that of Caxton's version of the *Polychronicon*, published 2 July 1482 (for a misinterpretation of the colophon by Professor Lander see n. 63 below). Although in general Warkworth's chronicle seems to follow Caxton's *Brut*, in places it corresponds with Caxton's *Polychronicon*: only full collation would reveal to what extent it is a conflation of the works.

[62] The scribal notes are cited in *JW*, pp. xxiii, xxiv, 1. They are reproduced in facsimile in *JW*, opposite p. 1.

[63] Professor Lander erroneously attributes the colophon to the scribe of Warkworth's chronicle, thereby reaching the conclusion that the Peterhouse MS. was finished on 2 July 1482 (from which he deduces that the first edition, which was published in 1480, of Caxton's *Brut* was used); J. R. Lander, 'The treason and death of the duke of Clarence: a re-interpretation' in *Canadian Journal of History*, ii, no. 2 (1967), pp. 21–2 n. 86.

[64] *JW*, p. 15. Cf. Lander, op. cit., p. 21 n. 86.

[65] *JW* p. xxv n. *.

[66] Peterhouse MS. 190, back of front flyleaf. Printed *JW*, p. xxiv.

author were Warkworth and if he took his name from Warkworth in Northumberland. (However, there is also a Warkworth in Northampton-shire.)

Since Warkworth's chronicle was written under a Yorkist king, its pro-Lancastrian bias cannot be attributed to government propaganda. The author was not a fanatic, but was mildly sympathetic to Henry VI and critical of Edward IV. On Henry's release from captivity in 1470, he comments that the king 'was not worshipfully arrayed as a prince, and not so cleanly kept as should seem such a prince.' He asserts that 'all his good lovers were full glad, and the more part of [the] people' rejoiced at his restoration, and attributes the evils of the reign to the 'mischievous people that were about the king', who were greedy and added nothing to his prestige or prosperity or to the welfare of the country. In addition these 'false lords' were responsible for the loss of Normandy, Gascony and Guienne.[67] The chronicler has a moving though restrained account of Henry's end:[68]

> And the same night that King Edward came to London, King Harry, being inward in prison in the Tower of London, was put to death, the twenty first day of May, on a Tuesday night, betwixt eleven and twelve of the clock, being then at the Tower the duke of Gloucester, brother to King Edward, and many other; and on the morrow he was chested and brought to [St] Paul's, and his face was open that every man might see him; and in his lying he bled on the pavement there; and afterward at the Black Friars was brought, and there he bled new and fresh; and from thence he was carried to Chertsey abbey in a boat, and buried there in our Lady chapel.

The chronicler hated the hardships caused by the Wars of the Roses, and blamed Edward IV for failing to fulfil men's expectation that he would establish peace and prosperity. Instead there was 'one battle after another, and much trouble and great loss of goods among the common people'. He also criticized Edward for the heavy taxation and for demanding military service outside men's own counties and at their own expense. As a result England was 'brought right low', and Edward 'had much blame' for damaging trade and for the loss by the English merchants of credit both at home and abroad.[69]

While admitting the Lancastrian bias of Warkworth's chronicle, its value must be recognized, because it is a well informed, contemporary and generally moderate account of the period. Besides the evidence it provides

[67] *JW*, pp. 11–12.
[68] *JW*, p. 21.
[69] *JW*, p. 12.

about the condition of England during the Wars of the Roses, it is a reliable authority for a number of details, some of which are not found elsewhere. For example, it attributes the Lincolnshire rising of 1470 (which it describes at length) to a conspiracy of the duke of Clarence and the earl of Warwick; the only other early chronicle to make the same statement is the *Chronicle of the Rebellion in Lincolnshire*, which was commissioned by the Yorkist régime, and cannot, therefore, be regarded as authoritative on such a contentious point.[70] Warkworth's chronicle alone gives the information, in the vivid description of the battle of Tewkesbury, that Edward, prince of Wales, before his death cried to Clarence for help.[71] And it has the most detailed and graphic account of the arrest of the chancellor George Neville, archbishop of York, on his manor of Moor Park in Hertfordshire.[72]

Warkworth's chronicle is the only chronicle of this period which has special knowledge of events in the north. It gives, for example, details concerning Edward IV's subjugation of Northumberland after his accession. Edward's army laid siege to certain castles (including that of Warkworth) which were being held by Queen Margaret's supporters, but the besiegers retreated when a force of French and Scots approached to relieve the garrison. However, the Scots, mistaking this for a ruse, were afraid to advance—had they done so they must have defeated Edward's men who 'had laid there so long in the field, and were [so] grieved with cold and rain, that they had no courage to fight.'[73]

The chronicle describes Edward's campaign of 1463 in the north,[74] and has a well informed account of the rising of Robin of Redesdale.[75] It gives an exact description of Henry VI's capture in 1465, in Ribblesdale near Clitheroe:[76]

> King Henry was taken beside a house of religion in Lancashire, by the men of a black monk of Abingdon, in a wood called Clitherwood, beside Bungerly [*sic* for Brungerley] Hippingstones, by Thomas Talbot, son and heir to Sir Edmund Talbot of Bashall, and John Talbot his cousin of Salesbury, with other more; which deceived, being at his dinner at Waddington Hall, and carried to London on horseback, and his leg bound to the stirrup.

Another passage which shows the author's detailed knowledge of events in the north, is the account of Edward IV's landing at Holderness in 1471 and entry into York. It relates that Edward said he came only

[70] *JW*, p. 8. Cf. pp. 261–2 passim below.
[71] *JW*, p. 18. Cf. Kingsford, *Hist. Lit.* p. 172.
[72] *JW*, pp. 24–6.
[73] *JW*, p. 2.
[74] *JW*, p. 4.
[75] *JW*, pp. 6–7.
[76] *JW*, p. 5.

against the earl of Warwick, not to claim the crown, and 'afore all the people he cried "A King Harry! A king and Prince Edward!" and weared an ostrich feather, Prince Edward's livery.'[77]

The next group of chronicles to be considered are those by authors who were closely associated with the government. Firstly there are the two 'official' histories, the *Chronicle of the Rebellion in Lincolnshire* and the *History of the Arrival in England of Edward IV*. Then there is the second continuation of the Crowland chronicle, which, although not commissioned by the government, was obviously by someone who either was at the time of writing, or had previously been, in royal service.

The *Chronicle of the Rebellion* and the *Arrival* are political tracts designed as government propaganda. Any kind of official history was rare in medieval England,[78] but the literary form of these examples was almost unprecedented; the only known tract resembling them appears to be Thomas Favent's *History . . . of the Wonderful Parliament* written in support of the lords appellant; Favent's style, however, is much more florid and blatantly propagandist.[79]

The purpose of the *Chronicle of the Rebellion* was to discredit the duke of Clarence and the earl of Warwick by proving that they had instigated the revolt in Lincolnshire, and the purpose of the *Arrival* was to record Edward's readeption in terms most flattering to the king. Internal evidence suggests that the author of the *Chronicle of the Rebellion* was connected with the privy seal office in chancery. The *Chronicle* is especially detailed concerning the king's correspondence, For example it records that on 13 March the king wrote two letters in his own hand to the earl of Warwick and duke of Clarence, which were delivered by one of his esquires, John Doune, announcing his victory over the rebels. Similarly the *Chronicle* gives the names of those who carried letters from the earl and the duke to the king.[80] It also records that the king sent them summonses by Garter King of Arms 'under privy seal', to answer the accusation of complicity made against them by the rebel leader, Sir Robert Welles, and cites the text.[81] There is no specific evidence indicating with which administrative office the author of the *Arrival* was connected. The opening paragraph, however, states that he was 'a servant of the king's, that presently saw in effect a great

---

[77] *JW*, p. 14. Edward was referring, of course, to Henry VI's son, Edward of Westminster.

[78] See A. Gransden, 'Propaganda in English medieval historiography' in *Journal of Medieval History*, i (1975), pp. 363–82 passim.

[79] P. 252 above. At about the same time as the *Chronicle of the Rebellion in Lincolnshire* was composed, the duke of Clarence and the earl of Warwick, then in opposition to Edward IV, produced their propaganda tract, a factual piece of work, to justify their acts and inform the public, *The Manner and Guiding of the Earl of Warwick at Angers . . .* ; see p. 252 and n. 21 above.

[80] *Chronicle of the Rebellion*, pp. 10–11, 12, 14–16.

[81] Ibid., pp. 12–13.

part of his exploits, and the residue knew by the true relation of them that were present at every time.'[82] The evidence on the authorship of the two works does not preclude the possibility, which is supported by their style, that they were by the same author.[83]

Both works are biased in the Yorkist interest. The *Chronicle* argues as persuasively and authoritatively as possible that Clarence and Warwick were implicated in the rebellion. It states that in the battle the rebels cried 'A Clarence! A Clarence! A Warwick!' and many, including Sir Robert Welles, wore Clarence's livery.[84] It asserts that a 'casket' was discovered belonging to Sir Robert Welles 'wherein were found many marvellous bills, containing matter of the great sedition, and the very subversion of the king and the common weal of all this land, with the most abominable treason that ever were seen or attempted within the same, as they be ready to be showed.'[85] No doubt the exact details of the king's correspondence concerning the rebellion, with the text of the summonses, were intended to add the weight of documentary evidence to the argument. And finally the author appeals to the authority of the confessions made by Sir Robert Welles and others. He emphasizes that they, 'of their own free wills, uncompelled, not for fear of death nor otherwise stirred, knowledged and confessed the said duke and earl to be partners and chief provokers of all their treasons.'[86]

The bias in the *Arrival* partly consists of the reiteration of Edward's right to rule as opposed to the illegal claim of Henry VI, and partly in eulogy of Edward which involves glossing over discordant facts. The author's intention is announced in the prologue:[87]

> Hereafter followeth the manner how the most noble and right victorious prince Edward, by the grace of God, king of England and of France, and lord of Ireland, in the year of grace 1471 ... arrived in England, and, by his force and valiance, of new reduced and reconquered the said realm, upon and against the earl of Warwick, his traitor and rebel, calling himself lieutenant of England, by the pretensed authority of the usurper Henry. ...

Henry is regularly referred to as a usurper[88] and his son Edward's title of prince of Wales impugned.[89] The author ends with Edward IV's recovery of his 'just title and right ... to his realm and crown' with the

---

[82] *Arrival*, p. 1.
[83] See also p. 270 below.
[84] *Chronicle of the Rebellion*, p. 10.
[85] Ibid., p. 10.
[86] Ibid., p. 11. For mention of the confessions of other conspirators see ibid., p. 17–18.
[87] *Arrival*, p. 1.
[88] Ibid., pp. 1, 2, 8, 13.
[89] Ibid., pp. 14, 30.

help of God and 'by his full noble and knightly courage'.[90] God's favour—and St Anne's—was demonstrated by a miracle which was interpreted as a prophecy of Edward's success. The *Arrival* relates that on his way south Edward attended divine service on Palm Sunday in the parish church at Daventry. The statue of St Anne, for whom Edward had an especial veneration, was boarded up (because, as the author explains, all statues in churches are shut from view from Ash Wednesday until Easter Sunday);[91] but when the king honoured the rood, the boards burst open.[92]

The *Arrival* praises not only Edward's courage,[93] but also his piety[94] and love of peace.[95] Queen Elizabeth is also praised: she endured her time in sanctuary 'in right great trouble, sorrow, and heaviness ... with all manner patience that belonged to any creature, and as constantly as hath been seen at any time. ... '[96] Presumably to suppress possible criticism of Edward IV no details are given concerning how Edward prince of Wales was killed at Tewkesbury,[97] while Henry VI's death is passed over with the explanation that on learning of the total defeat of his party 'he took it to so great despite, ire, and indignation that, of pure displeasure, and melancholy, he died the twenty third day of the month of May.'[98]

Despite the propagandist nature of the *Chronicle of the Rebellion* and the *Arrival* they are useful historical sources because they were written very soon after the events they describe in such detail, by authors (or an author) who were (was) at the centre of affairs. In general they read like authoritative records, almost like diaries of the acts and movements of the king and his party. The *Chronicle* is well documented, while the *Arrival* often gives a credible cause for an event—even a number of causes. Thus the author of the *Arrival* explains why Edward was not opposed in the north when he landed: Lord Montagu had too few soldiers; the common people loved Edward; the earl of Northumberland, who remained neutral, was a powerful influence; and Edward's own excellently equipped force inspired fear.[99]

Both the *Chronicle* and the *Arrival* have much reportage which relates them in genre to contemporary newsletters. The *Arrival* has, for example, a graphic account of the battle of Tewkesbury and its preliminaries, which includes this description of where the enemy struck camp:[100]

[90] Ibid., p. 39.
[91] For the veiling of statues, relics, pictures, etc. during Passiontide see Herbert Thurston, *Lent and Holy Week* (London 1904), pp. 100–1, 103.
[92] *Arrival*, p. 13.
[93] Ibid., pp. 19, 29, 39.
[94] Ibid., pp. 13, 19, 29, 30–1.
[95] Ibid., pp. 9–10, 39–40.
[96] Ibid., p. 17.
[97] Ibid., p. 30.
[98] Ibid., p. 38.
[99] Ibid., pp. 6–7. For the approximate date when the *Arrival* was composed see p. 264 below.
[100] Ibid., p. 28.

they put them[selves] in a field, in a close even at the town's end; the town, and the abbey, at their backs; afore them, and upon every hand of them, foul lanes, and deep dykes, and many hedges, with hills, and valleys, a right evil place to approach, as could well have been devised.

These two works were intended to bring news of Edward's triumph not only to his own subjects in England,[101] but also to his allies abroad. Little is known about the dissemination of the *Chronicle* on the continent, but its presence, presumably in a French translation, is proved by the fact that Jean de Waurin used a copy for his *Recueil des Croniques*.[102] Waurin must have had contacts with the Yorkist court, for he presented a splendid copy of his own work to Edward IV.[103] Rather more information is available concerning the *Arrival*: two versions gained currency:[104] one was the version in English which is discussed above. This version was used by Waurin, who included a French translation of it in his *Croniques*.[105] The other version, which was in French, was shorter and was used by Thomas Basin for his history of the reign of Louis XI.[106] There is evidence suggesting that this short version, four copies of which are known to survive on the continent, was composed before the longer English one. Possibly it was based on some brief newsletter in English sent abroad by Edward IV almost immediately after his restoration.[107] This newsletter may well have been sent to Edward's brother-in-law, Charles the Bold, duke of Burgundy, and another copy of it to the burgesses of Bruges. An appropriate covering letter was probably enclosed with each. Copies of two letters which could well have been sent with such a newsletter still survive; a copy of one or other accompanies three of the extant texts of the short (French) version. If this hypothesis is correct, the original newsletter was probably written between 26 and 28 May 1471. This is suggested by the fact that the last event mentioned in the short version is of 26 May, while Edward's letter to Charles the Bold is dated 28 May (the letter to the burgesses of Bruges is dated 29 May). Internal evidence proves that the short version itself was composed before March 1472.

---

[101] For the possible use of the *Chronicle of the Rebellion* and the *Arrival* by a chronicler in England see pp. 269–70 below.

[102] *Waurin*, v. 589–602 (*Chronicle of the Rebellion*, pp. 6 et seq.). For Waurin's chronicle see pp. 289–93 below; for the printed text see p. 288 n. 2.

[103] See p. 291 and n. 20 below.

[104] For the dissemination of the *Arrival* abroad see J. A. F. Thomson, '"The Arrival of Edward IV"—the development of the text' in *Speculum*, xlvi (1971), pp. 84–93. For a suggestion as to when the *Arrival* was taken abroad see p. 270 below.

[105] *Waurin*, v. 640–75. For variants in Waurin from the extant texts see Thomson, op. cit., pp. 84–6.

[106] *Basin*, ii. 64–94. See Thomson, op. cit., pp. 84–93 passim. For the chronicle of Thomas Basin see p. 294 and n. *39* below.

[107] See Thomson, op. cit., pp. 86–93.

Edward apparently had *de luxe* copies of the short version especially made in Flanders for distribution to important people: two of the extant copies are lavishly illuminated; the text is divided into four chapters, instead of being continuous as it is in the other two copies, and each chapter is preceded by a miniature of an important event leading to Edward's readeption (see the picture of the battle of Barnet, Plate VIII below). One of these illuminated copies has a transcript of the king's letter to the burgesses of Bruges. The other was owned by Jean Spifame, secretary to Charles VIII of France.[108]

Unlike the chronicle of the *Rebellion* and the *Arrival*, the second continuation of the Crowland chronicle was not commissioned by the government, although at least part of it was by a royal official and reflects the government's point of view. The second continuation supplements as well as continues the first continuation of the Crowland chronicle.[109] The first continuator (who was the prior)[110] ended with the death of Abbot John Littlington in 1470. The second continuator begins by stating that he will add information omitted by his predecessor 'because of his ignorance of worldly matters and for the sake of brevity'; therefore, to make the course of events clear, he will begin a little before the accession of Edward IV, with the battle of Ludlow.[111]

The second continuation comprises two ingredients. The principal one is a political memoir (comparable, for example, to that of Philippe de Commynes) rather than a chronicle in the strict sense of the word. It was conceived as a whole; the author states his intention of continuing until the death of Richard III[112]—although in fact he ended with the accession of Henry VII. The other ingredient of the second continuation is a history of Crowland abbey. Internal evidence suggests that this chronicle was composed about three years after Edward IV's death, probably late in April and early in May 1486.[113] The succession and death of each abbot is

---

[108] For the manuscripts of the *Arrival* see pp. 481–9 Appendix B, below.

[109] The Crowland chronicle is printed in *Rerum Anglicarum Scriptorum Veterum Tom.* I ed. William Fulman (Oxford 1684). It comprises: two forged chronicles which together consecutively cover the period from 616 to 1117, by a pseudo-Ingulf and a pseudo-Peter of Blois, for which see pp. 400, 490–1, Appendix C, below; a first continuation for the years 1149–1470 (Fulman, pp. 451–546); a second continuation, with which we are concerned here, covering the years 1459–86 (Fulman, pp. 549–78); a third continuation, covering the years 1485–86 (Fulman, pp. 581–93). The structure of the Crowland chronicle is described in J. G. Edwards, 'The "second" continuation of the Crowland chronicle: was it written "in ten days"?' in *BIHR*, xxxix (1966), p. 117. The first and third continuations are discussed pp. 408–12 below. A new edition of the second continuation is being prepared by Mr Nicholas Pronay for the series Oxford Medieval Texts. Mr Pronay kindly allowed me to read his introduction, to which I refer below, in typescript.

[110] The first continuator states: 'prioris officium, ... indigne et perfunctorie duntaxat administramus'; CC, p. 545.

[111] *CC*, p. 549.

[112] *CC*, pp. 570, 575, 577.

[113] For this date see pp. 491–2, Appendix C, below.

recorded in its proper chronological place, even at the expense of inter-rupting the narrative of national events. The notices of the succession of John of Wisbech in 1470 and that of Richard of Crowland in 1476 include promises that these abbots' achievements will be fully discussed when their deaths are recorded—promises duly fulfilled. (Lambert Fossdike's succes-sion, death and achievements are dealt with in one entry, presumably because he ruled for less than two years.) No such promise occurs in the notice of Edmund Thorpe's succession in 1485; he was still alive at the time of writing (he died in 1497).[114]

The name of the author of the political memoir is not known. However, a marginal note possibly provides a clue to his identity. In considering this marginal note, it must be borne in mind that the manuscript text of the second continuation of the Crowland chronicle, together with that of rest of the chronicle, was irretrievably damaged by the fire of 1731 in the Cottonian library, and that the student has to rely on the text printed by William Fulman in 1684.[115] Therefore, it can only be assumed that the marginal note in question was in the manuscript. Accepting this assump-tion, the note apparently reveals the author's status. It reads 'ille qui hanc historiam compilavit' ('he who compiled this history'), and occurs next to a passage in the text recording that after his readeption in 1471 Edward IV sent 'one of the councillors of the king, a doctor in canon law' as an ambassador to Charles the Bold to negotiate a treaty against France.[116] This evidence suggests that the author was a cleric and an administrator close to the king, a class of officials often used on diplomatic missions. The contents of the chronicle corroborate this view. The author was clearly interested in diplomacy, particularly in England's relations with Bur-gundy. He not only describes the mission of 1471,[117] but also Edward's efforts to raise money in parliament for the war against France in 1474,[118] his meeting with Charles the Bold at Calais in 1474 to discuss the conduct of the war,[119] his treaty with France at Picquigny in the following year and King Louis's ultimate betrayal of the terms of that treaty.[120]

Moreover, the memorialist was concerned about church affairs, and was very indignant at oppressive taxation. He bursts out with a tirade

[114] *CC*, 552, 553, 560–1, 569–70, 576–7.

[115] For the manuscript see Edwards, op. cit., p. 117 n. 1, and p. 490 Appendix C, below.

[116] *CC*, p. 557. I here, in agreement with Mr Pronay and with Mrs Hanham (*Richard III and his Early Historians 1483–1535* (Oxford 1975), pp. 86–7), accept Kingsford's assumption (*Hist. Lit.* pp. 181–2) that the marginal note refers to the author of the chronicle. Edwards challenges this opinion both because it cannot be proved that the marginal note was in the manuscript, and because the word *historia* can be taken to indicate merely the 'story' of the embassy, not the whole 'history' as recounted in the chronicle; Edwards, op. cit., pp. 126–9.

[117] *CC*, pp. 556–7. For the author's knowledge of the political repercussions in England of Charles the Bold's marriage to Edward IV's sister Margaret see p. 269 below.

[118] *CC*, p. 558.

[119] *CC*, pp. 558–9.

[120] *CC*, pp. 559, 562, 563.

against convocation's grant, in response to a royal demand, of a tenth in 1483:[121]

> Oh! how abject! what pernicious ruin of the church! May God prevent all succeeding kings from treating such an act as a precedent, lest worse evils than they can imagine should befall them — indeed these soon most unhappily befell this king and his most illustrious progeny!

The memorialist's clerical affiliations also appear in his interest in chronology; he explains that the papal curia dates the year from 1 January, while the church in England starts at the Annunciation (25 March).[122] His status as a royal administrator is reflected in his knowledge of the neighbourhood in London where such men lived, near London bridge in Bishopsgate and Southwark. Describing the damage done by the 'malignants' who rose in support of the Bastard of Fauconberg, he writes:[123]

> Marks of their misdeeds can be seen on the bridge to this day; all those houses built at great expense, which lie between the drawbridge and the outer gate which dominates the high street of Southwark, were burnt.

Although the memorialist was one of the king's councillors, he was not of the inner council. This is indicated by the fact that on one occasion he admits ignorance of a 'state secret'. Recording the advance of the armies of Edward IV and Charles duke of Burgundy against the French in 1475, he notes that 'a suggestion reached us from the enemy, I know not how, for entering into peace negotiations.'[124] Other evidence in the chronicle indicates that the author worked in chancery. He has a number of references to chancery and its personnel which show both interest and knowledge. He gives the form of dating by regnal year used on letters patent and the like, which Henry VI adopted on his restoration in 1470,[125] and he notes that Edward IV in 1476 examined 'the registers and rolls of chancery' in order to discover the names of those who had illegally occupied property.[126] He comments on the chancellors who presided successively over parliament in 1473 and 1474:[127]

> At the beginning there was Robert bishop of Bath who did nothing except through his pupil John Alcock bishop of Worcester[*sic*]; second there was Lawrence bishop of Durham who exhausted himself

---

[121] *CC*, p. 563. For knowledge of particular bishops see below and *CC*, p. 574.
[122] *CC*, pp. 552–3.
[123] *CC*, p. 556.
[124] *CC*, p. 558.
[125] *CC*, p. 554.
[126] *CC*, p. 559.
[127] *CC*, p. 557.

> with indescribable industry, and third, there was Thomas bishop
> of Lincoln who brought matters to a conclusion.

And the memorialist notes the presence at Bosworth Field of Robert Morton, master of the rolls, and of two chancery clerks, Christopher Urswick and Richard Fox.[128]

It can, therefore, be accepted that the author of the memoir in the second continuation of the Crowland chronicle was, during the period about which he wrote, one of the class of clerical administrators in chancery, councillors of the king and occasional diplomats. The question arises how his memoir found a place in the chronicle of Crowland abbey. Three possibilities may be suggested: first, that he wrote it in retirement as a monk at Crowland; second, that he wrote when on a visit to the abbey; and third, that the monks acquired a copy of his memoir and incorporated it in their monastic chronicle.

If the memorialist took the habit at Crowland after a life in royal service, a parallel to his career would be that of Thomas Wykes; the latter had a busy secular life, possibly working for Richard of Cornwall, until in 1282, at the age of sixty, he became a canon of Osney, where he wrote his chronicle.[129] On the other hand, a passage in the Crowland continuation could be used in support of the suggestion that the author was a visitor: the concluding verses in praise of Crowland comment on the monks' generous hospitality which 'we ourselves have seen.'[130] This view might also account for the fact that the third continuator of the Crowland chronicle did not know the name of the previous writer.[131] If the memoir was by a royal servant in retirement at Crowland or by a visitor, it seems likely that he used a pre-existing abbatial history for the sections on the abbots; this would account for the piecemeal method of composition.

The third possibility, that the monks of Crowland obtained the memoir which already existed as an independent work, remains to be considered.[132] If this hypothesis is the true one, the memoir was presumably actually written in chancery, with which as has been seen the author was connected.[133] The Crowland monks must have obtained a copy, and one of them written the passage introducing the second continuation, transcribed the memoir, and inserted the sections on abbatial history. This hypothesis, like the previous one, might explain the third continuator's ignorance of

---

[128] *CC*, p. 574.
[129] See Gransden, *Historical Writing*, i. 463–4.
[130] *CC*, p. 578.
[131] *CC*, p. 581.
[132] This is the view taken by Mrs Hanham (op. cit., pp. 78–85), who does not, however, mention the memorialist's apparent use of the *Chronicle of the Rebellion* and the *Arrival* (see below).
[133] P. 267 above.

the name of his predecessor (that is of the memorialist).[134]

Of the three hypotheses, the last best explains the apparent use by the memorialist of the *Chronicle of the Rebellion in Lincolnshire* and the *History of the Arrival of Edward IV*.[135] His use of the earlier works is indicated by the fact that his outlook and in places his subject matter resemble theirs (although it is hard to compare a general history in Latin with detailed monographs in English). The memorialist's approach to history is very like that found in the *Arrival*. He often gives long rational explanations of events. For example he dismisses the suggestion that the quarrel between Edward IV and the earl of Warwick in 1467 was the result of the king's marriage to Elizabeth Woodville, for, the memorialist points out, the earl had agreed to the marriage in council: rather the breach was caused by Edward's negotiations for the marriage of his sister Margaret to Charles the Bold; this destroyed Warwick's plans for her marriage to the dauphin which was to cement an Anglo-French alliance.[136]

There are also specific resemblances in subject matter between the Crowland memoir and the *Chronicle of the Rebellion* and the *Arrival*. The memorialist mentions the complicity of Clarence and Warwick in the Lincolnshire rebellion, the theme of the *Chronicle*.[137] Moreover, the memorialist remarks that after the revolt, although Edward executed the leaders, he spared the ordinary folk ('rudi atque innocenti multitudini gratiam fecit'),[138] while the *Chronicle* has the same statement expressed in English (Edward 'plentifully [used] his mercy in saving of the lives of his poor and wretched commons').[139] The Crowland memoir and *Arrival* share three statements: both comment on the fact that Edward's landing place, Holderness, was the same as Henry Bolingbroke's in 1399; both stress that Edward came to claim only his duchy, not the crown; and both describe how the earl of Warwick misjudged Edward in supposing he would be at his devotions on Easter Saturday and so exposed to a surprise attack, when in fact Edward was marching towards Barnet, ready to do battle.[140]

If, as seems likely, the memorialist used the *Chronicle of the Rebellion* and the *Arrival* as sources, this would corroborate the hypothesis that he wrote near the seat of government rather than at Crowland, because copies of both works were presumably preserved in chancery or by someone con-

---

[134] Mrs Hanham suggests that the third continuator was the monk who incorporated the memoir into the abbatial history to form the second continuation; Hanham, op. cit., p. 84.

[135] Similarly, if Mrs Hanham's view that Polydore Vergil used the memoir now preserved in the Crowland chronicle (Hanham, op. cit., pp. 96, 97, 135–42) is right, this would strengthen the case for its composition in London rather than at Crowland. However, Mrs Hanham's arguments, which are based on occasional resemblances between the continuation and Vergil's work, are not conclusive. Cf. p. 442 n. 114 below.

[136] *CC*, p. 551. For an example from the *Arrival* see p. 263 above.

[137] *CC*, p. 553. Cf. pp. 261–2 above.

[138] *CC*, p. 553.

[139] *Chronicle of the Rebellion*, p. 10.

[140] *CC*, pp. 554–5; *Arrival*, pp. 2, 4, 17–18.

nected with it. Furthermore, if at the time of writing the memorialist himself was still employed in chancery (as he had been during Edward IV's reign),[141] his use of the two official histories would be even more easily explained. Nor should the possibility be overlooked that the memorialist himself may have written the monographs fifteen years previously.[142]

In addition, it should be noted that the memorialist himself records how Charles the Bold received the news of Edward IV's readeption. He was overjoyed and immediately sent ambassadors to congratulate Edward and to remind him of Louis XI's hostility, urging Edward to avenge himself and regain his lost rights in France, for which enterprise he promised help.[143] Edward, therefore, sent an embassy that summer to discover exactly what Charles had in mind; it was on this occasion, as noted above, that the memorialist was probably one of the ambassadors.[144] The news was probably first conveyed to Charles by means of the newsletter which, as suggested above, formed the basis of the extant versions of the *Arrival*. It seems possible that the *Arrival* itself and the short French version were taken to the continent by the summer embassy. The object of giving Charles full details of the readeption was no doubt partly to assure him that Edward, being secure on his throne, could negotiate from a position of strength and was a worthwhile ally.

Recent scholars have put forward two candidates for the authorship of the memoir. Mr Pronay argues in favour of Master Henry Sharp; the few known facts of his life fit those of the author's.[145] On the other hand Mrs Hanham, following P. M. Kendall,[146] argues that the author was John Russell, bishop of Lincoln. He was a doctor of canon law, and was secondary of the privy seal office from 1469 to 1474, keeper of the privy seal from 1474 to 1483, and chancellor under Richard III until his dismissal in 1485.[147] There is evidence suggesting that he may have gone on an

---

[141] P. 267 above.

[142] Kingsford (*Hist. Lit.* p. 183) suggested that the second Crowland continuator might have been the author of the *Arrival*, but his suggestion has not been taken up by later scholars, who indeed do not even remark on the parallels between the Crowland continuation, and the *Chronicle of the Rebellion* and the *Arrival*. Cf. p. 269 above.

[143] *CC*, pp. 556–7.

[144] See p. 266 above.

[145] Mr Nicholas Pronay's arguments are in the introduction to his forthcoming edition of the second continuation (see p. 265 n. 109 above).

[146] Hanham, op. cit., pp. 88–95; P. M. Kendall, *Richard III* (London 1955), p. 432. Russell's authorship is accepted without question by Professor Ross; Ross, *Edward IV*, p. 352.

[147] For Russell's career see Emden, *Biographical Register*, iii. 1608–11. Sir Thomas More described him as one of the most learned men of his time. Russell owned a number of humanist texts, and the speeches he prepared for Edward V's parliament include quotations from classical and humanist authors. See Weiss, *Humanism in England*, pp. 171, 177. If Russell was the author of the second continuation of the Crowland chronicle, his humanist interests might help account for the attribution of some events recorded in it to natural causes (see p. 269 above), since natural causation was a feature of humanist historiography; see p. 427 and n. 20 below. (The same comment applies if he wrote the *Arrival*.)

embassy to Charles the Bold soon after the readeption.[148] Russell might, therefore, have written the memoir and given a copy to the monks of Crowland when he visited the abbey fifteen years later.[149] However, it is hard to see why, if he were the author, the third Crowland continuator, who recorded his visit, was ignorant of the fact.[150] This suggests the possibility that one of his entourage wrote the work.

The memoir is a valuable source because it was written at the centre of affairs by an intelligent, well educated man who, despite his bias in favour of the government, was capable of rationally analysing the causes and consequences of events. He preserves information on, and interpretations of events not found elsewhere, and some of his observations must be eyewitness. There is for example, the description of the clothes Edward IV wore for the Christmas festivities in 1482:[151]

> He was usually dressed in a variety of costly clothes, in quite
> another fashion than we had seen before in our time. The sleeves
> of his cloak hung in ample folds like those of a monk's frock, lined
> inside with the richest furs and rolled on the shoulders. Thus the
> prince, who was of imposing build, taller than others, presented
> a novel and remarkable spectacle.

The memorialist comments in general terms on the king's love of luxury,[152] but is more specific on the financial expedients which enabled Edward to accumulate the vast treasure which was later taken over by Richard III. For example, he describes how in 1476 after the failure of the French expedition, Edward resumed royal lands which had been alienated, engaged in commerce, exacted payment before handing over temporalities, and fined anyone who illegally occupied property.[153] The memorialist also has a unique account of the postal system established by Edward at the time of the Scottish war: 'riders were deployed at intervals of twenty miles; these, riding at speed but not beyond their limits, could carry news

---

[148] Miss Scofield asserts that Russell was on the second embassy, on the evidence of a payment to him as ambassador to the duke of Burgundy, entered on the issue roll of Easter, 11 Edward IV (E 403/844 in the Public Record Office); C. L. Scofield. *The Life and Reign of Edward IV* (London 1923, 2 vols), ii. 16 and n. 2. However, Easter 11 Edward IV (i.e. 14 April 1471) is too early a date for payment for the embassy in question which did not take place until the summer. Nevertheless, in view of Russell's previous employment as an ambassador to the duke of Burgundy (see Scofield, op. cit., i. 430–2, 455, 507), it is not unlikely that he was 'the king's councillor and doctor of canon law' mentioned in the Crowland memoir (p. 266 above) as having been chosen on that occasion. Miss Scofield suggests that the author of the memoir accompanied Russell on the embassy (cf. my suggestion below, that the author was one of Russell's entourage); ibid., ii. 16 n. 2.

[149] See p. 491, Appendix C, below.

[150] See p. 268 and n. 131 above.

[151] *CC*, p. 563. (Cf. Commynes's comments on Edward IV's appearance and character; p. 298 below.) For comments on the clothes worn by Queen Anne and Princess Elizabeth at Richard III's Christmas celebrations see *CC*, p. 572.

[152] *CC*, p. 564. Cited Ross, *Edward IV*, p. 86.

[153] *CC*, p. 559. See Ross, op. cit., p. 352.

200 miles within two days, passing the letters from hand to hand.'[154]

Similarly the chronicle is an important authority for Richard III's reign. In at least one instance its information antedates Tudor propaganda. It gives details of Richard's attempt to prove his hereditary right to the throne by means of a propagandist story.[155] This states that Edward IV's children by his queen, Elizabeth, were bastards because he had previously contracted a marriage with Eleanor Butler. Therefore, since the duke of Clarence had been attainted, Richard's was the only 'certain and uncorrupt blood' of the Yorkist line. The story was made public, the chronicle explains, by means of a petition on 'a certain parchment roll' presented to the meeting of lords and commons in June 1483, just after Richard III's coup.[156] Since this assembly was not a properly constituted parliament, the parliament held in January 1484 passed an act stating Richard's title in full, in order to remove 'diverse doubts, questions and ambiguities'; the roll itself was cited in the act and so copied on to the parliament rolls. By recording this story the memorialist was responsible for the preservation of a piece of propaganda unacceptable to the Tudors (because one corollary of the story was that Henry VII's queen, Edward IV's daughter Elizabeth, was illegitimate). In 1485 parliament repealed the act of 1484.[157]

The memorialist clearly understood that the story was a piece of propaganda: it provided, he writes, 'the colour for an act of usurpation'. However, his inclusion of the story is the only demonstrable instance when he departed from the Tudor view of the events of the Wars of the Roses; elsewhere his picture roughly corresponds with that of the Tudor historians. Indeed, because the memoir was not used as a source by the Tudor writers (with the possible exception of Polydore Vergil),[158] it provides important evidence showing that the legend which dominated the Tudors' view of fifteenth century history had a very early origin.

The memorialist saw the Wars of the Roses as a dynastic struggle, begun by the claim to the throne of Richard duke of York (1432–60), which was based on his descent from Lionel duke of Clarence. (The claim of the descendants of Lionel's elder brother John of Gaunt, duke of Lancaster, was vitiated by the unjust usurpation of the latter's son, Henry Bolingbroke.)[159] The memorialist favoured Henry VI whose 'innocent life, love

[154] *CC*, p. 571.

[155] *CC*, p. 567. This story is fully discussed, with reference to the Crowland continuation, the only known chronicle source for it, by Mortimer Levine, 'Richard III—usurper or lawful king?' in *Speculum*, xxxiv (1959), pp. 391–401; cf. J. R. Lander, 'The treason and death of the duke of Clarence: a re-interpretation' (see p. 258 n. 63 above), p. 26 and n. 106.

[156] *Rot. Parl.* vi. 240–1. For other propagandist fabrications copied on to the rolls of parliament in the late fourteenth century and in the fifteenth century see Lander, op. cit., p. 19 and n. 77.

[157] *Rot. Parl.* vi. 289.

[158] See p. 269 n. 135 above.

[159] *CC*, p. 550.

of God and the church, patience in adversity and other remarkable virtues' and his posthumous miracles 'earned for him the title of glorious martyr.'[160] His attitude to Edward IV is ambivalent, at once approving and critical. He admired Edward because he was born an outstanding conqueror and monarch, and asserted that the king's praises, as a result of his 'prompt and speedy' triumph in 1471, 'resounded through all lands.'[161] The memorialist also applauded the successful mediation by this 'most loving' prince in the quarrel between the duke of Clarence and the duke of Gloucester in 1473—such family quarrels exacerbated the conflict during the Wars of the Roses.[162] And he praised Edward with patriotic fervour for the 'honourable' treaty he made with France in 1475.[163] On the other hand the memorialist considered that Edward's glory was clouded, and the peace he had established in England threatened by his quarrel with Clarence in 1476.[164] In his view Edward recognized no limits to royal power after Clarence's murder in 1478; 'he was feared by all, but seemed himself to fear no one.' The king planted spies throughout the kingdom to check rebellion (he also had spies abroad), raised money under the name of 'benevolences',[165] which he spent prodigally, and his subsequent Scottish campaign achieved nothing except the capture of Berwick, which was more a loss than a gain because of the great expense of its defence.[166]

The memorialist regarded Richard III's reign as the culminating disaster in the Wars of the Roses. Like the Tudor writers he emphasized Richard's deceitfulness (his obsequious manner to the little princes while he was plotting their destruction),[167] and his astuteness (he divided the council so that one part did not know what the other was doing).[168] Richard ruled without respect for law or justice; he was a tyrant, trying to establish his power without God's help.[169]

The account of the battle of Bosworth, written less than a year after the event, is both detailed and moving, and supports later descriptions. The memorialist relates that Richard's sleep on the previous night was disturbed by 'a terrible dream in which he was surrounded, as it seemed, by a multitude of demons.' In the morning the king could find no priest ready to celebrate mass, took no breakfast 'to refresh his ailing spirits' and faced the enemy looking 'deathly pale'. The memorialist does justice to Richard's personal bravery, but regards the victory of Henry Tudor,

[160] *CC*, p. 556.
[161] *CC*, p. 556.
[162] *CC*, p. 557.
[163] *CC*, p. 559.
[164] *CC*, p. 562.
[165] For the memorialist's dislike of Edward's financial impositions see also pp. 266–7 above.
[166] *CC*, pp. 562–3. Cf. Ross, op. cit., pp. 245, 421.
[167] *CC*, p. 564.
[168] *CC*, p. 566.
[169] *CC*, pp. 566, 570, 571.

whose triumph was symbolized by Henry's discovery of the crown which had fallen from Richard's head in the fighting, as a gift from heaven.[170] To the memorialist Henry's accession marked the end of the civil war, and his marriage with Elizabeth united the rival royal houses:[171]

> Henry was praised by all as an angel sent from heaven, through whom God deigned to visit his people and free them from the evils which had so afflicted them.

The chivalric type of chronicle did not flourish in fifteenth century England, as indeed the Flemish chronicler Jean de Waurin observed.[172] Although romance literature influenced the biographies of Henry V and the narrative of the French war from 1415 to 1429,[173] the only work wholly in the chivalric style was the chronicle in English verse by John Hardyng.

John Hardyng was born in 1378 in the north of England.[174] Like Waurin he began his career as a soldier and ended it writing history. At the age of twelve he joined the household of Sir Henry Percy ('Hotspur'), eldest son of the earl of Northumberland.[175] There he would have received the military training which he was later to describe.[176] He also took part in border warfare—he attended Henry Percy, as he says, 'at divers roads and fields'[177] and was clearly in Percy's confidence.[178] He finally saw him fall at the battle of Shrewsbury.[179] After the pardon of Percy's followers Hardyng entered the service of Sir Robert Umfraville, who was the grandson of Gilbert, earl of Angus, and uncle of Gilbert Umfraville, titular earl of Kyme in Lincolnshire. Hardyng had previously fought with Sir Robert

---

[170] CC, p. 574.

[171] CC, pp. 574–5.

[172] See p. 288 below.

[173] See Chapter 7 passim above and pp. 329–30 below.

[174] The best account of Hardyng's life, based on his chronicle and other sources, is by C. L. Kingsford, 'The first version of Hardyng's chronicle' in EHR, xxvii (1912), pp. 462–9. As will be seen, Hardyng's chronicle survives in two versions (for a discussion of the versions see pp. 276–9 and nn. below). The second version is printed The Chronicle of John Hardyng, ed. Henry Ellis (London 1812, reprinted New York 1974). Ellis based his text on the edition Richard Grafton printed in 1543 (Grafton added a prose continuation to 1543); Ellis collated Grafton's text with two manuscripts of the second version, BL MS. Harley 661 and Selden MS. B. 10, in the Bodleian Library, Oxford; he printed extracts in his preface and at the end of the volume (see p. 286 n. 278 below) from the earliest and fullest surviving version of the chronicle, in BL MS. Lansdowne 204. The Lansdowne text is discussed by Kingsford, op. cit., pp. 469–82; its dedication, proem, eulogy of Henry V, the concluding sections on Sir Robert Umfraville and Hardyng's grievances, and the envoy are printed in ibid., pp. 740–53. For the text of the chronicle printed by Grafton see Kingsford, op. cit., pp. 481–2, and for Grafton's continuation, in so far as it relates to the pre-Tudor period, see Kingsford, Hist. Lit. pp. 187–8, 259, 263, 270. Ellis prints Grafton's dedication and preface (both in verse) and the continuation; JH, pp. 1–13, 434–607.

[175] See Hardyng's prose addition to his chronicle; JH, p. 351.

[176] See JH, p. i n.†. See p. 278 n. 213 below.

[177] JH, p. 351 (prose addition).

[178] Kingsford, 'Hardyng's chronicle', p. 463.

[179] JH, pp. 351, 353 (prose addition).

Umfraville at Homildon, and now accompanied him on the French campaign: he was at the siege of Harfleur and at the battle of Agincourt.[180] He then fought with Umfraville in the Scottish marches, probably taking part in the 'foul raid' of 1417,[181] and stayed with him in London.[182] Umfraville died in 1436, having rewarded Hardyng well for his services; he had first made him constable of Warkworth castle[183] and then of Kyme[184] which remained Hardyng's home until his own death in about 1465.[185]

At some stage Hardyng attracted Henry V's notice. Henry was interested in renewing the claims of the English crown to overlordship of Scotland. Scottish independence had never been secure since the death of Bruce in 1329, and throughout the fifteenth century the kings of England sporadically asserted their right and contemplated enforcing it.[186] Presumably because Hardyng combined north country connections with literary interests, Henry sent him to Scotland early in 1418 'to spy with all kinds of diligence' the best way of invading that country, and to collect evidence on the English claim to sovereignty.[187] Hardyng stayed there for more than three years, probably not returning to England until the summer of 1421, and subsequently again visited Scotland at least once,[188] apparently at considerable personal risk.[189] He delivered the first batch of 'evidences' to Henry V at Bois de Vincennes in 1422;[190] he handed over another batch to Henry VI at Easthampsted in 1440;[191] and he delivered a further batch to Edward IV at Leicester in 1463.[192] Modern research has shown that seventeen of the nineteen documents which are known to have passed through Hardyng's hands are forgeries—the other two were probably genuine copies.[193] And it is fairly certain that Hardyng himself was the forger.[194]

[180] *JH*, pp. iii, 351 (prose addition), 373, 375.
[181] *JH*, pp. 380–2.
[182] *JH*, p. 20.
[183] *JH*, p. 361.
[184] Kingsford, 'Hardyng's chronicle', p. 465. Robert inherited Kyme on Gilbert's death in 1421.
[185] Ibid., p. 466.
[186] See *Anglo-Scottish Relations 1174–1328, some selected Documents*, ed. E. L. G. Stones (Nelson's Medieval Texts 1965, reprinted Oxford 1970), pp. xxx-xxxi.
[187] Kingsford, 'Hardyng's chronicle', pp. 741–2, 751.
[188] Ibid., pp. 464–5.
[189] Hardyng was apparently 'maimed' in Henry V's service; ibid., p. 743, and *CPR, 1452–1461*, p. 393.
[190] *JH*, pp. 293, 306. Kingsford, 'Hardyng's chronicle', pp. 464, 467.
[191] Kingsford, op. cit., p. 741; confirming *CPR, 1436–1441*, pp. 431, 484, 490. Cf. Kingsford, op. cit., pp. 464–5, 467.
[192] *JH*, p. 317.
[193] Palgrave prints those documents, eight in number, which are extant and are preserved in the Public Record Office; *Documents and Records illustrating the History of Scotland*, ed. Francis Palgrave (London 1837, 1 vol. only printed), i. 367–76. Cf. Kingsford, 'Hardyng's chronicle', p. 468, and with particular reference to the documents relating to the Great Cause of 1291–2, *Edward I and the Throne of Scotland, 1290–1296: an Edition of the Record Sources for the Great Cause*, ed. E. L. G. Stones and G. G. Simpson (Glasgow 1978, 2 vols), i. 385–7, and p. 276 n. 203 below.
[194] Palgrave, op. cit., i. ccxvi, ccxxiii; Kingsford, op. cit., p. 468.

There can be no doubt that Hardyng's desire to promote his own career provided a strong motive for research into the claim of the kings of England to overlordship of Scotland, and he must have forged the documents to make the case more convincing. He expected and gained reward for his labours: in 1440 he was granted £10 a year from the manor or preceptory of Willoughton,[195] and in 1457 he was given £20.[196] However, Hardyng was not satisfied. It seems that Henry V promised in 1422 at Bois de Vincennes to give him the manor of Geddington in Northamptonshire, but after the king's death the promise was not honoured; the chancellor Cardinal Beaufort, bishop of Winchester, gave it to the queen as part of her dower.[197] Hardyng persistently pressed his claim, reinforcing his arguments with a document purporting to prove that he had resisted an attempt by James I of Scotland to deflect his loyalty—a forged safe conduct, dated March 1434, with an offer to pay 1,000 marks in return for the surrender of his 'evidences'.[198]

Hardyng's chronicle can be regarded from one point of view as a by-product of his Scottish researches and his desire for reward. He began writing the chronicle, a history of England from Brutus to 1437, in about 1440 while at Kyme, and in 1457 presented a copy to Henry VI,[199] to whom he addressed the proem.[200] He inserted every 'proof' he knew why the kings of England were overlords of Scotland; he asserted that Brutus' son Albanact did homage as king of Scotland to his eldest brother Locrine, king of England,[201] and worked through the occasions after the Norman Conquest when the Scottish kings had done homage,[202] culminating in John Balliol's submission to Edward I.[203] Hardyng exhorted Henry VI in the proem to reconquer Scotland as Edward I had done, and, in order

---

[195] *CPR, 1436–1441*, pp. 431, 484, 490, 557.

[196] *CPR, 1452–1461*, p. 393.

[197] *JH*, p. 292.

[198] Palgrave, op. cit., i. 376. This document is mentioned in the letters patent of 1457 granting Hardyng £20; *CPR, 1452–1461*, p. 393. Cf. Kingsford, 'Hardyng's chronicle', pp. 464–6 passim.

[199] Ibid., p. 465.

[200] Ibid., pp. 740–4.

[201] *JH*, pp. 42–3.

[202] See *JH*, pp. 42–3, 159, 166, 210, 211, 212, 223, 228, 235–6, 240, 243, 247, 253–4, 256, 262, 269, 270, 276, 283, 294, 296, 299, 323. Cf. ibid., p. 87.

[203] *JH*, pp. 293–4. (For later evidence relating to the English claim to overlordship of Scotland see *JH*, pp. 295–300 passim, 306.) Professor Stones and Dr Simpson point out that Hardyng's details on the Great Cause suggest that he had read John of Caen's or Andrew de Tange's Great Rolls as well as the submissions of the competitors. They also consider it very unlikely that copies of the submissions were preserved among the Scottish records. Therefore, Hardyng presumably acquired them from the English treasury—Professor Stones and Dr Simpson suggest that Hardyng stole them, but it seems equally possible that they were shown to him by treasury officials in his capacity as an 'official' historian. See Stones and Simpson, op. cit., i. 387.

to help him in his campaign, appended an itinerary and topographical maps of Scotland.[204]

Hardyng not only repeatedly reverts to the question of the overlordship of Scotland, but also to his own grievance—the inadequate reward of his labours. He virtually began and ended with petitions to Henry VI to honour his father's promise of the manor of Geddington, emphasizing the dangers he had undergone and the expenses he had incurred to obtain the 'evidences':[205] Henry V, he asserts, would never have broken his word. He relates in detail how his efforts to acquire the manor were thwarted when on the brink of success by the chancellor who[206]

> ... rather would, ere I had Geddington,
> Ye should lose your royal sovereignty
> Of Scotland, which long to your royalty.

Poverty, he explains, prevented him from pursuing the case further[207]— so he wrote his chronicle instead. However, he remained dissatisfied, and soon began to rewrite his work, this time dedicating it to Richard duke of York. In its final form the second recension continued the narrative to 1464, at the end of which year Hardyng stopped revision. But Richard of York died in 1460, and Hardyng added an invocation to Edward IV,[208] to whom he probably presented a copy at Leicester in 1463 together with the documents on the overlordship of Scotland.[209]

Change of patrons meant change of political outlook. Hardyng had written the original recension of the chronicle to please Henry VI and the Lancastrian faction; he wrote the second to please the Yorkists. His theme was in harmony with the neo-imperialism of the fifteenth century Lancastrians. Besides arguing in favour of the reconquest of Scotland, he demonstrates the right of the kings of England to France 'by succession of blood and generation': he points out that Edward III was the first English king to have the right, and praises the victories of that 'prince peerless', that 'flower of earthly worthiness [who] to the height of knighthood [did] aspire.'[210]

Hardyng's attitude to Henry VI in the first recension of his chronicle is tinged with disapproval because Henry had not kept his father's promise

---

[204] Kingsford, 'Hardyng's chronicle', pp. 740–2. For the itinerary and maps see pp. 285–7 below.

[205] Kingsford, op. cit., pp. 743, 751–2.

[206] Ibid., p. 752.

[207] Ibid., p. 743.

[208] *JH*, pp. 409–15. For Hardyng's revisions of the chronicle see Kingsford, op. cit., p. 466.

[209] This suggestion is made by Kingsford op. cit., p. 466.

[210] *JH*, pp. 335–6. The version of the chronicle in Harley MS. 661 gives the genealogical descent of the English kings from St Louis, with a prose explanation of their right to the French crown; ibid., p. 336 n. 1.

to give him Geddington.[211] However, he writes of Henry V with fulsome eulogy. He praises him for regaining his inheritance in France, 'as chroniclers have made remembrance', and for uniting England and France. He also praises him for enforcing order at home; even when fighting abroad[212]

> His shadow so obumbered all England
> That peace and law were kept continuant.

When Hardyng rewrote the chronicle in the Yorkist interest, he cut the eulogy of Henry V,[213] and inserted lines impugning Henry IV's right to the throne: Henry obtained the crown[214]

> Not for desert nor yet for any wit,
> Or might of himself. . . .

Henry's coup cast a shadow on his grandson's position, so that many said[215]

> The third heir should not [re]joice, but be uncrowned,
> And deposed of all regality.

Hardyng added criticism of Henry VI, describing him as 'of small intelligence'.[216] And in the proem he sets out the claims of Richard duke of York to his titles at home (besides the duchy, he had inherited the earldoms of Cambridge, March and Ulster) and, less convincingly, to various foreign kingdoms[217] (the crowns of France, Spain, Portugal, Italy, Jerusalem and 'other lands'—indeed he ought to rule 'all Europe . . . without any strife').[218] Hardyng especially elaborated on Richard's right to the English crown (as nephew and heir to Edmund Mortimer, earl of March) by descent through the female line from Edward III's second son Lionel: he compared his right to that of Jesus to be king of the Jews as Mary's heir.[219] Hardyng demonstrates in similar detail that Edward IV had a legitimate title to the English crown.[220]

---

[211] Kingsford, 'Hardyng's chronicle', pp. 743, 752; cf. ibid., pp. 475, 480.

[212] Kingsford, op. cit., pp. 744–5. 'Obumbered' ('aboumbred' in Hardyng) here means to overshadow; see *NED*, vii. pt i. 40, under 'obumber' 1.

[213] Compare Kingsford, 'Hardyng's chronicle', pp. 744–5, with *JH*, pp. 387–8. For Hardyng's change of viewpoint see Kingsford, op. cit., pp. 475, 480. Hardyng's second version omits his account of the education of a young warrior (see p. 274 and n. 176 above), besides the passages printed by Kingsford as peculiar to Lansdowne MS. 204 (see p. 274 n. 174 above).

[214] *JH*, p. 409; cf. *JH*, pp. 369, 371.

[215] *JH*, p. 18.

[216] *JH*, p. 410. Professor Storey uses this comment as evidence that Henry VI was a 'simpleton'; R. L. Storey, *The End of the House of Lancaster* (London 1966), p. 33. However, in view of the anti-Lancastrian bias of this version of Hardyng's chronicle, perhaps such an interpretation is rash. See pp. 497–8 and n. 1, Appendix G, below.

[217] *JH*, pp. 16–20 passim.

[218] *JH*, p. 17.

[219] *JH*, p. 17.

[220] *JH*, pp. 415–20.

Hardyng further undermined the Lancastrian claim to the throne by inserting in a long prose addition a story, which cast discredit on a member of the house of Lancaster, John of Gaunt, and showed to what lengths Gaunt was forced to go in order to establish that his son Henry Bolingbroke had any valid claim to the crown. Hardyng asserts that Gaunt fabricated evidence to prove that Bolingbroke had a hereditary right.[221] Gaunt had tried in the first place to persuade parliament to admit Henry as Richard II's heir, but he had failed because Roger Mortimer, earl of March, was heir by 'full descent of blood'. Therefore, Gaunt forged a chronicle which alleged that Henry III's second son Edmund, earl of Lancaster, was in fact his eldest son, but had been passed over in favour of Edward because he was a humpback: since the Lancastrians descended from Edmund this would have given Henry the right to the throne. Gaunt sent copies of this forgery to various religious houses, and (according to Hardyng) Henry produced it in the deposition parliament as proof of his hereditary right; however, it was 'annulled and reproved' because the evidence of reputable chronicles proved beyond doubt that King Edward was the eldest brother. ('All the chronicles of Westminster and of all other notable monasteries' were brought to Westminster 'and examined among the lords').

Nevertheless, Hardyng's chronicle does not wholly reflect Yorkist propaganda. He shows no indignation at Humphrey duke of Gloucester's fall, and condemns the duke of Suffolk's murder.[222] His attitude to Henry VI remains mildly sympathetic. He urged Edward IV in a moving invocation, written at the time when Henry, Queen Margaret and Prince Edward had taken refuge in Scotland, to treat Henry and his family leniently on account of his 'benign innocence' and his family's courage in adversity — and because it was wiser to secure their loyalty than to drive them into an alliance with France.[223]

Hardyng did not only write to please the reigning king, but also in honour of his other patrons. He praises his first patron, Henry Percy, earl of Northumberland, as a bulwark against the Scots,[224] and in the second version of the chronicle introduces a long section in prose exonerating the Percys from complicity in the Lancastrian coup of 1399.[225] Hardyng writes

---

[221] *JH*, pp. 353–4. Cf. p. 186 above.

[222] *JH*, pp. 400, 401.

[223] *JH*, pp. 410–11.

[224] See *JH*, p. 380. Hardyng also gives the descent of Lady Percy; see p. 281 and n. 244 below. In addition, he urges Richard, duke of York, to treat the Percys well because they were descendants of the earl of March: 'Your right might all been his, as now is yours: Through God's might, make them your successors'; *JH*, pp. 18–19. One fifteenth century manuscript of the second version of Hardyng's chronicle, Selden MS. B. 10, in the Bodleian Library, was owned by Henry Percy, fifth earl of Northumberland (1489–1527); his arms are on folio 198ᵛ: see *JH*, p. xv, and F. Madan et al. *Summary Catalogue of Western Manuscripts in the Bodleian Library* (Oxford 1895–1953, 7 vols in 8), ii. 617 (no. 3356).

[225] *JH*, pp. 351–4 (prose addition).

that he intends to establish the truth for all time because 'many men marvel greatly why the earl of Northumberland and Sir Henry Percy his first gotten son, and Sir Thomas Percy earl of Worcester, were supporters to King Henry the fourth, to have his heritage and to take King Richard to have depose him by strong hand.'[226] He appeals for credence to his long service in Sir Henry Percy's household, by virtue of which he had access not only to family archives,[227] but also to verbal information from the earl of Northumberland himself.[228] He asserts that the Percys sincerely believed that Henry Bolingbroke would keep the oath he had taken at Doncaster by which he promised to claim only his and his wife's inheritance, and, therefore, Northumberland, on Hotspur's advice, sent his forces home.[229] Hardyng also relates that Henry had forced Richard to renounce his right, and had been crowned 'against the will and counsel' of the earl of Northumberland and his son.[230] An account of how Henry 'unjustly, without title of law but by deceit and force' seized the throne is in the Percys' 'diffidatio' delivered before the battle of Shrewsbury, the text of which Hardyng recites.[231] The Percys' 'quarrel' with Henry in 1403 was, Hardyng asserts, both 'sweet' and 'devout', and they rebelled on the advice of Richard Scrope archbishop of York,[232] that hero of Yorkist propaganda and symbol of opposition to Lancastrian rule.[233]

Hardyng is warm in his praise of his second patron, Sir Robert Umfraville. Clearly, although Sir Robert had been dead twenty years at the time of writing, Hardyng remembered him with admiration and affection. Sir Robert had taken a vigorous part in fighting the Scots, and had also held the offices of sheriff of Northumberland,-vice admiral of the north, chamberlain of Berwick, warden of Roxburgh castle and finally warden of Berwick. Hardyng records Sir Robert's military triumphs in the course of the chronicle,[234] and has three chapters depicting him as a perfect knight.[235] He writes of him:[236]

> Of sapience and very gentleness,
> Of liberal heart and knightly governance,

[226] *JH*, p. 351 (prose addition).
[227] *JH*, pp. 351–2 (prose addition).
[228] *JH*, pp. 353–4 (prose addition).
[229] *JH*, p. 352 (prose addition).
[230] *JH*, 353 (prose addition).
[231] *JH*, pp. 352–3 (prose addition).
[232] *JH*, p. 351 (prose addition).
[233] For the Yorkist cult of Richard Scrope see J. W. McKenna, 'Popular canonization as political propaganda' (see p. 251 n. 17 above), pp. 608–23.
[234] *JH*, pp. 342, 344, 355, 357, 361, 365, 367, 373, 380–2 passim. Hardyng also records some of Sir Robert's opinions; pp. 74, 408.
[235] Kingsford, 'Hardyng's chronicle', pp. 746–8. Hardyng omitted this passage from the second version of his chronicle; ibid., p. 480.
[236] Kingsford, op. cit., p. 748. For another reference of this eulogy see p. 283 and n. 256 below.

> Of hardiment, of truth and great gladness,
> Of honest mirth without any grievance,
> Of gentle bourds[237] and knightly dalliance
> He hath no make: I dare right well avow;
> Now is he gone, I may not gloss him now. . . .
> Truly he was a jewel for a king
> In wise counsel and knightly deed of war.

Hardyng's patrons all belonged to the chivalric class, and he wrote in an appropriate style. He recounts heroic deeds—because[238]

> Old knights' acts with minstrel's tongue stir
> The new courage in young knights. . . .

He not only describes the training of a young knight,[239] but also has a chapter on the 'house of fame' ('where knights be rewarded, after the merits in arms, by Mars, the god of arms').[240] He expatiates on the exploits of King Arthur:[241]

> The hardiest man and most courageous,
> In acts martial most victorious.
> In him was never a drop of cowardice,
> Nor in his heart a point of covetise.

The tone of Hardyng's chronicle is warlike, in accordance with the tradition of romance literature. Although Hardyng regarded peace at home as desirable, this was partly because it made conquest abroad easier.[242] No doubt Hardyng's audience also appreciated his careful heraldic descriptions—for example he describes the (fictional) arms of Brutus and St George, and the (genuine) arms of Edmund of Lancaster.[243] The family pedigrees (for example the descent of Hotspur's wife Elizabeth from Lionel duke of Clarence)[244] must have had a similar appeal. Nor were women to be excluded from the pleasures of the book, which indeed begins with a tale about women—Albina and her sisters, who first came to this island, and, having been made pregnant by spirits, peopled it with giants. The original version was not only addressed to Henry VI,[245] but also to Queen Margaret, for her 'consolation'. And the proem to the second version, which is addressed to Richard duke of York, states that Hardyng wrote[246]

---

[237] Bourd: a jest, a joke; *NED*, i. pt ii. 1025, under 'bourd' *sb.*
[238] *JH*, p. 32.
[239] See p. 274 and n. 176 above.
[240] *JH*, pp. 36–9 (Chapter X).
[241] *JH*, p. 148.
[242] See pp. 282–3 below. On the desirability of peace in general see *JH*, p. 155.
[243] *JH*, pp. 39, 84, 286.
[244] *JH*, pp. 332–3.
[245] Kingsford, 'Hardyng's chronicle', p. 740.
[246] *JH*, p. 23. Cf. Hardyng's remark that 'women desire of all things sovereignty, and, to my

> To the entent to please both God and man:
> And even to please good femininity,
> Of my lady your wife dame Cecily.

Hardyng points out that he has written in English for her benefit because, although Duke Richard with his 'great intelligence' knows Latin well, 'my lady that is under your protection' has little knowledge of it. Finally Hardyng included Edward IV's wife Elizabeth in his invocation addressed to that king. Women, he writes, like 'to know all things [be]longing to their husbands', so that they can understand them properly, and the queen especially would rejoice in Edward's noble ancestors and their success.[247]

Hardyng's chronicle is much more than an exhortation to Henry VI and Edward IV to reconquer Scotland, a petition for reward, a memorial to his patrons and a catalogue of heroic deeds. Hardyng was interested in his own times for their own sake, and was especially concerned for good government. Therefore, he often adopted an exemplary tone. Addressing Richard duke of York he writes that he will recall the rule and misrule of the duke's forebears,[248]

> By which knowledge your discreet sapience,
> All vice evermore destroy may and reprove,
> By virtuous and blessedful diligence,
> And virtue love, that may not aught grieve,
> How ye shall rule your subjects, while ye live,
> In law, and peace, and all tranquillity,
> Which been the flowers of all regality.

And Richard of York should teach his son and heir, the earl of March, how to rule.[249] Hardyng constantly recurs to the duty of 'lords and princes' to keep law and order—an obvious allusion to the lawlessness and disorder of his own day. He points the moral from British history. King Keredic had fomented civil disorder and been forced to flee, with the result that Britain was left to the ravages of civil war for many years.[250] Cadwallader's failure to enforce his authority resulted not only in his own 'disinheritance' but also in his peoples' expulsion from Britain.[251] Disunity at home exposed a country to defeat by its enemies—France fell to Henry V because of internal division.[252] Moreover, as Hardyng emphasized in turn to Henry VI

concept, more in this land than in any other; for they have it of the nature of the said sisters' (that is of Albina and her sisters); *JH*, p. 26.
[247] *JH*, pp. 421–2.
[248] *JH*, p. 16.
[249] *JH*, pp. 180–1.
[250] *JH*, pp. 154–5 (Hardyng calls Keredic Carreis or Careys). Cf. Geoffrey of Monmouth, *Historia Regum Britanniae*, bk XI, cap. viii; ed. Acton Griscom (London 1929), pp. 504–5.
[251] *JH*, p. 179; cf. *JH*, pp. 175–9.
[252] *JH*, p. 180.

and Edward IV, civil war makes foreign conquest impossible.[253] History had shown that neither Scotland nor France were ever conquered by treaty or bribery, but always by military victory—which could only be achieved by a united nation.[254]

In the course of urging Henry VI, Duke Richard and Edward IV to learn the lesson of history on the necessity of keeping law and order, Hardyng describes the condition of England in his day. Particularly valuable is his account of the lawlessness during Henry VI's reign, written before he was influenced by Yorkist propaganda. He enjoins Henry to suppress the 'misrule and violence' which pervade the country, and to 'chastise well ... rioters ... and all their maintainers'.[255] The same impression of lawlessness is implied by the eulogy of Sir Robert Umfraville: he, a loyal subject of the king, was 'a true justice of peace in his country', who kept law and order with such impartiality that even the Scots beyond the Firth of Forth came to Berwick 'to stand to his decree'; he was no 'rioter' and never drew sword or knife on a fellow Englishman.[256]

Besides having an interest in the present, Hardyng was a conscientious researcher into past history. He used a wide range of sources, both oral and written. He informs the reader that he not only acquired information verbally from the earl of Northumberland[257] and Sir Robert Umfraville,[258] but also learnt of the extravagance and depravity of Richard II's court from 'Robert Ireleffe, a clerk of the green cloth'.[259] The number of his written sources, both continental and of English origin, is impressive. For example he cites Apuleius,[260] 'Hugh de Genesis, a Roman historiographer',[261] and Bartholomew Anglicus' *De Proprietatibus Rerum*.[262] Among English authorities he used Nennius,[263] Bede,[264] Florence of Worcester (whom he refers to as Marianus Scotus),[265] the *Flores Historiarum*[266] and at least one version of the *Brut*.[267] In addition, he is the only fifteenth century

---

[253] Kingsford, 'Hardyng's chronicle', p. 750–1; *JH*, p. 413.

[254] *JH*, p. 413.

[255] Kingsford, op. cit., pp. 749–50; cf. Kingsford, *Hist. Lit.* pp. 145–6.

[256] Kingsford, 'Hardyng's chronicle', pp. 746–7.

[257] See p. 280 and n. 228 above

[258] *JH*, p. 408.

[259] *JH*, p. 346. This passage is noted by T. F. Tout, *Chapters in the Administrative History of Mediaeval England* (Manchester 1920–33, 6 vols), iv. 46 n. 2, who erroneously calls Robert Ireleffe Richard Ireleffe. Tout accuses Hardyng, perhaps in excessively disparaging terms, of grossly exaggerating the extravagance of Richard II's household. For the 'board of green cloth' see ibid., ii. 41 and n. 1.

[260] *JH*, p. 115.

[261] E.g. *JH*, pp. 26–9 passim.

[262] E.g. *JH*, p. 30.

[263] E.g. *JH*, p. 85.

[264] E.g. *JH*, pp. 157, 186, 195.

[265] E.g. *JH*, pp. 29, 30, 39.

[266] E.g. *JH*, pp. 167, 191, 193.

[267] Kingsford points out that 'the main thread of Hardyng's whole history from 1399–1437 was derived, whether directly or through an intermediary, from some version of the *Brut*';

author besides Thomas Elmham known to have used the *Gesta Henrici Quinti*.[268] Once he describes how he obtained access to a book: through the influence of Cardinal Beaufort he obtained daily instruction in Justin's Epitome of Pompeius Trogus from Julian Caesarini, then auditor of Pope Martin's chamber, probably when Caesarini was in London as papal envoy in 1426–7.[269]

Hardyng also consulted documents, citing them to give added authority to his statements. He records both that he used the Percy archives,[270] and that Sir Robert Umfraville showed him in London the sealed agreement between John of Gaunt and Edmund of Langley, duke of York (d. 1402), for the latter's marriage to Peter of Castile's daughter Isabella. (Umfraville had apparently borrowed the document from Edmund.) Hardyng read it to Umfraville, and cites it in his chronicle as evidence that Duke Richard, being Edmund's nephew and heir, had a claim to Castile and Leon, because Isabella had inherited them in accordance with the terms of the marriage settlement.[271]

Hardyng's work has a noticeably antiquarian element, and he can be regarded as a forerunner of John Rous and William Worcester. His interest in heraldry is demonstrated by his descriptions of coats-of-arms,[272] but

---

Kingsford, 'Hardyng's chronicle', p. 478. He also concludes that the 'chronicle of Master Norham' which Hardyng cites in marginal notes in the Lansdowne MS. at the beginning of the reigns of Henry IV, Henry V and Henry VI, was a version of the Latin *Brut*; ibid., pp. 476 and n. 69, 477–8. Cf. *JH*, p. xiv.

[268] Hardyng borrows, making small additions, his account of the siege of Harfleur and the battle of Agincourt mainly from the *Gesta Henrici Quinti*; *JH*, pp. 389–91 (Latin prose addition). Cf. Kingsford, 'Hardyng's chronicle', p. 463, *GH V*, p. xlix (Hardyng's additions are noted in *GH V*, pp. 23 n. 3, 33 n. 3. 47 n. 1, 59 n. 6), and J. H. Wylie, *The Reign of Henry V* (Cambridge 1914–29, 3 vols), ii. 87. For Elmham's use of the *Gesta* see pp. 206–7 above.

[269] See *JH*, p. vii, and Kingsford, 'Hardyng's chronicle', p. 464 and n. 13. Julian Caesarini was made a cardinal in 1430, presided over the Council of Basle, was bishop of Grosseto 1439–44, and cardinal bishop of Frascati 1444 (d. 1444). For his patronage of humanism see L. F. A. Pastor, *History of the Popes from the Close of the Middle Ages*, ed., and translated into English, F. I. Antrobus and others (London 1891–1953, 40 vols), i. 268. For his mission to England see *Cal. Papal Registers, 1417–1431*, pp. 16, 34, 36.

[270] See p. 280 and n. 227 above.

[271] *JH*, pp. 20–1. For Isabella's marriage to Edmund of Langley see P. E. Russell, *The English Intervention in Spain and Portugal in the Time of Edward III and Richard II* (Oxford 1955), p. 176. In reply to a letter of mine Professor Russell informed me (24 February 1976) that he has never come across any trace of an agreement of the kind mentioned by Hardyng. He writes: 'In Spanish terms the agreement would lack any validity since Salic law did not of course apply in Castile and any child of John of Gaunt and Constance would have been, from the legitimist point of view, the heir to the throne irrespective of sex . . . .' But Professor Russell continues that the lack of evidence does not, 'of course, cast any real doubt on the supposed agreement between John of Gaunt and Edmund except in the sense that, if it was as set out, it would add a new dimension of unreality to the Lancastrian intervention in Castile. Certainly, however, John of Gaunt must have learnt better later on, as there is no mention whatever of Edmund Langley's children in the final settlement, which is entirely based on the acceptance by both sides that Constance was the legitimist heiress to the throne.' For the agreement making Constance heiress see ibid., pp. 173–5.

[272] See p. 281 above.

his antiquarianism can best be seen in his research on Scottish history. He gives an etymology of the name of the Scots—it derived, he asserts, from the word for a gathering of the people, a 'scotte', though one chronicler alleges that it came from the name of Scota, daughter of King Pharaoh, an early settler in Scotland.[273] He gives the history of the stone of Scone,[274] and correctly points out that until Henry V's reign the king's head on Scottish coins faced sideways ('to his sovereign lord of England as I see'), while thereafter it looked straight ahead, symbolizing, in Hardyng's opinion, the equality the kings of Scotland then presumed to claim with their lord.[275] Even Hardyng's forgeries, which were intended to prove the right of the English kings to overlordship of Scotland, can be regarded as illustrations of his antiquarianism. Sir Francis Palgrave wrote:[276]

> [Hardyng] was a diligent antiquary, a collector of ancient documents, and the style of the forgeries is just such as would result from an individual possessing archaeological knowledge, and yet using it according to the uncritical character of his age.

Most remarkable is Hardyng's interest in the topography of Scotland. Although the knowledge he acquired is far from accurate, it was the result of considerable research. He compiled the itinerary and drew the maps at the command of Henry V, so that the king would know where his fleet might harbour and where his army could march and find food, shelter, 'guns and ordinance'.[277] Hardyng appended the itinerary in verse and the maps, which occupy three pages, to the earliest recension of his chron-

---

[273] *JH*, p. 86. Scotland takes its name from the Scotti of Ireland who settled Argyle in the sixth century. The derivation of the name Scot itself is obscure; see *NED*, viii. pt ii. 246, under 'Scot' *sb*. Hardyng's 'scotte' is presumably related to the 'scot' as in 'scotale'; ibid., viii. pt ii. 247, under 'scotale'.

[274] *JH*, p. 87.

[275] *JH*, pp. 87–8. Coins were first minted in Scotland in the reign of David I (1124–53); the bust of the king on the obverse was in profile until the reign of Robert III (1390–1406) when the full-face portrait was adopted (which continued until the reign of James V, 1514–42): see H. A. Grueber, *Handbook of the Coins of Great Britain and Ireland in the British Museum* (revised edition, London 1970), pp. 170 et seq., and P. F. Purvey, *Coins and Tokens of Scotland*, *Seaby's Standard Catalogue of British Coins*, iv (Seaby's Numismatic Publications Ltd, London 1972) pp. 13–34. (The full-face portrait may, however, have been introduced at the end of the reign of Robert II, 1371–90; see Edward Burns, *The Coinage of Scotland* (Edinburgh 1887, 3 vols), i. 364.) Although Scottish coins in general approximate to the English ones (see Burns, op. cit., i. 3), with regard to the royal bust their practice diverges; in the twelfth century some English coins have the portrait in profile, some full-face, but from the thirteenth until the late fifteenth century the portrait is full-face. Perhaps Scottish moneyers retained the profile portrait in the thirteenth and fourteenth centuries in order to distinguish their coins from the English ones; or perhaps they were more influenced than English moneyers by Roman prototypes (the full-face portrait belongs to the Byzantine tradition).

[276] *Documents and Records illustrating the History of Scotland*, ed. Palgrave, p. ccxxiii. Palgrave was here referring to the content of the forgeries, not of their style and handwriting which belong to Hardyng's own time.

[277] Kingsford, 'Hardyng's chronicle', p. 742.

icle; he gives the itinerary in prose in the second recension.[278] His declared purpose was to help Henry VI and Edward IV in the conquest of Scotland. The route indicated from Berwick to Edinburgh and then on to Ross, was that taken by Henry IV in 1400 ('as I well kenned').[279] Hardyng names the towns, gives the mileage between them (in the margins), and has brief topographical notes and advice on how to conduct the campaign. The first page of the maps covers the lowlands; it sketches the seas and rivers and has the names of the places with conventional pictures of fortifications. The second is of the highlands and marks the seas and principal rivers with topographical notes useful for an invading army. Hardyng writes, for example, that there are[280]

> the castle of Kildrummy and many good castles and villages with victual in which is corn, cattle and grass [in] great plenty to the east sea, and on a sea side a good merchant town, Aberdeen, where ships may meet you on the east sea.

The top third of the next page completes the highlands to Sutherland and Caithness. Hardyng's map of the lowlands is moderately accurate. His map of the highlands is less so. It is very sketchy, and he inadvertently transposed east and west: it may be suggested that he drew the map on information derived from itineraries.

The bottom two thirds of the final page devoted to the map of Scotland are occupied by three stanzas framed by the towers of a castle which in their turn are surrounded by the four infernal rivers. In the verses Hardyng uses a simile to reinforce his invective against the Scots, and to emphasize the necessity of subduing them. He compares Scotland with Hades where Pluto reigns in the palace of pride. The four infernal rivers flow continually and the wind blows misrule throughout the land ('as scripture saith *a*

---

[278] Ellis prints the verse version of the itinerary from Lansdowne MS. 204 in his text; *JH*, pp. 422–9: he prints the prose version from Harley MS. 661 in a footnote; ibid., pp. 414–20 n. 12. Three copies of Hardyng's map are known. One is in the first version of the chronicle Lansdowne MS. 204, ff. 226ᵛ, 227; reproduced D. G. Moir, *The Early Maps of Scotland to 1850* (Royal Scottish Geographical Society, Edinburgh 1973), facing p. 5. The two others are in the second version of the chronicle, Harley MS. 661, ff. 187–8 (a page is reproduced Plate XI), and Selden MS. B 10, ff. 184–5 (reproduced in R[ichard] G[ough], *British Topography* (London 1780, 2 vols), ii. 579, and in *Facsimiles of National Manuscripts of Scotland*, photozincographed by Colonel Sir Henry James (Record Publications, Edinburgh, 1867–72, 3 pts), pt ii. For the value of Hardyng's maps see Moir, op. cit., pp. 6, 163. Cf. *JH*, pp. xiv-xvi, and Kingsford, 'Hardyng's chronicle', p. 476.

[279] *JH*, p. 414 n. 12.

[280] Harley MS. 661, f. 187ᵛ. For Kildrummy Hardyng writes Mundromy (the same reading occurs in Selden MS. B 10, f. 184ᵛ). Professor Stones, however, confirmed the identification which I had suggested with Kildrummy in a letter to me, pointing out that, as it is spelt Kyndromyn in one Scottish document, the substitution of 'n' for 'l' is not without precedent (see *Anglo-Scottish Relations 1174–1328: Some Selected Documents*, ed. Stones, p. 255); the misreading of the first two letters could well be the result of English ignorance of Scottish place-names.

borea omne malum'). The wild Scots live in the highlands, their own 'mansion' (presumably the castle of the picture),[281]

> And the wilder they been without regiment
> The sooner must they be meeked and tamed.

There can be no doubt that Hardyng's hatred of the Scots was genuine and that his desire for their defeat was sincere. He abuses them in traditional north country style, as Guisborough and Langtoft had done before him; the Scots were perennial rebels and robbers, ever crafty and treacherous.[282] Nevertheless, the care he expended on Scottish topography suggests that his interest in Scotland was partly objective, especially as neither Henry VI nor Edward IV had any immediate plans for invasion. Richard Grafton, the first editor of the *Chronicle*, paid tribute to Hardyng in his verse preface:[283]

> Neither is there any that ever wrote,
> Which in matters of Scotland could better skill, . . .
> Or better knew water, wood, town, vale and hill.

---

[281] *JH*, p. 420 n. For the image of the castle as the devil's fortress in sermon literature see G. R. Owst, *Literature and the Pulpit in Medieval England* (second edition, Oxford 1961), pp. 81–4. The analogy of a castle with hell or Hades occurs in romance literature (for the equation of hell with Hades see Rosemond Tuve, *Allegorical Literature* (Princeton 1966), pp. 228–9). See, for example, Perlesvaus' defeat of the black knights in the castle (identified as hell) of the Black Hermit (identified as Lucifer), an episode based on the 'harrowing of hell'; *Le Haut Livre du Graal Perlesvaus*, ed. W. A. Nitze and T. A. Jenkins (Chicago 1932–7, 2 vols), i. 54–5, 63, 109, 401–2 (lines 757–65, 966, 2180–3, 9942 et seq.); ii. 233–4. For another possible example see Sir Orfeo's rescue of his wife from the fairy castle which some scholars identify as Hades: *Sir Orfeo*, ed. A. J. Bliss (Oxford 1966), pp. 34–5; cf. G. V. Smithers, 'Story-patterns in some Breton lays' in *Medium Ævum*, xxii (1953), pp. 85–8, and Constance Davies, 'Classical threads in "Orfeo"' in *Modern Language Review*, lvi (1961), pp. 161–6.

[282] See e.g. *JH*, p. 414. For the views of Guisborough and Langtoft see Gransden, *Historical Writing*, i. 475.

[283] *JH*, p. 11. For Grafton's edition see p. 274 n. 174 above.

10

Chroniclers of the Wars of the Roses: Foreign

Abroad England was news. The Hundred Years' War had of course always attracted attention, and this interest extended to other aspects of English affairs. The prowess of Englishmen in France was but an expression of their chivalric tradition at home, a subject which might well arouse the curiosity of knights and nobles on the continent. Moreover, dramatic and bloody events exercise a perennial fascination, whether the deposition of Richard II,[1] the battles of the Wars of the Roses, Richard III's usurpation, or the murder of the little princes in the Tower. And continental statesmen needed accurate information on the political situation in England because she was part of the European diplomatic scene.

We have remarked above that chivalric historiography did not flourish in fifteenth century England. The fact that the valiant deeds of British and English heroes were not adequately recorded was lamented by one foreign chronicler, the Fleming Jean de Waurin, lord of Forestal.[2] Waurin was born in about 1394, an illegitimate member of a noble family of Artois.[3] As a young man he entered the service of John the Fearless, duke of Burgundy, fighting in the duke's army and with his English allies. He fought at Agin-

---

[1] For accounts of Richard II's deposition and death written in France see pp. 161–2, 188–9 above. For French interest in the English as regicides see p. 189 n. 189 above.

[2] The part of Waurin's chronicle from Albina to 688 and 1399–1471 is printed *Recueil des Croniques et Anchiennes Istories de la Grant Bretaigne, a present nomme Engleterre, par Jehan de Waurin*, ed. William Hardy and E. L. C. P. Hardy (RS 1864–91, 5 vols), the edition cited below. The part 1325–1471 is printed *Anchiennes Cronicques d'Engleterre par Jehan de Waurin*, ed. L. E. E. Dupont (Soc. de l'Histoire de France 1858, 3 vols). An English translation of the part from Albina to 688 and 1399–1431 is by William Hardy and E.L.C.P. Hardy (RS 1864–91, 3 vols). Waurin himself divided his chronicle into six volumes (see p. 289 and n. 14 below), subdivided into books and chapters (references to these are given below in brackets). The Hardys' volumes do not correspond to Waurin's; a list of the chapter headings, under volume and book headings, in those parts of Waurin's work which the Hardys print, excluding Waurin's volume VI, together with volume and page references to the Hardys' edition, are in *Waurin*, i. ccxxi-ccxxxiv; iv. xiii-xliii. For Waurin's comment on the lack of histories of England in the chivalric style see p. 274.

[3] *Waurin*, i. xxi; cf. *Waurin*, 1.3 (prologue). For Waurin's life, with quotations translated into English from his chronicle, see *Waurin*, i. xv-xlvi; cf. Dupont, op. cit., i. xiii-xxxvi.

Synopsis

The marriage of Margaret of Anjou to Lancastrian King Henry VI of England is arranged as part of a peace treaty between England and France. A proxy engagement and marriage is performed in 1445 at Nancy, the duke of Suffolk, standing in for King Henry. As celebrations are taking place, King Charles of France is re-organizing his army into efficient units of operation.

Chapters two to six of Part One define the political situation in England. The Yorkists claim

court[4] and in other battles against the French.[5] After the treaty of Arras in 1435, which ended the Anglo-Burgundian alliance, Waurin retired from the army, though he served John's successor, Philip the Good, and then Charles the Bold in other capacities.[6] He was the dukes' councillor and chamberlain,[7] and spent some of his time at the ducal court. Already by 1442 it seems that Duke Philip had rewarded Waurin for his services with the seigneuries of Forestal and Fontaine.[8] At least once Philip the Good sent Waurin on a diplomatic mission; in 1463 he was one of an embassy to Pope Pius II to discuss how to combat the Turks.[9] In 1467 he accompanied the duke's illegitimate son Anthony, count de la Roche, to England where the count was to joust with Lord Scales, but the occasion was interrupted by news of Philip's death.[10] Waurin also served Charles the Bold; in 1469 he was with Charles's court when he met the earl of Warwick at Calais.[11] But despite Waurin's active public career, he spent much time settled at Lille after his marriage in about 1437 to Marguerite Hangouart, the widow of a burgess.[12]

Waurin probably began writing history in 1446, with an account of the naval expedition sent by Duke Philip to Constantinople to fight the Turks in 1444. The fleet was commanded by Waurin's nephew and former companion in arms, Waleran lord of Waurin. The clarity and detail of the narrative and the prominence given to Waleran's exploits suggest that Waurin must have written on Waleran's information and probably at his request.[13] Waleran certainly asked him to write his larger project, the *Recueil des Croniques et Anchiennes Istories de la Grant Bretaigne, a present nomme Engleterre*, a chronicle of England from Brutus until originally the death of Henry V, in four volumes. Waurin seems to have started collecting material for the chronicle at about the same time as he wrote the narrative of the expedition against the Turks, and he completed it in 1455. However, soon after Edward IV's accession in 1461, Waurin added another volume bringing the chronicle down to 1443. Then he added a sixth volume which continued to Edward's readeption in 1471.[14] Finally he revised this last

---

[4] Waurin mentions his own presence at Agincourt; *Waurin*, ii. 229 (vol. V, bk I, c. 14), iii. 109 (vol. V, bk III, c. 29). Cf. *Waurin*, i. xxiv and n. 1.

[5] For references to Waurin's presence see e.g. *Waurin*, iii. 70, 101, 109 (vol. V, bk III, cc. 17, 28, 29), and p. 292 below. For further examples see *Waurin*, i. xxvii-xl.

[6] *Waurin*, i. xxxix-xlvi.

[7] *Waurin*, i. xlv n. 1.

[8] See *Waurin*, i. xli and n. 2.

[9] *Waurin*, i. xlii and n. 2, and Dupont, op. cit., i. xxxi and n. 37. The embassy is noticed in the continuation of Monstrelet, s.a. 1463; *Chroniques d'Enguerran de Monstrelet* (Paris 1895, 3 vols), iii. 98.

[10] *Waurin*, v. 542–3 (vol. VI, bk V, c. 26).

[11] *Waurin*, v. 578 (vol. VI, bk V, c. 45).

[12] *Waurin*, i. xli.

[13] *Waurin*, i. xli-xlii. See p. 290 and n. 15 below.

[14] For the arrangement and composition of the chronicle see *Waurin*, i. xlvii-xlix. A synopsis of the contents of Waurin's six volumes is in *Waurin*, i. xlix-li.

volume and incorporated his piece on the expedition against the Turks.[15]

Waurin gives his initial motives for writing the chronicle in the prologue.[16] He asserts that after Waleran's return from Constantinople, they often discussed together the heroic deeds of the Trojans, Greeks, Romans and others in ancient times, and equally of the French and their neighbours in their own day whose 'prowess and renown deserve perpetual remembrance.' Waurin and Waleran particularly talked about 'that noble and ancient kingdom of Britain', and were amazed that no Englishman had adequately commemorated the 'lofty enterprises' achieved by the valour of the 'excellent and powerful kings and princes ... and by the many noble knights'. Therefore Waurin, encouraged by Waleran's promise of 'aid and counsel', and in order to avoid idleness now that he was too old to pursue the profession of arms, undertook to remedy the deficiency.

Waurin's interest in the history of England no doubt originated in the days when he fought with the English against the French. It must have been fostered by his service in the Burgundian court; like Commynes he came into contact with the rival English kings and with members of the nobility when they were in exile on the continent or engaged on diplomatic missions. Whenever possible he seems to have taken the opportunity to pursue his historical studies. After visiting Calais in 1469 in the entourage of Charles the Bold, he returned there because the earl of Warwick had promised to put him in touch with a man who could supply him with information he needed for his chronicle:[17]

> So I went to visit him, and he entertained me for nine days with good cheer and much honour; but I obtained very little of the information I sought, though he promised that if I came back at the end of two months he would supply me with part of what I wanted; and on my taking leave of him, he paid all my expenses and gave me a fine saddle horse. I saw plainly that he was busy with other important matters.

Charles the Bold was obviously interested in Waurin's work. Knowing of the earl of Warwick's promise to help, he gave him permission for the visit to Calais,[18] and it was from the ducal archives that Waurin obtained the copy of the *Arrival of Edward IV*, and perhaps of the *Chronicle of the Rebellion in Lincolnshire*, both of which he transcribed into his chronicle.[19]

Clearly Waurin wrote for a wider audience than just his immediate patron, Waleran. There must once have been a copy of his chronicle made for presentation to Charles the Bold, and perhaps one also for Philip the

[15] *Waurin*, v. 5–119 (vol. VI, bk I, cc. 2–19).
[16] *Waurin*, i. 1–3.
[17] *Waurin*, v. 578–9 (vol. VI, bk V, c. 45); cf. *Waurin*, i. xlv-xlvi.
[18] *Waurin*, v. 578 (vol. VI, bk V, c. 45).
[19] See p. 264 and nn. 102, 105 above.

Good. The extant manuscripts show that both royalty and the nobility acquired copies. Those surviving are all richly illuminated with excellent miniatures. A particularly fine copy was made for Edward IV;[20] another was owned by Louis de Bruges, seigneur de Gruthuyse and earl of Winchester (1472–92),[21] and another by the counts of Marche.[22] And there is also a copy which has a shield with arms surmounted by a marquis's coronet in many of the illuminated vignettes.[23]

Waurin provided a very readable history of England in the romance style, equally suitable for reading privately or aloud to a chivalric audience.[24] He used a variety of sources, both English and continental, acknowledging some by name. However, he acknowledges others in general terms (for example 'the chronicles of Scotland' and 'the chronicles of France'[25]), which, combined with the fact that he usually paraphrased his sources, makes identification difficult.[26] His principal source for the early part, the British history, and for the history of England until the beginning of the fourteenth century, was a lost version (or versions) of the *Brut*.[27] For

[20] BL MS. Royal 15 E IV contains volume I of the chronicle written for presentation to Edward IV. Volume III is BL MS. Royal 14 E IV. The other volumes are lost. The text has its own distinctive prologue addressed to Edward IV, in place of the prologue in the other manuscripts: the Hardys suggest that it may be a pirated copy, but there seems no good reason to doubt Waurin's authorship. See *Waurin*, i. ccxiii–ccxiv and n. 2, ccxv, and, for a printed text of the prologue, ibid., i. 608–11. See also Margaret Kekewich, 'Edward IV, William Caxton and literary patronage in Yorkist England' in *Modern Language Review*, lxvi (1971), pp. 484–5, and p. 264 above and Plate IX.

[21] Bibliothèque Nationale MSS. fr. 6748–59. This is the only known complete manuscript of the chronicle and was the Hardys' exemplar; *Waurin*, i. xvi and n. 1, ccxi–ccxiii, ccxvi. Louis de Bruges, seigneur de Gruthuyse, the duke of Burgundy's governor in Holland, befriended Edward IV when he was in exile in 1470; the king and part of his entourage stayed with Louis in the Hôtel de Gruthuyse at Bruges from January to February, 1471. After his readeption Edward rewarded Louis for his services with a grand welcome in London in 1472, and the earldom of Winchester: Frederic Madden in *Archaeologia*, xxvi (1835), pp. 265–84; G. W. Watson in the *Genealogist*, new series, xiv (1898), pp. 73–6. Louis was a patron of letters and had a magnificent library; see Madden, op. cit., pp. 271–4, and, with a catalogue of his books, J. Van Praet, *Recherches sur Louis de Bruges* (Paris 1831), pp. 81–324 (for Louis's copy of Waurin see ibid., pp. 241–8, no. 95). His example no doubt encouraged Edward IV to build up his own library; the king commissioned numerous manuscripts to be executed for him in Flanders, such as the above mentioned copy of Waurin, and that of Froissart (p. 90 n. 199)—besides those of the *Arrival* (pp. 265 above, 481–4, Appendix B, below). Cf. C. A. J. Armstrong, 'L' échange culturel entre le cours d'Angleterre et de Bourgogne à l'époque de Charles le Téméraire' in *500ᵉ Anniversaire de la Bataille de Nancy (1477). Actes du colloque organisé par l'Institut de recherche régionale en sciences sociales, humaines et économiques de l'Université de Nancy II (Nancy, 22–24 Sept. 1977)* (Nancy 1979), pp. 43–4. I owe this reference to Dr Malcolm Vale.

[22] Bibliothèque Nationale MSS. fr. 6746, 6747 (vols I and II of the chronicle). See *Waurin*, i. ccxiii.

[23] Bibliothèque Nationale MS. fr. 6761 (vol. II of the chronicle). See *Waurin*, i. ccxiii.

[24] In the prologue Waurin begs all who 'read or hear' the chronicle to improve and correct it, *Waurin*, i. 3.

[25] *Waurin*, i. xcv, clii; Waurin, vol. I, bk IV, c. 52 (not in printed text); *Waurin*, iv. 385 (vol. V, bk VI, c. 20).

[26] The Hardys review at length the sources used by Waurin; *Waurin*, i. li–ccx. It seems likely that further research would lead to the identification of even more.

[27] *Waurin*, i. lix–xcvi passim.

the fourteenth century he used mainly Froissart, and for the fifteenth century until 1444 his chronicle is related to the chronicle by the Picard noble, Enguerran de Monstrelet (which covers the years from 1400 to 1444 and includes details of the English campaigns and diplomacy in the Hundred Years' War).[28]

As the fifteenth century proceeds, Waurin adds an increasing amount of material independent of all known chronicles, and after Monstrelet ends he is wholly independent except for the sections on the Lincolnshire rebellion and on Edward IV's readeption.[29] Waurin based his original passages on his own experience and observation, from what he heard, and no doubt from newsletters. He is often inaccurate, but does on occasion record vivid impressions and interesting opinions. There is, for example, a first hand account of the battle of Verneuil (in 1424) which includes this description of the duke of Bedford's bravery:[30]

> The duke of Bedford, as I heard say (for I could not see or understand everything, because I was pretty well occupied defending myself) performed marvellous feats of arms and slew many a man. He laid about him with his axe which he held in both hands—there was nothing he did not strike down; he was a man of great physical strength, with very powerful limbs, and both prudent and fearless in arms.

Waurin gives a full account of the Wars of the Roses with detailed descriptions of the battles, based at least in part on oral information.[31] Nor was he only interested in military history. He also comments on the personalities of the times and tries to interpret the political scene. For example he describes how the earl of Warwick consolidated his power:[32]

> This earl of Warwick had in great measure the voice of the people, because he knew how to persuade them with beautiful soft speeches; he was conversable and talked familiarly with them— subtle, as it were, in order to gain his ends. He gave them to understand that he would promote the prosperity of the kingdom and defend the interests of the people with all his power, and that as long as he lived he would never do otherwise. Thus he acquired

[28] From 1400 to 1443 Waurin either used Monstrelet's chronicle or a common source; see *Waurin*, i. xii and n. 1, cxxxiii-cxlii. Waurin could have known Monstrelet, who died in 1453, personally; see *Waurin*, i. xii n. 1. Monstrelet's chronicle is printed *La Chronique d'Enguerran de Monstrelet en deux Livres avec piëces justificatives, 1400–1444*, ed. L. Douet-D'Arcq (Soc. de l'Histoire de France 1857–62, 6 vols). For Monstrelet's life and work see A. M. L. E. Molinier, *Les Sources de l'Histoire de France des Origines aux Guerres d'Italie, 1494* (Manuels de Bibliographie Historiques, no. 3, 1901, 5 vols), iv. 192–4 (no. 3946).

[29] P. 264 and nn. 102, 105 above.

[30] *Waurin*, iii. 114 (vol. V, bk III, c. 38).

[31] For his use of oral information for the first battle of St Albans and for the battle of Towton see *Waurin*, v. 268, 341 (vol. VI, bk III, c. 9; vol. VI, bk III, c. 48), respectively; cf. *Waurin*, i. clxxiii, clxxxiii.

[32] *Waurin*, v. 319 (vol. VI, bk III, c. 36).

the goodwill of the people of England to such an extent that he was the prince whom they held in the highest esteem, and on whom they placed the greatest faith and reliance.

An example of Waurin's analysis of political motivation is the reason he gives for the opposition of Edward IV's counsellors to the king's marriage with Elizabeth Woodville—an explanation which a recent scholar accepts as probable.[33] When Edward put his plan to them,[34]

> they told him that she was not his match; however good and fair she might be, he must know well that she was no wife for so high a prince as himself; she was not the daughter of a duke or earl, but her mother, the duchess of Bedford, had married a knight by whom she had had two children before her marriage. Therefore, although she was the daughter of the duchess of Bedford and the niece of the count of St Pol, she was not, all things considered, a suitable wife for him, nor a woman of the kind who ought to belong to such a prince.

The large quantity of diplomatic correspondence produced in the fifteenth century demonstrates the importance to rulers of information about events abroad. The ambassadors of Francesco Sforza, duke of Milan, and his successors sent back regular newsletters.[35] Thus Prospero di Camulio kept the duke informed of events in England. Besides general comment on the violence of the English, he weighed the relative strength of the political factions and estimated King Edward's chances of success.[36] Nor was Francesco's interest merely the result of love of colourful news. He needed to know Edward's strength before inducing him to undertake the reconquest of England's continental possessions—in order to distract the French from his own schemes in Naples (he planned to help the Aragonese dynasty against the Angevin one which was backed by Charles VII of France).[37]

The French kings and nobility were interested in English affairs as combatants in the Hundred Years' War, and because of the Anglo-Burgundian alliance. This concern is reflected by the French chroniclers, the most important of whom wrote either while in, or after retirement from royal or ducal service. For example Jean de Roye, the author of the 'scandalous chronicle' covering the years from 1460 to 1483, was secretary of the duke of Bourbon;[38] Thomas Basin, bishop of Lisieux, born of a bourgeois

---

[33] Charles Ross, *Edward IV* (London 1974), p. 89.

[34] *Waurin*, v. 455 (vol. VI, bk IV, c. 34).

[35] See *Calendar of State Papers and Manuscripts existing in the Archives and Collections of Milan*, i, *1385–1618*, ed. A. B. Hinds (London 1913), pp. ix-xxxix, 20–245 passim.

[36] Ibid., pp. 59–60.

[37] Ibid., pp. ix-x.

[38] His chronicle is printed *Journal de Jean de Roye connu sous le nom de Chronique Scandaleuse, 1460–1483*, ed. Bernard de Mandrot (Soc. de l'Histoire de France 1894–6, 2 vols). For his life and work see the introduction to ibid. and Molinier, op. cit., v. 24–5 (no. 4666).

Norman family, whose history covers the reigns of Charles VII and Louis XI, was a councillor of King Charles and took an active part in public life under him and then under Louis, until royal disfavour forced him to retire to Utrecht, where he lived under Burgundian protection and wrote his history;[39] and Jean Molinet, born at Desvres, Pas-de-Calais, wrote his chronicle of the years from 1474 to 1506 while employed as the official historiographer of the duke of Burgundy.[40] None of these writers is very reliable for events in England and their statements are sometimes based on wild rumour—Molinet for instance asserts that Richard III made Edward IV's eldest daughter Elizabeth, Henry VII's future queen, pregnant.[41]

However, two works written in France are of more importance for English history: one is the *Mémoires* of Philippe de Commynes, for the years from 1464 to 1498;[42] the other is Dominic Mancini's *De Occupatione Regni Anglie* (*On the Usurpation of the Kingdom of England*),[43] an account of Richard III's seizure of power in 1483. Both were dedicated to Angelo Cato, archbishop of Vienne.[44] Cato was born in Benevento before 1440, studied at the university of Naples and became physician and librarian to King Ferrante. Regarding the advent of printing 'as a gift of God', he began to edit and publish texts (mainly on medicine) in 1474. In 1475 he went with the king's son Frederick prince of Taranto to the court of Charles the Bold of Burgundy. There he apparently stayed until 1479 or 1480, when he joined the court of Louis XI, becoming the king's physician, councillor and confidant, and was rewarded with the arch-

---

[39] His chronicle is printed *Histoire de Charles VII*, ed., with a French translation, Charles Samaran and Henry de Surirey de Saint-Rémy (Les Classiques de l'Histoire de France au Moyen Age 1934–44, 2 vols), and *Histoire de Louis XI*, ed., with a French translation, Charles Samaran and M. C. Garand (Les Classiques de l'Histoire de France au Moyen Age 1963–72, 3 vols). For Basin's life and work see the introduction to Samaran and Garand, op. cit., i. vii–xxii, and Molinier, op. cit., iv. 245–7 (no. 4137).

[40] His chronicle is printed *Chroniques de Jean Molinet, 1474–1506*, ed. G. Doutrepont and O. Jodogne (Académie Royale Belgique, Classe des Lettres et des Sciences Morales et Politiques, Collection des Anciens Auteurs Belges, Brussels 1935–7, 3 vols). For his life and work see the introduction to ibid., iii. 15–56.

[41] *Chroniques de Jean Molinet*, i. 432. For the prevalence of unfounded rumours abroad see Ross, *Edward IV*, p. 433. Commynes himself told Warwick's supporters in Calais in 1470 that Edward IV was dead although, as he confesses, he knew the statement to be false; *PC*, i. 209 (bk III, c. 6). For Commynes's *Mémoires* see below and the next note.

[42] The standard edition, that used here, is *Philippe de Commynes, Mémoires*, ed. J. L. A. Calmette and G. Durville (Les Classiques de l'Histoire de France au Moyen Age 1924–5, 3 vols). Another good edition is by L. M. E. Dupont; see p. 484, Appendix B, below. A recent English translation of the memoirs for the reign of Louis XI, with a useful introduction on Commynes's life and work, is by Michael Jones (Penguin Books 1972).

[43] Printed *The Usurpation of Richard III*, ed., with an English translation, C. A. J. Armstrong (Oxford 1936; second edition, that used here unless otherwise stated, Oxford 1969).

[44] *PC*, i. xii and n. 2, 1 (prologue). For Cato as Mancini's patron see p. 301 below. For Cato's life and works see *Usurpation*, pp. 26–50.

bishopric of Vienne in 1482. After Louis's death he served his successor Charles VIII. As a resident in Paris he became one of a group of humanist scholars. Meanwhile his position at court involved him in politics. He developed a keen interest in contemporary affairs and recent history. Shortly after he became archbishop he asked Mancini to inform him about events in England, when Mancini had returned from a visit he planned to make there: his enthusiasm for news was such that he required Mancini's written account almost immediately he arrived back. Meanwhile Cato collected official documents and letters relating to continental politics, and by 1489 had decided to write a Life of Louis XI. To do so he commissioned Commynes to record his recollections of the reign. Cato planned to add his own observations and turn the whole into elegant Latin. However, he never fulfilled his purpose: what remains of the scheme are Commynes's *Mémoires*. These will be discussed first, before Mancini's work, because although written later they partly concern an earlier period.

Philippe de Commynes was born in about 1447 in the castle of Renescure in Flanders.[45] His family had risen in the service of the counts of Flanders and of their successors, the dukes of Burgundy. He himself entered the service of Charles the Bold, count of Charolais, son and heir of Philip the Good, duke of Burgundy, in 1464. Charles succeeded Philip in 1467, and Commynes was knighted in 1468, taking part in the jousts held to celebrate Charles's marriage to Edward IV's sister Margaret in that year. Commynes became Charles's chamberlain and served him as an administrator and diplomat. Nevertheless, despite his success at the Burgundian court, in 1472 Commynes transferred his loyalty to Louis XI, soon gaining his confidence, and becoming important in the royal service, mainly as a diplomat. His career in the French court suffered various vicissitudes: his influence over Louis reached its height in 1477, but then his power temporarily declined. Thereafter until Louis's death in 1483, he was sometimes with the king and sometimes on embassies, but he was held in less favour than formerly. With the accession of Charles VIII, court factions aggravated his troubles and he was exiled to Dreux in 1489. He subsequently managed to regain some favour but his part in public life steadily lessened until his death in 1511; he spent an increasing amount of time on his own affairs and on the *Mémoires*, which he started while in exile at Dreux and continued writing until 1496 (he was still revising them in 1498).[46]

Commynes's career brought him into close touch with the English. He negotiated with them in his diplomatic capacity, and met those in exile on the continent, notably at the Burgundian court. Thus he acquired an interest in and knowledge of England's foreign relations which is fully

---

[45] A useful account of Commynes's life is in Michael Jones's translation of the *Mémoires* (see p. 294 n. 42 above), pp. 11–26.
[46] For the date of the composition of the *Mémoires* see *PC*, i. xii–xv.

reflected in the *Mémoires*. Charles the Bold sent Commynes to Calais in 1470 at the time of the earl of Warwick's coup and Henry VI's restoration. Warwick was captain of Calais, and the purpose of Commynes's visit, which lasted about two months, was to ensure the loyalty to Edward IV of Warwick's lieutenant, Lord John Wenlock. The latter, as Commynes describes, successfully played a double game, convincing King Edward of his loyalty and yet secretly negotiating with his enemies.[47]

Commynes had just left Calais and joined Charles at Boulogne when the news of Edward's defeat and flight reached the duke—at first it was rumoured that Edward was dead. Commynes was sent back to Calais, not without misgivings, where he found the English wearing Warwick's emblem of the ragged staff, and the doors of his own lodgings covered with graffiti—white crosses and rhymes on the good relations established between the king of France and the earl of Warwick. He succeeded in his mission, reaching an agreement with the English; the duke of Burgundy was to retain his alliance with the kingdom of England, only now it would be with Henry VI instead of Edward IV.[48] Later Commynes was with Charles when he met Edward at St Pol.[49]

Commynes again took part in diplomacy with England in 1475, this time on behalf of Louis XI of France. He was at the French court when Garter King of Arms arrived to deliver Edward's letter of defiance (which was composed 'in fine language and elegant style'), claiming the realm of France. He describes the herald's polite reception by Louis. Afterwards, Commynes writes, 'Louis called me in and told me to entertain the herald until an escort had been found to accompany him back, so that no one could speak to him, and that I should give him thirty ells of crimson velvet, which I did.'[50]

After the failure of King Edward's campaign, Commynes helped negotiate the treaty of Picquigny in 1475. He gives a detailed account of the transactions, in the course of which Louis summoned Commynes and asked Edward whether he recognized him. Edward replied 'that he did, and mentioned the places where he had seen me, and that previously I had taken much trouble serving him at Calais at the time when I was still with the duke of Burgundy.'[51] Perhaps it was on this occasion that Edward gave Commynes information about his expulsion from England in 1470, and mentioned his practice of sparing the ordinary soldiers of an enemy army when he won a battle.[52]

---

[47] *PC*, i. 190–6 (bk III, c. 4); cf. C. L. Scofield, *The Life and Reign of Edward IV* (London 1923, 2 vols), i. 521, 533, 550–3.
[48] *PC*, i. 206–12 (bk III, c. 5).
[49] *PC*, i. 139 (bk II, c. 8).
[50] *PC*, ii. 32 (bk IV, c. 5); cf. Scofield, op. cit., ii. 130–1.
[51] *PC*, ii. 66 (bk IV, c. 10); cf. Scofield, op. cit., ii. 144–5, and Ross, *Edward IV*, pp. 232–3.
[52] *PC*, i. 201, 202 (bk III, c. 5).

Commynes did not confine himself to King Edward's activities abroad. He was also concerned with English domestic history, with the intention of giving his readers an understanding of the situation in England. His motive was partly patriotic—to supply background knowledge for French diplomacy:[53]

> It is necessary for our king [Louis XI], when he is waging war, to know what is going on in many parts of his realm and in neighbouring territories. In particular he must be able to satisfy the king of England or to divert his attention by embassies, presents and fine words, so that he will not interfere in our affairs.

As a source for English history the *Mémoires* have limitations. They are in places inaccurate because Commynes wrote much later than most of the events he described, and sometimes his narrative is misleading owing to his bias in favour of Burgundy and France.[54] For example, the immediate cause to which he ascribes Edward IV's death reflects his own patriotism rather than the truth. He attributes Edward IV's death to grief at the rebuff he received from Charles VIII who failed to keep the terms of the treaty of Picquigny: instead of Edward's daughter Elizabeth, Charles married Marguerite of Austria, and stopped paying Edward the pension (which, Commynes asserts, Edward wrongly called 'tribute').[55]

Nevertheless, Commynes's involvement in diplomacy and contact with the English exiles at the Burgundian court enabled him to describe a number of leading figures at first hand, and to form some general assessment of the English and of affairs in England. He knew personally some of the nobility who fell during the Wars of the Roses, and heard of others who died from Englishmen at the Burgundian court.[56] Besides meeting King Edward there, he saw other leading figures, notably the duke of Clarence and the duke of Gloucester ('who later had himself called King Richard').[57] He also spoke with Henry Tudor at the court of Francis duke of Brittany: Henry told him that since his flight from England at the age of five with

---

[53] *PC*, ii. 240 (bk VI, c. 1).

[54] Commynes is used extensively as a source for Edward IV's reign, particularly for events in Calais in 1470 and for the English invasion of France and subsequent peace negotiations in 1475, by Scofield, op. cit. and Ross, op. cit; for references see the indices to both works. (Cf. p. 296 and nn. 47, 50, 51 above.) Although Miss Scofield remarks on one misleading passage (op. cit., i. 552–3), she otherwise tends to take Commynes's statements at face value. Professor Ross on the other hand is critical of Commynes's hostile attitude to Edward IV (Ross, op. cit., pp. 86, 148, 294, 307, 418–19, 429, 433–4, and see p. 298 below). For Commynes's view of Edward see also Jean Dufournet, *La Destruction des Mythes dans les Mémoires de Ph. de Commynes* (Geneva 1966), pp. 506–7. For the reliability of Commynes in general, with further references, see Jones, op. cit., pp. 40–2.

[55] *PC*, ii. 231 (bk V, c. 20). For another example of Commynes's patriotism, where he states that France is the most favoured land in the world, see ibid., ii. 38 (bk IV, c. 6).

[56] *PC*, i. 54 (bk I, c. 7); cf. *PC*, i. 191 (bk III, c. 4).

[57] *PC*, ii. 157 (bk V, c. 9).

his uncle the earl of Pembroke 'he had been guarded like a fugitive, or kept in prison.'[58]

Commynes left a first hand description of Edward IV:[59]

> King Edward was not outstanding as a man but he was a very handsome prince, more handsome than any other I saw at that time, and he was very valiant.

However, Commynes did not in general have a favourable opinion of King Edward. In home affairs Edward was avaricious,[60] and lacked foresight in dealing with his Lancastrian opponents,[61] and despite his courage, 'he was not suited to endure all the toil necessary for a king of England to make conquests in France.'[62] Above all Commynes emphasizes Edward's self indulgence:[63]

> He was accustomed . . . to more luxuries and pleasures than any prince of his day because he thought of nothing but women (far more than is reasonable), hunting and looking after himself. During the hunting season he had many tents brought along for the ladies.

Commynes's attitude to Richard III was hostile, no doubt reflecting opinion at the French court. He records that King Louis considered Richard 'very cruel and evil', and was unwilling to reply to his letters or listen to his envoy.[64] On the other hand he approved of Henry Tudor, who fought for the crown (to which, Commynes believed, he had no right) without money 'nor any reputation except what his own person and honesty gave him.'[65]

Commynes has a number of references to the characteristics of the English. He considered them courteous,[66] but hot tempered and bellicose.[67] They were always ready to fight in France, 'under colour of the claims they pretend to have to it and for hope of gain.'[68] As soldiers, they needed training in continental methods of warfare, but once taught they made 'very good, brave soldiers'.[69] He attributed the origin of the Wars of the Roses to the warlike propensities of the English. When, because of

---

[58] *PC*, ii. 233 (bk V, c. 20).
[59] *PC*, i. 197 (bk III, c. 5); cf. Ross, op. cit., pp. 10, 232–3.
[60] *PC*, ii. 76 (bk IV, c. 11); ii. 246 (bk VI, c. 1).
[61] *PC*, i. 200–1, 204–5 (bk III, c. 5).
[62] *PC*, ii. 77 (bk IV, c. 11). For Commynes's bias against Edward IV see p. 297 n. 54 above.
[63] *PC*, i. 203 (bk III, c. 5); cf. *PC*, ii. 245–6 (bk VI, c. 1).
[64] *PC*, ii. 305 (bk VI, c. 8). Commynes has the 'precontract' story: *PC*, ii. 305 (bk VI, c. 8); cf. p. 272 and n. 155 above.
[65] *PC*, ii. 306 (bk VI, c. 8).
[66] *PC*, i. 206 (bk III, c. 6).
[67] *PC*, i. 217 (bk III, c. 7).
[68] *PC*, ii. 240 (bk VI, c. 1).
[69] *PC*, ii. 29 (bk IV, c. 5).

the loss of their continental possessions, they could no longer campaign in France, they began fighting each other, in order to retain their status and way of life.[70] This conflict was exacerbated by the dynastic dispute[71] and resulted in 'full-scale and bloody battles'.[72] 'And so,' writes Commynes, 'within my memory more than eighty members of the English royal family, some of whom I knew, were killed in these disturbances.'[73]

However, Commynes's estimate of the English was by no means wholly adverse. He asserts that the horrors of civil war were mitigated by the fact that the English did not slaughter the common people, destroy the countryside or demolish and burn buildings.[74] But perhaps what impressed him most was the institution of parliament:[75]

> The king cannot undertake [a campaign] without assembling his parliament, which is like our Three Estates. It is a very just and laudable institution, and, therefore, the kings are stronger and better served when they [consult parliament] on such a matter. When these estates are assembled [the king] declares his intentions and asks for aid from his subjects; he cannot raise any tax in England except for an expedition to France or Scotland or some other comparable cause. They will grant them very willingly and liberally—especially for crossing to France!

To a certain extent Commynes's approach to history was traditional. He saw events as demonstrating God's power on earth: the Wars of the Roses were divine retribution on the kings of England for allowing rivalries to develop at home, and for the injuries done by their ancestors to France.[76] Richard III's death and Henry Tudor's triumph were God's punishment for Richard's wickedness.[77] Moreover, Commynes had an exemplary purpose. His work was partly intended to instruct princes how to behave, and is, therefore, in the long established medieval tradition of exemplary literature, a tradition which was continued by the humanists. Commynes saw the Wars of the Roses partly as a lesson to princes—they should prevent faction in their households lest it spread further afield.[78] Again, the treacherous trick played by Lord John Wenlock at Calais on King Edward and Charles the Bold should warn princes to be always on their guard against deception.[79] Edward IV himself was an example of a prince

---

[70] *PC*, i. 52–3 (bk I, c. 7).
[71] *PC*, ii. 230–5 (bk V, c. 20).
[72] *PC*, i. 217 (bk III, c. 7).
[73] *PC*, i. 54 (bk I, c. 7); cf. *PC*, i. 191 (bk III, c. 4).
[74] *PC*, ii. 218 (bk V, c. 19); ii. 231 (bk V, c. 20).
[75] *PC*, ii. 8 and n. 4 (bk IV, c. 1).
[76] *PC*, i. 54 (bk 1, c. 7), 192 (bk III, c. 4).
[77] *PC*, ii. 235 (bk V, c. 20), 306 (bk VI, c. 8).
[78] *PC*, i. 54 (bk I, c. 7).
[79] *PC*, i. 195–6 (bk III, c. 4).

whose life was shortened and soul endangered by self indulgence and the struggle for worldly power.[80]

A distinctive feature of Commynes's historiography is his attempt at rational analysis of cause and effect—his propensity for ascribing events to psychological or political motives. Such a characteristic is particularly associated with some of the humanist historians.[81] However, it is more likely that Commynes acquired this method of interpreting events from his diplomatic experience than from the influence of humanists: diplomatic skill presupposes the ability to disentangle rationally the causes and effects of a situation. In his attempt at political analysis Commynes resembles the authors of three English chronicles—the second continuation of the Crowland chronicle, the *Chronicle of the Rebellion in Lincolnshire*, and the *Arrival of Edward IV*; the author of the first was probably a diplomat, while the two other works were written at least in part for reasons of diplomacy—as propaganda to strengthen Edward IV's position abroad.

Commynes's use of natural explanations appears in a number of contexts. He uses psychology to explain the ambivalent attitude of Charles the Bold to the royal houses of England. Charles's strongest sympathies were with the Lancastrians because he himself as the great grandson of John of Gaunt was descended on his mother's side from that family. But while openly supporting Henry, Charles secretly helped Edward IV, mainly on account of his marriage to Edward's sister Margaret. He also had political reasons for supporting both kings: he tended to favour Edward because he disliked the earl of Warwick's power over Henry's government, but in 1470 he supported the restoration of Henry because he did not want to have to fight the English as well as the French.[82] Similarly Commynes gives political motives for Edward's French expedition in 1475: the king undertook it partly to please his subjects who wanted a campaign like one in the good old days of the Hundred Years' War, partly as a result of the duke of Burgundy's importunity, and partly because he wanted to keep the money he had raised for the expedition.[83]

Of all events in fifteenth century England, none created such a sensation abroad as the usurpation of Richard III. Stories soon reached the continent, some brought by those who were visiting England at the time. One such visitor was Dominic Mancini. He arrived in London in the autumn of 1482 and returned to France on 6 July 1483: he was therefore in London during the crucial months of April, May and June (Richard was crowned on 26 June).

Mancini, who was born in Rome some time after 1434, was by 1482

[80] *PC*, ii. 332–4 (bk VI, c. 12).
[81] See p. 427 and n. 20 below.
[82] *PC*, i. 44 (bk I, c. 5), 212 (bk III, c. 6).
[83] *PC*, ii. 231 (bk V, c. 20).

living in Paris.[84] He was a priest, probably a member of a religious order, perhaps an Augustinian friar. He had humanists among his acquaintance—a close friend was the historian Robert Gaguin—and he was in touch with the French court. He wrote numerous works in elegant Latin verse, on religious, edificatory, congratulatory and political subjects, dedicating some to important people at court. Why he visited England is not clear. He may have come to find employment, perhaps some post connected with the court. One of his friends, Pietro Carmeliano, was in London, possibly working in Rolls House.[85] Petrus himself was a friend of Sir Robert Brackenbury, who became constable of the Tower under King Richard, and perhaps introduced Mancini to the court circle. Alternatively, Mancini may have already been in the service of Angelo Cato, and visited England at his request.

On his return Mancini entered Cato's household in Vienne, and regaled his patron with stories of the usurpation. It is likely that he also talked about it to other people. (The chancellor of France, Guillaume de Roche-fort, was in the neighbourhood; in January of the next year, when he addressed the Estates General at Tours, he accused Richard III of murdering the little princes.)[86] Mancini was soon asked by Cato to commit his information to writing. He completed the *De Occupatione Regni Anglie* in less than six months, on 1 December 1483.[87] By that time he was no longer with Cato; he concluded the work at Beaugency in the county of Orléans. Mancini's dedication begins thus:[88]

> You have often besought me, Angelo Cato, most reverend father in God, to write down by what machinations Richard III, who is now reigning in England, attained the high degree of kingship, a story which I had repeatedly gone over in your presence.

Mancini had no experience as an historian but he produced a work of high quality. The *De Occupatione* derived its merits partly from Mancini's personal gifts, intelligence and powers of observation, but it also benefited from the successful combination of two contemporary literary genres, that of contemporary humanist historiography and that of the diplomatic newsletter. These genres overlapped, but generally speaking the work owes its Latin, structure and interest in psychological motivation to humanism, and its factual content and rational analysis of cause and effects to the newsletter.[89]

---

[84] For what is known of Mancini's life and works see the introduction to *Usurpation*, pp. 1–26. See also Alison Hanham, *Richard III and his Early Historians 1483–1535* (Oxford 1975), pp. 65–73.

[85] *Usurpation*, p. 19 and n. 1.

[86] Ibid., pp. 22–3.

[87] Ibid., pp. 5, 23, 104.

[88] Ibid., p. 56.

[89] See pp. 263, 269, 300 above, 427 below. See also *Usurpation*, pp. 16–17.

Classicisms occur in the Latin itself. Thus Mancini calls England 'Britannia' and France 'Gallia,' and the English 'Britanni' (but the French are 'Franci').[90] However, much of the Latin is archaic, retaining ecclesiastical elements and having affinities with Italian: it is reminiscent of fourteenth rather than fifteenth century style. The structure of the work shows more signs of classical influence: Mancini achieves unity by means of a consistent theme which he underlines by using dramatic devices. He starts by describing the principal characters—Edward IV, the queen's brother, Anthony, Earl Rivers, and others.[91] Richard himself dominates the stage, and the narrative tells how he gradually gained power: his driving force was ambition and his instrument duplicity.

Mancini remarks in the first chapter that Richard was moved by ambition,[92] and, after describing the murder of the loyal and unsuspecting Hastings, he comments: 'whom will insane lust for power spare, if it dares violate the ties of kin and friendship?'[93] Richard's duplicity appears in a number of passages. For example in Edward IV's reign Richard dissembled his disapproval of the king's marriage with the low-born Elizabeth, and won popular favour by a show of rectitude in public and private life.[94] To avoid odium for Hastings' murder, he pretended Hastings had plotted treason: to substantiate the story, which was proclaimed by a herald, he exhibited wagon loads of arms ostensibly collected for the rebellion.[95] But Richard's deceit appears against a backcloth of popular scepticism. It was widely known that the wagon loads of arms were intended for the Scottish war,[96] and at Richard's coronation 'some people understood his ambition and duplicity and were always suspicious as to where his schemes would lead.'[97]

The theme of ambition pursued in an atmosphere of corruption and subterfuge was of course well known in classical literature. In this respect the *De Occupatione* is reminiscent of Sallust's *Catiline*. Of contemporary humanist works it probably has the nearest affinities with Angelo Poliziano's *De Pactiana Conjuratione* (*Concerning the Conspiracy of the Pazzi*) which was published in 1478.[98]

The classical tradition also encouraged Mancini's taste for exact descriptions. He gives a character sketch of Edward IV with realistic details,[99]

---

[90] See ibid., pp. 53–4.
[91] Ibid., pp. 64–8 passim (cf. p. 21). Sir Thomas More, a product of the renaissance, similarly used a consistent theme to give unity to his *History of Richard III*; see pp. 444–51 below.
[92] *Usurpation*, p. 61.
[93] Ibid., p. 90.
[94] Ibid., pp. 62–4.
[95] Ibid., p. 82.
[96] Ibid., p. 82.
[97] Ibid., p. 82.
[98] See *Usurpation*, ed. Armstrong (Oxford 1936), p. 20
[99] *Usurpation*, pp. 64–6.

which bears comparison with Suetonius' descriptions of the Caesars. He relates that Edward was very approachable, in fact so friendly that 'if he saw a stranger daunted by his appearance, he would lay a kindly hand on his shoulder to put him more at his ease.' Although Edward was normally gentle and cheerful, when roused to anger he was terrifying. He acquired a reputation for avarice: he wheedled money from his subjects in 'an assembly of the whole kingdom', by explaining that he had incurred expenses in their defence and that they, therefore, should foot the bill. He drank and ate to excess ('it was his habit, so I learnt, to take an emetic so that he could gorge the more'). He 'seized any opportunity to flaunt his fine stature', and was very licentious, 'most insolent to many women' both married and unmarried; having seduced a woman with money and promises, he would heartlessly abandon her to the pleasure of others at court.

Equally graphic is Mancini's description of London,[100] and again there are classical prototypes.[101] (It is noteworthy that during the twelfth century renaissance a Londoner, William Fitz Stephen, had written a detailed account of the capital, both its topography and the social customs of the inhabitants.)[102] Mancini was much impressed by the wealth and magnificence of the capital, and ends his book with the description, lest otherwise readers might consider it incomplete, because London 'is so famous throughout the world.' He describes the general topography of the city (identifying by name, however, only the Thames and the Tower), giving particular detail about London bridge, the docks and the commercial quarters. Of the two last features he writes:[103]

> On the banks of the Thames are huge warehouses for imports, and numerous cranes of remarkable size to unload merchandise from the ships. From the district on the east, adjacent to the Tower, three paved streets lead towards the other quarter in the direction of the walls on the west: they are almost straight and are the busiest streets in the city. The one closest to the river, below the others, is devoted to various staple commodities, both liquid and solid—minerals, wines, honey, pitch, wax, flax, robes, thread, grain, fish, and other rather sordid goods. In the street running between the other two you will find hardly anything for sale

---

[100] Ibid., pp. 100–4.

[101] For an example of a laudatory description of a city in classical literature see Aelius Aristides' *Roman Oration*, printed in translation by J. H. Oliver, *The Ruling Power* (Transactions of the American Philosophical Society, new series, xliii, pt 4, 1953), pp. 895–907. For a satirical description of Rome see Juvenal's *Satire III*.

[102] Printed in translation by H. E. Butler, 'A description of London by William Fitz Stephen' in F. M. Stenton, *Norman London* (Historical Association leaflets, nos 93, 94, 1934), pp. 25–35. See also Gransden, *Historical Writing*, i. 307–8.

[103] *Usurpation*, p. 102.

except cloths. And in the third street, which is level and touches the centre of the town, the traffic is in more precious goods such as gold and silver cups, dyed stuffs, various silks, carpets, tapestry, and much other exotic merchandise. ... There are also many other populous districts with numerous trades, for whatever there is in the city it all belongs to craftsmen and merchants. Their houses are not, as is usually the case, encumbered with merchandise only at the entrance, but there are spacious depositories in the inmost areas where goods are heaped, stowed and packed away like honey in a cone.

Such exact detail was not only the result of classical influence. Mancini's purpose to provide information, a newsletter as it were, for his patron encouraged the same taste. And besides Cato, he wrote specifically to inform at least one other foreigner. As he states in his dedication to Cato: 'you considered that you would be doing Frederick, prince of Taranto, a favour if you gave him the story to read which you had so enjoyed hearing.'[104] His work must also have been intended for the households and friends of Cato and Frederick, but since only one manuscript is known to have survived, it probably did not have a wide circulation.[105] Mancini, like Commynes, had to inform readers comparatively ignorant of England and the English. Besides the description of London, he included for their benefit an account of the equipment used by English soldiers—a digression introduced on the pretext that Richard brought many troops to London for his coronation.[106] And Mancini explains the meaning of the title prince of Wales: 'the province (*provincia*) of Wales, which lies 200 miles from the capital, is always given to the kings' eldest sons, and from it they take their title.'[107]

Despite such digressions Mancini's primary purpose was to record Richard's rise to power in the context of contemporary politics. He intended to tell the truth and refrains from elaborating if his information is inadequate. He writes in the dedication:[108]

I decided that I ought not to expatiate as freely in writing as in talking, for although I would not shirk the labour on your account, I have not enough knowledge of the names of those to be described, of the intervals of time, nor of men's secret designs in this whole affair.

[104] Ibid., p. 56. For Cato's connection with Frederick see p. 294 above.
[105] The surviving manuscript of the *De Occupatione* is now in the Bibliothèque Municipale at Lille, fonds Godefroy MS. 129. The Lille MS. is a late fifteenth century copy and was owned by Paulus Aemilius Veronensis, a humanist who came to France in 1483 and wrote on the antiquities of Gaul. See *Usurpation*, p. 51 and nn. 6, 7.
[106] Ibid., pp. 98–100.
[107] Ibid., p. 70.
[108] Ibid., p. 56.

And he concludes his narrative at the point when he left England because he had not discovered how Richard III ruled, 'and yet rules,' after the usurpation.[109] Mancini was not tempted to deviate from the truth on account of bias, because, as a foreigner, he was not involved in English politics.

The factual and rational elements predominate in the account of politics in the *De Occupatione*. Mancini dwells neither on classical virtues and vices (as was fashionable among humanists), nor on Christian values, and gives precise details whenever he can. He records, for instance, that until Hastings' murder official documents still bore the name and title of Edward V,[110] but that afterwards Richard changed the royal seals and titles, and carried on government in his own name, repealing or suspending Edward V's acts.[111] Mancini may have derived this information from public records. However, although he never names his informers, it is clear that his principal sources were oral.[112] Except for a few mistakes venal in a foreigner (and one whose direct acquaintance with England was limited apparently to a single visit to London),[113] Mancini was, as far as can be ascertained by comparison with other authorities, remarkably accurate.[114] (As Mancini's narrative is almost certainly independent of the accounts of the usurpation written in England, its evidence can be corroborated by the English authorities, notably Sir Thomas More's *History of Richard III*.)[115]

Mancini's approach to causation was rational. He does not attribute events to divine intervention, nor does he produce a stereotype on the classical model by ascribing them without distinction to ambition.[116] Rather his study of ambition led him to consider other psychological motives. For instance he asserts that the duke of Buckingham hated the party of Edward IV's queen, Elizabeth, because he had been forced to marry her sister, whose ignoble birth he despised.[117] Mancini is even

---

[109] Ibid., p. 105.

[110] Ibid., pp. 92, 126–7 n. 86. John Rous, *Historia Regum Anglie* (for which see p. 313 n. 7 below), p. 213, has a similar statement, which is correct.

[111] *Usurpation*, pp. 96, 131–2 n. 103. The statement is correct.

[112] See ibid., pp. 60 ('men say'), 70–2 ('it is said'). His information on the fate of the little princes derived ultimately from 'a doctor from Strasbourg'; see p. 306 and n. 124 below.

[113] An example of a mistake Mancini made because he was a foreigner is the statement that Richard at the time of Edward IV's death was staying 'on the Gloucester estates'; in fact he was on his Yorkshire ones. Clearly Mancini thought that like a member of the French royal family he would have had his property in the place from which he took his title. Ibid., pp. 70, 113 n. 36. For Mancini's ignorance of English topography see ibid., p. 116 n. 46, and of English institutions, ibid., p. 131 n. 102.

[114] For examples of Mancini's accuracy see above and n. 111 and p. 306 and n. 119 below. See also *Usurpation*, pp. 110 n. 16, 111 n. 22, 112 n. 25, 120 n. 61, 135 n. 118.

[115] For the similarity of More's narrative with Mancini's see pp. 450 n. 168, 452 below. For the probable mutual independence of the two writers see Hanham, op. cit., pp. 71–2.

[116] See Armstrong's introduction, *Usurpation*, pp. 14–16.

[117] Ibid., p. 74.

[305]

prepared to attribute a good motive to Richard: his enmity to Queen Elizabeth was the result not only of ambition, but also of grief at Clarence's murder and the desire for revenge.[118] Some events Mancini attributes to more mundane causes. He alleges that Edward IV would not help the Flemings against Louis XI because he was reluctant to lose the annual pension of 50,000 écus paid by the French king.[119] And he ascribes Edward's death to a cold caught when, with excessive enthusiasm, 'he went one day in a boat to watch the sport of some men whom he had sent out fishing.'[120]

The *De Occupatione*, as a fairly accurate and almost contemporary account of events and opinion in London during the months when Richard seized power, is an authority of primary importance.[121] It has some statements which, although they do not tally with the evidence of other authorities, may well be correct. For example, it asserts that on the eve of Richard's coup the young king's friends consulted in their own homes (not in Baynard's castle as was later supposed).[122] Mancini's silence raises a doubt concerning the physical deformity attributed to Richard by other early writers.[123] And Mancini gives the earliest indication of the fate of the little princes, together with a character sketch of Edward V:[124]

> After Hastings had been removed, all attendants who had waited upon the king were debarred access to him. He and his brother were withdrawn into the inner apartments of the Tower proper, and day by day began to be seen more rarely behind the bars and windows, till at length they ceased to appear altogether. A Strasbourg doctor, the last of his attendants whose services the king enjoyed, reported that the young king, like a victim prepared for sacrifice, sought remission for his sins by daily

---

[118] Ibid., p. 62.

[119] Ibid., p. 66. The sum given by Mancini is correct; see ibid., p. 122 n. 27.

[120] Ibid., p. 58.

[121] The *De Occupatione* was unknown to English historians until C. A. J. Armstrong wrote about it to *The Times*, 26 May 1934, preliminary to the publication of his edition in 1936. It was not, therefore, used by James Gairdner, *History of the Life and Reign of Richard the Third* (revised edition, Cambridge 1898).

[122] *Usurpation*, pp. 90, 125 n. 80. For examples of information only known from Mancini see ibid., pp. 108–9 n. 10, 119–20 n. 58.

[123] John Rous (*Rous*, p. 216) and Polydore Vergil (see p. 440 and n. 104 below) allege that Richard's shoulders were unequal. Sir Thomas More adds that he had a crooked back (see p. 453 and nn. below); hence Shakespeare was to describe him as having a humped back. It seems reasonable to conclude that the story of Richard's deformity was the result of later rumour and propaganda. This view is supported by the fact that a German traveller, Nicolas von Poppelau, who visited England in 1484 and wrote a description of Richard, noticed no deformity (see *Usurpation*, pp. 16 n. 2, 136–8). It is also noteworthy that Mancini makes no reference to the (allegedly) strange circumstances of Richard's birth, which both Rous (see p. 316 below) and More (see p. 453 below) mention.

[124] *Usurpation*, p. 92. For other early accounts of Edward V see ibid., p. 127 nn. 88–90.

confession and penance, because he believed that death faced him.

Here it seems relevant to comment on the youth's talents. But so much is told of his words and acts, of his kindness and courtesy—or rather prudence—far beyond his years, that much labour would be needed to record them, and I can justifiably excuse myself the task. However, there is one thing I cannot omit, his special knowledge of literature which enabled him to discourse elegantly, and to understand fully and expound most excellently whatever work came to hand, whether in prose or verse, unless it were by one of the more abstruse authors. He had such dignity of presence and such charm of expression, that those who set eyes on him were never tired of looking.

11

The Antiquaries: John Rous and William Worcester

A useful definition of the word antiquary has been supplied by Professor Momigliano:[1]

> I assume that to many of us the word 'antiquary' suggests the notion of a student of the past who is not quite a historian because: (1) historians write in a chronological order; antiquaries write in a systematic order: (2) historians produce those facts which serve to illustrate or explain a certain situation; antiquaries collect all the items that are connected with a certain subject, whether they help to solve a problem or not. The subject-matter contributes to the distinction between historians and antiquaries only in so far as certain subjects (such as political institutions, religion, private life) have traditionally been considered more suitable for systematic description than for a chronological account.

Among the subjects regarded as particularly suitable for systematic treatment is of course the study of antiquities, that is of buildings, 'objets d'art' and other material remains of past generations. It is with this branch of antiquarianism that we are here concerned. The term will be used also to include topography, that is the siting of man-made and natural features in the countryside. This kind of antiquarianism had a vigorous tradition in medieval England, especially among the monks during the twelfth century. William of Malmesbury described both new and old churches throughout England, and Gervase of Canterbury traced in detail the architectural history of Canterbury cathedral, while the city of Chester was described by the monk Lucian. And castles attracted the attention of the secular clerk who wrote the *Gesta Stephani*.[2]

Antiquarian studies underwent a remarkable development in the fifteenth century. As will be seen they left traces in some monastic produc-

---

[1] Arnaldo Momigliano, 'Ancient history and the antiquarian' in *Journal of the Warburg and Courtauld Institutes*, xiii (1950), pp. 286–7.
[2] See Gransden, *Historical Writing*, i. 174–5, 185, 255–6, 362, 376, and R. W. Southern, 'Aspects of the European tradition of historical writing: 4. The sense of the past' in *TRHS*, fifth series, xxiii (1973), pp. 246–56.

tions, notably in the history of St Augustine's, Canterbury, by Thomas Elmham and in the chronicle of Meaux by Thomas Burton.[3] But interest spread to a wider range of people. John Hardyng, a layman, included much topographical material in his chronicle.[4] And two scholars who lived late in the century, a secular clerk, John Rous, and a 'gentleman bureaucrat',[5] William Worcester, have earned reputations primarily as antiquaries.

In considering fifteenth century antiquarianism, it should be remembered that it developed despite the concurrent elaboration of the legends of British history—of Brutus and King Arthur—first popularized by Geoffrey of Monmouth. Those engaged on antiquarian studies apparently saw no conflict with them, and never suspected that the accumulation of data by them and their successors would in the end make the legends untenable. On the contrary, the British History, by firing enthusiasm for the past in general and for any place or relic particularly associated with the legends, stimulated their researches. Thus the tradition of medieval antiquarianism was transmitted to the post-reformation period, together with the British History, to be further developed by subsequent scholars.[6]

A discussion of John Rous and William Worcester necessitates a comprehensive treatment of their work. Neither was exclusively occupied with antiquarian studies; each was also concerned with the contemporary world and was influenced by his patron. Their various interests and opinions were interrelated, and all must be taken into account in order to give a complete picture.

John Rous was born near Warwick in about 1411.[7] He was educated at Oxford university,[8] leaving in about 1445 to become a chaplain of the chapel of St Mary Magdalen at Guy's Cliff, two miles from Warwick.[9] The chapel had been founded by Richard Beauchamp, earl of Warwick from 1403 to 1439, for two priests who were to sing mass for him, his wife, parents and friends. It was beside a hermitage reputedly occupied in

---

[3] See pp. 350–5, 361–6 passim below.

[4] See pp. 284–7 above.

[5] The term is McFarlane's. See K. B. McFarlane, 'William Worcester: a preliminary survey' in *Studies presented to Sir Hilary Jenkinson*, ed. J. Conway Davies (Oxford 1957), p. 199. Cf. p. 328 below.

[6] For the growth of the legends and how they were ultimately discredited see T. D. Kendrick, *British Antiquity* (London 1950). See also pp. 436–9, 471–2 below.

[7] Good accounts of Rous's life and work are in Courthorpe's introduction to his edition of Rous's 'Yorkist' roll (for which see p. 311 n. 18 below), and in Kendrick, op. cit., pp. 19–29. Most of the information derives from Rous himself, in his *Historia*. The latter is printed *Joannis Rossi Antiquarii Warwicensis Historia Regum Angliae*, ed. Thomas Hearne (Oxford 1716).

[8] See Emden, *Biographical Register*, iii. 1596–7.

[9] For an account of the chapel and its foundation see *Rous*, pp. xxiv, citing William Dugdale, *The Antiquities of Warwickshire* (London 1656), p. 192. See also the life of Richard Beauchamp in Rous's 'Yorkist' roll, for which see p. 311 and n. 18 below (Richard Beauchamp is no. 50 in *Rows rol*).

Anglo-Saxon times first by St Dubritius and then by Guy, the giant who according to legend was the first earl of Warwick. The place is still one of natural beauty; the chapel stands at the foot of the cliff facing the river Avon and the water meadows. Richard Beauchamp's foundation became the venue of pilgrims and was described by John Leland in the sixteenth century:[10]

> [Earl Richard] set up there an image of Earl Guy, giantlike, and enclosed the silver wells in the meadow with pure white slick[11] stones like marble, and there set up a pretty house open like a cage covered only to keep comers thither from the rain. He also made there a pretty house of stone for the chantry priests by the chapel. The lands he gave it lie about the house. It is a house of pleasure, a place meet for the muses. There is silence, a pretty wood ... , the river rolling over the stones with a pretty noise. ...

Here Rous spent his life under the patronage of the Beauchamps and later of the Nevilles (Richard Neville, the 'Kingmaker', succeeded to the earldom of Warwick in 1449 by right of his wife Anne, Richard Beauchamp's daughter). Rous lived quietly, sometimes travelling in southern England and Wales.[12] But occasionally he asserted himself in public affairs: in 1459 he petitioned parliament when it met at Coventry against enclosures, and apparently petitioned subsequent parliaments on the same subject, always without success.[13] He died in 1491.

Rous collected a good library at Guy's Cliff which was housed over the south porch. Here Leland saw the books, among them Rous's own works on history and antiquities.[14] Rous produced a number of works— on family history, local history and general history. Some of them are now lost. For example one on the antiquities of Guy's Cliff and another on the history of the town of Warwick are no longer known to survive.[15] Nevertheless there are enough extant to show Rous's achievement as an historian and antiquary. They demonstrate both his enthusiasm and talent for historical and antiquarian studies, and also his considerable artistic gifts. Among his drawings is a self portrait, a tinted picture of himself in his later years, a clean shaven rather fat man with a gentle expression,

---

[10] *Rous*, p. xxiv, citing Leland's *Itinerary*; *The Itinerary of John Leland*, ed. Thomas Hearne (Oxford 1710–12, 9 vols), iv. 50.

[11] Slick: smooth; *NED*, ix. pt i. 204, under slick *a*, 3.

[12] See p. 322 below.

[13] P. 314 and n. 34 below.

[14] *Commentarii de Scriptoribus Britannicis, auctore Joanne Lelando*, ed. Anthony Hall (Oxford 1709, 2 vols), pp. 474–5; cited *Rous*, pp. xxvi-xxvii. For Rous's recognition of the importance of 'libraries for students' see *Rous*, p. 130.

[15] See the list of works given by Leland, *Commentarii*, p. 474; cf. Kendrick, *British Antiquity*, p. 19.

seated writing or drawing on a roll at his desk; a shield bearing his arms is attached to the back of the chair.[16]

Rous's loyalty to his patrons is expressed in his two pictorial rolls containing the history of the earls of Warwick. He wrote and illustrated the earliest, the so-called 'Lancastrian' roll, between 1477 and the death of Richard III in 1485, though he revised it after the accession of Henry VII.[17] It gives a drawing of each earl in chronological sequence (starting with the legendary Guy) together with his arms and a brief account of his life in Latin. The other roll, the so-called 'Yorkist' roll, was executed a little later but during the reign of Richard III. It is similar to the 'Lancastrian' roll although its text is in English.[18]

Rous executed these rolls partly as a result of his connection with the earls of Warwick, who apparently were interested in his historical researches. Rous records that once while at St Albans he transcribed an account of the (legendary) origins of the town of Warwick from Matthew Paris' *Gesta Abbatum*, and sent it to Richard Neville. He also records that 'on various occasions' the earls of Warwick, who were hereditary chamberlains of the royal exchequer, gave him permission to consult a law book in their office.[19]

[16] Rous's self portrait (see Kendrick, op. cit., Plate II *a*) is on the back of his 'Lancastrian' roll (for which see below and the next note); see the introduction to *Rows Rol* (for which see n. 18 below), Kendrick, op. cit., pp. 27–8, and A. G. B. Russell, 'The Rous Roll' in *Burlington Magazine*, xxx (1917), p. 31 and Plate 1.

[17] The 'Lancastrian' roll, now preserved in the College of Arms, has not been printed in full but its text, which is in Latin, is printed in the footnotes to the description of the Plates in *Rows Rol*, ed. Courthope (for which see the next note). For reproductions of some of the pictures see Plate XII(f) below, and Kendrick, op. cit., Plates IIb-IV, Russell, op. cit., Plates II and III, and J. G. Mann, 'Instances of antiquarian feeling in medieval and renaissance art' in *Archaeological Journal*, lxxxix (1932), Plates II (2), III, IV, opposite pp. 259, 260, 261, respectively. With regard to Rous's reputation as an artist it should be noted that Dr C. E. Wright doubts whether Rous drew the pictures on the 'Yorkist' roll (for which see below and the next note), which implies that he did not draw those on the 'Lancastrian' roll either; C. E. Wright, 'The Rous Roll: the English version' in *British Museum Quarterly*, xx (1955–6), p. 79. The best account of the 'Lancastrian' roll, with full references to copies and printed notices, is in A. R. Wagner, *A Catalogue of English Mediaeval Rolls of Arms* (Harleian Soc., c, 1948, and Oxford 1950), pp. 116–18.

[18] BL MS. Additional 48976. Printed *This rol was laburd and finished by Master John Rows of Warrewyk*, ed. William Courthope (London 1845–59). The volume is not paginated but the line reproductions of the pictures are numbered and Rous's descriptive captions, which are printed all together before the pictures, are correspondingly numbered. An Elizabethan copy of the captions, now BL MS. Lansdowne 882, is printed in *Historia Vitae et Regni Ricardi II*, ed. Thomas Hearne (Oxford 1729), with the exception of those numbered in Courthope's edition 13–17 (some of the kings of England from Edward the Confessor to King John, and the empress Matilda) and 43 to 46 (Richard III, Queen Anne and their son Edward). For a full description of the 'Yorkist' roll, with further references, see Wagner, op. cit., pp. 118–20; it should be noted that Wagner wrote before the rediscovery of the roll in 1954 (its whereabouts from 1870 to 1954 were unknown), in which year it was acquired by the British Museum; see Wright, op. cit., pp. 77–80. Illustrations in the 'Yorkist' roll are reproduced Plate XII (a)-(e) below, and in Wright, op. cit., Plates XXVI, XXVII. [Note: Since this chapter went to press, Courthope's edition of the 'Yorkist' roll has been reprinted, with an introduction by Charles Ross (Gloucester 1980).]

[19] Rous records these examples of his scholarly contacts with the earls of Warwick in the *Historia; Rous*, pp. 64, 86.

Another strong motive for producing the rolls was Rous's love of the town of Warwick. He begins with the (legendary) history of its foundation, and proceeds to give many details concerning its development: he depicts a number of the town's benefactors and devotes especial attention in the text to the contributions of the earls of Warwick to the town's prosperity— whether a pious endowment, the strengthening of the castle, or some improvement to the market.[20] Many of the figures hold emblems of their benefactions, a church or a charter.

Rous expresses particular admiration for Richard Beauchamp, who besides being founder of St Mary Magdalen's chapel at Guy's Cliff, was a leading councillor, diplomat and soldier during Henry VI's minority.[21] Richard was the subject of a work which, though in book form, is similar in literary and artistic style to Rous's Warwick rolls, the *Pageant of the Birth, Life and Death of Richard Beauchamp Earl of Warwick*. This book was executed between 1485 and 1490 probably for Richard's daughter Anne, countess of Warwick and wife of Richard Neville, who died in 1493.[22] It comprises fifty three pencil drawings, the best of which are of excellent quality, with descriptive captions in English, illustrating the earl's life from the cradle to the grave. It ends with two family trees, one of Richard Beauchamp and his two wives, and their children, the other of Anne and Richard Neville, and their children and grandchildren.

The *Pageant* is a eulogy in the chivalric style. Although it records the main facts of Richard Beauchamp's life, it concentrates on his 'notable acts of chivalry'.[23] Some statements seem to reflect the author's desire to praise rather than a respect for truth. He asserts, for example, that once when the emperor Sigismund visited Henry V at Calais, of which Richard was captain, he said to the king that no other Christian prince had such a knight as the earl of Warwick, 'for wisdom, nurture and manhood'. Sigismund added that 'if all courtesy were lost, yet might it be found again in him'; and so, the author comments, for 'ever after by the emperor's authority, [he] was called the father of courtesy.'[24] Nor does the author neglect Richard's ancestry. When he refers to Guy, the legendary first earl of Warwick and the hermit of Guy's Cliff, he alleges that the sultan's lieutenant 'Sir Baltirdam' was particularly delighted to meet Richard on his visit to Jerusalem in 1408, because he had heard that he was a descendant

[20] See, e.g., *Rous Rol*, nos 15, 16, 32, 47, 50, 59.

[21] Ibid., no. 50.

[22] Printed *Pageant of the Birth, Life and Death of Richard Beauchamp Earl of Warwick K.G. 1389–1439*, ed. Viscount Dillon and W. H. St John Hope (London 1914). This is the edition cited here; another is *The Pageants of Richard Beauchamp Earl of Warwick*, ed. William, earl of Carysfort (Roxburghe Club, Oxford 1908). The suggestion that the *Pageant* was executed for Anne was first made by E. Maunde Thompson, 'The Pageants of Richard Beauchamp, earl of Warwick' in *Burlington Magazine*, i (1903), p. 160.

[23] *Pageant*, p. 1.

[24] *Pageant*, p. 69.

of 'the noble Sir Guy of Warwick whose Life they had there in books of their language.'[25]

Formerly the *Pageant* was attributed to Rous, but nowadays scholars agree that he was not the artist;[26] nor is it at all certain that he was the author of the text.[27] Nevertheless it is related to the Warwick rolls. The theme itself, the eulogy of Richard, and the particular references to Earl Guy and Guy's Cliff,[28] would have been congenial to him. And two passages resemble the 'Yorkist' roll so closely that even if they were not written by Rous himself, they must have been copied from his work. One refers to Guy's Cliff: it asserts that Dame Emma Raughton, a recluse 'of All Hallows, Northgate street, York', in obedience to a command from the Virgin Mary as revealed to her in a vision, proclaimed the incomparable virtues of Earl Richard, commending him especially for his benefactions to Guy's Cliff 'which in process of time shall grow to a place of great worship, one of the most famed in England.'[29] The other passage records that Richard's grandfather Thomas earl of Warwick, having visited eastern Europe, brought the son of the king of Lithuania back to London, where he had him christened Thomas after himself.[30] It seems likely, therefore, that the *Pageant* was either executed under Rous's supervision or that the text was composed by someone with similar interests and who had access to the 'Yorkist' roll.

Rous's most substantial work remains to be considered. It is the *Historia Regum Anglie* (*The History of the Kings of England*), a general history of England from Brutus (with a brief introductory section from the Creation

---

[25] *Pageant*, p. 36. The reference must be to some version of the romance Life of Guy of Warwick. The original Life was in Anglo-Norman, but versions in Middle English were based on it. See C. W. Dunn in *A Manual of the Writings in Middle English 1050–1500*, i, ed. J. B. Severs (New Haven, Connecticut 1967), pp. 27–31, and L. H. Loomis, *Medieval Romance in England* (Oxford 1924), pp. 137–8. See also, with further references, D. N. Klausner, 'Didacticism and Drama in *Guy of Warwick*' in *Medievalia et Humanistica*, new series, vi (1975), pp. 103–19, and Lewis Thorpe's review of *Le rommant de Guy de Warwik et de Herolt d'Ardenne*, ed. D. J. Conlon (University of North Carolina Studies in the Romance Languages and Literature, no. 102, Chapel Hill 1971) in *Medium Ævum*, xlii (1973), pp. 65–7. For the popularity of the romance of Guy of Warwick from the fifteenth to the eighteenth century see R. S. Crane, 'The vogue of *Guy of Warwick* from the close of the middle ages to the romantic revival' in *Publications of the Modern Language Association of America*, xxx (1915), pp. 125–95. For Lives of Guy in Latin prose see pp. 322 and n. 87, 493 Appendix D, below.

[26] The pictures in the *Pageant* are not in the same style as those in the Warwick rolls; see Thompson, op. cit., p. 159, Russell, op. cit., p. 23, and Wright, op. cit., p. 80. (The editors of the *Pageant* (p. vi) do not commit themselves on this matter.) However, the conclusion that Rous cannot have illustrated the *Pageant* presupposes that he was the artist of the Warwick rolls, which Dr Wright does not accept without question; see p. 311 n. 16 above.

[27] The conclusion that Rous did not compose the text is based on its dissimilarity in style and content from his known works; Thompson, op. cit., p. 159.

[28] Pp. 312–13 and n. 25 above, and the next note. For a reference to Guy in the *Historia* see p. 493, Appendix D, below.

[29] *Pageant*, p. 93; *Rows Rol*, no. 50.

[30] *Pageant*, p. 44; *Rows Rol*, no. 47.

of the world) until the accession of Henry VII.[31] Rous collected the material and wrote it between 1480 and 1486. It is not a chronicle in the true sense of the word; no part of it is a contemporary record of events. Rather it is a composition written 'at a sitting', and resembles a common-place book in one respect—there are long digressions breaking the chronological sequence on topics in which Rous had a special interest.

Neither loyalty to his patrons nor local patriotism, the principal motives for Rous's other works, provided the initial incentive for the *Historia*. He explains why he started research for it. He makes the general remark that the erection of statues is one way to commemorate the founders of churches, cities, towns and the like. Then he turns to the case of the 'newly built college at Windsor' (that is St George's chapel) where many niches had been prepared for such statues. And he states:[32]

> I was asked by the venerable man, master of the said works, Master John Seymour,[33] in the last days of King Edward IV of famous memory, that, to please the said lord king, I should write a little work on the kings, the princes of the church and the founders of cities, so that statues of them could be honourably placed in the niches for the perpetual remembrance of their names. At the instance of the said worthy man, formerly a fellow scholar of mine at Oxford, and mainly to please the said most noble king and for the delight of his successors, I began this little book. However, I did not continue with it because other matters intervened.

Nevertheless, as Rous explains, he later took up the work again. This time he was impelled by another motive—indignation at the enclosure movement. His anger was no doubt increased by his love of his own neighbourhood, because he could see the hardship caused by enclosures in Warwickshire. After he had petitioned successive parliaments in vain against enclosures, the 'clamour and complaints' of the people had grown, and, he writes, 'I was urged by many to raise my voice and pen against them.'[34]

---

[31] For the printed edition see p. 309 n. 7 above. The text survives in BL MS. Cotton Vespasian A XII, which is apparently a fair copy made by a scribe in the reign of Henry VII; the handwriting is not the same as that of the Rous rolls.

[32] *Rous*, p. 120. John Seymour was a canon of St George's chapel, Windsor. There is no evidence supporting Rous's statement that Seymour was 'master of the works' at the chapel at the end of the reign of Edward IV; he was, however, surveyor early in Henry VII's reign. See *The History of the King's Works*, ed. H. M. Colvin (London 1963–76, vols i-iii, v, vi, and a volume of plans published to date), iii. pt i. 305–6.

[33] *Rous*, p. 120.

[34] *Rous*, pp. 120–1. Cf. p. 317 n. 44 below. For Rous's petition to the parliament which met in Coventry in 1459 see Maurice Beresford, *The Lost Villages of England* (London 1954), p. 102, and *The Agrarian History of England and Wales*, ed. H. P. R. Finberg, iv, *1500–1640*, ed. Joan Thirsk (Cambridge 1967), pp. 213–14.

Rous, therefore, had two reasons for undertaking the *Historia*. One, the commemorative, turned his mind back to the past; the other, his concern for a social ill, drew his attention to the present. The result was that Rous did research into the past, besides commenting on the contemporary scene. However, it would be a mistake to suppose that Rous's sole interest in his own times was in the enclosure movement. Inevitably, as a chaplain to the earls of Warwick, he was concerned with national politics. In discussing both aspects of Rous's work, his study of the past and his comments on the present, his two rolls on the history of the earls of Warwick, which show the same dual preoccupation, must be taken into account. Before turning to our main subject, Rous's study of antiquities, we will discuss his contribution to contemporary historiography.

As a historian of his own times Rous had to come to terms with the political situation. Like the other writers he showed no constant attachment to either Lancastrian or Yorkist dynasty: he favoured whichever was in power. Thus for most of his life he supported the house of York. His connections with it were particularly close because of the patronage of Richard Neville, earl of Warwick from 1449 to 1471. The latter was a Yorkist until briefly almost at the end of his career, in 1470, he espoused Henry VI's cause and his daughter Anne married Henry's son and heir, Edward of Westminster. However, in the spring of 1471 Neville was killed at the battle of Barnet and Prince Edward was killed at the battle of Tewkesbury. In the next year Anne was married to the duke of Gloucester, the future Richard III, after whose accession the royal couple paid a state visit to Warwick castle.[35]

It is not, therefore, surprising that Rous expressed Yorkist sympathies in the two Warwick rolls which, as has been seen, he executed in Richard's reign. (He treats Neville's brief Lancastrian apostasy as an unhappy aberration.)[36] He included Richard III because of his marriage to Anne Neville, and the 'Yorkist' roll has a eulogy on him. The entry reads:[37]

> The most mighty prince Richard by the grace of God king of England and of France and lord of Ireland by very matrimony without discontinuance or any defiling in the law by heir male lineally descending from King Harry the Second, all avarice set aside, ruled his subjects in his realm full commendably, punishing offenders of his laws, especially extortioners and oppressors of his commons, and cherishing tho[se] that were virtuous; by the which discreet guiding he got great thank of God and love of all his subjects rich and poor and great laud of the people of all other lands about him.

[35] *Rous*, pp. 216–17.
[36] *Rows Rol*, no. 57.
[37] *Rows Rol*, no. 63.

The 'Lancastrian' roll (in Latin) must originally have had a similar panegyric on King Richard. However, when Rous revised it early in Henry VII's reign he altered it to suit the new dynasty, replacing the Yorkist bias with a Lancastrian one. He cut out the portrait of King Richard from among the benefactors of Warwick and refers to him merely as the unhappy husband of Anne, omitting the eulogy. Anne herself loses her royal insignia, and her first husband, Edward of Westminster, Henry VI's son, is inserted with a eulogistic caption. Rous also removed the portrait of the other Yorkist king, Edward IV,[38] whom he had included as a benefactor of Warwick, substituting one of Edward III.

Similarly Rous expresses enthusiasm for the new dynasty in the *Historia*: Henry VII is praised; Richard III is denigrated. Fired by the 'ardour of love', Rous addresses himself in the last paragraph to King Henry. He describes him as sent by God, and asserts that in accordance with a prophecy Henry would be remembered with great honour by future generations. He ends with a reference to Henry's eldest son and heir Arthur, 'who will by divine providence inherit the worth of the other great Arthur.'[39]

Rous describes Richard III as a tyrant incited by Antichrist.[40] He alleges that he was born after being in his mother's womb for two years, and that he already had teeth and hair reaching down to his legs. As an adult Richard was small and his right shoulder was higher than the left. He was cruel beyond belief: among his victims were the two princes; having welcomed them with kisses and embraces, he killed them within three months or little more. Rous also accuses Richard of poisoning his queen, Anne— besides criticizing him for imprisoning his mother-in-law, Anne, countess of Warwick. But his worst crime was his responsibility for Henry VI's death:[41]

> And what was most detestable to God, to the English, and to all nations that had news of it, was that he killed that most saintly man King Henry VI, either by means of others, or, as many believe, with his own hands.

Rous records that when Henry's body was disinterred from its burial place (in Chertsey abbey) for removal to Windsor, it was found to be almost incorrupt, though the face was emaciated, and smelling sweetly—'certainly not from spices since he was buried by his enemies and tormentors.' The body was buried with due solemnity in the new chapel of St George's,

---

[38] See *Rows Rol*, the introduction and notes to the descriptions of the Plates illustrating nos 16, 17, 62, 63. Cf. Kendrick, op. cit., p. 21.

[39] *Rous*, pp. 218–19.

[40] *Rous*, p. 218. For the character-sketch of Richard see *Rous*, pp. 215–16. Alison Hanham, *Richard III and his Early Historians 1483–1535* (Oxford 1975), pp. 118–24, translates Rous's account of Richard and his reign. For the legend of the curious circumstances of Richard's birth and of his physical deformity see p. 453 and n. 190 below.

[41] *Rous*, p. 215.

on the south side of the high altar, and at once began to work miracles in witness of Henry's sanctity, 'as writings there make sufficiently apparent.'[42] However, although Rous reflects early Tudor propaganda, he does make some attempt to be fair to Richard. He comments favourably on his building activities in a number of cities, for which Richard refused payment because, he said, he preferred to have his subjects' hearts rather than their money. And Rous does justice to Richard's bravery at Bosworth:[43]

> If I would speak the truth in his honour, [I must say] that he bore himself with great distinction like a noble knight despite his small body and slight strength, most honourably defending himself to his last breath.

Perhaps it was caution, perhaps distaste at his own *volte-face*, which caused Rous to be brief and reserved on the politics of his day. Certainly they did not stir him to the passionate eloquence and rational argument which enclosures evoked. Writing of his crusade against the enclosure movement Rous says: 'I have no doubt that I am a soldier of Christ, fighting for Him and in His cause, and for the whole church and for the common-wealth of England. ... I pray for God's help against the enemy.'[44] His purpose was not only to stimulate opinion against enclosures and shame the enclosers into repentance, but also to persuade the king to remedy the evil by legislation. Parliament had regulated such trivialities as dress and games. Why should it not prohibit the wanton destruction of villages?[45]

Since the enclosure movement belonged to no one year, Rous faced a problem how to insert his apologia into a chronicle. It is true that he noted in their correct chronological place occasions in the past when kings had enclosed in order to create forests or parks. But his polemic occurs in three long excursuses introduced into the narrative on various pretexts. The first follows an account of the ancient philosophers and of the growth of knowledge; this leads to reflections on virtue in relation to political organization, and so to enclosures as a violation of social order.[46] The second excursus is in the entry about King Alfred as a great lawgiver; Rous then writes on law in general and so introduces enclosures because, he argues, they were contrary to law.[47] The third excursus occurs after the remark that William the Conqueror destroyed villages when he

---

[42] *Rous*, p. 217.

[43] *Rous*, p. 218.

[44] *Rous*, p. 137. Rous, in the introductory passage to his discussion of law (which leads to an excursus on enclosures, for which see below), denies that he undertook his research for its own sake, but states that 'pro certo nunquam aliud intendebam quam honorem dei, et regis et totius rei publicae proficuum, ut deus novit'; *Rous*, p. 86.

[45] *Rous*, p. 136.

[46] *Rous*, pp. 37–43.

[47] *Rous*, pp. 87–96.

created the New Forest; many people, Rous alleges, say that the deaths there of William's sons William Rufus and Richard, and of his grandson Richard, were the results of divine vengeance. Rous proceeds to explain why God was equally displeased with the enclosers of his own day.[48]

The tone which Rous adopts in his rhetoric suggests that he was moved at least in part by humanitarian feelings. 'God delights more in many just and pious families, with wives, children and households, although poor ... than in three or so greedy men thoughtlessly consuming the goods of Christ's faithful to the destruction of the commonwealth.'[49] And Rous deplores the misery caused by unemployment and by worry about the necessities of life, which result in children being neglected.[50]

No doubt Rous's concern for the poor was a consequence of his clerical status. Another consequence was the homiletic nature of his tirades. He invokes the culprits, those 'lovers of the world, enemies of the commonwealth, blatant torturers and oppressors of the people, destroyers of villages',[51] to leave their evil ways and make peace with God rather than suffer eternal damnation for the sin of avarice.[52] He reinforces his polemic with numerous biblical citations and allusions. For example, he exhorts the 'destroyers' to 'love thy neighbour as thyself,[53] and compares them with the sons of Cain (although, alas! they had not been wiped out by a flood).[54] He threatens them with divine vengeance—they will be punished even more severely than Ahab, Jezebel and Naboth because they refused to learn from the fates of these biblical personages.[55] Moreover, in true preaching style, Rous tells exemplary stories. To demonstrate that a man might suffer corporally if he seizes another's property, he tells how Philip Augustus buried alive a *praepositus* of Paris because he had forcibly occupied a vineyard.[56] And to show that a man might suffer spiritually, he relates how Louis landgrave of Thuringia, a tyrannical oppressor of the poor, had to suffer the torments of hell until one of his sons, on becoming a Cistercian monk, relinquished his father's ill gotten gains.[57]

Rous uses cogent argument as well as homiletic rhetoric. He demonstrates at length that enclosures are contrary to natural, divine and human law.

[48] *Rous*, pp. 112–37.
[49] *Rous*, p. 116.
[50] *Rous*, p. 125.
[51] *Rous*, p. 95.
[52] *Rous*, pp. 41, 87, 113, 116, 118–19, 128–9.
[53] *Rous*, p. 39.
[54] *Rous*, p. 127.
[55] *Rous*, p. 90.
[56] *Rous*, pp. 90–2. For this story Rous acknowledges the authority of Caesarius of Heisterbach's *Dialogus*, distinction vi, cap. xxiii; see *Caesarii Heisterbacensis Monachi Ordinis Cisterciensis Dialogus Miraculorum*, ed. Joseph Strange (Cologne 1851, 2 vols), i. 375–6.
[57] *Rous*, pp. 92–5. Rous again acknowledges the authority of Caesarius, distinction i, caps xxvii, xxxiv; Strange, op. cit., i. 32–4, 40–3.

Citing St Augustine's *City of God*,[58] he asserts that the interests of the community should be preferred to those of the individual; the commonwealth is a community of people under the law which the ruler should enforce; in this way each element, the upper, middle and lower ranks of society could be kept in accord, each fulfilling its functions; but the enclosers had destroyed the harmony, preferring private profit to the public good, and illegally attacking instead of helping other members of the community. Rous strengthens this argument with an elaborate simile in five parts, comparing the commonwealth with the human body.[59]

Rous's arguments on the illegality of enclosure are carefully reasoned and supported by tags from the bible, the fathers and the jurists. He argues with equal force and some ingenuity that they were contrary to the country's interests. Enclosures created povery, even famine, by destroying villages and depriving ordinary people of their homes.[60] The heirs of the enclosures themselves suffered because the property they inherited was less valuable.[61] The population declined because people reduced the size of their families in order to survive; therefore, the defence of the kingdom was imperilled because there were fewer able bodied men for the army.[62] Trade suffered since villagers had no produce to sell and were too poor to buy, and so towns declined.[63] Trade also was impaired because enclosures made travel difficult and dangerous:[64]

---

[58] *Rous*, pp. 37–8. Rous cites St Augustine, *De Civitate Dei*, II. 19, and V. 18. These references do not correspond with the modern divisions of the work (for the problem of the medieval chapter divisions of *De Civ. Dei* see H. I. Marrou, 'La division en chapitres des livres de *La Cité de Dieu*' in *Mélanges J. de Ghellinck*, i (Gembloux 1951), pp. 235–49). In terms of the modern divisions, Rous's references seem to be to *De Civ. Dei*, II. 21, and perhaps to XV. 8; for these chapters see H. A. Deane, *The Political and Social Ideas of St Augustine* (Columbia 1963), pp. 118 and nn. 4–7, 119, 123 and n. 20. It should be noted, however, that *De Civ. Dei*, XIX. 21 and 23 also deal with the nature of the *res publica*. The latter chapter, which compares the *civitas obediens* with a just man (see the next note for the analogy of the state with the human body), is cited in a similar context by Sir John Fortescue; *De Laudibus Legum Angliae*, ed., with an English translation, S. B. Chrimes (Cambridge 1949), p. 30.

[59] *Rous*, pp. 39–44. The analogy of the state with the human body was a commonplace in the middle ages. It is fully discussed, but without reference to Rous, in E. H. Kantorowicz, *The King's Two Bodies, a Study in Medieval Political Theology* (Princeton 1957), pp. 207–32. (For the related idea of the *corpus ecclesiae mysticum* see ibid., pp. 194–206.) The concept appears in John of Salisbury's *Policraticus* (see p. 45 and n. 12 above) and was elaborated by Sir John Fortescue: *De Laudibus Legum Angliae*, Chap. XIII (ed. Chrimes, pp. 30–3); cf. Kantorowicz, op. cit., pp. 223–4. It also figures prominently in the sermon delivered by John Russell, bishop of Lincoln, to parliament in 1483: see ibid., p. 225; various drafts of his sermon are printed in S. B. Chrimes, *English Constitutional Ideas in the Fifteenth Century* (Cambridge 1936), pp. 168–91. Russell's treatment of the analogy, with numerous biblical quotations, resembles Rous's. Moreover, like Rous, Russell accuses enclosers of causing the decay of 'the common and public body of the realm'—they were 'rotten members' of the community; ibid., pp. 180–1.

[60] *Rous*, pp. 121–5 passim.

[61] *Rous*, p. 116.

[62] *Rous*, pp. 116, 124.

[63] *Rous*, p. 124.

[64] *Rous*, pp. 126, 125.

In many places long established royal roads are obstructed by enclosure for parks and great meadows. Now men and women on horseback, especially the old and the weak, are harassed because they have to dismount to open gates where formerly they could proceed without hindrance. People on foot and some riding along other roads have to use byways and roundabout routes before they can gain access to an enclosed road, no doubt meanwhile cursing such enclosures. Moreover, streams are obstructed by enclosures and make roads almost impassable in many places, particularly around gateways. Woods and undergrowth grow and in them rooks flourish as never before, constantly consuming all kinds of grain crop; they also provide congenial lairs for wild beasts such as wolves and foxes which eat sheep, rabbits and birds. ... And where royal roads leading to various cities and fine villages run through destroyed villages, often by the gate or in some place suitable for thieves, the most savage robbers lurk, who rob men and rape women; they also ambush, seize, rob, beat, wound, tie up and, alas!, brutally take captive, mutilate without mercy, and kill God's faithful flock and the king's subjects, without regard for sex or age.

In addition enclosures harmed the church. Some churches were actually destroyed and others were impoverished by the decrease in tithes resulting from depopulation.[65] Similarly reduction in income injured schools and colleges, together with their libraries. Therefore, the clergy were less educated, God less well served and the battle against heresy impaired.[66]

Rous did not confine himself to such generalizations. He supported his argument that the condition of the country had deteriorated with scholarly research. He examined the villages in his own neighbourhood near Warwick. He listed fifty eight of them, and, in order to discover the extent of the depopulation, he studied twelve in more detail,[67] comparing their present state with what it had been in the time of Edward I, as recorded in the hundred rolls.[68] Nor did he cite only documentary evidence; for one village, Fulbrook, he also used the observations of his own eyes to provide evidence of decline since enclosure:[69]

At Fulbrook, where there was formerly a rectory, the church is destroyed, the villeins fled, and only the manor remains. The rest

[65] *Rous*, pp. 115–16, 118.
[66] *Rous*, p. 130.
[67] *Rous*, pp. 122–4.
[68] *Rous*, p. 123. Rous was a pioneer in his use of the hundred rolls; see Beresford, *Lost Villages of England*, p. 282. Rous also cites Domesday book as evidence; *Rous*, p. 107.
[69] *Rous*, pp. 123–4; cf. *VCH*, *Warwick*, iii. 91–2 (where this passage is cited). For Joan, Lady Bergavenny (d. 1435), wife of William Beauchamp, Lord Bergavenny (1392–1411) see *G.E.C.*, *Complete Peerage*, i. 26.

was enclosed for a park by John duke of Bedford, brother of King Henry V, who built a noble square tower for the castle, but now almost nothing is there. Also Joan, Lady Bergavenny, built a splendid gate-house inside the park fence, suitable to welcome her noble lord—to please him on arrival; now this gate-house is destroyed.

Rous was a pioneer in his research on enclosures.[70] No one previously had tried to assess their extent and results, and it was not until the early sixteenth century that the government undertook a comparable inquiry.[71] Here Rous showed his gift for historical and antiquarian research which is so remarkable a feature of his study of the more remote past.

As already mentioned, Rous began the *Historia* in order to commemorate kings, great ecclesiastics and the founders of cities. In fact the founders of other places besides cities (and towns) attracted his attention—churches, monasteries, castles and especially universities. His interest in founders was stimulated by patriotism and by love of his own locality: the older an institution, the greater its venerability. Therefore, he did not want only to commemorate the achievements of founders, but also by so doing to prove the antiquity of what they had founded. He asserts, for example, that Paris university owed its origin to four Englishmen, pupils of Bede,[72] and that Warwick was named after an early Anglo-Saxon king called Warremund who had restored the town.[73]

In order to write the history of England from the earliest times Rous used numerous standard sources, both English and continental. Among the former he cites Bede,[74] Florence of Worcester,[75] William of Malmesbury,[76] Henry of Huntingdon,[77] Ralph Diceto,[78] William of Newburgh,[79] Roger of Howden,[80] Gerald of Wales,[81] Matthew Paris,[82] Nicholas Trevet,[83]

---

[70] For the importance of Rous's researches to the historian today see Beresford, op. cit., pp. 81–2, 117, 148–9, 269 (Rous's list of depopulated villages is reproduced in ibid., Plate IX), and *Deserted Medieval Villages*, ed. Maurice Beresford and J. G. Hurst (London 1971), p. 11.

[71] See Ephraim Lipson, *An Introduction to the Economic History of England* (ninth edition, London 1947), i. 142, 151, 175–8, 180–1.

[72] *Rous*, p. 68.

[73] *Rous*, p. 60.

[74] E.g. *Rous*, pp. 48, 67.

[75] E.g. *Rous*, pp. 78, 139 (Florence of Worcester is referred to as Marianus Scotus; for the relationship between the Worcester chronicle and Marianus' see Gransden, *Historical Writing*, i. 145).

[76] E.g. *Rous*, pp. 67, 73.

[77] E.g. *Rous*, pp. 18, 59.

[78] E.g. *Rous*, pp. 69, 188.

[79] E.g. *Rous*, pp. 145, 148.

[80] E.g. *Rous*, p. 188.

[81] E.g. *Rous*, pp. 98, 143.

[82] E.g. *Rous*, pp. 101, 102.

[83] E.g. *Rous*, pp. 38, 142.

Ranulf Higden[84] and John Mandeville.[85] He also used the *Brut*,[86] besides some less known works—a Life (apparently lost) of Earl Guy of Warwick,[87] the *Gesta Abbatum* of St Albans,[88] a chronicle of Osney abbey,[89] the chronicle of John Strecche[90] and John Hardyng's chronicle.[91] His continental sources include Bernard de Breydenbach,[92] Caesarius of Heisterbach,[93] Martinus Polonus[94] and Vincent of Beauvais.[95] Among the non-historical writers to whom he refers are Cicero,[96] St Augustine[97] and Bracton.[98]

Rous recognized the importance of libraries,[99] but although he built up a good one himself, he did not have at hand the resources of one of the famous libraries of his day. Therefore he had to travel to consult books. He records that he visited north Wales and Anglesey to consult chronicles.[100] He also read in the university library at Oxford,[101] and in London he used a book on law in the office of the king's chamberlain, one entitled *De Aquis Thamesiae* in the Guildhall[102] and Diceto's chronicle at St Paul's.[103] Besides visiting St Albans where he consulted the *Gesta Abbatum*, and Osney abbey where he consulted its chronicle,[104] he went to Winchester: there in Hyde abbey he not only copied 'a certain ancient *tabula*', but also saw 'a noble chronicle which had been transcribed in a modern, clear script from an ancient manuscript lest it perished';[105] and at St Swithun's he talked to the monk Thomas Rudborne, himself a chronicler and 'the most learned man of his times in the chronicles of the English'.[106]

[84] E.g. *Rous*, pp. 10, 141.

[85] E.g. *Rous*, pp. 4, 16.

[86] Rous's use of the *Brut* is shown, for instance, by his narration of the Brutus legend. He cites Geoffrey of Monmouth; e.g. *Rous*, pp. 18, 26.

[87] *Rous*, p. 54. For a Life of Guy of Warwick in Latin prose attributed to Girardus Cornubiensis, see p. 493, Appendix D, below. For another Life of Guy, now lost but presumably in Latin prose, attributed to Walter of Exeter, see Hardy, *Cat.* iii. 373. For the romance Lives of Guy of Warwick, in Anglo-Norman and English, see p. 313 n. 25 above.

[88] *Rous*, p. 60.

[89] *Rous*, p. 203.

[90] *Rous*, p. 98 (Rous calls him Strench).

[91] E.g. *Rous*, pp. 19, 23.

[92] E.g. *Rous*, pp. 3–4, 5; cf. p. 324 and n. 118 below.

[93] See p. 318 nn. 56, 57 above.

[94] *Rous*, p. 73.

[95] Eg. *Rous*, pp. 68, 151.

[96] *Rous*, p. 39.

[97] E.g. *Rous*, pp. 17, 34; see also p. 319 and n. 58 above.

[98] *Rous*, p. 38.

[99] He deplores the damage done to resources for the upkeep of libraries, which he asserts was an indirect result of enclosures; *Rous*, p. 130.

[100] *Rous*, p. 54.

[101] *Rows Rol*, no. 8. Cf. *Rous*, p. 208.

[102] *Rous*, p. 200.

[103] *Rous*, p. 69.

[104] Nn. 88, 89 above.

[105] *Rous*, p. 96.

[106] *Rous*, p. 73. For the historical works of Thomas Rudborne, monk of St Swithun's, Winchester, see pp. 394–8, 493–4, Appendix D, below. Rous cites his *Historia Major*; *Rous*,

Rous read widely but was undiscriminating in the use of sources, accepting legend and credible history with equal satisfaction. When dealing with legend, he even weighs one source against another to give added authority to his narrative,[107] and explicitly defends Mandeville's veracity.[108] He borrows the legendary history of early Britain mainly from Geoffrey of Monmouth and John Hardyng and shares their taste for false etymologies of place-names—which were particularly congenial to his interest in origins.[109] He liked the legends of foreign countries as well as those of Britain. He was particularly fascinated by giants (no doubt because Guy, the legendary first earl of Warwick, was one), and wrote a book, now lost, about them.[110] He tells of the giants in Albion to whom Albina and her sisters gave birth,[111] and of those abroad who inhabited Palestine before the Flood. Of the latter he writes:[112]

> [In] Jaffa (so called after Japhet son of Noah, who built it and named it after himself) great poles may be seen to this day, which seem to hang from a certain cliff, and to which boats were moored. There also are chains of amazing size where a giant named Andromadus was held captive, one of whose ribs extended in length to forty feet, as can still be seen. That worthy man Bernard [de Breydenbach] saw this rib on the first of July 1483.
> ... I also remember reading in the *Travels* of John Mandeville (an Englishman born at St Albans and a doctor of medicine) that he had seen this same rib of the giant Andromadus.

Rous's failure to distinguish the credible from the incredible is well illustrated by his propensity for combining first hand observation with legendary origins. For example he remarks correctly that wallwort, which he found in villages around Warwick, is a reddish plant, but asserts that it was thus coloured by blood shed during the Danish wars.[113] He

---

pp. 78, 82, 96, 98. In addition, Rous mentions Rudborne's namesake who was a fellow of Merton College, chaplain to Henry V, and bishop of St Davids (d. 1442); *Rous*, p. 208. This Rudborne is supposed to have written a chronicle which is now lost; see Emden, *Biographical Register*, iii. 1582–3. Doubt has been expressed whether in fact he did; see J. H. Wylie and W. T. Waugh, *The Reign of Henry the Fifth* (Cambridge 1914–29, 3 vols), ii. 80 and n. 4. However, since the Winchester Rudborne cites a chronicle by his namesake (see Hardy, *Cat.* iii. 78), the possibility cannot be dismissed, although it should be borne in mind that the Winchester Rudborne was not scrupulously meticulous in the ascription of sources, and used at least one work, in this case probably a forgery, apparently under a bogus name (see pp. 493–4 Appendix D, below).

[107] See, for example, Rous's treatment of the 'evidence' for predeluvian history: *Rous*, pp. 3–5.
[108] *Rous*, p. 4.
[109] *Rous*, pp. 18–19.
[110] Rous mentions his own book on giants; *Rous*, p. 18.
[111] *Rous*, pp. 10, 14.
[112] *Rous*, p. 4. Cf. *Mandeville's Travels*, ed. M. C. Seymour (Oxford 1967), p. 21, and p. 127 and n. 69 above.
[113] *Rous*, p. 104. For Wallwort (*Sambucus ebulus*), also called Danwort, Danes' blood and Daneweed, see *NED*, x. pt ii. 56, under 'wallwort' 1 (which cites this passage by Rous).

mentions in the Warwick rolls that he had seen the cup in the treasury of Warwick castle formerly owned by Eneas, a (legendary) ancestor of the earls of Warwick ('I have drunk of the same [cup, so] I dare the better write about it'): Eneas, Rous relates, had been given a shield by an angel to defend his mother against his wicked stepmother, who had turned his brothers into swans and bound them with collars and chains; the cup was made of their chains.[114] Similarly, Rous follows his account of the supposed foundation of Oxford university by King Alfred with careful topographical references to the students' halls.[115]

Rous is chiefly famous as an antiquary, and his love of legend should not be allowed to detract from this reputation. The results of his antiquarian inquiries can easily be distinguished from those of his credulity. Indeed legends in one respect had a beneficial effect on his work; they roused his curiosity about the past in general and about any object of legendary significance in particular. His interest in history was also influenced by the works of such 'encyclopaedic' historians as Ranulf Higden and by travel writers such as John Mandeville; to them he partly owed his broad view which included not just the acts of famous men, but such topics as social customs.

Rous's powers of exact observation of individual objects were a by-product of his artistic abilities.[116] The illustrations on the two Warwick rolls show that he had considerable talent.[117] Moreover, he recognized the value of art as a means of recording anything of historical or social interest. Here he claims to have forestalled Bernard of Breydenbach who took an artist with him to the Holy Land; Rous had earlier urged John Tiptoft, earl of Worcester ('a fellow scholar whom I had known at Oxford, a very well read man'), to include an artist in his entourage when he visited the Holy Land, to draw whatever caught his attention, and so provide a souvenir for his return.[118]

The breadth of Rous's antiquarian interests is very evident. He gives a detailed account of the origin of shires and their organization in Anglo-Saxon times, derived at least in part from charter evidence.[119] He discusses

---

[114] See *Rows Rol*, no. 18.

[115] *Rous*, pp. 77–8. Cf. p. 325 and n. 123 below. For Oxford's antiquities see also *Rous*, pp. 201–2.

[116] In this respect Rous resembled Matthew Paris; see Gransden, *Historical Writing*, i. 364–6.

[117] See, however, p. 311 n. 17 above.

[118] *Rous*, p. 5. For the life of Bernard de Breydenbach, dean of Mainz, see H. W. Davies, *Bernhard von Breydenbach and his Journey to the Holy Land 1483–4* (London 1911; reprinted Utrecht 1968), p. i–iii. The artist who accompanied him on his pilgrimage and drew views of the places seen on the journey, was Erhard Reuwich of Utrecht; see ibid., pp. iii, xxi, and J. R. Mitchell, *John Tiptoft, 1427–1470* (London 1938), p. 28. Rous's acquaintance with Tiptoft may well have been helped by Tiptoft's marriage in 1449 to Cecily daughter of Richard Neville, earl of Salisbury, sister of Richard Neville, earl of Warwick, and widow of Henry Beauchamp, duke of Warwick (d. 1446); although Cecily died after a year of marriage, Tiptoft's connection with the earl of Warwick continued; see ibid., p. 19.

[119] *Rous*, p. 66.

the decline of the English language after the Norman Conquest,[120] and considers the possibility, because of his surname, that he himself was descended from William Rufus (he decides, however, that this was unlikely because most families who came over with William the Conqueror had a member with that cognomen).[121] As the family historian of the earls of Warwick, Rous was conscientious and rational once he emerged from their legendary past into the post-Conquest period.

Rous's use of visual evidence is illustrated in a number of passages in the *Historia*. He includes topographical descriptions: his comments on the villages and roads of Warwickshire have already been referred to, and he also has a good description of the town of Warwick itself. He was interested not only in the topography of Warwick as it existed in his own day, but also, as in the case of neighbouring villages and roads, in what was once there. Thus he explains exactly where in relation to the streets and buildings of his own day, a monastery and nunnery were situated, one in the town and the other in the suburbs, before their destruction by the Danes.[122] The evidence of the *Historia* alone would establish Rous's claim to be a topographer of ability. There is, however, additional evidence. His other place of residence, Oxford, elicited a topographical study. His account of the halls has been mentioned above, but he gave more detail in a separate survey which he made some time between 1440 and 1450, before he left the university to take up the chaplaincy of Guy's Cliff. Having listed the sixteen colleges, Rous lists over sixty halls grouped according to their locations. Then he lists six halls which were destroyed 'before my time', and six more destroyed 'in my time in Cat street for [All] Souls college'.[123]

It is clear from the *Historia* that Rous also examined other types of material objects with a discriminating eye, and drew reasonable conclusions from his observations. He notes more or less correctly that Henry I started the practice of sealing documents with wax seals; previously the kings of England had authenticated them with a cross and sign manual (he cites examples of royal charters).[124] He also remarks that 'after the

---

[120] *Rous*, pp. 138–9.

[121] *Rous*, p. 110.

[122] *Rous*, p. 104.

[123] No holograph manuscript of Rous's list survives. However, there are a number of copies, the best of which is printed in '*Survey of the Antiquities of the City of Oxford*' composed in 1661–6 by *Anthony Wood*, i. *The City and Suburbs*, ed. Andrew Clark (Oxford Historical Soc., xv, 1889), pp. 638–41. For a recent discussion of Rous's list and of its value, with further references, see T. H. Aston, 'Oxford's medieval alumni' in *Past and Present*, no. 74 (1977), pp. 36–8 and nn. To this period belongs the bird's eye view of New College by the warden, Thomas Chandler; A. H. Smith, *New College Oxford and its Buildings* (Oxford 1952), pp. 43, 49, 109, 179 and frontispiece.

[124] *Rous*, p. 138. Edward the Confessor was the first king to use a great seal (which was of wax); see *Facsimiles of English Royal Writs to A.D. 1100 presented to Vivian Hunter Galbraith*, ed. T. A. M. Bishop and Pierre Chaplais (Oxford 1957), pp. xix, xxii, and Pierre Chaplais,

capture of John king of France' (in 1356) the English nobility replaced the equestrian figures on their seals by coats-of-arms.[125] To reach these conclusions Rous must have examined the charters in the archives of the earls of Warwick. His interest in heraldry appears mainly in the Warwick rolls, in which he describes and depicts the arms of the figures commemorated.[126]

Rous's interest in the history of costume is evident in all his works. The *Historia* has numerous references to varieties of dress through the ages. He describes what people wore in Anglo-Saxon times, under William Rufus and under Richard II.[127] He describes what the Jews used to wear when they lived in England before their expulsion by Edward I,[128] and the habits worn by the regular canons of St Sepulchre in Jerusalem.[129] And he had given the dress of his contemporaries careful consideration: he inveighs against frivolous modern fashions, in traditional homiletic style.[130]

His interest in dress dominates the Warwick rolls. Here he tried to transpose into artistic form what he had learnt on the subject.[131] The ladies on the rolls wear old fashioned styles, accurately copied but not appropriate to the times when they lived. Thus King Alfred's daughter Æthelfrida is dressed in a costume similar to that of the effigy of Katherine, wife of Thomas Beauchamp, earl of Warwick from 1329 to 1369, in St Mary's, Warwick.[132]

More remarkable is Rous's attempt to indicate the development of medieval armour. He probably obtained his information from seals,

---

English Royal Documents, King John to Henry VI, 1199–1461 (Oxford 1971), p. 2. Rous may have attributed the introduction of the use of a royal seal in wax to Henry I because surviving examples are more numerous for Henry I's reign than for the preceding reigns; see W. de G. Birch, *Catalogue of Seals in the Department of Manuscripts in the British Museum* (London 1887–1900, 6 vols), i. 2–8.

[125] *Rous*, p. 204. Rous's general statement that armorial seals replaced equestrian ones is correct, but his dating is wrong; the change took place in the early thirteenth century. Moreover, from the same period some of the greater barons used two faced seals, with an equestrian figure on the obverse, and a shield of arms on the reverse; see C. H. Hunter Blair, 'Armorials upon English seals from the twelfth to the sixteenth centuries' in *Archaeologia*, lxxxix (1943), pp. 1–26 passim.

[126] P. 311 above. For a notice of arms in the *Historia* see *Rous*, pp. 142–3.

[127] *Rous*, pp. 106, 110, 205. Rous also notes the introduction of the side-saddle by Richard II's queen, Anne of Bohemia; *Rous*, p. 205.

[128] *Rous*, p. 202.

[129] *Rous*, pp. 139–40.

[130] *Rous*, 131. For tirades against contemporary fashions in dress by other chroniclers see pp. 104–6 passim above.

[131] Rous's pictorial contribution to the history of armour is discussed in Mann, 'Instances of antiquarian feeling in medieval and renaissance art', p. 262, and in Kendrick, *British Antiquity*, pp. 28–9, who also discusses his representations of ladies' dress. For references to reproduction of some of the pictures see p. 311 n. 17 above.

[132] For an engraving of Katherine's effigy, which is next to her husband's, see, for example, [Richard Gough], *Description of the Beauchamp Chapel* ... (London 1804).

effigies and wall paintings, and perhaps from a collection of old armour in Warwick castle. As a result of this research he established a chronology which is in a very general sense correct.[133] He portrays the legendary founders of the house and the early Anglo-Saxon earls in the long mail hauberks which were used from the seventh to the eleventh centuries. The late Anglo-Saxon earls have short hauberks. Most of the late eleventh century earls have a ribbed helm chained to the pommel of the sword (probably a misunderstanding of the sword chained to the hauberk which appears on medieval Beauchamp seals).[134] The thirteenth century earls wear armorial surcoats; the late thirteenth and early fourteenth century earls wear mixed mail and plate, and then the full-plate armour begins. Rous's representation of fourteenth century armour is fairly accurate, and indeed the picture of the suit of Thomas Beauchamp, who died in 1369, so closely resembles that on his effigy in St Mary's, that it must either have been copied from it or from the armour itself. In the same way the drawing of Richard Beauchamp shows a suit like that of his effigy.[135]

It can, therefore, be seen that Rous continued and developed the medieval antiquarian tradition. Nevertheless, the amount of space in his main historical work the *Historia* devoted to antiquities is small, much smaller than that spent on legends: and the proportion which concerns topography in particular is even less.

In contrast to Rous's *Historia*, William Worcester's principal work, the *Itinerarium* (the *Itinerary*) is almost exclusively antiquarian in content. This was partly the result of Worcester's absorption in such studies in his later years, and partly because of the nature of the book: it is not a history circumscribed by medieval forms but a notebook of an antiquary's travels. However, before discussing the *Itinerary* in detail, Worcester's life and other works must be considered.[136]

---

[133] For reproductions see Plate XII below and the plates in the works by T. D. Kendrick, J. G. Mann and C. E. Wright cited above (see p. 311 nn. 17, 18). For twelfth century full mail with long hauberks and coifs in one piece, resembling that worn by Rous's legendary earls of the British period, see G. F. Laking, *A Record of European Armour and Arms through Seven Centuries* (London 1920–2, 5 vols), i. 66–70. For a reconstruction of an Anglo-Saxon warrior, closely resembling Rous's portraits see ibid., i. 31, fig. 39. For an Anglo-Saxon ribbed helm, like those depicted by *Rous*, see ibid. i., 8, fig. 11. For war hats in the middle ages see ibid., ii. 57–66. For the introduction of surcoats in the early thirteenth century see ibid., i. 124. For the introduction of mixed mail and plate in the mid-thirteenth century see ibid., i. 121 et seq., and for its increased use in the fourteenth century see ibid., i. 145. It will be noticed that Rous represents Waleran de Newburgh (d. 1203 or 1204) in a helm with a nasal (Plate XII (d)): nasals were apparently introduced into England by the Normans; see ibid., i. 39, fig. 45, 42, 57 fig. 71. For a more detailed discussion of Rous's representation of the evolution of medieval armour see A. Gransden, 'Antiquarian studies in fifteenth century England' in *Antiquaries Journal*, lx, pt i (1980).
[134] See, for example, the seal (1343–4) of Thomas Beauchamp; BL Seal no. xliii. 18.
[135] For Richard Beauchamp's effigy see Laking, op. cit., i. 163–5.
[136] The best account of Worcester's life and work is by McFarlane, 'William Worcester', pp. 196–221.

William Worcester was born in Bristol in 1415, and was a student at Oxford by 1432. He had entered the service of Sir John Fastolf by 1438, and acted as his secretary until Fastolf's death in November 1459. A recent scholar has described him as one of the new class of 'gentlemen bureaucrats';[137] such men grew up in the service of literate laymen, acted as amanuenses, helped to run their employers' estates, and engaged in legal and other business. At first Worcester acted as the surveyor of Fastolf's manor of Castle Combe in Wiltshire,[138] but then he lived mainly in London until 1454, when he moved to Fastolf's home at Caister in Norfolk.[139] He was nearly always in his master's company. However, he went on business journeys on his own in England and also in Normandy, partly on Fastolf's family business, and partly on business connected with John duke of Bedford, the king's lieutenant in Normandy from 1422 until his death in 1435, of whose household Fastolf was master.[140] Occasionally Worcester visited his home in Bristol and at some date he married, probably rather late in life. He looked after Fastolf in his old age, acting both as secretary and as physician.

Nor was Worcester freed from his duties by Fastolf's death.[141] The latter left his business affairs in confusion, and Worcester spent nearly twenty years trying to carry out Fastolf's intentions and defending his rights at law. He himself was harassed by poverty and fought for the reward that was his due: in 1470 lack of money compelled him to stop his business journeys and to settle in Cambridge. It was not until 1474 that he considered his labours adequately recompensed, but he was still sporadically engaged on his old master's affairs until 1478. He died in 1482. Worcester, therefore, never had the opportunity of being a full time scholar. The study of history and antiquities was the occupation of his limited leisure hours and of the few years remaining to him after his final retirement.

Nevertheless, although Fastolf worked Worcester so hard and left him so poor, a career in his service had some advantages for a would-be historian and antiquary. Worcester lived in a circle which had some interest in learning. Fastolf's master, John duke of Bedford, was, like many of the Lancastrian nobility, a patron of letters; he bought 843 books from the French royal library which had been built up by Charles V and Charles VI.[142] Fastolf himself, though not a learned man, was interested in literature. He owned books,[143] one of which, Christine de Pisan's

---

[137] Ibid., p. 199.

[138] Ibid., pp. 199 n. 7, 200 and n. 9.

[139] Ibid., p. 200.

[140] Ibid., p. 200 and n. 6.

[141] Ibid., pp. 201–3.

[142] See J. H. Wylie, *History of England under Henry IV* (London 1884–98, 4 vols; reprinted New York 1969), iv. 135 and n. 9, 136 and n. 1.

[143] An inventory of Fastolf's books drawn up in about 1450 is printed in *Historical Manuscripts Commission, Appendix to the Eighth Report*, p. 268 a (from the papers in Magdalen College,

Epistle of Othea to Hector, had been written and illuminated especially for him (in 1450).[144] Six of his dependants, including Worcester, are known to have written literary works. His stepson Stephen Scrope translated the *Epistle of Othea* from French into English with a long dedication to him.[145] Furthermore, Fastolf commissioned Worcester to render into English the French translation of Cicero's *De Senectute*.[146] While in Fastolf's household Worcester studied a number of classical authors besides Cicero, for example Ovid, Virgil, Lucan, Seneca and Suetonius.[147] He studied these authors, and also Orosius, in French translations, but he made his own translation of Cicero's *De Amicitia* direct from the Latin.[148] However, despite his knowledge of classical writers who were masters of style, he did not use them to classicize his Latin which remained a rough instrument of his meaning without literary polish (with grammatical mistakes and English words interspersed). Rather he used the classics to provide him with moral dicta to add weight to the subject matter of his prose.[149]

As an inmate of Fastolf's household Worcester had access to his master's archives. He was also able to consult those of John duke of Bedford in Normandy, when Fastolf sent him there in 1442 to try to straighten out the late duke's affairs. This visit made it possible for him to learn about Fastolf's career, and about the Hundred Years' War and the English administration in Normandy. By these means and by talking to members of the household Worcester accumulated material for his (now lost) *Acta Domini Johannis Fastolf* (*The Deeds of Sir John Fastolf*), an account of Fastolf's family and career.[150] He started this work in the year of his master's death, perhaps for the amusement of the invalid, but only finished it later.

Chivalric ideals must have been paramount in Fastolf's household which included old soldiers who had fought in the Hundred Years' War. Two of these men, Philip Basset and Christopher Hanson, who had served Fastolf when he was governor of Maine and Anjou, composed a short chronicle of the war (covering the years from 1415 to 1429) for their master.[151]

Oxford). Cf. K. B. McFarlane, *The Nobility of Later Medieval England* (Oxford 1973), p. 237 and n. 6. Worcester himself transcribed part of Fastolf's copy of Cristoforo Buondel-monte's *Liber Insularum Archipelagi*; see *WW*, pp. xxi, xxiii, 372 and n. *c*.

[144] Bodleian Library, Oxford, MS. Laud Misc. 570; see Kathleen Chesney, 'Two Manuscripts of Christine de Pisan' in *Medium Ævum*, i (1932), pp. 38–41.

[145] *The Epistle of Othea to Hector, or the Boke of Knyghthode M Translated from the French of Christine de Pisan. With a Dedication to Sir John Fastolf, K. G. By Stephen Scrope Esquire*, ed. G. F. Warner (Roxburghe Club, London 1904).

[146] McFarlane, 'William Worcester', pp. 215–16. Worcester mentions in his *Itinerary* that in 1472 he presented a copy of his translation of the *De Senectute* to William Wainfleet, bishop of Winchester, but received no reward; *WW*, p. 252.

[147] For Worcester's use of classical authors see McFarlane, op. cit., pp. 214, 215–16.

[148] Ibid., pp. 215–16 and n. 4.

[149] For Worcester's Latin see ibid., pp. 212, 214, 219.

[150] Ibid., pp. 208–10.

[151] Fully discussed and extracts printed from the manuscript (College of Arms MS. 9) in

They wrote in French, helped by one of Fastolf's chaplains, a Frenchman called Luke Nantron. The work has recently been aptly described as 'a plain soldierly account of the wars in which Fastolf had played so leading a part, intended to please the old man by awakening memories of his past adventures. It is rich in the names of those companions in arms and well-tried foes whom Fastolf would delight to recall.'[152]

In view of the milieu in which Worcester lived it is hardly surprising that he accepted chivalric values. Indeed he had some hand in the composition of Basset's and Hanson's chronicle: he made additions in Latin, (including a preface which states that the work was compiled 'through the diligence of William Worcester, secretary of the said Sir John Fastolf'.[153] Moreover, the fact that Worcester's military companions were frustrated by the end of the Hundred Years' War must help account for his consistently pro-war attitude: he advocated the renewal of the war as a solution to England's ills. This view, which influenced his historical studies, gives him an affinity with John Hardyng, but divided him intellectually from his acquaintance Sir John Fortescue, who favoured peace with France.[154]

Worcester's opinion in favour of war is most clearly expressed in the *Boke of Noblesse*.[155] He began this work soon after 1451[156] perhaps partly to please Fastolf, but his principal purpose was to persuade Henry VI to enforce the just claims of the English crown in France. He urges the king to 'the repairing and winning again, upon a new conquest to be had for your very right and true title in the inheritance of the said Realm of France and the Duchy of Normandy.'[157] He recalls the spectacular conquests achieved by the descendants of Brutus, and the deeds of the famous heroes of the English nation. He gives advice on the conduct of war in general (quoting standard works on chivalry[158] and also some of Fastolf's dicta[159]) and on how England's continental possessions should be adminis-

---

B. J. H. Rowe, 'A contemporary account of the Hundred Years' War from 1415 to 1429' in *EHR*, xli (1926), pp. 504–13. See also McFarlane, 'William Worcester', pp. 207–8.

[152] Rowe, op. cit., p. 513.

[153] A transcription of the preface is in Rowe, op. cit., p. 506, but a slightly better transcription is in McFarlane, op. cit., pp. 207–8.

[154] See *The Governance of England ... by Sir John Fortescue. Kt.*, ed. Charles Plummer (Oxford 1885), pp. 68–9 and nn. For Worcester's acquaintance with Fortescue see McFarlane, op. cit., p. 214 and n. 1.

[155] Printed *The Boke of Noblesse*, ed. J. G. Nichols (Roxburghe Club, London 1860, reprinted New York 1972). For the popularity of military manuals in fifteenth century England, with a survey of the surviving examples, see Diane Bornstein, 'Military manuals in fifteenth-century England' in *Mediaeval Studies*, xxxviii (1975), pp. 468–77 (for Worcester's *Boke* see ibid., pp. 473–5). For the significance of the *Boke* as part of the revival of the chivalric ideal in the last half of the fifteenth century see A. B. Ferguson, *The Indian Summer of English Chivalry* (Durham, North Carolina, 1960), pp. 144–53, and pp. 475–6 below.

[156] McFarlane, op. cit., pp. 211–12.

[157] *Boke of Noblesse*, p. 3.

[158] For Worcester's sources see ibid., pp. iii–x passim. They include Vegetius' *De Re Militari*, of which a copy, in French translation, occurs in Fastolf's book list; see p. 328 n. 143 above.

[159] *Boke of Noblesse*, pp. v, x, xiv, 16, 64–5, 77; for another mention of Fastolf see ibid., pp. xi, 68.

tered, with especial reference to the regency of John duke of Bedford.[160]

Most remarkable is the amount of research Worcester did for the *Boke of Noblesse*. He consulted books in the libraries of London and Cambridge, and made extracts relating to events in ancient and modern history which could be used to support his argument.[161] Furthermore, he provided scholarly documentation, primarily to illustrate the duke of Bedford's success. No doubt making full use of Bedford's archives, he collected the relevant documents together into a 'codicil', a short volume of *additamenta*.[162] Subsequently Worcester seems to have presented a copy of the *Boke* and its 'codicil' to Edward IV on the eve of his French campaign of 1475. For this purpose he apparently adapted the preface to the 'codicil', addressing it to Edward instead of to Henry VI. (Later still his son, also called William, was to adapt it for presentation to Richard III.)[163]

Worcester's interest in contemporary history extended little beyond Anglo-French relations. He makes few references to the Wars of the Roses in his most famous work the *Itinerary*[164] with which we are concerned below. However, he does describe in it three instances of lawlessness in Norfolk (all indirectly connected with Fastolf or his family), and remarks: 'thus neither the law of England nor King Henry VI was held in respect; and in this way the realm of England began to fall to ruin.'[165]

Worcester's principal concern was with antiquities. For his antiquarian studies his career in Fastolf's service had some advantages, as it did for his other intellectual activities.[166] Business journeys must have cultivated his taste for travel; responsibility for Fastolf's property must have trained him to look carefully at buildings; and the duty of keeping accounts taught him to think in figures, a skill he turned to good use as an antiquary. Nevertheless, as has been seen, while he was engaged on Fastolf's affairs, antiquarianism could occupy only a small part of his time: it was not until after 1477, less than five years before his death, that he was able to indulge his interest freely. Almost at once he set out on his antiquarian travels. The longest was in 1478, lasting from 17 August until 8 October.

---

[160] Ibid., pp. v–vi, 17–19, 28, 31, 44–5, 47, 72.

[161] McFarlane, op. cit., pp. 212 and n. 7, 213 and n. 1.

[162] The book of documents with their preface (Lambeth MS. 506) are printed in *Letters and Papers illustrative of the Wars of the English in France*, ed. Joseph Stevenson (RS 1861–4, 2 vols in 3 pts), ii. pt ii. 521–742. For Stevenson's edition see McFarlane, op. cit., p. 213 n. 4.

[163] For the date of the work see McFarlane, op. cit., p. 210. For the revision of the preface see ibid., p. 210, and Stevenson, op. cit., ii. pt ii. 521–2. A parallel instance of revision is provided by Fortescue's *Governance of England*. If Plummer's first interpretation of the evidence is accepted, the revision of the *Governance* would exactly correspond with the revision of Worcester's *Boke* as postulated by McFarlane. However, Plummer suggests alternatively that the *Governance* was first addressed to Richard III, and then revised in Tudor times to make Edward IV the dedicatee; he offers the same suggestion with regard to the revision of Worcester's *Boke*; Plummer, op. cit., p. 95 and n. 4.

[164] Printed *William Worcestre Itineraries*, ed., with an English translation, J. H. Harvey (Oxford Medieval Texts 1969).

[166] *WW*, pp. 190, 252, and see p. 334 and n. 198 below.

[166] Pp. 328–9 above.

He travelled from Norwich to London, then on to Bristol via Southampton, Salisbury and Castle Combe; from Bristol he proceeded to St Michael's Mount via Wells, Taunton and Okehampton; he returned to London again through Bristol, but varied his route considerably from that taken on the way. In the summer of 1479 he travelled in Norfolk (in the neighbourhood of Norwich), and also visited Thetford and Bury St Edmunds in Suffolk. And in August 1480 he travelled from London to Glastonbury, via Oxford, Castle Combe and Bristol.[167]

Wherever he went Worcester carried folded sheets of paper for notes, probably in his saddle bags. These were later bound into a book, a long narrow volume, which still survives (Corpus Christi College, Cambridge, MS. 210). This book is the *Itinerary*.[168] It contains a jumble of entries, material relating to the journeys themselves, and miscellaneous jottings mainly concerning what Worcester saw. It is in no sense finished work and Worcester can never have intended it for publication. It falls into the same category as two of his other extant notebooks, his common-place book and medical collections.[169] (Also surviving is a volume of his accounts relating to his surveyorship of Castle Combe.)[170]

It is uncertain whether Worcester's *Itinerary* represents notes made in preparation for a finished book on the antiquities of England. Indeed such a work, the *Antiquitates Anglie* (*The Antiquities of England*), in three volumes, has been attributed to Worcester, but no copy has survived, nor is there any conclusive evidence that it was ever written. Possibly it merely comprised three notebooks, the *Itinerary* being the only one now extant.[171] There is rather more evidence that Worcester completed and published another antiquarian work, the *De Agri Norfolcensis Familiis Antiquis* (*On the Ancient Families of Norfolk*). This is not now known, but there is evidence dating from the sixteenth century onwards that it once existed. It was apparently a collection for family history, containing lists and genealogies of the East Anglian nobility and gentry.[172]

The *Itinerary* has features of a common-place book and reflects Worcester's varied interests. There are scattered through it, besides miscellaneous historical notes, proverbs,[173] lines from classical authors,[174] notes on the etymology of Greek words,[175] and also on the divisions of time[176] and on

---

[167] For a map of Worcester's itineraries see *WW*, at the end of the volume.

[168] For a description of the manuscript see ibid., pp. xviii-xxi. See also Plate XIII above.

[169] BL MSS. Cotton Julius F VII and Sloane 4, respectively; see *WW*, p. xx. Another medical notebook is apparently lost; see McFarlane, 'William Worcester', p. 216. Cf. *WW*, pp. 90, 125 n. 4.

[170] BL MS. Additional 28208.

[171] See McFarlane, op. cit., pp. 216–18, and *WW*, p. xi.

[172] McFarlane, op. cit., pp. 216–17.

[173] *WW*, p. 324.

[174] *WW*, pp. 154, 391.

[175] *WW*, pp. 64, 66.

[176] *WW*, pp. 238, 240.

astrology.[177] Worcester's interest in botany (no doubt connected with his medical interests) and zoology is also evident: he mentions that sage and bindweed have flowers like bells, and that percepier grows in the Cotswolds[178] and on the walls of Dover castle,[179] and he lists the fishes in the river Wye,[180] and often records what birds and animals inhabited islands— for example 'birds called puffins' lived on Tresco Island, gannets, gulls and sea mews on Pentyver's Rock, sheep and rabbits on Sheep Island, and rats and mice on St Tudwal's.[181]

Nevertheless, despite its miscellaneous character, Worcester's journeys themselves impose some unity on the *Itinerary*. It has entries relating to the mechanics, so to speak, of travel. There are useful routes described, for example the route taken by Thomas Clerk of Ware from Ware to St Michael's Mount.[182] Often the route is given together with the mileage (which Worcester estimated with varying degrees of accuracy) between the towns—for instance from Oxford to St Michael's Mount.[183] In the absence of road maps such mileages were of course very useful to a rider. It seems that in a day Worcester covered on an average just over twenty one miles, riding for between four and six hours (sometimes more).[184] Some of the entries are diaries of his journey. He records, for example: 'a certain man called Philip Pure of his courtesy put me up for the night' in Salisbury;[185] in Bristol Thomas Yong and his wife 'kindly made me good cheer for his father's sake';[186] he was arrested near Warminster in Wiltshire (the cause is not given);[187] and his horse fell on Bodmin moor.[188] He also notes some of his expenses. Thus he records that while visiting Bristol from 1 September until 9 September in 1478 he made a six day expedition to Tintern which cost him 3s 2d. In addition he paid: 'For wax candles 2d. For a bill of the forest 8d. For paper ½d. For wine and meals 3d. For house fodder 1d. For shoeing 1d. Also for repairs to the saddle and other things 6d. For horse medicine 2d. Total 1 s½d [sic]'.[189]

Worcester must have had more than one reason for setting out on his travels. He undoubtedly had a religious motive. His longest journey was to St Michael's Mount, an ancient place of pilgrimage, and he also visited

[177] *WW*, p. 84.
[178] *WW*, pp. 124, 125 n. 4.
[179] *WW*, pp. 368, 369 n. 1.
[180] *WW*, p. 68.
[181] *WW*, pp. 24, 110, 132, 136.
[182] *WW*, p. 12.
[183] See, for example, *WW*, pp. 34–8 passim.
[184] See *WW*, p. xvii.
[185] *WW*, p. 36.
[186] *WW*, p. 262.
[187] *WW*, pp. 40, 130. He was also apparently arrested in 1475; *WW*, p. 252.
[188] *WW*, p. 38.
[189] *WW*, p. 40; see also *WW*, pp. 262–6 passim.

the shrines at Bury St Edmunds and Walsingham.[190] He visited numerous religious houses and conversed with the inmates.[191] And he notes occasions when he attended mass—for example that of St Edith at Wilton[192]—and has much information about the burial places, miracles and feast days of saints, especially those of Cornwall.[193]

Furthermore, Worcester transacted business. He has a memorandum that he must speak to Master William Paston concerning the tenancy of a house in Tresawle in Cornwall, held by one Davy Trewlyfyk of Trevithick.[194] At Bedminster he spoke to 'Justice John' Choke (?a mistake for Sir Richard) in order to establish his sister's claim to two acres of land, and to obtain rents of which Sir John Choke had wrongly deprived him.[195] And in Bristol he made arrangements for the purchase from a potter of 'two pots like the last but with a smaller mouth by ¼in. according to this wooden measure whose breadth the mouth is to have.'[196]

Worcester had another reason at least for his travels in Norfolk; affection for his old master, Sir John Fastolf. A number of entries relate to Fastolf. There are the obits of members of his family, generally dated from Fastolf's death, and their burial places at St Benet of Hulme and Yarmouth.[197] Worcester was interested in property having some connection with Fastolf. For example, he gives details of the siege of the castle at Caistor in 1469 by John duke of Norfolk, who claimed to have bought it from one of Fastolf's executors.[198] Similarly the full description of Sir Andrew Ogard's castle and property at Buckenham may be accounted for by a fact, which Worcester notes, that Fastolf had had the option of buying it should Ogard die without an heir.[199] Worcester was also interested in his own family, and when he visited Bristol he questioned relatives about it.[200]

However, such entries occupy only a small proportion of the *Itinerary*: clearly neither his piety nor his business interests nor the desire to discover information about Fastolf's family or his own, was the predominant motive. Indeed Worcester's principal reason for travelling was curiosity—the wish to know about England, its towns and countryside and their history. Perhaps the passage which most vividly conveys Worcester's love of sightseeing is his description of Wookey Hole in Somerset. To cite an extract:[201]

[190] See *WW*, pp. xiii-iv, 160, 174.

[191] See, for example, his notes on visits to Norwich priory (*WW*, pp. 238, 240), to the Charterhouse at Sheen (*WW*, p. 270), and to Glastonbury abbey (*WW*, pp. 296, 298; and see p. 340 and nn. 254, 255 below).

[192] *WW*, p. 36.

[193] See e.g. *WW*, pp. 62, 64, 86.

[194] *WW*, p. 18.

[195] *WW*, p. 260.

[196] *WW*, p. 76. For another notice of a business transaction see *WW*, p. 36.

[197] *WW*, pp. 180, 184, 220. For events dated from Fastolf's death see also *WW*, pp. 24, 182.

[198] *WW*, pp. 186, 188.

[199] *WW*, p. 48. For other entries relating to Fastolf see pp. 160, 222, 322, 334.

[200] *WW*, pp. 308, 310 (cf. *WW*, p. 306), 312.

[201] *WW*, p. 290.

Wookey Hole is half a mile from Wells and within the parish. At the mouth of its narrow entrance is the image of a man called the porter, and it is necessary to ask leave of him to enter the hall of Wookey. People carry what is called in English 'sheaves' of sedge reed to light the hall which is as large as Westminster hall, and from the vault, wonderfully arched in stone, hang stalactites. The passage leading from the door to the hall is about half a furlong in length, and is likewise arched with smooth stones hung with stalactites. There is a broad lake between the passage and the hall, crossed by 500 stepping stones, each about four feet wide, and if a man slips off a stone he falls into the water which is about five or six feet deep on all sides. The kitchen before the entrance of the hall is covered with a vault of stone whose span is beyond estimation. And there is a room called in English 'an oast' (intended for the drying of barley for making ale, etc.). In it is the figure of a woman, clothed and spinning with what is called in English a 'distaff' beneath her girdle. From here people cross another alleyway about 100 paces long; a man can easily cross dry footed on the stepping stones. Next comes a room called the parlour; it is round, built of great rocks and about twenty paces across. On the north side of this parlour is a 'holy hole', so-called in English; this well, which is beautifully arched over, is full of water, and none can say how deep the water is.

However, Worcester's description of Wookey is hardly typical of his writing. In general his entries are short and factual, expressing neither wonder nor admiration. To take for example one of his many descriptions of river courses, that of the Otter in Devon:[202]

There is a bridge over the river in Ottery St Mary which is [12 miles] from Exeter, going towards Axminster and Taunton. Its source is at Otterford, 4 [sic] miles north of Ottery St Mary, and falls into the harbour of Ottermouth haven after flowing through about 9 miles of country.

Worcester did not rely entirely on what he saw for his descriptions of natural features. He made some use of literary works (he cites Gerald of Wales for his description of the islands off the coast of north Wales),[203] but his main additional source was oral information, which he used both to learn about places where he had never been and to supplement the evidence of his own eyes. He frequently gives the name of his informant in scholarly fashion. Thus his kinsman Robert Bracy of Fowey told him

[202] WW, p. 18.
[203] WW, pp. 118, 120.

about the rivers of Cornwall,[204] and Sir Roger Kynaston of Shrewsbury about those of the Welsh border country and of north west England.[205] Worcester learnt in particular about the Wye and the Usk from 'N. a servant in the wardrobe of the last duke of Exeter, at Cambridge on 1 January 1475/6, who was born a gentleman's son in "Herefordeest" [Hereford? Haverfordwest?]'.[206] He obtained most of his information about the islands off the British coasts by word of mouth. Thus he heard about the islands off the Cornish coast from Robert Bracy,[207] and those off southern Scotland from a seaman of Bristol called Slaterbarow 'who had been there'.[208] A 'youngish merchant of the city of Dublin' called Bartholomew 'Rossynell' described the Isle of Man while riding with him from London to Walsingham on 10 July 1479.[209] And he learnt details concerning access to the port of Bristol, the distance of Bristol by sea from Land's End, and the distances between various places on the way, from 'a sailor, a ferryman who keeps the "ferry" (so-called in English) across the Avon and Frome for those coming from Bristol, at Rownham, going and coming in a small skiff.'[210]

Worcester's method of combining his own observations with what he was told is well illustrated by his description of Ghyston Cliff, on the Avon near Bristol:[211]

> On Sunday 24 September [1480] I went to Ghyston Cliff and measured the depth of the rock as far as the Hermitage [and found it to be] 20 fathoms deep. And a young man, a blacksmith by trade, told me on that day that the rest of the rock measured from the chapel of the Hermitage up to the water level called in English 'ebbing water' is 44 fathoms deep. And so the total depth is 64 fathoms.

Worcester used the same method to describe buildings as natural features. His architectural descriptions are equally businesslike, and show a similar tendency to arid brevity. He describes numerous churches and some secular buildings, principally manor houses. (His interest in castles is mainly expressed by a list of those in Cornwall, with short notes on the foundation, owner and state of repair of some of them.)[212] And he describes one town, Bristol, with exhaustive thoroughness.[213]

[204] *WW*, p. 108.
[205] *WW*, p. 66.
[206] *WW*, p. 198.
[207] *WW*, p. 106.
[208] *WW*, p. 132.
[209] *WW*, pp. 168, 169 n. 1.
[210] *WW*, p. 302.
[211] *WW*, p. 262.
[212] *WW*, pp. 20, 22.
[213] Worcester's survey of Bristol, which is in the same manuscript as the *Itinerary*, is not printed by Harvey (see *WW*, p. xxiii), but by James Dallaway, *Antiquities of Bristowe* (Bristol 1834).

Most characteristic of his descriptions are the innumerable measurements he gives; it seems that whenever he set foot in a building he immediately paced it out. He records the measurements in his own paces; his stride was about three feet long (but few of the measurements are exact on this calculation).[214] The abundance of architectural dimensions in the *Itinerary* was without precedent: virtually no previous antiquary had recorded any measurements at all, nor did anyone subsequently record them until comparatively modern times.[215] Worcester's preoccupation with measurements appears in other contexts in the *Itinerary*, for instance in his exact commission, already cited, to the potter in Bristol,[216] and in a note on units of measurement used by the exchequer (which he copied from a book in St Stephen's church in Bristol).[217] It is likely that Worcester acquired this interest as a result of his business career for Fastolf. His work, particularly as surveyor of Castle Combe, involved keeping accounts, and cost and size are often intimately connected. (Today, for example, the quantity surveyor and the carpet fitter estimate cost from linear measurements.) Worcester was probably conscious of this connection, though he very rarely gives the cost of a building as well as its dimensions.[218]

A typical example of Worcester's method of describing a church is his account of Old St Paul's:[219]

> The length of the nave of the church of St Paul's, measured in my 'steps' (as is said in English) is 180 paces.
> The width of the transepts from south to north is 160 of my 'steps'.
> The width of the nave with its two side aisles is 48 of my paces.
> The length of the choir with the chapel of St Mary is 130 of my paces.
> The width of the choir is 48 of my paces.

Worcester's description of Bristol was the first full topographical description of a city. (William Fitz Stephen's account of London, written in the late twelfth century, is more concerned with the citizens' social customs than with the layout of the streets, and the description of Chester by Fitz Stephen's contemporary Lucian is very brief.)[220] His survey was the precursor of John Stow's *Survey of London*. Some idea of its detail is

---

[214] See *WW*, p. xv. Cf. the description of Ghyston Cliff cited on p. 336 above.

[215] See *WW*, pp. xi-xii.

[216] See p. 334 above.

[217] *WW*, pp. 130, 314.

[218] See, however, for notices of the cost of a building as well as its measurements, *WW*, pp. 46, 48.

[219] *WW*, pp. 152, 154.

[220] See A. Gransden, 'Realistic observation in twelfth-century England' in *Speculum*, xlvii (1972), pp. 46–7.

given by the following extract:[221]

> The width of the road of the quay running from the custom-house directly to an alleyway (which begins at the back of Shipward's house and leads to the west door of St Stephen's church) [is] 34 paces. [It runs] towards the open space by the quay, which is drained in the middle by a channel of freestone. The alleyway immediately next to it (which crosses into the cemetery by a stile) starts on the east side of the church of St Stephen, and passes directly through the southern part of the cemetery of that church as far as the quay; [it] is 30 paces long through the cemetery, and then where it crosses directly by the west part of the church to the place called the quay, is 90 paces long: but dray horses cannot use this alleyway.

However, Worcester by no means confined himself to pacing out buildings and streets. His curiosity extended to whatever he saw. Thus he was the only man in medieval England known to have described an architectural detail exactly; he describes the mouldings on the door of the south porch of St Stephen's in Bristol, carved, as he records by 'Benedict the freemason' (Benedict Crosse), complete with drawing of a cross section (perhaps contributed by Crosse himself).[222] Worcester also read epitaphs (he transcribes, for example, Sir William Elmham's in the abbey church at Bury St Edmunds).[223] And he copied or noted any other writing set up in a church which caught his eye—the account of St Henry bishop of Uppsala and St Henry emperor of Germany in St Henry's chapel in the Carmelite priory at Yarmouth,[224] the history of the order of St John of Jerusalem in the Temple church in London,[225] and the pious Latin verses in the abbey church at Tavistock.[226] Similarly he transcribed the (spurious) papal bull pinned to the door at St Michael's Mount,[227] and comments that the thirty four or so devotional tablets in the London Charterhouse ('in a good text hand and in bastard letter') made the best such display he had ever seen.[228]

Moreover, Worcester questioned people for extra information about buildings, in the same way as he did to discover more about natural features. Even some of his measurements were probably acquired at second hand[229]

---

[221] Dallaway, op. cit., pp. 101–2. The meaning of some sentences is obscured by Worcester's bad Latin and by the fact that they are merely notebook jottings.

[222] WW, pp. xiii, 314, 316. See Plate XIII above. For Benedict Crosse see J. H. Harvey, English Medieval Architects (London 1954), p. 79.

[223] WW, pp. 162, 163 n. 2.

[224] WW, p. 186.

[225] WW, p. 312.

[226] WW, p. 112.

[227] WW, pp. 100, 101 n. 1.

[228] WW, p. 270.

[229] See e.g. WW, pp. 270, 272.

(this is suggested by his occasional use of feet and yards instead of paces).[230]
He often acknowledges his authority by name. He states that Master
Brewster, the receiver-general of Richard Beauchamp earl of Warwick,
provided him with his details about the earl's building activities,[231] and
that Humphrey Paris 'of the office of the wardrobe' of Sir William Oldhall
told him the cost of Sir William's manor at Hunsdon.[232] In the same way
the context suggests that Sir Ralph Cromwell's herald informed him about
Sir Ralph's wealth and about the manors he built.[233] He learnt the date
of the foundation of Syon abbey from Nicholas Burton of Bristol,[234] and
about Cornish saints from Thomas Peperelle of Tavistock, a papal notary.[235]
Similarly he sometimes names his authority for his few entries on general
history: he heard about the taking of Caen (1417) from Sir Thomas
Fastolf,[236] and about the battle of Verneuil (1424) from Ireland king of
arms.[237] On occasion he mentions a conversation but not its subject (at
Launceston 'I talked with Dr Ewen and certain canons', at Ottery St Mary
'I talked and drank with Master Cornwall, priest').[238]

Nor did Worcester neglect books, and his work throws light on the
book traffic. He himself lent books: he has a memorandum that he must
get back his grammar book from John Sowle, a Carmelite friar;[239] and
he notes that he spoke with Thomas Yong for the return of 'a large book
of Ethics and another in a red cover called Le Myrrour de Dames'.[240]
But above all he made a tireless search for books to satisfy his curiosity,
especially for calendars and martyrologies (from which he copied feast
days, obits and miscellaneous notes), registers and chronicles. Acquaintances, whose help he meticulously acknowledges, provided him with access
to a number of books. A 'scrivener text writer dwelling at St Mary-le-
Strand' let him consult a calendar in his possession.[241] Dr Ewen showed him
a copy of Gerald of Wales's *Itinerary of Wales*,[242] John Burton, a priest of
St Thomas's, Bristol, showed him 'a great paper book of chronicles'[243]
and Richard Vowell, master of the borough of Wells, let him inspect a

---

[230] See e. g. *WW*, p. 46.
[231] *WW*, p. 218. Master Brewster is not among Richard Beauchamp's receiver-generals
mentioned in Charles Ross, *The Estates and Finances of Richard Beauchamp Earl of Warwick*
(Dugdale Society Occasional Papers, no. 12, 1956).
[232] *WW*, p. 50.
[233] *WW*, pp. 72, 73 n. 5.
[234] *WW*, p. 334.
[235] *WW*, pp. 114, 115 n. 2.
[236] *WW*, p. 352.
[237] *WW*, p. 2.
[238] *WW*, p. 38; cf. *WW*, pp. 116, 118, 119 n. 1.
[239] *WW*, p. 312 and n. 1.
[240] *WW*, p. 262.
[241] *WW*, p. 150.
[242] *WW*, p. 118.
[243] *WW*, p. 322 and n. 1; cf. *WW*, p. 326.

chronicle on the bishops of Bath and Wells.[244] Similarly Master Brewster allowed him to make extracts from a chronicle in his keeping which recorded Henry V's campaigns in France, with particular references to his employer, Richard Beauchamp, earl of Warwick.[245]

Worcester found many of the books he needed in churches and monasteries, and refers specifically to some libraries, for example those of All Saints' church in Bristol, and of Brecon priory (which included twelve books 'made' by that 'best of clerks', Odo bishop of Bayeux).[246] He cites calendars owned by the Augustinian friars of Norwich and by Tavistock abbey,[247] a martyrology owned by Newenham abbey,[248] registers at St Benet of Hulme,[249] and chronicles at Thetford,[250] Hyde[251] and Glastonbury.[252]

The trouble Worcester took to gain access to the chronicles of Glastonbury abbey is recorded in the *Itinerary*. Among the notes of his 1478 journey is a reminder 'to speak with Master [Thomas] Dapirfelde the prior and with Dr [William] Frampton of Glastonbury to have sight of the chronicles on the recommendation of Richard Vowell.'[253] Then in 1480 he entered a reminder 'to speak with Dom Kanyngton of Glastonbury abbey about seeing the chronicles; also with Master Rolee, secretary to the lord abbot, for the acts of King Arthur.' There follows another note to ask one of the monks, Dom John Murlage, 'for the names of the historians of King Arthur and others, with the authors' names and the incipits of their works'.[254] Worcester also records a conversation he had with Murlage on his arrival at Glastonbury on 29 August 1480, about the chronicles and acts of King Arthur and about Geoffrey of Monmouth's *Historia Regum Britanniae*.[255]

The evidence of Worcester's researches at Glastonbury and that supplied by other entries in the *Itinerary* leave no doubt that he accepted the Arthurian legends together with the traditional British History.[256] Despite his powers of exact observation, and his enthusiasm and assiduity in pursuit of antiquarian knowledge, Worcester rarely shows critical ability. He does indeed once suggest on rational grounds the provenance of a breviary belonging to William Hunt, a carver of Kingston Sheen; he thought,

---

[244] *WW*, pp. 79, 79 n. 4; for Richard Vowell see also below.

[245] *WW*, pp. 208–16 passim, Cf. p. 339 above.

[246] *WW*, pp. 316, 156, respectively.

[247] *WW*, pp. 236, 112, respectively.

[248] *WW*, p. 122.

[249] *WW*, p. 224.

[250] *WW*, p. 164.

[251] *WW*, p. 148.

[252] See below.

[253] *WW*, p. 78.

[254] *WW*, pp. 292, 293 n. 2. For Dom John Murlage or Murelege (i.e. Moorlynch) see *WW*, p. 261 n. 1.

[255] *WW*, p. 260.

[256] See e.g. *WW*, pp. 44, 94, 176.

apparently on the evidence of its calendar, that it came from Bayonne or Bordeaux (in fact he was probably right on its French origin, but as the feasts he copied from it include that of the relics of Bayeux, it probably came from there).[257] But this is an isolated instance of rationality, and in general Worcester was credulous.

Worcester's credulity not only enabled him to accept the British History, but also left its traces on his topographical studies. He repeats hagiographical miracles which were associated with particular places. For example, anyone who said the Lord's prayer or drank at a certain well near Brecon where 'St Elevetha' was beheaded, would find a hair from her head.[258] Some of his best descriptive passages include superstitious tales. Thus he has in his exact account of the course of the river Wye the statement that in Dimin Dale 'spirits suffer torment and there is a marvellous entrance into the earth of the Peak where souls are tortured.'[259] Similarly his excellent description of Wookey Hole is followed by a miracle. After describing the caves he turns to the stream flowing from them to Mere; it was full of fish—'trout, coles called miller's thumbs, loaches, flukes, pickerel, minnows, prides (which are like lampreys), crawfish and "dewdows"'; this abundance, Worcester remarks, was of great benefit to the people of Wells and the neighbourhood. However, on one occasion Thomas Beckington, bishop of Bath and Wells, tried to arrogate the fishing for his own use. Immediately the supply of fish miraculously ceased, and was not restored until two years later when the bishop again allowed the populace to fish freely.[260]

However, although Worcester shared the superstitious beliefs of his contemporaries, the legend and folklore in the *Itinerary* can easily be distinguished from the bulk of the entries which were the result of his own observation or of reliable information. He provided material which contributed to the foundations of future studies, and his methods, like those of John Hardyng and John Rous, pointed the way for subsequent antiquaries.

---

[257] *WW*, pp. x, 268, 269 n. 4.
[258] *WW*, p. 154; cf. *WW*, pp. 64, 120.
[259] *WW*, p. 68.
[260] *WW*, p. 292.

12

The End of the Monastic Tradition of Historiography: Thomas Elmham, Thomas Burton, and John Whethamsted

In the two centuries preceding the dissolution of the monasteries only St Albans retained importance as a centre of historical writing, first with Thomas Walsingham (d. 1422) and then with Abbot John Whethamsted (d. 1467). Nor did the tradition of the monastic chronicle, a full account of general and local history kept up fairly contemporarily with the events recorded, survive to any appreciable extent in the fifteenth century. Nevertheless, the period produced three outstanding writers, besides many lesser ones who will be considered in the next chapter. Thomas Elmham, Thomas Burton and John Whethamsted were all pre-eminent as local historians. Thomas Elmham, monk of St Augustine's, Canterbury (who became a Cluniac in 1414, and wrote the *Liber Metricus de Henrico Quinto*), was concerned only with local history in his *Speculum Augustinianum* (*The Mirror of St Augustine's*).[1] Thomas Burton's history of his house, the Cistercian abbey of Meaux in the East Riding of Yorkshire, from its foundation until the late fourteenth century, has sections on general history but is of interest mainly as a local history.[2] John Whethamsted's historical works are in the form of two registers, each covering one of his two abbatiates (he ruled St Albans from 1420 until 1440, and then again from 1452 until 1465).[3] These may be described as 'historicized' registers and, of course, relate to local history, although they contain passages of interest

[1] Printed *Historia Monasterii S. Augustini Cantuariensis*, ed. Charles Hardwick (RS 1858). The original title, *Speculum Augustinianum*, was discovered by Mr Taylor; Frank Taylor, 'A note on Rolls Series 8' in *BJRL*, xx (1936), pp. 379–82. For the manuscript see p. 353 and n. 60 below. For Elmham's later career and the *Liber Metricus de Henrico Quinto* see pp. 206–10 above.

[2] Printed *Chronica Monasterii de Melsa*, ed. E. A. Bond (RS 1866–8, 3 vols).

[3] Whethamsted's two registers (see below pp. 373 et seq.) are printed respectively as follows: *Annales Monasterii S. Albani a Johanne Amundesham, Monacho*, ed. H. T. Riley (RS 1870–1, 2 vols); *Registrum Abbatiae Johannis Whethamstede*, ed. H. T. Riley (RS 1872–3, 2 vols). They are referred to in the footnotes below as *Reg. I* and *Reg. II*.

for national history, notably the accounts of two battles of St Albans.

The same motives inspired Elmham, Burton and Whethamsted as caused the lesser monastic chroniclers to write local histories. The monks wrote to defend their order and their houses against enemies and critics. For at least three centuries the monks had been on the defensive. They found critics among their rivals, the regular and secular canons and the mendicants. Criticism was particularly virulent in the late fourteenth century, when a new enemy emerged, the Lollards. Individually each monastery had enemies, actual or potential: the diocesan, royal and papal agents (especially tax collectors), and neighbouring landlords. Nor were the monks harassed only by external enemies: a number of houses, including St Albans and Meaux, were torn by internal strife.

As in earlier times, the monks wrote to strengthen their position. Their objective was partly to increase the prestige of the monastic order and of individual houses, by proving that they had long and glorious pasts. To defend the order as a whole treatises were composed on the history of monasticism.[4] The prototype of these treatises appears to have been one composed at Bury St Edmunds in the first half of the fourteenth century. It traced, by means of research on the bible, the Fathers and other early sources, the beginnings of the monastic movement, well before the time of St Benedict, thus establishing that its origins predated those of the Augustinian canons who claimed foundation by St Augustine of Hippo. And it defended the right of monasteries to own property, in order to disprove the mendicants' assertions to the contrary. This work gained popularity: it was revised at Bury itself, and copies went to Durham, St Albans, Glastonbury, Winchester and elsewhere. The treatise and the ideas expressed in it were influential. Even Henry V when he harangued the monks at the meeting held at Westminster in 1421, spoke of the ancient tradition of monasticism, and of the devotion of the early monks and their benefactors; modern laxity and worldliness marked a sad decline.[5]

Meanwhile a number of monks wrote to prove the antiquity of their own monasteries. Interest in a house's early history might result in antiquarianism: indeed antiquarian investigation often extended beyond the circumstances of foundation to the origins of the estates, privileges, administrative organization, buildings and treasures. And at the same time the chroniclers sought to record the achievements of distinguished members

---

[4] These tracts are fully discussed by W. A. Pantin, 'Some medieval English treatises on the origins of monasticism' in *Medieval Studies presented to Rose Graham*, ed. Veronica Ruffer and A. J. Taylor (Oxford 1950), pp. 189–215. For the contribution of John Wessington, prior of Durham (1416–46), for whom see pp. 392–3, 403–4 below, to this historiographical genre see R. B. Dobson, *Durham Priory 1400–1450* (Cambridge 1973), pp. 381–2.

[5] See Pantin, op. cit., p. 209, citing *Documents illustrating the Activities of the General and Provincial Chapters of the English Black Monks 1215–1540*, ed. W. A. Pantin (Camden Soc., third series, xlv, xlvii, liv, 1931–7, 3 vols), ii. 99; Thomas Walsingham, *HA*, ii. 337.

of their communities and the generosity of benefactors; this was done partly to increase the reputation of the house, and partly as an act of piety, to preserve remembrance of such people. Once a monastery's history had been established, a suitable narrative might be composed for display to the public on a board in the church.[6]

The most ambitious work written as a result of the desire to substantiate the early history of a religious house was Thomas Elmham's *Speculum Augustinianum*. Elmham's object was to strengthen his abbey's defences by writing an authoritative account of its history from the beginning in the conversion period—a period from which authentic documents no longer survived. To do so he undertook a considerable amount of research. He described his house's treasures and also commemorated the notable people connected with it. Thomas Burton did not face the same problem as Elmham with regard to his house's origin, because Meaux, having been founded after the Norman Conquest, was of comparatively recent date and the facts were adequately documented. Nevertheless, he did much research and gives a detailed account of Meaux's foundation. He then proceeded with the abbey's later history, noting its antiquities, outstanding monks and its benefactors. (John Whethamsted's registers, because of their genre, do not concern St Albans' early history or antiquities, but they make due recognition of the abbey's benefactors.)

Elmham, Burton and Whethamsted were all concerned to put on record their houses' victories over their enemies, or, if a case had been decided against them, at least the course of the quarrel. Elmham records St Augustine's disputes with the archbishops of Canterbury, Burton records Meaux's disputes with the archbishop of York, the papacy and the king, and Whethamsted his abbey's conflicts with neighbouring landlords. Burton and Whethamsted also give careful details of internal quarrels from which both suffered personally; Burton, who was elected to the abbacy in 1396, was forced to resign in 1399, and one reason for Whethamsted's resignation in 1440 was undoubtedly the hostility of some of his monks. Burton describes the disputes at Meaux from the mid-fourteenth century over abbatial elections and between abbot and convent, while one of Whethamsted's objectives in writing was to prove the iniquity of his enemies.

Both Elmham and Burton wrote at great length and arranged their chronicles elaborately: possibly in these respects they were influenced by Higden's *Polychronicon* and by the *Historia Aurea* ascribed to John of Tynemouth.[7] Burton was the last great monastic local historian. Writing

---

[6] For such *tabulae* see below p. 495, Appendix E.

[7] The *Historia Aurea* has not been printed in full. It is a massive work in twenty three books mainly derived to 1327 from the *Polychronicon*. For the identity of John of Tynemouth and for his work see V. H. Galbraith, 'The *Historia Aurea* of John, vicar of Tynemouth, and the sources of the St Albans chronicle (1327–77)' in *Essays in History presented to Reginald Lane*

in a remote area, he retained the old fashioned virtues; he provides a careful record in straightforward Latin. Elmham's work, like Burton's, is outstanding as a piece of research, but it has stylistic traits typical of the fifteenth century. In places its Latin is distinguished by the literary flamboyance which was to be a feature of his *Liber Metricus de Henrico Quinto*.

Florid Latin became popular among the fifteenth century intelligentsia, and it is a marked characteristic of John Whethamsted's registers. Of the three writers Whethamsted departed most from the usual monastic style, embellishing his Latin with all sorts of literary devices—word-play, biblical and classical allegory, and the like. His knowledge of the classics was considerable, and it has been claimed that he was an early humanist. However, as will be seen, he never succeeded in freeing himself from the mental habits of a monk, and despite his pretensions to classical learning, he remains a typical medieval figure.

Thomas Elmham, Thomas Burton and John Whethamsted will be considered in turn.

Thomas Elmham wrote the *Speculum Augustinianum* while a monk of St Augustine's where he probably professed in 1379.[8] He was treasurer in 1407, and studied at Oxford apparently later in that year and also in 1408. It is likely that he wrote the *Speculum* shortly before he joined the Cluniac order and was elected prior of Lenton (in 1414). He conceived his work on a massive scale, and to make it easier to use he prefixed an elaborate table in nine columns.[9] The first column gives the dates from A.D. 597 (the year of the abbey's foundation) to 1418, and four others contain chronological data (the year of St Augustine's arrival in England, the Dominical letters, the lunar cycle and the indiction); the remaining columns have historical synopses, serving as a table of contents and an indication of the kind of material to be included in the chronicle. They contain: the succession of popes and the bulls they granted to St Augustine's abbey; the succession of the archbishops of Canterbury, miscellaneous notes about them and their charters to St Augustine's; the succession of the kings of England, with brief notes, and their charters to St Augustine's;[10] and the succession of the abbots of St Augustine's, some of their acts and their burial places.

Poole, ed. H. W. C. Davis (Oxford 1927, reprinted 1969), pp. 379–98. For passages of interest not derived from any known literary source see the same author's 'Extracts from the *Historia Aurea* and a French "Brut" (1317–47)' in *EHR*, xlii (1928), pp. 203–17.

[8] For Elmham's career see Taylor, 'A note on Rolls Series 8', p. 382, p. 206 above and n. 10 below.

[9] *SA*, pp. 2–73.

[10] This column has s.a. 1407 a note concerning Thomas Elmham (*SA*, p. 72). It states that he, then treasurer, was arrested at the suit of Henry Somerset for distraining for certain rents in London, but recovered the rents by means of an assize (*per assisam*).

Elmham intended to follow the table with a section (a 'titulus') on each of the sixty one abbots who had ruled from the abbey's foundation until his own day, but he only completed the sections on the first fourteen abbots, bringing the history down to 806.[11] The rest of the work is a preparatory collectanea, containing brief particulars to 1089 and then documents to about 1192. Possibly his work was only this far advanced by 1414 when he left St Augustine's for Lenton.

As Elmham states at the beginning of his narrative, his principal sources were Bede's *Ecclesiastical History* and the *Gesta Pontificum* of William of Malmesbury (whose authority 'no one in England can dispute').[12] He also acknowledges the help of earlier historians of St Augustine's, citing two by name, Thomas Sprott and William Thorne. Sprott's chronicle is now lost, but it was used by Thorne as well as by Elmham, and apparently ended in 1228. Thorne revised Sprott's work[13] and continued to 1397; he took as his theme the rivalry between St Augustine's and Christ Church, Canterbury, presenting his abbey's case with eloquence and substantiating it with numerous documents. It seems likely that Elmham derived the idea of an introductory table partly from his two predecessors. Sprott arranged his work by abbots and archbishops.[14] And although Thorne arranged his material chronologically, he states in his preface that he will mark references to three classes of persons conspicuously in the margins, kings of England, abbots of St Augustine's and archbishops of Canterbury (he adopted these categories because the abbey had been endowed by kings, protected by its abbots, and often attacked by the archbishops).[15]

Beside literary sources Elmham made extensive use of documents. He clearly indicates the value of documentary evidence. He writes that when the guiding light of Bede failed he found better guidance than that enjoyed by most of his predecessors. This was provided by papal and royal documents—bulls and charters, sealed and indented.[16]

Although the *Speculum* is a monastic chronicle it is not in the pedestrian style usual to the genre. There are a few scattered verses, but, more distinctive, much of the prose is inflated with rhetorical flourishes and literary mannerisms: stylistically the work is a precursor in prose of Elmham's

---

[11] *SA*, p. 344.

[12] *SA*, p. 77. For another of Elmham's literary sources see p. 348 and n. 37 below.

[13] For a discussion of Sprott's chronicle and its use by Thorne see *William Thorne's Chronicle of Saint Augustine's Abbey Canterbury*, translated by A. H. Davis, with a preface by A. Hamilton Thompson (Oxford 1934), pp. xx-xxvi passim. See also the Latin text of Thorne's chronicle in Roger Twysden, *Historiae Anglicanae Scriptores Decem* (London 1652), cols 1753-2202.

[14] *Thorne's Chron.* p. xxvi.

[15] *WT*, col. 1758; *Thorne's Chron.* p. 2.

[16] *SA*, pp. 309-10. For a discussion of Elmham's extensive use of documents in the *Speculum Augustinianum*, together with a table of the literary and documentary sources of each titulus, see J. P. Genet, 'Cartulaires, registres et histoire: l'exemple anglais' in *Le Métier d'historien au moyen âge*, ed. Bernard Guenée (Publications de la Sorbonne, série 'Études', xiii, Paris 1977), pp. 112-16.

later *Liber Metricus de Henrico Quinto*.[17] It invokes the reader,[18] expatiates on good and inveighs against evil.[19] It uses symbolism, for example comparing the first seven abbots with the Seven Days of the Creation—the seventh, Abbot Hadrian, who deserved even greater praise than the other six, represented the Seventh Day, the day of completion and of rest.[20]

Elmham reveals his own name in an acrostic, in the verses which conclude the introductory section.[21] He also uses word-play[22] and alliteration, for instance in a passage concerning a Dane called Thunor who, according to legend, tried to prevent King Egbert giving land to the nunnery of Minster in Thanet. The king promised Dompneva, the first abbess, the area delineated by the course of a hind as it ran from one side of the island to the other, but Thunor, wanting the lands himself, waited on his horse in order to stop it. His evil intention was frustrated because the earth opened and swallowed him up. Egbert, therefore, then listened to 'the sane counsel of the theologians Archbishop Theodore and Abbot Hadrian instead of to the thunderings of the torrid Thunor'.[23] Elmham links Thunor with two other assailants of monastic property whose names began with 'Th', Theutbald, an enemy of St Vedast's,[24] and Thurstan, an enemy of St Albans.[25] Together with Thunor they formed 'a nefarious trinity', and God punished them all with death. They and their like were the forerunners of the dispossessioners of Elmham's day—especially the Lollards.[26] The latter, he alleges, derived their name either from *lolium*, a tare, or from *loligo*, a cuttle fish, which 'has a jet black tumour and a very bitter flavour'.[27] The Lollards were to be a favourite theme of the *Liber Metricus*.[28] Elmham writes of Thunor's fate in similar style, with biblical allusions, as he later employed for Sir John Oldcastle's: 'the earth could no longer bear to have [Thunor] on it, so Behemoth committed that satellite of Satan, like a drop of the infernal river, to the whirlpool of Orcus, the dragon.'[29]

---

[17] Pp. 206–10 above.

[18] See e.g. *SA*, pp. 79, 84.

[19] See e.g. *SA*, pp. 135–6, 208 et seq., 243.

[20] *SA*, pp. 200–1; cf. *SA*, pp. 242–3.

[21] *SA*, p. 93. Elmham also uses chronograms; see *SA*, p. 73 (s.a. 1415, 1418). For his use of an acrostic and chronograms in the *Liber Metricus* see pp. 207–8 above. For the use of acrostics in other historical works see pp. 47 and n. 18, 94, 159–60 above and 405 below.

[22] See his play on the name 'Lollards' mentioned below.

[23] *SA*, p. 214.

[24] *SA*, pp. 210–11. The passage in Elmham is substantially the same as that printed from the Miracles of St Vedast by the Bollandists in *Acta Sanctorum*, February, i. 807–8.

[25] *SA*, pp. 211–13. The gist of the story told by Elmham concerning the official called Thurstan, who was miraculously punished by St Alban for refusing to pay rent to the abbey some time during the archiepiscopate of Stigand (1052–70), is in the *Nova Legenda Anglie* (ed. Carl Horstmann (Oxford 1901, 2 vols), i. 36).

[26] *SA*, pp. 213–14.

[27] *SA*, p. 209.

[28] P. 207 above.

[29] *SA*, p. 209. Cf. Job, xl-xli, and p. 209 above.

Elmham was acutely aware of the hostility surrounding the religious houses in general and St Augustine's in particular. He writes of monasticism in a defensive tone. He has a long eulogy,[30] and emphasizes the preponderance of monks among the early archbishops and the high respect in which they were held.[31] Elmham probably had a homiletic intention in stressing primitive virtue. He deplored the degeneracy of the abbots and prelates of his own day who occupied themselves with secular matters and trivialities, and lived in comfort while their subjects were ill fed and oppressed.[32] He may have considered that if they could be persuaded to reform, the monks would be less vulnerable to criticism.

Elmham's most eloquent writing was reserved for the defence of St Augustine's itself. The abbey's principal enemy had always been the archbishop of Canterbury, who periodically attacked its privilege of exemption from episcopal control.[33] It also suffered from the rivalry of the canons of St Gregory's, Canterbury.[34] Elmham counters some specific attacks in detail. He alleges that certain trouble makers and scandal mongers had scoffed at the verses on a plaque by the tomb of St Augustine: the verses concerned the saint and the abbey's foundation, asserting that St Augustine's was the first monastery to be founded in England, and that the abbot was, as it were, the archbishop's brother and colleague.[35] Similarly, Elmham alleges that people had been misled by Higden's statement that the king of Kent made Benedict Biscop abbot of St Augustine's, a statement which in itself was false. Therefore, the abbey's detractors asserted that Archbishop Theodore had first given the abbacy to Benedict Biscop, his chaplain, and subsequently to Hadrian, another of his chaplains. (Such a view implied the abbey's subjection to the archbishop.) Elmham on the other hand argued that Theodore never made Benedict Biscop abbot. And he contended that although Theodore appointed Hadrian, he did so in his capacity as papal legate, not as archbishop, and chose Hadrian not because he was his chaplain but as a brother and colleague.[36] Elmham also mentions an attack by the canons of St Gregory's who, as they had done since the early twelfth century, claimed to have the relics of Dompneva's daughter, St Mildred. He dismisses their claim, recapitulating the arguments used three centuries earlier by the hagiographer Goscelin.[37]

[30] *SA*, pp. 133–6.
[31] *SA*, pp. 134–5, 243–4, 292.
[32] *SA*, pp. 199–200. This passage is translated in *Thorne's Chron.* pp. xxxvii–xxxviii.
[33] For a synopsis of the causes of contention between St Augustine's and the archbishops of Canterbury see Wilhelm Levison, *England and the Continent in the Eighth Century* (Oxford 1946), pp. 182–3. For the claim to exemption by St Augustine's which was one of the principal causes of friction, see M. D. Knowles, 'Essays in monastic history,' iv. the growth of exemption' in *Downside Review*, 1 (1932), pp. 401–15.
[34] See below and n. 37.
[35] *SA*, pp. 87–8.
[36] *SA*, pp. 185–6, 202–5. Elmham gives the correct reference to Higden's *Polychronicon*, bk V, c. 16; *Poly.* vi. 78.
[37] *SA*, pp. 218, 225–6. Goscelin's *Libellus contra inanes s. uirginis usurpatores Mildrethae* is edited

In order to prove its priority Elmham gives a detailed account of the foundation of St Augustine's. He concludes that from the evidence 'anyone of sane mind must see that ours was the first community of monks established in England; the monastery was founded from no other monastery establish-ed earlier elsewhere in England, but all others derived from it.'[38] He deals severely with the pretensions of the monks of Glastonbury.[39] He states that their house was founded by King Ine, pointing out that it could not have been founded, as the monks claimed, at the time of the birth of Christ because there was no evidence in the chronicles of any monastic foundation before the time of King Lucius. Possibly their claim to endow-ment by King Arthur was justified, because Edward I had opened the tomb and seen the body at Glastonbury in 1278;[40] this, however, did not prove the existence of a monastery there in or before King Arthur's time. Having discussed the foundation of St Augustine's Elmham later in the chronicle gives examples of the precedence allowed to the abbot,[41] and emphasizes his good relations with the archbishop in the early Anglo-Saxon period.[42]

The main facts of the foundation and of the early history of St Augustine's were reasonably well known, and based on the authority of Bede. Elmham, therefore, could argue the abbey's case without diverging too much from the truth, and had little need of legend to strengthen its defences. However, he probably cited the story of Dompneva's hind, whose course determined the boundaries of the Minster's estates, to fortify St Augustine's property rights: King Canute had given the Minster's estates to the abbey, the original nunnery having been destroyed in the Danish invasions,[43] and on occasion the monks had to defend their claim.[44]

It is clear that Elmham included the formidable array of spurious charters in order to defend the abbey. St Augustine's had emerged from the Anglo-Saxon period with numerous privileges (including that of exemption from subjection to the archbishop) which were respected because they were customary, but which were unwritten. In order to counter the archbishops' attacks, the monks in about 1070 forged appropri-ate charters,[45] the authenticity of which was periodically challenged in

---

by M. C. Colker, 'A hagiographic polemic' in *Mediaeval Studies*, xxxix (Toronto 1977), pp. 60–108.

[38] *SA*, p. 82.

[39] *SA*, pp. 264–5.

[40] For Edward I's visit to Glastonbury in 1278 see A. Gransden, 'The growth of the Glaston-bury traditions and legends in the twelfth century' in *Journal of Ecclesiastical History*, xxvii (1976), p. 355.

[41] *SA*, pp. 88–90.

[42] See e.g. *SA*, pp. 148, 204.

[43] *WT*, col. 1783. For Elmham's map of Thanet see p. 355 and n. 72 below.

[44] For example in 1294 Edward I tried to obtain the manor of Minster (*WT*, col. 1962), and in 1318 the tenants rose against the abbot's claims (*WT*, cols 2034–5; cf. *Thorne's Chron.* pp. xxxix–xlv passim).

[45] See Levison, *England and the Continent in the Eighth Century*, pp. 205–6.

the middle ages, notably in the reigns of Henry II and Henry III.[46] It is hardly surprising that the abbey's official historians accepted them without question as indispensable evidence. Therefore, by treating the forgeries as genuine, Elmham was merely following the example of his predecessors.

There can be no doubt that Elmham's propagandist intention, the desire to substantiate the claim of St Augustine's to a long and glorious past, was a powerful incentive to his study of the abbey's early history. Nevertheless, Elmham showed impressive ability as a research worker and antiquary. His scholarship no doubt owed much to the influence of Bede for whom he expresses the highest admiration. Concurring with William of Malmesbury, he laments that no Anglo-Saxon after Bede bothered to continue the tradition of recording English history.[47] 'The lazy', he writes, 'were followed by the lazier': he adds that this trend had continued up to his own day; 'the very lazy have been succeeded by those lazier still . . . , and all enthusiasm for study has cooled among our people.'

Apart from his uncritical acceptance of the abbey's forged charters, Elmham's attitude to documents was judicious. He was able to read Anglo-Saxon charters (he copies a passage in Anglo-Saxon from a charter, supplying a Latin translation).[48] And he reflects (with disapproval) on the Anglo-Saxon practice of corrupting personal names, and uses the correct grammatical terms to denote the categories of corruption (metathesis, syncope, apocope, epenthesis and paragoge): thus Ethelbert was spelt Egbrith, Egbert or Edbert, and Thomas became Thomme or Tomlin, and John, Jankin or Jakke.[49]

Elmham regarded documents as more authoritative than literary sources on matters of fact. He twice corrects the accepted estimate of the length of a king's reign (Ethelbert's and Egbert's) on charter evidence.[50] Moreover, he explicitly states that an original document was of superior authority to a copy. Having accepted this rule, he collated two originals with copies in registers, and discovered discrepancies resulting 'either from the carelessness of the scribes, or from the lack of skill of the compiler in reading Anglo-Saxon handwriting'. Elmham, therefore, transcribed the material omitted in the copies—a passage of several lines from one charter (he indicated with signs where it should be inserted), and the name of a witness (whom he identified) from the other.[51]

Elmham's interest in charters led to an interest in seals. During the

---

[46] See Knowles, 'Essays in monastic history, iv. the growth of exemption', p. 414 and nn.; SA, pp. xxviii-xxxiv; Thorne's Chron. pp. liv-lvi, 116 et seq.

[47] SA, p. 309, citing 'Willelmus Malmesberiensis, lib. i. cap. xlviii ' Elmham cites the Gesta Regum (bk I, c. 62, in the most recent printed edition) partly verbatim; Willelmi Malmesbiriensis monachi de Gestis Regum Anglorum, ed. William Stubbs (RS 1887-9, 2 vols), i. 66-7.

[48] SA, p. 332.

[49] SA, p. 338.

[50] SA, pp. 137, 324.

[51] SA, pp. 233, 237-8.

abbey's struggle with Richard of Dover archbishop of Canterbury (1173–84), one of the objections brought against its most important 'privilege', the (forged) grant of immunity by St Augustine, was that it had a leaden bull attached; the archbishop's party pointed out that only popes, not bishops, employed such bulls.[52] Elmham considers this objection, and counters it by asserting that St Augustine, being a Roman and a papal legate, might have used a leaden bull. He argues that in later times popes had occasionally granted a bishop the right to use one. To demonstrate his point, he records that when Archbishop Richard rejected the bull as a fake, Philip count of Flanders sent the abbot a bull to use in evidence; he claimed that it was given him by a bishop, who had alleged that he and his predecessors had used it.[53]

It had also been objected that the charters granted by King Ethelbert to St Augustine's had no seals. Elmham answers this objection by stating, more or less correctly, that the practice of sealing documents was not introduced until after the Norman Conquest. Previously only King Canute, a foreigner, had used a seal.[54] Other kings of the Anglo-Saxon period had used the sign of the cross as authentication. In Elmham's view this was a superior method: coining a metaphor from diplomatic, he writes that the sign of the cross was 'the first public instrument of our salvation after the cyrograph of damnation had been torn up.' Such a sign was sufficient in those pious days, and, moreover, it lasted for ever, while a seal might be lost or turn to dust with age.

Close study of documents and seals resulted in antiquarian observation of their physical appearance. Thus Elmham looked more closely at the bull sent by the count of Flanders (which was 'preserved with our muniments') than the mere question of the authenticity of the Augustinian bull demanded. He decided that it was not a bishop's bull at all, but an abbot's: it bore the effigy of an abbot; moreover, the inscription revealed that he was abbot of a house dedicated to St Stephen.[55] In writing on the subject of seals in general, Elmham describes two curious examples, apparently from his own observation.[56] One, the seal of William first earl of Warenne,

---

[52] *SA*, pp. 122–4. Elmham erroneously dates the dispute in which the leaden bulla was called in question to Henry III's reign, presumably because he identified Archbishop Richard as Richard Grant, archbishop 1229–31. However, the reference (see below) to Philip count of Flanders (1168–91) makes it clear that the archbishop concerned was Richard of Dover. Moreover, Gervase of Canterbury testifies to the dispute over the leaden bulla under the latter archbishop; *The Historical Works of Gervase of Canterbury*, ed. William Stubbs (RS 1879–80, 2 vols), i. 296–7.

[53] *SA*, p. 123. See also p. 353 below.

[54] *SA*, p. 118. See the somewhat similar statement by John Rous; p. 325 and n. 124 above.

[55] *SA*, p. 123.

[56] *SA*, pp. 118–19. The charter of William de Warenne, first earl of Surrey (d. 1088), is printed in *Early Yorkshire Charters*, ed. C. T. Clay (Yorkshire Archaeological Soc., record series, extra series, 1935–65, 10 vols), viii. 54–5, no. 2. There is no reference to the presence of his hair in the seal. It may be noted, however, that the confirmation issued by William de

attached to a charter preserved in the priory of St Pancras at Lewes, contained some of the earl's hair; the other, the earl of Lincoln's seal, attached to a charter at Castleacre in Norfolk, bore the imprint of the earl's teeth—the charter itself had the subscription 'In evidence of this I have impressed the seal with my teeth, as Muriel my wife witnesses.'

Elmham's antiquarianism appears elsewhere in his work. He gives an account of eight books still surviving in the abbey which according to tradition had been given by St Augustine himself. He lists their contents, remarks on any striking features, and describes their bindings.[57] One, for example, was a bible in two volumes which had tinted pages, some purple and some pink, at the beginning of each book. Another was a psalter, which lay on the high altar and had a binding bearing an image of Christ in silver with the four evangelists. Elmham notes that St Augustine also gave precious vessels. These, however, had all been lost, and opinions varied as to their fate: they were hidden during the Danish raids; they formed part of Richard I's ransom; Abbot Egelsin absconded with them when he fled abroad after the Conquest.[58] Moreover, the ancient church interested Elmham. He discovered as much as he could about its plan from Bede, and compared it with the church of his own day: he concluded that it was narrower than the latter, that the altar of St Gregory was almost in the middle, and that the porticus of St Martin was on the south side.[59]

Elmham's powers of observation were supported by ability as a graphic artist. His awareness of the physical appearance of documents, seals and the like is well expressed in the pictures with which he illustrated his work. Because he appreciated that different scripts were written at different periods, he copied St Augustines's four (purportedly) earliest charters in duplicate, once in the hand of his own day and once in 'facsimile'. Thus he gives the privilege of St Augustine and the third charter of King Ethel-

---

Warenne, third earl of Surrey (1138–48), on the occasion of the dedication of Lewes priory, which endowed it with a tenth penny of his rents, records that he gave seizin 'by hair of his own head and that of Ralph de Warenne his brother, cut with a knife by Henry, bishop of Winchester, before the altar'; printed ibid., viii. 84–5, no. 32. This instance is noticed in V. H. Galbraith, 'Monastic foundation charters of the eleventh and twelfth centuries' in *Cambridge Historical Journal*, iv (1934), p. 211.

[57] *SA*, pp. 96–9. The passage is discussed, with an English translation, in M. R. James, *The Ancient Libraries of Canterbury and Dover* (Cambridge 1903), pp. lviii–lxiv. James identifies with fair certainty one of the volumes Elmham describes with the psalter now BL MS. Cotton Vespasian A. I, an eighth century manuscript in uncials. This identification, first proposed by Humphrey Wanley in 1705, is accepted in *The Vespasian Psalter*, ed. D. H. Wright (Copenhagen 1967), pp. 37–43. James also tentatively suggests an identification of the other psalter in Elmham's list, with Corpus Christi College, Cambridge, MS. 286, a late sixth century manuscript in uncials (James, op.cit., pp. lxvii–lxviii). Cf. p. 354 n. 66 below. Both manuscripts were owned by St Augustine's in the middle ages. It will be noted that both post-date St Augustine and, therefore, cannot have been given to the abbey by him.

[58] *SA*, p. 101.

[59] *SA*, pp. 132–3. For the church built by King Ethelbert for St Augustine see H. M. Taylor and Joan Taylor, *Anglo-Saxon Architecture* (Cambridge 1965, 2 vols), i. 135–7.

bert in uncials, and Ethelbert's first and second charters in Anglo-Saxon script.[60] Similarly, Elmham illustrates his discussion of bulls and seals with carefully drawn pen-and-ink pictures. He gives an exact reproduction of the obverse and reverse of St Augustine's leaden bull, with an explanatory note and copy of the inscription.[61] He also has a picture of both sides of the (forged) leaden bull attached to the privilege of Boniface IV.[62]

Undoubtedly the principal reason why Elmham reproduced the archaic scripts of the abbey's earliest charters and drew the authenticating devices was to give these documents added authority, and thus to substantiate St Augustine's claims to privilege. The same motive must have made him include a stylized copy of the *bene valete* and *rota* of the bull of Lucius II (granted to the abbey in 1144), and exact copies of the devices, subscriptions and closing formulae of the bulls of Innocent II (of 1139) and Eugenius III (of 1146).[63] However, the care which Elmham expended on his 'facsimiles' indicates that he was partly moved by objective antiquarian curiosity. This suggestion is supported by the fact that he drew the obverse of the seal of the abbot of the unidentified monastery dedicated to St Stephen, which the count of Flanders had presented to the monks—but which had no direct bearing on their privileges.[64] He added the comment that the image of the Virgin and Child on the reverse was hardly distinguishable because of age, and that the inscription was totally illegible.

The question arises whether Elmham was the first man to produce 'facsimiles' of St Augustine's 'earliest' charters. As the original eleventh

---

[60] Elmham's facsimiles (see *SA*, pp. 109 and n. 4, 110, 111 and n. 1, 112–13, 114 and n. 1, 115–16, 119 and n. 3, 120–1) can be seen in the splendid manuscript of the *Speculum Augustinianum*, written at St Augustine's and now in Trinity Hall, Cambridge, folios 21ᵛ, 22, 23, 24. There seems no reason to doubt that the manuscript is Elmham's autograph comparable to the illustrated manuscripts of Matthew Paris, for which see Gransden, *Historical Writing*, i. 364–6. It measures about 22 in. by 14 in. and is beautifully written in two columns, decorated and illustrated (see the description in M.R. James, *A Descriptive Catalogue of the Manuscripts in the Library of Trinity Hall, Cambridge* (Cambridge 1907), pp. 1–3. The facsimiles are described and some reproduced in Michael Hunter, 'The facsimiles in Thomas Elmham's History of St. Augustine's, Canterbury' in *The Library*, fifth series, xxviii (1973), pp. 215–20. For reproductions of Elmham's 'facsimile' of St Augustine's privilege to St Augustine's see the next note.

[61] Trinity Hall MS. f. 24. Reproduced Hunter, op. cit., Plate III, and Plate X below. The description reads: 'Ex una parte istius signi beati Augustini descripcio est ista ut patet . : . *Augustini episcopi* et hec est scriptura in exteriori circumferencia. In medio signi est forma unius ecclesie, et supra eamdem scribitur *ecclesia*, subtus *Christi*, a dextris ponitur una litera scilicet *M*, a sinistris *P*, per *M* monasterium, per *P* Petri intellige, quod bene cum prima carta fundacionis presentis monasterii concordat, in qua solummodo Petri apostoli mencio annotatur, sed in carta secunda et tercia fit mencio de utrisque uidelicet Petro et Paulo. Ex altera parte istius signi descripcio est ista. In exteriori circumferencia scribitur + *signum sancti saluatoris*. In medio est ymago salutoris ab umbilico sursum. A dextris scribitur *Jesus*, a sinistris *Christus*.'

[62] Trinity Hall MS. f. 26ᵛ.

[63] Trinity Hall MS. ff. 90ᵛ, 86, 92ᵛ, respectively; *SA*, pp. 386–9, 369–71, 392–6, respectively. Reproduced Hunter, op. cit., Plates Ib, IV, V, respectively.

[64] Trinity Hall MS. f. 24ᵛ; *SA*, p. 123.

century forgeries are lost, this question cannot be answered with certainty. The forgeries themselves may have been in 'facsimile'. Examples of the imitation of archaic scripts can be found from the tenth century onwards.[65] (At St Augustine's palaeographical models were readily available among the abbey's early books and charters.)[66] Similarly, authenticating devices were sometimes copied—a twelfth century cartulary of St Augustine's itself has copies of three papal devices from two bulls.[67] (There were numerous examples among the abbey's archives.) There was, however, as far as is known, no precedent in England for Elmham's reproduction of the total format of documents, complete with their authenticating devices, not just the handwriting and devices in isolation. Possibly the answer to the question is that Elmham improved on the work of the forgers, referring afresh to the models to produce 'facsimiles' with convincing details.

Elmham used his talent as a graphic artist to provide illustrations for other aspects of his research. He was a notable cartographer. Two of the five surviving antiquarian plans and local maps to be produced in England before 1500 were by Elmham.[68] He has a diagrammatic picture of the high altar in the abbey church, and of the shrines containing the relics of saints in the sanctuary.[69] He includes notes on the dates of the dedications of the altars, and on the resting places of St Augustine before the final translation of his relics and those of the other saints by Abbot Wido in 1091. Elmham intended this picture to illustrate an account of the translation in Titulus XLIV, the section on Abbot Wido, but he never fulfilled his purpose— his completed text ends early in Wido's abbatiate. However, he inserted the picture at the end of the unfinished titulus.[70] The picture, which combines plan with elevation in a typically medieval fashion, has attempts

[65] See Mr N. R. Ker's remarks in Margaret Deanesly, 'The court of King Æthelberht of Kent' in *Cambridge Historical Journal*, vii (1942), p. 107 n. 11.

[66] Two examples of ancient manuscripts in uncials which were owned by St Augustine's have been noted above (p. 352 n. 57), and at least one of them figures in Elmham's library list. For the school of uncial writing at Canterbury, c. 700, see Maunde Thompson, *An Introduction to Greek and Latin Palaeography*, p. 384. Professor Deanesly's contention that Elmham's facsimiles of King Ethelbert's first and second charters to St Augustine's are in Merovingian script, and were based on genuine documents (Deanesly, op. cit., pp. 53–66 passim) cannot be sustained; see Levison, *England and the Continent in the Eighth Century*, pp. 174 et seq.

[67] BL MS. Cotton Vitellius A II. See Hunter, op. cit., p. 218, and Plate VI. For the reproduction of a *rota* by a chronicler, 'Benedict of Peterborough', see A. Gransden, 'Realistic observation in twelfth century England' in *Speculum*, xlvii (1972), p. 38 and Fig. I.

[68] See Professor Harvey's introduction to *Local Maps and Plans from England*, ed. R. A. Skelton and P. D. A. Harvey (Oxford, forthcoming); I am very grateful to Professor Harvey, and to Dr Hull and the late Dr Urry (see nn. 69, 71–3 below), for allowing me to see the typescripts of their respective contributions to this volume before publication.

[69] Trinity Hall MS. f. 63. The plan is fully discussed by W.G. Urry and reproduced (with references in an appendix to previous reproductions) in Skelton and Harvey, op.cit.

[70] See *SA*, pp. 286 n. 1, 346 n. 1.

at perspective: these suggest that Elmham made his sketch from above, perhaps from the west side of the choir gallery. There is no reason to distrust the accuracy of the work, and it provides valuable evidence for the disposition of the altars and shrines in the fifteenth century.[71]

The final example of Elmham's graphic skill is his map of Thanet.[72] He drew the map to illustrate, as he explains in the text, the legend of Dompneva's hind; it marks the hind's course and the spot where Thunor disappeared into the earth. But it includes additional information; for example it plots the churches assigned to the sacristy of St Augustine's, giving pictorial representations of them. Recent research has shown that the map is not purely diagrammatic or pictorial. Although the shape of Thanet (which is orientated to the east) is inaccurate, the relative positions of the churches and the sketches of them are, in respect of those which can be checked, remarkably exact: this encourages the present day scholar to accept its evidence for the information it contains (for example on the place-names of Thanet) which can no longer be verified.[73] Moreover, whatever the truth of the story of the hind, there was certainly in Elmham's time a linch dividing the lands of St Augustine's from those of Christ Church, which roughly followed the hind's run as plotted on the map; and there was also probably some sort of pit on the spot where, according to tradition, Thunor vanished. Elmham's map, therefore, reinforces his claim to being an observant and competent antiquary.

Thus Thomas Elmham has merits as an historian: he arranged his work well; he used critical judgment in his research on documents; he showed antiquarian curiosity and made intelligent use of visual evidence. Less attractive aspects of his work are his florid style and his constantly reiterated theme, the rights of St Augustine's.

It can be argued that Thomas Burton, the historian of the Cistercian abbey of Meaux, had the same merits as Elmham, but in greater measure, and was free from his shortcomings: he wrote clear, simple Latin, and although he supports his own abbey on any particular issue, the tone of his work is not predominantly contentious.

Meaux's position was very different from that of St Augustine's. It was not an ancient foundation, nor was it highly privileged. It had been founded in 1150 by William le Gros, count of Aumale, and was settled by twelve monks from Fountains.[74] It lay in the lordship of Holderness which was held by the counts of Aumale. They and their successors as lords of Holderness (the line of the counts of Aumale became extinct in 1296) had close

---

[71] See Skelton and Harvey, op. cit.
[72] Trinity Hall MS. f. xxviii^v. Reproduced in *SA*, frontispiece. It is also reproduced, and fully discussed by Felix Hull, in Skelton and Harvey, op. cit.
[73] See Hull, op. cit.
[74] The foundation of Meaux is fully described by Burton; *TB*, i. 73 et seq.

connections with the abbey as patrons.[75] Moreover, being a Cistercian monastery, the abbot of the mother house, in this case Fountains, had supervisory authority.[76] In general Meaux's relations with its patrons and mother house, and with its neighbours, the local gentry, were good. Its main enemies were the archbishop of York and the king's officials. The pope had granted the abbey exemption from the payment of tithes on its estates,[77] and the monks were frequently engaged in lawsuits to defend its right.[78] In addition, their property had suffered badly from flooding and erosion by the Humber and its tributary the Hull, and by the sea:[79] the abbey struggled to gain relief from assessment for taxation by the central government on the lands it had lost.[80]

Thomas Burton's chronicle of Meaux covers the period from the foundation of the abbey up to the resignation of the eighteenth abbot, William of Scarborough, in 1396, and includes general as well as local history. Burton himself was a monk of the abbey from the late fourteenth century until his death in 1437.[81] Little is known of his early monastic career, but he appears in two lists of the monks at Meaux which he himself compiled in 1394 and 1396 respectively.[82] In the first list, which has twenty eight monks, he has the number twenty two prefixed to his name to indicate his place in the convent, and in the second he has the number twenty one, marking an advance in his seniority as a result of the removal of the name of one monk from the list. The fact that Burton was low in seniority suggests that he had not been a professed monk for long. The first list describes him as 'bursar and sergeant (*servitor*) of the abbot', and a note records that he was removed from office in 1394, and two other monks appointed instead. The second list ascribes no office to him.

Burton emerges from obscurity in 1396 when he was elected abbot. The election was disputed, the rival candidate being the prior, William of Wendover, a man of greater experience.[83] A faction in the convent accused Burton of obtaining the abbacy through the undue influence of the patron Thomas of Woodstock, duke of Gloucester (to whom Richard II granted the lordship of Holderness in 1394),[84] and the abbot of Foun-

---

[75] See e.g. *TB*, i. 362; ii. 6, 29, 35, 47, 90; iii. 262; pp.356–7, 362–3, 368 below.

[76] See e.g. *TB*, i. 327; iii. 93, 107; pp. 356–7, 367 below..

[77] *TB*, i. 109, 381–3.

[78] See e.g. *TB*, i. 311, 320; ii. 12 et seq., 51, 76 et seq., 174; iii. 189–9. Cf. p. 361 below.

[79] *TB*, i. 169; ii. 30, 91, 300–1; iii. 16, 79, 102–3, 120–2, 182–5; pp. 364, 365 below.

[80] *TB*, iii. 123, 247 et seq., 279 et seq.; p. 361 below.

[81] For Burton's life see *TB*, i. lviii-lxx.

[82] The 1394 list is in the same manuscript as one of the two texts of Burton's chronicle (see p. 358 and n. 96 below); it is on folio 175ᵛ of BL MS. Egerton 1141. The 1396 list is on folio 234 of Burton's collectanea in BL MS. Cotton Vitellius C VI (see p. 361 and n. 121 below). Both lists are printed in *TB*, i. lx n. 1.

[83] A full account of the disputed election is in the continuation of Burton's chronicle (see p. 357 below); *TB*, iii. 239–40, 258–71, 274–5; cf. *TB*, i. lxii-lxix.

[84] Burton gives an accurate account, obviously based on documents, of the acquisition by

tains.[85] The case went to the Roman curia, but although an arbitration award was eventually given in Burton's favour, dissension continued within the abbey. In 1399 Burton resigned to avoid further litigation. He was succeeded by Wendover.

A full account of the dispute and of Burton's brief abbatiate was added to his chronicle by a continuator.[86] This writer describes Burton as a 'pious and well educated' man,[87] and records that he went to Vienna to attend the general chapter of the Cistercian order.[88] He also notes that Burton resigned in the chapter house at Fountains,[89] and that the abbot of Fountains conceded that he should have an annual pension of 40s. and a chamber in the monks' infirmary at Meaux.[90] The continuator praises Burton for resigning: 'the greatest benefit he bestowed on the monastery was to resign rather than burden it with the expense of further litigation against his false and lying enemies.'[91] He asserts that during his retirement Burton wrote his chronicle 'for the profit of his successors'.[92] In fact Burton had written nearly all of it earlier. He was blind for the last eight years or more of his life.[93]

Thomas of Woodstock of the lordship of Holderness. He states, giving details (*TB*, iii. 219–20), that Richard II in his thirteenth year granted the reversion of the lordship to Thomas on the death of the then holder, Queen Anne. In the first version of the chronicle Burton includes the date of the grant, 12 June (*TB*, iii. 219 n. 10). A grant of the reversion of the manor, 6 May 1390, is enrolled on the patent rolls (*CPR, 1388–1392*, p. 255) but cancelled 'because the king granted the premises to hold under another form, 12 June, 13 Richard II.' Richard II originally granted the reversion as part of the annuity given to Thomas of Woodstock, earl of Buckingham, at the coronation: *Reports . . . touching the Dignity of a Peer* (London, 1820–9, 5 vols), v. 101 (the terms are recapitulated in a charter of 15 February 1392; *Cal. Charter Rolls, 1341–1417*, pp. 330–1). Burton notes that Thomas, now duke of Gloucester, obtained seizin on Queen Anne's death in Richard's seventeenth year 'at about Pentecost' (7 June 1394, the date of Anne's death). A mandate of 10 June on the patent rolls orders that the duke be given seizin; *CPR, 1391–1396*, p. 420. See also p. 363 below.

[85] For the interference of Thomas duke of Gloucester, and the abbot of Fountains, see *TB*, iii. 240, 259–62 passim. After Duke Thomas's death in 1397, his successor as lord of Holderness, Edward, earl of Rutland (d. 1415), who succeeded to the dukedom of Aumale in 1397 (*G. E. C., Peerage*, i. 357), tried to settle the dispute; *TB*, iii. 262–3. Burton calls him Edmund duke of Aumale, probably confusing him with his father Edmund of Langley, duke of York.

[86] Printed in *TB*, iii. 237–76. Cf. *TB*, i. xlviii–xlix.

[87] *TB*, iii. 239.

[88] *TB*, iii. 266–7. The general chapter was held in Vienna instead of at Cîteaux on account of the schism: England and most of Germany adhered to Boniface IX, and, therefore, the Cistercians in those regions could not attend a general chapter at Cîteaux, which, being in France, adhered to the pope at Avignon, Benedict XIII. The general chapter which Thomas Burton attended, and for which his chronicle is apparently the sole literary authority, met in September 1397. See P. B. Griesser, 'Statuten von Generalkapiteln ausserhalb Cîteaux, Wien 1393 and Heilbronn 1398' in *Cistercienser-Chronik*, lxii (1955), pp. 68–9, and see also H. Tüchle, 'Generalkapitel ausserhalb Cîteaux im grossen Schisma' in *Cistercienser-Chronik*, lxiv (1957), pp. 21–2 passim.

[89] *TB*, iii. 274.

[90] *TB*, iii. 275.

[91] *TB*, iii. 271.

[92] *TB*, iii. 276.

[93] *TB*, iii. 276.

The chronicle is divided into sections, one for each abbot, and each section is divided into two subsections, one for local history and one for general history. The subject matter is again divided within the subsections. The local history subsections deal in turn with: the abbot's election; business transactions during his rule; his building activities, gifts to the church and the like; his death; and (from 1286)[94] the exact debts and assets he left to the abbey. The general history subsections deal in turn with: papal history; European history; the history of the archbishopric of York; and English history. In order to help the reader Burton prefixed two lists and two tables.[95] There is a list of the chapter headings occurring in the sections on each abbot, and a list of the abbots themselves, each with length of rule and date of death. And there is a table denoting what properties were held under the individual abbots, arranged under abbots, and a similar table arranged under properties.

Burton's chronicle survives in two versions. One is an early draft and the other a revised text.[96] The principal difference between them is that the revised version omits the list of abbots from the preliminary tables, and has much shorter subsections on general history. Moreover, only the manuscript of the revised version has the continuation. It is possible to draw some conclusions concerning the evolution of the text. Burton apparently began the chronicle in about 1388, and had more or less completed it by 1396, adding the three final chapters, the preliminary lists and table, and revising the whole rather later, probably between 1397 and 1402.[97] The continuation was written under Abbot John Hoton (1445).[98] Besides the account of Burton's abbatiate the continuation contains part of William of Wendover's, and ends with numerous documents relating to the monks' proceedings in the royal exchequer from 1396 to 1418 to gain exemption from taxation for lands wasted by the Humber, the Hull and the sea.[99] The continuator does not include general history: he explains that he had no source from which to copy it.[100]

Burton's subsections on general history were compiled from a variety of sources,[101] many of them among those named in the list of books in the

---

[94] The death of Abbot Richard de Barton (1280–6); *TB*, ii. 176.

[95] *TB*, i. 3–69.

[96] The early version of Burton's chronicle and the revised version survive in two early manuscripts, John Rylands Library, Manchester, MS. Lat. 219 (formerly Phillipps MS. 6478) and BL MS. Egerton 1141 respectively. Hardwick prints the sections on local history from the Egerton MS., giving various readings from the Phillipps MS. in the footnotes. He prints the sections on general history from the Phillipps MS., giving those in the Egerton MS. in Appendices. See *TB*, i. xlv–lviii.

[97] For the dates of composition see *TB*, i. xliv–xlv, l–li.

[98] Printed and described in *TB*, i. xlviii–l passim; iii. xxxiii–xxxiv, 237–314.

[99] See p. 361 and n. 124 below.

[100] *TB*, iii. 238.

[101] Many of Burton's chronicle sources are identified and passages copied *verbatim* printed in small type in *TB* passim. See also *TB*, i. lxxiv–lxxxi; ii. xxxii–xxxiv.

abbey library which Burton himself drew up.[102] His principal sources were Higden, John Brompton,[103] Martinus Polonus and (for the history of the archbishopric of York) Thomas Stubbs.[104] He also used Nennius (or Geoffrey of Monmouth), the *Brut*, Gerald of Wales, the *Quadrilogus* for the life of Thomas Becket, besides other well known works.

However, not all Burton's sources are so easily identified. From the beginning of Edward II's reign until 1334 he used some now lost Cistercian chronicle, which was also used by the chronicler of Woburn abbey.[105] From 1334 until 1338 Burton's narrative is closely related to the chronicle of Bridlington.[106] He gives a full account of Edward III's French campaigns until the siege of Calais in 1347 (thereafter he is noticeably less well informed on the wars).[107] He has some information not found in the other chronicles. There is a joke about the great number of the enemy slain and drowned during the battle at Sluys: the estuary was so full of corpses that it was said that if God were to grant the fish the power of speech, they would talk French.[108] And there is a description of the gold noble issued by Edward III to commemorate the victory.[109]

Another passage with unique information relates to a man born in the neighbourhood of Meaux, at Ruston near Nafferton,[110] who had lived in France for sixteen years: before the battle of Crécy he guided the English army safely across a ford 'in the towns of St Valery and Crotoy'.[111] The fact that this last passage has a local connection suggests the possibility

---

[102] Burton's library list is in his collectanea (see pp. 361–2 and n. below), BL MS. Cotton Vitellius C VI, ff. 241ᵛ–5. Printed as an appendix in *TB*, iii. lxxxiii-c. The works in it used by Burton for his chronicle are listed in *TB*, i. lxxix-lxxx. See also *TB*, iii. lxxii-lxxiii.

[103] *TB*, i. lxxvi. The so-called chronicle of John Brompton (Corpus Christi College, Cambridge, MS. 96) covers the years from A.D. 588 to 1199. It is an anonymous compilation, a copy of which was acquired by John Brompton, abbot of Jervaulx (1436–c. 1464), for the abbey library. It is printed in Twysden's *Scriptores Decem*, pp. 721–1284. See Hardy, *Cat*. ii. 539–41, M. R. James, *A Descriptive Catalogue of the Manuscripts in the Library of Corpus Christi College, Cambridge* (Cambridge 1909–12, 2 vols), i. 183–4, and Emden, *Biographical Register*, i. 277. Cf. pp. 56–7 above.

[104] *TB*, i. lxxiv. Thomas Stubb's history of the church of York covers the years from 1147 to 1373. It is printed and described in *Historians of the Church of York and its Archbishops*, ed. James Raine (RS 1879–94, 3 vols), iii. xxi-xxiv, 388–421.

[105] See *TB*, ii. xxxiv-xxxv.

[106] See *TB*, ii. xli-xlii, *Chrons Edw. I and II*, ii. xxvii-xxviii, and pp. 2 and n. 7, 9–12, 113–15 above. The Bridlington chronicle was still unpublished at the time of Bond's edition of Burton's chronicle.

[107] See *TB*, iii. xxxi-xxxiii.

[108] *TB*, iii. 45.

[109] *TB*, iii. 45. Burton is apparently the authority for the statement that Edward put the words 'Jesus autem transiens per medium illorum ibat' on the noble to commemorate his escape from danger when 'breaking the line' of the French fleet; Charles Oman, *The Coinage of England* (Oxford 1931), pp. 171–2 (and cf. H. A. Grueber, *Handbook of the Coins of Great Britain and Ireland in the British Museum* (London 1899, reprinted 1970), p. 48).

[110] Ruston Parva is about two miles from Nafferton, which lies nine and a half miles south west of Bridlington.

[111] *TB*, iii. 57–8.

that to 1348 Burton used some lost monastic chronicle written at Meaux in the mid-fourteenth century.[112]

Nevertheless, although Burton devoted considerable space to general history, his main concern was his own abbey. Its affairs increasingly pre-occupied him: the early version of his chronicle contains nearly as much general as local history, but, as has been seen, in revision he drastically reduced the length of the subsections on general history. Furthermore, the subsections on local history contain some of the most valuable informa-tion on national affairs: this is because Meaux and its neighbourhood sometimes became involved in them. Those passages which are of partic-ular interest to the social and economic historian will be discussed later, but one passage relating directly to political events may be mentioned here. Burton records that on one occasion during the reign of Henry III, the king's eldest son, the Lord Edward, planned to subdue Scotland, and summoned all the knights and free men of Holderness to serve in the army.[113] But they were unwilling to go, and sent the subprior of Meaux to offer their excuses. Later Edward repeated his demand, and again the subprior took the excuses to him; as a result King Henry, 'who was holding a great parliament in London', sent an army to reduce the rebels. The sheriff and men of Holderness quickly broke the bridge over the Hull, retreated to the abbey's grange at Sutton and held counsel in its chapel in the wood.[114] The monks, fearing damage to their property, placated the intruders with gifts of food and by feasting them in the abbey—'never was seen such a multitude dining our house'. Meanwhile the subprior acted as a go-between; he rode to and fro between the parties so often that 'he slept hardly twice in six days, and in one day and night changed horses three times because they were exhausted by the hard work.' Eventually he was successful and peace was made. 'And so by God's favour, we avoided death and arson, and the whole neighbourhood was forever in our debt'.

---

[112] There is another piece of evidence which could be interpreted as supporting the view that Burton used an earlier chronicle of Meaux. The earliest known draft of the chronicle (the John Rylands MS.) records an earthquake in the abbey church in 1349, in the sub-section on general history. The revised version of his chronicle (the Egerton MS.) has the same entry in the subsection on local history. (*TB*, iii. 37 and n. 12, 69). This suggests the possibility that Burton was using a typical monastic chronicle written at Meaux, in which the local and general history were intermixed in the usual way, and, therefore, inadvertently copied local history into the subsection on general history, and only sub-sequently removed it to the appropriate place. For another example of a local entry in a general subsection see the account of King John's treatment of the abbey in 1207, although in this case Burton left the entry in the general subsection in the revised version, as well as including it in the local subsections in both versions; *TB*, i. 326, 346, 352. It should also be noted that Burton gives a number of references to chronicles of the monastery in his tract on tithes (see *TB*, i. lxxii, lxxiii, and p. 361 and n. 123 below).

[113] *TB*, ii. 106–8. Burton does not give a specific date for this occurrence, but there is evidence suggesting that it may have taken place in the spring of 1268. See p. 496, Appendix F, below.

[114] For the chapel of St Mary by the bridge in the wood see p. 362 n. 129 below.

Burton initially wrote the chronicle, as he states in the preface, because he saw 'the memory of those illustrious men, the abbots of Meaux, almost lost on account of the sloth of the negligent, and I grieve that their light is obscured.'[115] To remedy the deficiency he undertook extensive research on written sources, mainly documents, besides using oral information and his own observation. 'No one', he writes, 'who finds anything in what follows which he did not know before, should think that I invented it; he must rest assured that I have only included what I have found written in other works or in a variety of documents, or have heard from reliable witnesses, or have myself seen.'[116] The result of his research was a work of scholarship unrivalled in depth and scope by any other chronicle written in England in his time.

Burton used some narrative sources. His account of the foundation of Meaux[117] was almost certainly taken from a foundation history of the kind produced by the north country Cistercian houses in the late twelfth century; such a work is mentioned in Burton's library list.[118] He probably also used at least one monastic chronicle composed in the abbey.[119] But more remarkable is his use of documents. As he explains: 'I collected together many ancient documents and long forgotten parchments; I found some which had been exposed to the rain, and others put aside for the fire.'[120]

Burton's recognition of the value of documents as historical sources was no doubt partly the result of his work as bursar. The office gave him access to documents and a training in their use. His interest in and knowledge of documents appears not only in his chronicle, but also in collectanea he compiled both before he became abbot and after his retirement. These comprise a register[121] and documentary material he appended to the revised version of the chronicle.[122] Among the items are: a digest of grants of lands and rents to the monastery arranged under parishes; notes on grants made for special purposes; notes on royal charters of confirmation; papal privileges and Cistercian constitutions (1389–1404) arranged under subjects and ending with an index of papal bulls; a tract on the exemption of the abbey's churches from payment of tithes;[123] and a tract on the abbey's attempt to gain exemption from tax on lands wasted by floods, 1396–1418[124]

---

[115] *TB*, i. 71.
[116] *TB*, i. 72–3.
[117] *TB*, i. 73 et seq.
[118] *TB*, i. lxxiii; iii. lxxxiv.
[119] See pp. 359–60 and n. 112 above.
[120] *TB*, i. 71.
[121] BL MS. Cotton Vitellius C VI. Described in *TB*, i. lvi-lviii, and pp. 356 and n. 82, 359 n. 102 above.
[122] Described in *TB*, i. liii-liv.
[123] These items are all in BL MS. Cotton Vitellius C VI, and are included in the description in *TB*, i. lvii.
[124] This tract is among the material appended to the revised version of the chronicle (Egerton MS. 1141). See *TB*, i. liii-liv.

(this work formed the basis of the account of the struggle by Burton's continuator).[125]

Burton's method of using documents was more sophisticated than that of most chroniclers. He did not, as was usual, copy them in full with brief explanatory notes. As he states in his preface, 'I have abridged their great length and illuminated their obscurities; I have read through the registers and added from the original documents whatever they omit; and finally I have combined the total results into this one volume with the greatest care.'[126]

The substratum of documentary evidence in Burton's chronicle juts out in many places. There are numerous references to charters as the authority for the detailed accounts of business transactions,[127] and in some instances there are references to the absence of charters.[128] In cases where comparison can be made between the text of the chronicle and the original charter, it is possible to demonstrate how closely Burton followed the document: an example is Burton's account of the abbey's foundation, the particulars of which are corroborated by the count of Aumale's foundation charter.[129]

Burton's preoccupation with documents is well illustrated by a number of passages in his chronicle. Documents were the crucial evidence in the disputes between the abbey and the secular church, particularly as represented by the archbishop of York, which Burton describes in full. For instance, when Archbishop Alexander Neville (1374–88) claimed and seized the manor of Wawne, the monks were worried because they could not find the agreement previously drawn up between Archbishop Walter Gray and Abbot Richard de Ottringham (1221–35), or any record or copy of it.[130] Eventually they discovered it, the chronicle alleges, with fourteen seals appended, in their muniment room; it was not in the bags containing charters but in a hole or gap between the ceiling and the roof, together with a charter of Henry II. Marvellously enough, they were quite undamaged though hidden and forgotten for so long.[131] Charters were also at issue, as Burton explains, when Archbishop Thomas Arundel allowed a rumour to circulate that he was the abbey's patron. This dis-

[125] See p. 358 above.
[126] *TB*, i. 71.
[127] See e.g. *TB*, i. 77, 175, 416; ii. 65. See also pp. 369–70 below.
[128] See e.g. *TB*, i. 96.
[129] *TB*, i. 81; for the charter itself see *Early Yorkshire Charters*, ed. William Farrer, (Edinburgh 1914–16, 3 vols), iii. 89–90, 93. Similarly, Burton's detailed account of the foundation by Sir Peter de Mauley of a chantry in Meaux's chapel of St Mary 'by the bridge in the wood' is confirmed by an inspeximus of 1238, which was enrolled on the charter rolls in chancery: *TB*, ii. 59–61 (cf. p. 367 and n. 155 below); *Cal. Charter Rolls*, i. 233–4. For Burton's competent use of documentary evidence see also his account of Thomas duke of Gloucester's acquisition of the lordship of Holderness; p. 357 n. 84 above.
[130] *TB*, iii. 174–5; for the earlier agreement see *TB*, i. 407–8.
[131] See *TB*, iii. 175.

turbed Thomas of Woodstock, duke of Gloucester, who, on succeeding to the lordship of Holderness, claimed the right of patronage. Therefore, when he visited the abbey in September 1394, he asked to see the foundation charters to verify his claim and to discover whether he was entitled to any dues from the monks. It was established that although he was rightly patron, the abbey owed him nothing because it held in free alms.[132]

Similarly, documents are an important feature in Burton's detailed account of a dispute with 'certain clerks' who tried to obtain two of the abbey's churches, Easington and Keyingham, by means of papal provision. The monks appealed to the curia, then resident at Avignon, but were unwilling to send the original charters of appropriation for the case. They, therefore, had copies made, with authenticating seal, in the consistory at York by a public notary. But the curia would not admit the copies as evidence, and the monks had most reluctantly to send the originals, which they conveyed abroad hidden in two flasks. Burton explains a further obstacle which they encountered: Gregory XI would not accept the royal title as set forth in the charters, 'Edward king of England and France', which would have to be recited in full in the papal confirmations. The notary could not in all conscience suppress the phrase 'of France', and the pope did not want to alienate his French allies by its inclusion. Eventually a compromise was reached; the title stood, but the papal seal in green wax was stamped over the offending words.[133]

Burton has some good stories which may well derive from oral tradition — though he could equally well have copied the earlier ones from a pre-existing chronicle of Meaux. He relates, for example, that when William Fossard, heir to a nearby barony, was living as a ward in the household of William le Gros, count of Aumale, he seduced the count's sister. He then fled abroad, and in revenge the count, with the king's permission, sacked his castle at Mountferaunt. The castle, Burton writes, had a wooden tower and according to common report. supplied Sir Robert de Stutville with the timber which he gave to the monks to construct domestic buildings.[134] There is also the story of a bondman, Richard de Aldwyn, and the 'crows'.[135] In the time of Abbot Michael de Brun (1235–49), Richard

---

[132] *TB*, iii. 219–21. The year of Gloucester's visit is fixed by Burton's statement that it took place in the September after the duke obtained seizin of the lordship of Holderness, which he did in 1394; see pp. 356–7 n. 84 above.

[133] *TB*, iii. 186–91. The monks' intermediary at the papal curia was Cardinal Jean de Bussières, abbot of Cîteaux (*TB*, iii. 189). This dates the case to the period between 20 December 1375, when de Bussières was created cardinal-priest of St Laurence in Lucina, and 4 September 1376, when he died; Denis de Sainte-Marthe *et al.*, *Gallia Christiana* (Paris 1715–1865, 16 vols), iv. 1001.

[134] *TB*, i. 104–5. See *Early Yorkshire Charters*, ed. Farrer, ii. 328.

[135] *corvi*; *TB*, ii. 48–9. No doubt 'rooks' are meant but 'crows' seems right here (a 'rook' is called a 'crow' in the north of England). The story may be true and possibly was thought to explain the place-name 'Croo', or perhaps it was invented for that purpose. (A. H. Smith, *The Place-Names of the East Riding of Yorkshire and York* (English Place-Name Soc., xiv, 1937), pp. 81, 127, suggests derivation from 'croh', a bend, nook or corner.)

lived on the grange of 'Croo'(its lands were in Beeford and Dringhoe), and suffered from the caws of the 'crows'. Therefore, he obtained the abbot's permission to cut down the surrounding oaks, ashes and other fine trees; 'and so to this day the grange is deprived of the shade of a single tree.' In the same way hearsay was probably the source of the description of the carving of the crucifix for the laybrothers' church under Abbot Hugh de Leven (1339–49): the sculptor would only carve on Friday when fasting on bread and water, and he used a naked man as a model ('by this means he embellished the image with even greater beauty'). The crucifix worked miracles, and to 'encourage devotion and otherwise benefit the monastery' the monks applied to the abbot of Cîteaux for permission to admit 'men and respectable women' to see it.[136]

Since the date of Thomas Burton's birth, the place where he spent his early life, and exactly when he joined the community at Meaux are unknown, it is not certain in all instances whether he acquired information at first hand or by oral transmission. The chronicle gives, for example, two vivid descriptions of the flooding of Ravenser Odd, which was situated on the extreme edge of Holderness, once during the abbatiate of William de Dringhoe (1349–53) and once during that of Robert de Beverley (1356–67). The first flood devastated the abbey's church there, washing the bodies and bones of the dead from their graves in the cemetery— 'a horrible sight'.[137] On the second occasion the village was surrounded by 'a towering wall of water'. The inhabitants, already scared by previous high tides, fled with their belongings to Kingston-upon-Hull and other coastal towns, where they settled.[138]

It is very likely that Burton actually experienced the fire which broke out during the rule of Abbot William de Dringhoe and which he describes in graphic terms. One morning before cockcrow lightning struck the leaden roof of the church, setting alight the timbers underneath in three places 'above the crucifix on the south side'. Luckily a tailor rising early saw the fire and wakened a monk who was sleeping outside the dormitory. The monk roused the others by hammering on the dormitory door with such violence that 'they thought the whole church was ablaze around them.' The monks leapt scarcely dressed from their beds, pulled on tunics and cloaks, and rushed to seize 'golden vessels and other receptacles' of such size that normally they could hardly be lifted even when empty. They carried these full of water up into the roof, along beams which miraculously bore their weight although considered safe only for a child, and extinguished the flames.[139]

[136] *TB*, iii. 35–6.
[137] *TB*, iii. 79.
[138] *TB*, iii. 120–1. This passage is noticed by N. Denholm-Young in his account of Ravenser Odd: 'The Yorkshire estates of Isabella de Fortibus' in *Yorkshire Archaeological Journal*, xxxi (1934), p. 404 n. 2.
[139] *TB*, iii. 166.

There can be little doubt that Burton himself examined the havoc caused by a storm to the abbey's church of Keyingham in 1396. He describes how the windows were shattered as if by hammer blows, and the panes, though themselves intact, together with small stones from walls and tower, were blown to a distance of up to thirty feet. And the solid oak doors were so cracked that 'you could put your hand through'.[140]

Some of Burton's first hand observations show his antiquarian interests. It is clear that he had studied both the topography of the abbey's estates, and some of its 'ancient monuments'. He describes the original boundaries of the manor of Meaux, using charter evidence. The boundary was marked by a mound in the form of a kiln, a large stone under a bridge, a buried cow and holes in the ground three feet wide and a stone's throw apart. 'But', Burton comments, 'as the marks are now wholly unknown, we must examine the boundary as it exists today.'[141]

Burton was particularly interested in the topographical changes which had resulted from silting and erosion in the flat levels of Holderness. He explains how the vill of Wick, which was washed on one side by the Humber and on another by the Old Hull, was once in Holderness but became part of Harthill: the New Hull to the east of Wick had grown in size, while the Old Hull had been reduced to a mere trickle ('hardly deserving to be called a drain'), so that the New Hull 'now divides Holderness and Harthill', leaving Wick on the Harthill side. In Burton's day the abbey's grange at Wick ('now called Grangewick') had been abandoned, though 'its ruins can still easily be seen.'[142] The lost Ravenser Odd also attracted Burton's attention. First he carefully explains the distinction between Old Ravenser, a manor in his day set back from the Humber and the sea, and Ravenser Odd which had disappeared into the Humber—its ruins were a danger to sailors. He gives an exact description of the remains of the road which once led to Ravenser Odd from Old Ravenser, explaining that it could still be used on foot or on horseback except for its last half mile which was sunk in the Humber:[143] 'it is sandy and scattered with round, yellow pebbles, and is raised very little above water level, and is hardly a bowshot in width, but has resisted the flooding of the sea on the east and the battering of the Humber on the west in a truly wonderful fashion.'

Burton has a number of entries on the history of the abbey's buildings, one of which shows antiquarian interest. He records that Abbot Hugh de Leven did not complete the chantry chapel which his predecessor had begun to construct above the great gate, either because he did not think it important, or because he had not the means. Abbot Hugh demolished

---

[140] *TB*, iii. 193–4.
[141] *TB*, i. 78–81. Cf. *TB*, iii. 1 and n. 2.
[142] *TB*, i. 168–9; for Wick, later the site of Kingston-upon-Hull, see *TB*, ii. 186, 192, and p. 369 and n. 171 below.
[143] The passage occurs twice in the chronicle: *TB*, ii. 30; iii. 121–2.

what had been built already except for part of the foundations ('which can be seen to this day'), and used the stone to improve the brewery, making a handsome tank next to the malt kiln for the fermentation of the malt and barley.[144] Burton has little on the antiquities of the church itself, apart from the usual record of the burial places of abbots and benefactors,[145] but he does note that the dates on the epitaph for Abbot Robert de Beverley were wrong—because, he asserts, the sculptor lost the sheet provided for him to copy, and so invented them.[146]

The subsections on local history are of exceptional value because of Burton's careful use of sources,[147] many of them otherwise irretrievable. Nor did Burton limit himself narrowly to the abbey's immediate concerns, but has interesting excurses on related subjects. As a monastic history his chronicle is unrivalled in the period, except by the *Gesta Abbatum* of St Albans. It is in a sense complementary to the latter work which gives a picture of a prosperous Benedictine house in the south of England and one in the current of contemporary affairs; the chronicle of Meaux, on the other hand, portrays a north country Cistercian monastery, struggling with poverty and remote from the centres of national politics.

Burton throws light on the nature of the community at Meaux. He records that when the abbey was founded there were forty monks.[148] He also cites evidence proving that before the middle of the thirteenth century the number, having at some time previously been fixed at fifty, was raised to fifty one; how long this quota lasted Burton admits he had no means of knowing.[149] In the mid-thirteenth century he records that there were sixty monks and ninety laybrothers,[150] but when the Black Death reached the monastery in 1349 numbers had again fallen; there were forty two monks excluding the abbot and only seven laybrothers.[151] The impact of the plague itself was devastating—the abbot, thirty two monks and all the laybrothers died ('on one day', Burton writes, 'the abbot and five monks lay unburied'). The community seems never to have recovered: among the dead were the senior monks and obedientiaries, and those who survived did not have the experience and administrative knowledge to run the estates competently. In addition, the monastery faced a decrease in rents and possessions resulting from the death of tenants.[152]

---

[144] *TB*, iii. 36.
[145] For the burial places of the abbots see e.g. *TB*, i. 107, 234, 380; ii. 119, 157; iii. 167, 234. For the burial places of laymen see p. 370 and n. 177 below. For a brief description of vestments see *TB*, iii. 167.
[146] *TB*, iii. 152.
[147] For examples see pp. 356 n. 84, 362 and n. 129 above.
[148] *TB*, i. 107.
[149] *TB*, ii. 28–9, 51.
[150] *TB*, ii. 65.
[151] *TB*, iii. 36.
[152] For the effects of the plague on the abbey see *TB*, iii. 36–7.

At the end of the abbatiate of William de Scarborough in 1396, there were twenty six monks and no laybrothers.[153]

Burton gives the impression that observance in the abbey was better in the thirteenth century than in the fourteenth, and that in his own time life in the convent became progressively less harmonious. The most elaborate arrangements for the distribution of alms at the gates are recorded during the rule of Abbot Michael de Brun (1235–49). The abbot allocated revenues for the purpose: the tannery was to supply the porter with twenty cured ox- and cow-hides for the repair of old shoes and for the making of new ones; the woolshop was to provide cloth; and the two dairies specified were to contribute a tenth of their cheese.[154]

The chronicle records in detail the endowment of a number of chantries in the abbey. For example in 1293 Richard de Ottringham, rector of Shelford (in the diocese of Ely), founded a chantry chapel outside the gates, served by six monks and a secular priest, to pray for the soul of his uncle, John de Ottringham, his own soul, and for the souls of other members of the family.[155] Although such endowments increased the abbey's property, they could result in problems over the discipline of the monks appointed to serve in the chantry. Thus Abbot Adam de Skyrne (1310–39) had to move the Ottringham chantry to a chapel inside the precincts because of the scandalous lives of the six monks;[156] and by the mid-fourteenth century divine service in the chantry had stopped altogether.[157]

In the last half of the fourteenth century dissension grew. John de Rislay (1353–6) was imposed on the convent by the abbot of Fountains without its assent and after a disputed election. He was forced to resign after an appeal to Rome because of his highhanded actions and his squandering of the abbey's resources: Burton comments that John did not deserve to be numbered among the abbots, because he acquired his position by simony, and ruled to the detriment of the monks.[158]

The last years of William de Scarborough, who ruled from 1372 to 1396, were marked by discord. The pope appointed as prior one of the monks who represented the community in the papal curia, but his nominee

---

[153] *TB*, iii. 234. For the history of the laybrothers (*conversi*) at Meaux, based on the figures and other information given by Burton, see R. H. Snape, *English Monastic Finances in the Later Middle Ages* (Cambridge 1926), pp. 8–9.

[154] *TB*, ii. 64–5.

[155] *TB*, ii. 192–205. Burton includes the text of the abbot's regulations for the six monks serving the chapel and a full account of the difficulty he had in obtaining a licence to alienate in mortmain from the provost of Beverley, of which college some of the endowments were held; see (citing Burton) K. L. Wood-Legh, *Perpetual Chantries in Britain* (Cambridge 1965), p. 311. For details of other chantries see *TB*, ii. 59–61 (cf. p. 362 n. 129 above); iii. 11–13, 18–20, 163–5, and p. 369 and n. 168 below.

[156] *TB*, ii. 294–6.

[157] *TB*, iii. 82.

[158] *TB*, iii. 93–4, 109–11; cf. *TB*, iii. 151.

met such bitter opposition that he was forced to resign.[159] Abbot William himself with the support of Thomas of Woodstock, duke of Gloucester, offered his resignation to the abbot of Fountains, because of the community's intransigence and his own decrepitude: but the convent, fearing the precedent of interference by the patron, would not agree. A year later William renewed his request, and again the monks resisted. Thomas of Woodstock attributed their opposition to 'the desire to freely indulge their excesses contrary to the discipline of the order'; he wrote to persuade the abbot of Fountains to accept William's resignation, and also obtained the support of neighbouring lords.[160]

When finally in 1396 William was allowed to resign, the election of a successor brought further disorder. It was on this occasion that Burton himself was elected, but, as has been seen, his election was opposed by a faction in the convent which supported the candidature of the prior, William of Wendover. During the conflict Thomas of Woodstock and the abbot of Fountains were accused of using force to support Burton. The two monks deputed to lay the convent's complaints before the meeting of the general chapter of the Cistercian order in London were imprisoned. Subsequently they feared to return, but wandered from place to place dressed as laymen, 'to the great injury of our order's reputation',[161] until a settlement was reached. And eventually Burton felt compelled to resign the abbacy because of hostility among his monks.[162]

The abbey also had trouble with the laybrothers. Because of their 'duplicity and impudence' Abbot Richard (1221–35) moved them from the granges, employing them instead in the monastery itself as masons, carpenters, glaziers and plumbers, and to look after the animals.[163] One tenant at Wawne gave up his property because of the laybrothers' bad behaviour, and Burton attributed the burning down of a granary full of corn at Skerne to their drunken negligence.[164]

Nor were the abbey's relations with its bondmen always good. During the rule of Abbot Robert de Beverley (1356–67) the bondmen of Wawne revolted, claiming to be the king's villeins, not the abbot's.[165] (Doubtless

---

[159] *TB*, iii. 191.
[160] *TB*, iii. 229–33.
[161] *TB*, iii. 262.
[162] *TB*, iii. 271. The continuator (see p. 357 above) gives a full account of Burton's election, rule and resignation.
[163] *TB*, i. 432. See Snape, *Monastic Finances*, pp. 8, 12, and J. S. Donnelly, *The Decline of the Medieval Cistercian Laybrotherhood* (New York 1949), pp. 36 and n. 82, 54 and n. 69, 74.
[164] *TB*, ii. 4, 109–10.
[165] Burton gives a full account of the case; *TB*, iii. 127–42, and see pp. 370–1 below. The case is noticed in R. H. Hilton, 'Peasant movements in England before 1381' in *Essays in Economic History*, ed. E. M. Carus-Wilson (London, 1954–62, 2 vols), ii, p. 89, and in the same author's *The Decline of Serfdom in Medieval England* (London-New York 1964), pp. 37–8. Burton also records the unsuccessful attempt of a bondman to grant the abbey some land during the rule of Abbot Michael (1235–49); *TB*, ii. 34.

they hoped that a more distant lord would be less oppressive than a nearby one.) Abbot Robert imprisoned three or four, and the king appointed a commission of inquiry. The abbot only obtained a favourable judgment after expensive litigation: Burton alleges that during the proceedings 'all the king's ministers and officials did whatever injury they could to our abbot, except the chancellor who as a result of bribery inclined slightly to his side.'[166]

Burton's chronicle is especially remarkable as a business record. In accordance with his training as bursar, Burton gives numerous figures.[167] He calculates as far as possible any financial loss in a particular deal. Thus he explains at length that the cost of maintaining two chantries founded in the mid-fourteenth century exceeded the income obtained by the convent from the initial endowment.[168] Similarly he explains that the annual revenue of 5s. from the mills in Wawne was quite inadequate to cover the expenses of repairs and of dredging the dykes which served them.[169] And he demonstrates arithmetically how the merchants to whom Abbot Robert de Beverley sold the abbey's wool clip in advance, made a profit of £645 at the abbey's expense.[170] His taste for figures resulted in him giving exact details concerning the foundation of Kingston-upon-Hull by Edward I. In order to found the town, the king acquired the abbey's manors of Wick and Myton. He gave various other properties in exchange, but, according to Burton's calculations, the monks lost badly on the transaction—and their attempts at recompense were thwarted by 'the malice of a valuer'.[171]

The use of Burton's chronicle to the social and economic historian extends beyond his record of figures. He has, for example, much other information on the founding of Kingston-upon-Hull,[172] and throws light on a number of aspects of life in his locality. Thus he provides evidence of a customary payment in the East Riding of Yorkshire. He explains that four measures (thraves) of corn had to be paid annually from every carucate to feed the royal horses. This due, which dated back to the reign of King Athelstan, was rightly called 'hestcorn', but the word had been changed 'by certain ill-disposed people' to 'bestcorn'.[173]

---

[166] *TB*, iii. 141.

[167] For Burton's exact record of the debts left by the abbots from 1286 onwards see p. 358 and n. 94 above. Some of Burton's figures, both in the chronicle and in his collectanea, are cited by Snape, *Monastic Finances*, pp. 93, 130, 137, 138, 166, 167.

[168] I.e. the chantries at Fulstow and Winestead; see *TB*, iii. 13, 20, and, with reference to Burton's calculations, Wood-Legh, *Perpetual Chantries in Britain*, pp. 153 and n. 4, 154 and n. 1. For other references to these chantries, based on bishops' registers, see ibid., pp. 45, 144, 145 and n. 1, 146 and n. 2.

[169] *TB*, ii. 84.

[170] *TB*, iii. 144–5. For the practice of advance selling, common among religious houses, with reference to Meaux, on Burton's evidence, see Snape, *Monastic Finances*, p. 137.

[171] *TB*, ii. 190–1. Cited *VCH York, East Riding*, i. 16.

[172] See ibid., i. 1–21 and nn., passim.

[173] *TB*, ii. 236. See *Early Yorkshire Charters*, ed. Farrer, i. 95.

Burton was very well informed about the business transactions of the Yorkshire nobility with the Jews. The abbey, like many other north country monasteries, sometimes acquired property from laymen by buying up unredeemed Jewish bonds at a discount. Such deals could lead to difficulty. For instance, the monks took over debts owed by William Fossard to Aaron of Lincoln,[174] in exchange receiving the manors of Bainton and Neswick. Subsequently they paid the total amount, as they thought, to Richard I, in response to a royal ordinance, but on Aaron's death a charter was discovered by which it appeared they still owed over £500. However, after much trouble and expense they found an acquittance; this 'was read before the barons of the exchequer and copied on to a roll, but not the great roll, and then copied on to the abbot's great roll.'[175] Burton disliked the Jews. He considered them untrustworthy, and attributed to them the ruin of many a noble and gentle family: 'nobles and those of lesser estate were reduced to penury by debts to the Jews, who distrained their property and patrimony.'[176]

Burton's sympathies lay with the local nobility, and he was very well informed about them. He notes the burial of a local lord in the abbey church,[177] and in order to record for whom Richard de Ottringham's chantry is to pray, he lists Richard's close relatives and descendants.[178] Similarly, he names any local lord who became a novice at Meaux— and so endowed the monastery with his property.[179] But most important he records many property transactions between the nobility and the abbey. Moreover, in order to show that a grant was valid, he had to demonstrate that the grantor had an indisputable title. This led him to trace the genealogies of families and the descent of their properties, recording any other gifts to the abbey, often from as far back as the evidence permitted and up to his own day.[180] He even gives the genealogy of the leader of the

---

[174] For William Fossard's indebtedness to the Jews see R. B. Dobson, *The Jews of Medieval York and the Massacre of March 1190* (Borthwick Papers, no. 45, York 1974), p. 10.

[175] *TB*, i. 173–4, 177–8. This transaction is fully explained in Joseph Jacobs, 'Aaron of Lincoln' in *Transactions of the Jewish Historical Society of England*, iii (1899), pp. 163–4. For other business dealings connected with the Jews see *TB*, i. 306, 367, 374–5, 377; ii. 12, 55, 109, 116. See also Dobson, op. cit., p. 41 and n. 133.

[176] *TB*, i. 244. Professor Dobson (op. cit., p. 20 n. 68) notes the anti-Jewish attitude of the Meaux chronicle.

[177] *TB*, i. 260. For the burial place of William le Gros see *TB*, i. 212. For the burial of the heart of William de Forz, count of Aumale 1241–60, in the church at Meaux see *TB*, ii. 106.

[178] *TB*, ii. 194.

[179] See e.g. *TB*, i. 233; ii. 5–6, 28, 45.

[180] His pedigree of the Etton family of Gilling and history of the family's estates (*TB*, i. 316–18), and scattered references (see the index to *TB*, iii, under Etton) provided much of the information used by John Bilson, 'Gilling castle' in *Yorkshire Archaeological Journal*, xix (1907), pp. 105–92 passim. For other examples of pedigrees see the accounts of the families of Sayers (*TB*, i. 96), Scures (*TB*, i. 97–8), Fossard (*TB*, i. 104), Sculcottes (*TB*, i. 169–70) and Routh (*TB*, ii. 92). Burton also gives the genealogy of the Forz family (the counts of Aumale), and the descent of the honour and of the lordship of Holderness; *TB*, i. 89–93.

rebel bondman, Richard de Aldwyn, to prove that he belonged to the abbot. (Richard himself gave a genealogy to prove that he belonged to the king.)[181] And Burton includes biographical anecdotes concerning members of the families. The detail of such family and property histories seems to exceed the needs of a business record and suggests objective interest.

William de la Pole, first mayor of Hull, receives special attention. He was 'second to none' as an English merchant. He had strong local connections: he 'learnt the art of commerce' at Ravenser Odd, and Edward I granted him the abbey's former manors of Wick and Myton. Burton notes that his eldest son was Michael de la Pole, earl of Suffolk (1385), who lent the king 'many thousand pounds', was appointed a baron of the exchequer, and was granted among other royal properties, the lordship of Holderness.[182]

If the Latin prose style of Thomas Burton is compared with that of Thomas Elmham, the difference will be noticed. Burton, who was the earlier writer of the two, and apparently lacked a university education, wrote simply, without literary embellishment. Although much of Elmham's history of St Augustine's is in similar style, some passages are, as has been explained above, in the flowery prose favoured by fifteenth century *littérateurs*. Elmham, a product of an Oxford education, subsequently wrote the Life of Henry V in Latin verse in a more markedly florid style. John Whethamsted, who had also studied at Oxford and wrote later still in the fifteenth century, is an even more extreme case, and indeed stands in a category apart: he wrote both prose and verse in predominantly flowery Latin.

The date when John Whethamsted (*alias* Bostock), son of Hugh and Margaret Bostock of Wheathampstead in Hertfordshire, professed at St Albans is unknown, but it was certainly before the death of Thomas Walsingham.[183] He studied at Oxford and was prior of the house of the Benedictines of the southern province, Gloucester college, from 1414 to 1417. He incepted in theology in 1417. He became abbot of St Albans in 1420, and in 1423 was chosen by convocation to represent the English

---

[181] *TB*, iii. 126, 130, 134.

[182] *TB*, i. 170; iii. 47–9.

[183] For a survey of Whethamsted's life and significance in fifteenth century culture see: David Knowles, *The Religious Orders in England*, ii (Cambridge 1955), pp. 193–7; E. F. Jacob, 'Verborum florida venustas' in his *Essays in the Conciliar Epoch* (second edition, Manchester 1953), pp. 187–96 (this article is reprinted with revision from *BJRL*, xvii (1933), pp. 264–90); R. Weiss, *Humanism in England during the Fifteenth Century* (second edition, Oxford 1957), pp. 30–8; Emden, *Biographical Register*, iii. 2032–4. These authors refer to an unpublished Manchester thesis by Miss Esther Hodge, 'The Abbey of St. Albans under John of Whethamstede'. Unfortunately I was unable to consult this because Manchester University Library reports that it has been mislaid. Whethamsted is also discussed in W. F. Schirmer, *Der Englische Frühhumanismus* (Leipzig 1931), pp. 82–98, 143–5.

Benedictines at the council of Pavia.[184] He attended the council, which moved to Siena, and visited Rome, where he had an audience with Pope Martin V, to whom he successfully presented a petition on behalf of St Albans.[185] In 1440 he resigned the abbacy giving ill health as his principal reason, though it seems likely that dissension in the convent and the debts which he had contracted were contributory factors.[186] In 1452 he was again elected abbot and ruled until his death in 1465.

As a scholar and man of letters Whethamsted achieved some fame. Three main factors influenced his intellectual development: his education at Oxford; his friendship with Humphrey duke of Gloucester; and his monastic background. After his return from university to St Albans and his election to the abbacy, Whethamsted retained a close connection with Oxford, and whenever possible promoted the interests of Gloucester college. When he dissolved the abbey's cell of Beaulieu, he put the revenues towards the expenses of the St Albans monks studying at Oxford.[187] On his re-election to the abbacy in 1453 he was distressed to find that the standard of learning in the monastery had fallen. Since he thought that 'ignorance of letters and neglect of study relegates monks to obscurity', and that 'the worst evil to overtake a community is blindness of intellect', he increased the number of his monks at the university from one to four.[188] He also gave £108 towards the cost of building a new library, chapel and wall around the garden at Gloucester college.[189]

Besides the education Whethamsted received in the schools, he benefited from contact with Humphrey, duke of Gloucester, the patron of a circle of scholars engaged on classical studies.[190] Duke Humphrey was a benefactor of[191] and frequent visitor to St Albans, where he was ultimately buried.[192] He was on friendly terms with Whethamsted. When on retiring from office in ·1440 Whethamsted quarrelled with his successor, Abbot John

---

[184] *Reg. I*, i. 99. Whethamsted's account of his visit is discussed in E. F. Jacob, 'Englishmen and the General Councils of the fifteenth century' in *Essays in the Conciliar Epoch*, pp. 44–6 (this article is reprinted with revision from *History*, xxiv (1939), pp. 206–19). See also pp. 385–6 below.

[185] *Reg. I*, i. 153–8.

[186] See p. 380 below.

[187] *Reg. I*, ii. 107–8.

[188] *Reg. II*, i. 24–5.

[189] *Reg. I*, ii. 200, 264. For gifts to the Benedictine scholars of Gloucester college see *Reg. I*, ii. 256. For letters from Whethamsted to the prior of Gloucester college see *Reg. II*, ii. 416–17, and to the scholars see *Reg. II*, ii. 382–3, 419. Whethamsted obtained papal permission to use a portable altar while in Oxford; *Reg. I*, i. 154.

[190] For Duke Humphrey as the patron of humanist scholars see Weiss, *Humanism in England*, Chaps III and IV. For his friendship with Whethamsted see ibid., pp. 26, 33–4, 40.

[191] See *Reg. I*, ii. 187–90; *Reg. II*, i. 26, 92–4. For Duke Humphrey's friendship with St Albans see K. H. Vickers, *Humphrey Duke of Gloucester* (London 1907), pp. 329–31.

[192] A number of Duke Humphrey's visits are noticed in the *Annales Sancti Albani* (for which see p. 412 and n. 147 below), pp. 4, 8–9 passim, 12–13, 19, 25. For his burial at St Albans see Vickers, op. cit., pp. 294, 331–2, 439–41 (Appendix C).

Stokes, over his living allowance, the duke arbitrated the case.[193] His friendship with Whethamsted is witnessed by the latter's gift of books to him. These books included a copy of Cato[194] and a Latin translation of Plato, besides some of Whethamsted's own works.[195] Through his contact with Duke Humphrey, Whethamsted made the acquaintance of the Italian humanist Piero del Monte. The latter wrote a dialogue on the vices and virtues which he dedicated to Duke Humphrey, and sent a copy to Whethamsted for his criticism. He also introduced Whethamsted to the works of Plutarch, and borrowed books from him.[196]

Whethamsted was quite a prolific author, and wrote two kinds of works, encyclopaedias and histories. He composed four encyclopaedias entitled *Granarium*, *Palearium*, *Pabularium poetarum*, and *Propinarium*.[197] The last two are not known to survive, but two parts (I and II) of the four which originally comprised the *Granarium*, and the complete *Palearium* are extant. The latter is a dictionary of classical history and mythology. The *Granarium* is a more ambitious work. Part I is a detailed dictionary of ancient and medieval historians and their works, and of historical topics; the various opinions on historians are discussed, and Whethamsted expresses his own views with sober judgment. Part II is a dictionary of the heroes of classical antiquity, with appropriate moral adages. For both encyclopaedias Whethamsted made extensive use of classical works. Most were ones well known in the middle ages, but a few were less usual: for example, he drew on Lactantius' commentary on Statius, the *Satyricon* of Petronius, Martial, Quintilian's *Institutiones* and the *Bucolics* of Calpurnius.[198] He had also read Plato, Aristotle, Xenophon and Plutarch in Latin translations,[199] and when in Pavia he seems to have seen Petrarch's copy of the Latin version of Homer's *Iliad* by Leontius Pilatus.[200]

Whethamsted's historical works comprise two 'registers', one for each of his abbatiates. The first covers the complete period of his rule from 1420 to 1440.[201] The second starts at his accession but ends in 1461, three years before his death.[202] Already at the end of 1458 he had intended to stop writing the second register because of sickness and old age.[203] Nevertheless, he continued for another three years finally ending with a colophon, and some verses saying that he has put down his pen because sight and hearing

---

[193] *Reg. I*, ii. 278–90.
[194] *Reg. I*, ii. 256, and Weiss, *Humanism in England*, p. 33 n. 9.
[195] See ibid., pp. 33 and nn. 9, 10, 34 and n. 1.
[196] Ibid., pp. 27 and n. 4, 34 and n. 4.
[197] For these works see Jacob, '*Verborum florida venustas*', pp. 193–6.
[198] Weiss, *Humanism in England*, p. 35.
[199] Ibid., pp. 35–6.
[200] Ibid., p. 32 n. 8.
[201] BL MS. Cotton Claudius D I. For the printed edition see p. 342 n. 3 above
[202] Arundel MS. 3 in the College of Arms. For the printed edition see p. 342 n. 3 above.
[203] *Reg. II*, i. 322.

have failed, his hands are crippled with arthritis, and death awaits him.[204]

Whethamsted wrote the two registers in order to record his acts and present them in as favourable a light as possible.[205] He probably wanted to justify himself partly on account of the opposition he had met in the convent. He had particular trouble at the outset of his second abbatiate. He quarrelled with one of the two rival candidates for election as abbot, William Wallingford, who held the offices of cellarer, subcellarer, bursar, forester and chamberlain. Whethamsted accused him of withholding money bequeathed on his deathbed by Abbot John Stokes for the benefit of the abbey. He writes of Wallingford in the bitterest terms: he was a second Ananias; he 'cultivated the idol of avarice, and made friends with the mammon of unrighteousness.' It seems likely that Whethamsted was trying to blacken Wallingford's reputation so that he would not succeed him as abbot.[206] (In fact his successor was William Albon, but Wallingford became prior and in 1476 was elected abbot.)

The distinguishing feature of Whethamsted's registers is, as mentioned above, their literary style. They are in the flowery Latin fashionable among men of letters in his day, a style which was a branch of the medieval rhetorical tradition. Whethamsted clearly admired those proficient in this kind of prose. Writing of Francis de Coppinis, bishop of Terni, a papal legate, who visited St Albans in 1459, he describes him as 'short and insignificant to look at, but of very lively talents, a most eloquent man; words flowed from his lips like dew.'[207] Whethamsted himself acquired a national reputation for his elegant style: in 1427 Archbishop Chichele asked him to write on behalf of the English church to Pope Martin V (probably concerning the statute of provisors).[208]

Whethamsted's registers, as would be expected, include numerous

---

[204] *Reg. II*, i. 420.

[205] Riley points out that there was once another register covering Whethamsted's second abbatiate. This is proved by three passages in the extant register referring the reader for further details to the other register (*Reg. II*, i. 375, 383, 420). Riley argues that although Whethamsted wrote this lost register, it is most unlikely that he wrote the extant one. Riley bases his argument mainly on the boastful tone of the extant register (see p. 379 below) and on the scurrilous passages about William Wallingford (see below); he contends that the abbot would never have written in such a way (*Reg. II*, i. xiv-xviii). However, his views are not convincing. Bearing in mind the stylistic unity of Whethamsted's two surviving registers, for his first and second abbatiates (see pp. 375 and nn. 210–11, 214, 376 and nn. 215–17, 379 and n. 236, 381 and nn. 243–5 below), it seems most probable that he wrote the extant register for his second abbatiate as well as the lost one.

[206] *Reg. II* i. xv-xvi, xviii-xix, 102–35. For evidence of discord in the abbey during Whethamsted's first abbatiate see *Reg. I*, i. 176, 187–94 passim; ii. 211–12.

[207] *Reg. II*, i. 331. Francis de Coppinis, bishop of Terni, was appointed papal legate and commissary in England and Ireland on 4 December 1459, and collector in England, Scotland and Ireland of the tenth imposed on 18 February 1460, for the campaign against the Turks; see *Calendar of Entries in the Papal Registers relating to Great Britain and Ireland, Papal Letters*, xi, *1455–1464*, pp. 397–403 passim.

[208] *Reg. I*, i. 17; cf. Jacob, '*Verborum florida venustas*', p. 189.

business documents copied *verbatim*, but the copies of Whethamsted's own letters, the connecting prose, the passages of narrative and the verses which end each annal are in florid Latin.[209] The result is a hybrid between a factual record and a literary work. The stylistic mannerisms had various functions. They were partly intended to amuse the reader. Whethamsted liked word-play: he was, for example, fond of puns.[210] He plays on the name of the heretic, Reginald Pecock, bishop of Chichester.[211]

> in looks and action he was like a peacock, with splendid feathers and bright colours to attract the multitude, but he had a horrible voice with which to proclaim and publicize his opinions.

Of Pecock's disgrace and recantation Whethamsted writes:[212]

> Thus was the peacock deplumed and despoiled,
> Thus was his ugly voice silenced,
> Thus this bird, once honourably named,
> Came to be called owl, not peacock.

At the beginning of each annal Whethamsted often, particularly in his second register, engages the reader's attention by general reflections on the time of the year or by setting the scene so that the reader can, as it were, participate in the action. Sometimes the season is denoted by astrological references ('the sun, descending from Cancer, turned its course towards Capricorn'),[213] and sometimes in terms of classical exemplar:[214]

> In the evening of [Whethamsted's] fifth year [as abbot], Phoebus in his golden chariot had descended to his sister Thetis and stabled his horses for one night; then in the morning of his sixth year he harnessed his horses again to the chariot and began his upward climb, higher and higher, until he reached that height in the heavens when on earth below the turtle dove coos, the flowers of the vine give forth their odour, and the birds sing sweetly in hedgerow and thicket. . . .

Other introductory passages allow the reader to feel that he sees Whethamsted at work and even to enter into his thoughts. 'The abbot sat alone in his study pondering, like Martha (Luke x. 41), how to protect

---

[209] See e.g. Whethamsted's letter to Archbishop Chichele and the letters he wrote to the convent when he was abroad: *Reg. I*, i. 118–19, 126–7; cf. Jacob, op. cit., pp. 190–1.

[210] See also his use of alliteration, e.g.: *Reg. I*, i. 196 ('doctor plus doctus disquietare quietos quam docere'); *Reg. II*, i. 166 ('Stabimus nos sub jactu aleae, alearisque potius quam aularis, sive animalis, erit nobis vita nostra').

[211] *Reg. II*, i. 279–80. For other examples of play on names see *Reg. I*, i. 364, 366–7; ii. xlviii-xlix. For Elmham's word-play see pp. 208–9, 347 above.

[212] *Reg. I*, i. 288.

[213] *Reg. II*, i. 186. Cf. *Reg. II*, i. 199, 268, 330.

[214] *Reg. II*, i. 264. For a very similar opening passage see *Reg. I*, ii. 203.

his church from injury or loss caused by the greed of laymen.'[215] And again, 'the abbot sat among his disciples inquiring what had happened in his absence' (while he was attending the council of Pavia and Siena).[216] Sometimes the reader's participation is illusory, because the abbot's actions are described allegorically. One annal, for example, records a visitation carried out by Whethamsted of the abbey's cells (the dependent priories) during his second abbatiate:[217]

> The abbot went down into his garden of fruit trees, to inspect the apple orchards, and to see if the vines were in flower, and whether the pomegranates would germinate and bear fruit—he visited, I mean to say, the garden of his cells, to inspect the lives and conduct of the brethren, and to see if the vine of religion was in flower and would be fruitful in the way it should.

Whethamsted's purpose in adopting this style of writing was not merely to entertain. He also wanted to reveal his opinions and make general moral observations, and to persuade his readers of the truth of both. To achieve these ends he combined biblical and classical allegory, and used various other rhetorical devices.

He used the bible to reinforce his arguments by analogy, so that people of his day might assume the *personae* of biblical figures, and contemporary events might acquire the importance of those which happened in biblical times. For example, he himself might become the type of Job. He describes a dispute with Archbishop Chichele over the latter's attempt to include St Albans in a metropolitan visitation. Whethamsted, pleading the abbey's privilege of exemption, refused to admit the priest appointed to visit the religious houses in Hertfordshire. He bases his account on the Book of Job i–iii; he begins with an imaginary conversation derived partly from the Lord's conversation with Satan when He gave him permission to tempt Job (the passages from Job i. 7–12 are in italics).[218]

> *And the Lord* [i.e. the archbishop] *said unto* [Satan] *'whence comest thou?'* And he *answered, 'From going to and fro in the earth, and from walking up and down in* the county of Hertford, and I have corrected what you ordered, but not as fully as you wished'. And the archbishop *said unto* him, but ironically, *'Hast thou considered my* brother, the abbot of St Albans [*my servant, Job,* in the bible], that *there is none like him in the* whole county, *a perfect and an upright man, one that . . . escheweth evil?'*

[215] *Reg. II*, i. 186.
[216] *Reg. I*, i. 187.
[217] *Reg. I*, ii. 105. For a very similar opening passage see *Reg. II*, i. 216–17.
[218] *Reg. I*, i. 195. For references to earlier examples of the same style of writing see p. 209 and n. 105 above, p. 385 and nn. 276, 278 below.

Whethamsted also identifies himself with the good servant of Luke xix. 15–17, who increased tenfold the pieces of money committed to him. To demonstrate this he enumerates in the annal for 1438 ten properties (representing the ten pounds in the parable) which he had acquired for the abbey, citing relevant documents.[219] Congratulating himself on his success in increasing the abbey's prosperity (with an allusion to Luke xix. 23), he called to mind those magnates and others who had used the talents entrusted to them by the Lord (here the allusion is to Matthew xxv. 14–30) well—that is for the benefit of St Albans. He lists five such benefactors, on the analogy of the five talents in the parable, starting with Humphrey, duke of Gloucester, and records their gifts to the abbey.[220]

Whethamsted also used biblical allegory to give added meaning to his narrative of general history. His account of the summary execution of Richard duke of York in 1460 has citations from and allusions to the crucifixion as described in Matthew xxvii. 29. The duke's enemies made him stand on an anthill and crowned him with a vile garland of reeds, and then bent their knees before him, 'just like the Jews before Our Lord', and mocked him saying 'Hail king without sway! Hail king without a kingdom! Hail duke and prince without followers or possessions!'[221] And after the Yorkist defeat Whethamsted exhorts the people to assuage God's anger and avert his vengeance by repentance—like the Ninevehites they must humble themselves in sackcloth and ashes (Jonah iii. 5, 6).[222]

In order to convey his opinions and persuade the reader Whethamsted adopted a number of other rhetorical devices. For example, to express his approval of, and justify the clemency shown by King Henry to his defeated opponents in 1459, he personifies Justice and Mercy, making each defend its point of view at length.[223] He also includes numerous set speeches purporting to have been delivered by the great men of his day, and even occasionally undertakes to reveal their thoughts. The meaning of both speeches and thoughts is reinforced by allusions to the bible and the classics, and to more recent works.

Whethamsted describes Richard duke of York as addressing his troops before the first battle of St Albans with a panoply of biblical and classical allusions, besides a reference to one of St Augustine's letters. The duke, like Joab, and King Henry, like King David, have raised arms against the wicked duke of Somerset (according to St Augustine's letter to Count

---

[219] *Reg. I*, ii. 159–85.
[220] *Reg. I*, ii. 186–96.
[221] *Reg. II*, i. 382.
[222] *Reg. II*, i. 385.
[223] *Reg. II*, i. 345–55. It seems likely that in writing a dialogue between Justice and Mercy, Whethamsted was influenced by Piero del Monte's dialogue on the virtues and vices, a copy of which del Monte sent to Whethamsted for comment; see p. 373 and n. 196 above, and Weiss, *Humanism in England*, p. 25 and n. 3. For the use of similar rhetorical devices by the Pseudo-Elmham see pp. 213–14 above.

Boniface, there can never be peace until the sons of perdition are totally vanquished); the duke of Somerset was responsible, among other ills, for the death in battle of John Talbot, earl of Shrewsbury, that flower of English knighthood, a very Hector in strength, an Ajax in bravery and an Achilles in ferocity.[224]

Whethamsted reinforces his arguments with moral *dicta* and adages drawn from the bible and classical literature. Thus Henry VI, reflecting on the necessity of a reconciliation between the warring factions in 1458, recalled the words of St Matthew (xii. 25) that 'every kingdom divided against itself is brought to desolation.'[225] And before the battle of Ludlow he remembered Seneca's adage that it was bravery not numbers which decided a battle.[226] The truth of a moral dictum might be driven home by an appeal to a precedent in ancient history: it is better to conciliate the great than to give offence by plain speaking—Callisthenes was condemned to death for it, and Seneca forced to kill himself.[227]

Whethamsted frequently appealed to *exempla* from ancient and biblical history. King Henry remembered the disasters which had befallen the Thebans, Romans and Jews as a result of discord.[228] Rivalry, the cause of the ruin and death of Humphrey duke of Gloucester, had taken its toll in classical times; because of it Julius Caesar had been murdered, Ptolemy drowned, Tarquin driven out and Tydeus exiled.[229] And Whethamsted cites similar precedents in a rhetorical speech which he claims to have delivered to Duke Richard after the first battle of St Albans, asking him for permission to bury the dead: Whethamsted pleads that the duke should show the same mercy in victory as did Aeneas, Achilles and Julius Caesar, capping his argument with an adage from Ovid's *Tristia*—that nothing should be sought in addition to victory.[230]

Whethamsted's style illustrates contemporary literary tastes, but is an obstacle to the use of his registers as historical sources. His high flown language leaves down-to-earth reality far behind. His very prolixity makes the texture of his works so loose that the information in them is hard to isolate, and his preference for conventional stereotypes to first hand observation often almost totally obscures the actual facts. Indeed Whethamsted's primary purpose was not to record facts, but to persuade the reader

---

[224] *Reg. II*, i. 164–6. For other examples of rhetorical speeches see *Reg. II*, i. 176–7, 368–9, and below and n. 230.
[225] *Reg. II*, i. 296.
[226] *Reg. II*, i. 338–9. I have failed to trace this dictum in Seneca, but the idea occurs in Vegetius, *De Re Militari*, III, xxvi (ed. Charles Lang (Teubner, Leipzig 1885), p. 121); 'Occasio in bello amplius solet iuuare quam virtus.' Cf. also 1 Maccabees iii. 18–20, and the *GH V*, p. 78). I owe these references to Dr C. T. Allmand.
[227] *Reg. II*, i. 247.
[228] *Reg. II*, i. 297.
[229] *Reg. II*, i. 182.
[230] *Reg. II*, i. 176 and nn. 5, 6.

to accept his idealized view of people and events. Nevertheless, the registers are of value to the historian today: they reveal a certain amount concerning Whethamsted himself, both his personality and outlook, and also his opinions, and in addition they contain factual information, mostly relating to local history, not found elsewhere.

Whethamsted shows traces of family feeling and humanity. His affection for and pride in his family appears in the joy he expressed when John of Bamburgh, subprior of Tynemouth priory (one of the cells of St Albans) brought 'forth out of his treasure things new and old' (Matthew xiii. 52) — an excellent Life of Whethamsted's uncle, John Mackrey, formerly prior of Tynemouth. Whethamsted wrote the author an effusive letter of thanks: now his uncle's light, which had been hidden under a bushel for forty years or more (an allusion to Matthew v. 15), would illuminate this vale of tears.[231] That Whethamsted was humane is suggested by the fact that he pleaded for the burial of the dead after the first battle of St Albans.[232] Moreover, after the famine of 1437, moved by considerations of gratitude and by a sense of responsibility, he refused to follow the example of others by reducing the number of servants in his household.[233] And when his clerk, Matthew Bepset, tried on his deathbed to put his total property at the abbot's disposal, Whethamsted insisted he left the greater part to his wife and children.[234]

A less attractive side of Whethamsted's character was a tendency to boast. It should, however, be borne in mind that the boasting in the registers must partly be attributed to Whethamsted's self-justificatory intention in writing them. He himself had considered the morality of recording his acts. One must not be, he writes, like the scribes and the Pharisees who do 'all their works ... for to be seen of men: they make broad their phylacteries, and enlarge the borders of their garments' (Matthew xxiii. 5). On the other hand it is necessary to 'let your light shine before men, that they may see your good works, and glorify your Father which is in heaven' (Matthew v. 16). Because of the transitory nature of human affairs, Whethamsted decides for the latter view: he will record his acts for the benefit of posterity and to the glory of God; and in case he arouses envy or a carping spirit in the reader he adds some verses of exhortation.[235] In the course of his registers Whethamsted compares himself explicitly or by implication not only with Christ, but also with Moses, Job, Martha, Mary, St Paul, St Benedict, St Martin and the good servant.[236]

---

[231] *Reg. II*, i. 311–16.
[232] See p. 378 and n. 230 above.
[233] *Reg. I*, ii. 157.
[234] *Reg. II*, i. 157–8.
[235] *Reg. I*, ii. 201–2.
[236] See *Reg. I*, i. 187, 265, 275; ii. 185, 201, 211, 237, 238; *Reg. II*, i. 20. See also pp. 375–6 and nn. 215, 218 above.

To emphasize his popularity he recites the expostulations and describes the grief of the monks—and of the abbey's servants, villeins, tenants and neighbours—on his resignation in 1440.[237]

Three of the six reasons Whethamsted gives for resigning may strike the modern reader as odd.[238] They give the impression that the abbot was eccentric. He asserts that he was a very timid person, and during his rule was utterly exhausted by the constant fear and trembling in which he lived on account of the hazards of fortune. He claims to have been exceptionally shy and bashful, finding it the worst sort of punishment to appear in public and meet strange people in the course of his administrative duties. He was more embarrassed than a girl if he saw or heard anything obscene: 'he suffered badly among the domestics, worse among outsiders, and worst of all among magnates.' Whethamsted is here alluding to Psalm lxix. 7 ('shame hath covered my face'), and it is not clear whether this was an actual character trait (perhaps itself encouraged by the psalmist), or a stereotype intended to put him in a flattering light and at the same time helping to justify his resignation.

Whethamsted also pleads ill health:

> He was so feeble in body and so sad at heart that there was no health in him from the soles of his feet to the top of his head. He suffered in the spleen, he suffered in the kidneys, he suffered in the liver, and he suffered in the bowels—he suffered indeed in every part of his body so that it would be an insupportable burden to bear the pastoral staff any longer.

Whethamsted refers to his health a number of times in his second register.[239] As he wrote it late in life these references probably record genuine debility. However, one passage suggests that he may have been preoccupied with his health at an earlier age. The first register records a visit made on his Italian journey to a physician in Florence in order to obtain a remedy against the effects of the sun.[240] Other passages show an interest in health and medicine in general. He mentions that the spring of 1455 was particularly unhealthy, and gives advice on how to keep well: talk less, and eat and drink less, so that by drunken frivolity you do not acquire a bloated body and a fuddled head—moderation is the secret of longevity.[241] He holds up his clerk, Matthew Bepset (who 'preferred the tavern to the tabernacle') as an example of a man who died 'of overindulgence in food and drink, especially drink'.[242]

---

[237] *Reg. I*, ii. 237–8.
[238] *Reg. I*, ii. 233–4.
[239] *Reg. II*, i. 264, 324, 332. See also pp. 373 and n. 203, 374 and n. 204 above.
[240] *Reg. I*, i. 135. See p. 386 and n. 280 below.
[241] *Reg. II*, i. 156.
[242] *Reg. II*, i. 156.

Whethamsted makes frequent use of medical imagery: he takes quick action in a legal suit because to cure a patient a remedy must be applied promptly;[243] alternatively, he delays action because given time an illness may cure itself;[244] and in 1461, when Edward IV reduced York, the king treated the citizens like a wise surgeon, applying mild remedies to those who could be cured, and only using the knife on hopeless cases (that is, he punished mildly all whom he could win over to his side, and executed only the obdurate).[245]

Whethamsted's expression of his political views is muted: discretion probably discouraged him from being more explicit. Citing Proverbs xvi. 14 ('the wrath of a king is as messengers of death'), he states that he will omit common gossip concerning Henry VI, 'by which people, disregarding the said proverb, are wont to denigrate the king', and will keep to the essentials necessary for understanding Henry's character.[246] Such views as are apparent show clearly that he was influenced by local loyalty, moral considerations, expediency and, to a lesser degree, his own observations.

In general Whethamsted's sympathies were with the Yorkists. Gratitude for benefactions to St Albans accounts for his eulogy on Humphrey duke of Gloucester. This is inserted in the annal for 1455, when parliament cleared Duke Humphrey's name of the charge of high treason for which he was arrested in 1447, imprisoned and murdered. Whethamsted abuses those 'satellites of Satan' who had poisoned King Henry's mind against a man 'so respected and loved by the people, so faithful to the king'. The duke had been to the king like David to Saul; he was his right hand, a tower of strength, his defender against enemies at home and abroad.[247]

Whethamsted notes that the reinstatement of Duke Humphrey was brought about by Richard duke of York.[248] He supports the duke of York's cause, but with reservations. He justifies in detail Duke Richard's hostility to the duke of Somerset, asserting that it originated because Somerset ousted Richard from the governorship of Normandy, although Richard had ruled well.[249] Whethamsted notes with approval Richard's attempt to negotiate peace with the Lancastrians in 1455,[250] and says that when Richard fled to Ireland in 1459, he was received like another Messiah—

---

[243] *Reg. I*, ii. 120–1. Cf. *Reg. I*, ii. 126.

[244] *Reg. II*, i. 204.

[245] *Reg. II*, 411. For other examples of medical imagery see *Reg. II*, i. 141, 265, 349.

[246] *Reg. II*, i. 248. It may be noted that Whethamsted advised the three monks of Cluny who visited him in London (pp. 383–4 below) to 'keep silent or give a good report' on their return home, although their mission to the king had been unsuccessful; *Reg. II*, i. 322.

[247] See *Reg. II*, i. 178–83. For Whethamsted's friendship with Humphrey, duke of Gloucester, and the duke's close relations with the abbey see pp. 372 and nn. 190–2, 373 above.

[248] *Reg. II*, i. 181.

[249] *Reg. II*, i. 159–60.

[250] *Reg. II*, i. 184–5.

and like Ulysses he longed to return home.[251] Whethamsted implies a comparison of Richard with Christ by representing the duke's execution as an analogue of the crucifixion.[252] And he has an eloquent passage on the people's grief at his death.[253]

On the other hand Whethamsted criticizes Richard of York on moral grounds. He asserts that in his vendetta against the duke of Somerset, Richard was unmindful that revenge is wrong.[254] He also criticizes Richard for aspiring to the crown in 1460: the duke's claim was caused by the sin of pride, and opened him to the charge of perjury, because he had sworn that his only intention in opposing the king was to reform the government. (However, Richard subsequently acted with greater humility and respect for his monarch.)[255]

Whethamsted's Yorkist sympathies were also tempered by his local loyalties. He was outraged by the plundering and destruction which accompanied both battles of St Albans. Despite the fact that God prohibits theft, the victorious Yorkist soldiers took everything they could lay hands on. The abbey itself was in danger: in 1455 it was only saved, Whethamsted asserts, because King Henry, his councillors and armed retinue, inevitably the focus of the Yorkists' attack, kept clear of the abbey when they came to St Albans, moving instead to the centre of the town;[256] in 1460, although Edward, at the abbot's request, forbade looting,[257] the monks' property was so badly damaged that the community had to disperse for a while, and Whethamsted himself had to go to one of his manors, 'well away from any royal road', where he could live more economically.[258]

These crises led Whethamsted to reflect on the horrors of civil war in general,[259] and more particularly on the conflict between the southerners of Henry's army and the northerners of Edward's. He contrasts the natures of the two peoples: the southerners tended to be effete ('resembling Paris rather than Hector'), and were often treacherous and cowardly; the northerners were loud-mouthed and boastful, fierce and warlike, with a propensity for unbridled looting. Whethamsted attributed their love of spoil to the austere conditions which they endured at home. There they had only the bare necessities of life ('barley, oats, rye and wheat'), and not its luxuries ('oysters and ebony, gold and silver', and the like).[260]

---

[251] *Reg. II*, i. 367, 371.
[252] See p. 377 above.
[253] *Reg. II*, i. 384–6.
[254] *Reg. II*, i. 161.
[255] *Reg. II*, i. 376–81.
[256] *Reg. II*, i. 173–4. Cited C. A. J. Armstrong, 'Politics and the battle of St Albans, 1455' in *BIHR*, xxxiii (1960), p. 28 n. 7. See also ibid., pp. 40, 46–8 passim.
[257] *Reg. II*, i. 394.
[258] *Reg. II*, i. 396–9.
[259] *Reg. II*, i. 172, 385–90 passim. Cf. Armstrong, op. cit., p. 47.
[260] *Reg. II*, i. 168–9, 171–2, 391–5 passim.

Whethamsted had considerable admiration for Henry VI as a person. The king was 'blessed and modest, gentle and pious' (he neither 'standeth in the way of sinners, nor sitteth in the seat of the scornful'; Psalm i. 1).[261] He was 'guileless and upright',[262] and a man of peace.[263] On the other hand Whethamsted could not approve of Henry as a military commander or as a ruler. He was a poor soldier,[264] and was too gullible and easily influenced:[265] evil counsellors persuaded him that Duke Humphrey was a traitor, and they so impressed on him the idea that a king must be generous that he squandered the resources of the crown, reducing it to poverty and making oppressive taxes necessary.[266] Ultimately Whethamsted (perhaps motivated in part by the expediency of supporting the reigning king) welcomed Edward IV's accession: he praises Edward for ending the civil war and restoring law and order,[267] and emphasizes his right to rule, both because of his hereditary claim (which is explained in detail), and because he was acclaimed by the people.[268]

Whethamsted had excellent opportunities for obtaining news. He often visited London, where he had the use of a house owned by the abbey. St Albans itself, besides being the site of two important battles, was, because of its proximity to London and situation on a royal road, the venue of kings, magnates and ecclesiastics. In 1456 a priest from Hungary came to the abbey with three letters concerning the Hungarian crusade against the Turks. One was from the sultan of Egypt to the pope expostulating at the Christian attack; another was the pope's reply, abusing the Turks for their pride; and the third was an account of the campaign from a Dominican friar. No doubt the letters were primarily intended to raise religious enthusiasm, but Whethamsted seems to have been regarded as a fitting recipient of historical material. He copied the letters into his register 'to the praise, glory and honour of the Hungarians, and to the discredit of the Turks'.[269] In 1458 when Whethamsted was staying in London he was visited by three monks of Cluny, who had come to England

---

[261] *Reg. II*, i. 248, 378.

[262] *Reg. II*, i. 248. I here concur with the general meaning of the phrase 'simplex et rectus' given by Dr Wolffe who renders it as 'honest and upright'; B. P. Wolffe, 'The personal rule of Henry VI' in *Fifteenth-Century England, 1399–1509*, ed. S. B. Chrimes, C. D. Ross and R. A. Griffiths (Manchester 1972), p. 37. Whethamsted also uses the phrase of Henry in the speech which he puts into the mouth of Richard duke of York exhorting his followers to reform the kingdom in 1455; *Reg. II*, i. 164. For the significance of the translation of the phrase in any estimate of Henry VI's character see pp. 497–8, Appendix G, below.

[263] *Reg. II*, i. 162, 295–8. Henry was also merciful; *Reg. II*, i. 356.

[264] *Reg. II*, i. 415.

[265] *Reg. II*, i. 179, 415 (at the latter reference Whethamsted describes Henry as 'in factis nimiae vir simplicitatis'; cf. n. 262 above and p. 497, Appendix G, below).

[266] *Reg. II*, i. 248–9.

[267] *Reg. II*, i. 412–15.

[268] *Reg. II*, i. 402–7.

[269] *Reg. II*, i. 268–79.

to speak to the king on the business affairs of their order. On leaving, the monks gave Whethamsted a tract on knighthood in England, which the eldest, a doctor of theology, had written for the king and his nobles.[270]

Whethamsted's registers have some information which is of value to the historian today. There are, for example, the details about the battles of St Albans. There is also a revealing account of the illness to which King Henry succumbed in 1453:[271]

> A disease and disorder of such a sort overcame the king that he lost his wits and memory for a time, and nearly all his body was so unco-ordinated and out of control that he could neither walk, nor hold his head upright, nor easily move from where he sat.

However, as sources for political history the registers are disappointing. Their account of national events is only exceptionally specific enough to be useful to the historian today. As repositories of facts they are chiefly of value for local history. St Albans was Whethamsted's centre of interest, and his writing on local events has a greater sense of immediacy than it does for national ones. He manages to sandwich straightforward factual narrative of the abbey's domestic affairs, besides copies of numerous documents, between introductory and concluding passages in florid prose or verse. An example of this mixture of styles is the account of the quarrel between the abbey and the town after Whethamsted's return from Italy. Whethamsted relates that the townsmen came to him and accused the monks of usurping their liberties, but he found 'no cause of death' (Luke xxiii. 22). He then describes the dispute: the townsmen claimed certain common pastures, but the abbot's councillors discovered that their demands were the same as those made at St Albans during the Peasants' Revolt of 1381. Therefore, they produced the royal statute annulling all concessions extorted by violence at that time. The townsmen were amazed 'like the accusers of the woman taken in adultery' (an allusion to John viii. 3–11), and retreated without a word. Whethamsted gently reproved the monks, saying that since their accusers had abandoned the case, 'neither do I condemn thee: go, and sin no more' (John viii. 11).[272]

Some of Whethamsted's local material has a wider relevance. For example he tells a story about Henry VI which illustrates the king's unthinking generosity. When he visited St Albans in 1459 he ordered his

---

[270] *Reg. II*, i. 317–22. See also p. 381 n. 246 above.

[271] *Reg. II*, i. 163. For a notice of this passage and references to other chroniclers who record Henry's mental breakdown, see J. R. Lander, 'Henry VI and the duke of York's second protectorate, 1455 to 1456' in *BJRL*, xliii (1960), pp. 46 and n. 3, 47 and n. 1. See p. 498, Appendix G, below. For the value of Whethamsted's narrative for the first battle of St Albans and its aftermath see Armstrong, 'Politics and the battle of St Albans, 1455', pp. 28 and n. 7, 40, 42 and nn. 5, 8, 44 and n. 4, 45 and n. 3, 46 and nn. 2–7.

[272] *Reg. I*, i. 187–94.

best robe to be given to the prior, but the lord treasurer on hearing of this redeemed it for fifty marks because it was the only robe suitable for Henry's regal estate. The king reluctantly concurred with his decision, and told the abbot to collect the money in London. When he did so, Henry gave him a warrant for the wardrobe, where he received a length of gold cloth to be made into vestments for the high altar.[273]

In his choice of factual material and in his historical interpretations Whethamsted differed little if at all from many previous chroniclers. Even his egoism was not unprecedented: Gerald of Wales at least equalled him in boastfulness, and excelled him in the quantity of autobiographical material.[274] Similarly, his encyclopaedias belong to a well established medieval genre exemplified by Isidore of Seville and Vincent of Beauvais.[275] Furthermore, many features of his style were traditional. Biblical allegory had been used in a number of earlier chronicles: it is particularly characteristic of the early fourteenth century continuation of the *Flores Historiarum* written at Westminster abbey[276] and of the metrical Life of Henry V by Whethamsted's near contemporary, Thomas Elmham.[277] And again the use of classical typology and rhetoric was common among the twelfth century chroniclers.[278]

Nevertheless, Whethamsted's taste for imagery based on classical models, the wide knowledge of classical literature evident especially in his encyclopaedias, combined with his known contact with the humanist Piero del Monte, have raised the question whether he can be classed as an early humanist. Such a classification would, however, be misleading. Whethamsted used classical literature in the same way as he used the bible and Christian works, to provide allegories and adages enabling him to moralize more elegantly and persuasively. And he used it to embellish his writing according to the tastes of the age—his prose shows no trace of the Ciceronian Latin of the renaissance. The most that can be claimed for him is that, without himself catching the spirit of the antique, he helped habituate scholars to classical texts, and so contributed to the foundations on which the later humanists were to build.[279]

Whethamsted's place in the history of English humanism can be illustrated by an incident which took place during his visit to Italy. He records

---

[273] *Reg. II*, i. 324–5.

[274] See the autobiography of Gerald of Wales compiled from extracts from his own works; *The Autobiography of Giraldus Cambrensis*, ed. and translated by H. E. Butler, with an introduction by C. H. Williams (London 1937).

[275] See Jacob, '*Verborum florida venustas*', pp. 194–6 passim.

[276] See A. Gransden, 'The continuations of the *Flores Historiarum* from 1265 to 1327' in *Mediaeval Siudies*, xxxvi (Toronto 1974), pp. 477–8.

[277] See p. 209 and n. 105 above.

[278] See e.g. Gransden, *Historical Writing*, i. 190, 214, 215, 235, 241, 382.

[279] I here concur with the conclusions of Jacob, '*Verborum florida venustas*', pp. 192–4, and Weiss, *Humanism in England*, pp. 30, 37–8.

that in order to obtain the name of a physician in Florence he asked a fellow traveller (whom he never names), 'a Venetian gentleman, a man of distinguished appearance, well spoken and courteous'. The gentleman gave him a name and wrote a letter of introduction. Later Whethamsted asked the physician the identity of the gentleman who had so kindly written a recommendation for him, a foreign and unknown abbot. The physician replied: 'The gentleman is of the highest education, of such refined eloquence and outstanding learning that he can dispute with any master in any of the liberal arts, and has vanquished many by the force of reason.' The abbot bewailed his previous ignorance, and composed a letter of lament addressed to the humanist in full grandiloquent style.[280]

[280] *Reg. I*, i. 135–8. See Jacob, op. cit., p. 192.

13

The End of the Monastic
Tradition of Historiography:
Minor Works

The same reasons which led Thomas Elmham and Thomas Burton to write their histories, caused many lesser men to compose historical narratives and monographs. As pointed out at the beginning of the previous chapter, monks wrote to defend their houses against enemies and critics. They tried to strengthen monastic defences by increasing prestige. This could be done by proving a house's great antiquity, and by calling attention to its rich treasures, laudable inmates and generous benefactors. (The record of facts about benefactors had also a pious motive—to ensure that monks knew something about those whom they commemorated liturgically.) Moreover, the monks armed themselves by defining their house's rights to privilege and property. And if a monastery's claims were in dispute, the chronicler would present its case as convincingly as possible. He might even produce a tract, a *pièce justificative*, for information or for actual use in a court case. The preparation of the chronicles and tracts written for these reasons often involved considerable research, and sometimes the authors show genuine antiquarian interest. Indeed, in some instances it is clear that propaganda was not the motive: the chronicler undertook his research to satisfy his own curiosity and that of his readers. As will be seen, this must have been the principal reason for the compilation of the Thornton annals. And the author might even simply intend his work to be useful: the topo-bibliographer Henry Kirkstead at Bury St Edmunds was concerned to reorganize the monastic library and provide biblio-graphical aids for readers.

A number of monks besides Elmham and Burton were interested in the origins and early histories of their houses. Most wrote on a modest scale, but the works of some, notably John Wessington at Durham and John Flete at Westminster, are massive undertakings, which rival in size if not in quality Elmham's and Burton's chronicles. A few of the writers, for example the annalists of Bermondsey and Thornton, approached their subject in a scholarly way. If, however, an abbey's early history was obscur-ed by the passage of time, the chronicler might well resort to fiction and forgery, to supply the necessary glorious past. Hence, some chroniclers associated the origins of their houses with such legends as that of Brutus the founder of Britain, and of King Arthur, the British hero. An example is John of Glastonbury who elaborated the already partly legendary history of Glastonbury abbey to create a truly flamboyant narrative. An even more extreme case is that of the monks of Crowland who produced a chronicle of their abbey from its foundation until 1148 which is spurious from beginning to end.

Meanwhile, the practice of keeping a monastic chronicle, in the sense of a full-scale narrative combining general and local history, written up fairly contemporarily with the events recorded, had virtually fallen into abeyance. Few of the monastic chronicles of Richard II's reign continue beyond the turn of the century. The anonymous continuation of the *Eulogium Historiarum* ends in 1413, and Thomas Walsingham's chronicle in 1422. In fact only two chronicles were written in the fifteenth century which belong even approximately to this category. One is the chronicle of John Strecche, canon of Kenilworth, which covers the period from Brutus to the death of Henry V, and the other is the continuation of the chronicle of Crowland abbey from 1149 to 1470. Neither compares in quality with the best monastic chronicles of the thirteenth century, nor even with those of the fourteenth century. Strecche was much influenced by secular historiography, and the Crowland chronicler was mainly interested in local affairs.

There seems to be no obvious reason for the lack of a revival of the monastic chronicle in the fifteenth century. It may be suggested, however, that the popularity of the *Brut*, and to a lesser extent of the London chronicles, with the monks, removed the necessity of providing their own account of current affairs. Moreover, potential chroniclers may have been discouraged by the tensions of the period: perhaps they were inhibited by divided loyalties, first on account of the political turmoils of the Wars of the Roses, and then of the religious upheavals of the reformation. Indiscretion could lead to the alienation of friends or even to retributive action.

In such difficult times religious houses could not afford to alienate important people; rather they needed whenever possible to acquire allies. Historical writing could be used to win friends as well as to ward off enemies. The period was marked by the rise of a small group of university educated religious who wrote for members of the nobility and for royalty. · Humphrey

---

[1] For Whethamsted's association with Humphrey, duke of Gloucester, see pp. 372–3 above. For John Lydgate see W. F. Schirmer, *John Lydgate, a Study in the Culture of the Fifteenth Century*, translated by A. E. Keep (London 1961). For the saints' Lives which Matthew Paris wrote for the aristocracy see Gransden, *Historical Writing*, i, pp. 358–9 and nn. 18–20. For Walsingham's *Ypodigma Neustriae* see p. 126 above, and for Elmham's *Liber Metricus* see pp. 206–10 above. Capgrave's historical works are printed: *Johannis Capgrave Liber de Illustribus Henricis*,

duke of Gloucester's patronage of John Whethamsted as a man of learning was discussed in the last chapter, but the most famous member of this group was John Lydgate, monk of Bury St Edmunds, poet and friend of Chaucer. He wrote for the Lancastrian kings and for various noble men (including Duke Humphrey) and women. Although his works throw much light on the politics and society of his day he was primarily a literary figure.

However, some of the religious who wrote for royal and noble patrons were chroniclers. Already in the thirteenth century Matthew Paris had written saints' lives for such patrons, but in the fifteenth century actual chronicles were written for them by members of the religious orders. As has been seen, Matthew Paris' successor at St Albans, Thomas Walsingham, wrote his *Ypodigma Neustriae* for Henry V, in about 1420. We have also discussed the *Liber Metricus de Henrico Quinto* written at about the same time by Elmham, after he had joined the Cluniac order, and dedicated to the same king: this, besides being a polemic against Lollardy, is a royal panegyric.

John Capgrave, prior of the Augustinian friary at Lynn (he was elected prior provincial in 1453) can be regarded as Elmham's successor as a royal panegyrist. He wrote the *Liber de Illustribus Henricis* (*The Book of Illustrious Henries*) for Henry VI late in 1446 or early in 1447. It is in three books, the first two containing six chapters, and the last twelve chapters. Each chapter comprises a eulogistic biography of someone distinguished called Henry: emperors are in the first book; kings, including the English Henries, in the second; and a miscellaneous selection of other well known Henries in the third. The chapter on Henry VI is a fulsome panegyric in florid style, which though in prose is reminiscent of that employed by Elmham in the *Liber Metricus*. Capgrave's debt to Elmham is shown by the fact that the *Liber Metricus* was his principal literary source for his account of Henry V.

Capgrave may have been commissioned by Henry VI to write the *Liber de Illustribus Henricis*. He had good reason for wishing to please the king. The latter had visited the Augustinian friary at Lynn in 1446. There he was welcomed by Capgrave as prior, and he was made patron of the house. The only original information on Henry in the *Liber de Illustribus Henricis* (apart from a brief account of his foundation of Eton) is the description of this visit. Capgrave mentions that some of the friars opposed accepting

---

ed. F. C. Hingeston (RS 1858); and *The Chronicle of England*, ed. F. C. Hingeston (RS 1858). For their literary sources see Kingsford, *Hist. Lit.* pp. 38–9. For Capgrave's political apostasy, which resembles that of John Hardyng and John Rous (see pp. 277–9, 313–17 above respectively), see L. D. Duls, *Richard II in the Early Chronicles* (The Hague-Paris 1975), pp. 218–19. (For the change of allegiance of Sir John Fortescue see p. 252 n. 24 above.) For Capgrave's life and works in general see Alberic de Meijer, 'John Capgrave, O.E.S.A.' in *Augustiniana* (Louvain) v (1955), pp. 400–40; vii (1957), pp. 118–48, 531–75, and J. P. Lucas, 'John Capgrave, O.S.A. (1393–1464), scribe and "publisher"' in *Transactions of the Cambridge Bibliographical Soc.* v (1969), pp. 1–35 (see ibid., p. 1 n. 2 for further references).

Henry as patron because, they argued, the house had had a patron, or patrons, since the time of its foundation. Capgrave refutes this argument with careful reference to the house's early charters. Undoubtedly he partly wrote to convince Henry that he was the one and only true patron.

Capgrave had an established reputation as a writer. Besides dedicating the *Liber de Illustribus Henricis* to Henry VI, he wrote a variety of religious works for a number of patrons, among them Humphrey, duke of Gloucester, and William Gray, bishop of Ely. It is not, therefore, surprising that when Edward IV came to the throne he should try to attract his favour, for his own sake and for that of his friary, by dedicating a work to him. This was *The Chronicle of England*, which covers the period from the Creation until 1417. It ends incomplete: possibly Capgrave intended to continue it up to Edward's accession but was prevented by his own death (in 1464). The *Chronicle*, a compilation almost entirely from Walsingham, has no value as a source to the historian today. Its interest lies in its political outlook. For Capgrave, having adopted the official Lancastrian view of events in the *Liber de Illustribus Henricis*, now supported the Yorkist cause: having previously eulogized Henry IV, he now in his dedication calls him a usurper.

These full-blown royal panegyrics are far removed from the traditional monastic chronicles. The writers (and their communities) ran no political risk provided they were prepared, if necessary, to change their political affiliations. It can be argued that at the other end of the scale the simple monastic annalists shared their immunity. The author of brief, factual annals, without editorial 'comment', could escape the problem of making up his mind on contemporary political and religious issues, and the danger incurred by expressing his sympathies. Indeed, in the fifteenth century a number of houses produced annals. Despite their circumscribed scope, these reveal something of the authors' outlook, and inadvertently throw light on current events. Those of Butley priory continue to the eve of the dissolution, while the annals of the Grey friars of Newgate, London, were continued after the friary was dissolved, to as late as 1556.

The four main categories of works will be considered in turn. First, the narratives of monastic foundations and early history, starting with those based on sound research, and proceeding to those which include fictional material. Second, the tracts relating to monastic treasures, legal disputes and the like. Third, the two chronicles. And fourth, the annals.

Shortly after 1432 a monk of the Cluniac priory of Bermondsey compiled a chronicle of the history of his house from its foundation in 1042 to his own day (he also included a few entries on general history derived from a number of well known chronicle sources).[2] He gives a record of the priory's

---

[2] Printed in *Annales Monastici*, ed. H. R. Luard (RS 1864–9, 5 vols), iii. 423–87. Miss Graham suggests that the Bermondsey annals were compiled in connection with a visit in 1432 by

endowment which he derived from Domesday book and from charters. He probably also used some now lost annals of the house for the details about the weather, and perhaps for the succession of the priors and, after the priory became an abbey, of the abbots.[3]

A similar work is the chronicle of St Peter's, Gloucester, compiled during the abbatiate of Walter Frocester (1382–1412), perhaps by the abbot himself or at least at his command.[4] The author made extensive use of charter evidence, although apparently he drew mainly on a register of charters rather than on the original texts themselves. This register was probably in the form of a chronicle. It is evident that for the period from 1072 to 1139 or later, the author used a substantial, but now lost, chronicle of St Peter's, which recorded among other things benefactions to the abbey in chronological order.[5] The author's interest in charters is demonstrated by the fact that he prefixed his chronicle to a register of the abbey's properties, to which he gives occasional references. The register is arranged alphabetically, and records the circumstances of the acquisition of each property, in a manner reminiscent of Thomas Burton. It is noteworthy that Frocester himself 'renewed' the registers of St Peter's.[6] The Gloucester chronicler, like the Bermondsey one, copied some information on national events, derived from standard authorities, into the account of his abbey's history.

Another chronicle of rather the same type as that of Gloucester is the so-called Book of Hyde, a chronicle of Hyde abbey near Winchester, which was written probably towards the middle of the fifteenth century.[7] It is

---

Theodore Douet, prior of La Charité-sur-Loire, the mother house of Bermondsey, as vicar-general of the abbot of Cluny. Miss Graham points out that the annals are an unreliable source for the history of the priory. See Rose Graham, 'The priory of La Charité-sur-Loire and the monastery of Bermondsey' in the same author's *English Ecclesiastical Studies* (London 1929), pp. 93 et seq., and the next note. For the sources of the entries on general history see *Berm.* pp. xxxvii–xxxviii.

[3] The use of charters is apparent throughout in the record of Bermondsey's acquisition of property, etc.; for explicit references to charters see *Berm.* pp. 447, 467, 486. For details of the weather during the late twelfth and thirteenth centuries see *Berm.* pp. 448, 450, 455. The succession of the priors of Bermondsey given in the chronicle is extremely inaccurate; see Graham, op. cit., pp. 99–100, 121–4.

[4] Printed in *Historia et Cartularium Monasterii Sancti Petri Gloucestriae*, ed. W. H. Hart (RS 1863–7, 3 vols), i. 3–58. For Frocester's responsibility for the chronicle see C. N. L. Brooke, 'St Peter of Gloucester and St Cadoc of Llancarfan' in *Celt and Saxon, Studies in the early British Border*, ed. N. K. Chadwick (Cambridge 1963), p. 260 and n. 3. For the composition and value of the chronicle see ibid., pp. 260–9. For a chronicle on general history written at St Peter's, Gloucester, in the fifteenth century see p. 412 and n. 153 below.

[5] See Brooke, op. cit., pp. 264–9. For the relationship of *HG* to Florence of Worcester see ibid., pp. 277–9, Appendix I.

[6] *HG*, i. 50. For Thomas Burton's careful record of Meaux's acquisition of properties see p. 370 above.

[7] Printed *Liber Monasterii de Hyda*, ed. Edward Edwards (RS 1866). The only medieval manuscript of the *Liber* is owned by the earl of Macclesfield, and is in the library of Shirburn Castle; see G. R. C. Davis, *Medieval Cartularies of Great Britain* (London 1958), p. 121 no. 1051. The editor of the *Liber* does not commit himself as to the date of composition beyond pointing out that it must be after 1354 (see Edwards, op. cit., p. xxiii). The handwriting of the MS.

a general history compiled from various sources, some well known, some now lost, covering the period from Brutus to 1023 (the manuscript ends incomplete), into which is fitted the domestic history of the abbey. From the time of King Ethelwulf until that of Canute the chronicle is arranged under the reigns of kings. To each section are appended copies of charters granted to Hyde during the reign. The chronicler's interest in and knowledge of charters is indicated by the fact that he provides translations of the Anglo-Saxon charters into both Latin and middle English. (Similarly, when a monk of Evesham brought the chronicle of his abbey's history up to date, continuing it from 1214 to 1418, he made extensive use of charters and other documents.)[8]

More remarkable as examples of research are the brief, unpretentious annals of Thornton[9] written just before the dissolution of the monasteries (Thornton was dissolved in 1539). The author tabulated his pages, arranging his material under abbots, from the foundation of the house in 1139 to 1532 (the latest entry is for 1526). His main interest was in the fabric and ornaments of the church, and in the conventual buildings. In order to collect material he used the records of the various monastic officials. Thus under 1264 he notes: 'In this year I find the first mention in the accounts of the office of master of the fabric.'[10] He follows the annals with lists of obedientiaries, including the masters of the fabric, and usually by a specimen of their accounts.[11]

These local histories are on a modest scale. They are monastic records, without propaganda intention, and show antiquarian predilections. However, as mentioned above, a number of writers besides Thomas Elmham and Thomas Burton aspired to write local history on a grand scale. At Durham the prior, John Wessington, who ruled from 1416 to 1446,[12]

---

could well be of the first half of the fifteenth century. I suggest towards the middle of the century because of the work's affinities with Thomas Rudborne's history of St Swithun's, Winchester (for which see below); this also raises the possibility that Rudborne had some hand in its production. See p. 395 n. 30 below. John Rous saw the manuscript, which, he alleges, had been newly copied from a manuscript in an ancient hand, at Hyde. He refers to the account of the foundation of Cambridge university in it (Edwards, op. cit., p. 11), which, he states, was 'in dicta abbathia [de Hyda] in quadam bene indictata nobili Chronica, quae de vetusta et antiqua manu iterum, ne periret, nova manu et placida scripta est, ut egomet vidi benevola licentia domini abbatis ejusdem loci'; *JR*, p. 96.

[8] Printed in *Chronicon Abbatiae de Evesham*, ed. W. D. Macray (RS 1863), pp. 260–310; cf. *Eve.* p. xxxv. A translation is in D. C. Cox, *The Chronicle of Evesham Abbey* (Vale of Evesham Historical Soc., Evesham 1964), pp. 35–65. For specific references to documents see for example *Eve.* pp. 301, 302.

[9] Discussed and extracts printed Kathleen Major, 'The Thornton abbey chronicle (Bodleian Library, Tanner MS. 166), with extracts relating to the fabric of the abbey' in *Archaeological Journal*, ciii (1946), pp. 174–8. See p. 413 below.

[10] *Thornton*, p. 175. See V. H. Galbraith, *Historical Research in Medieval England* (London 1951), p. 43.

[11] For the list of the masters of the fabric and a specimen of their accounts see *Thornton*, pp. 177–8.

[12] For Wessington's career see Emden, *Biographical Register*, iii. 2018, David Knowles, *The*

produced what he no doubt hoped would become the standard history of St Cuthbert's see, the *Libellus de exordio et statu ecclesie cathedralis quondam Lindisfarnensis, post Conchestrensis, demum Dunelmensis, ac de gestis pontificum eiusdem* (*A Little Book on the Beginnings and Status of the Cathedral Church first of Lindisfarne, then of Chester-le-Street, and finally of Durham, and the Deeds of Its Pontiffs*).[13] Wessington reached 1362, about fifty years before his time of writing.[14] He compiled his work from the previous histories of Durham (by Symeon, Geoffrey de Coldingham, Robert de Graystanes and others) and from standard authorities such as Bede, William of Malmesbury, Henry of Huntingdon and John of Tynemouth's *Historia Aurea*, appending a list of literary sources for the history of Durham. He also copied charters (some of them spurious) and other documents from cartularies and registers.[15] A recent scholar sees him 'sitting down, with a pile of manuscripts from the conventual library at his elbow, to compile a history of his monastery'.[16]

John Flete's history of Westminster abbey[17] resembles Wessington's *Libellus*. Flete was a monk of Westminster from 1420 to 1465, and like Wessington held official positions in his community.[18] From 1443 to 1446 he was one of the wardens of Queen Eleanor's manors, and was probably responsible for drawing up a survey of some of the abbey's estates. He was 'warden of the new work' (that is he was in charge of the new work on the church) from 1445 to 1446, treasurer from 1449 to 1450, and in about 1457 he became prior. His history of Westminster is divided into four sections: the abbey's foundation story; copies of its charters of privilege; a list of its relics and indulgences; and Lives of the abbots up to the death of Nicholas Littlington in 1386 (again like Wessington, Flete failed to bring his work up to date).[19]

Religious Orders in England, ii (Cambridge 1955), pp. 190–3, and R. B. Dobson, *Durham Priory 1400–1450* (Cambridge 1973), pp. 89–113. For his work as an historian and antiquary see H. S. Offler, *Medieval Historians of Durham* (Durham 1958), p. 17, and Dobson, op. cit., pp. 378–86.

[13] The *Libellus* is known to survive in three manuscripts: Bodleian Library MS. Laud Misc. 748; Lincoln's Inn Library MS. Hales 114; BL MS. Cotton Claudius D IV. All three were written at Durham and the first is probably Wessington's autograph. The manuscripts are fully described in H. H. E. Craster, 'The Red Book of Durham' in *EHR*, xl (1925), pp. 504–14 passim. The *Libellus* is unprinted but an epitome of the text in a now lost manuscript previously owned by John Leland is in Leland's *Collectanea*, ed. Thomas Hearne (Oxford 1715, 6 vols), ii. 365–92. For the failure of the *Libellus* to become the standard history at Durham see Offler, op. cit., p. 17. See also Dobson, op. cit., pp. 379–81.

[14] Craster, op. cit., p. 114.

[15] For Wessington's literary sources see ibid., pp. 516–17 (for his appendix see ibid., pp. 514, 516).

[16] Ibid., p. 514.

[17] Printed *The History of Westminster Abbey by John Flete*, ed. J. Armitage Robinson (Cambridge 1909). See also B. F. Harvey, *Westminster Abbey and its Estates in the Middle Ages* (Oxford 1977), pp. 12–18.

[18] For Flete's career see *Flete*, pp. 1–2.

[19] For the value of Flete for the succession of the abbots see *Flete*, pp. 140–4.

The circumstances of the abbey's foundation were unknown, and the evidence for its early history was sparse. Therefore for this period Flete relied on literary authorities and on the charters of privilege, some of which were forgeries.[20] He borrowed his account of the foundation from three eleventh century writers (a lost chronicle of Westminster, Sulcard's chronicle and the *Life of St Mellitus* by the hagiographer Goscelin),[21] and from a now lost work, the *Liber Regius (Royal Book)*, which was written at Bury St Edmunds during the reign of Richard II.[22] The story claimed that the abbey was founded in A.D. 184 by King Lucius, but was destroyed during the Diocletian persecution; it was refounded by King Sebert (d. 616), and consecrated by St Peter in the spirit.

More evidence was available for the post-Conquest period, and Flete's treatment of it was scholarly. To write the lives of the abbots he used documents (charters, obedientiaries' accounts[23] and public records[24]), many of which he cites in full. He also used his own observation of antiquities. He notes the exact burial places of the abbots and copies the epitaphs; his work has enabled modern scholars to attribute with a fair degree of certainty some of the surviving graves and effigies to individual abbots of the twelfth and thirteenth centuries.[25] In addition, he mentions notable features in the church, for example the tapestries depicting the histories of Our Lord and of Edward the Confessor,[26] and the sumptuous mosaic pavement before the high altar.[27]

At about the same time as Durham and Westminster produced official accounts of their foundations and early histories, a similar narrative was written at Winchester. Thomas Rudborne, a monk of St Swithun's, wrote his *Historia Major ... Ecclesiae Wintoniensis (The Greater History ... of the Church of Winchester)* in the mid-fifteenth century.[28] The *Historia* is primarily a history of the Old Minster (the dedication to St Swithun dates probably from after the refoundation of the cathedral priory by

---

[20] For a discussion of charters of privilege transcribed by Flete see *Flete*, pp. 12–18.
[21] See *Flete*, pp. 2–11 passim.
[22] See *Flete*, pp. 3–4, 11.
[23] See e.g. *Flete*, p. 98.
[24] See e.g. *Flete*, p. 138.
[25] See *Flete*, pp. 22–4.
[26] *Flete*, p. 105. A copy of the wording on the tapestries still survives; see *Flete*, pp. 24–29.
[27] *Flete*, p. 113.
[28] Printed in Wharton, *Anglia Sacra*, i. 179–286. Wharton used Lambeth Palace Library MS. 183 as the basis of his text. I owe this information to Margaret Cash, County Archivist of Hampshire. As the manuscript, however, is incomplete at the beginning and end, Wharton supplemented it from the *Epitome Historiae Majoris Ecclesiae Wintoniensis* (see Wharton, op. cit. i. xxvi, 179–81, 285–6, and n. 30 below). It should be noted that the titles given here of the works are all post-reformation. In general I have followed Wharton's account of Rudborne's works. However, the attributions and identifications of Wharton and later scholars stand in need of revision, and I am deeply indebted to Professor D. J. Sheerin, of the University of North Carolina, for putting the results of his researches at my disposal (see pp. 395 n. 30 and 493–4, Appendix D, below).

St Ethelwold in 964), and covers the period from A.D. 164 until 1138.[29] It also includes much general history and is arranged from early Saxon times under the reigns of kings; from the beginning of Book III one chapter is devoted to each king, starting with Egbert. Rudborne may also have been the author of some other chronicles, that is: the *Epitome Historiae Majoris* (*The Epitome of the Greater History*), a chronicle of England, with especial reference to Winchester, from Brutus until the reign of Henry VI,[30] the *Historia Minor* (*The Lesser History*), which covers the period from Brutus to 1234;[31] and a brief history of Durham to 1083, commissioned by Robert Neville, bishop of Durham (1438–57).[32]

Unlike Wessington and Flete Rudborne includes general as well as local history in the *Historia Major*. Moreover, his work is more literary in tone than theirs. On occasion he writes in rhetorical style. For instance, he alleges that King Edwin eventually became chaste because he decided to follow the examples of Alexander the Great, Scipio and Nospurna— whose chastity Rudborne demonstrates with references to Vegetius[33]

---

[29] Wharton, *Anglia Sacra*, i. xxvi.

[30] The *Epitome* is unprinted except for the beginning and end published by Wharton to supplement his text of the *Historia Major* (see p. 394 n. 28 above). Wharton used the text in BL MS. Cotton Galba A XV, item 2, which is now seriously mutilated owing to damage in the fire of 1731 in the Cottonian library. A number of other copies survive: All Souls, Oxford, MS. 114, ff. 6 et seq. (see H. O. Coxe, *Catalogue of MSS. in the Library of All Souls College* (Oxford 1842), p. 35); a copy of the latter, Corpus Christi College, Cambridge, MS. 110, pp. 260 et seq. (see M. R. James, *A Descriptive Catalogue of Manuscripts in the Library of Corpus Christi College, Cambridge* (Cambridge 1909–12, 2 vols), i. 234); BL MS. Cotton Vespasian D IX, ff. 12–24 (imperfect); BL MS. Additional 29436, ff. 4–9^v (imperfect). On the basis of a colophon dated 1531 in the All Souls and Corpus MSS. the *Epitome* was attributed by Professor Willis to John of Exeter, a monk of St Swithun's at the time of the dissolution of the monasteries; R. Willis, 'Architectural history of Winchester cathedral' in *Proceedings of the Royal Architectural Institute, Winchester* (1845), p. 3 n.a. His view has been accepted by R. N. Quirk, 'Winchester cathedral in the tenth century' in *Archaeological Journal*, cxiv (1957), p. 28 n. 1. The colophon reads: 'Liber historialis et antiquitatum domus S. Swithuni Wintonie Iohannis Exeter eiusdem loci commonachi propriis manibus descriptus anno dominicae incarnationis millesimo quingentesimo trecesimo primo.' This colophon could refer of course to the scribe and not to the author. Professor Sheerin is of the opinion that the work is by Rudborne. Nor should the possibility be overlooked that besides the *Epitome* and the next two works to be mentioned, Rudborne may have written, or at least supervised the writing of the historical narrative in the Book of Hyde (see p. 391 and n. 7 above). It will be noticed that the arrangement of the *Liber* under kings closely resembles that of the *Historia Major*. In addition, the *Liber* uses two of the now unidentified sources cited by Rudborne—Girardus Cornubiensis, *De Gestis Regum West-Saxonum*, and 'Vigilantius'; see Edwards, op. cit., p. xxi, and below pp. 396 and nn. 38, 39, 493–4, Appendix D, below. Possibly further research would result in a firm conclusion.

[31] BL MS. Nero A XVII. Unpublished. See Wharton, *Anglia Sacra*, i. xxvii, and Hardy, *Cat.* iii. 78–9. M. R. James, op. cit., i. 235, suggests that the chronicle from the foundation of the Old Minster by King Lucius to the beginning of Henry VI's reign in Corpus Christi College, Cambridge, MS. 110, pp. 314 et seq. is another copy of the *Historia Minor*. But see Quirk, op. cit., p. 57 n. 1.

[32] See Wharton, op. cit., i. xxviii.

[33] *TR*, p. 216. The reference to Vegetius is erroneous; the passage is in fact from Frontinus, *Stratagemata*, II. xi, 6 (ed., with an English translation, C. E. Bennett (Loeb Classical

and Valerius Maximus.[34] He liked word-play,[35] and had a taste for false etymologies: he debates whether the Isle of Wight derived its Latin name Vecta from the past participle of *vehere* (to carry), because no one could reach it unless carried in a boat, or from *vectigalia* (a tax), because it paid tribute to the Romans.[36]

Rudborne leant heavily on literary sources. He cites numerous authorities ranging in date from the late Roman to the late medieval period. He names them meticulously, and often cites long passages *verbatim*. His sources include the standard English chronicles (William of Malmesbury, Matthew Paris, Higden and the like), and continental works (such as Marianus Scotus and Martinus Polonus), besides encyclopaedias and earlier histories of Winchester.[37]

Most of Rudborne's notices of the architectural history of the Old Minster in Anglo-Saxon times are based on earlier sources. He cites, for example, a lost work (or forgery), Vigilantius' *De Basilica Petri* (*On the Church of* [*St*] *Peter*),[38] for the minster's early history, including the locations of the burial places of Anglo-Saxon kings and bishops. Thus, following Vigilantius, he states that St Ethelwold, bishop of Winchester from 963 to 984, translated the body of St Birinus from Dorchester to the cathedral where it was interred 'to the north of the high altar'.[39] His reliance on written authorities had the result that he incorporated much legendary material—for example the dimensions of the church built by King Lucius.[40] However, occasionally Rudborne used his own first hand observation of the few remains of the pre-Conquest monastery. He records that St Swithun's original burial place was marked by a chapel 'which can be seen to this day by the north door of the nave of the church.'[41] (For the architectural history of the cathedral in the post-Conquest period Rudborne continues to rely on literary sources and to a lesser extent on his own observation.)[42]

Rudborne made relatively little use of documents. Nevertheless, he

---

Library 1925), p. 192; cf. p. 190). The attributions of *bons mots* derived from Frontinus to Vegetius was not uncommon. I owe this reference to Dr C. T. Allmand.

[34] I have failed to trace this reference.

[35] See his play on the name of St Benedict; *TR*, p. 222.

[36] *TR*, p. 189.

[37] Not all Rudborne's sources have been identified and more work needs to be done on them. See pp. 493–4, Appendix D, below.

[38] For Vigilantius see pp. 493–4, Appendix D, below.

[39] *TR*, p. 223. For other references to Vigilantius see e.g. *TR*, pp. 181, 186, 199.

[40] *TR*, p. 185.

[41] *TR*, p. 203. See Quirk, 'Winchester cathedral in the tenth century', p. 65 and n. 6, and Martin Biddle and R. N. Quirk, 'Excavations near Winchester Cathedral, 1961' in *Archaeological Journal*, cxix (1962), p. 174 and n. 6.

[42] For example Rudborne's explanation of the fall of the Norman tower is taken from literary sources (*TR*, pp. 270–1), but his description of some of the tombs and transcriptions of epitaphs in the cathedral may well have been the result of his own observation (see e.g. *TR*, pp. 256, 279).

copies some charters (including forgeries) in full, and shows some interest in diplomatic. He defines the units of land measurement employed in Domesday book,[43] and also comments on the means of calculating regnal years: he alleges that many historians had made the mistake of including the year of a king's accession in the calculation (such a year should not be included because it was incomplete).[44] His recognition of the importance of documentary evidence is indicated by the fact that he obtained Bishop Neville's permission to consult the archives at Durham for his history of St Cuthbert's.[45]

Rudborne was more interested in origins than either Wessington or Flete, and the propagandist element in his work is stronger. He adopted the foundation story probably concocted at St Swithun's in the late thirteenth and early fourteenth century.[46] This story relates that monks were first established in the Old Minster in British times, and that, therefore, the monastery antedated the community of secular canons which at some unspecified date replaced the monks. This meant that when King Edgar expelled the canons in 964 and introduced monks into the cathedral, he was merely restoring the ancient foundation. Rudborne embellished this tale with the statement that the first monastery was built by King Lucius who established 250 monks there, and gave the church the right of sanctuary in the suburbs of the city, to be held 'with the privilege of Dunvallo Molmutius'. His foundation was dedicated by the missionaries, Phagan and Deruvian.[47] These details were inspired by Geoffrey of Monmouth: Geoffrey related that the pious Lucius founded and endowed numerous churches, besides persuading Pope Eleutherius to send Phagan and Deruvian;[48] and Geoffrey alleged that Dunvallo Molmutius instituted laws among the Britons, which included the right of sanctuary for temples and cities.[49]

Rudborne's interest in the monastic origins of the Old Minster was accompanied by an interest in monastic origins generally. He has a long excursus on the origins of monasticism, which soon turns into an account of the origin of the order of St Benedict: monasticism was as old as Christi-

---

[43] *TR*, p. 257.

[44] *TR*, p. 284.

[45] See Wharton, *Anglia Sacra*, p. xxviii, citing BL MS. Galba A XV, for which see p. 395 n. 30 above.

[46] The monks' account of the 'British history' of the Old Minster, designed to prove that the kings, not the bishops, were its patrons, is in *Registrum Johannis de Pontissara Episcopi Wintoniensis*, ed. Cecil Deedes (Canterbury and York Soc., xix, xxx, 1915, 1924, 2 vols), ii. 609–15. For the conflict between the bishop and his chapter see ibid., i. xv, xx–xxii; ii. 676–94. For the monks' earlier falsification of the Old Minster's history see H. P. R. Finberg, *The Early Charters of Wessex* (Leicester 1964), pp. 226–44 passim.

[47] *TR*, pp. 181–2.

[48] *The Historia Regum Britanniae of Geoffrey of Monmouth*, ed. Acton Griscom (London 1929), pp. 328–30 (bk IV, c. xix).

[49] Ibid., p. 275 (bk II, c. xvii).

anity, and Benedictinism incorporated all that was best in the earlier rules.[50] No doubt Rudborne wrote partly to defend the Benedictine order from its detractors. (He also wrote as a patriotic Englishman: in his account of the conversion of Britain to Christianity, he comments that although Britain resembled other countries in so far as it was converted by an apostle of Christ, it alone remained free of apostasy).[51]

Besides expounding the ancient origins of the Old Minster, Rudborne emphasizes the power and prestige of the bishop. He demonstrates the miraculous power of St Swithun,[52] and the bishops' right to precedence: he points out that at an ecclesiastical council the bishop should sit third or fourth from the archbishop of Canterbury, regardless of the date of ordination which determined the precedence of other bishops.[53] Rudborne argues that the bishop of Winchester perhaps had a better claim to be a primate than the archbishop of York: his see was established by a papal legate, St Birinus, while a missionary, Paulinus, sent by St Augustine and not directly by the pope, established the see at York.[54]

It is likely that Rudborne wrote some passages with the pretensions of the monks of Glastonbury in mind. The Glastonbury monks claimed that the abbey was originally founded by St Joseph of Arimathea, that, having subsequently fallen into decay, it was refounded by Phagan and Deruvian,[55] and that its site was the ancient Avalon, the burial place of King Arthur.[56] Rudborne states categorically that Glastonbury abbey was founded by Ine king of Wessex (688–c. 726).[57] As has been seen, he connects Phagan and Deruvian particularly with Winchester itself, asserting that they consecrated the Old Minster.[58] Moreover, he writes slightingly of the Arthurian legends. It was no credit to King Arthur that he concentrated on foreign conquest and brutally subdued the English; as a result the latter rebelled and slew their oppressors. And the legends themselves were historically unsound: for example, Arthur could not have defeated an emperor called Lucius, because no emperor of that name ruled in his time (as Rudborne demonstrates with references to literary sources).[59]

Flete's and Rudborne's use of legend pales in comparison with John of

---

[50] *TR*, pp. 220–2. Noticed in W. A. Pantin, 'Some medieval English treatises on the origins of monasticism' in *Medieval Studies presented to Rose Graham*, ed. Veronica Ruffer and A. J. Taylor (Oxford 1950), p. 199. See p. 343 above.

[51] *TR*, pp. 177–8.

[52] *TR*, pp. 223, 234–5.

[53] *TR*, pp. 254–5.

[54] *TR*, pp. 190–1.

[55] For the Glastonbury legends see pp. 399 and n. 65, 400 and n. 68 below.

[56] *Adami de Domerham Historia de Rebus gestis Glastoniensibus*, ed. Thomas Hearne (Oxford 1727), i. 19–20. See J. Armitage Robinson, 'William of Malmesbury "On the Antiquity of Glastonbury"' in *Somerset Historical Essays* (London 1921), pp. 6–7.

[57] *TR*, p. 194.

[58] See p. 397 and n. 47 above.

[59] *TR*, pp. 187–8.

Glastonbury's. In about 1400 John produced a definitive chronicle of his abbey down to 1342.[60] He explains his immediate motive for writing in the preface;[61] it was to counter an assertion by Ranulf Higden in the *Polychronicon* that the St Patrick buried at Glastonbury was not the apostle of Ireland (who, the Glastonbury monks claimed, became their house's first abbot after retiring from his missionary work), but a ninth century abbot of that name.[62] John tried to demonstrate the falsity of Higden's allegation by putting forward various arguments. He gives in addition another reason for his work; he intended to show that formerly the abbey had enjoyed many liberties and possessions—that it had been the most privileged foundation in England—which had now been lost through the neglect of 'certain prelates', the depredations of the Danish and Norman invasions, and because of the bishop of Bath's oppressions.[63] John concludes his preface with a prayer for the restoration of the abbey's prosperity. And no doubt he hoped that his propagandist chronicle would contribute to that end.

John was little more than a compiler. As he himself admits, the basis of his chronicle to 1290 was that of Adam of Domerham, which he abbreviated because he considered it too prolix.[64] Adam's chronicle in its turn had incorporated the *De Antiquitate Glastoniensis Ecclesiae* (*On the Antiquity of the Church of Glastonbury*) by William of Malmesbury. The Glastonbury monks had interpolated both chronicles with more legends, which they had borrowed from various sources. They adapted and elaborated these sources in order to increase the abbey's prestige—and thus its pilgrim trade and prosperity.[65] John also states that, for the convenience of the reader, he had collected material from saints' Lives and other 'ancient books'.[66] He continued the chronicle to 1342, giving an account of each abbot in turn.

The result of John of Glastonbury's labours, the culmination, as it were, of the work of his predecessors, was a chronicle which in its early part is mainly legendary. The legends had been developed at Glastonbury under the influence of hagiography and romance literature. The principal ones

---

[60] Printed *John of Glastonbury, Cronica sive Antiquitates Glastoniensis Ecclesie*, ed. J. P. Carley, British Archaeological Reports, xlvii (i and ii, 1978, 2 vols). For this edition and the editor's conclusions about the chronicle, some of which are unconvincing, see the review in *EHR*, xcv (1980), pp. 358–63.

[61] *JG*, i. 7–8.

[62] *Poly.* v. 304, 306.

[63] *JG*, i. 8.

[64] *JG*, i. 5–6.

[65] The interpolation by William of Malmesbury is fully discussed by W. W. Newell, 'William of Malmesbury on the Antiquity of Glastonbury' in *Publications of the Modern Language Association of America*, xviii (1903), pp. 459–512, and, independently, by Armitage Robinson, 'William of Malmesbury "On the Antiquity of Glastonbury"', pp. 1–25. See also A. Gransden, 'The growth of the Glastonbury traditions and legends in the twelfth century' in *Journal of Ecclesiastical History*, xxvii (1976), pp. 342 and n. 5, 349, 356, 358, and p. 398 above.

[66] *JG*, i. 7.

relate to Joseph of Arimathea and King Arthur; John now linked the saint and the hero of romance together as blood relatives by means of a genealogy.[67] This corpus of legends endowed not only the abbey itself, but also some of its treasures and estates, with holy and romantic associations.[68]

The monks of Crowland excelled even those of Glastonbury in the art of fabrication. They produced an official chronicle of the abbey's early history which was a total forgery.[69] The first part (to 1089) masquerades as the work of Ingulf, abbot of Crowland from 1085/6 to 1109, and the 'continuation' (to 1148) as that of the well known twelfth century writer Peter of Blois. The intention of the forger (or forgers) was to substantiate the abbey's claims to privilege and property (the chronicle begins with a long series of spurious charters), and in general to increase its prestige: this was to be done by describing the circumstances of the abbey's foundation and by proving that it had an uninterrupted history from its original foundation by King Ethelbald of Mercia (716–57): in fact the abbey had been destroyed by the Danes and refounded in 966, in the reign of King Edred.

A number of tracts on local history were written in the last half of the fourteenth century and the first half of the fifteenth, which reflect the distinctive preoccupations of the times. Concern for prestige and the commemorative intention were probably the principal motives for the composition of two tracts at St Albans, one on the pictures and images in the abbey church,[70] and the other on its altars, monuments and graves.[71] Both involved some research and include antiquarian observations. The tract on the pictures and images, having explained the utility of such visual aids in promoting piety among laymen, describes the pictures and expounds their iconographical significance. In discussing the statues of St Lawrence and St Grimbald in the chapel of St Lawrence, the author shows his interest in history. He explains that previously the almonry chapel had contained statues of St Lawrence and St Grimbald, but that these had been removed when the chapel was destroyed to make room for the new gatehouse and infirmary. However, 'in accordance with the tenor of the constitution then drawn up', the statues had been moved to their present place, so that these saints might be venerated as before. The writer concludes by asking for prayers for those responsible, 'whose names and works he had noted on a roll', especially for William Wintershull, the almoner,

---

[67] *JG*, i. 68–9.
[68] The legends in John of Glastonbury are discussed in J. Armitage Robinson, *Two Glastonbury Legends: King Arthur and St Joseph of Arimathea* (Cambridge 1926) passim.
[69] For the forged Crowland chronicle see pp. 490–1, Appendix C, below.
[70] Printed in *Amund.* i. 418–30. Described *Amund.* ii. lviii-lix.
[71] Printed in *Amund.* i. 431–49. Described *Amund.* ii. lix-lxii.

and Thomas Houghton, the sacrist, whose grave was in front of the altar in the chapel, and 'whose good deeds are recorded elsewhere'.[72]

The tract on the altars, monuments and graves records the names of those buried (abbots, priors, obedientiaries, local clergy, benefactors and the like) and the exact location of their tombs. To identify the people the author used 'the Book of Benefactors on the high altar',[73] archives preserved by William Wintershull (including a roll of benefactors)[74] and the *Gesta Abbatum*.[75] To describe the tombs themselves, the author clearly used his own observation. As in the case of the previous tract, the author was interested in earlier arrangements. In writing of the altar in the chapel of the Virgin Mary, he used written evidence and pictures to discover where her cult was observed before the construction of the existing chapel: masses to her were said in a chapel dedicated to St Blaise; this was formerly situated by the entrance to the cemetery, though no trace of it remained in the author's day.[76]

A similar interest in the ornaments and contents of churches was shown elsewhere. At Christ Church, Canterbury, William Glastonbury described the scenes in the twelve windows of the choir; although he partly made use of a description written a century earlier,[77] he seems to have relied to some extent on his own observation.[78] At Durham Prior Wessington copied, and gave the scriptural references to the inscriptions beneath the images (or pictures) of monks, numbering 148 in all, at the altar of SS Jerome and Benedict, and named some of the hitherto unidentified figures.[79] He also worked on the books in the cloister and in the library; he listed the commentaries on the books of the bible and the works of the fathers, stating in which volumes they were to be found.[80]

The monk who contributed most in this period to bibliographical studies was Henry Kirkstead of Bury St Edmunds. He was successively novice master, armarius and subprior in the reign of Edward III and early

---

[72] *Amund.* i. 421.

[73] *Amund.* i. 431–2; cf. *Amund.* pp. 434–41 passim. Perhaps this was Thomas Walsingham's *Book of Benefactors*, now BL MS. Cotton Nero D VII; see p. 123 and n. 52 above.

[74] *Amund.* i. 448.

[75] *Amund.* i. 433–4.

[76] *Amund.* i. 445–6.

[77] Printed *The Verses formerly inscribed on twelve Windows in the Choir of Canterbury Cathedral*, ed. M. R. James (Cambridge Antiquarian Soc., octavo series, xxxviii, 1901).

[78] See 'The chronicle of William Glastynbury, monk of the priory of Christ Church, Canterbury, 1419–1448', ed. C. E. Woodruff in *Archaeologia Cantiana*, xxxvii (1925), pp. 123, 138, 139–51 (Appendix). For a notice of William Glastonbury's annals, see p. 415 below.

[79] The tract is in Durham cathedral library MS. B III 30, the first part of which comprises Wessington's collectanea. It is on folios 6–25ᵛ and part is printed in *Rites of Durham*, ed. J. T. Fowler (Surtees Soc., cvii, 1903), pp. 124–36. Cf. *Historiae Dunelmensis Scriptores Tres, Gaufridus de Coldingham, Robertus de Graystanes, et Willielmus de Chambre*, ed. James Raine, sn. (Surtees Soc., ix, 1839), p. cclxix, Pantin, 'Some medieval English treatises on the origins of monasticism', p. 200; and Dobson, *Durham Priory 1400–1450*, p. 382.

[80] See Raine, op. cit., p. cclxx.

in Richard II's reign.[81] The wide range of his antiquarian interests is shown by numerous notes in manuscripts surviving from St Edmund's abbey.[82] For example he annotated the thirteenth century tract on the dedications of chapels and altars in the abbey,[83] and also an early fourteenth century list of benefactors, to which he added the dates of each benefactor and stated whether his or her charter to St Edmund's was still extant.[84] But his principal energies were devoted to the organization of the abbey library. He inserted classmarks in the volumes, probably to facilitate the compilation of inventories and the recording of loans;[85] he listed the contents on the fly-leaves, noted incipits and explicits, and marked book and chapter divisions. He often also noted if the text were incomplete and stated where a better copy might be found.[86]

Kirkstead's great work was a catalogue, described by a recent scholar as a 'bio-bibliographic union catalogue'.[87] This vast work, beginning with an exposition on the genuine and apocryphal books of the bible and on the fathers whose writings were accepted by the church, gives a numbered list of 195 monastic libraries. It then has a list, arranged mainly in alphabetical order, of 674 authors, with a short biography of each and a list of his works; in most cases it gives the incipit and explicit of each work, and indicates by means of the numbered references libraries in which the work is to be found. Kirkstead relied mainly on earlier catalogues for the biographies of authors and the lists of their works, but his research on the location of copies was new. He travelled from monastery to monastery examining the volumes in their libraries; as a 'topo-bibliographer' he was a forerunner of the fifteenth century antiquaries, John Rous and William Worcester (neither of whom, however, organized their findings into a catalogue). The purpose of his catalogue was, according to the preface, to provide information 'for the use and convenience of students and preach-

---

[81] His life and work are fully discussed by R. H. Rouse, 'Bostonus Buriensis and the author of the *Catalogus Scriptorum Ecclesiae*' in *Speculum*, xli (1966), pp. 471–99 passim.

[82] Some of these notes are reproduced in ibid., Plates I-XIV.

[83] BL MS. Harley 1005, ff. 217ᵛ–18ᵛ. Printed (including Kirkstead's marginalia) in *The Customary of the Benedictine Abbey of Bury St Edmunds in Suffolk*, ed. A. Gransden (Henry Bradshaw Society, xcix, 1973), pp. 114–21. See also Gransden, *Historical Writing*, i. 390 and n. 71, 393–4. Cf. Rouse, op. cit., p. 484.

[84] BL MS. Harley 1005, ff. 81–3. Cf. Rouse, op. cit., p. 484.

[85] Ibid., pp. 488–9.

[86] Ibid., pp. 490–3.

[87] Ibid., p. 472. The *Catalogus Scriptorum Ecclesiae* is described in ibid., pp. 471–2, and the portions for which Kirkstead's preliminary notes survive printed in ibid., pp. 495–9 (Appendix). For further references to modern work on it see ibid., p. 471 n. 1. The *Catalogus* survives in a late seventeenth century transcript by Thomas Tanner, CUL MS. Additional 3470. The entries for English authors are printed in Thomas Tanner, *Bibliotheca Britannico-Hibernica sive de Scriptoribus*, ed. David Wilkins (London 1748), pp. xvii-xliii. Professor Rouse completed a preliminary edition of the whole as a doctoral dissertation in 1962; see Rouse (op. cit., p. 471 n. 1), and informed me in a letter of 1 December 1976 that he is now engaged on editing the *Catalogus*.

ers'; its value for the historian today is the data it preserves on the contents and distributions of medieval books.[88]

The works discussed so far relate to the cultural and intellectual life of the monks. But at least equally typical of the age were the tracts about important events in the history of individual houses, particularly those connected with their privileges and property rights. Good examples of such tracts survive from Bury St Edmunds, and continue the series started in the abbey in the early thirteenth century. There are: the account of the disputed election of John Timworth to the abbacy on the death of John Brinkley in 1379 (the dispute lasted until 1384);[89] the *Visitatio Thome de Arundel* (*The Visitation of Thomas Arundel*), written soon after 1400 and describing how the archbishop was entertained (with lavish hospitality) when he arrived unexpected at the abbey;[90] the *Contentio cum Episcopo Eliensi* (*The Dispute with the Bishop of Ely*), a narrative with documents relating to litigation between the abbot of St Edmunds and the bishop of Ely over the return of writs (1410–25);[91] the *Pensio de Woolpet* (*Concerning the Woolpit Pension*) compiled at about the same time, and comprising mainly documents (eleventh to fourteenth century) used in evidence in the prolonged dispute over the payment of twenty marks due to the abbey from the vicarage of Woolpit;[92] and the *Incensum Ecclesie* (*The Burning of the Church*), an account of the fire which destroyed the abbey church in 1465.[93] These tracts are primarily records. Although the last is purely reportage, the purpose of such works was usually to prove that the author's community was in the right, and also to establish precedents: as the author of the *Visitatio* (who wrote to demonstrate that the abbey's privilege of exemption was not infringed by the archbishop's visit) expressed it:[94]

> I have been led to commend to memory, according to my ability, what is written above, so that our posterity should learn and know how to behave to archbishops of Canterbury in case in like manner they wish to come to our monastery.

As in the past monks produced *pièces justificatives* to prove the legitimacy of their claims. At least forty such tracts were written at Durham, probably all of them by the prior, John Wessington. Wessington was trained primarily as an administrator. While studying at Oxford, he was bursar of Durham College, and he learnt more about business affairs when he

---

[88] Rouse, op. cit., p. 493.
[89] Printed in *Memorials of St Edmund's Abbey*, ed. Thomas Arnold (RS 1890–6, 3 vols), iii. 113–37. For the thirteenth century tracts from Bury St Edmunds see Gransden, *Historical Writing*, i. 385–95. Cf. p. 166 n. 45 above.
[90] Printed in *Memorials of St Edmund's Abbey*, ed. Arnold, iii. 183–8.
[91] Printed in ibid., iii. 188–211.
[92] Printed in ibid., iii. 78–112.
[93] Printed in ibid., iii. 283–7.
[94] Ibid., iii. 188.

served his own monastery as sacrist.[95] A contemporary at Durham listed some of his tracts on a roll with the comment that Prior Wessington 'compiled them not without labour and study, for the perpetual preservation and defence of the rights, liberties and possessions of the church of Durham against the malice and machinations of would-be molesters.'[96]

The majority of the tracts were designed for use in legal proceedings: they were to be studied in private for information, or to be actually read aloud in court. And all were preserved with the cathedral muniments in case of future need. The prior's method was to defend the monastery's rights by tracing the history of whichever was in question and citing precedents. In this way, for example, he defended in one tract the cathedral's right of sanctuary, and in another the prior's archidiaconal jurisdiction over his churches (this tract, the scribe comments, 'would be of value against the archdeacon of Durham').

Sometimes Wessington's appeals to history to justify the priory's claims are inapposite. But sometimes he approached his subject in a scholarly fashion. One tract, the *Jurisdictio Spiritualis* (*Spiritual Jurisdiction*),[97] which, though not in the list of Wessington's works, is undoubtedly by him,[98] shows that Wessington did a considerable amount of sound research not only on literary sources but also on original documents. He combined evidence from Robert de Graystanes's history of Durham with that from documents among the archives of the prior and chapter; he cites an indenture 'with the seals of Archbishop John, Anthony bishop of Durham, Ralph bishop of Carlisle, and the chapter of York',[99] and a certificate of the archdeacon of Northumberland, which had 'many seals'.[100]

The purpose of the *Jurisdictio Spiritualis* was to try to solve the problem whether during a vacancy the see of Durham's spiritual jurisdiction should be administered by the cathedral chapter or by the archbishop. Unlike most of Wessington's tracts, it was not, therefore, primarily contentious, but was intended to establish the truth. Similarly, a monk of St Albans wrote a tract explaining how the abbot of St Albans lost his right to pre-

---

[95] See Emden, *Biographical Register*, iii. 2018 (for further references to modern work on Wessington see p. 392 n. 12 above).

[96] Three copies of the roll are preserved in Durham cathedral library; see Dobson, *Durham Priory 1400–1450*, p. 379 and n. 2. One of the texts is printed in *Historiae Dunelmensis Scriptores Tres*, ed. Raine, pp. cclxviii–cclxxi. See also H. H. E. Craster, 'The Red Book of Durham', p. 515 and n. 2.

[97] Durham Dean and Chapter Archives, Register III, ff. 211–11v. This tract is discussed and printed by Robert Brentano, 'The *Jurisdictio Spiritualis*: an example of fifteenth-century English historiography' in *Speculum*, xxxii (1957), pp. 326–32.

[98] Professor Brentano (op. cit., p. 327) ascribes the work only tentatively to Wessington, but Wessington's authorship is accepted by Professor Dobson (op. cit., p. 386), who takes a less favourable view of the tract than does Professor Brentano.

[99] This indenture with the seals still survives at Durham. See Brentano, op. cit., p. 331 n.g. Cf. ibid., pp. 327–8.

[100] Ibid., p. 331.

cedence in parliament during the reign of Richard II: Abbot John Moote failed to press his claims for a variety of reasons—humility, ignorance, the desire for royal favour (King Richard supported the claims of Westminster), and finally the inability to attend because of illness in old age. And so under Henry IV the abbot of Westminster and the prior of Christ Church, Canterbury, ousted the abbot of St Albans.[101]

To turn now to the two surviving examples of works which equate at least to some extent with the traditional monastic chronicle, that by John Strecche, and the chronicle of Crowland abbey. Virtually nothing is known about the life of John Strecche except that he was a canon of the Augustinian priory of St Mary's, Kenilworth, in the first quarter of the fifteenth century, and had literary interests.[102] He put together a collection of romances and historical pieces which is now Additional MS. 35295 in the British Library. His collectanea includes a history of England; this begins with a brief history from Brutus, and then deals with the period from Anglo-Saxon times until the death of Henry V (folios 228^v-97^v).[103] The history is divided into five books; Strecche's name appears in an acrostic in the initial letters of the chapters of the first three books, as stated in a note on folio 246.[104] His name in an acrostic and his monogram also occur elsewhere in the volume.[105] The early part of the chronicle is derived from the *Brut*, but the section for Strecche's own times is apparently almost entirely independent of known sources, and was written shortly after the events it records took place.

Perhaps of all the monastic chroniclers of the period Strecche was the most influenced by the secular world. His enthusiasm was concentrated on Henry V and the French war. He may well have acquired his distinctive attitude from a rather closer knowledge of king and court than that possessed by most of the religious. Henry was often at Kenilworth: he recuperated in the castle in 1403 after being wounded in the battle of Shrewsbury, [106] and was there again in the spring of 1408;[107] in 1414 he

---

[101] Printed in *Amund.* i. 414–17.

[102] For what is known of Strecche's life and works see Frank Taylor, 'The chronicle of John Strecche for the reign of Henry V (1414–1422)' in *BJRL*, xvi (1932), pp. 137–9.

[103] Strecche's chronicle, BL MS. Additional 35295, has never been printed complete but it is discussed and most of bk v (folios 265–97^v) printed in Taylor, op. cit. (henceforth referred to as *Strecche*), pp. 139–87. An extract from folio 260 is printed in M. V. Clarke and V. H. Galbraith, 'The deposition of Richard II' in *BJRL*, xiv (1930), pp. 163–4, and folios 264^v–5 are printed in *The First English Life of Henry the Fifth*, ed. C. L. Kingsford (Oxford 1911), p. xxviii.

[104] The note is printed in Kingsford, *Hist. Lit.* p. 40 n. 1. Cf. *Strecche*, p. 137 n. 10.

[105] Strecche's name in acrostic appears in two lines of verse on folio 2^v with his monogram above; his monogram is also on folio 6.

[106] BL MS. 35295, f. 263^v. See J. H. Wylie, *History of England under Henry IV* (London 1884–98, 4 vols), i. 362, and J. H. Wylie and W. T. Waugh *The Reign of Henry the Fifth* (Cambridge 1914–29, 3 vols), i. 190 and n. 7.

[107] Wylie, *Henry IV*, iii. 118.

supervised the building of a great hall in the castle to house a meeting of parliament (Strecche gives the exact measurements);[108] in 1416 Henry was at Kenilworth before leaving for his French campaign,[109] and also in 1421 in the course of his itinerary of southern England.[110] The royalist tone of Strecche's chronicle resembles that of Elmham's metrical Life of Henry V, and even foreshadows Capgrave's treatment of Henry VI in his *Liber de Illustribus Henricis*.[111]

Strecche has nothing but praise for Henry V (he does not mention his wild youth). King Henry had the character of Augustus, the wisdom of Solomon, the good looks of Paris, and the loving heart of Troilus.[112] In battle he was as strong as Achilles and fearless as Hector: in command he was far-seeing and invincible.[113] Strecche's patriotism pervades his account of Henry's campaigns in France, sometimes leading to obvious misrepresentation. He tends to exaggerate the odds against the English, and to minimize their losses in contrast to those of the French. At Pont de l'Arche a small English force defeated an army of 50,000, and at Valmont the French, again with vastly superior numbers, lost 2,000 men while not one Englishman was even wounded.[114] Similarly, Strecche makes the serious reverse suffered by the English at Baugé in 1421 appear a minor incident: the duke of Clarence's defeat and death were the result, Strecche asserts, of the treachery of a mercenary whom Clarence had previously alienated by depriving him of booty.[115]

Strecche loves a good story and tells a number, some bordering on the legendary, about the French war; perhaps he heard them from members of Henry's entourage when they were at Kenilworth. Two relate specifically to Henry V. Strecche is the earliest authority for the tennis ball story, which also occurs in Elmham's metrical Life.[116] He recounts that when in 1415 Henry was attempting to negotiate a marriage with Katherine, the French, 'blinded by pride' and on account of the king's youth, told his emissaries that they would send the king tennis balls to play with, and soft pillows on which he could sleep until he grew to manhood. Henry exclaimed angrily:[117]

[108] *Strecche*, p. 147.

[109] *HA*, ii. 317.

[110] *Strecche*, p. 184.

[111] See pp. 206, 389–90 above. There are direct parallels between Strecche's chronicle and Elmham's *Liber Metricus de Henrico Quinto*. Both authors give their names in an acrostic (p. 207); Elmham has a similar acrostic in his history of St Augustine's (p. 347 and n. 21). For other parallels, including the tennis ball story (see below), see *Strecche*, pp. 145 and n. 6 (the death of Sir John Oldcastle), 145 and nn. 9, 11 (the tennis ball story), 155 and nn. 7, 8 (the emperor Sigismund's departure from England).

[112] *Strecche*, p. 187.

[113] *Strecche*, pp. 147, 187.

[114] *Strecche*, pp. 166, 156, respectively. Cf. *Strecche*, pp. 153, 164.

[115] *Strecche*, pp. 142–3, 178–80, 184–5.

[116] *TE*, p. 101.

[117] *Strecche*, pp. 145, 150.

If by God's will I keep in good health, within a few months I shall play a game with the French on their own territory with such balls that they will stop joking, and their mock will turn to moan; and if they sleep too long on their pillows, I shall rouse them one morning from their slumbers sooner than they like.

The other anecdote about Henry, which also has a legendary ring, is less famous. One day during the siege of Louviers the king was standing in the earl of Salisbury's tent next to the central pole, 'having a secret discussion with the earl'. Suddenly a stone thrown by an enemy mangonel struck the pole, shattering it to splinters. By a miracle the king was unhurt, and thanking God he calmly ordered the tent to be re-erected.[118]

Despite Strecche's taste for good stories, his chronicle is a useful source for the French war. He has a number of details not found elsewhere. He gives, for example, the fullest extant account of Henry's itinerary in England in 1421.[119] And he is the only authority for the information that the Londoners gave the king a gun for the siege of Melun, which terrified the citizens into submission. He describes the gun's performance:[120]

As soon as this gun, called the 'London', arrived, the king ordered it to be loaded with powder and a great stone to be placed in its mouth, and [the powder] to be lit. At once the huge stone was hurled against the city, striking and demolishing a row of houses nearly a quarter of mile long; the explosion itself split the gun and almost broke it in pieces.

Strecche's preoccupation with the French war left him little space for anything else. However, like Thomas Elmham, he is venomous on the subject of the Lollards, and gives an account of the execution of Sir John Oldcastle similar to Elmham's.[121] He also shows some interest in the origins of his order and in the foundation of his house. He wrote a tract demonstrating that the order of Augustinian canons was older than that of the Augustinian friars.[122] And he gives a detailed description of the discovery of the tomb of the founder of the priory at Kenilworth, Geoffrey de Clinton, who had been Henry I's chamberlain and treasurer. The canons had undertaken to refurbish the chapel which housed the tombs of the patrons. On removing the wood on the tombs, they found three marble slabs. They lifted up the middle one and beneath they saw Sir Geoffrey's body, 'lying complete in a sweet scented grave'. When the canons had touched the body,

---

[118] *Strecche*, p. 163.
[119] *Strecche*, pp. 143, 184.
[120] *Strecche*, pp. 144, 183.
[121] See pp. 209–10, 406 n. 111 above.
[122] This tract is in the same volume (BL MS. Additional 35295) as his chronicle; *Strecche*, p. 139.

the slab was replaced and adorned with an effigy. Strecche follows this description with verses he had composed in praise of Sir Geoffrey.[123]

Apart from this one entry, Strecche has little on the priory's domestic history. His work is not in fact a typical monastic chronicle. The chronicle of Crowland abbey is nearer to the traditional form. Shortly after the death of Abbot John Littlington in January 1470, the prior composed a continuation to Crowland's official (but forged) chronicle, from 1149 until Abbot John's death.[124] Later the monks added as a second continuation the political memoir for the years from 1459 to 1486 discussed above, into which they interpolated local material.[125] And finally an anonymous monk added a third continuation, which in its extant form covers the years 1485 and 1486 (for this period it supplements the previous continuation), and breaks off incomplete. This last continuation is of minor interest,[126] and it is with the first, the prior's, continuation that we are concerned here.

The tone of the prior's work is, in contrast to Strecche's, pious. His centre of concern is the abbey, and to some extent his interest in general history radiates from this focal point. He cares about the abbey's spiritual prestige: he tells a long story concerning an unrepentant sinner who was eventually persuaded by one of the monks of Crowland to confess his crime, and out of gratitude to God, the Blessed Virgin and St Guthlac, became a regular visitor to the abbey;[127] and he tells how twice the saint's intercession saved the abbey from pillage by marauding armies, in 1461 and 1469, so that it became, as the prior puts it, with a reference to the Book of Genesis (xix. 20), 'another little Zoar'.[128]

The author in common with a number of monastic chroniclers belittles his own achievement. He compares the Crowland chronicle with the image in the Book of Daniel (ii. 33): the 'Ingulf' section is the head of fine gold; the 'Peter of Blois' section is the breast of silver; and his own continuation the feet of iron and clay. He intimates, however, that he might

---

[123] *Strecche*, pp. 159–61. For the foundation of Kenilworth priory by Sir Geoffrey de Clinton see J. C. Dickinson, *The Origins of the Austin Canons and their Introduction into England* (London 1950), pp. 122 and n. 7, 126. For Sir Geoffrey see R. W. Southern, *Medieval Humanism and Other Studies* (Oxford 1970) pp. 214–18.

[124] For the manuscript and printed edition of this and the subsequent continuations see p. 265 n. 109 above.

[125] Pp. 265–74 above.

[126] The third continuator begins with a brief account of political events (he includes, however, a description of the death of Cardinal Henry Beaufort, bishop of Winchester, in 1447, which the author asserts he copied from some narrative by an eyewitness and inserted because of its intrinsic interest, *CC*, p. 582). He then proceeds to concentrate on the abbey's business affairs, transcribing the notarial record of the proceedings relating to the appropriation of Bringhurst (see J. G. Edwards, 'The "second" continuation of the Crowland chronicle: was it written "in ten days"?' in *BIHR*, xxxix (1966), pp. 122–3, and p. 265 and n. 109 above).

[127] *CC*, pp. 536–9.

[128] *CC*, pp. 531, 543. See also pp. 410–11 below.

have done better if he had had more time. The demands of administration and of regular observance prevented him concentrating his slender talents on the work; he had written it at odd moments as occasion offered.[129]

Unlike Strecche, the prior was not fascinated by warfare. Indeed some of his most eloquent passages deplore the sufferings of civil war. Speaking of the breach between Henry VI and Richard duke of York he writes that as a result 'dissension, which is to be detested above all things, broke out, never to be quelled; on the contrary nearly all the great men of the realm were to suffer death.' In civil war, he continues, alluding to the gospels (Matthew x. 21, Mark xiii. 12), brother is divided against brother, father against son; and in England even communities—chapters, colleges and convents—were rent in two, so that 'friend scarcely dared confide in friend, and none could speak his mind without fear of scandal.'[130] The prior describes the slaughter caused by Edward's defeat of Henry VI at Towton in 1461 in graphic terms: 'The blood of the slain mixed with the snow, which covered the land at that time, and when the snow melted it flowed into furrows and ditches over an area of two or three miles in a most gruesome fashion.'[131]

To write his chronicle the prior used, as he acknowledges, reliable informants, his own observation and old, decaying documents.[132] His work is a careful record of the abbey's property transactions and its litigation, comprising documents cited *in extenso* and narrative. He also intended to commemorate the contributions of some of the monks to the abbey's prosperity and to its spiritual and cultural life.[133] The prior's fullest praise is expended on the abbot, John Littlington. He follows the notice of Abbot John's death with a panegyric in verse, and meticulously records his untiring energy in the abbey's service, his business dealings, his struggles in the law courts, his building activities and his gifts to the community.[134] Some of the prior's most vivid prose occurs in this section. He describes, for example, how Abbot John had five bells cast for the church and the accident which happened at the first attempt to hang them:[135]

> So that nothing should remain undone which could contribute to the praise of God, [Abbot John] had five beautiful bells of most harmonious tone cast in London, to replace the three old bells. He himself met the cost which, including the expense of transport to Crowland by land and sea, amounted to £160. While the bells

[129] *CC*, pp. 545–6.
[130] *CC*, pp. 529–30.
[131] *CC*, p. 533.
[132] *CC*, p. 545.
[133] *CC*, p. 536.
[134] *CC*, pp. 534–6, 544–5.
[135] *CC*, pp. 540–1.

were still on the ground before being hung, they were solemnly consecrated by Nicholas bishop of Elphin, then suffragan of our father in Christ, John bishop of Lincoln. They were all inscribed, from smallest to largest, with the names of our patron saints, in whose honour they were so devoutly dedicated, that is of Guthlac, Bartholomew, Michael, Mary and the Holy Trinity. ... The great tower on the western side of the church, in which the bells were to be hung by the skill of the carpenters, had only just been built, and had as yet no roof and no floors. When [the workmen] had built a kind of machine for winding and lifting, they tried by means of pulleys and ropes to fix to the top of the walls a huge beam to support the whole works. After a great struggle the men winding managed to raise the beam nearly fifty feet from the ground, but all at once the machinery, unable to bear the immense weight, began to fail. At the same moment the ropes snapped and the beam crashed to the ground with a terrible noise, shattering everything constructed beneath it.

By a miracle, for which the prior thanks God and St Guthlac, none of the twenty workmen was injured.

Until about 1461 the prior has little on general history, but thereafter he devotes an increasing amount of space to it. His attention may have been drawn to national events partly because the abbey could not remain isolated from them. He mentions a visit from Henry VI in 1460, recording that the king was admitted to confraternity and that he granted a charter of liberties to the vill (the text is cited *verbatim*).[136] The prior also gives a vivid description of Edward IV's visit in 1469 on his way north. The king approached the abbey with 200 horse along the foss, from which all defensive barriers had been removed. He greatly enjoyed the quiet and the kind hospitality of the monks. The next day he went on foot to the west side of the town in order to set out by boat, and expressed great admiration for the stone bridge and houses.[137]

But in 1461 Crowland's contact with the outside world was less pleasant. The prior describes in moving terms the terror of the monks on hearing that the northern army was sweeping south after the Lancastrian victory at Wakefield. It was accompanied by 'an infinite number of paupers and beggars ... who had emerged like mice from their holes'—a crowd over thirty miles wide. This mob 'robbed and pillaged without restraint, regardless of person or place'; it looted churches and indulged in unspeakable crimes—'murdering anyone, including clergy, who resisted, and robbing the rest, even digging up valuables whose whereabouts they discovered by threats of death.' The monks' terror was the greater because their

136 *CC*, p. 530.
137 *CC*, p. 542.

neighbours had brought their treasures to the abbey for safekeeping. They protected themselves as best they could, as the prior describes:[138]

> We collected together our precious vestments and other treasures, and our silver vessels, besides all our charters and muniments, and hid them in the most secret places within the walls. And every day the convent held processions, and each night after matins we poured forth prayers and tears, in the spirit of humility and contrition, with the utmost devotion, at the tomb of our saintly father and protector, Guthlac, to seek divine mercy through his intervention. Moreover, all the gates of the monastery and town, both the watergates and those on dry land, were guarded day and night. And all the open stretches of water in the streams and dikes surrounding the town, by which there could be any sort of access, were strongly defended with stakes and pales, so that none could leave without licence, nor outsiders be admitted. Our causeways and embankments, which had clear open footpaths along them, were blocked—the trees strewn across them were a formidable obstacle to anyone approaching.

By grace of God the marauding enemy passed them by, with a margin of six miles. The monks had a similar scare in 1469, after King Edward's visit; they feared an attack, because they heard that a rumour had reached the earl of Warwick of traitors and treasure hidden at Crowland; but again the monks were spared.[139]

On the Wars of the Roses in general the prior's continuation of the Crowland chronicle has virtually nothing to add to the other sources. It has even been suggested that the prior derived some of his information from the *Brut*.[140] His attitude to politics was typical of most other writers of the period: he had Yorkist sympathies but was tolerant of Henry VI. He considered that Henry was led astray, and power taken from him, by evil men on account of his 'simplicity'.[141] He asserts that the nobles turned from Henry in 1461 because he had abandoned them by going north at the persuasion of Queen Margaret: she had prevailed 'because the king had already for many years suffered from an infirmity of mind on account of an illness which had overtaken him; this mental weakness lasted for a long time, and he was ruler of the kingdom only in name.'[142] The prior approves of Edward IV's (allegedly) courteous treatment of Henry when he captured him in 1465.[143] He welcomes Edward's accession

[138] *CC*, p. 531.
[139] *CC*, p. 543.
[140] Kingsford, *Hist. Lit.* p. 179.
[141] *CC*, p. 521. See pp. 497–8, Appendix G, below.
[142] *CC*, p. 532. See p. 498, Appendix G, below.
[143] *CC*, p. 539.

because of his hereditary right to the throne, which the prior explains at some length, and because he was the right age for fighting (and so could end the anarchy which followed the battle of Wakefield), and well suited to govern.[144]

Of the fairly numerous monastic annals produced in the period from the late fourteenth century to the sixteenth century, probably the best known are: Dieulacres (Cistercian abbey), 1337–1403;[145] Louth Park (Cistercian abbey), Brutus–1413;[146] St Albans, 1422–31;[147] Bermondsey (Cluniac priory, then, 1399, abbey), 1042–1432;[148] the annals of William Glastonbury, monk of Christ Church, Canterbury, 1419–48;[149] Waltham (Augustinian abbey), from the Norman Conquest to 1447;[150] Sherborne (Benedictine abbey), Brutus to 1456;[151] Ely (Benedictine abbey), 1307–1462;[152] St Peter's, Gloucester (Benedictine abbey), from the Creation to 1469;[153] the annals of John Stone, monk of Christ Church, Canterbury, 1415–71;[154] Tewkesbury (Benedictine abbey), to 1471;[155] Bury St Edmunds (Benedictine abbey), 1020–1471;[156] Glastonbury (Benedictine abbey), from its

[144] *CC*, pp. 532–3.
[145] See pp. 159 and n. 7, 186 above. For a chronicle to 1400 from the Cistercian abbey of Kirkstall see pp. 159 and n. 6, 186–7 above, and for one to 1430 from the Cistercian abbey of Whalley p. 159 and n. 8 above.
[146] Printed from 1066, *Chronicon Abbatiae de Parco Ludae: The Chronicle of Louth Park Abbey*, ed. Edmund Venables, with a translation by A. R. Maddison (Lincolnshire Record Soc., Horncastle 1891).
[147] Printed in *Amund.* i. 3–64.
[148] See pp. 390 and n. 2, 391 above.
[149] William Glastonbury's annals are described and extracts printed by C. E. Woodruff; see p. 401 and n. 78 above.
[150] The Waltham annals are mainly derived from the *Brut*. They may also be indebted to the London chronicles. The annals are discussed and those from 1422 printed in Kingsford, *Hist. Lit.* pp. 160–1, 350–4.
[151] Discussed and printed from 1437 in ibid., pp. 158, 346–9.
[152] Printed from 1422 in *Three Fifteenth Century Chronicles*, ed. James Gairdner (Camden Soc., new series, xxviii, 1880), pp. 148–63. To 1459 the annals have little of interest and are mainly derived from a London chronicle. Thereafter they record contemporary news and some are in English. See Kingsford, *Hist. Lit.* p. 161.
[153] Discussed and printed in ibid., pp. 161–2, 355–7. For a chronicle of the abbey's domestic history written in the late fourteenth or early fifteenth century see p. 391 and n. 4 above.
[154] Printed *The Chronicle of John Stone, monk of Christ Church, Canterbury, 1415–1471*, ed. W. G. Searle (Cambridge Antiquarian Soc. 1902).
[155] The original of the Tewkesbury annals is apparently lost. Kingsford prints the annal for 1471 from Stow's *Annales; Kingsford, Hist. Lit.* pp. 376–8 (cf. ibid., p. 179).
[156] St John's College, Oxford, MS. 209. This diminutive volume contains a miscellaneous collection of historical, liturgical and hagiographical material. It was written after 1479; the list of abbots on folio 133[v] records the succession of Thomas Rattlesden (1479–97), with the note 'Christo vivat pius abbas.' The author may have been a monk called Thomas Croftis. This is suggested by a note on folio 35[v]: 'Anno Domini M. cccc. lviij. in festo apostolorum Philippi et Jacobi Thomas Croftis habitum recepit cum aliis tribus.' Much of the contents are extracted from well known sources: the St Albans chronicles; John of Tynemouth's *Historia Aurea;* the lost chronicle of St Benet of Hulme (for a passage on the foundation of St Edmund's abbey and its friendship with St Benet's, see ff. 99[v]–101; cf.

legendary foundation to 1493;[157] Hickling (Augustinian priory), 1297–1503;[158] Thornton (Augustinian priory, then, 1148, abbey), Brutus to 1526;[159] Butley (Augustinian priory), 1509–35;[160] St Augustine's, Canterbury (Benedictine abbey), 1532–7;[161] and Grey Friars, Newgate, London, 1189–1556.[162]

Nearly all these annals contain the traditional mixture of local and general history, but they reflect new historiographical developments: a number, it will be noticed, are continuations of the *Brut*, and one set of annals, those of the Grey friars of Newgate, is a continuation of a version (or versions) of the London chronicle which it also used throughout the fifteenth century and perhaps later; and both the Grey friars' annals and those of St Augustine's are in English. The later entries in most of the annals were written contemporarily with events they record. (The annals of Bermondsey and Thornton, are exceptions; they were composed after the date of their last entries, and have been discussed already, as examples of antiquarianism.)[163] Many, however, are very brief and only three seem distinguished enough to merit separate discussion. They are the annals of John Stone, the annals of Butley priory in Suffolk, and those of Grey Friars, Newgate. These three works are of particular interest because they throw light on religious history. John Stone gives a picture of the state of monasticism in a great Benedictine foundation in the fifteenth century; the Butley annalist depicts life in a less important house on the eve of the reformation.[164] And the Grey friars' annals, which bridge the reformation, give some idea of the impression made by the religious changes on at least one individual.

A. Gransden, 'The "Cronica Buriensis" and the abbey of St Benet of Hulme' in *BIHR*, xxxvi (1963), p. 78); and the chronicle of Bury St Edmunds (ed. A. Gransden, Nelson's Medieval Texts 1964). Extracts from the annals from 1263 to 1471, which derive from no known source, and other material are printed in *Memorials of St Edmund's Abbey*, ed. Thomas Arnold (RS 1890–6, 3 vols), iii. 291–300. Other narrative passages which are apparently original and unprinted may be noted: an account of Abbot Anselm (1121–48), ff. 33ᵛ–35ᵛ; an account of Abbot Robert de Ixworth (1469–74), ff. 94–95ᵛ; two passages on John of Gaunt's friendship with the abbey, ff. 97–99.

[157] See pp. 399 and n. 60, 400 above.

[158] Discussed and printed *Chronica Johannis de Oxenedes*, ed. Henry Ellis (RS 1859), pp. xxxvi–xxxviii, 437–9.

[159] See p. 392 and n. 8 above.

[160] Printed *The Register or Chronicle of Butley Priory, Suffolk, 1510–1535*, ed. A. G. Dickens (Winchester 1951). (For the editor's introduction see *But.* pp. 1–23). See pp. 417–21 below.

[161] Printed *Chronicle of the Years 1532–1537, written by a Monk of St. Augustine's, Canterbury* in *Narratives of the Days of the Reformation*, ed. J. G. Nichols (Camden Soc., original series, lxxvii, 1859), pp. 279–86. See n. 164 below.

[162] Printed *Chronicon ab anno 1189 ad 1556, ex Registro Fratrum Minorum Londoniae* in *Monumenta Franciscana*, ed. Richard Howlett (RS 1882, 2 vols), ii. 143–260. This is the edition used here. An earlier edition is by J. G. Nichols (Camden Soc., original series, liii, 1852). See pp. 421–4 below.

[163] Pp. 390–1, 392 above.

[164] The annals of St Augustine's (see above and n. 161) have a similar interest for the five years they cover.

John Stone, who came from the village of Stone on the island of Oxney,[165] records the outlines of his career in his chronicle. He professed as a monk of Christ Church on 13 December 1418.[166] In 1451 he, then refectorar, was present at the blessing of bells;[167] in 1452 he was promoted to sit at the first table;[168] in 1457 he was subsacrist and *magister ordinis* (the official in charge of discipline);[169] in 1461 he was third prior, and was, therefore, on one occasion in the subprior's absence responsible for appointing a new keeper of St Thomas Becket's tomb;[170] and in 1467 the prior made him 'head of the choir'.[171] Stone also records two occasions when he was concerned with the cathedral's relics: in 1448 he helped move the relics of St Feologild, archbishop of Canterbury (in 832), from the shrine at the high altar to a reliquary 'placed on a beam between the tomb and *corona* of St Thomas',[172] and in 1457 he received a bone of the arm of St Osmund from two of the monks who had attended the translation of the saint at Salisbury.[173]

John Stone notes that he wrote his chronicle in 1467.[174] It is likely that he added the entries for the last three years, until the end in 1471, contemporaneously with events. He used various written sources—he mentions registers,[175] ordinances of the prior and chapter,[176] letters[177] and a martyrology.[178] He must also have used oral information and his own observation. His use of the latter is particularly apparent in the annals for the last ten years. He must surely have written some of the exact details from personal observation. For example, the snow in the spring of 1460 was the worst anyone could remember;[179] again on Christmas day, 1465, the snow was so bad that the monks could not go in procession through the cloisters, but instead had to reach St Thomas's shrine by way of 'le hake' (praise God, a thaw began on 10 February);[180] in 1466 wind and rain prevented the monks from attending a burial in the cemetery.[181] And in January 1468 the crypt was flooded for four weeks, right up to the tomb

---

[165] His chronicle has a reference to a fire which burnt the church and houses at Stone in 1463; *JS*, p. 89.
[166] *JS*, p. 5.
[167] *JS*, p. 51.
[168] *JS*, p. 56.
[169] *JS*, p. 71.
[170] *JS*, p. 84.
[171] *JS*, p. 107.
[172] *JS*, p. 44.
[173] *JS*, p. 71. St Osmund was canonized by Calixtus III on 1 January 1457.
[174] *JS*, p. 3. For another reference to Stone's authorship see *JS*, p. 107.
[175] See *JS*, p. 32.
[176] *JS*, p. 98.
[177] See p. 417 and nn. 193, 194 below.
[178] *JS*, p. 97.
[179] *JS*, p. 78.
[180] *JS*, pp. 90–1.
[181] *JS*, p. 96.

of St Thomas, so that the convent could not process there and instead passed by the statue of the Blessed Virgin near the dormitory, between the altars of St Martin and St Stephen; however, candles were kept alight in the crypt during the procession, and the convent stood there after second vespers on the vigil of the Purification and on the feast itself.[182]

The facts of John Stone's career make it evident that his concern was with the liturgical life of the cathedral, not with the abbey's administration of its estates and dealings with outsiders. Indeed, his chronicle is an unusual record of the routine of the monastic observance, a routine varied by funerals and enlivened by the visits of the great. Although it bears some similarity with the annals of Butley, its closest parallel is another work from Christ Church, the annals of William Glastonbury, who (as William himself notes in the entry for 1438) held the office of fourth prior.[183] His choice of subject matter is more or less identical with Stone's, and the period he covers corresponds with the first half of Stone's annals. However, there is little duplication because Stone wrote fairly briefly at the beginning, progressively increasing the detail as he neared the time of writing; William Glastonbury supplements Stone's narrative by including some events which Stone does not mention, and by giving more information about others.

John Stone records the community's liturgical life with meticulous care, expressing no emotion stronger than mild surprise (for example at the novel decision of the archbishop of York to carry his cross erect within the metropolitan see of Canterbury).[184] He has entries on the enthronement of the archbishops, the appointment of the priors, the reception of novices, the profession of monks, the conferment of orders, the blessing of holy oil and vestments (specified in one instance as 'the blue ones with embroidered griffins'),[185] always giving the date and often noting what vestments were worn, what respond sung, who preached the sermon and on what theme, and so on.

Obits, mostly of monks but a few of laymen, occupy a large part of the annals; in fact Stone may have begun his annals in order to commemorate the dead.[186] A typical obit reads:[187]

> In the year of the Lord 1457 on the fourth Sunday in Lent, at lunchtime in the twelfth hour, died Brother Walter Broke, a professed monk of the church of Christ at Canterbury; and he lay in the choir throughout the night, and had fifty psalms; [he died] in the twenty fifth year of his monkhood.

[182] *JS*, p. 102.
[183] *WG*, pp. 130–1.
[184] *JS*, p. 109.
[185] *JS*, p. 47.
[186] The early entries in the annals are all of obits; *JS*, pp. 7–17.
[187] *JS*, p. 66.

Occasionally a biographical note is added, especially if the monk were important,[188] or his life was marked by some unusual circumstance— there was, for example, Brother Nicholas 'Winchelsey who 'had been born at sea sailing to France.'[189] These obits assume a more than local interest when they are of victims of the plague (who died 'ex vehementi pestilencia' as Stone puts it). They indicate that the community suffered severe epidemics in 1457 and 1471.[190] On each occasion the monks held a procession carrying the relics of St Ouen in order to end the epidemic: in 1471 Stone records that each monk was given a candle at mass which he could offer wherever he chose, and that in this instance the measures were effective.

Visitors are John Stone's other main preoccupation. He notes innumerable visits (and some gifts) from a variety of people. Many came primarily as pilgrims; Stone mentions both ecclesiastics and monks—among them the archbishop of York, the cardinal bishop of Winchester, the bishops of Ely and Chichester, the abbots of Evesham, Hyde, Gloucester, Abingdon and Ramsey, and the abbess of Shaftesbury. Others came because Canterbury was on the road from London to the channel port of Sandwich. Stone records visits from papal legates and ambassadors (both of the king of England and of the king of France), who were engaged in peace negotiations. But he pays most attention to visits by royalty. First Henry VI and then Edward IV and their queens were frequent visitors. Stone describes with brevity but with meticulous details how they were received, and how they spent their time, in so far as they were occupied with religious observances. For example, King Henry arrived on 2 August 1460. He was received at the gate by the archbishop and the prior and convent wearing green copes and singing the respond 'Summe Trinitati'. On the same day he attended vespers, and on the next day joined the monks' procession (the convent was not vested); and he watched the novices take communion on both Sundays of his stay. On 8 August he was again in the monks' procession, and on 14 August was at vespers, in the procession, and at mass, not wearing his crown. He left for London on 18 August.[191]

Although these numerous visits by important people gave John Stone the opportunity of obtaining news of the outside world, he made little use of it. It is true that he notices the main battles of the Wars of the Roses, but he does so only briefly; he is slightly fuller on the battle of Northampton which the archbishop watched from the top of a hill, and gives the exact location of the battlefield.[192] But otherwise his record of national events tends to be incidental to his local interests. He describes the services of

---

[188] *JS*, pp. 71, 115.
[189] *JS*, p. 117.
[190] *JS*, pp. 67–70, 115–17. For the death of a monk from plague in 1465 see *JS*, p. 92.
[191] *JS*, p. 81.
[192] *JS*, p. 80. For notices of other battles see *JS*, pp. 64 (St Albans I), 83 (Towton), 115–16 (Barnet), 116 (Tewkesbury).

thanksgiving which followed the reception of a letter from Henry VI announcing the birth of his son Edward in 1453,[193] and of one from Edward IV announcing King Henry's capture in 1465.[194] He mentions that Henry held a council in the prior's chapel in 1451[195] and that Edward held one in the prior's house of Master Homer in 1470 (for each he gives the exact dates and a list of those present).[196] And he notes the itinerary of the earl of Warwick as he passed to and fro through Canterbury when engaged on negotiations with the French in the summer of 1467.[197]

Clearly Stone was not much concerned about general history, and it was not his primary purpose to record it. He wrote to commemorate those who had contributed to the religious life of the cathedral. He may also have intended his annals to serve as a precedent book of liturgical observance, at least for himself.[198] Whether he meant his work to be useful to others is hard to say. There is no direct evidence that it was an official production; in fact like the annals of William Glastonbury it resembles a diary, even a common-place book, intended for private use. In this respect it differs from the annals of Butley priory which were almost certainly written as an official record.

The annals of Butley only survive in an eighteenth century transcript which is obviously not complete.[199] Exactly what the copyist omitted is unknown, but it is clear that the annals once had copies of more documents than are to be found in the present text. This is indicated by the fact that they have references to documents, copies of which are not now included.[200] Indeed, the work must in its original form have been more like a register than it is in the extant text. The author himself calls it a register.[201] The identity of the author is unknown, but the modern editor suggests that he was the subprior, William Woodbridge (1504–32) who, as an entry testifies, copied one of the documents into the work.[202] If he were the author, it is necessary to accept a break in authorship on his death in 1532; a more abrupt style and an increase in carelessness could indicate that the entries for the last three years were not by the original author.[203]

The annals begin in 1509, the year of the succession of Prior Alexander

---

[193] *JS*, p. 87.
[194] *JS*, pp. 93–4.
[195] *JS*, p. 52.
[196] *JS*, pp. 113–14. For the prior's house of Master Homer, which was within the precincts, see R. A. L. Smith, *Canterbury Cathedral Priory* (Cambridge 1943), pp. 69 n. 7,200 n. 2.
[197] *JS*, pp. 99–101 passim.
[198] See for example the descriptions of the enthroning of archbishops which refer to the precedent of previous enthronizations; *JS*, pp. 55–6, 64.
[199] The manuscript (Bodleian Library MS. Tanner XC, ff. 24–67) and its probable relationship to the original text are fully discussed in *But*. pp. 2–5.
[200] See *But*. pp. 4, 57, 58.
[201] *But*. p. 58 (cf. *But*. p. 4).
[202] *But*. pp. 5–7, 27.
[203] *But*. p. 6.

Rivers. The fact that they give full coverage to his priorate suggests the possibility that he commissioned them.[204] The author used the priory's archives and probably obtained some of his information directly from the prior. For example, his account of the funeral of Thomas duke of Norfolk at Thetford in 1524 could well have been derived from Rivers, who read the epistle on that occasion.[205] Similarly, Rivers's successor, Prior Thomas Sudbourne, may have told him about the burial of Mary Tudor (widow of Louis of France and duchess of Suffolk) at Bury St Edmunds in 1533, which he attended.[206] Clearly the annalist made considerable use of oral information.[207] He no doubt relied on his own observation for the priory's domestic affairs.

Alexander Rivers, who took over after the suicide of his predecessor, Robert Brommer, was a fairly successful prior. Both the annals themselves and the records of four visitations held by Richard Nix, bishop of Norwich, and his commissaries in 1514, 1520, 1526 and 1532, indicate that the priory was reasonably prosperous and well ordered.[208] Nevertheless, without a doubt life in a moderate sized house with little tradition was more humdrum, less rigidly institutionalized, than in a great cathedral like Christ Church. Therefore, it is not surprising that the author was less preoccupied with ritual and more outward looking and self expressive than was John Stone.

The Butley annalist appears to have been pious and rather naive. He thinks ill of Robert Brommer ('who miserably killed himself')[209] and of one of the canons, Thomas Orford, 'an elegant person', who travelled westward accompanied by another canon, a disreputable fellow previously imprisoned at Melford for theft, to seek his fortune in the form of a rich preferment.[210] And the annalist approves of the abbot of Leiston, who left his house in order to become an anchorite.[211] He is consistently loyal to Henry VIII despite his government's ecclesiastical policy.[212] He loves resounding titles and epithets: Henry is 'the most serene king, the most faithful defender of the faith, and most serene suppressor and destroyer of heretics and all other malefactors';[213] Charles V 'the most illustrious and fear inspiring emperor, and time honoured Augustus';[214] Mary

[204] This suggestion is made by the editor; *But.* p. 7.
[205] *But*, p. 44.
[206] *But.* p. 60 and n. 8.
[207] The author uses the phrases 'quidam dicit' (*But.* p. 29), 'ut dicitur' (*But.* p. 48), 'ut aiunt' (*But.* pp. 41, 54, 59), and 'ut fertur' (p. 48). See also p. 420 and n. 230 below. Sometimes he admits his ignorance (e.g. pp. 51, 69).
[208] *But.* pp. 8–17.
[209] *But.* p. 25.
[210] *But.* pp. 10, 49–50.
[211] *But.* p. 59 and n. 5.
[212] *But.* p. 20.
[213] *But.* p. 58 (cf. *But.* p. 20).
[214] *But.* p. 40.

[418]

Tudor 'the most excellent Lady Mary, queen of France, most beautiful sister of our invincible King Henry VIII, and most beloved wife of that very renowned warrior Charles Brandon, duke of Suffolk';[215] and even Wolsey has his string of titles and eulogistic epithets.[216]

The annalist took a simple delight in the visits of the great. Butley was visited by the duke of Norfolk and, most frequently, by Mary Tudor. In some respects the author's descriptions of such visits resemble John Stone's. He relates, for example, exactly how Lady Mary was received in 1516. She was met by the prior and convent in silk copes, sprinkled with holy water, censed, and received the kiss of peace, and the antiphon 'Regina coeli' was sung at the high altar. Lady Mary then knelt on two silk cushions placed before a bench draped with a silk pall, and gave one golden noble, and the 'Te Deum' was sung. Next day she attended mass and gave another golden noble.[217] The Butley annalist also likes to give the precise itineraries of visitors just as John Stone had done. Thus he records that Lady Mary arrived with her husband, Charles, duke of Suffolk, on 12 July 1527 and stayed until 22 August. On 17 July they rode to Benhall and Letheringham to hunt, returning on 18 July. On 22 July the duke left to join the royal court, and on 15 August Lady Mary rode to Sir John Glemham's and stayed overnight.[218]

However, some of the Butley writer's descriptions have a human touch absent from John Stone's. He tells how Lady Mary during her visit in 1527 often had supper out of doors, in the garden 'to the east of the chapter house', in the prior's garden, and in 'Brother Nicholas's garden on the north side of the church'; on one occasion it started raining so she was obliged to finish her meal in the church.[219] Another time, in September 1528, she and the duke went hunting in Staverton Park, and had a 'merry picnic under the oak trees with good jokes and jolly games'.[220] The prior himself liked to join such hunting expeditions,[221] and apparently the annalist saw no objection to prolonged visits by the nobility (he records without comment a stay of nearly eight months by the duke of Suffolk's chaplains and nine choir boys, at the prior's expense).[222]

The Butley annalist gives one description of a funeral (the duke of Norfolk's),[223] which bears comparison with John Stone's funeral accounts, but unlike Stone, he is more interested in the exact location of a burial place than in the liturgical minutiae of the service. He records, for instance,

---

[215] *But.* p. 33.
[216] See e.g. *But.* pp. 39, 42, 58.
[217] *But.* p. 33.
[218] *But.* pp. 51–2.
[219] *But.* p. 52.
[220] *But.* p. 54.
[221] See the account of Thomas duke of Norfolk's visit in 1525; *But.* p. 50.
[222] *But.* p. 68.
[223] *But.* p. 44.

that William Lord Willoughby was buried in a chapel in Mettingham castle, in front of the high altar, the tomb of one of his relatives having been moved to leave room.[224] The annalist's almost antiquarian interest in buildings and their contents appears in his careful record of the buildings erected under Prior Rivers, which included 'a new kitchen with three fireplaces in one chimney, two ovens and boilers, ... built at great expense by the prior'.[225] He also mentions church furnishings, the making of a crucifix,[226] the painting of statues[227] and the construction of two organs, one with two stops, the other with five and 'a good tone'.[228]

But the annalist's interests were by no means confined to his own house. He gave whatever news he could of national events—and even had interests further afield, noting the capture of Rhodes by the Turks.[229] He had some knowledge of the war in France, but was better informed about the naval battles off the south east coast, probably obtaining his information from Suffolk sailors.[230] However, he is of most value to the present day historian for his account of the ecclesiastical history of East Anglia.[231] He records the dissolution by Wolsey of a number of small houses in 1524 and 1527,[232] and is the only authority for an outbreak of iconoclasm in Ipswich, Bury St Edmunds 'and elsewhere' ('wicked men cut the heads and arms from statues of the Blessed Mary ... ').[233]

More important than the facts the annalist records is the state of mind he betrays. Writing of Wolsey's dissolution of religious houses, he exclaims that it was 'to the scandal, dissipation and ruin not only of our religion but also of monks and nuns'.[234] However, his worst forebodings came later. Under 1534 he notes without comment that all swore to the act of succession, and cites the letters patent ordering this to be done (he gives three texts, one in Latin and two in English).[235] He also records that 'Convocation made the king the supreme head of the church of England, and this was afterwards confirmed by parliament', again with no comment.[236] But under 1535 he bursts out:[237]

> In this year there were terrible winds and torrential rain with
> thunder and lightning, especially in the summer, and every month

---

[224] *But.* pp. 50–1. See also the account of the successive burial places of Prior Robert Brommer; *But.* pp. 25–6. Cf. *But.* p. 60.
[225] *But.* p. 35. See also *But.* pp. 28, 49, 58.
[226] *But.* p. 47.
[227] *But.* p. 59.
[228] *But.* pp. 28, 66.
[229] *But.* p. 40.
[230] For information perhaps acquired by word of mouth from sailors see *But.* pp. 33, 49.
[231] See *But.* p. 21.
[232] *But.* pp. 46–7, 58.
[233] *But.* p. 60.
[234] *But.* p. 47.
[235] *But.* pp. 61–5.
[236] *But.* p. 66.
[237] *But.* p. 67. Cf. *But.* p. 60.

people suddenly died of languor; charity froze, love and devotion stagnated, and false opinions and heresy rose against the holy sacraments.

And so after a few more desultory entries, the Butley annalist ends.

The annalist of Grey Friars, Newgate, London, wrote during the period when events gave substance to the Butley writer's forebodings. The Grey friars' annals were started in the late fifteenth century. The author copied a version of the London chronicle from 1189, which had an ecclesiastical bias and a few entries relating to the Franciscan order (which, however, the author himself may have added to his exemplar's text). The manuscript is a fair copy until early in Henry VIII's reign:[238] then there are numerous changes of ink, corrections, blanks left for names, and marginal additions; it is impossible to be certain where and how often the handwriting changes. The fair copy may have been the work of a friar called Andrew Bavard. It is in a volume containing a number of other items, mostly relating to Grey Friars, Newgate, and many of historical content (there is, for example, a list of the tombs in Grey Friars' church, and a copy of Thomas Eccleston's chronicle).[239] Included is a note dated 1494 in the same hand which wrote the annals until the early sixteenth century, stating that he, Andrew Bavard, a professor of theology, seeing that the church had few choir books, had had some (which are specified) copied for it. It seems likely, therefore, that Bavard was the compiler of the chronicle as far as the early sixteenth century. However, who wrote the annals from the date when Bavard's text ended is unknown, though clearly the author was an inmate of Grey Friars. From the 1520s the entries were probably made fairly contemporarily with the events they record.

The Grey friars' annals are in many respects a typical London chronicle. They reflect the gaiety of London life with its celebrations—the processions and pageants, the bonfires and bunting. They also reflect its grimness, the sequence of executions, death by beheading, death by hanging (with drawing and quartering), death by burning and even, in the case of poisoners, by boiling (a cook was boiled in a cauldron for planning to poison the bishop of Rochester and his servants—he 'was locked in a chain and pulled up and down with a gibbet at divers times till he was dead'):[240] Grey Friars' proximity to Newgate prison provided abundant material for the annalist's interest in such matters.

---

[238] BL MS. Cotton Vitellius F XII. See Plate XIV. For a brief description see *GFC*, pp. li-lii, and C. L. Kingsford, *The Grey Friars of London* (Aberdeen 1915), pp. 1–2.

[239] Nichols and Howlett tentatively suggest that the volume was compiled by Brother Andrew Bavard (d. 1508), guardian of the friary 1498–1508, who promoted learning in the convent; see *Chronicle of the Grey Friars of London*, ed. Nichols, pp. xxxiii–xxxiv, and *GFC*, pp. lii-liii. Kingsford, however, treats the compilation as the work of an anonymous friar; Kingsford, *Grey Friars of London*, pp. 1–2 (for Bavard see ibid., pp. 23, 60, 107, 171).

[240] *GFC*, p. 194. Cf. ibid., p. 204.

Detailed references to the friary itself begin in the reign of Henry VIII. Under 1522 the annalist, having recorded the execution of Lady Agnes Hungerford at Tyburn, notes that she was buried at Grey Friars 'in the nether end of the midd[le] of the church on the north side'.[241] Under 1525 he records that one of the Observant friars of Greenwich, who fled from an episcopal visitation, was imprisoned at Grey Friars before he submitted, and also that when 'the king came out of his chamber to come to Grey Friars, tiding was brought to him that the king of France was taken by the duke of Burgundy.'[242] And under 1534 and 1537 the annalist notes, with details, the burial in Grey Friars of some of the victims of public executions.[243]

The friary was dissolved in 1538. The annals do not record this event, but there is no break in style or handwriting (see Plate XIV above) to suggest a change of authorship. Nor does interest in Grey Friars, though now without a community, lessen. The annalist records that in 1545 the large quantity of wine looted from French ships was 'laid in the church sometime the Grey Friars, all the church [being] full in every place of it', and that later in the same year the steeple was taken down.[244] Under 1547 it is noticed that the church was reopened; 'mass [was] said at the altars with divers priests, and it was named Christ Church of the foundation of King Henry the VIIIth.'[245] But immediately after Edward VI's accession 'all the tombs, great stones, all the altars, with the stalls and walls of the choir' were dismantled and sold, and the church made smaller.[246] And then in 1552, the annals note, 'children were put in the house that was sometime the Grey Friars.'[247] Thus was founded the school for fatherless and poor men's children, Christ's Hospital.

It seems likely, therefore, that the annals were continued after the dissolution by a former friar of the house. The annals also suggest that he found employment in St Paul's. As they proceed they are increasingly preoccupied with the affairs of St Paul's, often giving specific details. Many entries relate to the religious changes, notably the reforms of Edward VI's reign—for example, the removal of images and rood screen (two labourers were killed and many others injured at the task), the

---

[241] Ibid. p. 189. Lady Alice Hungerford's grave is included in the list of monuments in Grey Friars in Vitellius F. XII, f. 295ᵛ. Cf. Stow's copy of this list; *A Survey of London by John Stow*, ed. C. L. Kingsford (Oxford 1908, 2 vols), i. 322 (for the shortcomings of Stow's copy see ibid., ii. 345).

[242] *GFC*, p. 190.

[243] *GFC*, pp. 197, 201.

[244] *GFC*, pp. 208, 209. See *Survey of London*, ed. Kingsford, i. 318. For his account of Grey Friars Stow made some use of Vitellius F XII; see n. 241 above.

[245] *GFC*, p. 213. See *Survey of London*, ed. Kingsford, i. 318–19, and *Letters and Papers, Foreign and Domestic, of the Reign of Henry VIII, 1546–1547*, nos 698, 771 (14).

[246] *GFC*, p. 215.

[247] *GFC*, p. 238. A fuller account is in *Survey of London*, ed. Kingsford, i. 319.

blocking of the grates beside the high altar, so that 'the people should not look in at the time of the communion', and the first use of the 'book of the new service of bread and wine' (on which occasion the bishop preached 'in a rochet and nothing else on him').[248]

Some of the entries relate to more worldly aspects of life in St Paul's. Under 1548 the annalist notes that there was 'much controversy and much business in Paul's every Sunday, and sitting in the church, and of none that were honest persons, but boys and persons of little reputation; and would have been much more if they had not away been taken.'[249] Under 1551 he mentions the 'many [af]frays in Paul's church and nothing said on to them; and one man fell down in Paul's church and broke his neck for catching of pigeons in the night the fourth day of December.'[250] And he records that on Sunday, 10 June 1553 'was a gun shot near Paul's churchyard [so] that the pellet came near the preacher's face that preached at Paul's Cross.'[251]

The annalist does not write down his reflections on the political and religious changes through which he lived. He makes no comment, for example, on the execution either of Sir Thomas More or of Anne Boleyn.[252] But, though he does little more than record the facts, there can be no doubt where his sympathies lay; they were, predictably, with the old order. This is apparent in his account, for instance, of the disgrace and subsequent reinstatement of Edmund Bonner, bishop of London. Recording Bonner's imprisonment in 1550 he writes:[253]

> Item, of the great gentleness that was showed unto the bishop of London E[dmund] Bonner, being prisoner in the marshalsea; the 8th day of January of the knight marshal taking away his bed ... so that he had no more to lie in but the straw and a cover-let for the space of eight days, for because he would not give the knight marshal £10 or a gown of that price.

And he describes the public rejoicing at Bonner's release in 1553:[254]

> [and the 5th day] of August at 7 o'clock at night came home Edmund Bonner, bishop, from the marshalsea, like a bishop, that all the people by the way bade him welcome home ... and as many of the women as might kissed him; and so [he] came to Paul's and knelt on the steps and said his prayers; then the people rang the bells for joy.

---

[248] GFC, pp. 215, 230, 238, respectively. Cf. VCH, London, i. 429 n. 438.
[249] GFC, p. 217. For the secular use of St Paul's see Survey of London, ed. Kingsford, i. 225, 335; ii. 316, 349, 361.
[250] GFC, p. 229.
[251] GFC, p. 252.
[252] GFC, pp. 197, 198.
[253] GFC, p. 226.
[254] GFC, p. 244.

The annalist regarded the accession of Mary as the beginning of a new era. At St Paul's the choir sang the 'Te Deum', 'with organs going, with the bells ringing'.[255] He describes in detail the queen's reception when she visited St Paul's, the grand pageant put on in her honour. A man stood on a castle constructed above the steeple holding a flag with 'eight flags hanging beside', and in the church was a pageant 'made of rosemary with all her arms and a crown in the midst', which she stood looking at for a a long time.[256] But soon the record of the execution of traitors and the burning of heretics starts again, and the annals end in 1556 on a sombre note: 'Item, the 5th day of September was brought through Cheapside tied in ropes twenty four tied together as heretics, and so unto the Lollards' tower.'[257]

Because of the Grey friars' annals it could perhaps be argued that the tradition of the monastic chronicle survived the reformation. However, such a view would be misleading. The Grey friars' annals must be regarded as exceptional, and were, moreover, virtually a London chronicle. The conclusion cannot be avoided that the chronicle tradition of the religious houses was all but dead well before the end of the fifteenth century.

[255] *GFC*, p. 242.
[256] *GFC*, pp. 246–7.
[257] *GFC*, p. 260.

14

The Humanist Historians: Thomas More and Polydore Vergil

Sir Thomas More's *History of King Richard III*[1] and Polydore Vergil's *Anglica Historia (English History)*[2] are the only two humanist histories written in England. The term 'humanist' presents problems. Perhaps the most distinctive feature of the humanists was that they regarded themselves as humanists, and were so regarded by others. In addition they belonged to an international group drawing its principal inspiration from Italy. Contemporary rulers, noblemen and ecclesiastics recognized their identity, and often employed them as *littérateurs* in their courts. Indeed there was such a demand that many Italian and some French humanists found employment with patrons abroad.

The term 'humanism' has been variously defined,[3] but it can be regarded as the literary aspect of the fifteenth and sixteenth century renaissance. Humanist literature was based on the study of classical works, both Latin and Greek. Latin literature had of course been much studied in the middle

[1] The standard edition of the English and Latin texts is in *The Yale Edition of the Complete Works of St Thomas More*, ii. ed. R. S. Sylvester (New Haven-London 1963). A short edition of the English version with modern spelling, together with a selection of More's English poems, and Latin poems in the English prose translation by Leicester Bradner and C. A. Lynch (*The Latin Epigrams of Thomas More* (Chicago 1953)), is *St Thomas More: The History of King Richard III and Selections from the English and Latin Poems*, ed. R. S. Sylvester (New Haven-London 1976).

[2] No complete modern edition of the *Anglica Historia* exists. For the first three sixteenth century editions, published at Basle in 1534, 1546 and 1555, all during Vergil's lifetime (the first two with the text to 1509 and the third to 1537), see pp. 432–3. An edition of the last part of the text, which relates to the Tudors, is *The Anglica Historia of Polydore Vergil A.D. 1485–1537*, ed., with an English translation, Denys Hay (Camden Soc., new series, lxxiv, 1950). Professor Hay prints the text to 1513 from the earliest recension in the Vatican MSS. (see pp. 431–2 and n. 49 below), with full collation with the first three printed editions. He prints the continuation, 1513–37, from the Basle edition of 1555. Part of a mid-sixteenth century English translation of the 1546 edition which reaches to 1485 (see *AH*, ed. Hay, p. xvii) is published *Polydore Vergil's English History*, ed. Henry Ellis (Camden Soc., original series, xxix (1844), xxxvi (1846), 2 vols); vol. i covers bks XXIII–XXV, and vol. ii bks I–VIII.

[3] For a useful discussion of the term see P. O. Kristeller, *The Classics and Renaissance Thought* (Cambridge, Mass., 1955; reprinted as *Renaissance Thought*, Harper Torchbook, New York 1961), pp. 3–23.

ages, but during the renaissance it assumed a more dominant role. Owing to development in the book-trade, in part made possible by the invention of printing, those classical works already known in the middle ages were more widely disseminated, while others previously partially or totally unknown were now studied in full or for the first time. The study of Greek literature was virtually an innovation. The attitudes of the humanists tended to differ from those of their medieval predecessors: they studied the classics from the secular rather than the theological point of view, and Man rather than God increasingly absorbed their attention.[4]

Among the classical works to which renaissance scholars turned their attention were those of the historians. Lorenzo Valla emended the text of Livy. In 1452 he completed a Latin translation of Thucydides, and he then translated Herodotus.[5] By the early sixteenth century the standard classical histories were all available in print. Caesar was printed in Rome in 1469, and Livy probably in the same year.[6] In 1470 the first editions of Sallust[7] and Suetonius[8] were printed in Rome. In 1502 the Aldine press in Venice published editions of Herodotus and Thucydides.[9] Tacitus' works, except the *Agricola* and part of the *Annales*, were printed in Venice in about 1470, and the *Agricola* was printed, perhaps in Milan, in about 1482. The full text of the *Annales* was not known until the early sixteenth century when Books I–VI were discovered: a complete edition of Tacitus' works was printed in Rome in 1515.[10]

The effects of humanism in general, and of the study of the classical historians in particular, on historical writing were complex and various.[11] There was no abrupt break with the medieval tradition which itself had developed under the influence of Latin classical literature. The humanists accepted past views and methods, contributing their own predilections. The movement must not be seen as a revolution but as an acceleration of existing trends combined with a gradual shift of emphasis. Its influence is apparent in the style and structure of historical works, and also in their content.

[4] Cf. p. 469 below.
[5] See J. E. Sandys, *A History of Classical Scholarship* (Cambridge 1906–8, 3 vols), ii. 69.
[6] Ibid., ii. 73, 97, 103.
[7] Ibid., ii. 103.
[8] Ibid., ii. 73, 97, 103.
[9] Ibid., ii. 98, 104.
[10] Ibid., 103, 108, and *R III*, pp. lxxxix-xc.
[11] This subject is discussed in detail in its various aspects, with illustrative extracts, in Peter Burke, *The Renaissance Sense of the Past* (London 1969). A useful short survey, arranged under countries and authors is B. R. Reynolds, 'Latin historiography: a survey, 1400–1600' in *Studies in the Renaissance*, ii (New York 1955), pp. 7–66. See also Herbert Weisinger, 'Ideas of history during the Renaissance' in *Journal of the History of Ideas*, vi (1945), pp. 415–35 (reprinted in *Renaissance Essays*, ed. P. O. Kristeller and P. P. Wiener (Harper Torchbook, New York 1968), pp. 74–94), and J. R. Hale, *The Evolution of British Historiography* (London-Melbourne 1967), pp. 9–11.

With regard to style, humanism fostered the medieval rhetorical tradition. Rhetoric was a necessary part of medieval education,[12] and a number of chroniclers had tried to write in elegant Latin, with rhetorical set speeches.[13] During the renaissance this style was developed on the model of antique writers, especially of Cicero.[14] Some writers concentrated almost exclusively on the stylistic aspect of humanist historiography. In England it was typified by the visiting Italian Titus Livius, and by the Pseudo-Elmham in their biographies of Henry V,[15] and by John Whethamsted.[16] With regard to structure, humanism encouraged the composition of history in literary form; a work should have a sustained theme. Titus Livius achieved this in his Life of Henry V. However, it should be borne in mind that a non-humanist writer might compose a unitary work, especially if he had a propagandist intention. (For example Thomas Favent's account of the Merciless Parliament, the *Chronicle of the Rebellion in Lincolnshire*, and the *History of the Arrival of Edward IV*,[17] besides some tracts on local history,[18] are in the form of monographs.)

The content of humanist histories resembles in many respects that of those written within the medieval tradition. The humanists, like their medieval predecessors, saw history as the manifestation of God's will on earth; the future was predicted by prodigies and portents, and the Wheel of Fortune continued to turn. But the humanists laid greater emphasis on natural causation: God remained the prime mover of events, but usually worked through secondary, natural causes. This view led to careful analysis of motives, especially of psychological, but also of political ones.[19] The only medieval chroniclers undertaking comparable analysis were those who wrote in connection with diplomacy—some of whom may well have been subject to humanist influence.[20]

---

[12] See Kristeller, *The Classics and Renaissance Thought*, pp. 11–13.

[13] For the rhetorical tradition in early medieval historiography, see R. W. Southern, 'Aspects of the European tradition of historical writing. 1. The classical tradition from Einhard to Geoffrey of Monmouth' in *TRHS*, fifth series, xx (1970), pp. 178–88.

[14] For the humanists' use of rhetoric see Reynolds, op. cit., pp. 8–9, 18, 44, and Burke, op. cit., pp. 132–3.

[15] See pp. 210–13 above.

[16] See pp. 213–17 above.

[17] See pp. 373, 385–6 above.

[18] For examples from Durham and Bury St Edmunds see Gransden, *Historical Writing*, i. 122–3, 126–7.

[19] See L. F. Dean, *Tudor Theories of History Writing* (University of Michigan Contributions in Modern Philology, no. i, April 1947), pp. 10–21, and Burke, op. cit., pp. 77–89.

[20] For rational causation in: Commynes's *Mémoires*, see p. 300 above; the *Arrival of Edward IV*, see p. 263 above; the second continuation of the Crowland chronicle, see p. 269 above. For the possibility that the author of the latter work (who may also have written the *Arrival*) was John Russell, bishop of Lincoln, who had humanist interests, see p. 270 and n. 147 above. It is noteworthy that a number of humanists acted as diplomats. It was as a diplomat that Machiavelli developed his interest in psychological motivation; see Frederico Chabod, *Machiavelli and the Renaissance*, translated by David Moore (Harper Torchbook, New York 1965), p. 7. A number of the fifteenth century humanists in England served as diplomats;

The humanists stressed the importance of truth as the historian's objective. To discover the truth they used a wide range of literary sources, weighing one authority against another and sometimes deciding in favour of a particular account because it seemed the most probable.[21] Some also searched for record material, subjecting documents to critical examination: a famous example of the detection of a forgery by a humanist is Lorenzo Valla's strictures on the Donation of Constantine.[22] The humanist historians exploited the evidence of topography and antiquities, including ancient buildings, archaeological remains and coins—particularly those of the classical period. Gradually the idea of 'anachronism'—that the past was different from the present—gained ground.[23] The study of literary sources, documents, topography and antiquities had of course a continuous tradition in the middle ages: monks had written local histories based on the study of this type of evidence,[24] while the fifteenth century had produced non-monastic antiquaries, notably William Worcester and John Rous. The humanists' contribution was to reinforce the existing interest and to direct especial attention to classical remains.

The humanists continued the medieval tradition of treating history as a repository of *exempla*, although with a slight change of attitude. The humanists tended to concentrate less on examples for moral behaviour than on those for political behaviour, and they increasingly became more interested in man as a social, political being, than in his prospects of salvation. In time political expediency replaced abstract morality as the criterion of virtuous behaviour, a development which reached its final definition in Machiavelli's *Prince*.[25] This exemplary view of history could run counter to the humanists' intention of discovering the truth: a writer might distort his narrative of events in order to prove that moral virtue had been rewarded or sin punished (even though in actuality this had not been the case), or that a certain course of action was successful or unsuccessful (when this was false or only partly true).[26]

---

see F. J. Levy, *Tudor Historical Thought* (California 1967), p. 40. For Polydore Vergil's diplomatic activity see p. 430, and for Sir Thomas More's p. 444, below.

[21] See Burke, *The Renaissance Sense of the Past*, pp. 50–76, and Denys Hay, 'Flavio Biondo and the Middle Ages' in *Proceedings of the British Academy*, xlv (1959), pp. 117–18.

[22] Burke, op. cit., p. 55, and Arnaldo Momigliano, 'Ancient history and the antiquarian' in *Journal of the Warburg and Courtauld Institutes*, xiii (1950), pp. 289–92. For Biondo see Hay, op. cit., pp. 102, 111–12.

[23] For the idea of 'anachronism' in the middle ages see pp. 454 n. 3, 463 and nn. 55, 56, 464–5 and n. 66 below.

[24] For a comparison of the monastic local historians with the Tudor antiquaries see R. W. Southern, 'Aspects of the European tradition of historical writing. 4. The sense of the past' in *TRHS*, fifth series, xxiii (1973), pp. 246–63.

[25] P. O. Kristeller, 'The moral thought of renaissance humanism' in *Chapters in Western Civilization*, ed. Contemporary Civilization staff of Columbia College (Columbia 1961), p. 312. (The article is reprinted in the same author's *Renaissance Thought II* (Harper Torchbook, New York 1965); see p. 45.) Cf. p. 435 and n. 62 below.

[26] See Dean, *Tudor Theories of History Writing*, p. 12.

The search for truth was hindered by another factor, patronage. Patrons, who were usually, but not always, kings or other rulers, often commissioned humanists to write histories of their countries. Most of these official historiographers were Italians, but a few were Frenchmen, and they were domiciled in foreign courts. Thus Aeneas Silvius Piccolomini (later Pius II, d. 1464), when a courtier in Vienna, wrote a history for the emperor Frederick III,[27] Paolo Emilio of Verona (d. 1529) wrote a history of France for Louis XII,[28] Giovanni Nanni (Annius) of Viterbo (d. 1502) wrote a history of Spain for Ferdinand and Isabella,[29] and Antonio Bonfini (d. 1505) wrote a history of Hungary for the king, Matthias Corvinus.[30] In England Titus Livius wrote the Life of Henry V for Humphrey duke of Gloucester,[31] Bernard André wrote a biography of Henry VII, for that king,[32] and, as will be seen, Polydore Vergil also wrote for Henry VII, for whom he undertook his history of England.

In order to please a patron the humanist historian gave a eulogistic account of him and his family. Moreover, he had to accommodate to his patron's patriotism. A patriotic bias also served to make a book generally acceptable in a country. As a result a number of humanists retold and elaborated national foundation myths.[33] These not only conflicted with the truth, but might prove irreconcilable with another humanist ideal, veneration of the classical past. Writers who succumbed to patriotic sentiment might resent the dominance of Italy and seek pre-classical origins for their countries. Such an anti-classical attitude could have one beneficial effect: it might divert attention to the dark and middle ages.[34]

Modern scholars have tended to divide the humanist historians into two main groups: Leonardo Bruni (d. 1444), who concentrated on style and structure, characterizes one group, and Flavio Biondo (d. 1463), who was notable for his criticism of sources and antiquarian zeal, characterizes the other. The so-called school of **Bruni** flourished in the fifteenth century, while that of Biondo gained importance in the sixteenth. However,

---

[27] Reynolds, 'Latin historiography: a survey, 1400–1600', p. 12.

[28] Ibid., p. 28.

[29] R. B. Tate, 'Mythology in Spanish historiography of the middle ages and renaissance' in *Hispanic Review*, xxii (1954), pp. 11–12.

[30] Reynolds, op. cit., p. 39.

[31] See pp. 210–11 above.

[32] Bernard André's biography, which is a eulogy and survives in only one manuscript, is printed *Historia Regis Henrici Septimi a Bernardo Andrea Tholosate conscripta*, ed. James Gairdner (RS 1858). It is discussed in G. B. Churchill, *Richard III up to Shakespeare* (*Palaestra*, x, Berlin 1900), pp. 59–64.

[33] See Reynolds, op. cit., pp. 20–2, 27–8. For early criticism of these myths see Burke, *The Renaissance Sense of the Past*, pp. 69–76. For the foundation myths of Spain see Tate, op. cit., pp. 1–18 passim.

[34] Biondo has been described as 'the first medieval historian'; Hay, 'Flavio Biondo and the Middle Ages', pp. 116–17. For resentment of Italian cultural dominance by some Spanish historians see Tate, op.cit., pp. 11–14 passim.

no rigid distinction can be maintained; style and structure can rarely be dissociated from content. Biondo himself, although mainly preoccupied with the study of written sources and antiquities, tried to give literary form to his *Decades historiarum ab inclinatione Romani imperii* (*History of the Decades from the Fall of the Roman Empire*), and also used rhetorical devices.[35]

It is against this background that the only two purely humanist historians who wrote in England, Polydore Vergil and Thomas More, must be considered.

Vergil and More belonged to the humanist circle in London. Both were members of Doctors' Commons, a club for learned men,[36] and included among their friends and acquaintances leading scholars such as John Colet, William Grocyn, William Lily, Christopher Urswick, Cuthbert Tunstall, and Henry VII's Latin secretary, the Italian, Andrea Ammonio.[37] Both became friendly with Erasmus during his visits to England,[38] and corresponded with other continental humanists, for example with the French scholar Guillaume Budé.[39]

Polydore Vergil himself was a native of Urbino and came to England in 1502 with his patron Adriano de Castello of Corneto who had been pre-ferred to the see of Hereford.[40] Castello was collector of Peter's Pence, and Vergil was appointed his deputy in the collectorship. Vergil enjoyed a favourable position in England because his patron was a man of influence. Castello became a cardinal in 1503, and in 1504 was translated to the see of Bath and Wells. He was one of the king's most valued agents in Rome until his disgrace in 1517. Vergil obtained various preferments in the church, and in 1508 was appointed archdeacon of Wells. He acted as an ecclesiastical diplomat for the English court and visited Italy in 1514, probably in connection with Wolsey's attempts to be raised to the cardi-nalate. On his return from Italy Vergil's fortunes suffered a reverse, and Wolsey had him put in the Tower. His imprisonment was partly the result of the enmity of Ammonio, his rival for the post of deputy collector of Peter's Pence. But it was mainly owing to his involvement with Wolsey's schemes. The archbishop used the imprisonment as a means of bringing

---

[35] See Hay, op. cit., pp. 98–9, 124–5.

[36] Doctors' Commons is discussed in William Senior, *Doctors' Commons and the Old Court of Admiralty* (London, 1922), pp. 59–83, and in E. J. Davis, 'Doctors' Commons, its title and topography' in *London Topographical Record*, xv (1931), pp. 36–50.

[37] See Denys Hay, *Polydore Vergil, Renaissance Historian and Man of Letters* (Oxford 1952), pp. 19–20.

[38] Ibid., pp. 13, 18–19; R. W. Chambers, *Thomas More* (London 1938), pp. 70, 119–20, etc.

[39] For the probability that Vergil corresponded with Budé see Hay, op. cit., p. 18 and n. 7. For More's acquaintance with him see Chambers, op. cit., p. 217, and *R III*, pp. xlii n. 2, lxxv.

[40] For Vergil's life see Hay, op. cit., pp. 1–21 (reprinted with some additions and alterations from Denys Hay, 'The life of Polydore Vergil of Urbino' in *Journal of the Warburg and Courtauld Institutes*, xii (1949), pp. 132–51), and *AH*, ed. Hay, pp. ix–xi.

pressure to bear on Vergil's friends in Rome, so that they would promote his own interests. Vergil was released when Wolsey obtained a cardinal's hat, but at the same time Wolsey procured the disgrace of his patron, Cardinal Castello. Vergil visited Italy again in 1516 and 1517. Subsequently he lived quietly in England, taking no part in ecclesiastical politics, but engaged on his clerical duties and scholarly interests. He was frequently in London, but although he attended convocation, his part in the reformation was nominal; while remaining a Catholic he ostensibly subscribed to the new order. He finally left England in 1553 and died at Urbino in 1555.

The books which Vergil regarded as his most important and which formed the basis of his reputation were the *Proverbiorum Libellus* (*Book of Proverbs*), also called the *Adagia* (*Adages*), and the *De Inventoribus Rerum* (*Concerning the Originators of Things*). He composed both while still resident in Italy, and they were first printed in Venice, the *Proverbiorum Libellus* in 1498 and the *De Inventoribus Rerum* in 1499, but they were so popular that when Vergil was settled in England he enlarged them; they appeared in numerous editions, in Latin and in translation, in the course of the sixteenth century. The *Proverbiorum Libellus* is a collection of proverbs from classical authors, to which in 1521 Vergil added saying from the bible, comparable to Erasmus's *Adagia*.[41] The *De Inventoribus Rerum* describes in three books the origins of all aspects of human life, for example, religions, customs, art, learning and commerce. A fourth book, which Vergil appended in 1521, comprises information on Christian origins.[42] While in England Vergil wrote, besides the *Anglica Historia*, a number of dialogues in accordance with renaissance taste, designed primarily to display his skill as a latinist. Most concern religious and moral topics, but one is on the then popular subject of prodigies.[43] Vergil also translated Chrysostom's *De Perfecto Monacho* (*On the Perfect Monk*) into Latin.[44] And in connection with his research on early English history he published in 1525 the first printed edition of Gildas's *De Excidio Britanniae*.[45]

Vergil began his historical research soon after he arrived in England, and at the same time he apparently kept some sort of diary of current events. But it was as a result of a commission from Henry VII that he started work on a comprehensive history.[46] In 1531 he completed the first version of the *Anglica Historia*, which carries the narrative to 1513,

[41] For the *Proverbiorum Libellus* see Hay, *Polydore Vergil*, pp. 22–9.
[42] For the *De Inventoribus* see ibid., pp. 52–78. Cf. John Ferguson, *Hand List of Editions of Polydore Vergil's De Inventoribus Rerum* . . . , ed. J. F. Fulton and C. H. Peters (New Haven, Conn. 1944).
[43] For Vergil's dialogues see Hay *Polydore Vergil*, pp. 34–51. The dialogue on prodigies was first printed as *Dialogorum de prodigiis libri tres* (Basle 1531).
[44] Ibid., pp. 50–1. Printed as *Divi Johannis Chrysostomi Comparatio regii potentatus et divitiarum* . . . (1533).
[45] The edition was probably published in Antwerp; see Hay, op. cit., p. 30 and n. 1. For its value see ibid., pp. 29–31.
[46] See *AH*, ed. Hay, p. xx and n. 1.

and dedicated it to the new king, Henry VIII.[47] An autograph manuscript, in two volumes, of this version still survives, in the Urbino collection in the Vatican library. Vergil took the manuscript to Italy in 1514, probably so that the famous copyist, Frederigo Veterani, could prepare a presentation copy (which is no longer extant) for Henry VIII.[48] Veterani's colophon and annotations are in the manuscript.[49]

Vergil wrote for a wide audience as well as for the king. He intended the *Historia* to be read both in England and on the continent. The first printed edition appeared at Basle in 1534, the delay in publication being no doubt owing to the political situation. Vergil probably took the manuscript for this edition to the continent in 1533, when the crises preceding Henry VIII's marriage to Anne Boleyn seemed to have been resolved by the marriage itself. The text ends in 1509, with the death of Henry VII; possibly Vergil wrote a continuation to about 1530, which includes the rise and fall of Wolsey, but did not publish it because he was afraid of offending important political figures. (It will be seen that Thomas More did not publish the *History of King Richard III* because of a similar circumspect attitude to those in power.)[50] The text is virtually a rewrite of the original version. Vergil revised the history not only to improve the Latin style, but also to alter its political viewpoint. He modified his strictures on Henry VII and his government. This was partly because Vergil had changed his opinion: his initial enthusiasm for Henry VIII had given way to disenchantment, and no doubt he thought, in the light of Henry's oppressive rule, that his criticism of Henry VII was too severe. Another reason for such revision was caution: it was probably owing to respect for Thomas Cromwell's influence that Vergil dealt with Henry VII's notorious officials, Richard Empson and Edmund Dudley, more mildly in the first printed edition than in the manuscript version. It is likely that the revised text was prepared in the years from 1521 to 1524, but publication was delayed because Vergil regarded the political climate as unfavourable.

[47] The dedication to Henry VIII is fuller in the manuscript version than in the subsequent printed editions. It is summarized in Hay, *Polydore Vergil*, pp. 152–3, and in *AH*, ed. Hay, pp. xxviii–xxix. The dedication is on pages 1–2 in the early printed editions (for which see below and n. 49).

[48] Ibid., pp. xiii–xv.

[49] *AH*, ed. Hay, pp. xiv, xl, 221 n. The Vatican MS. has never been printed complete but the section from 1485 to 1513 is printed in *AH*, ed. Hay; see p. 425 n. 2 above. The printed editions of the subsequent recensions (see below) are hereafter referred to as follows: Basle 1534, *AH¹*; Basle 1546, *AH²*; Basle 1555, *AH³*. In the footnotes I have mainly cited *AH²* because it was the first revised version to be printed and was little altered for the 1555 edition. In the extracts from *AH* I cite in the text I have followed the sixteenth century translation (PV, *EH*), for which see p. 425 n. 2 above, whenever possible. Otherwise I have in the main followed Professor Hay's translation, with his kind permission and that of the Royal Historical Society.

[50] For the political background to the composition of the various recensions of the *Anglica Historia* see *AH*, ed. Hay, pp. xvi–xvii, xxii–xxiii. For More's non-publication of *Richard III* see pp. 443–4 below.

The second edition of the *Anglica Historia*, which like the first ends in 1509, was published at Basle in 1546. It seems likely that Vergil prepared a continuation to the birth of Edward VI in 1537, incorporating a revised version of the previous continuation, but again caution prevented him from publishing it. As in the case of the first edition, he revised the content, improving the Latin and altering politically dangerous passages. Vergil's final edition was published at Basle in 1555, the year of his death. This contains further stylistic revision but little alteration in content. Vergil published it when he left England for the last time, after the accession of Queen Mary. At last the political situation seemed propitious for the publication of the continuation to 1537: it is for this continuation that the third edition is mainly valuable.

Vergil's historiography, like that of most renaissance historians, was a mixture of the medieval and the humanist. He made extensive use of classical authorities and his humanist training appeared both in the style and in the content of his work. He wrote in classical Latin (and included rhetorical speeches), which he revised in the successive editions of the *Historia* to make it more eloquent.[51] He gave his work a coherent structure and, to a certain extent, a unitary theme. His approach to his subject was often critical, he had strong antiquarian interests, and attributed many events to natural causes. In all these respects he had medieval antecedents, and his work does not mark a distinct break with the medieval tradition. Nevertheless, as a result of his study of the classics, Vergil's historiography was an advance on that of his predecessors.

To a certain extent Vergil tried to impose unity on his work by means of its structure. Having begun with a survey of the geography and social customs of England, he proceeds in the first eight books to give a chronological account of English history until 1066. But then he adopts a more ambitious arrangement. Under the influence of Suetonius' *Lives of the Caesars*, William of Malmesbury's *Gesta Regum*, and Platina's *Lives of the Popes*, he arranged the rest of his history biographically.[52] Each book covers the reign of one king, and is itself arranged in accordance with the Suetonian system: it begins with a chronological narrative of the king's public life, and follows this with an account of his character and family. A section on famous men is sometimes appended. Vergil discusses particular topics (for example the Becket controversy) *en bloc*. Although there was little actually new in this arrangement,[53] Vergil adhered to it more

---

[51] See *AH*, ed. Hay, pp. xvi, xxiii. For Vergil's use of rhetorical speeches see Hay, *Polydore Vergil*, pp. 105–6.

[52] For the structure of the *Anglica Historia* see ibid., pp. 95–103.

[53] Not only William of Malmesbury (for the structure of whose *Gesta Regum* see Gransden, *Historical Writing*, i. 170–1), but also the authors of histories of abbeys, and of archbishoprics and bishoprics, had used the biographical arrangement throughout the middle ages. Roger of Howden is an example of a medieval chronicler who treated subjects *en bloc*; see ibid., i. 229.

consistently than his predecessors had done, and his choice of a structure based on secular divisions was rare in the middle ages. Moreover, Vergil concluded the work with a novel feature, an index: he probably borrowed the idea from other kinds of contemporary books, for example lexicons and collections of the complete works of classical authors.[54]

In his dedication to Henry VIII Vergil states his objectives.[55] He deplores the fact that there was no adequate history of England—he regarded the monastic chronicles as 'bald, uncouth, chaotic and deceitful', although he appreciated William of Malmesbury and Matthew Paris. Vergil undertook to remedy this want with a history which was both true and edifying. History 'is the only unique, certain and faithful witness of times and things, redounding as much to the glory of the author as to the usefulness of posterity.'

Vergil explicitly declares his intention to tell the truth both in the dedication and elsewhere in his work. 'I hope', he writes 'that it will be to my advantage that I write as an Italian, and relate everything with truthfulness.'[56] He states that it is a law in history that the writer should never be 'so bold as to open any false thing, nor so remiss as not to utter any truth'.[57] A tendentious narrative is to be avoided: the historian must stick to the truth without favour or envy.[58] Vergil particularly deplores guesswork: 'an history is a full rehearsal and declaration of things done, not a guess or divination.'[59] He laments the proclivity of some patriotic writers to attribute legendary origins to their countries:[60]

> for the most part all countries [are] wont to draw their pedigree either from the gods or from heroical nobles, to the end that they which afterward being not easy of belief minded to scan and derive them, when they should hardly find anything of more certainty, they should rather be constrained to believe it firmly than any further to labour vainly ... , so easily is truth always discoloured from feigned fantasies.

Vergil is equally explicit about the edificatory intention of his book. History, he asserts in the dedication, should record both good and bad deeds so that 'it displays eternally to the living those events which would be an example and those which should be a warning.' In the course of the *Historia* Vergil provides instances demonstrating the power of divine providence over human affairs, and the vagaries of fortune—which illus-

---

[54] Hay, op. cit., pp. 102–3.
[55] See *AH*, ed. Hay, pp. xiii–xv.
[56] *AH*, ed. Hay, p. xxviii.
[57] *AH²*, p. 17 (lines 25–6); PV, *EH*, i. 30.
[58] See *AH²*, p. 53 (line 35); PV, *EH*, i. 107.
[59] *AH²*, p. 15 (lines 41–2); PV, *EH*, i. 26.
[60] See *AH²*, p. 53 (lines 18–21, 37–8); PV, *EH*, i. 107.

trate the transitory nature of all human achievement.[61] Vergil hoped by such *exempla* to teach all his readers, but he had princes especially in mind.[62]

Similarly, Vergil included wise sayings for the instruction of his readers. (As has been mentioned, he published a collection of such adages.)[63] Thus he states: 'we find by experience that friends do very seldom answer like for like, yea rather unthankful minds do requite much good with great evil';[64] 'a guilty conscience causeth the offenders to have due punishment alway in imagination before his eyes',[65] and fear 'seldom causeth continuance of dutiful dealing.'[66] One of the adages, perhaps intended particularly for a prince, shows that Vergil was aware of the potential conflict between moral virtue and political expediency, a problem which engaged later humanists; 'the better part of high estates are wont often times rather in the end to follow that serveth for their present profit, than that which is honest and honourable.'[67]

The contents of the *Historia* can conveniently be considered in two parts, taking the year 1400 as the dividing line. In the part before the end of the fourteenth century Vergil writes fairly objectively and makes a genuine attempt to discover the truth, as he had promised. But thereafter his work is heavily biased, which results in some wilful misrepresentation.

Vergil was able to approach the period before 1400 with considerable objectivity because he was a foreigner. He was not moved by patriotism,[68] the cause of bias in many renaissance histories.[69] (Nor does he seem to have regarded it as necessary to adopt the patriotism of the English in order to please his royal patrons.) He was, indeed, positively hostile to patriotic sentiment. Commenting on England's loss of Aquitaine, he deplores the 'venom' of nationalism, which disrupts 'the common society of mankind' and 'hath already a good while since infected much people, so as that (to be silent of others) it cannot be brought to pass by any mean that a Frenchman born will much love an Englishman, or, contrary, that an English will love a Frenchman.'[70]

To discover the truth about English history before 1400 Vergil used numerous written sources, subjecting them to critical, even sceptical,

---

[61] E.g. *AH* [2,3], p. 531 (line 18), *AH²*, p. 558 (lines 43–5); PV, *EH*, ii. 191, 201; *AH*, ed. Hay, pp. 8, 332. See Hay, *Polydore Vergil*, pp. 135, 141–3.

[62] See, e.g., *AH²*, pp. 439–40; PV, *EH*, ii. 166. Cf. *AH*, ed. Hay, p. xxxi, and Hay, *Polydore Vergil*, pp. 140–1.

[63] p. 431 above.

[64] *AH²*, p. 514 (lines 10–11); PV, *EH*, ii. 117.

[65] *AH²*, p. 542 (lines 25–6); PV, *EH*, ii. 178–9.

[66] *AH²*, p. 548 (lines 36–7); PV, *EH*, ii. 192.

[67] *AH²*, p. 537 (lines 45–6); PV, *EH*, ii. 169. See p. 428 above.

[68] See p. 437 below.

[69] Hay, op. cit., p. 150.

[70] *AH²*, p. 497 (lines 28–31); PV, *EH*, ii. 82. Cited Hay, op. cit., p. 116–17. See also ibid., p. 136, and *AH*, ed. Hay, p. xxxi.

examination.[71] He compares accounts of events in different literary works, and when the truth was hard to discover cites all narratives.[72] (As has been already mentioned Thomas Rudborne and John Rous had adopted this method.)[73] Vergil also applies the test of common sense: if a statement in a source seems improbable, he dismisses it or at least warns the reader.[74] In addition, he tries to evaluate the sources as evidence: he grasped the basic principle that sources written closest in time to the events recorded are usually of more authority than later ones.

Vergil's recognition of the value of primary sources for medieval history is demonstrated by his edition of Gildas.[75] At that time only the *Brut* and *Polychronicon* were in print; the next chronicle to go to press was 'Matthew of Westminster', which Archbishop Parker published in 1567. Vergil virtually discovered Gildas. His attention was drawn to Gildas's work by references in Bede and William of Newburgh. He found one manuscript of the text, and later Cuthbert Tunstall provided him with another and allowed him the help of his own chaplain, Robert Ridley. Modern scholars consider the edition excellent by the standards of Vergil's day and respectable by those of more recent times. Apart from rearranging some words in the interests of clarity and suppressing a few anti-clerical passages, Vergil printed the text as it stood.

Vergil edited Gildas in order to substantiate his conclusions on the earliest habitation of Britain.[76] The passage in the *Anglica Historia* on the origins of the Britons illustrates Vergil's critical ability at its best.[77] (However, Vergil's debt to William of Newburgh should not be forgotten; William, besides introducing him to the *De Excidio*, pointed the way for scholarly criticism of Geoffrey of Monmouth's account of early British history.)[78]

No period, Vergil asserts, is more obscure than that of early Britain, a country distant from and long unknown to the Greeks and Romans. Gildas had stated that, since the native chronicles were destroyed, only foreign sources survived for the Roman period. Vergil challenges the Brutus story, because it was not mentioned by such writers as Livy and Dionysius of Halicarnassus. Moreover, it seemed most unlikely that Britain lacked inhabitants until the arrival of Brutus because the coast could be

---

[71] See, for example, *AH²*, pp. 52–3; PV, *EH*, i. 105–7. See also Hay, *Polydore Vergil*, pp. 107–9. For Vergil's authorities for the fifteenth and sixteenth centuries see p. 442 and n. 114 below.

[72] See, for example, *AH²*, pp. 55–60; PV, *EH*, i. 112–21.

[73] See pp. 398, 323, respectively, above.

[74] For an example see below.

[75] For his edition see Hay, *Polydore Vergil*, pp. 29–31.

[76] Vergil states that he has arranged to publish Gildas in order to refute the 'erroneous fables' of more recent writers; *AH²*, p. 16 (line 43); PV, *EH*, i. 28.

[77] *AH²*, pp. 15–19; PV, *EH*, i. 26–33.

[78] For a reference to William of Newburgh's authority see *AH²*, p. 17 (line 3). For Newburgh on Geoffrey of Monmouth, see Gransden, *Historical Writing*, i. 264–5.

seen from France on a clear day.[79] On the popularity of such legends Vergil writes:

> In the old time they did presume on this franchise and liberty that many nations were so bold as to derive the beginning of their stock from the gods (as especially the Romans did), to the intent the original of their people and cities might be the more princely and prosperous, which things, albeit they sounded more like fables than the sincere witnesses of noble acts, yet were they received for truth.

In Vergil's view the history of Britain began in Roman times. He quotes Caesar and Tacitus; and he cites Bede ('than whom I have seen nothing more sound, sincere, or true'), but preferred Gildas ('who, exiling all fables, most earnestly embraceth the truth'), the source of Bede's information.[80] In his treatment of the Arthurian legends Vergil vehemently attacks Geoffrey of Monmouth, who adopted 'both the colour of Latin speech and the honest pretext of a history', in order to extol the Britons 'above the nobleness of the Romans and Macedonians, enhancing them with most impudent lying'—although Gildas had shown them to be 'neither stout in battle nor faithful in peace'.[81] Nevertheless, out of respect for the tastes of ordinary people, Vergil recites, with some corrections, the Brutus and Arthurian legends. The fables 'in the admiration of the common people (who always more regard novelties than truth) ... seem to be in heaven, where with a good will I will leave them, thinking it not good to debate the matter with them as touching those feigned trifles.'[82] Besides written sources Vergil used oral ones, treating them with similar discretion. A Scot, Gavin Douglas, bishop of Dunkeld, told him first by letter and then in conversation about the earliest settlers in Scotland. But Vergil despite his regard for the bishop, 'a sincere man', was forced to dismiss his legendary account because it was not corroborated by Caesar, Tacitus, Ptolemy or Pliny.[83]

Vergil's sources were not limited to written and oral ones, and the scope of his interests extended beyond political history. His antiquarianism appears in a number of contexts. He used the evidence of geography, topography, 'ancient monuments' and archaeology, and was interested in place-names, language and social history. In Book I he describes in detail the geography of England, Scotland and Wales, indicating the rivers and their sources, and in Book IV gives the boundaries of the seven king-

---

[79] *AH²*, pp. 17 (lines 45–6), 18 (lines 1–3); PV, *EH*, i. 31.
[80] *AH²*, p. 16 (lines 6–7, 15–17); PV, *EH*, i. 27.
[81] *AH²*, p. 17 (line 10): PV, *EH*, i. 29.
[82] *AH²*, p. 19 (lines 8–10); PV, *EH*, i. 33.
[83] *AH²*, pp. 52–3; PV, *EH*, i. 105–8.

doms of Anglo-Saxon England.[84] He observes, citing Tacitus, that although London in Roman times was the venue of merchants, it cannot have been important since it was not mentioned by Caesar. Now, however, it is 'the most princely city of all others, the head of the nation, the palace of kings, most abounding in riches'.[85] And Vergil gives a vivid topographical description of the Thames, including this account of London bridge:[86]

> In this most renowned city is there a bridge of stone of wondrous artificial workmanship, for therein are contained twenty piles of square stone, sixty foot of height, thirty of breadth, the one being distant from the other about twenty foot, yet knit and joined together with arches, in the top whereof houses on both sides are so subtly builded, that it rather representeth a street of great length than a bridge.

Although Vergil allowed himself to be misled by Geoffrey of Monmouth into stating that Caerleon was founded by Belinus, he adds an antiquarian observation: he remarks that vestiges of the houses were to be seen in his own day.[87] He debates whether Camulodunum was to be identified with Doncaster or Pontefract. The former had the strongest natural fortifications, but the latter was pleasanter. Moreover, Pontefract had a castle, and the ruins of a temple with two statues in it, one of the goddess Victory and the other of the emperor Claudius—Tacitus, Vergil notes, states that Camulodunum had a temple dedicated to Claudius.[88]

Vergil dismisses Geoffrey of Monmouth's false etymologies of names of British towns. He doubts the early existence of such towns as Canterbury, Bath and Carlisle, because they were not mentioned by Caesar, Tacitus, Strabo, Ptolemy or Pliny. He also points out that many place-names said to derive from the names of kings of ancient Britain were in fact of Anglo-Saxon, Danish or Norman derivation.[89] And although he admits he has not discovered the origin of the name Wales, he denies that it was from a bygone king or queen, as some had asserted.[90] Vergil's interest in language appears in his observation that the people of Cornwall spoke a language similar to that of the Bretons, which also resembled that of the Welsh, and was quite different from English.[91] He devotes considerable space in the introductory section to the social customs of the English, and comments on England's economy, remarking, for example, that wool

[84] *AH*[2], pp. 1–14, 63–92 passim; PV, *EH*, i. 1–19, 128–88 passim.
[85] *AH*[2], p. 25 (lines 41–3); PV, *EH*, i. 47.
[86] *AH*[2], p. 4 (lines 38–41); PV, *EH*, i. 3.
[87] *AH*[2], p. 25 (line 14); PV, *EH*, i. 46.
[88] *AH*[2], p. 34 (lines 5–12); PV, *EH*, i. 65–6.
[89] *AH*[2], p. 26 (lines 14–17); PV, *EH*, i. 48.
[90] *AH*[2], p. 8 (lines 41–4); PV, *EH*, i. 12–13.
[91] *AH*[2], p. 9 (lines 31–45); PV, *EH*, i. 14. See also Hay, *Polydore Vergil*, p. 91–2.

growing (which he thought was probably of post-Conquest origin) was the source of the country's prosperity.[92]

To turn now to the other part of the *Historia*, that for the period after 1400, which differs from the preceding section because of its strong bias. The bias is the result of two factors which influenced Vergil consecutively. In the first place there was his desire to please his royal patrons. This lasted until shortly after Henry VIII's accession. Thereafter until the end in 1537 Vergil, disillusioned with the king and his rule, expressed his personal principles and prejudices, though he was inhibited by caution.[93]

For the period from the end of the fourteenth century until 1509 Vergil produced an apologia for the house of Tudor. The *Historia* was intended to spread Tudor propaganda by means of the scholars whom it persuaded. Vergil's patrons, Henry VII and Henry VIII, especially needed an historian to write in their defence; their title to the throne was weak, and they had to combat sedition at home and hostility abroad.[94]

Vergil treated the fifteenth century as a prelude to the glorious accession of Henry VII. He could discern a pattern which began with the deposition and murder of Richard II without male issue: as a result England was ultimately torn between two factions supporting the rival dynasties of Lancaster and York.[95] Vergil inveighs against the horrors of civil war which is 'more hurtful to commonwealths than foreign war, than famine, or sickness'.[96] He writes:[97]

> Thus was the state of the realm, by reason of intestine hatred and divisions amongst the noble, most miserable, for churches and houses were everywhere spoiled, sword and fire raged all over, the realm was wholly replenished with harness and weapon, and slaughter, blood, and lamentation; the fields were wasted, town and city starved for hunger, and many other mischiefs happened, which proceed commonly from the rage of wars.

Throughout the fifteenth century each successive reign was overshadowed by the consequences of the guilt attached to Henry IV's illegal seizure of power.[98] Vergil detected that a particularly unhappy reign was followed by a more fortunate one, which in its turn was followed by another of ill omen. Thus Henry IV did not rule propitiously, while Henry V was successful in foreign conquest. Henry VI, although 'a man of mild and plain

---

[92] *AH²*, p. 13; PV, *EH*, i. 21.
[93] Pp. 432–3 above.
[94] *AH*, ed. Hay, pp. vii–viii, 9, 154, 166.
[95] *AH*, ed. Hay, p. 148.
[96] *AH²*, p. 498 (lines 15–16); PV, *EH*, ii. 83–4.
[97] *AH²*, p. 518 (lines 5–9); PV, *EH*, ii. 126.
[98] *AH²*, p. 531 (lines 18–22); PV, *EH*, ii. 154. See also Hay, *Polydore Vergil*, p. 143. John Hardyng made the same statement; see p. 278 above.

dealing disposition', universally loved for his 'liberality, clemency, integrity, and fortitude',[99] was cursed with civil strife and eventually deprived of his kingdom. ('Such was the pleasure of God, that King Henry, a most holy man, should by so many calamities, wherewithall he was continually afflicted, be deprived of his earthly kingdom, to enjoy forthwith the everlasting [one].')[100] Edward IV, on the other hand, though less praiseworthy than Henry as a person (he was given to lust and to excessive familiarity with his friends), 'appeased all intestine division [and] left a most wealthy realm abounding in all things, which by reason of civil wars he had received almost utterly void as well of able men as money.'[101]

The evil of the time was epitomized in Richard III, who pursued his ambition by means of deception, 'in most crafty and subtle manner',[102] without sparing 'the blood of his own house'.[103] Vergil gave a portrait of Richard's appearance, idiosyncrasies and character which helped to fix for later generations their view of the king:[104]

> He was little of stature, deformed of body, the one shoulder being higher than the other, a short and sour countenance, which seemed to savour of mischief, and utter evidently craft and deceit. The while he was thinking of any matter, he did continually bite his nether lip, as though that cruel nature of his did so rage against itself in that little carcass. Also he was wont to be ever with his right hand pulling out of the sheath to the midst, and putting in again, the dagger which he did alway wear. Truly he had a sharp wit, provident and subtle, apt both to counterfeit and dissemble. . . .

In writing of Henry VII's accession Vergil makes a case for its legality. Henry was crowned at Bosworth 'as though he had been already by commandment of the people proclaimed king after the manner of his ancestors, and that was the first sign of prosperity.'[105] Having entered London 'like a triumphing general', Henry 'acquired the kingdom, an event of which foreknowledge had been possible both many centuries earlier and also soon after his birth.' Vergil relates that Cadwallader, the last king of the Britons (Vergil had already mentioned him earlier in his history),[106] had had a vision which predicted that his descendants would recover the land—

---

[99] *AH²*, pp. 492 (line 10, 'Erat Henricus rex uir miti, simplicique ingenio. . .'), 510 (lines 29–31); PV, *EH*, ii. 70, 110.

[100] *AH²*, p. 509 (lines 23–4); PV, *EH*, ii. 108.

[101] *AH²*, p. 539 (lines 26–8); PV, *EH*, ii. 172.

[102] *AH²*, p. 542 (lines 29–30); PV, *EH*, ii. 179.

[103] *AH²*, p. 544 (line 27); PV, *EH*, ii. 183.

[104] *AH²*, p. 565 (lines 3–9); PV, *EH*, ii. 226–7. See also p. 453 below.

[105] *AH²*, p. 564 (lines 40–2); PV, *EH*, ii. 226.

[106] *AH²*, p. 61 (line 23).

and Henry traced his ancestry back to Cadwallader;[107] this prophecy had also been made to Henry when a child by Henry VI.[108]

Vergil's attitude to Henry VII's rule was not, as has been seen;[109] wholly favourable. His hopes centred on Henry VIII, the offspring of the union of the houses of Lancaster and York. On the marriage of Henry VII with Elizabeth of York Vergil writes:[110]

> It is legitimate to attribute this [marriage] to divine intervention, for plainly by it all things which nourished the two most ruinous factions were utterly removed, by it the two houses of Lancaster and York were united, and from the union the true and established royal line emerged which now reigns.

Of Henry VIII himself Vergil writes:[111]

> everybody loved him; and their affections were not half-hearted, because the king on his father's side descended from Henry VI and on his mother's from Edward IV. For just as Edward was the most warmly thought of by the English people among all English kings, so this successor of his, Henry, was very like him in general appearance, in greatness of mind and generosity and for that reason was the more acclaimed and approved of by all.

Having established Henry's right to the throne, Vergil proceeds with a fulsome eulogy:[112]

> Henry was recommended by his handsome bearing, his comely and manly features, showing authority as well as good will, his outstanding physical strength, remarkable memory, aptness at all the arts of both war and peace, skill in arms and on horseback, scholarship of no mean order, thorough knowledge of music, and by his humanity, benevolence and self-control.

However, as remarked above, Vergil's attitude to Henry VIII soon changed, and with it the opinions he expressed in the *Historia*. His bias is now against the king and his ministers. In the continuation from 1509 to 1537 he scurrilously abuses Wolsey, the principal cause of his own fall from favour, and, because of his catholicism, suppresses mention of or deals briefly with the religious upheavals of the times.[113] How he revised the *Historia* in the successive editions and delayed publication for prudential reasons has already been explained.

---

[107] *AH*, ed. Hay, pp. 2,4.
[108] *AH*¹, p. 515 (lines 18–19); *AH*², p. 522 (lines 19–20).
[109] P. 432 above.
[110] *AH*, ed. Hay, p. 7.
[111] *AH*, ed. Hay, p. 150.
[112] *AH*, ed. Hay, p. 150.
[113] See *AH*, ed. Hay, pp. xxi, xxix-xxx, and Hay, *Polydore Vergil*, pp. 154, 159, 171–2.

The *Anglica Historia* is important to the student of English history on two accounts: it is a primary authority for the period from the mid-fifteenth century until it ends in 1537; and it was a formative influence on Tudor historiography. Although for the fifteenth century Vergil relied on a written source, a version of the London chronicle,[114] from the middle of the century he also drew on oral information, derived from important men (such as John Morton, Reginald Bray and Christopher Urswick),[115] and also cites popular opinion.[116]

Besides preserving some unique information, Vergil deals rationally with a number of events, suggesting natural causes for them (it is noteworthy that the events in question often relate to diplomacy). He gives political and economic causes: for example, he attributes the outbreak of civil war in 1452 to the fact that the nobility was no longer occupied fighting abroad,[117] and he asserts that the marriage planned between Edward IV's daughter Elizabeth and Louis XI's son Charles never took place because Louis, no longer fearing war, went back on the marriage agreement and failed to pay the tribute he owed to Edward.[118] Vergil was particularly interested in psychological motivation. For instance he asserts that Edward IV agreed to help Charles, duke of Burgundy, against Louis for two main reasons: because Louis had supported the earl of Warwick; and because Edward was grateful to the duke for 'manifold benefits' when he was forced to leave England.[119]

But the value of the *Historia* as a source is not confined to the facts it preserves, and the reasonable explanations it offers. It is also important as an indication of popular opinion. Even Vergil's caution is revealing— it is evidence of the awe in which the new monarchy was held, evidence corroborated by Thomas More who showed similar circumspection as an historian. A recent scholar has described Vergil's work as 'a comment on Tudor times ... sprinkled with observations of the England Vergil knew'.[120]

Many historians in the sixteenth century distrusted the *Anglica Historia*.[121] Scholars such as Leland and Bale objected to Vergil's sceptical treatment of the Brutus and Arthurian legends, which they attributed to his

---

[114] Mrs Hanham argues that besides using a version of the London chronicle Vergil used the memoir also used by the author of the second continuation of the Crowland chronicle, and cites a number of passages showing similarities between the two works. However, the evidence is inconclusive. See Alison Hanham, *Richard III and his Early Historians, 1483–1535* (Oxford 1975), pp. 135–42, 148–51. Cf. p. 269 n. 135 above.

[115] Vergil questions the veracity of current opinion on the death of Richard II; *AH*², p. 428 (lines 24–7). See also Hay, *Polydore Vergil*, p. 92.

[116] Ibid., p. 93.

[117] *AH*², p. 502 (lines 32–6); PV, *EH*, ii. 93.

[118] *AH*², pp. 537 (lines 43–6), 538 (lines 1–4); PV, *EH*, ii. 169.

[119] *AH*², p. 533 (lines 42–6); PV, *EH*, ii. 160.

[120] Hay, *Polydore Vergil*, p. 114.

[121] See ibid., pp. 157–65.

foreign birth. And Vergil was suspect because of his catholicism. Neverthe-less, the *Anglica Historia* was the recognized authority for English history. Its account of the dark and early middle ages was superseded by more up-to-date research in the seventeenth century, but for the fifteenth century and for the sixteenth century up to 1537 it retained its reputation until the nineteenth century. Vergil's interpretation of English history for this period became part of the canon of English historical literature. It was borrowed by Edward Hall who, by expressing it in more highly coloured terms and in the English language, ensured its further dissemination.[122] Thus it reached not only other historians but also the dramatists, notably Shake-speare: 'from the wicked uncle [Richard III] to the grasping prelate [Wolsey], Vergil's story has become part of the national myth.'[123] The black portrait of Richard III which Vergil bequeathed to posterity was in all essentials duplicated by that left by Sir Thomas More. However, the latter's *History of Richard III*, although like the *Anglica Historia* a product of the renaissance, belongs to a very different literary genre.

Sir Thomas More's *Richard III* was the first and the last humanist history written by an Englishman. More probably wrote it between 1510 and July 1518, concurrently with the *Utopia*.[124] He wrote two versions, one in English and the other in Latin: he composed them simultaneously and independently of each other (neither is a translation of other), intending the first for readers in England, and the second primarily for those abroad.[125] He completed neither version (the English one ends before the Latin), and though manuscript copies were in circulation in the 1530s, the work was not printed until after More's execution in 1535.[126] Richard Grafton appended the English version to his edition of John Hardyng's chronicle which he published in 1543; he printed it again in 1548 and 1550, this time with Edward Hall's chronicle. In 1557 William Rastell published a definitive edition, which was the basis of the later Elizabethan editions, in the collected works of Sir Thomas More. The Latin version was first printed in Louvain in 1565.

The reason why More never finished *Richard III* is obscure. Perhaps he was too preoccupied, wondering to what extent he should become involved in the royal government. And then he may have been too busy: in 1517 he became a member of the king's council and master of requests; in the following years he was appointed to a succession of public offices, culmina-

---

[122] See pp. 470–1 below.
[123] *AH*, ed. Hay, p. xxxix.
[124] *R III*, pp. lxiii-lxv.
[125] For the relationship between the versions see *R III*, pp. xviii-liv.
[126] For the manuscript copies see *R III*, p. xxvii, and for the early printed editions see *R III*, pp. xvii-xviii, and Hanham, *Richard III and his Early Historians*, pp. 198–219.

ting in the chancellorship in 1529, besides being engaged on various diplomatic missions.[127]

On the other hand prudence may have stopped More continuing work on *Richard III*, and also deterred him from publishing it. The point at which the English version ends is the account of the advice given by John Morton, then bishop of Ely, to Henry, the second duke of Buckingham, inciting him to rebel in order to press his claim to the crown. A record of this circumstance would not have pleased Henry VIII and his ministers. Already in 1514 Buckingham's son, the third duke, was ready to rise in defence of similar claims, and in 1521 he was executed for treason. More's faith in Henry VIII may initially have been shaken by the summary execution of Edmund de la Pole in 1513. The possibility should be borne in mind that in these circumstances he hesitated to strengthen the king's hand by providing him with historical proof that the Tudors' seizure of power was justified on the grounds that Richard III was the worst possible tyrant.

More's own works provide evidence of the sense of insecurity suffered by the writers in his day. In *Richard III* he puts these words into John Morton's mouth: 'I love not much to talk much of princes, as thing not all out of peril',[128] and in one of his Latin poems he comments on the danger a courtier incurs if he makes frivolous remarks to the king ('what was just now a game brings death. . . . As for me, let my pleasure be less great—and safe').[129] The same impression of the insecurity is given by a letter of Erasmus, dated 8 July 1517, to More asking for advice where to settle: 'As to England, I fear its tumults, and I have a horror of servitude.'[130]

Richard III is a renaissance product written under the influence of classical models.[131] However, as More followed no classical history closely, but adopted an eclectic, interpretative method, it is hard to isolate particular instances of borrowing. Plutarch's *Life of Pompey* may have helped shape the work, and perhaps More learnt about power politics from Thucydides. But he was most influenced by Sallust, Tacitus and Suetonius. Sallust's *Jugurtha* and *Catiline* both concern conspiracies, while More's use of anecdote and interest in characterization were probably encouraged

---

[127] For these suggestions why More left Richard III unfinished and unpublished see *R III*, p. lxix, ci, ciii. Professor Sylvester also suggests (*R III*, pp. cii-ciii) that More, alarmed at Henry VIII's growing autocracy, preferred not to provide the king with an *exemplum* (see below) on the methods available to an aspiring tyrant. This view is not very convincing: Professor Hay points out (Hay, *Polydore Vergil*, p. 166) that Henry probably regarded history as potential propaganda rather than as a means of self instruction. Moreover, even if Henry did read the work as an *exemplum*, he knew that Richard was doomed.

[128] *R III*, p. 92.

[129] The poem is printed in an English translation in *The History of King Richard III*, ed. Sylvester, pp. 148–9.

[130] 'Et Anglie motus timeo et seruitutem horreo': *Opus Epistolarum Des. Erasmi Roterodami*, ed. P. S. Allen, H. M. Allen *et al.* (Oxford 1906–58, 12 vols), iii. 6 (Ep. no. 597).

[131] *R III*, pp. lxxxii-xcviii.

by his reading of Suetonius. And both Suetonius and Tacitus provided patterns for the atmosphere of deception which pervades More's narrative of the politics of Richard's reign.

Although More was principally influenced by humanist scholarship, he also, like other renaissance historians, was indebted to the medieval tradition. He emphasizes the transitory nature of earthly prosperity, and his work is partly an *exemplum*. More explains that history teaches lessons: 'sithen things past cannot be gaincalled, much ought we the more beware, by what occasion we have taken so great hurt affore, that we eftsoons fall not in that occasion again.'[132] However, in renaissance fashion he concentrated on examples for political rather than moral behaviour.

Richard III is a piece of apologetic, not an objective history. But unlike most renaissance histories in this category, it is not an apologia for a particular ruler: it is not a work of propaganda written in the Tudor interest— in fact More was critical of Henry VII.[133] Rather *Richard III* is an apologia for an idea. More sought to demonstrate by means of an *exemplum* the nature of tyranny and its evil results. He had, as Erasmus remarked, 'a peculiar loathing of tyranny',[134] which he expressed in some of his poems as well as in *Richard III*.[135] To put his main theme in relief he starts with an account of the peace and harmony established by Edward IV. More writes:[136]

> In ... [King Edward's] later days this realm was in quiet and prosperous estate; no fear of outward enemies, no war in hand, nor none toward, but such as no man looked for: the people toward the prince, not in constrained fear, but in willing and loving obedience: among themselves, the commons in good peace.

And the (incomplete) end of the work depicts the beginning of the reassertion of natural order, with Buckingham plotting for Richard's overthrow.

Against this background More traces Richard's rise to power as a tyrant. Richard provides the structure of the work ('this duke's demeanour ministreth in effect all the whole matter whereof this book shall entreat').[137] The usurpation destroyed the kingdom's harmony: 'Now fell there mischiefs thick. And as the thing evil gotten is never well kept, through all the time of his reign, never ceased there cruel death and slaughter, till his own destruction ended it.'[138]

[132] *R III*, p. 13.

[133] See the criticism of Henry VII's reign in More's poem on the coronation of Henry VIII; *History of King Richard III*, ed. Sylvester, pp. 131, 133.

[134] '... quaeque prorsus absit ab omni specie tyrannidis': Allen and Allen, op. cit., iv. 15 (Ep. no. 999).

[135] See the poems in Sylvester, op. cit., pp. 137–41 passim.

[136] *R III*, p. 4.

[137] *R III*, p. 6.

[138] *R III*, p. 82.

Richard's character was the factor determining the course of events. Ambition was his motive force, and this by creating dissension destroyed the harmonious order of the kingdom:[139]

> Such a pestilent serpent is ambition and desire of vainglory and sovereignty, which among states where he once entreth creepeth forth so far, till with division and variance he turneth all to mischief. First longing to be next the best, afterward equal with the best, and at last the chief and above the best. Of which immoderate appetite of worship, and thereby of debate and dissension, what loss, what sorrow, what trouble hath within these few years grown in this realm, I pray God as well forget as we well remember.

Richard, who had a 'deep dissimul[at]ing nature',[140] pursued his goal by means of deception. For example, he deceived Edward IV's widow, Queen Elizabeth, by false assurances, into allowing her second son to be taken from her in the sanctuary of Westminster, ostensibly so that he could play with his brother. Richard took the prince in his arms and kissed him saying, 'Now welcome my lord even with all my very heart.'[141] Similarly, he lulled Hastings into a false sense of security until his arrest (Buckingham 'made very good semblance unto Lord Hastings; and kept him much in company').[142] More writes:[143]

> all things were in late days so covertly demeaned, one thing pretended and another meant, that there was nothing so plain and openly proved, but that yet for the common custom of close and covert dealing, men had it ever inwardly suspect, as many well counterfeited jewels make the true mistrusted.

Thus Richard's character in general determined the course of events. More was also interested in examining particular instances of psychological motivation. Such causal relationships had already been used by historians, notably by those writing in connection with diplomacy.[144] (It should be remembered that, as mentioned above, More himself acted occasionally as a diplomat.) For instance More gives psychological explanations for Queen Elizabeth's actions in the spring of 1483. She sent the prince with her brother to Wales, because she wanted him to learn at an early age to love her relatives and friends; but Gloucester defeated her with her own

---

[139] *R III*, pp. 12–13.
[140] *R III*, p. 90.
[141] *R III*, pp. 26–42.
[142] *R III*, p. 46.
[143] *R III*, p. 82.
[144] For example, by the author of the *Arrival*, by the memorialist in the second continuation of the Crowland chronicle, and by Commynes; see pp. 263, 269, 300 above.

weapons, stirring the great lords against her supporters, on the grounds that the lords themselves were excluded from the king's presence by these men of lesser birth.[145] Personal feelings might well influence public events ('private grudges [could be turned] into the common hurt').[146] More makes a number of wise observations on human nature, some in the form of adages. The queen, in her attempt to prevent Richard taking her second son from her, on the pretext that he should be able to play with other children, especially his own brother, says, 'As though princes as young as they be, could not play but with their peers, or children could not play but with their kindred, with whom, for the more part they agree much worse than with strangers.'[147] His adages include such sayings as: 'the common people ... oftentimes more esteem and take for greater kindness, a little courtesy, than a great benefit';[148] 'men use if they have an evil turn, to write it in marble; and whoso doth us a good turn, we write it in dust';[149] and 'evil opinion once fastened in men's hearts, hard it is to wrest out.'[150]

Perhaps More's most graphic description of human behaviour is his account of Richard's bad conscience after the murder of the little princes:[151]

> after this abominable deed done, he never had quiet in his mind, he never thought himself sure. Where he went abroad, his eyes whirled about, his body privily fenced, his hand ever on his dagger, his countenance and manner like one alway ready to strike again, he took ill rest a night, lay long waking and musing, sore worried with care and watch, rather slumbered than slept, troubled with fearful dreams, suddenly sometimes start up, leap out of his bed and run about the chamber, so was his restless heart continually tossed and tumbled with the tedious impression and stormy remembrance of his abominable deed.

Richard III owes its readability and persuasiveness to literary merit. More's descriptive talents was not confined to portraying individuals. He could equally well describe general scenes, for example the removal of Queen Elizabeth's luggage to the sanctuary at Westminster. The archbishop of York visited the queen:[152]

> About [her] he found much heaviness, rumble, haste and business, carriage and conveyance of her stuff into sanctuary—chests,

[145] *R III*, pp. 14–15.
[146] *R III*, p. 23.
[147] *R III*, p. 38.
[148] *R III*, p. 5.
[149] *R III*, p. 57.
[150] *R III*, p. 26.
[151] *R III*, p. 87.
[152] *R III*, p. 21.

coffers, packs, fardelles, trusses, all on men's backs, no man
unoccupied, some lading, some going, some discharging, some
coming for more, some breaking down the walls to bring in the
next way, and some yet drew to [i.e. followed] them that help[ed]
to carry a wrong way.

More includes homely details, witticisms and jokes.[153] He mentions
that when Richard met the lords in the Tower before the arrest of Hastings,
he asked the bishop of Ely to get 'a mass' of strawberries from his garden
at Holborn.[154] He writes a witty exchange between Edward IV and his
mother, the duchess of York, on the subject of the king's proposal to
marry Elizabeth, a commoner. The duchess, trying to dissuade him, said
that 'it was not princely to marry his own subject . . . but only, as it were,
a rich man that would marry his maid only for a little wanton dotage upon
her person.'[155] She also objected that Elizabeth was a widow with children,
to which Edward replied, 'she is a widow and hath already children, by
God's blessed lady, I am a bachelor and have some too, and so each of us
hath a proof that neither of us is like to be barren.'[156] Another example of
wit concludes the account of the sermons preached at St Paul's Cross by
Friar Thomas Penker and Dr Ralph Shaa in defence of Richard's hereditary
claim to the throne, on the alleged grounds that Edward IV and his offspring were all bastards: 'Penker in his sermon so lost his voice that he was
fain to leave off and come down in the midst; Dr Shaa by his sermon lost
his honesty, and soon after his life, for very shame of the world.'[157]

In common with some other renaissance writers More included descriptions of low life in his narrative of more weighty matters. He gives a moving
description of the courtesan, Jane Shore, a former mistress of Edward IV.
He uses her fate, in juxtaposition to the prosperity of the great, to typify
the double standards of the age, not only Richard's but also those of some of
his eminent subjects. Richard, accusing her of complicity in Hastings'
'conspiracy', despoiled her of her goods and made her do public penance.
By More's day she was reduced to beggary, and yet she had often interceded
with Edward IV for men then rich and famous. Her sins were venal compared with theirs: 'her doings were not much less, albeit they be much less
remembered because they were not so evil.'[158]

More includes in his account of Jane Shore the ironic comment that
Richard acted towards her 'as a goodly continent prince, clean and fault-
less himself, sent out of heaven into this vicious world for the amendment

---

[153] More also plays humorously on words. See, for example, his play on 'trusty' and 'trusting'
($R III$, p. 52), on 'kind', 'kindness', 'kindly' (p. 65), and on 'kinsmen' and 'kindly' (p. 83).
[154] $R III$, p. 47.
[155] $R III$, p. 62.
[156] $R III$, p. 64.
[157] $R III$, p. 59. For another joke see p. 450 and n. 172 below.
[158] $R III$, pp. 54–7.

of men's manners'.[159] This comment is typical of More's use of irony to add force to his argument. A few other examples may be cited: Buckingham in his speech at St Paul's Cross in support of Richard's claim to the throne refers his audience for better authority to Shaa's sermon, because Shaa was a virtuous man of God, and no honest man goes into a pulpit to tell lies.[160] Richard was much moved by the petition that he should take the crown, 'which else as every man may wit, would never of likelihood have inclined thereunto.'[161]

Irony and deception, both an important element in *Richard III*, involve the use of double meaning: what seems is contrasted to what is. The use of double meaning is a distinctive feature of the work, and gives the argument much of its persuasiveness. More's taste for this literary device was fostered by his interest in drama.[162] As a child he acted while in John Morton's household. His brother-in-law, John Rastell, had a stage in his country place. More was related by marriage to the playwright John Heywood, and, according to Erasmus, himself wrote plays.[163]

More presented the course of events to the readers in *Richard III* very much in the form of a play. King Richard himself made an excellent central character. More employed dialogue to good effect: his legal training and classical studies enabled him to write convincing speeches. He wrote neither an exact record of what was said nor rhetorical set pieces. His speeches are fictional representations of arguments cogently expressed. His characters voice with equal force opinions which More shared together with those with which he disagreed. An example of misdirected eloquence is the speech Buckingham addressed to Queen Elizabeth to persuade her that sanctuary was not appropriate for her second son:[164] the purpose of sanctuary was, he argued, to protect a person in danger—an innocent child neither needs nor can have such protection; all are protected against unlawful hurt.[165]

> I never heard erst of sanctuary children. And therefore as for the conclusion of my mind, who so may have deserved to need it, if they think it for their surety, let them keep it. But he can be no sanctuary man, that neither hath wisdom to desire it, nor malice to deserve it, whose life or liberty can by no lawful process stand in jeopardy.

---

[159] *R III*, p. 54.
[160] *R III*, p. 73.
[161] *R III*, p. 79.
[162] For More's interest in drama see A. N. Kincaid, 'The dramatic structure of Sir Thomas More's *History of King Richard III*' in *Studies in English Literature 1500–1900*, xii (1972), pp. 226–7.
[163] 'Adolescens comoediolas et scripsit et egit'; Allen and Allen, op. cit., iv. 16 (Ep. no. 999).
[164] *R III*, pp. 28–33.
[165] *R III*, p. 33.

More emphasizes the dramatic aspects of Richard's usurpation. There is no evidence that he invented incidents, but he treated them in such a way as to exploit their dramatic potential. An example occurs in the sermon Shaa delivered in support of Richard's hereditary claim to the throne. Part of his argument was that Edward IV's children were bastards, that Edward himself and Clarence were also probably bastards, and, therefore, that Richard was the only legitimate son of Richard duke of York. At this point Shaa was to pause and Richard himself appear to demonstrate that he was 'the sure undoubted image' of his father, but Richard missed his cue, arriving too late so that Shaa had to repeat his argument.[166] Stage management is again indicated in the description of Buckingham's meeting with the citizens in the Guildhall to persuade them to ask Richard to accept the crown. His speech, though repeated, failed to win applause, but eventually his supporters at the back of the hall cried 'King Richard! King Richard!'[167] Stage props are suggested by the reference to the 'barrels of harness' (i.e. armour), which Gloucester and Buckingham produced to convince the populace by 'colourable proof' that the queen's brother, Anthony Woodville, Lord Rivers, and her second son by her first marriage, Richard Grey, had plotted treason.[168] Theatrical costume seems implied by the detail that Buckingham appeared equipped with 'old ill-faring briginders' (i.e. body arms of foot-soldiers), as if he had arrived in an emergency, to announce to the specially assembled crowd that Hastings had conspired against him. (In fact Richard's plan was laid well beforehand).[169] And when finally Richard accepted the crown he appeared to the people on a gallery (reminiscent of a stage) outside Baynard's castle.[170]

Reader and Londoners alike are the audience. The reader is never deceived by events, but the Londoners at first are taken in by the subterfuge around them. Scepticism soon, however, prevails. No one believed Richard's accusation that his withered arm was the result of sorcery practised by the queen and Jane Shore—everyone knew he was born with it.[171] More jokes at the notion that the long proclamation, 'fair written on parchment', which was issued to justify Hastings' execution, could possibly have been composed within the two hours which had elapsed since that event: 'a schoolmaster of [St] Paul's, of chance standing by, and comparing the shortness of the time with the length of the matter, said unto them that stood about him, "Here is a gay, goodly cast [i.e. trick], foul cast away for haste"; and a merchant answered him that it was written by prophecy.'[172]

---

[166] *R III*, pp. 67–8.
[167] *R III*, p. 76.
[168] *R III*, p. 24. Mancini also mentions arms placed about the city in readiness for the Scottish war; *Usurpation*, p. 83.
[169] *R III*, p. 52.
[170] *R III*, p. 77.
[171] *R III*, p. 48.
[172] *R III*, p. 54.

When the Londoners had heard Shaa preach 'they stood as they had been turned into stones, for wonder of this shameful sermon',[173] and after listening to Buckingham's speech in the Guildhall they 'much marvelled ... and thought they never had in their lives heard so evil a tale so well told.'[174]

The climax of the work, Richard's acclamation as king, is also the climax of the dramatic structure. More points out that the Londoners were well aware that the performance in the Guildhall was pre-arranged, but disguised their knowledge. To explain the wisdom of their dissimulation More makes explicit use of theatrical imagery:[175]

> in a stage play all the people know right well, that he that playeth the sultan is percase a sowter [i.e. a shoemaker]. Yet if one should can so little good, to show out of season what acquaintance he hath with him, and call him by his own name while he standeth in his majesty, one of his tormentors might hap to break his head, and worthy for marring of the play. And so they said that these matters be kings' games, as it were stage plays, and for the more part played upon scaffolds, in which poor men be but the lookers-on. And they that wise be, will meddle no further.

The fact that More wrote *Richard III* in literary form does not mean that he did not regard it as a history. His interest in history is beyond doubt, and he was widely read in classical, medieval and renaissance historical works.[176] Besides writing *Richard III*, he intended to compose a history of Henry VII and one about Perkin Warbeck.[177]

Richard III is a valuable source for the period. It gives an account of the usurpation independent of all other known works.[178] More knew the verses of Pietro Carmeliano of Brescia, court scholar under Richard III and Henry VII, and those of Bernard André, court scholar under Henry VII, both of whom alternately praised and abused Richard. He may also have known André's *Life of Henry VII* which depicts Richard as a villain—but More did not borrow directly from it. And he may have used various biographies of Richard which were circulated in manuscript, and possibly a draft of Polydore Vergil's *Anglica Historia*; but there is no definite evidence of this.

Professor Pollard wrote that 'As history, More's book stands or falls by the value of its oral information.'[179] Only once does More give the name of an informant (perhaps he considered it politically dangerous to be specific):

[173] *R III*, p. 68.
[174] *R III*, p. 75.
[175] *R III*, p. 81.
[176] See *R III*, pp. lxxiii-lxxv, lxxxi-xcviii passim, 189–90.
[177] See *R III*, pp. 83, 262, 263.
[178] For the possible written sources of *Richard III* see *R III*, pp. lxx-lxxviii.
[179] A. F. Pollard, 'The making of Sir Thomas More's *Richard III*' in *Historical Essays in Honour of James Tait*, ed. J. G. Edwards *et al*. (Manchester 1933), p. 228.

he reports a piece of news on the authority of his father who heard it from a certain 'Mystlebrooke' who had it from 'one Pottyer dwelling in Red Cross street without Cripplegate'. 'Mystlebrooke' has been identified fairly certainly as William Mistlebrook (d. 1513), a servant successively of Edward IV, Richard III and Henry VII, and 'Pottyer' as Richard Potter, a servant of King Richard who was appointed an attorney in the chancery of the duchy of Lancaster in 1483.[180] Elsewhere More admits his use of oral information by some general phrase: 'it is for truth reported',[181] 'as the fame runneth',[182] 'this have I by credible information learned',[183] and 'as I have learned from them that much knew and little cause had to lie').[184] And he comments sceptically that 'evil words walk far.'[185]

More's possible sources of such information were excellent. He knew numerous important men.[186] One of his informants was of course his father, a judge of common pleas and then of king's bench, who could tell him at first hand about Richard's reign. But his principal informant was John Morton, in whose household he was educated. His father-in-law, John Roper, commissioner of array for Kent and then attorney general, was yet another of a number of men of affairs active in Richard III's reign whom More knew well. He may also have been acquainted with the antiquary John Rous through their mutual friend Richard Fox, later bishop of Winchester.[187]

In so far as the statements in *Richard III* can be checked, it seems, apart from a few curious errors, to be accurate.[188] Its narrative corresponds in all main particulars to that of Mancini, who wrote his objective account within a year of the events. This gives credence to the information in the work which is not found elsewhere, for example, the statement that Richard had 'forethought to be king' even before Edward IV's death,[189] and the details about Jane Shore.

Richard III is also a valuable source for opinions concerning Richard in the early Tudor period, and for the growth of the legend surrounding

---

[180] *R III*, pp. 9, 170.
[181] *R III*, p. 7.
[182] *R III*, p. 7.
[183] *R III*, p. 9.
[184] *R III*, p. 86.
[185] *R III*. p. 26.
[186] For the following and other of More's informants see *R III*, pp. lxviii-lxx passim. For the possibility that More knew John Russell, bishop of Lincoln, whose possible authorship of the memoir in the second continuation of the Crowland chronicle has been mentioned above (pp. 270–1); see *R III*, p. lxxii.
[187] *R III*, p. lxxii.
[188] See *R III*, p. lxxix, and A. F. Pollard, 'Sir Thomas More's "Richard III"' in *History*, xvii (1933), p. 320.
[189] *R III*, p. 8.

him.[190] More sketches Richard as wicked and ill-favoured:[191]

> Richard, [Richard duke of York's] third son, . . . was in wit and
> courage equal to either of [his brothers], in body and prowess far
> under them both: little of stature, ill-featured of limbs, crook-
> backed, his left shoulder much higher than his right, hard favour-
> ed of visage, and such as is in states [i.e. noblemen] called warly, in
> other men otherwise. He was malicious, wrathful, envious, and
> from afore his birth, ever froward. It is for truth reported that
> the duchess his mother had so much ado in her travail, that she
> could not be delivered of him uncut, and that he came into the
> world with the feet forward, as men be born outward, and (as the
> fame runneth) also not untoothed—whether men of hatred re-
> port above the truth, or else that nature changed her course in
> his beginning, which in the course of his life many things un-
> naturally committed. . . .

This legendary description of Richard (which More admits was based
at least in part on rumour) is corroborated by other writers. The description of his appearance and ill-nature resemble Vergil's sketch.[192] Both
Vergil and John Rous[193] mention Richard's unequal shoulders (Vergil
does not state which was the highest, but Rous alleges that it was the right
one). And Rous also notes the peculiar circumstances of Richard's birth.

More's literary interpretation of Richard's motivation, combined
with the legendary embellishments, provided the sixteenth and seventeenth
century dramatists with their model. Through them this portrait reached
an audience of ordinary people, while at the same time Vergil's narrative
was forming the opinion of the educated public. Together Vergil and More
created the 'saga of King Richard' which has become part of our national
myth.

---

[190] For the 'saga' of Richard III see A. R. Myers, 'Richard III and historical tradition' in
History, liii (1968), pp. 181–202.
[191] *R III*, pp. 7–8.
[192] See p. 440 above.
[193] For Rous's account of Richard see p. 316 above.

Epilogue

Having surveyed nearly 1,000 years of English historiography, it is appropriate to try to assess briefly the medieval achievement and its legacy to the later period. The main characteristics of medieval historiography, both that dealing with general and that dealing with local history, will be discussed: first, up to the end of the fourteenth century, and, second, as a prelude to the later age, in the fifteenth century; it will be necessary in these two sections to recapitulate apposite points made earlier in this survey. Finally, what happened to the medieval tradition of historical writing in the sixteenth century will be considered.

Much has been written on the idea of history in the middle ages.[1] The Christian concept was defined by Orosius: history demonstrated the workings of God's will on earth; as mankind proceeded towards its destiny, the last judgment and eternal life in heaven and hell, God rewarded virtue, punished vice and otherwise showed His omnipotence.[2] (The fact, however, that historians implicitly or explicitly interpreted events as manifestations of the divine will, did not preclude them from also attributing an event to a natural cause.)[3] Moreover, an historian might adopt a literary

---

[1] See, for example, Benedetto Croce, *Theory and History of Historiography*, translated by Douglas Ainslie (London 1921), pp. 200–23, R. G. Collingwood, *The Idea of History* (Oxford 1946), pp. 52–6; J. T. Shotwell, *An Introduction to the History of History*, i (New York 1922, revised edition New York 1939), pp. 255–377; B. M. Lacroix. 'The notion of history in early mediaeval historians' in *Mediaeval Studies*, x (Toronto, 1948), pp. 219–23; and the same author's *L'Historien au moyen âge* (Montreal-Paris 1971). For a lucid recent summary of medieval historiographical ideas see Beryl Smalley, *Historians in the Middle Ages* (London 1974), pp. 27–49.

[2] See p. 427 above.

[3] For examples of events attributed simultaneously to divine and natural causation see Bernard Guenée, 'Y a-t-il une historiographie médiévale?' in *Revue Historique*, cclviii (1977) pp. 262–3, and Gransden, *Historical Writing*, i. 20–1 and n. 68, 22. For examples of authors who clearly believed in divine causation, but who on occasion gave a natural cause, see ibid., i. 4, 32 and n. 17, 51 and n. 68, 176, 181–2 and n. 136. The opinion expressed by Peter Burke,

structure to reflect the divine scheme. St Augustine handed down to the middle ages two methods of dividing history into periods: there were the Seven Ages, corresponding with the seven days of the Creation;[4] and there were the Four Monarchies, derived from the apocalyptic visions in the Book of Daniel and the Book of Revelation.[5]

According to the Orosian concept the purpose of history was to edify the reader: it was to teach him by examples to appreciate that God rewards virtue and punishes vice, and to make him comprehend the divine power. To reinforce the edificatory content the writer might also include moral excursuses, sometimes launching into a full-scale tirade against the corruption of the times.

Although historians in medieval England took the Orosian doctrine for granted, they made slight use of it. They sporadically attributed events to divine intervention, but such attributions usually read more like pious exclamations than profound reflections.[6] And a few inveighed against contemporary depravity. But only Henry of Huntingdon, writing in homiletic vein, sustained a pious theme: he repeatedly emphasized the transitory nature of all earthly achievement and prosperity, and the mercilessness of death to the greatest and to the most humble alike.[7] In addition, Henry adopted divisions in his *Historia Anglorum* which illustrate God's retributive power: he divided English history into five sections, each beginning with a conquest—God's punishment for the sins of the people.[8] Henry's divisions were simple, but few other writers in medieval England used even such a rudimentary structure: the norm was a record of events (usually beginning at the Creation or the Norman Conquest) in chronological order, with only year divisions. An exception to this generalization is Ranulf Higden, who adopted an elaborate structure in order to fit all seven books of his *Polychronicon* (which, as a universal history in the encyclopaedic tradition, inevitably included geographical information and pagan material) into a biblical framework.[9]

The Renaissance Sense of the Past (London 1969), pp. 1–20, that historians in the middle ages did not give the causes of events, had no sense of anachronism and were not critical is, as Professor Guenée points out (op. cit., pp. 261–3), demonstrably false. See also pp. 463, and nn. 55, 56, 465 and n. 66 below.

[4] For the concept of the Seven Ages of the World see Augustine, *De Civ. Dei*, xxii. 30, and Auguste Luneau, *L'Histoire du salut chez les pères de l'église* (Paris 1964), pp. 285 et seq., 352 et seq., and C. A. Patrides, *The Grand Design of God* (London 1972), pp. 18–22 and nn.

[5] For the theory of the Four Monarchies, which goes back to biblical and classical times, see J.W. Swain, 'The theory of the Four Monarchies: opposition history under the Roman Empire' in *Classical Philology*, xxxv (1940), pp. 1–21, and H. L. Ginsberg, *Studies in Daniel* (New York 1948), pp. 5–23,

[6] In this view I agree with Professor Partner: see N. F. Partner, *Serious Entertainments: the Writing of History in Twelfth-Century England* (Chicago-London 1977), pp. 213–21 passim.

[7] See Gransden, *Historical Writing*, i. 197, and Partner, op. cit., pp. 28–40.

[8] See *Henrici Archidiaconi Huntendunensis Historia Anglorum*, ed. Thomas Arnold (RS 1879), p. 8. Cf. Partner, op. cit., pp. 22–8.

[9] See pp. 45–7 above, and A. Gransden, 'Silent meanings in Ranulf Higden's *Polychronicon*

There are of course other methods besides the use of literary structure by which a history can be given cohesion.[10] On a limited scale causality can unify: if a work's primary object is to show why and how an important event took place, and what its results were, it has a thematic structure. However, as has been seen, the workings of divine providence are only exceptionally demonstrated with enough consistency and frequency to give unity. Similarly, natural causation is far too rarely mentioned to serve the purpose.

A strong bias, based on well thought out views, is another means of imposing unity on a history. But such bias is not common in medieval English historiography. The typical chronicler was politically uncommitted. He put local interests first and, in a sporadic and unsystematic way, tended to be hostile to central authority, whether royal or papal, especially if it came into conflict with his own monastery or church. In the case of Matthew Paris this hostility is so persistent and so carefully considered that it can be said to constitute a unifying theme. Matthew derived his political attitudes partly from his predecessor at St Albans, Roger of Wendover, a bitter critic of King John, in whose reign he lived.[11] In the same way exceptional circumstances at other times produced consistent political attitudes. Most chroniclers who wrote during the Barons' War were ardent supporters of Simon de Montfort and his cause, some of the chronicles even having a propagandist tone in favour of the barons.[12] Furthermore, in the reign of Richard II an historical monograph was composed which is in fact a well argued propagandist pamphlet in support of the lords appellant: this is the account of the Merciless Parliament of 1388 by the civil servant Thomas Favent.[13]

Chronicles written in favour of the government, equally with those inimical to central authority, have a unitary theme. However, official history, in the sense of government commissioned history, was extremely rare in medieval England.[14] Indeed, no example of a chronicle with specific evidence of such a commission survives. Nevertheless, some chronicles represent the government's point of view so exactly that it seems almost certain or at least very likely that they were commissioned; and if they

---

and in Thomas Elmham's *Liber Metricus de Henrico Quinto*' in *Medium Ævum*, xlvi (1978), pp. 231–3.

[10] The literary structure of Einhard's *Life of Charlemagne* was to some extent reproduced in the surviving royal biographies written in the Anglo-Saxon period—Asser's *Life of King Alfred*, the Life of King Canute (the *Encomium Emmae*), and the *Life of King Edward* (the Confessor); see Gransden, *Historical Writing*, i. 51–2, 56, 60. For classical influence on these biographies see p. 458 and n. 25 below.

[11] See Gransden, *Historical Writing*, i. 367–74.

[12] Ibid., i. 407–36 passim.

[13] Pp. 185–6 above.

[14] See A. Gransden, 'Propaganda in English medieval historiography' in *Journal of Medieval History*, i (1975), pp. 363–82.

were not actually commissioned, they were certainly written to please the king. The Alfredian version of the Anglo-Saxon Chronicle, with its propaganda in favour of the royal house of Wessex, was probably written at the request of King Alfred.[15] The continuation composed under Edward the Elder, Alfred's son, maintains the official bias,[16] but thenceforth the Anglo-Saxon Chronicle became localized in the monasteries where it was continued, only retaining traces of central influence.[17]

For at least two centuries after the Norman Conquest no history was written in England which can even tentatively be called official. Meanwhile the genre was common on the continent. It is noteworthy that the two narratives of the Conquest itself which give the Norman version of events and justify Duke William's actions, were composed in Normandy by the Norman historians William of Jumièges and William of Poitiers.[18] But although traces of Norman propaganda in support of the invasion occur in the Anglo-Norman chronicles, notably in William of Malmesbury's,[19] no official *pièce justificative* is known to have been written in England.

It was apparently towards the end of the thirteenth century that the government began to fully appreciate the value of history as an instrument of propaganda. Edward I, in the trial of the claims of the competitors to the Scottish throne in 1291 and 1292, cited historical precedents to justify his own claim to overlordship of Scotland. To obtain evidence he ordered the monasteries to ransack their chronicles, and he had their findings entered on the official record of the proceedings. Moreover, he sent copies of the competitors' submissions to his judgment to the monasteries for transcription into their chronicles.[20] The inclusion of an isolated piece of government propaganda did not of course transform a monastic chronicle into an official history. However, to this period belongs one chronicle which has throughout the characteristics of an official history. This is the so-called 'Merton' *Flores Historiarum*, one of the continuations from 1265 to 1306 of Matthew Paris' *Flores*, which may have been written at Westminster and consistently eulogizes Edward I. Possibly this continuation of the *Flores* was written in response to a royal command, or at least it may have been written to please the king.[21]

The *Flores Historiarum* was later continued from 1307 to 1327 by Robert

---

[15] Gransden, *Historical Writing*, i. 34–5.

[16] Ibid., i. 35–6.

[17] Ibid., i. 38–41.

[18] Ibid., i. 94–102 passim.

[19] Ibid., i. 173–4.

[20] Ibid., i. 441–3, and E. L. G. Stones, 'The appeal to history in Anglo-Scottish relations between 1291 and 1401: Part I' in *Archives*, ix (1969), passim.

[21] Gransden, *Historical Writing*, i. 456–63. The 'Merton' *Flores* and the chronicle of Robert of Reading are discussed in some detail in A. Gransden, 'The continuations of the *Flores Historiarum* from 1265 to 1327' in *Mediaeval Studies*, xxxvi (Toronto 1974), pp. 472–92.

of Reading, a monk of Westminster. This continuation, like the previous one, reads like an official history, and may well have been written to justify the coup of Queen Isabella and Roger Mortimer in 1327: it systematically denigrates Edward II.[22] In the reign of Edward III Robert of Avesbury wrote of the king's military successes with such fulsome praise as to suggest the possibility that he wrote to please the king.[23] And in the reign of Henry IV government propaganda again influenced historiography: three important chroniclers, including Thomas Walsingham at St Albans, gave the Lancastrian version of Richard II's deposition, and copied extracts from the official account on the rolls of parliament.[24]

Despite the occasional use of chronicles to express the views of opponents of the central government and of the government itself, it cannot be claimed that bias played an important part in the development of thematic unity in chronicle writing. The case of the royal biography is different. This genre was not popular in medieval England. Indeed up to the end of the fourteenth century the only surviving examples were the three biographies written in the Anglo-Saxon period, Asser's *Life of King Alfred*, the Life of King Canute (the *Encomium Emmae*), and the *Life of King Edward* (the Confessor). These have some literary structure, which the *Life of King Alfred* certainly, and the *Encomium* and the *Life of King Edward* probably derived from Einhard and so ultimately from Suetonius. In addition, as Sir Richard Southern has pointed out, their prose style and theme give them 'artistic form'.[25] They were written in the tradition of classical rhetoric, the purpose of which was to persuade the reader of the truth of the author's point of view. To do so the author was not bound to be accurate on points of detail, only to convey a general truth. The royal biographies were intended to eulogize the kings in question, and are biased to that end. They have, therefore, thematic unity, but cannot be regarded as typical of the historical writing of medieval England.

The strength of the tradition of English medieval historiography lay not in the cultivation of abstract ideas about history, nor in the composition of works unified by literary structure or consistent theme. It lay in contemporary reportage—eyewitness accounts, accounts based on oral evidence[26] and on documents, put together piecemeal in chronological

---

[22] Pp. 17–22 above, and see the previous note.
[23] P. 68 above.
[24] Pp. 140, 187 above.
[25] For these biographies see A. Gransden, *Historical Writing*, i. 46–66. For Sir Richard Southern's views see R. W. Southern, 'Aspects of the European tradition of historical writing. 1. The classical tradition from Einhard to Geoffrey of Monmouth' in *TRHS*, fifth series, xx (1970), pp. 173–96 passim. Sir Richard points out that Geoffrey of Monmouth's *Historia Regum Britanniae* has 'artistic' form, because its powerful theme, the glorious history and destiny of an ancient and noble people from its origin in classical times, gives it unity; see Southern, op. cit., pp. 193–4.
[26] On the importance to the historian in the middle ages of oral evidence see Guenée, op. cit., p. 268.

order to create a serial, episodic narrative.[27] Sometimes the text was brief and bald, as in the case of the Anglo-Saxon chronicle, and sometimes it extended to flowing and colourful prose, as in the case of Matthew Paris' chronicles.

Although, as stated above, the primary intention of history written in the Christian mode established by Orosius was to edify the reader, in practice it served a variety of other purposes. Some works (especially royal biographies) were intended to provide rulers with examples of behaviour. The ruler should benefit morally from such examples, but he might also learn political lessons from them. Another purpose of historical works was to record events for the benefit of posterity. However, perhaps the most important purpose was to provide the reader with news—to satisfy his curiosity about current affairs. The reader might find the information useful, and he would certainly find it interesting and enjoyable. Nor should it be forgotten that the desire to entertain was itself often in the mind of the historian.

An historian's intention to entertain might find expression in the use of elegant Latin. But some authors, whose main object was to amuse, adopted for their contemporary history the chivalric values characteristic of romance literature. The taste for chivalric narratives received a vital stimulus in England from the publication in 1136 of Geoffrey of Monmouth's *Historia Regum Britanniae* (*History of the Kings of Britain*), a work which although almost wholly fictional, masqueraded as a true history.[28] This taste was most fully expressed in the *chansons de geste*, poems in French which told the stories of valiant heroes of past ages: the hero of a *chanson* was an historic figure, but the lengthy account of his deeds was the product of the author's imagination. In the course of the twelfth century the literary style of the *chanson* was adopted for authentic histories. The earliest history in the romance style was Geoffrey Gaimar's *Estoire des Engleis*, written within a decade of the British History, which was the source of its early part.[29] Gaimar only continued his work to 1100, but later histories belonging to this genre dealt with contemporary events. There was Jordan Fantosme's chronicle of the war between England and Scotland in 1173 and 1174,[30] Ambroise's narrative of the Third Crusade, in which Richard I is the hero,[31] the Life of William the Marshal by an anonymous trouvère,[32] and Chandos Herald's Life of the Black Prince.[33] Although the *Scalacronica*

---

[27] On the taste of the historian in the middle ages for disconnected narrative in chronological order see Bernard Guenée, 'Histoires, annales, chroniques. Essai sur les genres historiques au moyen âge' in *Annales Économies Sociétés Civilisations*, xxviii (1973), pp. 1008–10.

[28] Gransden, *Historical Writing*, i. 201–9. For its thematic unity see note 25 above.

[29] Ibid., i. 209–11.

[30] Ibid., i. 236–8.

[31] Ibid., i. 238–42.

[32] Ibid., i. 345–55.

[33] Pp. 97–100 above.

by Sir Thomas Gray of Heton is in French prose, not verse, it must, because of its chivalric tone, be grouped with the romance histories.[34]

It will be observed that of the authors mentioned only Jordan Fantosme (who was educated in France) and Sir Thomas Gray (whose chronicle is not a typical romance history as it is not in verse) were Englishmen; the rest were Normans. Indeed, romance historiography never took root in England. However, it should not be regarded as quite separate from the tradition of the Latin chronicles. Many of the latter were influenced by chivalric tastes, as can be seen, for example, from their graphic battle scenes. Moreover, the romance histories treated contemporary events in much the same way as the Latin writers, producing a disconnected sequence of facts and episodes.

Conditions were favourable to the composition of contemporary history in medieval England. News was normally conveyed by word of mouth, but as a means of transmitting it in writing the chronicle had virtually no competition until the newsletter began to gain currency in the late thirteenth century.[35] In general chroniclers seem to have felt free to express their opinions without fear of retributive action from those in power. This was no doubt partly because they usually wrote for a limited audience: monks wrote for their own communities and perhaps for others of their order; or, if the author had a patron, whether an ecclesiastic or a layman, he wrote primarily for that patron and his household. However, there is evidence that sometimes the chroniclers were cautious. William of Malmesbury commented on the difficulties faced by the historian of contemporary affairs because of the danger of offending the great, and possibly his revision of his chronicles to mitigate his censure of important people was partly the result of circumspection.[36] Similarly, Matthew Paris' revision of the *Chronica Majora* may have been owing to the desirability of placating the powerful.[37] There is some indication that chroniclers were affected by government censorship. At least one chronicle appears to have been revised to modify a reference to the posthumous cult of Simon de Montfort, presumably in response to the Dictum of Kenilworth (clause 8).[38] And as has been seen, government propaganda had an influence on the accounts in the chronicles of the Scottish succession case and of Richard II's deposition.

The contemporary historian in the middle ages was not hampered by the lack of research techniques—palaeography, diplomatic, philology, place-name study and archaeology—which obstructed inquiries into the more distant past. But the early periods could not be ignored. There was a theological reason for including them; history, seen as a manifestation

---

[34] Pp. 92–6 above.
[35] See Gransden, *Historical Writing*, i. 514.
[36] Ibid., i. 172, 181–2.
[37] Ibid., i. 370–1.
[38] Ibid., i. 396 and Plate XI. Cf. ibid., i. 401, 407 and n. 24.

of God's will on earth, started at the Creation of the world. In addition, there was a nationalistic motive for research into the remote past. Every country wanted to know its origins. This was partly the result of objective curiosity, but a more important motive was prestige—the more ancient a country's origins and the more glorious its history, the greater its reputation.

Since most chroniclers concentrated mainly on their own day, they tended to be perfunctory in their treatment of previous ages. In accordance with the dictates of Isidore of Seville they regarded history which they had not themselves experienced, as a vast expanse of time to be filled with a patchwork of extracts from the works of earlier and respected authorities.[39] Nevertheless, occasionally they compared literary accounts of an event and, in cases where evidence conflicted, might apply the test of common sense and decide in favour of the most likely version.[40]

The earliest historians in Britain showed a lively interest in their country's past. Gildas gave an account of Roman Britain, but his primary interest was in the history of Christianity, and so he included little pagan history and was not concerned with the original inhabitants.[41] On the other hand Bede in the *Ecclesiastical History* started at the beginning, with a geographical description of Britain and a brief history of the peoples who preceded the Anglo-Saxons.[42] Despite very limited information, his narrative is judicious. Nennius, writing a century later, was the first author to concentrate particularly on the ancient Britons, for whom he claimed a Trojan ancestry: the earliest settler was Brutus, son of Aeneas and a refugee from the fall of Troy. Thus Nennius introduced the element of myth into the history of British origins.[43] The writer, however, who finally supplied a detailed legendary history of the ancient Britons was Geoffrey of Monmouth.[44] His vivid narrative superseded Bede's brief but sensible few lines. With hardly a dissenting voice Geoffrey of Monmouth became the accepted authority, stifling further inquiry until the renaissance.[45]

Some research, however, was done after the Norman Conquest on the Anglo-Saxon period. The Conquest itself threatened the continuity of

---

[39] For Isidore's views on history see *Etymologiae*, bk I, caps xli–xliv.

[40] William of Newburgh's critique of Geoffrey of Monmouth is an excellent example of historical criticism in medieval England. See Gransden, *Historical Writing*, i. 264 and n. 137,265. See also pp. 49–50, 398 above. For the medieval historians' critical ability, with a continental example, see Guenée. 'Y a-t-il une historiographie médiévale?', p. 262.

[41] Gransden, *Historical Writing*, i. 3.

[42] Ibid., i. 16.

[43] Ibid., i. 11.

[44] See ibid., i. 204–5.

[45] There were, however, some medieval critics of Geoffrey of Monmouth; see ibid., i. 213, 246, and n. 40 above. For the influence of the British History in medieval England see T.D. Kendrick, *British Antiquity* (London 1950), pp. 1–17.

[461]

English history. Any cataclysm in the cultural tradition would deprive England of her famous past. Therefore, in the generation after the Conquest, historians attempted to write the history of the Anglo-Saxons. In the early twelfth century Florence of Worcester translated the Anglo-Saxon chronicle into Latin in order to form the early part of his chronicle.[46] William of Malmesbury, complaining that since Bede the Anglo-Saxons had neglected to record their history,[47] undertook more extensive research. He was particularly concerned with England's ecclesiastical past, discovering as much as he could about each bishopric and its bishops, each monastery and its saints.

William of Malmesbury's research was on a national scale: his *Gesta Pontificum*, which embodied the results, is virtually a survey of ecclesiastical England. But meanwhile similar investigations were proceeding at a local level.[48] The Conquest provided a variety of incentives for such research. Above all the monasteries had to reinforce their prestige. By so doing they could defend themselves more effectively against the alien rulers. The property of some was physically attacked. Others had to defend the reputations of their patron saints against the doubts cast on their sanctity by Anglo-Norman ecclesiastics.[49] And they had to compete with each other for status in the competitive society of the post-Conquest period. Prestige depended on a creditable past. The monks, therefore, wrote to prove that their houses had had praiseworthy and uninterrupted histories from the time of foundation.

A monk of Durham, perhaps Symeon, no doubt undertook to write a detailed history of the see of St Cuthbert because William the Conqueror harried the north, including estates belonging to Durham cathedral. The author used not only the cathedral archives but also his observation of antiquities.[50] A monastic writer tended to treat the patron saint of his monastery as the *persona* of that house, and in composing the saint's Life included much local history. Thus in the late eleventh century the hagiographer Goscelin undertook research on the early histories of the monasteries whose patron saints were the subjects of his Lives.[51] An example of

---

[46] Gransden, *Historical Writing*, i. 145. For other attempts of the monks of Worcester to establish the continuity of the history of their house from Anglo-Saxon times, see A. Gransden 'Cultural transition at Worcester in the Anglo-Norman period' in *The British Archaeological Association Conference Transactions: I. Medieval Art and Architecture at Worcester Cathedral* (1978), pp. 1–14.

[47] *Willelmi Malmesbiriensis Monachi de Gestis Pontificum Anglorum*, ed. N. E. S. A. Hamilton (RS, 1870), p. 4, and *Willelmi Malmesbiriensis Monachi de Gestis Regum Anglorum*, ed. William Stubbs (RS, 1887, 1889, 2 vols), i.2. Cf. Gransden, *Historical Writing*, i. 169.

[48] See Gransden, *Historical Writing*, i. 106, and R. W. Southern, 'Aspects of the European tradition of historical writing, 4. The sense of the past' in *TRHS*, fifth series, xxiii (1973), pp. 246–56.

[49] See Gransden, *Historical Writing*, i. 105–6.

[50] Ibid., i. 114–21.

[51] Ibid., i. 106–11.

research done as a result of rivalry between houses is William of Malmesbury's book on the antiquity of Glastonbury. This contains some of his best work and was written to defend Glastonbury against the allegation of the Canterbury hagiographer Osbern that Dunstan was the first abbot; William proved that the abbey had a far longer history.[52]

Research on the history of individual monasteries did not end immediately England recovered from the shock of the Norman settlement. Within less than a century the country suffered another, though a less traumatic and widespread upheaval, the anarchy of Stephen's reign. Again the monks resorted to their documents in order to strengthen the defences of their monasteries by means of historical writing.[53] They wanted to increase prestige in general, but, as the Ramsey chronicler explains, they also hoped to make rights to privilege and property more secure by defining them in detail and providing documentary evidence. Thus, in case of another period of disorder, the monks would be able to defend their houses more effectively. At Ramsey the chronicler, who can claim to be one of the first Anglo-Saxon scholars, did extensive work on the abbey's pre-Conquest charters, deciphering them and translating the English ones into Latin.[54]

Often a monastery's position was put in jeopardy not as a result of a national crisis, but for some local reason. For example, fire might damage its buildings and perhaps its relics and archives. This happened twice at Christ Church, Canterbury, in 1067 and again in 1174. A generation after the first fire Eadmer wrote an account of the architecture of the cathedral which had been destroyed, on the information of the monks who could remember it. His purpose was to describe the exact locations of the shrines housing the relics, and so to preserve the continuity of the cathedral's holy tradition from the period before the fire until his own day.[55] After the second fire another Canterbury monk, Gervase, wrote an architectural history of the cathedral, based partly on Eadmer, partly on oral information, and partly on his own observation. Again, his intention was to demonstrate that the relics had been saved and were preserved in the new choir.[56] The fire of 1184 in Glastonbury abbey resulted in a similar spate of local historiography. The purpose in this instance was more blatantly propagandist than at Canterbury. One means by which the monks sought to restore their finances was by boosting their pilgrim trade: they hoped to do this by proving that the abbey had an extremely long and extraordinarily holy past.[57]

[52] Ibid., i. 183–5. See also A. Gransden, 'The growth of the Glastonbury traditions and legends in the twelfth century' in *Journal of Ecclesiastical History*, xxvii (1976), pp. 341–6.
[53] Gransden, *Historical Writing*, i. 269–73 passim.
[54] Ibid., i. 274.
[55] Ibid., i. 131.
[56] Ibid., i. 255–6.
[57] Ibid., i. 184, and Gransden, 'The growth of the Glastonbury traditions and legends,' pp. 347 et seq.

Attacks by diocesan bishops were another reason why monks might do research on their house's history. Thus Gervase of Canterbury, in his account of the protracted dispute between the monks of Christ Church and Archbishop Baldwin (1184–90), made frequent appeals to historical precedents, reaching back to the time of St Augustine.[58] In the same way Thomas of Marlborough, a monk of Evesham, wrote a history of the abbey because of a dispute between the monks and Mauger, bishop of Worcester (1200–12), over the abbey's claim to exemption from episcopal authority; Thomas incorporated evidence relevant to the monks' case into his chronicle.[59]

Not all local histories were written as a result of disaster or contention. A number were composed primarily to instruct and entertain the inmates of religious houses. Matthew Paris' *Gesta Abbatum* comes into this category.[60] Such histories had the additional intention of enabling the well informed monk to impress pilgrims with the story of his abbey's past. They were also meant to edify the reader—to inspire the monks of the author's own day to emulate the spiritual and temporal achievement of their predecessors.[61] The foundation histories of the north country Cistercian abbeys have an edificatory tone, and at the same time express the piety of the early Cistercian monks.[62] Thomas of Eccleston's account of the arrival and early years of the Franciscan friars in England, though not a local history but the history of a religious order, had similar intentions— to instruct and edify the Franciscans themselves.[63]

There were, therefore, a number of reasons for research on local history. Some chroniclers (such as those at Glastonbury) resorted to legend in order to increase their abbey's prestige, and all were biased to a greater or lesser extent. Nevertheless, the reader is impressed less by their occasional credulity, wishful thinking and intellectual dishonesty, than by their frequently excellent scholarship. William of Malmesbury on the antiquity of Glastonbury, the Ramsey chronicler on the diplomatic of charters, and Gervase on the architectural history of Canterbury cathedral may be mentioned as outstanding, but there are many other examples of genuine antiquarian observation.[64] The conclusion is forced on the reader that at least some of this research was undertaken for its own sake, and was the result of objective curiosity.

In a few instances chroniclers make it clear that they had a sense of

---

[58] Gransden, *Historical Writing*, i. 253.
[59] Ibid., i. 519.
[60] Ibid., i. 374–7.
[61] Ibid., i. 375.
[62] Ibid., i. 270, 290–5.
[63] Ibid., i. 490–2.
[64] For references to examples see the index to ibid., i, under 'antiquarianism' and 'descriptions' passim.

anachronism—they understood that things in the past were different from those of their own times. Thus Gervase of Canterbury comments on the difference between the Norman style of architecture, as it existed in the cathedral choir before its destruction by the fire of 1174, and the Gothic style which replaced it.[65] And Matthew Paris describes the primitive shoes worn by earlier monks of St Albans (they were discovered when thirty bodies were exhumed in the cemetery);[66] he describes them, remarking that they could be worn on either foot and resembled those used by the poor in his own day.

It should also be remembered that to the late fourteenth century belongs the first 'topo-bibliographer', Henry Kirkstead, monk of St Edmunds. He not only meticulously listed and described the books in his own abbey's library, but also examined and made notes about those in other monastic libraries.[67]

It could be claimed that technically local historiography was in advance of the writing of general histories. As has been shown, more sound research into the remote past was done on local than on national history. In addition, competent local histories were written of contemporary affairs, containing good reportage and citations from documents; such works were usually factual and businesslike and were composed primarily as records.[68] It is also noteworthy that local histories, of both past and recent events, tended, unlike general histories, to have thematic unity. A theme could dominate them more easily than a general chronicle because of their limited scope. Many are monographs on some important event in a monastery's history— its foundation, the election of an abbot, or a legal dispute. Those which covered the whole of a monastery's history up to the author's own time were arranged as a series of abbatiates, which in turn were often subdivided according to subject, giving the whole some coherent structure.

The local histories of medieval England are not as well known as the general ones, and their significance is not perhaps sufficiently recognized, but they constitute an important element in the historiographical tradition of medieval England.

At the end of the fourteenth century the medieval tradition of historical writing was still intact. Contemporary history was being written by monks, secular clerks and laymen. The monks and secular clerks produced chronicles in Latin prose, and two laymen, Sir Thomas Gray and Chandos Herald continued the romance tradition of historiography in French. Indeed, in

---

[65] Ibid., i. 256 For the development of the sense of anachronism during the renaissance, see p. 428 above.
[66] Ibid., i. 372. For other examples of Matthew Paris' sense of anachronism see Guenée, 'Y a-t-il une historiographie médiévale?', pp. 261–2.
[67] Pp. 401–3 above.
[68] See for example those written in the abbey of Bury St Edmunds; Gransden, *Historical Writing*, i. 385–95.

the reign of Richard II there was a marked revival in the production of chronicles. Substantial works were written by Thomas Walsingham at St Albans, Henry Knighton at St Mary's, Leicester, and by anonymous chroniclers at Westminster, Canterbury and Evesham. An important secular chronicler of the period was Adam of Usk.

In the fifteenth century this picture changes. The tradition of romance historiography had only one follower, John Hardyng, and that of the monastic chronicle all but failed: John of Whethamsted's two 'registers', although they contain narratives of contemporary events, are not true chronicles,[69] and the best section of the Crowland chronicle, which relates to Edward IV's reign, is almost certainly a memoir by some layman (the rest of the chronicle mainly concerns local affairs).[70] A number of religious houses kept annals but most were brief and all were locally orientated. Nor did an abundance of chronicles by secular clerks compensate for the decline in the number of monastic ones. Moreover, the few secular chronicles which were written (notably John Benet's and John Warkworth's)[71] do not compare in fullness and quality with those of the previous era. The paucity of adequate contemporary histories is demonstrated by the importance scholars today have to place on works by foreigners—on the Life of Henry V by the Italian Titus Livius, written while Livius was resident in England,[72] and on the chronicle of England by the Fleming Jean de Waurin,[73] Philippe de Commynes's memoirs,[74] and Dominic Mancini's account of the usurpation of Richard III,[75] all written abroad.

Nevertheless, the fifteenth century is a significant period in the historiography of medieval England. In it there were developments which pointed the way to the future. The decline in the monastic and secular chronicle tradition was partly counterbalanced by the rise of the chronicles of London. The earliest known London chronicles, of the thirteenth and early fourteenth centuries, were in Latin, but those of the fifteenth century were in English. The annals are often short, but in general the London chronicles give a vivid account of life in the capital, and, because of the city's importance, are a valuable source for national history.[76] At the same time the *Brut* chronicles, some in Latin, some in French, but most in English, gained in popularity. At first they retained a chivalric tone, but as the century proceeded they came to resemble the London chronicles more and more closely.[77]

[69] Pp. 373–86 above.
[70] Pp. 265–74 above.
[71] Pp. 254–61 above.
[72] Pp. 210–13 above.
[73] Pp. 288–93 above.
[74] Pp. 295–300 above.
[75] Pp. 300–7 above.
[76] Pp. 227–45 above.
[77] Pp. 221–7 above.

The London chronicles, the *Brut* and Higden's *Polychronicon* were all fertile stock from which numerous continuations grew. In 1480 William Caxton printed a version of the *Brut* to 1461, and in 1482 he printed Trevisa's translation of the *Polychronicon*, to which he added his own continuation to 1460. Thus Caxton ensured the widespread dissemination and permanent influence of both works.[78]

Political propaganda left a deeper mark on fifteenth century historiography than it had on that of the preceding age. As has been seen, many of the accounts of Richard II's deposition written in Henry IV's reign have a strongly Lancastrian bias and include government propaganda.[79] Later in the fifteenth century this Lancastrian bias was replaced by one in favour of the house of York: almost without exception the chroniclers until the accession of Richard III supported the Yorkist cause, justifying the actions and the rule of the Yorkists in accordance with party propaganda.[80] The London chroniclers and the authors of the *Brut* continuations favoured the Yorkists because theirs was the party which promoted the war with France, a source of prosperity to the citizens of London. And any chronicler writing in the reign of Edward IV was moved by genuine enthusiasm for the king as well as by government propaganda to support the Yorkist cause. Yorkist propaganda not only contributed to the all pervasive bias in the chronicles, but also was responsible for the production of two monographs containing official history. These were the *Chronicle of the Rebellion in Lincolnshire* and the *History of the Arrival of Edward IV*, both written to justify Edward IV and his government; in order to rally support they were distributed on the continent as well as in England.[81]

In the fifteenth century the influence of humanism on English historiography can first be seen, although to a very limited extent. Humanism in fifteenth century England did not transform the concept of history, except perhaps in the case of *Arrival* and of the memoir in the Crowland chronicle relating to Edward IV's reign: it can be argued that both show a more rational approach to politics than any previous historical work; the authors' rationality may be ascribed to diplomatic training—which might well have resulted in contact with continental humanists.[82] Otherwise the medieval ideas about the causation of events survived unchanged. Nor did humanism result in the composition of well structured histories. The only fifteenth century chronicle with literary structure is Robert Fabyan's *New Chronicles of England and France* which is arranged in seven parts to correspond with the Seven Joys of the Virgin—a typically medieval piece of literary iconography.[83] And the only chronicles to have

---

[78] Pp. 221, 223 above.
[79] Pp. 140–3, 163–4, 178–88 passim above.
[80] Pp. 222, 225, 243, 251, 257, 277, 315, 411–12 above.
[81] Pp. 261–4 above.
[82] Pp. 263, 269 and n. 136, 427 and n. 20 above.

sufficient argument to give them thematic unity are the two Yorkist monographs, the chronicle on the Lincolnshire rebellion and that on Edward IV's arrival. It is not until the early sixteenth century that two truly humanist histories were composed, Polydore Vergil's *Historia Anglica* and Sir Thomas More's *History of Richard III*, the former being remarkable for its rationality, and the latter for its structural and thematic unity.

For the purpose of detecting the effect of humanism on historiography in the fifteenth century, it is necessary to consider not the structure and content of the historical works, but the style of the Latin prose in which they are written. In this respect three works are distinctive: they are written in Latin in accordance, the authors imagined, with the classical tradition. There are: Titus Livius' Life of Henry V; the Pseudo-Elmham, another Life of Henry V;[84] and the registers of John Whethamsted, abbot of St Albans.[85]

The fifteenth century, therefore, is a period of change and development in the writing of general history. It is also an important period in local historiography. Most of the monastic annals, as already noted, mainly concern local affairs. In addition works were written devoted exclusively or principally to the history of individual monasteries—Thomas Burton's history of the abbey of Meaux,[86] Thomas Elmham's history of St Augustine's, Canterbury,[87] John of Glastonbury's history of Glastonbury abbey,[88] the Crowland chronicle[89] and Thomas Rudborne's history of St Swithun's, Winchester.[90] Nearly all contain legends, occasionally to the almost total exclusion of the factual element—an extreme case is John of Glastonbury's flamboyant and largely fictional account of his abbey's early history. But equally most also include much sound research—Thomas Burton produced a remarkably scholarly and legend-free reconstruction of Meaux's past.

The chief merit of the histories by Thomas Burton and Thomas Elmham lies in their antiquarian observations. Indeed, the fifteenth century is remarkable for the flowering of the medieval antiquarian tradition. The two monks, Burton and Elmham, among others, applied their antiquarian zeal to the history of their own monasteries;[91] and two laymen, John Hardyng and William Worcester, applied theirs to a wider field. Hardyng mapped Scotland;[92] Rous studied a variety of antiquities but especially medieval armour, tracing its evolution;[93] and Worcester travelled southern

[83] P. 246 above.
[84] Pp. 210–17 above.
[85] Pp. 373–86 above.
[86] Pp. 355–71 above.
[87] Pp. 345–55 above.
[88] Pp. 398–400 above.
[89] Pp. 408–12 above.
[90] Pp. 394–8 above.
[91] Pp. 350–71 passim above.
[92] Pp. 285–7 above.
[93] Pp. 326–7 above.

England measuring churches and other buildings, and writing copious notes about whatever he saw of topographical interest.[94]

Thus the fifteenth century set the stage for the Tudor era.

The idea that the renaissance swept away the medieval tradition of historiography has long been discounted.[95] The two humanist histories written in England, Vergil's *Anglica Historia* and More's *Richard III*, stand outside the main stream of English historiography:[96] although the factual content of both was plundered by subsequent writers, the critical approach of the former and the literary form of the latter were not imitated. In the renaissance a new period of historiographical enlightenment did not suddenly dawn in England. The will of God was not immediately replaced by natural causation as the prime motive force in history. Histories did not all at once become secular instead of religious in tone. Nor were they transformed from annalistic chronicles into works with cohesive literary structure or thematic unity. The developments in these directions were slow and sporadic, and meanwhile medieval ideas and medieval techniques continued in most serviceable employment.

Initially historians turned to the medieval rather than to the classical historiographical tradition in order to equip themselves to meet the challenges of the times. And ultimately the alterations which took place in historical writing were less the result of ideas derived from the study of the classics, than of political and religious exigencies. Two factors profoundly affected the course of English historiography; the rule of the Tudor monarchs and the religious controversies of the sixteenth century.[97]

Henry VII's title to the throne was weak, and he and his successors needed whatever support propaganda could give them. The enthusiasm with which Henry's accession was welcomed by the historians who wrote shortly afterwards, John Rous and Robert Fabyan, was no doubt partly caused by genuine feeling but it was partly the result of government propaganda. Rous and Fabyan reflected the official Tudor viewpoint; they hailed Henry as the monarch who, by marrying Edward IV's eldest daughter Elizabeth and thus uniting the rival dynasties of Lancaster and York, finally ended the Wars of the Roses, and imposed law and order on the kingdom.[98] Bernard André, Henry VII's chaplain and biographer, wrote of the king in even more ecstatic terms.[99]

The historians' eulogy of Henry VII was not, however, the result only

---

[94] Pp. 331–41 above.
[95] Pp. 425–30 passim above.
[96] Chapter 14 above.
[97] Tudor historiography is the subject of two recent books. For a scholarly, factual study see May McKisack, *Medieval History in the Tudor Age* (Oxford 1971). For a more theoretical approach see F. J. Levy, *Tudor Historical Thought* (California 1967).
[98] Pp. 316, 247–8, respectively, above.
[99] P. 429 and n. 32 above.

of spontaneous enthusiasm and voluntary response to propaganda. It was also the result of fear. Writers had to be careful: as Sir Thomas More said, 'I love not much to talk of princes, as things not all out of peril', and his friend Erasmus too expressed unease.[100] Maybe caution engendered by insecurity prompted John Rous to remove the Yorkist bias from his Warwick roll and to substitute a Lancastrian one.[101] Fabyan may have had a similar reason for giving his chronicle throughout a bias in favour of the Lancastrians, although to do so he had to adapt what he borrowed from his principal source for English history, the London chronicles (which favoured the Yorkist cause).[102] There is no doubt that the desire to placate the ruling powers caused Polydore Vergil constantly to revise his *Anglica Historia* by modifying or removing contentious material.[103] Fear of reprisals could also result in delay in publication. More did not have his *Richard III* printed at all; it was first published eight years after his death.[104] Polydore Vergil did not publish the *Anglica Historia* for twenty years after he wrote it, and the continuation from 1509 to 1535, which he probably wrote in the 1540s, was not printed until 1555, the year of his death.[105] Both *Richard III* and the *Anglica Historia* were first printed abroad.

Although the repressive attitude of the Tudor government had an inhibiting effect on writers of contemporary history, its propaganda to some extent encouraged the study of the more distant past. The fifteenth century was treated as the prelude to the accession of Henry Tudor. Already John Hardyng had written of the doom which enshrouded the Lancastrian kings because of Henry Bolingbroke's illegal seizure of power and the murder of Richard II.[106] Polydore Vergil expanded this theme: he saw God's vengeance manifested in the alternation of an unhappy reign with a more propitious one, and regarded Richard III as the wickedest of kings.[107] This embryonic historiographical structure reached its full development in the chronicle of Edward Hall, completed in about 1532.[108] His work is divided into seven parts. He did not adopt the typically medieval divisions of the Seven Ages of the World, nor even, like Fabyan, of the Seven Joys of the Virgin Mary, but used secular divisions, namely the seven reigns of the kings of England from Henry IV to Henry VIII. Hall was an ardent

---

[100] Pp. 443–4 above.
[101] Pp. 316–17 above.
[102] P. 247 above.
[103] Pp. 432–3 above.
[104] P. 443 above.
[105] Pp. 432–3 above.
[106] P. 278 above.
[107] Pp. 439–41 above.
[108] The standard edition of Hall's chronicle is *Hall's Chronicle* . . . , ed. Henry Ellis (London 1809). Hall's chronicle is discussed in McKisack, op. cit., pp. 105–11, Levy, op. cit., pp. 173–9, and *AH*, ed. Hay, pp. xxxvi–xxxviii. For Hall's life, and for the date of composition of his chronicle and the independent value of the latter part, see A. F. Pollard, 'Edward Hall's will and chronicle' in *BIHR*, ix (1932), pp. 171–7.

patriot and wrote full-blooded prose in praise of the English in general and of the house of Tudor in particular. The evidence of God's vengeance—the reigns of disaster alternating with those of prosperity—is more marked in Hall's chronicle than in Vergil's, and assumes the power of a drama; the calamities of Richard III's reign have become the ultimate retribution, and the accession of Henry Tudor the dawning of a new era, now that God's anger was spent. Hall's view of the fifteenth century has been described as 'a dramatic progression from concord to discord and back to concord',[109] a theme which has a parallel in More's *Richard III*.[110]

In its emphasis on secular power and its predominantly secular tone, and in its literary and thematic unity, Hall's chronicle resembles a renaissance history. However, Hall's debt to his medieval predecessors is equally apparent. He derived nearly all his information from the fifteenth century chronicles, notably the chronicles of London. It is, therefore, hardly surprising that his work has medieval features: it is arranged in strictly chronological order, and its very theme derives from the idea of divine justice.

Tudor propaganda not only encouraged the study of fifteenth century history, but also contributed to enthusiasm for study of the very remote past. The history of the ancient Britons had a positive attraction for the Tudor dynasty. Henry VII, a Welshman, had fulfilled the prophecy of Cadwallader, the last British king who, according to Geoffrey of Monmouth, had predicted that a Briton would once again rule the land.[111] And if Henry himself was not the reimbodiment of King Arthur—legend related that Arthur was not dead but would return—perhaps his eldest son would be. When in 1486 a son was born to Henry, he was named Arthur. On the occasion of a visit by the young prince to Coventry in 1499, he was greeted by a pageant in which an actor played King Arthur and declared that the prince would equal that hero in might.[112]

In the sixteenth century the cult of King Arthur flourished as never before. Belief in the British History became an adjunct of patriotism. The legends provided the Tudors themselves with a long line of valiant ancestors and the country with a glorious past. They supplied poets with favourite themes, and were believed by reputable historians.[113] The antiquary John

---

[109] *AH*, ed. Hay, p. xxxvii. Cf. McKisack, op. cit., p. 110.

[110] See p. 445 above. It will be remembered that More's *Richard III*, like Hall's chronicle, has dramatic features.

[111] See Kendrick, *British Antiquity*, p. 35.

[112] Ibid., pp. 36–7 and n. 1. For the sixteenth century cult of the British History, and especially of King Arthur, see ibid., pp. 34–44. The use made by the Tudors of the British History for propaganda is discussed in Sydney Anglo, 'The *British History* in early Tudor propaganda' in *BJRL*, xliv (1961–2), pp. 17–48; Dr Anglo argues convincingly that after the initial enthusiasm of Henry VII, as a Welshman, for the British History (from which he acquired a genealogy back to Brutus, the idea of himself as the fulfiller of the prophecy of Cadwallader, and an association with King Arthur), he and the succeeding Tudor monarchs made progressively less use of it for propaganda purposes.

[113] The British History was believed, for example, by John Bale and John Stow; see Levy,

Leland was moved by patriotism and loyalty to Henry VIII and his dynasty, to publish a spirited defence of the British History against Polydore Vergil who had dared to cast doubts on it.[114] Indeed Vergil was widely abused for questioning such an essential part of the national heritage.[115]

By these means the Tudors tried to build a bridge connecting the present with the past, in order to strengthen their political position. At the end of the period the use which they had made of history was reflected in the works of Shakespeare. His history plays, written in the last decade of the sixteenth century, contain the Tudor view of the reign of Richard II, of the fifteenth century Lancastrian kings and of Richard III.[116] (In the early seventeenth century Shakespeare used two stories which he derived in part, either directly or indirectly, from the British History, for *King Lear* and *Cymbeline*.)[117]

The need to prove continuity between past and present was even greater in the religious than in the political sphere. The reformation threatened to disrupt the course of English religious history. The church of England, with its institutions and its dogmas, might well have found itself rootless, unable to derive either strength or prestige from the past. It was inevitable, therefore, that the reformation should have a powerful influence on historiography. History was used to provide specific precedents in the conflicts, to justify the allegations of the participants on particular points. But it was also used in a more general way, to prove, on the one hand, that the Catholic church in medieval times was corrupt, and, on the other hand, that the reformers of the sixteenth century had precursors in the earlier period. Henry VIII himself used historical evidence to justify his repudiation of papal authority.[118] Religious controversy provided an incentive to the researches of John Leland, the antiquary (d. 1552),[119] and of John

---

op. cit., pp. 132, 189. For the widespread belief in the British History and in similar legendary material in the sixteenth century see Kendrick, op. cit., pp. 65 et seq.

[114] Leland's critique of Vergil's views and defence of the Arthurian legends are in his *Assertio Inclytissimi Arturii* (London 1544). The *Assertio* is reprinted, together with a sixteenth century translation, in *The Famous Historie of Chinon of England*, ed. W. E. Mead (EETS, original series, clxv, 1925). See also Edwin Greenlaw, *Studies in Spenser's Historical Allegory* (Baltimore 1932), pp. 11–15, Kendrick, op. cit., pp. 85–98 passim, and Levy, op. cit., pp. 130–1.

[115] See *AH*, ed. Hay, p. xxxiv–xxxv.

[116] See E. M. W. Tillyard, *Shakespeare's History Plays* (London 1944), pp. 29–54, 59–64, and passim. For Shakespeare's *Henry V* see pp. 194–5 above, and for his view of English history in the late middle ages see p. 443 above.

[117] In the case of *King Lear*, Shakespeare's debt to Geoffrey of Monmouth may have been direct; in the case of *Cymbeline* he probably derived Geoffrey's story indirectly, from Holinshed. See Geoffrey Bullough, *Narrative and Dramatic Sources of Shakespeare* (London-New York 1957–73, 8 vols), vii. 272–3, 280, 281; viii. 7–8, 10, 11, 38 et seq.

[118] See J. J. Scarisbrick, *Henry VIII* (London 1968), p. 314. However, it was on canon law, not on historical precedent, that Henry VIII mainly based his case; ibid., Chap. VII passim, 255–6, 315.

[119] For John Leland's life and work see Kendrick, op. cit., pp. 45–64, Levy, op. cit., pp. 126–7, and McKisack, op. cit., pp. 1–11.

Bale, the topo-bibliographer (d. 1563).[120] When Leland set out in 1533, with a commission from Henry VIII, to examine the libraries of monasteries and colleges in search of 'ancient writers', one of his motives was religious. This is made clear in the progress report of his 'laborious journey', which he sent to the king in 1546 probably as a new year's gift, and, therefore, is called Leland's New Year's Gift. In it he describes his achievements and outlines his future plans.[121] He states that he had intended by salvaging the evidences of the medieval past, to ensure that 'the holy Scripture of God might both be sincerely taught and learned, all manner of superstition and craftily coloured doctrine of a rout of the Roman bishops totally expelled out of this your most catholic realm'.[122] And he claimed to have discovered 'full many things ... concerning the usurped authority of the Bishop of Rome and his complices, to the manifest and violent derogation of kingly dignity'.[123] (One of Leland's other works was a piece of apologetic in defence of Henry's assertion of royal supremacy against the pope.)[124]

John Bale, an ex-Carmelite who became a virulent protestant polemicist, began studying medieval history in order to find support, as a recent scholar asserts, for the pro-monarchical, anti-papal views of the Henrician apologists.[125] (His works include a play about King John in which the king,[126] depicted as a good ruler and a forerunner of the protestants, is the hero, and a chronicle denigrating and slandering English monasticism, which he published in 1546.)[127] Matthew Parker, archbishop of Canterbury (1559–75), quoted historical precedents in his arguments against both Calvinists and Catholics, and undertook his impressive research

---

[120] For John Bale's life and work see Levy, op. cit., pp. 89–97, and McKisack, op. cit., pp. 11–23.

[121] Leland's New Year's Gift is printed in *Itinerary of John Leland*, ed. L. Toulmin Smith (London 1907–10, 5 vols), i. xxxvi-xliii. See also ibid., p. xii, Kendrick, op. cit., pp. 47–8, and McKisack, op. cit., pp. 5–6. Bale published Leland's New Year's Gift in 1549 with a valuable commentary of his own; for a modern edition of Bale's text see p. 477 n. 145 below (for citations, etc. from it see pp. 477 and n. 145, 478 and nn. 148, 150 below).

[122] *Itinerary of John Leland*, ed. Toulmin Smith, i. xxxviii.

[123] Ibid., i. xxxix.

[124] Ibid., i. xv, xxxix.

[125] Levy, op. cit., p. 97.

[126] *King Johan*, ed. J. H. P. Pafford (Malone Soc., London 1931). See Levy, op. cit., p. 93. For Bale as a dramatist see T. B. Blatt, *The Plays of John Bale* (Copenhagen 1968).

[127] *The Actes of Englysh Votaryes* (Wesel 1546). See McKisack, op. cit., p. 13. Bale also wrote the Lives of protestant 'saints', Sir John Oldcastle and Mistress Anne Askew. The Lives are printed *A brefe Chronycle concernynge the Examinacyon and death of the blessed martyr of Christ syr Johan Oldecastell* (Antwerp 1544), *The first examinacyon of Anne Askewe* (Wesel 1546), and *The lattre examinacyon of Anne Askewe* (Wesel 1547). As a Protestant hagiographer Bale was indebted to the medieval hagiographical tradition (before his conversion to protestantism he had written lives of Catholic, especially Carmelite, saints), and was a forerunner of John Foxe. See L. P. Fairfield, 'John Bale and the development of Protestant hagiography in England' in *Journal of Ecclesiastical History*, xxiv (1973), pp. 145–60.

projects on medieval history in order to find historical justification for the Elizabethan church settlement.[128]

The need for precedents led to the careful examination of the chronicle sources. Towards the end of his life Bale compiled a list of manuscripts, which he sent with a letter to Parker, for the purpose of helping the archbishop in his studies. He commented on the particular interest of each. Of Matthew Paris' *Chronica Majora* he wrote: 'no chronicle painteth out the bishop of Rome in more lively colours, nor more lively declareth his execrable proceedings, than it doth.'[129] And the Catholic polemicist, Thomas Stapleton, translated Bede's *Ecclesiastical History* and had it printed in Antwerp in 1565, in order to provide clear proof that the church in England was of papal origin.[130]

Thus there were specific motives, both political and religious, for historical research during the Tudor period; there was also the motive of patriotism—and, to an indefinable degree, scholars felt the urge of objective curiosity. John Leland told Henry VIII in his New Year's Gift that one reason for his visits to libraries was to ensure that the 'ancient writers . . . of this your own province . . . receive like thanks of the posterity', as those of other lands had done. Another reason was to benefit learning.[131] Similarly, John Bale wrote his most famous work, the *Illustrium Maioris Britanniae Scriptorum Summarium* (*A Summary of the Famous Writers of Great Britain*) partly because of his love of his country and of letters.[132] To compile this book Bale ransacked the topo-bibliographical notes of Henry Kirkstead of Bury St Edmunds, and of John Leland, besides the libraries of his friends. His research makes it evident that he had, besides religious bigotry and patriotic feeling, a sincere love of learning. In the words of a recent scholar, he had 'a reverence and enthusiasm for the sources of English history which transcended religious controversy'.[133]

Topo-bibliography was only part of John Leland's work. He was primarily an antiquarian. Indeed he was the first of a distinguished series of sixteenth century antiquaries, which culminated in William Camden.

---

[128] See C. E. Wright, 'The dispersal of the monastic libraries and the beginning of Anglo-Saxon studies: Matthew Parker and his circle: a preliminary study' in *Transactions of the Cambridge Bibliographical Soc.*, i (1951), pp. 226–7, Levy, op. cit., pp. 114–15, and McKisack, op. cit., pp. 38–9. For Luther's interest in and use of history see Levy, op. cit., pp. 80–1.

[129] H. R. Luard, 'A letter from Bishop Bale to Archbishop Parker' in *Cambridge Antiquarian Communications*, iii (1879), pp. 172–3 (for Bale's letter to Parker see also p. 478 and n. 150 below). Similarly, John Leland was on the look out for evidence in support of royal supremacy in the church; see p. 243 above.

[130] Levy, op. cit., pp. 110–12, and McKisack, op. cit., p. 39. The first printed edition of Bede's *Ecclesiastical History* was published in 1475; see p. 479 below.

[131] *The Itinerary of John Leland*, ed. Toulmin Smith, i. xxxvii–xxxix.

[132] He gives among his motives 'literum cupiditas, atque vehementer naturalis et officiosus erga patriam amor'; *Illustrium Maioris Britanniae Scriptorum . . . Summarium* (Wesel 1548), f. 246ᵛ. Cf. McKisack, op. cit., p. 14.

[133] Levy, op. cit., p. 97.

Leland's study of topography and antiquities illustrates both his patriotism and his love of learning. He explains in his New Year's Gift to Henry VIII that when he had read all the chronicles of England which he could find, he decided to travel throughout the land recording whatever he saw of topographical and antiquarian interest. He writes:[134]

> I was totally inflamed with a love to see throughly all those parts
> of this your opulent and ample realm, that I had read of in the
> aforesaid writers.

Leland proceeds to tell the king that he planned to write a complete description of England—the history and geography of each county and outlying islands, and the genealogies of every important family. He never completed the project (he became insane towards the end of his life), and only his voluminous notes survive.

The sixteenth century antiquaries were no doubt influenced by the medieval antiquarian tradition. Indeed interest in the past and the consequent use of chronicles in the Tudor period ensured the survival of many elements of medieval historiography.[135] Medieval tastes and ideas influenced those of sixteenth century scholars and readers. Annals retained their popularity: the chronological arrangement of material was generally used, and John Stow's *Chronicles of England* has been described as 'a sort of re-edition of the old chronicles of London'.[136] (Having pillaged the London chronicles, Stow continued the annals up to his own day.) As has been seen, the Tudors adopted the medieval legends of Brutus and King Arthur for propaganda purposes, thus fostering interest in Britain's legendary past. The taste for such legends coincided with a love of chivalric literature. (The Arthurian cycle is distinguished by its brilliant battle scenes, and tales of valour and of chivalry.) It should be remembered that there was a revival of romance historiography under the Tudors. The chivalric code captured the imagination of Englishmen—the cult of chivalry blossomed at a time when all chance of its practical application

---

[134] *Itinerary of John Leland*, ed. Toulmin Smith, i. xli-xlii.

[135] The strength of the medieval antiquarian tradition has been underestimated by recent scholars, even by medievalists. Sir Thomas Kendrick asserts that Leland was 'medieval' in his belief in the British History (though the British History probably enjoyed more general popularity in the sixteenth century than it had in the middle ages) and treats Leland's antiquarianism as a product of the renaissance (though Sir Thomas himself devotes a chapter to John Rous and William Worcester). Kendrick, op. cit., p. 63. Professor McKisack ignores Leland's medieval precursors, describing him as 'a pioneer in the method of direct inquiry and first hand observation, the forerunner of Camden'; McKisack, op. cit., p. 11. Sir Richard Southern does full justice to the antiquarian studies of the early Anglo-Norman period, but claims that they were not continued later in the middle ages, thus ignoring antiquarian research during Henry II's reign and in the fifteenth century; 'Aspects of the European tradition of historical writing. 4. The sense of the past', p. 263. See A. Gransden, 'Antiquarian studies in fifteenth century England' in *Antiquaries Journal*, lx, pt i (1980), pp. 75–97.

[136] *Chronicles of London*, ed. C. L. Kingsford (Oxford 1905). p. xxxv. See also Levy, op. cit., p. 189, and McKisack, op. cit., p. 113.

[475]

had long since passed. In 1532 Lord Berners, captain of Calais, published his translation of Froissart, in which he caught the spirit of contemporary chivalry.[137] Battle scenes and chivalric episodes are a feature of a number of sixteenth century histories: Edward Hall, for example, loved to describe a battle in graphic terms, and he, in the same way as the romance historians of the previous age, wrote partly to 'enhance the fame' of the great men of the past.[138] At the same time the medieval rhetorical tradition, invigorated by the study of the classics, continued to leave its mark on historiography. Hall put fictitious speeches into the mouths of principal characters—a practice which was not uncommon among historians until the end of the eighteenth century.

However, it was not only the taste for medieval types of historiography which flourished in the sixteenth century: in addition, most historians continued to interpret events in a medieval manner. In fact one result of the religious preoccupations of the period was that the Christian concept of history acquired a renewed importance. Historians exploited the idea of history as the manifestation of God's will on earth more than they had done since the dark ages. This concept was, as has been shown above, the unifying theme in Edward Hall's chronicle. Both Richard Grafton and Sir Walter Raleigh divided their chronicles in accordance with the traditional Christian periods, the Seven Ages of the World,[139] while John Bale and John Foxe (whose *Actes and Monuments* was published in 1563) 'saw the hand of God in everything'.[140] History was regarded as a storehouse of moral examples, in typically medieval fashion. To Edward Hall it was 'the key to induce virtue and repress vice';[141] to Stow it provided 'persuasions to honesty, godliness, and virtue of all sort';[142] and Raphael Holinshed thought that chronicles (which 'next unto the holy scripture . . . do carry credit') were full of profitable lessons.[143]

Sixteenth century interest in the past gave primary importance to the

---

[137] For the works of Sir John Bourchier, Lord Berners, including his translation of Froissart, see N. F. Blake, 'Lord Berners: a survey' in *Medievalia et Humanistica*, new series, ii (1971), pp. 119–32. Like Lord Berners' translation of Froissart, the translation of Titus Livius' *Life of Henry V* made in 1513 or 1514 (see pp. 195–6 and n. 15 above), reflects the chivalric tastes of the age. The revival of the cult of chivalry in the last half of the fifteenth century and its popularity in the sixteenth are fully discussed in A. B. Ferguson, *The Indian Summer of English Chivalry* (Durham, North Carolina, 1960). One manifestation of the revival in the fifteenth century is William Worcester's *Boke of Noblesse*, for which see pp. 330–1 above.

[138] *Hall's Chronicle*, ed. Ellis, p.v. See McKisack, op. cit., pp. 105–6.

[139] See Levy, op. cit., pp. 179, 289.

[140] Ibid., p. 122.

[141] *Hall's Chronicle*, ed. Ellis, p. vi. See McKisack, op. cit., p. 106. Professor Hale perhaps gives the impression that the change was quicker and more complete than in fact it was, when he claims that in the sixteenth century the emphasis on what history taught shifted from morals to wisdom, especially political wisdom; J. R. Hale, *The Evolution of British Historiography* (London-Melbourne 1967), p. 10.

[142] *A Summarye of the Chronicles of Englande* (London 1570), f. iv ʳ; Levy, op. cit., pp. 168–9.

[143] *Holinshed's Chronicles of England, Scotland and Ireland* (London, 1807–8, 6 vols), i. 766.

availability and preservation of medieval texts. Especial value was placed on the chronicles. Scholars working in the first half of the century were not able to use a comprehensive range: Polydore Vergil, for example, had to rely mainly on fifteenth century sources. This was because chronicles were not yet easily accessible in libraries, and few had appeared in print. But as the century proceeded the situation improved and the number of available texts increased. Thus John Stow had access to many chronicles written in the middle ages. Besides the London chronicles he used, among others, Ralph Niger, Ralph Coggeshall, Walter of Coventry, Roger of Wendover, Matthew Paris, Thomas Walsingham, the *Brut*, Otterbourne, the Translator of Livius, John Hardyng, Robert Fabyan and Edward Hall—besides Geoffrey of Monmouth.[144]

The improvement in the availability of chronicles was largely the work of such dedicated men as John Leland, John Bale and Matthew Parker. They recognized that the fate of medieval books and documents hung in the balance because of the religious upheavals: fanaticism alone could cause the destruction or defacing of 'papistical' works, but a more serious threat came from the dissolution of the monasteries, which resulted in the dispersal of monastic libraries and archives. John Bale lamented the damage done by the greed of his contemporaries and their lack of concern over injury to their national heritage:[145]

> Avarice ... hath made an end both of our libraries and books. [In the past men's] labour was to hold things in remembrance, which otherwise had most wretchedly perished. Our practices now are, to do so much as in us lieth, to destroy their fruitful foundations. ... A few of us there be that would gladly save the most necessary monuments of their dispersed remnant. But wretched poverty will not permit us to show to our country such a natural and necessary benefit.

Leland had early recognized the danger to libraries posed by the dissolution of the monasteries. In all, acting on the commission Henry VIII gave him in 1533, he visited at least 137 monastic libraries out of a total of about 584. The copious notes he made on their contents show that he had examined manuscripts of Gildas, Bede, Nennius, Asser, Æthelweard, Eadmer (the *Historia Novorum*), Marianus Scotus, Symeon of Durham, William of Malmesbury (the *Gesta Regum*, the *Gesta Pontificum* and the *Historia Novella*), Geoffrey of Monmouth, Henry of Huntingdon, Roger of Howden, William

---

[144] See Levy, op. cit., pp. 191, 194. For Stow's belief in Geoffrey of Monmouth's British History see p. 471 n. 113 above.

[145] *The Laboryouse Journey and Serche of Johan Leylande, for Englandes Antiquitees* ... , ed. W. A. Copinger, pp. 16, 83–4, 95. Cf. McKisack, op. cit., pp. 17–18. On the subject of the dispersal of the monastic libraries and the efforts made to retrieve the damage, especially with regard to Anglo-Saxon manuscripts, see C. E. Wright, 'The dispersal of the monastic libraries and the beginning of Anglo-Saxon studies', pp. 208–27.

of Newburgh, Gerald of Wales, Walter of Coventry, Matthew Paris (the *Chronica Majora*), Walter of Guisborough, Adam Murimuth, the *Polychronicon*, the *Scalacronica*, Trevisa, the *Eulogium*, Thomas Walsingham, John Hardyng and Robert Fabyan.[146]

Leland claims in his New Year's Gift to Henry VIII to have 'conserved many good authors, the which otherwise had been like to have perished to no small inconvenience of good letters'. Some he acquired for the king, and some he kept.[147] John Bale, who continued Leland's work, was the first man to urge the necessity of founding a national library, or at least a public library in each county.[148] A plea for a national library was also made by the Cambridge scholar, John Dee, in a petition which he presented to Queen Mary in 1556, asking her to act 'for the recovery and preservation of ancient writers and monuments'.[149] However, nothing came of this farsighted idea, and the task of saving medieval manuscripts was in fact left to private individuals. Bale describes how, 'through much friendship, labour and expense', he accumulated manuscripts for his library:[150]

> Some I found in stationers' and bookbinders' store houses, some in grocers', soapsellers', taylors', and other occupiers' shops, some in ships ready to be carried over sea into Flanders to be sold — for in those uncircumspect and careless days, there was no quicker merchandise than library books, and all to destruction of learning. . . . Only conscience, with a fervent love of my country, moved me to save what might be saved.

Matthew Parker took similar trouble to preserve manuscripts from destruction, and employed people to search for them on his behalf.[151] A note by his secretary John Joscelyn in Parker's copy of Homer claims that it was found by the dean of Canterbury in the possession of a local baker who claimed to have rescued it from rubbish cleared out from St Augustine's.[152]

Bale's impressive library of medieval books did not survive: when he was appointed bishop of Ossory in 1552 he took it with him to Ireland;

---

[146] McKisack, op. cit., pp. 8–11.

[147] *Itinerary of John Leland*, ed. Toulmin Smith, p. xxxviii.

[148] *Laboryouse Journey*, ed. Copinger, pp. 16–18.

[149] Dr John Dee's petition to Queen Mary is printed in *Chetham Miscellanies*, i (Chetham Soc. 1851), item 5, pp. 46–7. See McKisack, op. cit., pp. 71–2.

[150] Luard, 'A letter from Bishop Bale to Archbishop Parker', p. 158. Bale also records that he found 'many notable antiquities' in the possession of stationers and book binders, and at Norwich Bale found that the contents of the libraries had been 'turned to the use of their grocers, candlemakers, soap sellers, and other worldly occupiers'; *Laboryouse Journey*, ed. Copinger, p. 110.

[151] For Parker as a collector see Wright, op. cit., pp. 211–27, Levy, op. cit., pp. 114–17, and McKisack, op. cit., pp. 27–9.

[152] Now Corpus Christi College, Cambridge, MS. 81; see M. R. James, *A Descriptive Catalogue of the Manuscripts in the Library of Corpus Christi College, Cambridge* (Cambridge 1909–12, 2 vols), i. 166.

and on being expelled from his see and from the country, his books were scattered.[153] Parker's magnificent collection, however, was more fortunate. It was preserved in Cambridge; Parker himself put some of the books in the University Library, but most he bequeathed to his old college, Corpus Christi.[154]

While these two scholars and many more whose names are less well known saved what medieval manuscripts they could, the process of editing and printing the chronicles gathered momentum. Already in the fifteenth century Bede's *Ecclesiastical History* had been printed in Strasburg (1475),[155] and Caxton had issued the *Brut* and the *Polychronicon* (in 1480 and 1482). Then in 1525 Polydore Vergil edited and printed Gildas's *De Excidio Britanniae*,[156] and in 1543 Richard Grafton, printer to the king, published John Hardyng's chronicle together with a continuation. But it was Matthew Parker who started the task of printing the chronicles in earnest. Between 1567 and 1574 he published 'Matthew of Westminster', Matthew Paris' *Chronica Majora*, Thomas Walsingham's *Historia Anglicana* and *Ypodigma Neustriae* and Asser's *Life of King Alfred*. Towards the end of the sixteenth century and in the early seventeenth other important chronicles appeared in print—Æthelweard, Eadmer, Florence of Worcester, William of Malmesbury, Henry of Huntingdon, Roger of Howden, Gerald of Wales and the Pseudo-Ingulf.[157]

In this way scholars in the sixteenth century saved the heritage of medieval historical writing. They digested its ideas, using them alongside those of the new age. The result was that the native tradition was not destroyed when towards the end of the century the impact of Italian and French historiography became irresistible: as a recent scholar has written, it was refined but not emasculated by their influence.[158] Therefore, the best elements of the old tradition were able to enrich the new developments. The antiquarian studies of the middle ages reinforced sixteenth and seventeenth century enthusiasm for and knowledge of antiquities. Probably the medieval chroniclers' gift for contemporary reportage taught their immediate successors (who were not primarily concerned with recording current events) little of value in technique: it did, however, bequeath to them and to posterity an inexhaustible store of information about events and people, and their opinions and feelings, without which the history of medieval England could not have been written.

[153] See Luard, 'A letter from Bishop Bale to Archbishop Parker', pp. 158–9; and Honor McCusker, *John Bale, Dramatist and Antiquary* (Bryn Mawr, Pennsylvania 1942), pp. 18–23, 29 et seq.
[154] See McKisack, op. cit., pp. 32–4.
[155] See E. P. Goldschmidt, *Medieval Texts and their First Appearance in Print* (*Transactions of the Bibliographical Soc., Supplement*, xvi, 1943), p. 74.
[156] See pp. 431, 436 above.
[157] See ibid., pp. 39–42, 61, 64–5, and Levy, op. cit., p. 134.
[158] Hale, *The Evolution of British Historiography*, p. 13.

Appendix A

The Chronicle of John Tiptoft

The chronicle attributed to John Tiptoft, earl of Worcester (born c. 1427, created earl 1449, executed 1470), formerly Phillipps MS. 11301, is apparently now lost (see p. 253 above). It was most recently known to have been in the hands of Maggs Bros (Cat. no. 838, item 44, 1956); for its provenance, as far back as the early nineteenth century, see R. J. Mitchell, *John Tiptoft, 1427–1470* (London 1938), pp. 195–6. As an assistant keeper in the department of manuscripts of the British Museum, I examined the chronicle at Maggs and wrote a report, dated 3 October 1956, for the departmental archive 'Notes on outside Collections', a copy of which the present deputy keeper, Mr D. H. Turner, has kindly sent me with permission to reproduce. The report is as follows:

> The volume is on vellum, octavo size, unfolioed (it is over one inch thick), and is written throughout in a cursive hand of the first half of the fifteenth century. The only content is a chronicle of England in Latin from Brutus (with a short account of the Creation, etc., at the beginning) to 1429. It begins (in red) 'de orbis indagacione facta per Iulium Ceasarem', (in black) 'Ex olim senatus consulto censuit Julius Cesar.' It is impossible to say without collation how much, if any, of the chronicle is not copied from known sources, but it appears to be a compilation from well-known works, notably the Brute chronicle. The last years, 1416–29, cover only nine folios.
>
> On the first folio is a title written in a late fifteenth century hand which states that the chronicle was compiled by John [Tiptoft], earl of Worcester, from the works of various historians. This title and the list of contents written in the same hand on the back of the page are signed 'Sheldwych'.

I concluded that perhaps Mitchell, op.cit., pp. 9–10, overestimates the source-value of the chronicle.

Appendix B

The Manuscripts of 'The Arrival of Edward IV'

A. INTRODUCTORY

No medieval copy of the long version (in English) of the *Arrival* has survived (see p. 264 above). However, in the sixteenth century a copy was owned by William Fleetwood, recorder of London, from which a copy, now in BL MS. Harley 542, was made by John Stow. See *Arrival*, pp. xiii.—xiv. For Fleetwood see May McKisack, *Medieval History in the Tudor Age* (Oxford 1971), pp. 68, 83, 131, 134.

Four manuscripts are known containing the short version (in French) of the *Arrival*. The text in two of them is illuminated: it is divided into four parts; each part begins with an illuminated initial and is preceded by a miniature. The text is followed by other relevant material, and both manuscripts end with a satirical epitaph, written in the Yorkist and Burgundian interest, on Richard Neville, earl of Warwick, who fell in the battle of Barnet. Both these manuscripts were executed in Flanders. (For other illuminated manuscripts executed in Flanders for Edward IV between 1470 and 1480 see pp. 90 n. 199, 291 nn. 20, 21 above.) The two other copies of the *Arrival* are of plain, unbroken texts.

Dr Thomson has discussed the relationship of the English version of the *Arrival* to the French one, and the relationship of three of the extant texts of the French version to each other. He has also considered the relationship of Waurin's copy to the extant text of the English version, and of Thomas Basin's copy to the extant texts of the French version (for these copies see p. 264 above). See J. A. F. Thomson, '"The Arrival of Edward IV"—the development of the text' in *Speculum*, xlvi (1971), pp. 84–93. However, he overlooked one manuscript of the French version, the Besançon MS., which will be discussed below.

A definitive edition of the French version, using all four manuscripts, is much to be desired. But meanwhile it may be useful to give brief descriptions of the manuscripts. It has also seemed worthwhile to print the satirical epitaph on the earl of Warwick. Its occurrence in two of the manuscripts also containing the French version of the *Arrival* and its propagandist tone link it with the *Arrival*. Nevertheless, although it is printed from the Ghent MS. by Giles (see p. 482 below), it is not mentioned by Jerningham (see below) or by Thomson. Finally, an attempt will be made to show what light the manuscripts throw on the methods of propaganda employed.

B. THE MSS. OF THE FRENCH VERSION OF THE 'ARRIVAL'

I. Illuminated Copies

1. The Ghent MS. (University Library, Ghent, MS. 236).

Contents:

1. The title of the *Arrival* in rubric, f. 1^v ;
2. The text of the *Arrival*, ff. 2–12;
3. Lists, respectively, of the Lancastrians killed, captured and wounded at the battle of Tewkesbury, ff. 12–13^v ;
4. Letter of Edward IV to the burgomaster and échevins of Bruges, 29 May, 1471, ff. 13^v–14^v ;
5. Satirical epitaph on Richard Neville, earl of Warwick, ff. 14^v–15^v.

Items 1–4 are printed by Edward Jerningham in *Archaeologia*, xxi (1825), pp. 11–23. A rendering in modern French of all the items is printed as *La Révolte du Comte de Warwick*, ed. J. A. Giles (Caxton Soc., 1849). A text of Edward's letters to the burgomaster and échevins of Bruges (for which see p. 264 above) is also given by Jean de Waurin (*Waurin*, v. 676), and in one of the plain copies of the *Arrival* (see p. 484 below). For the text of the *Arrival* in the Ghent MS. see Thomson, op.cit., pp. 86–92 passim.

Vellum; ff. 16. 276 mm × 201 mm. C. 1471. Executed in Flanders. The language is the Picard or Walloon dialect of French. Modern binding. In one book-hand. Four miniatures, of mediocre quality, as follows. (1) The battle of Barnet (Edward IV slays? the earl of Warwick), with an illuminated border, f. 2. (2) The battle of Tewkesbury (Edward IV, with the royal arms of France and England on his shield; a young knight,? Edward of Westminster, fallen, his head about to be struck off), f. 5. (3) The execution of the duke of Somerset (Edward IV watching, with shield as before), f. 7^v. (4) The attack on London by Thomas Neville, the 'Bastard of Fauconberg' (the Bastard's lance is broken and his men are retreating), f. 9^v. Described and reproduced in lithograph Jerningham, op.cit. pp. 12–

14, Plates I–IV. Reproduced Charles Ross, *The Wars of the Roses* (London 1976), pp. 108, 120, 127, 129. See also Plate VIII above. The manuscript was item 75 in the exhibition 'Treasures of Belgian Libraries' (held in Edinburgh in 1963; the catalogue is published).

2. The Besançon MS. (Bibliothèque Municipale, Besançon, MS. 1168).

Contents:

1. The title of the *Arrival* in rubric, f. 1ᵛ;
2. The text of the *Arrival*, ff. 2–10;
3. Lists, respectively, of the Lancastrians killed, captured and wounded at the battle of Tewkesbury, ff. 10ᵛ–10ᵛ;
4. Satirical epitaph on the earl of Warwick, ff. 10–11ᵛ.

Vellum (ff. 1–2) and paper (ff. 3–12); ff. 12. 241 mm × 185 mm. C. 1471. Executed in Flanders. The language is pure French. Original binding of vellum (without boards) with paper pastedowns and two vellum tie tabs (now broken). In one book-hand. There are two watermarks, as follows. (1) A dog with a collar and long, curly tail, resembling C. M. Briquet, *Les Filigranes* (Leipzig 1923, 4 vols), no. 3622 (Douai 1480; Bruges 1490; Laon 1479–81, Middlebourg 1478; L'Ecluse 1482; etc), f. 7. (2) A bear with a studded collar, which resembles closely none in Briquet, op.cit (it is most like no. 12330 (Geneva, 1558), but unlike the latter, does not have the letters G and B by it), f. 12. Four miniatures, as follows. (1) The battle of Barnet (the English soldiers have a golden rose on their backs and the Burgundians a golden baton), with illuminated border, f. 2. (2) The battle of Tewkesbury, f. 4ᵛ. (3) The execution of the duke of Somerset, f. 6ᵛ. (4) The attack on London by the Bastard of Fauconberg, f. 8. The miniatures are inferior in quality to, and the composition of the scenes is not identical with those in the Ghent MS. However, the general similarity of the scenes and their marked stylistic resemblances to the latter strongly suggests that they were executed in the same atelier. In the centre of the illuminated border on f. 2 is a coat of arms, apparently executed by the artist responsible for the rest of the border. The miniatures are described in *Catalogue général des Bibliothèques publiques de France, Departments*, t. xxxii, vol. i (Paris 1897), pp. 821–2, which identifies the arms as those of Jean Spifame, secretary to Charles VIII. For Jean Spifame III, who died in 1500 at Chalon-sur-Saône, see A. Lapeyre and R. Scheurer, *Les notaires et secretaires du roi sous les règnes de Louis XI, Charles VIII et Louis XII (1461–1515). Notices personnelles et généalogies* (Paris 1978, 2 vols), i. 299 and Plate LXXXIX. For the family of Spifame, many of whose members held important offices under the French crown, see André Delmas, 'Gaillard, Jacques et Raoul Spifame. Étude d'une famille au xviᵉ siècle' in *École Nationale des Chartes. Positions des Thèses* (1943), pp. 55–61, and Léon Mirot 'Études Lucquoises. Chapitre 1. La Colonie Lucquoise à Paris du XIII au XVᵉ siècle' in *Bibliothèque de l'École des Chartes. Revue d'Érudition*, lxxxviii (Paris 1927), pp. 82–3 and n. 1[1]. For the arms of Spifame (identical with those in the Besançon MS.) see J. B. Rietstap, *L'Armorial Général* (second edition, Gouda 1884–7, 2 vols), ii. 811.

II. *The Plain Copies*

1. Bibliothèque Nationale MS. française 3887, ff. 114–16ᵛ.

The text is discussed in Thomson, op. cit. pp. 86–92. It is followed by a copy in the same hand of Edward IV's covering letter to Charles the Bold, of 28 May 1471 (see p. 264 above), ff. 116ᵛ–17. Both this text of the *Arrival* and of the letter are printed in *Mémoires de Philippe de Commynes*, ed. L. M. E. Dupont (Soc. de l'Historie de France, 1840–7, 3 vols), iii. 281–91.

Paper. C. 1471. Written in Flanders or Burgundy. The language is the Picard or Walloon dialect of French (see Thomson, op. cit., p. 87 and n. 33). In a cursive hand on a gathering of four leaves in a composite volume. Watermark of a shield almost identical with Briquet, op. cit., no. 1650 (Arc-en-Barrois, 1459; variants Dijon, 1464; Cluny, 1465; Salins, 1466), ff. 116, 117.

2. Bibliothèque Nationale MS. française 11590, ff. 111–14.

The text is discussed by Thomson, op. cit. pp. 86–92 passim, who demonstrates that it is closely related to that in the Ghent MS. (ibid. pp. 87–9). It is incomplete at the end, lacking about twelve words. It is preceded by a copy of Edward IV's covering letter to the burgomaster and échevins of Bruges, 29 May 1471, f. 111. Paper. C. 1471. Written in ? Flanders. In a cursive hand on a gathering of six leaves (including three blank pages, ff. 114ᵛ–16) in a composite volume. There are two watermarks, as follows. (1) A paschal lamb, apparently identical with Briquet, op. cit. no. 44 (Luxembourg, Belgium, 1463; Mayence, 1468; Vienna, 1469; Nancy, 1471–2; Holland, 1459?), ff. 111, 115. (2) The letter P, identical with Briquet, op. cit. no. 8527 (Quievrain, Belgium, 1463–6; Darmstadt, 1464–8; Leyden, 1465–9; Decizes, 1466; Baden-Baden, 1467; Utrecht, 1468; etc.), f. 113.

---

[1] I owe the first two references on Jean Spifame and his family to Professeur Jean Philippe Genet, and the last one to Dr Michael Jones.

C. SATIRICAL EPITAPH ON RICHARD NEVILLE, EARL OF WARWICK

These propagandist verses are written from the Yorkist and Burgundian point of view.[2] They denigrate Warwick for his treachery to Edward IV, and as the architect of the English alliance with Louis XI against Burgundy.

The text below is printed from Ghent MS. 236, ff. 14ᵛ–15ᵛ, because it is in the Picard or Walloon dialect which is more typical of the manuscripts of the *Arrival* than the pure French one of the Besançon MS. Collation shows that the text in neither MS. is copied from the other.

Variations of words, but not of spellings, and of word order are noted from Besançon MS. 1168 (referred to as B), ff. 10ᵛ–11ᵛ. Punctuation, and the use of capitals, apostrophes and the vowel *u* and the consonant *v* are the editor's. Expanded abbreviations are in round brackets and letters supplied by the editor are in square brackets.

Ghent MS. 236[3]

f. 14ᵛ   Cyᵃ est escript de plume etᵇ non de graffe
Du conte de Warewick la dolant epitapheᶜ
[J]eᵈ Richard deᵉ Neufvilleᶠconte de Warewick
Et d'une aultre cont[r]e qui a nom Salberick.[4]
Je fus grant chambelan[5] du pais d'Angleterre,
De Callais capitaine[6] et de mainte aultre terre.
Ouᵍ je concquesta les chincq portz pour ma part,[7]
Et j'enʰ deboutay hors le bon roy Edouard.
Pour lequel despiter par mon oultrecuidance

ᵃ adds apres B
ᵇ omits et B
ᶜ The heading is in rubric, MS. and B
ᵈ J also omitted B
ᵉ adds vir deleted B
ᶠ adds fu B
ᵍ Ou] La ou B
ʰ j'en] en B

[2] The 'epitaph' may be compared with the propagandist verses written in support of Richard II after his deposition; see pp. 173 and n. 87, 188 and n. 181 above.
[3] I am indebted to my colleagues at Nottingham University, Dr Michael Johes and Mr. M. H. Offord, for reading my transcription and making corrections and suggestions.
[4] Warwick succeeded to the earldom of Salisbury in 1462; G. E. C., *Peerage*, xii. pt ii. 390.
[5] For Warwick's tenure of the office of chamberlain of England, see ibid. xii. pt ii. 386, 388, 389.
[6] For Warwick's tenure of the office of captain of Calais see ibid. xii. pt ii. 387, 389.
[7] Edward IV made Warwick warden of the Cinque Ports in 1461; ibid. xii. pt ii. 389.

Je mis discention entre le roy de France
Et le bon justicier Charles duc de Bourgongne.[8]
Lors fiz de droit[i] tort sans en prendre vergo(n)gne.
Les Franchois acointay mes anchiens ennemis,
Tant que par beau parler ils fure (nt) mes amys.
Entre eulz communicquay et menay sy gra(n)t bruit
Que le roy Edouard par armes s'enfuit.
Le francq duc de Bourgongne ou gist tout prouesse,
Le rechupt humblement pour l'honne(ur) de noblesse,
Son tresor lui ouvri, ses gens lui presenta.
Parquoy en[j] grant bruit sur la mer remonta.
Pe(n)dant ce temps je fuz en mes armes ca(m)pestre

f. 15   Tres bien acompaignie du noble duc d'Excestre,[9]
De mon frere et amy seigneur de Montagu,[10]
Du conte d'Occenfort,[11] qui fut plain[k] de vertu,
Et de maint chevalier digne de los et de pris.
J'avoie a dont voue a Dieu de paradis
Et au roy[l] Franchois qu'ava(n)t l'assention
Qu'Engleterre seroit en ma subgection.
S'ainsy fust advenu le roy de France et moy
Avions emprins de faire grant ennoy
Au duc des Bourgungno(n)s, qui est gra(n)t et courtois.
On lui devoit tollir Piccardie et Artois,
Et le despossesser d'Arras, Lille et Douay,[12]
Par le consentement des mentins de Tournay.[13]

---

[i] adds ung B
[j] adds tres B
[k] fut plain] plain fut B
[l] adds des B
[8] The verses here blame Warwick for exacerbating bad relations between Louis XI and Charles the Bold. In fact, they did come to an agreement shortly before the battle of Barnet; see J. Calmette and G. Périnelle, *Louis XI et l'Angleterre (1461-1483)* (Mémoires et documents publiés par la Société de l'Ecole des Chartes, xi, Paris 1930) pp. 138-9, and C. L. Scofied, *The Life and Reign of Edward IV* (London 1923, 2 vols), i. 577. Edward IV himself made a truce with Louis in the autumn of 1471; see Calmette and Périnelle, op. cit., p. 147, and Scofield, op. cit., ii. 18.
[9] Henry Holand, duke of Exeter (1450-61). Having been attainted in 1461, he returned to England on the temporary restoration of Henry VI in February 1471, and was severely wounded at the battle of Barnet. He died in 1475. See G.E.C., *Peerage*, v. 212-15.
[10] John Neville (brother of Richard Neville, earl of Warwick), earl of Northumberland (1464-70), marquess of Montagu (1470-1), killed at the battle of Barnet. Ibid. ix. 89-93.
[11] John de Vere, earl of Oxford (1462-75, 1485-1513). He fled after the battle of Barnet. Died 1513. Ibid. x. 239-44.
[12] The dismemberment of the Burgundian 'empire' was one of proposals agreed between Warwick and Louis XI during the negotiations of 1467; Calmette and Périnelle, op. cit., p. 82 and nn. 3, 4.
[13] For the loyalty of Tournai to Louis XI see Henri Sée, *Louis XI et les Villes* (Paris 1891, reprinted Geneva 1974), pp. 187-90. It was the subject of two hostile ballads produced by the Burgundians; see ibid., p. 190 n. 3, citing Leroux de Lincy, *Chants historiques et populaires du temps de Charles VII et de Louis XI* (Paris 1857), pp. 181 et seq.

La riviere de Somme estoit ja par divise
Subiecte a la couronne et contre droit remise.
Or est[m] retourne, car Edouard le preu
Me revint assaillir comme[n] ravissant leu.
Si grant assault me fist et sy bien si porta,
Que ma terre et la sienne acop reconcquesta.
En ung chasteau, m(ou)lt fort, il me voult assegier.
Attendre ne l'ozay com(m)e fol voulz widier.

f. 15[v]   A dont fuz assailliz de lances et de trait,
L'un de mes gens s'enfuit[o] et l'autre se retrait.
La fuz se fort constraint et de telle vertu
Que(n) fuiant je fuz prins et par terre abattu.
Tant de plaies rechups sur le corps et le chief
Que la voulsisse ou non, morus a gra(n)t meschief.
A dont consideray que ma perdition[p],
Et mon maulvais pechie plain de detration,
Aunsi me pugnissoit; car oncques en ma vie
A nul bien ne pensay sy non a tricherie.
Parquoy le jour de pasques[14] ou Dieu resussita,
Par armes Edouard m'occist et concquesta
Avec le duc d'Excestre[15]et mon frere marquis,
Et pluiseurs chevaliers, qui ne sont point cy mis[q],
Honteusement morus a[r] ma confusion
Sans avoir de nul prestre[s] quelq(ue) absolution,
Droit en l'an xv[c] xxix moins en nombre,
Non obstant priez Dieu q(ue) sathan ne m'enco(m)bre
Et me doinst par sa grace obtenir le royaulme,
Ou je le tiens et croy estre en corps et en ame.
Amen.

D. THE MSS. OF THE 'ARRIVAL' AS EVIDENCE FOR YORKIST PROPAGANDA METHODS.

The development of the text of the *Arrival* and how and when it reached the continent is discussed above (pp. 264–5, 270). Copies of the short French

[m] adds tout B
[n] adds ung B
[o] s'enfuit] fuyt B
[p] perdition] prodicion B
[q] ne sont point cy mis] pas ne sont cy mis B
[r] a] en B
[s] avoir de nul prestre] de nul prestre avoir B
[14] The battle of Barnet was fought on Easter Sunday, 14 April, 1471.
[15] In fact, Exeter was not killed at Barnet; see p. 486 n. 9 above.

version, which, as already mentioned, may have been composed before the long, English one, proliferated in Flanders. Three of the surviving four manuscripts are certainly of Flemish provenance: this is proved by an accumulation of evidence: firstly, the style of the miniatures in the Ghent and Besançon MSS.; secondly, the watermarks in the Besançon MS. and in BN MS. française 11590; and, thirdly, the language, the Picard or Walloon dialect, of the texts in the Ghent MS., and BN MS. française 11590.

The case with BN MS. française 3887 is not quite so clear. Although it is apparently in the Picard or Walloon dialect[16], its watermark links it with Burgundy. Therefore, either it was copied in Burgundy from a Flemish exemplar and/or by a Flemish scribe—who might even have rendered a French exemplar into his own dialect—or it was copied in Flanders on to paper brought from Burgundy. On the whole the latter alternative seems the most likely.

The Besançon MS. raises the question why a manuscript written in Flanders is in pure French. Perhaps it was copied by a French scribe. But there is another possibility; it may have been deliberately written in French to make it suitable for French readers.

The miniatures in the Ghent and Besançon MSS. obviously were intended to attract attention to, and emphasize the importance of the tale which the pamphlet had to tell. The pictures themselves are propagandist, containing political iconography favourable to the Yorkist cause. Besides recording in visual terms the victories which enabled Edward IV to reascend the throne, they have symbolic details. For example, in two of the pictures in the Ghent MS. the 'dual monarchy' is symbolized by Edward holding a shield on which are the arms of France and England. And, again, in the Besançon MS. the Anglo-Burgundian alliance is visually expressed in the picture of the battle of Barnet; the English identified by the golden rose and the Burgundians by the golden baton fight the Lancastrian army.

The question arises, how numerous were copies of the *Arrival*? There is only certain evidence of the existence of two copies of the English version, the copy used by Jean de Waurin and the one owned in the sixteenth century by William Fleetwood. Only two of the four surviving copies of the French version were made for propagandist dissemination: these are the illuminated texts; the two plain texts are clearly only transcripts. However, in addition, it is known that Thomas Basin had access to a copy.

Possibly the Besançon MS. contains evidence for the production of other similar copies. It will be observed that Jean Spifame's arms, in the border of the picture of the battle of Barnet, occur on the second of the two vellum leaves (a single sheet folded in two) at the front of the pamphlet; the title

---

[16] I deduce this from its textual similarity to the Ghent MS. demonstrated by Dr Thomson; see p. 484 above.

of the *Arrival* and the beginning of the text are also on the vellum leaves. Perhaps these leaves were affixed to the pamphlet after the rest of the text, on paper, had been completed. In this case a number of copies might have been put together in the same way, each bearing the arms of the individual who had ordered a copy or to whom one was to be presented.

The survival rate of such a pamphlet may well have been low. Its use and interest was ephemeral. (It may be noted that no medieval copy of Thomas Favent's propaganda tract written in support of the Appellants is known to survive.)[17] Probably very few were of sufficient quality as manuscripts to merit preservation: the Ghent MS. is a fairly handsome booklet—though certainly not of high quality—but the Besançon MS., with its crudely executed miniatures and coarse script, cannot be so described. In general, therefore, it seems likely that once the political circumstances which had given birth to the *Arrival* were past, there was no incentive to preserve copies of it.

[17] See p. 185 and n. 161 above.

Appendix C

The Crowland Chronicle

I. THE FORGED CHRONICLE

The only complete printed text of the forged Crowland chronicle (noticed p. 400 above) is in *Rerum Anglicarum Scriptorum Veterum Tom. I*, ed. William Fulman (Oxford 1684); 'Ingulf' is on pages 1–107, and 'Peter of Blois' on pages 108–32. Fulman also prints the rest of the Crowland chronicle; ibid., pp. 451–593 (see p. 265 n. 109 above). He apparently based his text on the fifteenth century manuscript now BL MS. Cotton Otho B XIII. This manuscript was badly burnt in the fire of 1731 in the Cottonian library. While the part of the text corresponding to Fulman pages 458–554 survives in a fairly legible state, there are only a few charred fragments of that corresponding to Fulman, pages 73–108 passim. Fragments of a seventeenth century copy (probably the printer's copy of Fulman's edition) are preserved in Corpus Christi College, Oxford, MS. B. 208 (see J. G. Edwards, 'The "second" continuation of the Crowland chronicle: was it written "in ten days"?' in *BIHR*, xxxix (1966), p. 117 n. 1). The 'Ingulf' and 'Peter of Blois' chronicles were apparently first detected as forgeries by Sir Francis Palgrave; see *Quarterly Review*, xxxiv (1826), pp. 289–98. His opinion has been confirmed by subsequent scholars: H. T. Riley 'The history and charters of Ingulfus considered' in *Archaeological Journal*, xix (1862), pp. 32–49, 114–33; Hardy, *Cat.* ii. 58–64; F. Liebermann, 'Ueber Ostenglische Geschichtsquellen des 12, 13, 14 Jahrhunderts, besonders den falschen Ingulf' in *Neues Archiv der Gesellschaft für ältere deutsche Geschichtskunde*, xviii (Hanover and Leipzig 1892), pp. 249–67; and W. G. Searle, *Ingulf and the Historia Croylandensis* (Cambridge Antiquarian Soc., octavo series, xxvii, 1894). Riley (op. cit., pp. 114–28) dates the forgery to about 1414, Liebermann (op.cit., pp. 262–3) to the mid-fourteenth century, and Searle (op.cit., p. 207) to the mid-fifteenth century.

If Searle's date is accepted, it seems likely that the Crowland forgery was written as a preliminary to Prior John's continuation. The forger did his best to make the work appear authentic. The 'Ingulf' chronicle begins by stating the author's intention to commemorate the abbey's founders and benefactors (Fulman, op.cit., p. 1), and to record its history and acquisition of property. Besides citing *in extenso* numerous (forged) charters to establish the abbey's rights to privilege and property, the author claims to have consulted Domesday book in London (ibid., p. 80: in fact the forger did not consult the original volumes of Domesday book; see Searle, op. cit., pp. 7–12). The 'Peter of Blois' chronicle opens with a letter from Henry de Longchamp, abbot of Crowland (1190–1236), to Peter asking him to continue Abbot Ingulf's chronicle, and undertaking to bring documents from the abbey's muniments to him in London (Fulman, op. cit., pp. 108–9). Peter's reply follows; he praises Crowland and Ingulf's work which he promises to correct, and says he will make use of the documents supplied (ibid., pp. 109–10).

For another possible example of a forged history, from St Swithun's, Winchester, see Appendix D below.

II. THE DATE OF THE SECOND CONTINUATION

It is suggested above (p. 265) that the second continuation of the Crowland chronicle, which incorporates the memoir on Edward IV's reign, was composed late in April and early in May 1486. This approximate date is indicated by the statement in the last paragraph (*CC*, p. 577), which precedes the concluding verses and colophon, that the peace achieved by the marriage of Henry VII and Elizabeth of York (18 January 1486) has been broken by a rising in the north. This is a reference to Lovell's rebellion which broke out early in April 1486. The continuator then adds verses on the patience and endurance necessary while waiting for the outcome. He does not mention the suppression of the rebellion which was completed by 22 April; see Gladys Temperley, *Henry VII* (London 1917), pp. 53–5. It seems probable that news of the rising was brought by John Russell, bishop of Lincoln, who arrived at Crowland on 16 April 1486 and stayed for about a month (Edwards, op. cit., p. 123 and n. 2; *CC*, p. 582). While at Crowland Russell arbitrated a legal dispute between Crowland and Peterborough abbey over the church of Bringhurst; the proceedings are briefly described in the second continuation, and the notarial record of the case is transcribed in the third continuation (*CC*, pp. 577, 582–93; cf. Edwards, op. cit., pp. 122–4). The conclusion on the date of the second continuation raises the problem of the meaning of the final colophon (*CC*, p. 578), which reads: 'Acta sunt haec et expleta apud Croylandiam, anno Domini millesimo quadringentesimo octogesimo sexto, per spatium decem dierum quorum postremus fuit ultimus dies mensis Aprilis ejusdem anni.' Sir Goronwy contends that the text of the second continuation is not now in its original order, and that the colophon records the date of the Bringhurst proceedings (Edwards, op.cit., pp. 118–26; Alison Hanham, *Richard III and his Early Historians 1483–1535* (Oxford

[491]

1975), p. 77, accepts this view). However, Mr Pronay (see p. 265 n. 109 above) is not convinced by Sir Goronwy's hypothesis, but argues that the second continuation retains its true order, and that the colophon records when the continuator wrote. Even if Sir Goronwy is right, the continuation was certainly written at about the date denoted by the colophon and within a short period.

Appendix D

Sources of Thomas Rudborne's
Historia Major

Thomas Rudborne used numerous written sources for his history of Winchester, the *Historia Major* (see pp. 394–8 above). Many of these have not apparently been identified. Among them is 'Girardus Cornubiensis', *De Gestis Britonum* (cited e.g. *TR*, pp. 181, 186, 189) and *De Gestis Regum West-Saxonum* (e.g. *TR*, pp. 189, 201, 204). Both works are now unidentified. A Life of Guy of Warwick is also attributed to 'Girardus'. Perhaps this is the work surviving in a fifteenth century copy, Magdalen College, Oxford, MS. 147, ff. 227–8, which is headed 'Narratio de Guidone Warwicensi auctore Gerardo Cornubiensi' (I am grateful to Dr Gerald Harriss for checking this for me), and is printed in *Chronicon . . . Prioratus de Dunstaple*, ed. Thomas Hearne (Oxford 1733, 2 vols), ii. 825–32, and cf. Hardy, *Cat.* iii. 50–1. Rudborne probably derived his account of the combat of Guy and the Danish giant Colbron directly or indirectly from this Life (his version is shorter); *TR*, pp. 211–12. Rous cites Rudborne among his authorities (which do not include Girardus) for the combat; *Rous*, pp. 97–8 (cf. *Rous*, p. 208). Another of Rudborne's sources was an historical concordance, *De Concordantiis Historiarum Angliae*, which he states was by a monk of Winchester: 'Ipse enim auctor multa scribit de ecclesia Wyntoniensi, in qua quondam nutritus erat'; *TR*, p. 271.

One of Rudborne's principal sources for the early history of the cathedral was the *De Basilica Petri* by 'Vigilantius'. He cites it in the *Historia Major* (see p. 396 and nn. 38, 39 above). In addition, 'Vigilantius' is cited in the following works written at Winchester in the late medieval period: the chronicle from Lucius to the beginning of Henry VI's reign in Corpus Christi College, Cambridge, MS. 110, pp. 314 et seq. (see p. 395 n. 31 above); the *Liber Monasterii de Hyda*, ed. Edward Edwards (RS 1866), pp. 7, 21, 181 (see pp. 391 and n. 7, 395 n. 30 above), and the *Epitome Historiae Majoris* (see p. 395 and n. 30 above). On the basis of Rudborne's citations from 'Vigilantius' the late Professor Robert Willis concluded that 'Vigilantius' wrote on the eve of the Norman Conquest (all Rudborne's citations and those in the other works listed refer to the pre-Conquest period), and regarded him as an important source for the architectural history of the Anglo-Saxon church at Winchester; R. Willis, 'Architectural history of Winchester cathedral' in *Proceedings of the Royal Architectural Institute, Winchester* (1845), p. 3 n. a. His view has been accepted by R. N.

Quirk, 'Winchester cathedral in the tenth century' in *Archaeological Journal*, cxiv (1957), p. 28 n. 1. However, Professor D. J. Sheerin (to whom I am indebted for allowing me to use his research notes on 'Vigilantius'), in a letter to me of 7 December 1976, argues convincingly that 'Vigilantius' was a late medieval forgery made at St Swithun's to substantiate its early history. The main basis of his argument is that some of the extant citations from 'Vigilantius' relate to the 'British history' of Winchester (see p. 397 and n. 46 above), which the monks concocted in the late thirteenth and early fourteenth centuries. However, 'Vigilantius' was probably written later: Rudborne himself, citing 'Vigilantius', is the earliest extant authority for the statement that King Lucius originally founded the Old Minster; if this legend existed in the late thirteenth and early fourteenth centuries it is surprising that it was not used by the monks who then wrote the Old Minster's legendary history.[1]

---

[1] It should be borne in mind that there may never have been an actual forgery under Vigilantius' name: he and his work may have 'existed' only in Rudborne's references to them. It may also be suggested that the works of 'Girardus Cornubiensis' were forgeries and/or that he was another fictional author invented by Rudborne: his name is suspiciously like that of Giraldus Cambrensis.

Since the above Appendix went to press, Dr A. R. Rumble, in a letter to me of 31 July 1981, has called my attention to an article on Rudborne's account in the *Historia Major* of the council of Florence; J. G. Greatrex, 'Thomas Rudborne, monk of Winchester, and the council of Florence', in *Studies in Church History*, ix (1972), pp. 171–6. I am also indebted to him for communicating the results of his own researches in so far as they relate to Rudborne. He writes: 'One of the marginal hands in the *Codex Wintoniensis* [BL MS. Additional 15350] may be that of Rudbourne; it is the same hand as that in BL MS. Additional 29436, ff. 4–9, a fifteenth century MS. of the foundation chronicle usually known as the *Epitome*, an extract of material from Rudbourne's *Historia Major*, attributed either to Rudbourne or to John of Exeter, a slightly later chronicler. The marginalia in the *Codex* are mostly to do with the history of the church of Winchester; they are listed on pp. 5–6 of vol. ii of my thesis (*The Structure and Reliability of the 'Codex Wintoniensis'*; London Ph.D., 1979), under the heading Annotator 10. I also found that Rudbourne quotes an interpolated version of document no. 39 from the *Codex* in his *Historia Major* (Book II, Chapter xii), surviving in Lambeth 183 (ff. 22–3). He was evidently one of the users of the *Codex* at the priory in the period before the Reformation. He is almost certainly the monk of St Swithun's mentioned in document no. 316 in Greatrex's book [*The Register of the Common Seal of the Priory of St Swithun, Winchester, 1345–1497*, ed. Joan Greatrex (Hampshire Record Series, ii, Winchester 1978)] dated 1447; one of the monks mentioned with him is William Basyng, the sacrist, whom I would identify as William Basinge, the owner of the foundation chronicle later copied by John Stowe in BL MS. Harley 539, ff. 114–16. This Basyng is subprior in 1457 (Greatrex, nos 332, 334–6). The chronicle copied by Stowe would seem to be that in Additional 29436 (above) and thus perhaps by Rudbourne, possibly made for the use of Basyng. In the sixteenth century at the time of the Reformation the *Epitome* was used by the prior in a certificate about the antiquity of the church of Winchester presented to Thomas Cromwell (see BL MS. Harley 358, ff. 16–17; apparently translated from the Latin of the *Epitome* (cf. text now in the same MS., ff. 61–62^v). Harley 358, ff. 27–70, are apparently part of a notebook of John Leland, who made use of the *Epitome*, and are now in a 'Misc. Ecclesiastical Collection' which also includes the prior's certificate mentioned above). The *Epitome* would appear to have been more used, or useful, than the *Historia Major* for the actual chronology of the foundations at the cathedral.' In addition, Dr Rumble writes: 'Annotator 10 of the *Codex* also wrote the 15th c. Winchester cathedral priory cartulary in ff. 49–70^v of BL MS. 29436; added rubrics and underlinings to the 13th c. priory cartulary in the same MS.; and was the second scribe of a roll of transcripts of papal bulls dating from 1144 to 1399 in BL Cotton Roll XIII. 16, mm. 6–7.'

Appendix E

Tabulae

A number of examples are known from the fourteenth, fifteenth and six-teenth centuries of *tabulae* hung in churches apparently intended primarily for the information of visitors (see p. 344 above). They were boards bearing the history of the church, legends associated with it, tracts on the origins of the order if the church were monastic, and the like. The purpose was to increase the church's prestige and perhaps encourage the visitors to give more generously. The example surviving from Glastonbury, now MS. Lat. hist. a. 2 in the Bodleian Library, is a folding wooden frame, 3 ft 8 in. high and when open 3 ft 6 in. broad. Inside are two smaller wooden boards, so that the whole when folded resembles a book. The six faces of the boards have parchment pasted on them, on which the legendary history of the abbey is written: the text is mainly derived from John of Glastonbury's chronicle (see pp. 398–400 above). This *tabula* is discussed and reproduced in J. A. Bennett, 'A Glastonbury relic' in *Proceedings of the Somerset Archaeological and Natural History Soc.*, xxxiv (1888), pp. 117–22, and in J. Armitage Robinson, *Two Glastonbury Legends: King Arthur and St Joseph of Arimathea* (Cambridge 1926), pp. 41–2.

Examples of *tabulae* from Stone priory in Staffordshire (*Mon. Angl.* vi. 230–1), St George's, Windsor (ibid., vi. 1364), Worksop priory in Nottinghamshire (ibid., vi. 122–4) are noticed, in addition to the Glaston-bury one, in G. H. Gerould, '"Tables" in medieval churches' in *Speculum*, i (1926), pp. 439–40. Further examples from the cathedrals of Durham, St Paul's, Lincoln and Lichfield are noticed in Noël Denholm-Young, 'The birth of chronicle' in *Bodleian Quarterly Record*, vii (1933), pp. 326 and n. 5, 237–8. A table like that from Glastonbury was in the south transept of Lichfield cathedral. It contained the story of the cathedral's foundation, a list of the bishops of Lichfield, and a list of the kings of Mercia, on folding boards. It was destroyed by the parliamentarians in 1643. See H. E. Savage, *The Lichfield Chronicles* (Lichfield 1915), pp. 8–10, 15–16. Another example from Durham, besides an example from Christ Church, Canterbury, and one from the abbey of St John the Baptist at Colchester are mentioned by W. A. Pantin, 'Some medieval English treatises on the origins of monasticism' in *Medieval Studies presented to Rose Graham*, ed. Veronica Ruffer and A. J. Taylor (Oxford 1950), pp. 200–1, 207–8.

The earliest example of a *tabula* which I have found is the late eleventh century one which was in the abbey church at Bury St Edmunds; *Memorials of St. Edmund's Abbey*, ed. Thomas Arnold (Rolls Series, 3 vols), i. 84.

[495]

Appendix F
Rebellion in Holderness (? 1268)

Thomas Burton gives no exact date for the rebellion in Holderness, which he describes in some detail (see p. 360 above). According to his narrative the sheriff, knights and free men of Holderness refused to obey the Lord Edward's summons to serve in Scotland. Henry III, therefore, sent an army to reduce the rebels, and peace was only made as a result of the tireless mediation of the subprior of Meaux.

Burton, having recorded the death of William de Forz, sixth count of Aumale, in 1260, and described the earl's arrangements for his burial and his bequests, proceeds with the narrative in question, which begins 'Et dum haec agerentur'. I have found no corroborative evidence that Edward embarked on a Scottish campaign at this time. In fact he seems to have been tourneying in France in 1260; Noël Denholm-Young, 'The tournament in the thirteenth century' in *Studies in Medieval History presented to F. M. Powicke*, ed. R. W. Hunt, W. A. Pantin and R. W. Southern (Oxford 1948), p. 259 n. 2. However, in February 1267 he was sent north partly to subdue the disinherited barons, and partly to get royalist and Scottish support for an attack on Ely; see F. M. Powicke, *King Henry III and the Lord Edward* (Oxford 1947, 2 vols), ii. 541 n. 1, 544. At just this time Holderness became the scene of disorder owing to a dispute between the joint administrators, Amice, countess of Devon (a royalist supporter), and her daughter Isabella, countess of Aumale (who sympathized with the barons): see Noël Denholm-Young, 'The Yorkshire estates of Isabella de Fortibus' in *Yorkshire Archaeological Journal*, xxxi (1934), pp. 410–11; *CPR, 1266–1272*, pp. 260, 275–6, 281–2, 296, 375–6.

Possibly Burton inserted the entry at this point in the chronicle because he associated 1260 with the Lord Edward; in that year Edward acquired the wardship of Holderness, which he sold to Amice and Isabella; *CPR, 1258–66*, pp. 97, 161; *CCR, 1259–61*, pp. 97–8; cf. Denholm-Young, op. cit., p. 390 n. 1. The parliament to which Burton refers (p. 360 above) could be identified with that summoned to meet at Westminster on 22 April 1268, to treat with the king 'on certain urgent business'. The gathering was obviously of some importance since the cities and boroughs were required to send representatives 'with full powers'. There is no direct evidence concerning the purpose of the assembly. However, it has been suggested that its intention was to help in the pacification of the kingdom, the government's main concern after the Dictum of Kenilworth. See G. O. Sayles, 'Representation of cities and boroughs in 1268' in *EHR*, xl (1925), pp. 581–5. If Burton's narrative does refer to this parliament, it corroborates Sayles's view.

Note: since this book went to press there has been published Barbara English, *The Lords of Holderness 1086–1260* (Oxford 1979). For a reference to the rebellion, dated *c.* 1260, see p. 74.

Appendix G

Henry VI the 'Simple' King

The biography of Henry VI by John Capgrave in *Liber de Illustribus Henricis*, and that by John Blacman, *De Virtutibus et Miraculis Henrici VI*, throw little light on Henry VI's character because they are pious eulogies. Blacman, a Carthusian and Henry's confessor, probably wrote his panegyric in connection with the suggested canonization of Henry in Henry VII's reign. For Capgrave's *Life* see pp. 389–90 above. The text of Blacman's work is printed *Duo Rerum Anglicarum Scriptores Veteres*, ed. Thomas Hearne (Oxford 1732, 2 vols), i. 285–307. See also *Henry the Sixth, a Reprint of John Blacman's Memoir*, with translation and notes by M. R. James (Cambridge 1919).

John Whethamsted twice uses the phrase 'simplex et rectus' to describe Henry VI's character, on both occasions s.a. 1455; *Reg. II*, i. 164, 248, and see p. 383 and n. 262 above.

The meaning of the word *simplex* which by the fifteenth century was equivalent to the English 'simple', is sometimes doubtful because of the variety of usage in the middle ages (see *NED*. ix. pt i. 63–5, under 'simple'). Two common medieval meanings shade into each other; it can mean innocent, honest, open, ingenuous and guileless, leading through uncalculating and unsuspicious to gullible, lacking in acuteness or learning— the latter meaning can imply humble in status or birth. Whethamsted uses the word at either end of the spectrum. In the phrase 'simplex et rectus' it undoubtedly has the flattering meaning. This use of *simplex*, in combination with *rectus*, is paralleled by the Evesham chronicler who writes of Abbot Roger Zatton (1380–1418): 'Iste abbas in conventu suo simplex et rectus et mitis semper apparuit, non nimis mundanus sed valde religiosus, nulli nocens sed omnes diligens et omnibus quantum potuit proficiens, semper Deo devotus'; *Eve.* p. 310.

Whethamsted, however, elsewhere uses *simplex* to denote unsuspiciousness and gullibility; *Reg.* I, i. 123, 203, 280. Thomas Elmham uses it in the latter sense; *SA*, pp. 317, 318, while Thomas Burton uses it to mean both gullibility and lack of learning; *TB*, i. 111, 258, 267, 279. It was with the rather pejorative sense of gullibility that Whethamsted applied the term *simplicitas* ('simplicity') to Henry. In his verses on Henry's fall in 1461, he describes him as 'of excessive simplicity in his acts'; *Reg.* II, i. 415, and see p. 383 and n. 265 above. Similarly the first Crowland continuator, s.a. 1446–7 (*CC*, p. 521), attributes the duke of Suffolk's influence over Henry to the king's 'simplicity' ('Qui in tantam Regis Henrici admissus est familiaritatem, ut ejus abutens simplicitate, omnia regni fere negotia ad suum disponere nutum arbitratur'). See p. 411 above.

It will be noticed that in none of the examples cited does *simplex* mean foolish or half-witted, nor does *simplicitas* mean idiocy. (The meaning of 'simple' as 'half-witted' apparently originated in the seventeenth century; see *NED*, ix. pt i. 64, under 'simple', 10.) It is true that John Hardyng (*JH*, p. 410) describes Henry as 'of small intelligence'. However, this description is in the last version of his chronicle, and could, therefore, be the result of anti-Lancastrian bias. The same version (*JH*, p. 394) describes Henry as a 'simplehead' who 'could little within his breast conceive. The good from evil he could uneth perceive' (cf. *JH*, p. 396). Again, this may be accounted for by anti-Lancastrian bias—but in addition it should be remembered that Hardyng was here referring to Henry when a child of nine years old.[1]

However, although the chroniclers do not depict Henry as a congenital idiot, a number notice his mental breakdown in 1453 (see p. 384 and n. 271 above), and the first Crowland continuator makes it clear that Henry remained mentally weakened for several years. Recording Henry's flight to the north in 1461 he writes: 'instintu Reginae se transtulerat; imo quia idem Rex ab annis jam multis ex accidente sibi aegritudine quandam animi incurrerat infirmitatem, et sic impos mentis permansit diutius; ac solo nomine regni gubernacula possidebat.' *CC*, p. 532, and see p. 411 above.

---

[1] R. L. Storey, *The End of the House of Lancaster* (London 1966), p. 33, asserts that 'those writing in the time of Edward IV referred to Henry as an idiot', and again that 'accounts of both friend and foes, indeed, disclose Henry as a devout and kindly simpleton.' In support of this contention Professor Storey cites Hardyng's comment that Henry was 'of small intelligence' (ibid., p. 33 and n. 7), and, more generally, 'the testimony of the Yorkist chronicles'. As has been seen, the evidence of the chronicles does not warrant such a definite conclusion. However, Professor Storey also cites the evidence of legal records which show that even before his breakdown a few of Henry's subjects spoke openly of him as childish or even lunatic—for which they were indicted. One such was a seditious yeoman of Britling, Sussex, who in 1450 was indicted for saying that 'the king was a natural fool, and would ofttimes hold a staff in his hands with a bird on the end, playing therewith as a fool' (ibid., p. 35). In this case at least there may be an explanation which does not involve believing that Henry was simple-minded; possibly the yeoman was making a joking reference to the fact that on state occasions Henry might hold the rod with the dove, part of the regalia (for which see L. G. Wickham Legg, *English Coronation Records* (Westminster 1901), pp. lii–liii).

Appendix H

Chronological Indices

1 THE PRINCIPAL LITERARY SOURCES FOR ENGLISH HISTORY, ARRANGED UNDER REIGNS 1307–1485

[499]

2 ANNALS (COMBINING LOCAL AND GENERAL HISTORY) OF THE FIFTEENTH CENTURY AND THE FIRST HALF OF THE SIXTEENTH CENTURY

3 LOCAL HISTORIES FROM THE LATE FOURTEENTH CENTURY TO THE EARLY SIXTEENTH CENTURY

4 ANTIQUARIAN WORKS OF THE FIFTEENTH CENTURY

(in order of composition)

Select Bibliography

1 TEXTS[1]

Amundesham, John, *Annales Monasterii S. Albani*, ed. H. T. Riley (RS 1870–1, 2 vols).

André, Bernard, *Historia Regis Henrici Septimi*, ed. James Gairdner (RS 1858).

Basin, Thomas, *Histoire de Charles VII*, ed., with a French translation, Charles Samaran and Henry de Surirey de Saint-Rémy (Les Classiques de l'Histoire de France au Moyen Age 1934–45, 2 vols).

—, *Histoire de Louis XI*, ed., with a French translation, Charles Samaran and M. C. Garand (Les Classiques de l'Histoire de France au Moyen Age, 1963–72, 3 vols).

Beauchamp, Richard: *The Pageants of Richard Beauchamp Earl of Warwick*, ed. William, earl of Carysfort (Roxburghe Club, Oxford 1908).

Bury St Edmunds, abbey of: *Memorials of St Edmund's Abbey*, ed. Thomas Arnold (RS 1890–6, 3 vols).

Canterbury, Christ Church: *The Verses formerly inscribed on twelve Windows in the Choir of Canterbury Cathedral*, ed. M. R. James (Cambridge Antiquarian Soc., Octavo series, xxxviii, 1901).

Canterbury, St Augustine's: *Chronicle of the Years 1532–1537, written by a Monk of St. Augustine's, Canterbury* in *Narratives of the Days of the Reformation*, ed. J. G. Nichols (Camden Soc., original series, lxxvii, 1859), pp. 279–86.

Capgrave, John, *The Chronicle of England*, ed F. C. Hingeston (RS 1858).

—, *Liber de Illustribus Henricis*, ed. F. C. Hingeston (RS 1858).

Chandos Herald: *Life of the Black Prince by the Herald of Sir John Chandos*, ed. M. K. Pope and E. C. Lodge (Oxford 1910).

Cheney, C. R. (ed.), see under Powicke, F. M.

Clifford, S. N. (ed.), 'An edition of 'the continuation of the *Eulogium Historiarum*, 1361–1413'' (M. Phil. thesis, University of Leeds 1975).

Commynes, Philippe de, *Mémoires*, ed. L. M. E. Dupont (Soc. de l'Histoire de France 1840–7, 3 vols).

Evesham abbey: *The Chronicle of Evesham Abbey*, translated by D. C. Cox (Vale of Evesham Historical Soc. 1965).

---

[1] The works are listed under the name of the author if this appears in the printed title or is well known. Otherwise chronicles are listed under the place of origin, biographies under the name of the subject, and works which can be put into none of these categories under the name of the editor. Texts which are in the list of Abbreviations at the beginning of this volume are not included here.

Domerham, Adam de, *Historia de Rebus gestis Glastoniensibus*, ed. Thomas Hearne (Oxford 1727).

Durham, cathedral priory: *Historiae Dunelmensis Scriptores Tres, Gaufridus de Coldingham, Robertus de Graystanes et Willielmus de Chambre*, ed. James Raine, sn. (Surtees Soc., ix, 1839).

Ellis, Henry (ed.), *The Manner and Guiding of the Earl of Warwick at Angers from the fifteenth day of July to the fourth of August, 1470, which day he departed from Angers* in *Original Letters illustrative of English History*, second series (London 1827, 4 vols), i. 135–7.

Fortescue, Sir John, *The Governance of England*, ed. Charles Plummer (Oxford 1885).

—, *De Laudibus Legum Angliae*, ed., with an English translation, S. B. Chrimes (Cambridge 1949).

Froissart, Jean, *Chroniques, Début du premier livre, Edition du manuscrit de Rome Reg. Lat. 869*, ed. G. T. Diller (Textes Littéraires Françaises, no. 194, Geneva 1972).

—, *Voyage en Béarn*, ed. A. H. Diverres (Manchester 1953).

Fulman, William (ed.), *Rerum Anglicarum Scriptorum Veterum Tom. I* (Oxford 1684).

Gairdner, James (ed.), *Three Fifteenth Century Chronicles* (Camden Soc., new series, xxviii, 1880).

Giles, J. A., *Incerti Scriptoris Chronicon Angliae de Regnis trium Regum Lancastrensium Henrici IV, Henrici V, et Henrici VI* (London 1848).

Grey Friars, Newgate, London: *Chronicle of the Grey Friars of London*, ed. J. G. Nichols (Camden Soc., original series, liii, 1852).

Hall, Edward: *Hall's Chronicle . . .* , ed. Henry Ellis (London 1809).

Haskins, G. L. (ed.), 'A chronicle of the civil wars of Edward II' in *Speculum*, xiv (1939), pp. 73–81.

Henry V: *The First English Life of Henry the Fifth*, ed. C. L. Kingsford (Oxford 1911).

Henry of Grosmont, duke of Lancaster, *Le Livre de Seyntz Medicines*, ed. E. J. Arnould (Anglo-Norman Text Soc., ii, 1940).

Jerningham, Edward (ed.), 'Account of Edward the Fourth's second invasion of England, in 1471, drawn up by one of his followers; with the king's letter to the inhabitants of Bruges upon his success: translated from a French manuscript in the Public Library at Ghent' in *Archaeologia*, xxi (1825), pp. 11–23.

Kirkstall abbey: *The Kirkstall Abbey Chronicles*, ed., with an English translation, John Taylor (Thoresby Soc., xlii, 1952).

Louth Park abbey: *Chronicon Abbatiae de Parco Ludae: the Chronicle of Louth Park Abbey*, ed. Edmund Venables, with a translation by A. R. Maddison (Lincolnshire Record Soc., Horncastle 1891).

Leland, John, *Commentarii de Scriptoribus Britannicis*, ed. Anthony Hall (Oxford 1709, 2 vols).

—, *The Itinerary*, ed. Thomas Hearne (Oxford 1710–12, 9 vols).

—, *The Itinerary*, ed. L. Toulmin Smith (London 1907–10, 5 vols).

Mandeville, Sir John: *Mandeville's Travels*, ed. M. C. Seymour (Oxford 1967).

Molinet, Jean, *Chroniques 1474–1506*, ed G. Doutrepont and O. Jodogne (Académie Royale Belgique, Classe des Lettres et des Sciences Morales et Politiques, Collection des Anciens Auteurs Belges, Brussels, 1935–7, 3 vols).

Monmouth, Geoffrey of, *Historia Regum Britanniae*, ed. Acton Griscom (London 1929).

Monstrelet, Enguerran de, *La Chronique . . . 1400–1444*, ed. L. Douet-D'Arcq (Soc. de l'Histoire de France 1857–62, 6 vols).

More, Thomas, *The History of King Richard III and Selections from the English and Latin Poems*, ed. R. S. Sylvester (New Haven-London 1976).

Nova Legenda Angliae, ed. Carl Horstmann (Oxford 1901, 2 vols).

Otterbourne, Thomas, chronicle of, in *Duo Rerum Anglicarum Scriptores Veteres viz. Thomas Otterbourne et Johannes Whethamstede*, ed. Thomas Hearne (Oxford 1732, 2 vols), i.

Powicke, F. M., and Cheney, C. R. (eds), *Councils and Synods, with other Documents relating to the English Church* (Oxford 1964, only vol. 2, in two pts, 1205–1313, published to date).

Rishanger, William, *Chronica et Annales*, ed. H. T. Riley (RS 1865).

—, *The Chronicle of the Barons' War. The Miracles of Simon de Montfort*, ed. J. O. Halliwell (Camden Soc. 1840).

Roye, Jean de, *Journal connu sous le Nom de Chronique Scandaleuse, 1460–1483*, ed. Bernard de Mandrot (Soc. de l'Histoire de France 1894–6, 2 vols).

Stevenson, Joseph (ed.), *Letters and Papers illustrative of the Wars of the English in France* (RS 1861–4, 2 vols in 3 parts).

Stow, John, *A Survey of London*, ed. C. L. Kingsford (Oxford 1908, 2 vols).

Stubbs, Thomas, *Chronica de Vitis Archiepiscoporum Eboracensium* in *Historians of the Church of York and its Archbishops*, ed. James Raine, jr. (RS 1879–94, 3 vols), ii. 388–421.

Wharton, Henry (ed.), *Anglia Sacra* (London 1691, 2 vols).

Worcester, William, *The Boke of Noblesse*, ed. J. G. Nichols (Roxburghe Club, London 1860, reprinted New York 1972).

—, description of Bristol, in James Dallaway, *Antiquities of Bristowe* (Bristol 1834).

York: *Historians of the Church of York and its Archbishops*, ed. James Raine, jr (RS 1879–94, 3 vols).

2 SECONDARY SOURCES[2]

Anglo, Sydney, 'The *British History* in early Tudor propaganda' in *BJRL*, xliv (1961–2), pp. 17–48.

Armstrong, C. A. J., 'Politics and the battle of St Albans, 1455' in *BIHR*, xxxiii (1960), pp. 1–72.

—, 'Some examples of the distribution and speed of news in England at the time of the Wars of the Roses' in *Studies in Medieval History presented to F. M. Powicke*, ed. R. W. Hunt, W. A. Pantin and R. W. Southern (Oxford 1948).

Arnould, E. J., *Études sur le Livre des Saintes Medecines du Duc Henri de Lancastre* (Paris 1948).

—, 'Henry of Lancaster and his *Livre des Seintes Medicines*' in *BJRL*, xxi (1937), pp. 352–86.

Bennett, J. A., 'A Glastonbury relic' in *Proceedings of the Somerset Archaeological and Natural History Soc.*, xxxiv (1888), pp. 117–22.

Blake, N. F., 'Lord Berners: a survey' in *Medievalia et Humanistica*, new series, ii (1971), pp. 119–32.

Brandt, W. J., *The Shape of Medieval History. Studies in Modes of Perception* (New Haven-London 1966).

Brentano, Robert, 'The *Jurisdictio Spiritualis*: an example of fifteenth-century English historiography' in *Speculum*, xxxii (1957), pp. 326–32.

Brie, F. W. D., *Geschichte und Quellen der mittelenglischen Prosachronik The Brute of England oder the Chronicles of England* (Marburg 1905).

Burke, Peter, *The Renaissance Sense of the Past* (London 1969).

---

[2] The works and articles included either relate wholly to historiography, or have been of significant help in the preparation of this book.

Chrimes, S. B., *English Constitutional Ideas in the Fifteenth Century* (Cambridge 1936).

Churchill, G. B., *Richard III up to Shakespeare* (*Palaestra*, x, Berlin 1900).

Clarke, M. V., 'Henry Knighton and the library catalogue of Leicester abbey' in *EHR*, xlv (1930) pp. 103–7, reprinted in the same author's *Fourteenth Century Studies*, ed. L. S. Sutherland and May McKisack (Oxford 1937), pp. 293–9.

Clarke, M. V., and Denholm-Young, Noël, 'The Kirkstall chronicle, 1355–1400' in *BJRL*, xv (1931), pp. 100–37, reprinted in Clarke, *Fourteenth Century Studies*, ed. Sutherland and McKisack, pp. 99–114.

Collingwood, R. G., *The Idea of History* (Oxford 1946).

Cox, D. C., 'The French chronicle of London' in *Medium Ævum*, xlv (1976), pp. 201–8.

Craster, H. H. E., 'The Red Book of Durham' in *EHR*, xl (1925), pp. 504–32.

Croce, Benedetto, *Theory and History of Historiography*, translated by Douglas Ainslie (London 1921).

Davies, H. W., *Bernhard von Breydenbach and his Journey to the Holy Land 1483–4* (London 1911, reprinted Utrecht 1968).

Davies, R. G. 'Some notes from the register of Henry de Wakefield, bishop of Worcester, on the political crisis of 1386–1388' in *EHR*, lxxxvi (1971), pp. 547–58.

Dean, L. F., *Tudor Theories of History Writing* (University of Michigan Contributions in Modern Philology, no. i, April 1947).

Denholm-Young, Noël, 'The birth of a chronicle' in *Bodleian Quarterly Record*, vii (1933), pp. 326–8.

—, see also under Clarke, M. V.

Diller, G. T., 'La dernière rédaction du premier livre de *Chroniques* de Froissart: une étude du Reg. Lat. 869' in *Le Moyen Age*, 4ᵉ série, xxv (1970), pp. 91–125.

Dobson, R. B., *Durham Priory 1400–1450* (Cambridge 1973).

Duls, L. D., *Richard II in the Early Chronicles* (The Hague-Paris 1975).

Edwards, J. G., 'The "second" continuation of the Crowland chronicle: was it written "in ten days"?' in *BIHR*, xxxix (1966), pp. 117–29.

—, 'Ranulf, monk of Chester' in *EHR*, xlvii (1932), p. 94.

Fairfield, L. P., 'John Bale and the development of Protestant hagiography in England' in *Journal of Ecclesiastical History*, xxiv (1973), pp. 145–60.

Ferguson, A. B., *The Indian Summer of English Chivalry. Studies in the Decline and Transformation of Chivalric Idealism* (Durham, North Carolina 1960).

Flenley, Ralph, *Six Town Chronicles of England* (Oxford 1911).

Fowler, D. C., 'John Trevisa and the English bible' in *Modern Philology*, lviii (1960), pp. 81–98.

—, 'New light on John Trevisa' in *Traditio*, xviii (1962), pp. 289–317.

Galbraith, V. H., 'An autograph MS. of Ranulph Higden's Polychronicon' in *Huntington Library Quarterly*, xxiii (1959–60), pp. 1–18.

—, 'The chronicle of Henry Knighton' in *Fritz Saxl 1890–1948: a Volume of Memorial Essays from his Friends in England*, ed. D. J. Gordon (London 1957), pp. 136–45.

—, 'Extracts from the *Historia Aurea* and a French "Brut" (1317–47)' in *EHR*, xliii (1928), pp. 203–17.

—, 'The *Historia Aurea* of John, Vicar of Tynemouth, and the sources of the St Albans chronicle (1327–77), in *Essays in History presented to Reginald Lane Poole*, ed. H. W.C. Davis (Oxford 1927), pp. 379–98.

—, *Historical Research in Medieval England* (London 1951).

—, 'Thomas Walsingham and the Saint Albans chronicle (1272–1422)' in *EHR*, xlvii (1932), pp. 12–30.

Genet, J. P., 'Cartulaires, registres et histoire: l'exemple anglais' in *Le Métier d' Historien au Moyen Age*, ed. Bernard Guenée (Publications de la Sorbonne, série 'Études', xiii, Paris 1977), pp. 95–129.

Gerould, G. H. '"Tables" in medieval churches' in *Speculum*, i (1926), pp. 439–40.

Giffin, M. E., 'A Wigmore manuscript at the University of Chicago' in *The National Library of Wales Journal*, vii (1951–2), pp. 316–25.

Gill, P. E., 'Politics and propaganda in fifteenth century England: the polemical writings of Sir John Fortescue' in *Speculum*, xlvi (1971), pp. 333–47.

Gransden, Antonia, 'Antiquarian studies in fifteenth century England' in *Antiquaries Journal*, lx, pt i (1980), pp. 75–97.

—, 'The continuations of the *Flores Historiarum* from 1265 to 1327' in *Mediaeval Studies*, xxxvi (Toronto 1974) pp. 472–92.

—, 'The "Cronica Buriensis" and the abbey of St Benet of Hulme' in *BIHR*, xxxvi (1963), pp. 77–82.

—, 'Propaganda in English medieval historiography' in *Journal of Medieval History*, i (1975), pp. 363–81.

—, 'Silent meanings in Ranulf Higden's *Polychronicon* and in Thomas Elmham's *Liber Metricus de Henrico Quinto*' in *Medium Ævum*, xlvi (1978), pp. 231–40.

—, Review of *JG*, in *EHR*, xcv (1980), pp. 358–63.

Greatrex, J. G., 'Thomas Rudborne, monk of Winchester, and the council of Florence' in *Studies in Church History*, ix (1972), pp. 171–6.

Gross, Charles, *A Bibliography of English History to 1485*, ed. E. B. Graves (Oxford 1975).

Guenée, Bernard, 'Histoires, annales, chroniques. Essai sur les genres historiques au moyen âge' in *Annales Économies Sociétés Civilisations*, xxviii (1973), pp. 997–1016.

—, 'Y a-t-il une historiographie médiévale?' in *Revue Historique*, cclviii (1977), pp. 261–75.

Hale, J. R., *The Evolution of British Historiography* (London-Melbourne 1967).

Hanham, Alison, *Richard III and his Early Historians 1483–1535* (Oxford 1975).

Hay, Denys, *Annalists and Historians, Western Historiography from the Eighth to the Eighteenth century* (London 1977).

—, 'Flavio Biondo and the Middle Ages' in *Proceedings of the British Academy*, xlv (1959), pp. 97–128.

—, 'History and historians in France and England during the fifteenth century' in *BIHR*, xxxv (1962), pp. 111–27.

—, *Polydore Vergil, Renaissance Historian and Man of Letters* (Oxford 1952).

Hunter, Michael, 'The facsimiles in Thomas Elmham's History of St. Augustine's, Canterbury' in *The Library*, fifth series, xxviii (1973), pp. 215–20.

Jacob, E. F. '*Verborum florida venustas*: some early examples of euphuism in England' in *BJRL*, xvii (1933), pp. 264–90, reprinted with revision in the same author's *Essays in the Conciliar Epoch* (second edition, Manchester 1953), pp. 185–206.

Jones, E. J., 'The authorship of the continuation of the *Eulogium Historiarum*: a suggestion' in *Speculum*, xii (1937), pp. 196–202.

—, 'An examination of the authorship of *The Deposition and Death of Richard II* attributed to Creton' in *Speculum*, xv (1940), pp. 460–77.

Kantorowicz, E. H., *The King's Two Bodies, A Study in Medieval Political Theology* (London-Princeton 1957).

Kekewich, Margaret, 'Edward IV, William Caxton and literary patronage in Yorkist England' in *Modern Language Review*, lxvi (1971), pp. 481–7.

Kendrick, T. D., *British Antiquity* (London 1950).

Kingsford, C. L., 'The early biographies of Henry V' in *EHR*, xxv (1910), pp. 58–92.

—, 'The first version of Hardyng's chronicle' in *EHR*, xxvii (1912), pp. 462–82, 740–53.

Kinkaid, A. N., 'The dramatic structure of Sir Thomas More's *History of King Richard III*' in *Studies in English Literature 1500–1900*, xii (1972), pp. 223–42.

Kliman, B. W., 'The idea of chivalry in John Barbour's *Bruce*' in *Mediaeval Studies*, xxxv (Toronto 1973), pp. 477–508.

Lacroix, B. M., *L'Historien au moyen âge* (Montreal-Paris 1971).

—, 'The notion of history in early mediaeval historians' in *Mediaeval Studies*, x (Toronto 1948), pp. 219–23.

Lander, J. R., 'The treason and death of the duke of Clarence: a re-interpretation' in *Canadian Journal of History*, ii, no. 2 (1967), pp. 1–28.

Lethbridge, C. L., 'Robert de Avesbury' in *EHR*, xxii (1907), p. 292.

Levine, Mortimer, 'Richard III—usurper or lawful king?' in *Speculum*, xxxiv (1959), pp. 391–401.

Levy, F. J., *Tudor Historical Thought* (Huntington Library, San Marino, California 1967).

Lewis, P. S., 'Two pieces of fifteenth-century iconography' in *Journal of the Warburg and Courtauld Institutes*, xxvii (1964), pp. 319–20.

—, 'War propaganda and historiography in fifteenth-century France and England' in *TRHS*, fifth series, xv (1965), pp. 1–21.

Liebermann, Felix, 'Ueber Ostenglische Geschichtsquellen des 12, 13, 14 Jahrhunderts, besonders den falschen Ingulf' in *Neues Archiv der Gesellschaft für ältere deutsche Geschichtskunde*, xviii (Hanover-Leipzig 1892), pp. 225–67.

McCusker, Honor, *John Bale, Dramatist and Antiquary* (Bryn Mawr, Pennsylvania, 1942).

McFarlane, K. B., 'William Worcester: a preliminary survey' in *Studies presented to Sir Hilary Jenkinson*, ed. J. Conway Davies (Oxford 1957), pp. 196–221.

McKenna, J. W., 'Henry VI of England and the dual monarchy: aspects of royal political propaganda, 1422–1432' in *Journal of the Warburg and Courtauld Institutes*, xxviii (1965), pp. 145–62.

—, 'Popular canonization as political propaganda: the cult of Archbishop Scrope' in *Speculum*, xlv (1970), pp. 608–23.

McKisack, May, *Medieval History in the Tudor Age* (Oxford 1971).

Mann, J. G., 'Instances of antiquarian feeling in medieval and renaissance art' in *Archaeological Journal*, lxxxix (1932), pp. 254–74.

Meyvaert, Paul, 'John Erghome and the *Vaticinium Roberti Bridlington*' in *Speculum*, xli (1966), pp. 656–64.

Mitchell, R. J., *John Tiptoft, 1427–1470* (London 1938).

Molinier, A. M. L. E., *Les Source de l'histoire de France des origines aux guerres d'Italie, 1494* (Manuels de Bibliographie Historiques, no. 3, 1901–6, 5 vols).

Momigliano, Arnaldo, 'Ancient history and the antiquarian' in *Journal of the Warburg and Courtauld Institutes*, xiii (1950), pp. 285–315.

Moranville, Henri, 'La Chronique du Religieux de Saint Denis, le Mémoires de Salmon et la Chronique de la Mort de Richard II' in *Bibliothèque de l'École des Chartes*, l (Paris 1889), pp. 5–40.

Myers, A. R., 'Richard III and historical tradition' in *History*, liii (1968), pp. 181–202.

Offler, H. S., *Medieval Historians of Durham* (Durham 1958).

Owst, G. R., *Literature and the Pulpit in Medieval England* (second edition, Oxford 1961).

Palmer, J. J. N., 'The authorship, date and historical value of the French chronicles on the Lancastrian revolution' in *BJRL*, lxi (1978–9), pp. 145–81, 398–421.

[—(ed.), *Froissart: Historian* (Bury St Edmunds 1981).] See p. 89 n. 198 above.

Pantin, W. A., 'Some medieval English treatises on the origins of monasticism' in *Medieval Studies presented to Rose Graham*, ed. Veronica Ruffer and A. J. Taylor (Oxford 1950), pp. 189–215.

Partner, N. F., *Serious Entertainments: the Writing of History in Twelfth-Century England* (Chicago-London 1977).

Piaget, Arthur, 'Le livre messire Geoffroi de Charny' in *Romania*, xxvi (1897), pp. 394–411.

Pollard, A. F., 'The authorship and value of the "Anonimalle" chronicle' in *EHR*, liii (1938), pp. 577–605.

—, 'Edward Hall's will and chronicle' in *BIHR*, ix (1932), pp. 171–7.

—, 'Sir Thomas More's "Richard III"' in *History*, xvii (1933), pp. 317–23.

—, 'The making of Sir Thomas More's *Richard III*' in *Historical Essays in Honour of James Tait*, ed. J. G. Edwards, V. H. Galbraith and E. F. Jacob (Manchester 1933), pp. 223–38.

Previté-Orton, C. W., 'The earlier career of Titus Livius Frulovisi' in *EHR*, xxx (1915), pp. 74–8.

Reid, R. R., 'The date and authorship of Redmayne's "Life of Henry V"' in *EHR*, xxx (1915), pp. 691–8.

Reiss, Edmund, 'Number symbolism and medieval literature' in *Medievalia et Humanistica*, new series, i (1970), pp. 161–74.

Reynolds, B. R., 'Latin historiography: a survey, 1400–1600' in *Studies in the Renaissance*, ii (New York 1955), pp. 7–66.

Richardson, H. G., 'The *Annales Paulini*' in *Speculum*, xxiii (1948), pp. 630–40.

Riley, H. T., 'The history and charters of Ingulfus considered' in *Archaeological Journal*, xix (1862), pp. 32–49, 114–33.

Robinson, J. Armitage, *Two Glastonbury Legends: King Arthur and St Joseph of Arimathea* (Cambridge 1926).

—, 'An unrecognized Westminster chronicler, 1381–1394' in *Proceedings of the British Academy*, iii (1907), pp. 61–92.

Roskell, J. S. and Taylor, Frank, 'The authorship and purpose of the *Gesta Henrici Quinti*', Part I and Part II, in *BJRL*, liii (1970–1), pp. 428–64; liv (1971–2), pp. 223–40.

Rouse, R. H., 'Bostonus Buriensis and the author of the *Catalogus Scriptorum Ecclesiae*' in *Speculum*, xli (1966), pp. 471–99.

Rowe, B. J. H., 'A contemporary account of the Hundred Years' War from 1415 to 1429' in *EHR*, xli (1926), pp. 504–13.

Russell, A. G. B., 'The Rous Roll' in *Burlington Magazine*, xxx (1917), pp. 23–31.

Sandys, J. E., *A History of Classical Scholarship* (Cambridge 1906–8, 3 vols).

Savage, H. E., *The Lichfield Chronicles* (Lichfield 1915).

Searle, W. G., *Ingulf and the Historia Croylandensis* (Cambridge Antiquarian Soc., octavo series, xxvii, 1894).

Shotwell, J. T., *An Introduction to the History of History* (New York 1922, revised edition 1939, 2 vols).

Smalley, Beryl, *Historians in the Middle Ages* (London 1974).

Smallwood, T. M., 'The text of Langtoft's chronicle' in *Medium Ævum*, xlvi (1977), pp. 219–30.

Southern, R. W., 'Aspects of the European tradition of historical writing. 1. The classical tradition from Einhard to Geoffrey of Monmouth' in *TRHS*, fifth series, xx (1970), pp. 173–96.

—, '2. Hugh of St Victor and the idea of historical development' in *TRHS*, fifth series, xxi (1971), pp. 159–79.

—, '3. History as prophecy' in *TRHS*, fifth series, xxii (1972), pp. 159–80.

—, '4. The sense of the past' in *TRHS*, fifth series, xxiii (1973), pp. 243–63.

Stow, G. B., jr, 'Some new manuscripts of the *Vita Ricardi Secundi*, 1377–1402' in *Manuscripta*, xix (1975), pp. 107–15.

—, 'Thomas Walsingham, John Malvern, and the *Vita Ricardi Secundi*, 1377–1381:

a reassessment' in *Mediaeval Studies*, xxxix (Toronto 1977), pp. 490–7.
—, 'The *Vita Ricardi* as a source for the reign of Richard II' in *Research Papers* (Vale of Evesham Historical Soc., iv, 1973), pp. 63–75.
Sudeley, Lord, 'Medieval Sudeley. Part I. The Sudeleys and Botelers of Sudeley Castle' in *Family History, the Journal of Heraldic and Genealogical Studies*, x (1977), pp. 9–20. See also under Winkless below.
Tait, James, 'On the date and authorship of the "Speculum Regis Edwardi"' in *EHR*, xvi (1901), pp. 110–15.
Tate, R. B., 'Mythology in Spanish historiography of the middle ages and renaissance' in *Hispanic Review*, xxii (1954), pp. 1–18.
Taylor, Frank, 'A note on Rolls Series 8' in *BJRL*, xx (1936), pp. 379–82.
—, see also under Roskell, J. S.
Taylor, John, 'The development of the *Polychronicon* continuation' in *EHR*, lxxvi (1961), pp. 20–36.
—, 'The French "Brut" and the reign of Edward II' in *EHR*, lxxii (1957), pp. 423–37.
—, 'Higden and Erghome: two fourteenth-century scholars' in *Économies et Sociétés au Moyen Age: Mélanges offerts à Edouard Perroy* (Publications de la Sorbonne, série 'Études', v, Paris 1973), pp. 644–9.
—, *The Kirkstall Abbey Chronicles* (Leeds 1952).
—, *Medieval Historical Writing in Yorkshire* (York 1961).
—, *The Universal Chronicle of Ranulf Higden* (Oxford 1966).
—, 'A Wigmore chronicle, 1355–77' in *Proceedings of the Leeds Philosophical and Literary Society (Literary and Historical Section)*, xi, pt v (1964), pp. 81–94.
Taylor, Rupert, *The Political Prophecy in England* (New York 1911).
Thompson, E. Maunde 'The Pageants of Richard Beauchamp, earl of Warwick' in *Burlington Magazine*, i (1903), pp. 151–64.
Thomson, J. A. F., '"The Arrival of Edward IV"—the development of the text' in *Speculum*, xlv (1971), pp. 84–93.
Three Fifteenth-Century Chronicles, ed. James Gairdner (Camden Soc., new series, xxviii, 1880).
Tout, T. F., 'The Westminster chronicle attributed to Robert of Reading' in *EHR*, xxxi (1916), pp. 450–64, reprinted in *The Collected Papers of T. F. Tout* (Manchester 1932–4, 3 vols), ii. 289–304.
Weisinger, Herbert, 'Ideas of history during the Renaissance' in *Journal of the History of Ideas*, vi (1945), pp. 415–35, reprinted in *Renaissance Essays*, ed. P. O. Kristeller and P. P. Wiener (Harper Torchbook, New York 1968), pp. 74–94.
Weiss, Roberto, 'Humphrey duke of Gloucester and Tito Livio Frulovisi' in *Fritz Saxl 1890–1948: a Volume of Memorial Essays from his Friends in England*, ed. D. J. Gordon (London 1957), pp. 218–27.
—, *Humanism in England during the Fifteenth Century* (second edition, Oxford 1957).
Winkless, D., 'Medieval Sudeley. Part II. The fifteenth century roll chronicle of the kings of England, with the Sudeley and Boteler pedigree. The Latin text and the roundels' in *Family History, the Journal of Heraldic and Genealogical Studies*, x (1977), pp. 21–39. See also under Sudeley, Lord, above.
Wood, C. T., 'The deposition of Edward V' in *Traditio*, xxxi (1975), pp. 247–86. (Discusses the contemporary and near contemporary authorities for Edward V's deposition.)
Wright, C. E., 'The dispersal of the monastic libraries and the beginning of Anglo-Saxon studies: Matthew Parker and his circle: a preliminary study' in *Transactions of the Cambridge Bibliographical Soc.*, i (1951), pp. 208–37.
—, 'The Rous Roll: the English version' in *British Museum Quarterly*, xx (1955–6), pp. 77–80.

3 SUPPLEMENT TO THE BIBLIOGRAPHICAL APPARATUS OF *HISTORICAL WRITING*, i[3]

Barnard, L. W., 'Bede and Eusebius as church historians' in *Famulus Christi*, ed. Gerald Bonner (q.v.), pp. 106–24.

Blair, P. Hunter, *The World of Bede* (London 1970). (Includes a good bibliography.)

—, 'The historical writings of Bede' in *La Storiografia altomedievale* (Settimane di studio del centro italiano di studi sull'alto Medioevo, xvii, Spoleto 1970), pp. 196–221.

Bonner, Gerald (ed.), *Famulus Christi, Essays in Commemoration of the Thirteenth Centenary of the Birth of the Venerable Bede* (London 1976). For articles particularly relevant to Bede's historiography see under Barnard, L. W., Ray, R. D., Wallace-Hadrill, J. M., and Ward, Benedicta.

Brooke, C. N. L., 'Historical writing in England between 850 and 1150' in *La Storiografia altomedievale* (Settimane di studio del centro italiano di studi sull'alto Medioevo, xvii, Spoleto 1970), pp. 223–47.

Campbell, James, 'The first century of Christianity in England' in *Ampleforth Journal*, lxxvi (1971), pp. 12–29.

—, 'Observations on the conversion of England' in *Ampleforth Journal*, lxxviii, pt ii (1973), pp. 12–26.

Colker, M. L. (ed.), 'A hagiographic polemic' in *Mediaeval Studies*, xxxix (Toronto 1977), pp. 60–108. The text of Goscelin's *Libellus contra inanes s. uirginis Mildrethae usurpatores* and the *Vita Sanctorum Aethelredi et Aethelberti Martirum et Sanctarum Virginum Miltrudis et Edburgis Idus Decembris*, with an introduction and summary in English of both works. Cf. Gransden, *Historical Writing*, i. 110–11.

—, 'Latin verses lamenting the death of Saint Wulfstan of Worcester' in *Analecta Bollandiana*, lxxxix (1971), pp. 319–22.

Conway Davies, James, 'Giraldus Cambrensis, 1146–1946' in *Archaeologia Cambrensis*, xcix (1947), pp. 85–108, 256–80.

Darlington, R. R., review of *The Life of King Edward the Confessor*, ed. Frank Barlow (Nelson's Medieval Texts 1962) in *EHR*, lxxix (1964), pp. 147–8.

Davis, R. H. C. 'The *Carmen de Hastingae Proelio*' in *EHR*, xciii (1978), pp. 241–61.

Dean, R. J., 'The manuscripts of Nicholas Trevet's Anglo-Norman *Cronicles*' in *Medievalia et Humanistica*, xiv (1962), pp. 95–105.

—, 'Nicholas Trevet, historian' in *Medieval Learning and Literature. Essays presented to Richard William Hunt*, ed. J. J. G. Alexander and M. T. Gibson (Oxford 1976), pp. 328–52.

Denton, J. H., 'The crisis of 1297 from the Evesham chronicle' in *EHR*, xciii (1978), pp. 560–79.

Druhan, D. R., *The Syntax of Bede's 'Historia Ecclesiastica'* (Catholic University Studies in Medieval and Renaissance Latin, viii, Washington D.C. 1938).

Dumville, D. N., 'Some aspects of the chronology of the *Historia Brittonum*' in *Bulletin of the Board of Celtic Studies*, xxv (1974), pp. 439–45.

—, 'Sub-Roman Britain: history and legend' in *History*, lxii (1977), pp. 173–92.

—, 'The Anglian collection of royal genealogies and regnal lists' in *Anglo-Saxon England*, v (1976), pp. 23–50.

—, 'The Corpus Christi "Nennius"' in *Bulletin of the Board of Celtic Studies*, xxv (1974), pp. 369–80.

---

[3] I have included works which appeared after 1968, from which year my typescript of *Historical Writing*, i, was in the hands of the publishers. (Sir Richard Southern's presidential addresses to the Royal Historical Society, which are listed in section 2 above, fall into this category.) I have also included a few works of earlier date which I inadvertently overlooked when preparing volume i. See also the corrigenda to *Historical Writing*, i, pp. 516 and n. 1, 517 below.

—, 'A new chronicle-fragment of early British history' in *EHR*, lxxviii (1973), pp. 312–14.

—, 'The *Liber Floridus* of Lambert of Saint-Omer and the *Historia Brittonum*' in *Bulletin of the Board of Celtic Studies*, xxvi (1975), pp. 103–22.

—, 'Nennius and the *Historia Brittonum*' in *Studia Celtica*, x–xi (1975–6), pp. 78–95.

—, 'On the North British section of the *Historia Brittonum*' in *Welsh History Review*, viii (1976–7), pp. 345–54.

Ditmas, E. M. R., 'A reappraisal of Geoffrey of Monmouth's allusions to Cornwall' in *Speculum*, xlviii (1973), pp. 510–24.

Farrell, R. T. (ed.), *Bede and Anglo-Saxon England* (British Archaeological Reports, xlvi, 1978). For articles particularly relevant to Bede's historiography see under Wetherbee, Winthrop, and Wormald, Patrick.

Flint, V. I. J., 'The date of the chronicle of "Florence" of Worcester' in *Revue Bénédictine*, lxxxvi (1976), pp. 115–19.

Goddu, A. A., see under Rouse, R. H.

Gransden, Antonia, 'The growth of the Glastonbury traditions and legends in the twelfth century' in *Journal of Ecclesiastical History*, xxvii (1976), pp. 337–58.

—, 'Cultural transition at Worcester in the Anglo-Norman period' in *The British Archaeological Association Conference Transactions: I. Medieval Art and Architecture at Worcester Cathedral* (1978), pp. 1–14.

Haahr, J. G., 'The concept of kingship in William of Malmesbury's *Gesta Regum* and *Historia Novella*' in *Medieval Studies*, xxxviii (Toronto 1976), pp. 351–71.

Harrison, Kenneth, 'Early Wessex annals in the Anglo-Saxon Chronicle' in *EHR*, lxxxvi (1971), pp. 527–33.

—, 'The beginning of the year in England, c. 500–900' in *Anglo-Saxon England*, ii (1973), pp. 51–70.

Hilpert, Hans-Eberhard, *Kaiser- und Papstbriefe in den Chronica majora des Matthaeus Paris* (Publications of the German Historical Institute London, ix, Stuttgart 1981).

Holmes, Urban T., 'The *Kambriae Descriptio* of Gerald the Welshman' in *Medievalia et Humanistica*, i (1970), pp. 217–31.

Hughes, Kathleen, 'The Welsh Latin chronicles: *Annales Cambrie* and related texts' in *Proceedings of the British Academy*, lix (1973), pp. 233–58.

Jenning, J. C., 'The writings of Prior Dominic of Evesham' in *EHR*, lxxvii (1962), pp. 298–304.

Jennings, Margaret, 'Monks and the *Artes praedicandi* in the time of Ranulf Higden' in *Revue Bénédictine*, lxxxvi (1976), 119–28.

Johnston, R. C., 'The historicity of Jordon Fantosme's *Chronicle*' in *Journal of Medieval History*, ii (1976), pp. 159–68.

—, *The Versification of Jordan Fantosme* (Oxford 1974).

Jones, C. W., 'Bede as early medieval historian' in *Medievalia et Humanistica*, iv (1946), pp. 26–36.

Keller, H. E., 'Two toponymical problems in Geoffrey of Monmouth and Wace: *Etrusia* and *Siesia*' in *Speculum*, xlix (1974), pp. 687–98.

Kirby, D. P., 'Bede's native sources for the "Historia Ecclesiastica"' in *BJRL*, xlviii (1966), pp. 341–71

—, *Saint Wilfrid of Hexham* (Newcastle-upon-Tyne 1974). (For Bede's sources for the *Historia Ecclesiastica* see pp. 1–34.)

Lagorio, V. M., 'The evolving legend of St Joseph of Glastonbury' in *Speculum*, xlvi (1971), pp. 209–31.

Lapidge, Michael, 'The hermeneutic style in tenth-century Anglo-Latin literature' in *Anglo-Saxon England*, iv (1975), pp. 67–111. Professor Lapidge includes a convincing argument that Byrhtferth of Ramsey was the author of both the anonymous *Life of St Oswald* and of the tenth century *Life of St Ecgwin*; ibid. pp. 91–3. Cf. *Historical Writing*, i, pp. 79, 80.

—, 'Some remnants of Bede's lost *Liber Epigrammaticus*' in *EHR*, xc (1975), pp. 798–820.

Leclercq, Jean, 'Monastic historiography from Leo IX to Callistus II' in *Studia Monastica*, xii (1970), pp. 57–86.

Leonardi, Claudio, 'Il Venerabile Beda e la cultra del seculo viii' in *I Problemi dell' Occidente nel secolo viii* (Settimane di studio de centro italiano di studi sull' alto Medioevo, xx, Spoleto 1973), pp. 603–58.

Markus, R. A., *Bede and the Tradition of Ecclesiastical Historiography* (Jarrow Lecture 1975).

Meyvaert, Paul, *Bede and Gregory the Great* (Jarrow Lecture 1964).

—, 'The Registrum of Gregory the Great and Bede' in *Revue Bénédictine*, lxxx (1970), pp. 162–6.

Miller, Molly, 'Bede's use of Gildas' in *EHR*, xc (1975), pp. 241–61.

Musca, G., *Il Venerabile Beda, storico dell'alto Medioevo* (Bari 1973).

Newell, W. W., 'William of Malmesbury on the antiquity of Glastonbury' in *Publications of the Modern Language Association of America*, xviii (1903), pp. 459–512.

Pafford, J. H. P., 'Robert of Gloucester's chronicle' in *Studies presented to Sir Hilary Jenkinson*, ed. J. Conway Davies (London 1957), pp. 304–19.

Ray, R. D., 'Bede, the exegete, as historian' in *Famulus Christi*, ed. Bonner, Gerald (q.v.), pp. 125–40.

—, 'Orderic Vitalis and his readers' in *Studia Monastica*, xiv (1972), pp. 17–33.

Rosenthal, J. T., 'Bede's use of miracles in "The Ecclesiastical History"' in *Traditio*, xxxi (1975), pp. 328–35.

—, 'Edward the Confessor and Robert the Pious: eleventh century kingship and biography' in *Mediaeval Studies*, xxxiii (Toronto 1971), pp. 7–20.

Round, J. H., 'Wace and his authorities' in J. H. Round, *Feudal England* (London 1895, repr. 1909, 1964), pp. 409–18.

Rouse, R. H., and Goddu, A. A., 'Gerald of Wales and the *Florilegum Anglicum*' in *Speculum*, lii (1977), pp. 488–521. For a bibliography of recent works on Gerald of Wales not listed here see ibid., p. 488 n. 1. For a bibliography of earlier works on Gerald see under Williams, E. A., below. In addition see under Davies, J. Conway, above.

Rousset, P., 'La description du monde chevaleresque chez Orderic Vital' in *Le Moyen Age*, xxiv (1969), pp. 427–44.

Schlauch, Margaret, 'Geoffrey of Monmouth and early Polish historiography: a supplement' in *Speculum*, xliv (1969), pp. 258–63.

Southern, R. W., 'Bede' in the same author's *Medieval Humanism and other Studies* (Oxford-New York 1970), pp. 1–8.

Stephens, J. N., 'Bede's *Ecclesiastical History*' in *History*, lxii (1977), pp. 1–14.

Stepsis, Robert, 'Pierre de Langtoft's chronicle: an essay in medieval historiography' in *Medievalia et Humanistica*, new series, iii (1972), pp. 51–73.

Taylor, H. M., 'The architectural interest of Æthelwulf's *De Abbatibus*' in *Anglo-Saxon England*, iii (1974), pp. 163–73.

Thomson, R. M., 'The reading of William of Malmesbury' in *Revue Bénédictine*, lxxxv (1975), pp. 362–402.

—, 'William of Malmesbury as historian and man of letters' in *Journal of Ecclesiastical History*, xxix (1978), pp. 387–413.

—, 'William of Malmesbury and some other western writers on Islam' in *Medievalia et Humanistica*, new series, vi (1976), pp. 179–87.

Wallace-Hadrill, J. M., 'Bede and Plummer' in *Famulus Christi*, ed. Bonner, Gerald (q.v.), pp. 366–85, and in the same author's *Early Medieval History* (Oxford 1975), pp. 76–95.

——, 'Gregory of Tours and Bede: their views on the personal qualities of kings' in *Frühmittelalterliche Studien*, ii (1968), pp. 31–44.

Ward, Benedicta, 'Miracles and History: a reconsideration of the miracle stories used by Bede' in *Famulus Christi*, ed. Bonner, Gerald (q.v.), pp. 70–6.

Werkmeister, O.K., 'The political ideology of the Bayeux Tapestry' in *Studi Medievali*, xvii (1976), pp. 535–95.

Wetherbee, Winthrop, 'Some implications of Bede's Latin style' in *Bede and Anglo-Saxon England*, ed. Farrell, R. T. (q.v.), pp. 23–31.

Williams, E. A., 'A bibliography of Giraldus Cambrensis' in *National Library of Wales Journal*, xii (1961), pp. 97–140.

Winterbottom, Michael, 'Three Lives of St Ethelwold' in *Medium Ævum*, xli (1972), pp. 191–201.

Wormald, Patrick, 'Bede, "Beowulf" and the conversion of the Anglo-Saxon aristocracy' in *Bede and Anglo-Saxon England*, ed. Farrell, R. T. (q.v.), pp. 32–90.

Zinn, G. A., jr, 'The influence of Hugh of St Victor's *Chronicon* on the *Abbreviationes Chronicorum* by Ralph of Diceto' in *Speculum*, lii (1977), pp. 38–61.

Addenda and Corrigenda to *Historical Writing*, i[1]

page xi, line 2 up, for 'historical works' read '*Annals*'

page xxi, line 1, for Chronica read *Chronica*

page xxii, insert after line 7, '—, *Historians of the Church of York: Historians of the Church of York*, ed. James Raine, sn. (RS, 1879–94, 3 vols).

page 5, line 18, for 'Britains' read 'Britons'

page 6, note 45, line 3, for 'probably from Hexham' read 'from Sawley'

— — — 4, for whole line read (2nd ed., Royal Historical Soc., 1964), p. 177.

page 10, line 5, for 'used' read 'given'

page 12, line 7, for 'Two' read 'Three'

page 13, line 3, for 'his contemporary' read 'a century later'

page 33, line 23, for 'the Russian chronicle of Novgorod.' read 'two Russian chronicles (of Kiev and Novgorod).'

—, note 24, insert 'A. G. Kuzmin, *Naczalnyje etapy drewnerusskogo letopisania* (Moscow 1977), pp. 104, 106, 110, 363, 367, and' after 'see'

page 52, note 69, line 4, for 'Alfred' read 'Alfredi'

page 54, note 93, line 2, for '315 n. 1' read '315–16'

page 79, note 92, line 2, for (London 1941) read (2nd ed., Royal Historical Soc., 1964)

page 86, n. 151, add 'However, it has been forcibly argued that the narrative into which the coronation *ordo* is inserted is an account of Edgar's marriage in 964; see H. G. Richardson and G. O. Sayles, *The Governance of Mediaeval England* (Edinburgh 1963), pp. 399–405.

page 89, note 171, lines 1–2, for 'xlvii (1938)' read 'xlviii (1933)'

page 95, line 1, for '966' read '996'

page 113, note 49, line 2, for 'history of' read 'history to'

page 130, line 3 up, for 'building' read 'buildings'

page 139, line 18, for '1197' read '1097'

page 144, note 53, for '161' read '159'

page 148, line 12, insert 'a' after 'adds'

page 178, line 9, for 'held' read 'had'

page 182, lines 12–13, for '"he did nothing that was not bad, nothing

---

[1] These corrections are confined to small mistakes. The more extensive revision made desirable in one or two places mainly because of the research of recent scholars has not been undertaken. However, some indication of such research is given in the bibliography above (pp. 512–15). For example my text treats the tenth century *Life of St. Ecgwin* and *Life of St. Oswald* as anonymous, although Professor Lapidge has now argued convincingly that both are by Byrhtferth.

that he had promised"' read '"there was no evil that he would not carry out, none that he would not threaten"'

page 184, line 9, for '1185' read '1184'

—, note 151, line 4, for '1185' read '1184'

page 202, line 1, for 'Europe' read 'libraries'

page 257, line 30, for 'in his last years that' read 'that in his last years'

page 263, note 130, for 'ibid.,' read 'WN, vol. i,'

page 316, lines 9–11, delete from 'This bible' to 'twelfth century.'

—, line 14, for 'were' read 'was'

—, note 150, add 'For this bible from Winchester see C. M. Kauffmann, *Romanesque Manuscripts 1066–1190* (London 1975), no. 83.

page 319, note 6, lines 5–6, for 'Cheney, 'The Dunstable annals', pp. 84–8, read C. R. Cheney, 'The Making of the Dunstable Annals, A. D. 33 to 1242' in *Essays in Medieval History presented to Bertie Wilkinson*, ed. T. A. Sandquist and M. R. Powicke (Toronto 1969), pp. 84–8 (this article is reprinted in C. R. Cheney, *Medieval Texts and Studies* (Oxford 1973), pp. 209–30).

— —, note 7, lines 4–5, for 'Denholm-Young, 'Winchester-Hyde chron.', p. 88 read 'Noël Denholm-Young, 'The Winchester-Hyde chronicle' in *EHR*, xlix (1934), p. 88 (this article is reprinted in the same author's *Collected Papers on Medieval Subjects* (Oxford 1946), pp. 86–95).

— —, line 3, add after bracket ', pp. 472–92'

page 364, line 7, for 'half-year' read 'fifty years'

page 427, line 22, for 'extortion' read 'protection'

page 456, note 146, lines 2–3, for 'The Westminster version of the *Flores Historiarum*' read 'The continuations of the *Flores Historiarum* from 1265 to 1327'

— —, line 3, add after bracket ', pp. 472–92'

page 458, line 13, for 'left' read 'right'

—, lines 14–15, delete passage in brackets

page 466, line 1, for 'Isabel' read 'Eleanor'

page 497, line 4 up, insert ', except Fitz Thedmar,' after 'chronicler'

page 507, note 181, insert a semi-colon after 'Walsingham'

page 539, column 2, line 28, for 'the' read 'from', and add 'and n. 150'

page 553, column 1, lines 14–15, for 'and n. 39' read 'n. 38'

page 555, column 2, line 6 up, insert '466, ' before '507'

page 561, column 2, line 35, for '1185' read '1184'

page 562, column 1, delete lines 36–7

— —, line 39, add ',166'

page 566, column 1, line 39, delete 'Nennius, 6 n. 45'

page 568, column 2, lines 33–4, delete ',466'

page 569, column 2, delete line 4

page 570, column 1, line 14, for '212, 354' read '211, 353'

—, column 2, after line 15, insert 'Kiev, chronicle of, 33'

page 571, column 2, line 11, delete '9'

page 583, column 2, lines 19–20, for '*De Moribus et Actis Primorum Norman-niae Ducum*' read 'St Quentin, Dudo of'

page 595, column 2, line 3 up, insert '391 and n.72' after 'abbey,'

page 602, column 1, line 36, for '370' read '369'

Plate IV, caption, line 1, delete comma after 'Vitalis's'

Ice cream
CONES

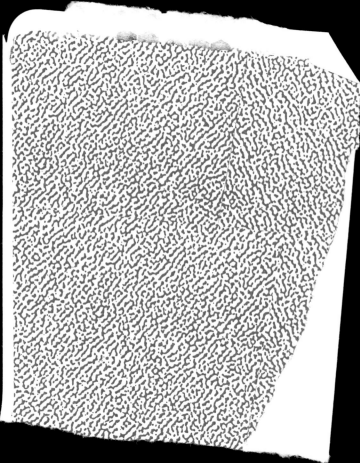

Index

Post-Conquest people are indexed under their second names if the second name can be regarded as a surname. However, if a person is commonly known by his or her first name, he or she is indexed under the first name, with a cross-reference. Moreover, if the second name is purely descriptive, the person is indexed under the first name.

Classical names, and names of the Anglo-Saxon period, are indexed under first names.

References to pages and notes are in italics if they cite printed editions of the works under discussion.

All animals (except for horses, which are indexed under 'horse' and 'horses'), birds and plants are grouped together under headings of those generic words. Mythical manlike monsters are treated similarly, being under 'monsters, mythical manlike'. The heading 'archives' has references only to passages of particular interest; chroniclers' routine use of documents is indexed in their own entries.

A

Aberdeen, 81, 82, 286
  archdeacon of, *see* Barbour, John
Abingdon, Berks., Benedictine abbey
  visitation of (*temp.* Edward III), 122 and n. 39
  owned copy of *Polychronicon*, 55
  abbot of, *see* Ashenden, William
  monks of, *see* Cantlow, William; Ildesle, Richard de
Abner, uncle of King Saul, 34
accounts, obedientiaries', in Thornton annals, 392 and n. 11
Achilles, 35
  Henry V compared to, 406
  John Talbot compared to, 378
acrostic, use of, for own signature, by
  Thomas Elmham, 207, 347
  John Erghome, 59 n. 4
  Sir Thomas Gray, 94
  Ranulf Higden, 44 and n. 6, 47
  Henry Knighton, 159–60
  John Strecche, 405 and n. 103
acrostics, as cryptograms, 209
adages, by
  John Whethamsted, 378 and n. 226
  Thomas More, 452
  see also dicta
Adam, first man, 169
  and Eve, Richard II's favourites compared to, 185

genealogy back to, 182
administration, royal
  chancery
    during Peasants' Revolt, 169
     great seal of, entrusted to Archbishop Arundel, 167
     'remembrancer' rolls of, destroyed, 166
    under Edward V, 305
    method of dating etc. of (*temp.* Henry VI and Edward IV), 267
    chroniclers connected with, 249–50, 261–2, 266–71. *See also Chronicle of the Rebellion in Lincolnshire*; Crowland, Benedictine abbey, chronicle, second continuation; *Historie of the Arrivall of Edward IV . . .*
    chancellors, *see* Alcock, John; Baldock, Robert; Beaufort, Henry; Booth, Lawrence; Bury, Richard de; More, Thomas; Rotherham (or Scot), Thomas; Russell, John; Scrope, Richard; Stillington, Robert; Stratford, John
    clerk in, wrote account of Peasants' Revolt, 160 and n. 17, 166 and n. 47, 167 and n. 48
     see also Ferriby, William
    clerk of the crown in, *see* Martin, Geoffrey
    spigurnel, *see* Wightman, William

IV

'Lancastrian' roll, 311 and n. *17*
  date of, 311
  originally Yorkist, 311, 316
  revised to suit Tudor dynasty, 311, 316
'Yorkist' roll, 309 and n. 9, 311 and n. *18*
  date of, 311
  Yorkist bias in, 316

ROUSE, R. H., on 'Bostonus Buriensis' and
  Henry Kirkstead, 402 nn. 81, 87
ROWE, BENEDICTA J. H., on chroniclers of
  Henry VI's reign, 249 and n. 1
Rownham, Bristol, ferryman at, 336
Roxburgh castle, warden of, *see* Umfraville,
  Sir Robert
Roye, Jean de, secretary of John II, duke
  of Bourbon, chronicle (1460–83), 293 n. *38*
  interest of, in English affairs, 293
Rudborne, Thomas, monk of St Swithun's
  (*fl.* mid–15th c.), 494 n. 1
  meets John Rous, 322
  reputation of, for knowledge of
    chronicles, 322
  annotates *Codex Wintoniensis*, 494 n. 1
  ?had hand in Book of Hyde, 392 n. 7,
    393 n. 30
  ascription of sources by, not to be relied
    on, 323 n. 106
  compares narratives of events in
    different literary authorities, 436
  works
  ?*Epitome Historiae Majoris* (Brutus–Henry
    VI), 395 and n. 30, 494 n. 1, 503
    attribution of, to John of Exeter, 395 n.
      30
    cites 'Vigilantius', 493
  Historia Major . . . Ecclesiae Wintoniensis
    (A.D. 164–1138), 394 and n. *28*, 395–8,
    468
    date of, 394
    includes general history, 395
    ?purpose of, partly to debunk
      Glastonbury legends, 398
    sources of, 493–4, 494 n. 1
      literary, include: *De Concordantiis
        Historiarum Angliae*, 493
      'Girardus Cornubiensis', 493, 494
        n. 1
      Geoffrey of Monmouth, 397
      'Vigilantius', 396, 493–4
    documentary, 396–7, 494 n. 1
    first-hand observation, 396 and nn.
      41, 42
    affinities of, with Book of Hyde, 392 n. 7
    literary tone of, 395–6
    legends in, 396, 397, 398
    scholarly observations in, 397
    on origins of: Old Minster, 397, 398
      monasticism, 397–8 and n. 50

patriotic tone of, 398
  on precedence of bishops of Winchester,
    398
  used by John Rous, 322 n. 106
?*Historia Minor* (Brutus–1234), 395 and n.
  31
?a history of Durham (to 1083), 395 and n.
  32
?Book of Hyde (Brutus–1023), 391, 395
  n. 30

Rudborne, Thomas, fellow of Merton
  College, bishop of St Davids 1434–42,
  322–3 n. 106
  chaplain of Henry V, 323 n. 106
  ?author of chronicle, 323 n. 106
Rudham, Walter de, of Huntingdon,
  defends bridge at Huntingdon during
  Peasants' Revolt, 167
RUMBLE, A. R., on Thomas Rudborne etc.,
  494 n. 1
Russell, John, secondary of privy seal office
  1469–74, keeper of privy seal 1474–83,
  bishop of Rochester 1476–80, bishop of
  Lincoln 1480–94, chancellor 1483–5
  on embassy to Charles the Bold (1471),
    270–1 and n. 148
  addresses parliament (1483), 319 n. 59
  uses analogy of kingdom with human
    body, 319 n. 59
  inveighs against enclosures in similar
    vein to John Rous, 319 n. 59
  visits Crowland abbey (1486), 271, 491
  humanist interests of, 270 n. 147
  ?knew Thomas More, 452
  ?author of: memoir in Crowland
    chronicle, 270 and n. 146, 271
    ?*Chronicle of Rebellion* and *Arrival of
      Edward IV*, 270–1 passim
  suffragan of, *see* O'Flanagan, Nicholas
RUSSELL, P. E., on John Hardyng on
  Lancastrian intervention in Castile, xv,
  284 n. 271
Ruste, Robert, sea captain (d. 1379),
  death of, by drowning described, 153–4
rustici, Thomas Walsingham's use of word,
  133
Ruston, nr Nafferton, Yorks., man from,
  guides English army before Crécy, 359
  and n. 110

S

St Albans, Herts., Benedictine abbey
  legend of foundation of, by King Offa,
    119
  Thurstan an enemy of (*c.* 1052–*c.* 1070),
    347
  relations of, with Edward II, 6
  negotiations at, for return of Piers

T

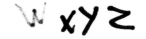